The Sino-Soviet Rift

Center for International Studies
Massachusetts Institute of Technology

STUDIES IN INTERNATIONAL COMMUNISM

Albania and the Sino-Soviet Rift
William E. Griffith

Communism in North Vietnam
P. J. Honey

The Sino-Soviet Rift
William E. Griffith

Communism in Europe, Vol. I
William E. Griffith

The Sino-Soviet Rift

Analysed and Documented by
WILLIAM E. GRIFFITH

THE M.I.T. PRESS
MASSACHUSETTS INSTITUTE OF TECHNOLOGY
CAMBRIDGE, MASSACHUSETTS

PUBLISHED IN COOPERATION WITH THE CHINA QUARTERLY

COPYRIGHT © 1964
BY
THE MASSACHUSETTS INSTITUTE OF TECHNOLOGY

ALL RIGHTS RESERVED

FIRST M.I.T. PRESS PAPERBACK EDITION, AUGUST, 1964
SECOND PAPERBACK PRINTING, OCTOBER, 1965
THIRD PAPERBACK PRINTING, MAY, 1968

LIBRARY OF CONGRESS CATALOG CARD NO.: 63-22708
PRINTED IN THE UNITED STATES OF AMERICA

PREFACE

FEW events in recent history have developed with such speed, have so rapidly become so complex, and have so largely confounded both the predictions of experts and the mythology of politicians as the Sino-Soviet dispute. To concentrate on one devil, "the international Communist conspiracy," is difficult enough, particularly amidst the distractions of Western affluent society and the intimations of atomic doom. But to cope with two if not more Communist devils is almost as confusing for most mortals as it must have been for the Chinese sages when they heard of the Protestant Reformation.

But we must not only daily conquer our freedom, as Goethe put it, but also strive to jettison outworn clichés in time, to absorb the veiled, diffuse, and contradictory contemporary Communist reality, and—such is the *hubris* of mankind—even to peer into the future of the Communist world. For Communists, of course, history is a weapon in the class struggle. Their arbitrary and continuous revision of the past does, however, at least enlighten the present and even gives some intimations of the future; and the stiff, Victorian sermons of Leninist secular messianism, when deprived of their ideological scaffolding, can reveal quite as much of the reality within as did theological controversies and Hippodrome feuds of the realities of power in Byzantium.

The decoding of Communist incantations is neither a counter-incantation nor a secret open only to the Communist high-priests who intone them. By now there has been much solid work done in this art, and much unravelled Communist history against which one can check it. True, we seldom know much more of that history than the part of the iceberg above the surface, and we must often wait years for a glimpse of the murky mass below. But Kremlinology and Pekinology—what is now fashionably called "the deciphering of esoteric communications"—while still, like all historical research, essentially an art, is one like art history and criticism; its tools are becoming burnished and tested even if its practitioners do not yet have the verbal facility of Burckhardt, Ruskin, Symons or Berenson.

This book has a much more modest and mundane purpose. It does not attempt to set up a theoretical model. The aim here is to summarise, document, and give a brief and—need one say?—preliminary analysis of the developments in Sino-Soviet relations from the late winter of 1962 through November 1963: what happened, what it revealed of the past and present, how it differs from the previous periods, and—

v

mixing inference with, I hope, not too much speculation—what it may possibly portend for the future.

Such a modest *vade mecum* may well serve some useful purpose for those who do not have access to, and means of filing, analysing, and putting together in some meaningful context, the flood of documentation that the Sino-Soviet rift has released. Like Welsh Calvinist preachers, Communists can talk—and write—nigh on forever; this may indeed be their unconscious but most effective secret weapon to prevent most non-Communists from ever understanding them.

Unlike most other analytical and documentary volumes so far published, therefore, the summary and analysis are complete in themselves; the documents serve as additional illustration and detail to the text. The limits of space plus the existence of documentary coverage for the earlier period (in particular, up to March 1963, in Dallin's *Diversity in International Communism*) have made it necessary to limit the documents to the period beginning with the exchange of letters between Moscow and Peking, i.e., March 1963. This later documentation is more complete, less esoteric, more illuminating, and historically more important than the previous material; it therefore must be given precedence.

This book, then, is one observer's narrow, winding path through the vast, gloomy forest of current Communist controversy, avoiding the trees, and, I hope, emerging on a view of the woods.

It is intended to follow in sequence both *The China Quarterly's* first documentary volume on this subject, *The Sino-Soviet Dispute*, and Professor Alexander Dallin's *Diversity in International Communism*. Because of the greatly increased complexity of recent Sino-Soviet developments, however, I feel that this volume has required the kind of detailed analysis without which documents alone may mystify rather than enlighten. The documents chosen are inevitably given space limits, only a part of what most students would probably consider essential; for that reason, and also because Sino-Soviet studies are still relatively new, I have given complete documentation in the footnotes.

Even more than most books on very recent developments, this study cannot hope to be definitive. As I have indicated in the introduction, existing studies of the Sino-Soviet dispute are already largely out of date, made so by subsequent revelations by Moscow and Peking; and the same may be expected to happen with this one. I hope, however, that for a time it may serve to enlighten both the specialist and the general reader, and that it may also encourage further research.

The texts of quotations and documents have when necessary been checked against the original languages. The transliteration system is based on that used by the Library of Congress, with some modifications;

for Chinese the standard Wade-Giles system has been used. I have devoted some attention to the problem of purposeful mistranslation and deliberately deceptive excerpting, which Moscow has recently resumed extensively. The reader of the footnotes will be aware that the study of contemporary developments in international communism requires the acquisition, cataloguing, filing and use of the most varied, voluminous, and geographically widespread sources; unfortunately, neither universities nor foundations have in my view yet realised the extent of this problem or begun to respond to it adequately.

The very variety and extent of the sources require many acknowledgments. My work has been made much easier by my research assistants, Joan Barth, Joan Gettig, Peter Prifti, Robin Remington, Rosemarie Sträussnigg, László Urban, and by my secretary, Mina Parks. Typing and retyping was faithfully done by Constance Boquist, Jane Gross, Martha Merrill, Lila Rose, and Doris Sigourney, and indexing by Peter Prifti, Joan Gettig, and Jane Gross. I have benefited greatly from comments and insights from many friends and colleagues in this field: Donald L. M. Blackmer, James F. Brown, Zbigniew Brzezinski, R. V. Burks, Christian Duevel, Joseph C. Kun, R. Rockingham Gill, Leopold Labedz, Wolfgang Leonhard, and my late friend and colleague, Herbert Ritvo. Its organisation and editing owe much to the Center's editors, Richard W. Hatch, Jean P. S. Clark, and to Donald L. M. Blackmer, as well as to *The China Quarterly's* editor, Roderick MacFarquhar. The errors and omissions, like the interpretations, are mine. Finally, this book would not have been possible without the resources for research afforded by the Center for International Studies and the encouragement and support of its Director, Max F. Millikan.

WILLIAM E. GRIFFITH

Center for International Studies
Massachusetts Institute of Technology
Cambridge, Massachusetts

November 27, 1963

CONTENTS

ix

DATE SUMMARY

1963	July 31	Chinese Government's Statement on Test Ban Treaty
1963	August 3	Soviet Statement on Chinese Position on Test Ban Treaty
1963	August 15	Chinese Reply to Soviet Statement of August 3
1963	August 21	Soviet Reply to Chinese Statement of August 15
1963	September 1	Chinese Answer Soviet Statement of August 21
1963	September 6	China Publishes "The Origin and Development of the Differences Between the Leadership of the CPSU and Ourselves—Comment on the Open Letter of the Central Committee of the CPSU"
1963	September 13	China Publishes "On the Question of Stalin—Comment on the Open Letter of the Central Committee of the CPSU (2)"
1963	September 21	Soviet Government Statement in Answer to Chinese Statement of September 1
1963	September 26	China Publishes "Is Yugoslavia a Socialist Country? —Comment on the Open Letter of the Central Committee of the CPSU (3)"
1963	September-October	Resolutions of Other Communist Parties Demanding an International Communist Meeting Begin Appearing in *Pravda*
1963	October 18	"Marxism-Leninism the Basis for the Unity of the Communist Movement" Published in *Kommunist*
1963	October 21	China Publishes "Apologists of Neo-Colonialism— Comment on the Open Letter of the Central Committee of the CPSU (4)"
1963	October 25	Khrushchev Again Calls for End of Polemics; Russians Apparently Drop Attempts to Organise International Meeting
1963	November 18	China Publishes "Two Different Lines on the Question of War and Peace—Comment on the Open Letter of the Central Committee of the CPSU (5)"
1963	December 12	China Publishes "Peaceful Coexistence—Two Diametrically Opposed Policies—Comment on the Open Letter of the CPSU Central Committee (6)"

ABBREVIATIONS

AAPSO	Afro-Asian Peoples' Solidarity Organisation
AFP	*Agence France Presse* (official French news agency)
Agerpress	Official Rumanian press agency
AKEL	Progressive Party of Working People of Cyprus (Communist)
BBC	British Broadcasting Corporation
BCP	Bulgarian Communist Party
CB	" Current Background " (U.S. Consulate-General, Hong Kong)
CC	Central Committee
CCP	Chinese Communist Party
CDSP	*Current Digest of the Soviet Press*
CGIL	*Confederazione Generale Italiana del Lavoro* (Italian PCI-PSO Trade Union Federation)
CMEA	Council for Mutual Economic Aid
CPB	Communist Party of Brazil
CPC	Communist Party of China (also CCP)
CPGB	Communist Party of Great Britain
CPI	Communist Party of India
CPR	Chinese People's Republic
CPSU	Communist Party of the Soviet Union
CPUSA	Communist Party of the United States
CRU	(British Broadcasting Corporation, Overseas Service), Central Research Unit
CSSR	*Ceskoslovenska socialisticka republika* (Czechoslovak Socialist Republic)
CTK	Czechoslovak News Agency
DDR	*Deutsche Demokratische Republik* (German Democratic Republic [East Germany])
ECMP	" Extracts from Chinese Mainland Publications " (U.S. Consulate-General, Hong Kong)
EE	East Europe
EEC	European Economic Community
FYP	Five-Year Plan
GMT	Greenwich Mean Time
ICBM	Intercontinental Ballistic Missile
IOJ	International Organisation of Journalists
IUS	International Union of Students
JCP	Japanese Communist Party
JPRS	Joint Publications Research Service (U.S. government translation service)
KPD	*Kommunistische Partei Deutschlands* (Communist Party of [West] Germany)
KSC	*Komunisticka strana Ceskoslovenska* (Communist Party of Czechoslovakia)
KSS	*Komunisticka strana Slovenska* (Communist Party of Slovakia).
LCY	League of Communists of Yugoslavia
NATO	North Atlantic Treaty Organisation
NCNA	New China News Agency (*Hsinhua*)
NEFA	North-East Frontier Area (of India)
NZCP	New Zealand Communist Party
PCB	*Parti communiste belgique* (Belgian Communist Party)
PCF	*Parti communiste français* (French Communist Party)
PCI	*Partito comunista italiano* (Italian Communist Party)
PKI	*Partai Komunis Indonesia* (Indonesian Communist Party)
PRC	People's Republic of China (also CPR)
PSI	*Partito socialista italiano* (Italian Socialist Party)
PSP	*Partido socialista popular* (Popular Socialist Party [of Cuba])
PURS	*Partido Unido de la Revolución Socialista* (United Party of the Socialist Revolution [of Cuba])

ABBREVIATIONS

PZPR	*Polska Zjednoczona Partia Robotnicza* (Polish United Workers' [Communist] Party)
SAC	Strategic Air Command
SAWPY	Socialist Alliance of the Working People of Yugoslavia
SBZ	*Sowjetische Besatzungszone* (Soviet Zone of Occupation [East Germany])
SCMP	" Survey of the China Mainland Press " (U.S. Consulate-General, Hong Kong)
SED	*Sozialistische Einheitspartei Deutschlands* (Socialist Unity [Communist] Party [of East Germany])
SKAF	Swedish Communist Workers' Federation
SFIO	*Section française de l'Internationale ouvrière* (French Socialist Party)
SOBSI	*Sentral Organisasi Buruh Seluruh Indonesia* (All-Indonesian Central Workers Organisation)
SOHYO	*Nihon-rodokumiai-sohyogikai* (Council of Japanese Trade Union Federations [Socialist])
SSSR	*Soyuz Sovetskikh Sotsialisticheskikh Respublik* (Union of Soviet Socialist Republics)
TANJUG	Official Yugoslav news agency
TASS	Official Soviet news agency
UAR	United Arab Republic
UEC	*Union des étudiants communiste* (French Communist Student Union)
UNR	*Union pour la nouvelle République* (Gaullist Party [France])
UPI	United Press International (news agency)
VNA	(North) Vietnam News Agency
VWP	Vietnamese Workers' Party
WFTU	World Federation of Trade Unions
WPC	World Peace Council
ZNP	Zanzibar Nationalist Party

Part 1

INTRODUCTION

Introduction: Background to the Break

WHEN little is certain one must scratch for every fact. The detailed treatment of the Sino-Soviet rift [1] in 1962 and most of 1963 which follows must therefore inevitably be a series of mosaics with an indeterminate number—but probably a majority—of the pieces in each one missing. Yet these mosaics are set against a background of general world affairs during this period, and that background, at least in its make-up if not in its meaning, is fairly clear, if not in our memories then at least in the contemporary record.

"It was the best of worlds, it was the worst of worlds." It saw the most critical post-war confrontation of the United States and the Soviet Union, the Cuban crisis of October 1962. It saw the Chinese invasion of India in the same month, the first time in centuries that a strong China threatened—and voluntarily but perhaps only temporarily desisted from—pouring down into the plains of India. It saw more Soviet and American successes in space; it saw America with renewed prosperity and with a boiling civil rights problem which bids fair to be the worst since the Civil War; it saw—as if that were new!—strife in Laos and guerila war in South Vietnam. It saw a fading Berlin crisis, particularly after the Soviet withdrawal of its missiles from Cuba. It witnessed a further surge of nationalism in the Middle East, Africa and Latin America, with present losses in the first two for the Soviet Union but, at least in southern Africa, with looming future dangers for Washington and tempting opportunities for Moscow and Peking. It saw continuing squabbles but no new major crisis in the UN, and the Congo crisis seemed—one hastens to add " at the time of writing "—to have subsided. It saw in the summer of 1963 the signature of the test ban treaty, one sign of a possible and partial East-West détente. Above all, it saw the end of the post-war era.

The post-war era was, as many eras after great wars are, primarily a bipolar one. The two super-Powers, the United States and the Soviet

[1] See Bibliography for full citations.

3

Union, at first loomed like two vast steaming volcanoes amid a range of small, arid, eroded hills. Western Europe was economically prostrate and militarily vulnerable to the Red Army; Japan, except for its protecting seas, was in the same state; China was more of a geographical expression than a major power; and Latin America, Africa, and the rest of Asia were made up of weak or at best nominally independent political and economic dependencies of the Western Powers.

By 1962 all this had changed. Western Europe's prosperity, like the Rabbi's dybbuk, had outgrown its American sponsor. Asia, Africa, and Latin America were demanding—and getting—a voice in world affairs far greater rather than, as always before, far less than their physical power entitled them to.

Furthermore, since 1962 Khrushchev has not done so well in these areas of the world. Since 1955 Soviet strategy there had been based on the assumption that the ebb of Western colonial power and the rise of radical young nationalisms could be manipulated to Soviet profit; and initially, in Cairo, Conakry and Djakarta, it certainly seemed the case. Yet when one looks at the picture today it has rather sharply changed to the Soviet Union's disfavour.

The Soviet aid programme to many of these areas continues, to Peking's fury and hardly to the liking of the Soviet and East European citizens, who like many Americans prefer to have their money spent at home. Yet Nasser is now stronger, less amenable to Soviet pressure, and more inclined to cross Soviet purposes than ever before; and the Algerian régime, to whom Moscow and Peking sent so many arms and supplies, has suppressed its Communist party, consolidated its position, relieved France of its last colonial cancer, and bids fair to compete with the Soviet Union and with Communist China for support of the radical anti-colonialists in Africa.

Black Africa has so far seen some of the most impressive Soviet losses of all: not only are French, West Germans and Americans now welcomed by Sekou Touré with open arms to Conakry, but the Soviet Ambassador there was publicly humiliated after two unsuccessful attempts to smuggle a recalcitrant Soviet teacher out of the country. Modibo Keita in Mali also seems to be moving away from pro-Soviet radicalism, and even Nkrumah, although increasingly radical, is not as yet a Soviet satellite. Thus the radical Casablanca grouping, the great Soviet hope in Africa, has proved ineffective, and the increasing current of African unity is led by such states as Nigeria, the Ivory Coast, Tanganyika, Ethiopia, and Algeria—none of them notable friends of the Soviet Union. Only in southern Africa, where a protracted period of bloody guerilla war seems likely before the South African white redoubt begins even to consider striking its flag, can Moscow still hope for future success.

4

In Asia, the Soviet Union has also been doing badly. The Chinese attack on India and Moscow's ambivalent attitude toward it, when contrasted with the West's immediate and massive aid, has caused Moscow's stock to slump briefly in India, and the resultant alienation of Pakistan from the West helps Peking, not Moscow. The massive Chinese military victory in India has tended to paralyse the South-East Asian neutrals, like so many birds transfixed by a yellow cobra, and to move them closer to the Chinese, not the Russians; and the controversy among Indonesia, the Philippines, and Malaysia is less favourable to Moscow than to Peking. In any case, the billion dollars worth of arms Moscow has sent to Indonesia, besides encouraging Sukarno to get more aid elsewhere, has certainly not led him to accede to all Soviet wishes. Yet in Asia as in Africa, the present régimes will not last forever: Nehru and Sukarno are both well along in years, and Moscow's plans, like those of all good Leninists, are designed for decades, not for days.

Surely the greatest single change in our decade, perhaps in our century, has been China's transformation from weakness, disunity, humiliation, and impotence into a new giant, the most powerful ground military force in Asia, and the most frustrated and certainly most populous nation in the world. When in early November 1962 the first soldier of the Chinese People's Army looked down on the plains of Assam, it finally became clear to the world that a power revolution was under way in Asia which future historians may compare with those set in motion by Alexander the Great and Ghenghis Khan. For our immediate purpose, that of sketching the background in world politics against which the Sino-Soviet developments of this period occurred, it is therefore best to begin with a more detailed consideration of the Sino-Indian problem.

THE SINO-INDIAN BORDER WAR [2]

When the British left in 1947 India proved unwilling to prevent resurgent Communist China from reoccupying Tibet. Indian protests at the loss of its rights there and later at the Chinese crushing of the 1959 Tibetan rebellion, as well as its granting of asylum to the Dalai Lama, infuriated but did not check the Chinese. In the fifties, Peking's determination to push into Indian border territory became increasingly clear. The first frontier incident occurred in 1954; in 1956–57 the Chinese built a strategic military road through East Ladakh; and in 1959, several months after the Chinese crushed the Tibetan rising, the Indians decided secretly to infiltrate and outflank the Chinese border posts in Ladakh.

[2] For documentation, see p. 56, note 1, *infra*.

When this began, in September 1959, the Chinese initiated the first serious Sino-Indian border clashes, to which the Russians responded with what amounted to a declaration of neutrality. In 1960, in spite of an abortive meeting between Nehru and Chou En-lai, the frontier incidents continued, and the Indians established new forward border posts in Ladakh.

From February 1962 onward, steadily more violent Chinese diplomatic notes to the Indians and propaganda attacks against them made clear that the Chinese would not tolerate these new Indian posts. In September the Chinese for the first time initiated border incidents along the McMahon Line in the (to India) more sensitive North-East Frontier Area (NEFA). In response Nehru on October 12 publicly ordered the Indian Army to drive the Chinese out of NEFA and back across the McMahon Line; but the Indians did not undertake any such operations. On October 20 the Chinese struck there and in Ladakh in full force.

In a month of fighting the Chinese overran the new Indian border posts in Ladakh and drove back the badly led, badly armed, and repeatedly outflanked Indian troops in NEFA to the foothills of Assam. Little remained between the Chinese army and Calcutta. Thus India was for the moment militarily exposed as a paper tiger, and the Chinese army was shown to be the decisive ground power in southern and South-East Asia. The already timorous South-East Asian neutrals adjusted their policies accordingly lest they too suffer India's fate, and Pakistan, jubilant at India's defeat and furious at America's aid to India, hastened to better its relations with Peking. India, desperate, turned to London and Washington; in effect it exchanged its non-alignment for what amounted to a military alliance with the West. Internally, in spite of his reluctant sacrifice of Krishna Menon, Nehru lost some of his popularity, but there was no other political alternative. More important, an enormous wave of patriotism swept over India.

Chinese objectives toward India were complex. Minimally, they wanted to push back the Indian counter-offensive in Ladakh and secure their strategic road there. Their maximum aims, an amalgam of Communist ideology and Chinese national interest, may be summarised as follows:

(1) Regaining territory they claim China lost to the imperialist British and thus restoring the prestige of China and of Chinese Communism in Asia, in the international Communist movement, particularly vis-à-vis the Soviet Union, and among the frightened in India itself.

(2) Destroying the "Indian alternative": its democracy, military power and economic growth, whose contrast with China's economic crisis made this the more necessary. Specifically, destroying

Nehru's prestige (although not his removal: his successor might be more hostile) and the discrediting of the Congress Party.

(3) Making the Indian northern frontier permanently vulnerable to a renewed Chinese attack.

(4) Splitting India from the effectively terrorised Asian neutrals and executing a rapprochement with Pakistan which would weaken U.S. alliances in Asia.

(5) To strengthen the position of the Party at home (as during the Korean War) by increased chauvinism and distraction from domestic woes without running the risk of a direct conflict with the United States or of being accused of invading a small country.

(6) Embarrassing Khrushchev and the Soviet Union in the international Communist movement, among underdeveloped countries, and in India itself, and demonstrating the independence of Peking from Moscow.

(7) By its probably always planned unilateral cease-fire, keeping India and the neutrals from organising any effective resistance and preventing massive Western intervention on India's behalf.

By late November 1962 the Chinese had achieved the greater part of these objectives. They had driven back the Indians and recovered the initial gains in Ladakh, for whose indefinite loss Delhi appears to be preparing the Indian people. They had shattered Indian military prestige and greatly raised their own among their neighbours and among all radical extremists in the international Communist movement. They had partially discredited Nehru in India and confronted Delhi with a choice between economic growth and military rearmament. They had retained excellent jump-off positions for a new offensive in NEFA even after post-cease-fire partial withdrawal. They had effectively split India from the neutralist South-East Asian countries, and they had carried out a considerable rapprochement with Pakistan and weakened the latter's ties with the West, which would probably not succeed in bringing about a Kashmir settlement. They had raised their prestige at home. They had lowered Khrushchev's prestige among all extremist Communists. Finally, their unilateral cease-fire had revived Indian hopes that China would not again attack and that the Soviet Union would continue minimal support. This in turn influenced India not to enter a complete military alliance with the West, which was itself reluctant to agree to the vast expenditure of funds and perhaps eventually of men which would be necessary to guarantee India's defence.

However, other results of the Chinese attack are not so favourable to Peking. The resultant great wave of patriotism in India temporarily united the country, and although renewed disunity has become evident, much of the patriotism still remains. India's desperate situation plus prompt and extensive Anglo-American aid, given without requiring

7

India officially to surrender its non-alignment, decisively and probably permanently changed relations between India and the West to the advantage of the latter and to the disadvantage of both Peking and Moscow. In the non-aligned countries not geographically close to China and therefore not so fearful of it, Chinese aggression and Soviet compromise have further discredited both Peking and Moscow. And finally, Sino-Soviet relations were further seriously exacerbated.

THE CUBAN CRISIS [3]

In September 1962 the Russians began placing medium-range guided missiles in Cuba, a fact confirmed by U.S. photographic reconnaissance in mid-October. On October 22 President Kennedy declared a " quarantine " of all " offensive weapons " entering Cuba. Soviet response was propagandistically violent but militarily cautious. Their ships reversed course en route and turned away from Cuba; and when it became increasingly clear that the United States would destroy the missile sites by bombing or invasion (and thus the Castro régime) unless they were removed, Khrushchev agreed to do so in return for a U.S. pledge not to invade the island.

The Russians withdrew their missiles and bombers from Cuba because the United States had and was prepared to use an overwhelming superiority of conventional (particularly naval and air) forces in the area; and the decisive American strategic superiority made a Soviet escalation to a thermonuclear exchange prohibitively risky. Furthermore, the American willingness to confine their demands to a limited objective enabled Khrushchev to salvage Castro, while his concessions to Washington " to save the peace " won him much support at home and in Eastern Europe. Yet the rise in American prestige and the demonstration of American superiority in weapons and will to use them outweighed this; Kennedy was the winner and Khrushchev the loser in this exchange.

The Cuban crisis was so serious, because it was a potentially thermonuclear Soviet-American confrontation, that for Khrushchev its negative effect on Sino-Soviet relations was probably a secondary element in Soviet considerations. What was it really about, and why was this so?

The 1962 Soviet-U.S. Cuban confrontation was primarily a strategic politico-military one, caused by a fast, potentially cheap, and certainly risky Soviet attempt to reverse the increasing American lead in thermonuclear missile and delivery systems. True, American hesitation at the 1961 Bay of Pigs invasion, agreement to the neutralisation of Laos and willingness to continue inconclusive conversations and apparently to

---

[3] For documentation, see p. 60, note 1, *infra*.

8

make peripheral concessions on Berlin had probably encouraged a higher level of Soviet risk-taking; but Khrushchev had badly miscalculated.

To understand Khrushchev's actions in the Cuban crisis, one must go back to 1957, the year of the first Soviet sputnik and ICBM, whose impact was so largely responsible for the initial deterioration of Sino-Soviet relations. Three aspects of these 1957 Soviet achievements must be distinguished: the events themselves and the Soviet and the American views of their significance. Both Moscow and Washington publicly overestimated their importance: Moscow in part deliberately and for propaganda purposes, Washington because it equated this irrefutable evidence of Soviet capability with probable Soviet intentions and performance. The subsequent November 1957 Soviet thesis that the strategic balance of power was changing in favour of the camp of socialism, a greatly exaggerated statement, became more menacing to the West because of its great propaganda and political effect throughout the world. Why Moscow did not build enough missiles, as it could have, to outstrip the U.S. is still unclear. Several reasons may be suggested: Khrushchev was probably unwilling to make the drastic necessary resource allocation changes away from consumer goods. Soviet missiles were so large, construction for them having begun early and therefore based on atomic rather than hydrogen bombs, that the production cost of enough of them to exploit fully the potential missile gap probably seemed prohibitory. (In addition, the necessarily large Soviet rocket thrust, so much superior to its American equivalents, guaranteed further Soviet space successes.) Furthermore, these heavy first-generation missiles, Moscow probably thought, would soon be outdated anyway. In any case, intermediate-range missile installations directed against Western Europe were chosen instead. Almost surely the Chinese were both opposed to and contemptuous of this decision.

The Soviet attainment of atomic and thermonuclear capacity in the late forties had led the Eisenhower administration in the early fifties to order crash development of a massive thermonuclear capacity. Since the U.S. already had the much smaller and lighter hydrogen bomb, its missile programme, contrary to the Soviets', needed much less rocket thrust; it could therefore produce smaller, lighter, and cheaper missiles. Furthermore, the American technological breakthroughs in invulnerable second-strike ICBM delivery systems (the Polaris submarine and the solid-fuel, hardened-site Minuteman), both initiated in the mid-fifties and beginning to come into operation in the early sixties, further worsened the Soviet strategic posture. Even so, in part because of domestic political considerations, the thesis of the " missile gap "—that the Soviets could and therefore presumably would outstrip the U.S. by the early sixties in deliverable thermonuclear capacity—had gained considerable support in the United States. When coupled with American public alarm over the alleged resultant decline in world-wide U.S. prestige, it had led to increased public pressure for effective U.S. countermeasures. Initially this resulted in the installation of a large number of intermediate-range U.S. missiles in England, Italy and Turkey in an attempt to counter the extensive Soviet intermediate-range missile programme. The late 1958 Berlin crisis was another factor favouring American rearmament.

By 1961 the " missile gap," plus the Soviet intensification of the Berlin crisis early that year led the new Kennedy administration sharply to increase U.S. strategic (thermonuclear) and conventional forces, particularly their invulnerable second-strike deterrent capacity, and publicly to make clear this continued and increasing U.S. superiority. Simultaneously, the Soviet first-generation missiles were becoming obsolete; in addition, although less importantly, the years of American U-2 flights had deprived the Soviet Union of their equivalent of the American hardened sites—the secrecy of their missile deployment. The Russians were thus threatened with a drastic increase in American strategic superiority and with a perhaps even more serious consequent loss of the world image of their military power and political prestige, one which would put them at a further disadvantage *vis-à-vis* the Chinese.

By late 1961, therefore, Khrushchev was probably convinced that drastic action was necessary. His long-term objective was to cut down and if possible to reverse the increasing U.S. strategic lead; to do this Soviet resources were reallocated at the end of the year. This was accompanied in September 1961 by the renewal of Soviet atomic testing, which he presumably felt imperative in order to produce lighter thermonuclear warheads and thus switch to lighter and cheaper missiles. The installation of Soviet missiles in Cuba would have accomplished the Soviet short-term objective: when fully operational, they could have destroyed almost all SAC bombers not in the air and thus have drastically cut U.S. second-strike retaliatory capacity. Although the Cubans may have urged Moscow to send the missiles during Raúl Castro's July 1962 visit to Moscow, with the purpose in part to deter a U.S. invasion, the initiative for their emplacement was apparently Soviet. As Castro has since indicated, Soviet objectives were primarily strategic and world-wide: they included: (1) cutting back the U.S. strategic lead, particularly its second-strike capacity, and (2) thus making the U.S. more likely, because of the resultant psychological shock, to submit to further nuclear blackmail, in particular in Berlin.

Yet for Khrushchev, as for Kennedy, political considerations predominated over military ones. The key to the rapid Soviet shifts from aggressiveness in Cuba in October 1962 to the signature of the test ban treaty and the subsequent partial Soviet-American détente must therefore be sought in Khrushchev's policies during the whole post-1957 period, *i.e.*, during his attempt to translate into political gains his missile and space victories. His utilisation of these was but one aspect of his over-all pre-October 1962 expansionist strategy. While continuing his attempts to reduce the risk of thermonuclear war, he was determined to expand Soviet influence, particularly in Central Europe and in the under-developed areas of Asia, Africa, and Latin America. He was encouraged to try not only by his missile and space successes but also by the revolutionary potential of decolonialisation, by his successful recon-solidation of East Europe, and by his domestic economic successes, while Sino-Soviet friction had not yet (in 1957) seriously inhibited his power and manoeuvrability.

Within the context of this Soviet forward strategy Khrushchev in November 1958 initiated the Berlin crisis. He had several objectives in so doing. The minimum one was (1) to force the West out of Berlin, or at least to weaken its position there, thus leading toward his maximum objectives; (2) to undermine the political situation in West Germany with a view toward its ultimate neutralisation; and thus (3) to split the NATO alliance and force the United States out of Europe. Later his unexpected success in Cuba (with Castro becoming pro-Soviet) made the Soviet leader hope that Havana could become the base for Communist revolutions in Latin America.

Yet, as has been outlined above, the political advantage of the Soviet missile successes turned out during the Cuban crisis to be overweighed by the political defeat resulting from the American military response to them. Furthermore, the other Soviet objectives in the forward strategy had not been achieved. Decolonisation in Asia and Africa had produced non-aligned rather than pro-Soviet régimes; the Sino-Soviet rift became progressively more serious, and relatively much more so than the dissension in NATO arising from General de Gaulle's policies and from Western disputes over Berlin; and the economic recovery of West Europe became steadily more impressive than CMEA's, so much so that were it to be translated into military terms, Moscow would deem it a serious danger to Soviet security.

THE TEST BAN TREATY AND THE SINO-SOVIET ATOMIC ISSUE [4]

The Cuban crisis thus became a major watershed in Soviet policy. By early 1963 its effect, together with the intensifying Sino-Soviet

[4] Richard Lowenthal, " The World Scene Transformed," *Encounter*, XXI, 4 (October 1963), pp. 3–10, " The End of an Illusion," *Problems of Communism*, XII, 1 (January–February 1963), pp. 1–9, and " The Rise and Decline of International Communism," *ibid.*, XII, 2 (March–April 1963); Helmut Sonnenfeldt, " Foreign Policy from Malenkov to Khrushchev," *ibid.*, pp. 9–18; Marshall Shulman, " Artificial

rift and Soviet economic problems, notably in agriculture, made Khrushchev decide that a relaxation of tension between Russia and the West was desirable. By June 1963 it must also have been clear to him that any hope of mending Sino-Soviet relations was illusory. He therefore needed to reinforce his image as the champion of peace as a weapon against the Chinese throughout the international Communist movement. Soviet agreement to a partial test ban treaty seemed the best way to do this, the more so because Khrushchev was by then committed not to give the Chinese atomic capacity.

Having decided by mid-1963 to sign a partial test ban treaty with the West as a part of his general strategy of easing tension, Khrushchev was further encouraged to maintain this strategy by the divisive impact of such a signature in the Western alliance, by France's refusal to sign the test ban treaty, and by the development of significant opposition to the signature in West Germany. Finally, given Moscow's domestic economic difficulties and the constantly increasing American strategic lead, the Soviet-American détente resulting from the test ban treaty was also insurance for the Russians against an American attempt to use its increasing superiority to consolidate and extend its gains in the Cuban crisis.

As the Chinese have now revealed and the Russians have not denied, whether Moscow would aid Peking to develop a thermonuclear capacity has been one of the key issues throughout the Sino-Soviet dispute. The initial October 1957 Soviet agreement to do so improved Sino-Soviet relations and prevented the Moscow November 1957 Sino-Soviet discussions from being much worse than they were. But in the late fifties Khrushchev intensified his efforts for a bilateral détente with the United States. China's shift to an extreme leftist course at home and abroad increased China's determination to prevent such a Soviet-American détente and to obtain its own atomic capacity. With Washington's determination to defend Formosa and the off-shore islands, Khrushchev refused to aid the Chinese militarily against the Americans and so the atomic issue became increasingly important for Moscow and Peking. The deterioration of Sino-Soviet and Sino-American relations in 1958 and early 1959, interacting with the improvement of Soviet-American relations, probably induced Khruschev in June 1959 to cancel his offer to Peking of atomic assistance. Whether intended by him as a threat or a sanction, this action further worsened Sino-Soviet relations and must have contributed largely to the Sino-Soviet dispute being made public in early 1960.

Tensions and the Test Ban," *The New Leader*, XLVI, 19 (September 16, 1963), pp. 8–11 ; Zbigniew Brzezinski, " After the Test Ban," *The New Republic*, CXLIX, 9–10 (August 31–September 7, 1963), pp. 18–20.

Yet the fundamental dilemmas of Soviet policy still remained. Too much détente with America could be dangerously reflected in internal pressure for liberalisation and in discontent among the more aggressive elements of international Communism (*e.g.*, Castro) for whose allegiance Khrushchev was bitterly competing with Mao. Khrushchev's centrist, pragmatic response to this dilemma could be seen in late 1963 in his contradictory cultural course at home, and abroad in his alternation of " soft " gestures toward America and (on the surface) toward China with such " hard " moves as the frequent Soviet stoppage of Allied traffic on the Berlin autobahn. His success or failure will be determined by his ability to solve his economic problems at home, by American power and will abroad, and by the success or failure of Mao's bid to replace him, and the Soviet Union, as the predominant power in world Communism.

THE SINO-SOVIET BORDER ISSUE

The Sino-Soviet border issue was referred to by the Chinese for the first time in March 1963, and then only indirectly.[5] Not until September 1963 did Chinese and then Soviet public charges and countercharges appear. Yet available evidence now indicates that their common border was a source of irritation as early as 1958 and had become a serious trouble spot by 1960. This is hardly surprising. Considering the long historical background of Sino-Soviet differences over the border, it would have been strange if the issue had not been revived in the context of the present dispute.

The Tsarist empire acquired what is now the Soviet Far Eastern Maritime Province by treaties forced on the declining Chinese empire in 1858 and 1860. Since that area did not become part of the Chinese empire until the Manchu conquest, it seems doubtful that Peking regards it as an immediate objective of Chinese policy—even though subsequent events have demonstrated that the Chinese are not adverse to keeping the issue open. The situation is more serious in Sinkiang. Here, after having annexed what is now Soviet Central Asia, the Tsarist empire acquired a border strip by military means in the 1860s. Subsequently Russia occupied the Ili valley region from 1871 to 1881 and even retained some of that area by the final settlement in 1881.

The nationality composition of Sinkiang intensified Russo-Chinese hostility over the region. Very few Chinese lived there; the great majority of nomads who roamed the area were Uighurs and, to a much lesser

---

5 " A Comment on the Statement of the Communist Party of the U.S.A.," *People's Daily*, March 8, 1963 (*Peking Review*, VI, 12, March 15, 1963, pp. 58–62). See p. 111, *infra*.

extent, Kazakhs of Turkic origin and Moslem religion, who naturally viewed the Chinese as an imperialistic colonial power. Feelings of kinship bound the Kazakhs to the far more numerous Kazakh population in Russian Central Asia; the Uighurs had fewer ethnic ties across the border, and only sharp pressure from Russians or Chinese could bridge, even temporarily, their mutual distrust. Ethnic and religious irredenta, always a classic cause of frictions between great or small powers, have thus played their familiar role in Sinkiang up to this day.

Geographic considerations were also favourable for Russian influence in Sinkiang. Mountain ranges isolated the province from China, making more accessible to the Russians its western areas, particularly the Ili valley, which is close to the important oil fields at Karamai to the north and at Wusu and Tushantse to the south, and may well be close to the probably existing Sinkiang uranium mines. The Turkestan-Siberian Railway, completed in 1930, further facilitated Soviet economic penetration.

Sinkiang has been free from Russo-Chinese rivalry only when both Russia and China have been weak. Moscow's influence over the warlords of Sinkiang rose during the early 1920s, at a time when the Soviet Union had re-established internal order and again become a Far Eastern power, while the Chinese central government remained weak. Once China was occupied with the war against Japan, Soviet influence grew steadily. In 1937 Stalin demonstrated that he was not willing to surrender this influence, even to the Chinese Communist Party, by vetoing CCP membership for the commander of the province, General Sheng Shih-ts'ai, and having him enrolled in the Soviet Communist Party.

During the 1942–44 period Soviet preoccupation with Nazi Germany and American support of Chiang Kai-shek's régime reversed the Sino-Soviet power relationship, and Chungking regained control of the province. However, economic chaos and local anti-Chinese resentments led to a serious rebellion there in late 1944, probably with Soviet support. The uprising centred in those areas of Sinkiang bordering the Soviet Union. Here an "Eastern Turkestan Republic" was set up which included the Ili valley and the Tushantse oil fields. In mid-1946 a Soviet-sponsored settlement guaranteed the Republic's political and cultural autonomy, leaving the door open to further Soviet economic penetration. Fighting began again in Sinkiang in 1947, again probably at Soviet instigation. The victory of the Chinese Communists in 1949, however, put an end to dominant Soviet influence in the area. Even so, one report indicates that Moscow unsuccessfully suggested to a Chinese nationalist general that he declare Sinkiang independent (and under Soviet influence) in order to keep out Mao's forces.

After the province fell to the Chinese Communists, another Kazakh revolt broke out in western Sinkiang and was not fully suppressed until 1953. From 1950 to 1954 joint Sino-Soviet stock companies permitted Soviet economic influence to continue in the province. These companies were liquidated as a result of the Khrushchev-Bulganin visit to Peking in 1954. Direct Soviet influence in Sinkiang thus presumably ceased. As the strength of Peking grew, its policies (especially after 1957) became more extreme. This caused a corresponding growth of Kazakh dissatisfaction in Sinkiang and thereby increased the attractiveness of the Soviet Union to the Kazakhs.[6]

Recent reports from Soviet and Western sources indicate that trouble began again in western Sinkiang in 1958, when the Chinese " great leap forward " and the people's communes led to economic distress, to general extremist and increasingly anti-Soviet policies, and to enforced sinification of the Turkic peoples. Chinese reports indicate that these troubles continued during 1959, and in 1960 further Soviet and Chinese reports indicate indirectly that some border guard clashes occurred in the Sinkiang and Amur River areas.[7]

We may turn from this briefly sketched background to the Sino-Soviet dispute. First, some general remarks, expanded upon and documented hereafter, on the history of the dispute and the course of Sino-Soviet relations in 1962 and the first ten months of 1963; thereafter some provisional remarks on the larger contours to whose illumination they have contributed.

6 Allen S. Whiting and General Sheng Shih-ts'ai, *Sinkiang: Pawn or Pivot?* (East Lansing: Michigan State Univ., 1958), *passim*; Allen S. Whiting, " Nationality Tensions in Sinkiang," *Far Eastern Survey*, XXV, 1 (January 1956), pp. 8–13; Oleh S. Fedyshyn, " Soviet Retreat in Sinkiang? Sino-Soviet Rivalry and Cooperation, 1950–1955," *American Slavic and East European Review*, XVI, 2 (April 1957), pp. 127–145; Mehnert, *Peking and Moscow*, pp. 269–273; " The Ethnography of Sinkiang and Tibet," *Central Asian Review*, VII, 1 (1959), pp. 84–92, at pp. 84–89; Hong Kong dispatch in *The Times* [London], October 18, 1963 ; and (for the Sinkiang uranium mines) George A. Modelski, *Atomic Energy in the Communist Bloc* (Melbourne: Melbourne University Press, 1959), pp. 181–184.

7 Robert Guillain, " La colonisation chinoise au Sinkiang rencontre une résistance active depuis 1958," *Le Monde*, September 8, 1963; Brian Crozier, " China's Soviet Border Problem," *Forum Service*, August 24, 1963; *Sotsialistikh Kazakhstan* (Alma Ata), summarised in *The New York Times*, October 20, 1963; " The Origin and Development of the Differences Between the Leadership of the CPSU and Ourselves," *People's Daily* and *Red Flag*, September 6, 1963, in *Peking Review*, No. 37, September 13, 1963, pp. 6–23, at p. 14, and Document 10; interview with Bukhara Tyshkanbaev (a Sinkiang Kazakh poet who fled to the Soviet Union) in *Literaturnaya Gazeta*, September 26, 1963; Zunun Taipov (a former Major-General in the Chinese People's Liberation Army, who returned to the Soviet Union in 1960), " On the Other Side of the Barricade," *Kazakhstanskaya Pravda*, September 29, 1963; Usman Mametov (a Uighur who returned to the Soviet Union from Sinkiang in 1959), " I Can't Be Silent!" *ibid*. September 22, 1963; O. Matskevich, " Along the Border," *ibid*. September 24, 1963. (The last three articles are translated in *CDSP*, XV, 38 [October 16, 1963], pp. 16–17, 24.)

NEW LIGHT ON THE SINO-SOVIET DISPUTE UP TO 1962

Recently published Chinese [8] (and to a lesser extent Soviet) [9] documents require some, though not fundamental, revision of the previously generally accepted history of the Sino-Soviet dispute.[10] Revision is mainly necessary in three areas: the 1956–57 period, the atomic issue, and the Sino-Soviet border issue. Limitations of space preclude any detailed treatment of the dispute's history in a book devoted primarily to the most recent period; furthermore, since Moscow and Peking will probably soon publish more hitherto secret documentation, such a treatment would be premature. The following sketch is therefore brief and provisional.

The new material indicates that Sino-Soviet differences first became serious in the spring of 1956,[11] immediately after the Twentieth Congress of the CPSU. They then involved Chinese objections (probably not as strong as Peking now maintains) to Khrushchev's denunciation of Stalin; to his emphasis on peaceful transition to socialism and on peaceful co-existence as the " general line " of the international Communist movement—*i.e.*, to his policy of détente with the United States; to his expansion of Soviet political and economic influence in the " zone of peace " and particularly in India (thus limiting Soviet economic aid to China while building up India against China); and to his failure to consult Mao, who, after the death of Stalin, considered himself the senior living Marxist-Leninist, on any of these decisions. Soviet difficulties in East Europe later that year apparently encouraged the Chinese to exert pressure on Moscow against Soviet intervention in Poland and in favour of it in Hungary (or so the Chinese claim), although such pressure can hardly have been, as the Chinese now maintain, decisive. Having thus tasted some success in intervening in East

[8] Notably " Statement by the Spokesman of the Chinese Government," *People's Daily*, August 15, 1963, and *Peking Review*, VI, 33 (August 16, 1963), pp. 7–15, and Document 7; " The Origin and Development of the Differences Between the Leadership of the CPSU and Ourselves," " by the Editorial Departments of *People's Daily* and *Red Flag*," *People's Daily* and *Red Flag*, September 6, 1963, and *Peking Review*, VI, 37 (September 13, 1963), pp. 6–23, and Document 10; and " The Truth About How the Leaders of the CPSU Have Allied Themselves with India Against China," *People's Daily*, November 2, 1963, and *Peking Review*, VI, 45 (November 8, 1963), pp. 18–27.
[9] Notably the July 14 Soviet " Open Letter," *Pravda*, July 14, 1963, and Document 3, the September 21 Soviet governmental statement, *ibid.* September 21 and 22, 1963, and Document 12.
[10] In particular in Zagoria, *The Sino-Soviet Conflict, passim.*
[11] The Chinese have recently stated that in 1954 they had made clear that they were unenthusiastic about Khrushchev's rapprochement with Tito. See " Is Yugoslavia a Socialist Country?" " by the Editorial Departments of *People's Daily* and *Red Flag*," *People's Daily* and *Red Flag*, September 20, 1963, and *Peking Review*, VI, 39 (September 27, 1963), pp. 14–27, and Document 13, citing and quoting a June 10, 1954, letter from the Chinese to the Soviet Central Committee. *Cf.* Zagoria, *op. cit.*, pp. 58–59.

Europe, the Chinese must have increased their pressure on the Russians, particularly in view of Khrushchev's difficulties after the Hungarian Revolution, and especially towards obtaining an atomic capacity. More importantly, the Soviet missile and sputnik launchings in the late summer and early autumn of 1957 convinced Mao, but not Khrushchev, of Soviet strategic superiority over the United States. Finally, inside China the short-lived " hundred flowers " period had given way in the autumn of 1957, under pressure of a domestic economic crisis, which Peking could not expect to be solved by massive Soviet economic aid, to the ascendancy of the left wing and to a new extremist domestic economic strategy.

On October 15, 1957, the Chinese have now stated, Moscow promised to aid them in obtaining an atomic capacity, a concession which the Russians may well have felt necessary in order to improve the atmosphere for the forthcoming November 1957 Moscow meeting. When one considers what the Chinese have now revealed of the stormy course of the dispute, it would seem doubtful if otherwise the Chinese would have compromised at all with the Russians at the meeting, particularly since Khrushchev had disposed of his own opponents the previous July and was certainly in no mood to capitulate to the Chinese.

For the November 1957 meeting we now have a detailed Chinese account but as yet no Soviet one. Mao, much more impressed than Khrushchev by Soviet strategic gains, felt that Moscow could and should now take much greater risks *vis-à-vis* Washington in order to achieve Chinese objectives in Formosa and the off-shore islands. The Chinese now maintain that the principal issue with the Russians at that meeting was the question of the peaceful transition to socialism and of the Soviet attempt to " impose " it and other conclusions of the Twentieth Congress upon the 1957 Moscow meeting. One may infer that this involved revolutionary strategy and tactics—*i.e.*, the whole of Khrushchev's innovations in foreign policy. The new Chinese material gives considerable detail on the various Soviet and Chinese draft resolutions and mutual concessions at the meeting, and one must now conclude that it saw a serious and essentially indecisive Sino-Soviet confrontation.

The Chinese probably also took a more anti-Yugoslav attitude in November 1957 than did the Russians—and they certainly did so in early 1958. Mao's insistence in November 1957 on the adoption of the formula " the socialist camp headed by the Soviet Union " was thus a more anti-Yugoslav than pro-Soviet one. In 1958 the Chinese also launched their " great leap forward " and the people's communes, which together were a desperate and ultimately unsuccessful attempt at rapid industrialisation and increased agricultural production without the massive economic aid which Moscow must already have denied them.

The communes also represented a Chinese claim to ideological primacy as the creators of a rapid and effective road to communism, particularly for the underdeveloped areas of Asia, Africa, and Latin America. Khrushchev unsuccessfully attempted to prevent these Chinese moves both by private representations and by having the communes ignored in Soviet public communications. In May 1958 Peking, fearing a successful Soviet-American détente, launched an earlier and much more violent assault against Belgrade than did Moscow. Moscow also unsuccessfully attempted, perhaps as a means of pressure, to obtain more military influence in China. The partial Sino-Soviet détente in late 1958 and early 1959 was minimal and short-lived.

By mid-1959, as Khrushchev's intention to work towards a détente with the United States became clear, and as the Chinese in spite of their economic failures refused to retreat from their separate economic, ideological, bloc, and political strategy, Khrushchev decided to force them to do so. In June, presumably both as penalty for the past and as threat for the future, he formally abrogated the Soviet commitment to give China aid in atomic weapons and he had some contact with Defence Minister P'eng Teh-huai and other Chinese leaders who opposed the Chinese extremist course at home and perhaps attacked even Mao himself. This attempt, however, was crushed by Mao at the Lushan Plenum in July and August,[12] and at the beginning of September the Chinese precipitated the first serious border incident with India (according to the Russians, in order to sabotage a Soviet-American détente; according to the Chinese, the Indians precipitated it) whereupon the Russians, in spite of repeated Chinese attempts to prevent them, publicly declared their neutrality on the issue. On September 12 the first over-all Khrushchevian (and thus anti-Chinese) ideological manual, *Osnovy Marksizma-Leniniszma* (*The Foundations of Marxism-Leninism*), the official elaboration and codification for the nuclear age of the Twentieth Congress's ideological innovations, was passed for the press. During Khrushchev's visit to Peking (after his trip to the United States) he tried (the Chinese now state) to persuade Peking to accept a " two Chinas policy "; the Russians retort that he only advocated a peaceful settlement of the Formosa issue.

The Lushan Plenum must thus in retrospect be considered probably the point of no return in Sino-Soviet relations; before it, some at least temporary compromise might still have been possible; after it, both sides, convinced that a break was probable, manoeuvred for position and allies and attempted to place the blame for the break on the other.

[12] See Charles, " The Dismissal of Marshal P'eng Teh-huai."

18

Peking's publication in April 1960 of "Long Live Leninism" brought the Sino-Soviet ideological controversy into the open. Chinese factional activity at the June 1960 WFTU meeting in Peking was its organisational counterpart and the first overt Chinese attempt to detach other Communist parties from Soviet control. That same month at Bucharest, Khrushchev launched a counter-offensive against the Chinese which resulted in violent verbal polemics with the Chinese delegate P'eng Chen. Thereafter Khrushchev recalled Soviet specialists from China, sharply reduced Soviet trade, and unsuccessfully tried to over-throw the pro-Chinese (because anti-Yugoslav) Albanian leadership. The Chinese have recently also accused the Russians of starting trouble along the Sino-Soviet border during this period. Thereafter China supported Albania politically and economically.[13]

The first major attempt to contain, if not to reconcile, the differences was the 81-party meeting in Moscow in November 1960, of which reliable accounts of practically the whole proceedings are now available.[14] The final unanimous communiqué was on balance a Soviet victory, but in fact the violent Sino-Soviet verbal polemics at Bucharest were exceeded at Moscow. The Chinese insisted upon continuing their factional activity in spite of the fact that the overwhelming pro-Soviet majority of parties demanded its cessation; and they proposed a kind of joint Sino-Soviet directorate for the whole movement—i.e., a continuing right of Chinese veto over Soviet policy while refusing to accept a Soviet veto over theirs. The lull which appeared to prevail after the Moscow meeting existed only on the surface. It concealed continuing controversy and increasing but still unsuccessful Soviet efforts to force Albania to capitulate. The false calm was shattered at the Twenty-second CPSU Congress in October 1961, where Khrushchev publicly denounced the Albanians and subsequently broke off diplomatic relations with Tirana. The new CPSU *Programme*, formally approved at this Congress, was in part the Soviet version of the transition to Communism, as opposed to the Chinese people's communes. This in turn was followed

13 See Griffith, *Albania and the Sino-Soviet Rift.*
14 See Griffith, " The November 1960 Moscow Meeting: A Preliminary Reconstruction," which, however, must now be supplemented by Edward Crankshaw, " The Split Between Russia and China," *Atlantic Monthly*, CCII, 5 (May 1963) pp. 60–65 (for speeches by the Latin American, Middle Eastern, Far Eastern and European delegates) and *The New Cold War: Moscow v. Pekin*, pp. 115–135 (for a detailed summary of Teng Hsiao-p'ing's two speeches); the full text of Maurice Thorez's December 15, 1960, report to the PCF CC, in *Problèmes du mouvement communiste international* (Paris: PCF, January 1963), of which the key new passages have been reproduced in *Est & Ouest*, XV (N.S.), 294 (February 16–28, 1963), pp. 4–7, and in JPRS 17, 772, February 21, 1963 (for the issue of " national Communism "); and " The Origin and Development of the Differences Between the Leadership of the CPSU and Our-selves," and Document 10, *op. cit.*, which reprinted part of the text of the September 10, 1960 CCP CC letter concerning the joint directorate.

in November and December 1961 and January 1962 by a new wave of Soviet-inspired anti-Chinese and anti-Albanian polemics and by even more violent Albanian attacks on Khrushchev.[15]

THE ISSUES IN DISPUTE [16]

For a Communist (as for St. Augustine or Calvin) there can be no separation between theory and practice. The Sino-Soviet dispute has therefore until very recently been carried on in public in an almost exclusively ideological context. Yet ideology made pragmatic compromise more difficult, and although it initially slowed down a total Sino-Soviet break, it has by now made it far more likely. The nationalistic, strategic, economic, and organisational differences between Moscow and Peking remained concealed until early 1963, when their emergence provided further confirmation of the now generally accepted techniques for deciphering esoteric Communist communications.[17] Even so, much of the story must still remain surmise and deduction.

Like all good Marxist-Leninists, the Russians and Chinese declare that the most important issue is " the fundamental nature of the present epoch." Moscow declares that " the socialist system is becoming," Peking that " it has become," the fundamental factor in international politics. For the Chinese ours is an " epoch of wars and revolutions "; for Moscow, an epoch of the forthcoming, and largely non-violent, victory of the " world socialist system." The main danger for Communism, Moscow implicitly declares, is " dogmatism and sectarianism " (*i.e.*, Chinese leftist views). Peking retorts that it remains " revisionism " (*i.e.*, the Soviet views).

Moscow has revised traditional Leninist doctrine on certain key ideological issues: it posits a " qualitative " (*i.e.*, decisive) change in the nature and destructiveness of thermonuclear war and a resultant change in the nature of imperialism, whose " sober circles " (*e.g.*, President Kennedy) also realise this and therefore also wish to avoid such a war. Moscow therefore declares that war is no longer inevitable, and that there now exists a possibility of avoiding war before the final victory of socialism and therefore of achieving general and complete disarmament. All these views the Chinese reject, their lip service to the non-inevitability of war notwithstanding.

Moscow uses these views to justify its " general line " of peaceful co-existence: the possibility and necessity of avoiding interstate conventional and thermonuclear wars (but not of " wars of national

---

[15] See Griffith, *Albania and the Sino-Soviet Rift.*
[16] My treatment owes much to Brzezinski's and Dallin's introduction to Dallin, *Diversity in International Communism*, pp. xxv–xxxvii.
[17] See *ibid.* pp. xxxvii–xliv, and references cited therein.

liberation ") *inter alia* by giving priority to the struggle for general and complete disarmament. The Chinese, while accepting peaceful co-existence in theory, declare it a tactic, not a strategy (" general line "), and insist that general and complete disarmament not be given priority over the " national liberation struggle," to which Moscow replies that the two are complementary, not contradictory. In late 1962 the Sino-Indian and Cuban crises and in mid–1963 the test ban treaty provided specific illustrations of differing Soviet and Chinese strategy and tactics on this range of issues.

Turning to clashes of state interests, China accuses the Soviet Union of failing to run sufficient risks in supporting her against the United States, specifically on the Taiwan and Quemoy-Matsu issues. Rather, Peking maintains, Moscow so desires a bilateral Soviet-American détente, as was shown by the Camp David Khrushchev-Eisenhower encounter and more recently by the test-ban treaty, that it will sacrifice for it the legitimate interests of China and of the world Communist revolution. Furthermore, Peking maintains, Moscow, after initially promising to do so refuses to aid China to obtain an atomic weapons capacity. Peking also has clearly implied that Moscow unjustly holds the territory annexed by the Tsars from the Chinese Empire: the Soviet Maritime Provinces, parts of Central Asia, and (as a Soviet sphere of influence) Outer Mongolia, and has declared that the Russians have enticed thousands of Chinese (Kazakhs) over the border for subversive purposes. Finally, Peking declares Moscow supports such pro-American and anti-Chinese states as India. The Russians deny all these charges, declaring that their policy towards Taiwan and their negotiations with the United States are the correct implementation of peaceful co-existence, that the Chinese territorial claims are the purest chauvinism, and that the Chinese have repeatedly violated the Sino-Soviet boundary. In response to the Soviet drive for increased economic integration of the pro-Soviet Communist states, the Chinese stress the necessity for the economic self-sufficiency of each socialist state, a move which the Russians characterise as economic chauvinism and a breach of proletarian internationalism.

Moscow has developed the doctrine of " national democracy " as a transitional phase to socialism in underdeveloped countries and as the more progressive part of the " zone of peace " (the non-aligned world); where it exists the national bourgeoisie, which there plays an " objectively progressive " role, must be given political and economic aid. While not explicitly rejecting this view, Peking takes a much more pessimistic view of the national bourgeoisie and prefers to support Communist parties; it also demands that Soviet economic aid be given to China and not to such " pro-imperialist " national bourgeois states as India.

21

Moscow emphasises the desirability of the peaceful and parliamentary transition to socialism, particularly in Western Europe; Peking, while not rejecting it in principle, argues that it has never occurred and that revolutionary violence must be assumed to be probable and therefore must be prepared for.

Moscow views the " inevitable " world-wide victory of socialism as resulting primarily from peaceful and successful economic competition with capitalism, while Peking insists it can come only through revolutionary struggle. The Chinese place overriding priority on the revolutionary struggle in Asia, Africa, and Latin America—*i.e.*, they favour reliance on the racism and xenophobia of the coloured peoples of the world, a context within which the Russians would have little role to play.

By mid-1963 the Chinese expanded their attack to include many of Khrushchev's main domestic policies: the denigration of Stalin and of the " cult of the personality " and the replacement of the dictatorship of the proletariat by the " all-peoples' state." Flatly and violently rejecting this attack, the Russians repeated their denunciation of the Chinese attempt to " leap over stages " by such measures as the people's communes.

The greatest Chinese challenges to the Soviet Union have been their attempt to bring about the removal of Khrushchev and the Soviet leadership (as Khrushchev had possibly hoped to do with the Chinese leadership in 1959) and displace Soviet ideological and organisational predominance within the international Communist movement. The Chinese support for Albania in 1960 and their penetration and splitting activities in European, Asian and Latin American Communism made clear the world-wide nature of Peking's challenge to Moscow: the Chinese are beginning to set up a new and implicitly racist Communist international.

Although Moscow exchanged its " leading " role for that of a " vanguard," it continues to claim international validity for Soviet pronouncements (*e.g.*, the 20th, 21st and 22nd CPSU Congresses and the CPSU *Programme*), which its supporters term the " general line " of world Communism, and it arrogates to itself the right to determine membership in the international Communist movement, through such measures as its excommunication of the Albanians and its reacceptance of the Yugoslavs.

Moscow founds these claims on its assured majority of parties in the international movement and tries to prohibit Chinese factionalism within it. The Chinese, however, insist that only unanimity can be binding, and that, failing that, they can and will continue to propagate their views until they are able to obtain majority international support

22

for them. Specifically, they blame Moscow (as Moscow blames them) for the Albanian affair; and they declare that the Yugoslavs are imperialist agents and Khrushchev's attempt to reintegrate them into the international movement is another proof of his plot (with the " U.S. imperialists ") against Marxism-Leninism. The Russians reply that, while " serious ideological differences " still exist with Belgrade, Yugoslavia is a socialist country and the differences with it are being gradually overcome.

Finally, on issues of procedure the Chinese consistently maintain that controversial ideological issues should neither be discussed in public nor extended to inter-state relations. Moscow, on the other hand, until recently generally took the initiative in publicising the differences and in (unsuccessfully) applying organisational and economic pressure against Peking.

When in early 1960 Sino-Soviet differences became overt, several factors in the dispute became increasingly clear. In the first place, the Russians (the reformist, stronger, challenged power—like Pope Leo X) were driven towards either forcing the Chinese to cease their ideological and organisational challenge to Soviet leadership or formally expelling them from the international movement. The Chinese (the orthodox, weaker, challenging power—like Luther) wished to remain within the movement, formally loosening its discipline and creating pro-Chinese factions in it. Secondly, as the dispute intensified, Soviet control over previously pro-Soviet parties lessened because Soviet need for their support against Peking increased the possibility for autonomy *vis-à-vis* Moscow. Other parties—Cuba, North Vietnam, Indonesia, North Korea—became " Communist neutralists " who treated Moscow and Peking equally in prestige accorded and space allotted, but who (except for the Cubans) supported the Chinese on the issues of unanimity, Albania, and Yugoslavia. The Chinese consistently increased their influence over the Asian parties; the Asian " Communist neutralists " became increasingly pro-Chinese, the North Koreans the earliest, the North Vietnamese last of all: thereafter only Cuba remained intermittently a true " Communist neutralist."

A third important element stems from the fact that pro-Soviet and pro-Chinese parties can both be divided into moderate and extremist groups. The former, while giving general policy support and organisational loyalty to the senior power, are so committed to the internationalist tradition of Communism and feel their interests so menaced by a total public Sino-Soviet rupture, which would create internal difficulties for them and limit their extent of manoeuvre in the international movement, that they put pressure on the senior partner to prevent it and try to limit the rift by mediating between the two giants. The latter, on the other hand, are divided in their support of extreme positions; the pro-Soviet ones favour an open rupture, the pro-Chinese ones the most extreme anti-Soviet and factionalist Chinese position. The pro-Soviet moderate parties are the Polish, Hungarian, Rumanian, Italian, Belgian, British, Scandinavian and Indian. (All of these except the Rumanian are also moderate in their domestic lines; and the Rumanian desire for more autonomy from Moscow is in part caused by their domestic Stalinism.) The extremist ones are the French, East German, Czechoslovak, and Bulgarian. The pro-Chinese moderates (now that the "Communist neutralist" category no longer exists in Asia) are the North Vietnamese, Indonesians, Japanese, and probably still the North Koreans; the pro-Chinese extremists are the Albanians, Malayans, Burmese, Thai, and New Zealand parties.

Finally, there is a limited community of interest between the pro-Soviet and the pro-Chinese moderates. Neither wants a total rupture although each supports the position of its senior partner on policy (as opposed to organisational) issues involved. Three times during 1962–63, at the beginning of 1962, the beginning of 1963, and in the autumn of 1963, these smaller parties played either substantial or (in the case of the French or New Zealand, for example) "surrogate" roles in attempting to influence Moscow and Peking. The line-up within the categories (except for the Asian "Communist neutralists" becoming pro-Chinese moderates) remained constant.

SINO-SOVIET RELATIONS 1962–63

Primarily, Sino-Soviet relations during the last two years encompassed another of the many failures to contain or even diminish the temperature of the controversy, followed, as also so often before, by signs of a slight détente. The first point to be made about this failure and the subsequent escalation is that they were not a result of the Sino-Indian and Cuban crises or the test ban treaty. On the contrary, they were well under way before these crises. Nevertheless, they doubtless greatly heightened the speed and extent of the escalation, and without them, especially the Soviet withdrawal in Cuba, Sino-Soviet relations would probably be quite different and considerably less in shreds than they are today.

The second point to be made is that the relative surface calm in Sino-Soviet relations during the spring and summer of 1962 (as during the same period in 1961) concealed an actual worsening. The Sino-Soviet agreement in the spring of 1962, reached largely under pressure from other Communist parties, was substantially only on the suspension of public polemics. Not only were the polemics immediately transferred to the more esoteric level (esoteric, that is, to a non-Communist, but hardly to the trained Marxist-Leninist), but both Moscow and Peking continued organisational as well as ideological moves which could not help but worsen Sino-Soviet relations. The Soviets publicly intensified their rapprochement with Yugoslavia and presumably undertook other unpublicised anti-Chinese acts as well; the Chinese publicly continued their support of Albania and their pressure on India. Finally, in September, the Chinese for the first time declared that capitalism had been restored in Yugoslavia, and the Albanians demanded that a line be drawn between the true Marxists-Leninists [*i.e.* the Chinese, the Albanians and their allies], and the " modern revisionists " [Khrushchev and his supporters], and to specialists the dispute was on again in earnest, a fact which became clear to the world when the Chinese invaded India.

We now know that one of the Chinese conditions in early 1962 for an over-all Sino-Soviet détente was that Khrushchev should take the initiative to go to an Albanian Canossa, hurling anathemas at Tito *en route*. Such a Soviet humiliation would demonstrate to other parties, firstly, that Moscow could be defied (as Tirana had) with impunity, or, as the Chinese self-righteously put it, that Moscow *nolens volens* endorsed " genuine equality " between Communist parties; secondly, that Moscow allowed Chinese factional activity to become institutionalised and permanent, and that, on the other hand, Khrushchev would never make up with Yugoslavia [*i.e.* the United States]. One of Khrushchev's conditions, on the other hand, was that Albania capitulate, with exactly the opposite consequences.

After the Sino-Indian and Cuban crises the Sino-Soviet dispute turned into an actual schism and moved ever closer toward an open, public, total break. The use of surrogates as targets (Albania by Moscow and Yugoslavia by Peking) gave way first to quoting explicitly anti-Soviet or anti-Chinese attacks by them and by others (North Korea quoted by Peking, the French Communist Party quoted by Moscow), and finally to increasingly broad, explicit Sino-Soviet polemics.

Furthermore several new issues appeared, some for the first time, others much more explicitly and completely, in the public controversy. The Chinese publicly stated their demand for a Soviet approach to Albania. The Russians publicly re-established full party relations with the Yugoslavs, whose internal problems made them anxious to accept the offer, and thus officially recognised the existence and permissibility of various ideological roads to socialism. The Chinese challenged the totality of post-Stalin Soviet domestic policies. The activity of the majority Dange faction of the Communist Party of India (CPI) became a matter of public Sino-Soviet controversy and was labelled by Peking, as it had earlier labelled the Albanian and Yugoslav issues, a decisive criterion of " revolutionary Marxist-Leninist orthodoxy." The Russians first implicitly, then clearly charged the Chinese with an attempt to remove Khrushchev, to which Peking replied with increasingly clear calls for his removal. The Chinese publicly raised the issue of the Tsarist annexations from the Chinese Empire of territory in the present Soviet Far Eastern Maritime provinces and Soviet Central Asia. The Chinese also publicly charged the Russians with the 1960 withdrawal of specialists from China and the cutting down of Soviet economic aid and trade, and they undertook increasingly extensive reorientation of their trade to the West. They tried hard, and with varying success, to pull Castro closer to them, using his fury over the Soviet missile withdrawal from Cuba and his fear of a Soviet-American détente. They gained considerable influence in the Japanese, North Vietnamese, and Indonesian Communist parties, and they consolidated their predominant influence in North Korea. They gained increasingly predominant influence in the Afro-Asian solidarity organisations and made quite clear their intent to concentrate on the coloured and underdeveloped areas of the world; and within this context, finally, they began organisational steps for detaching Communist parties and front organisations from Soviet organisational and ideological influence and control, or, failing this, splitting them and setting up new parties under Peking's aegis.

All this was accompanied by a rising demand in early 1963 from other Communist parties for another attempt at Sino-Soviet détente. The Chinese reiterated their demand for another meeting of parties from all over the world, where they could reasonably hope to make considerable hay among small radical Communist parties from underdeveloped areas. The Russians, on the other hand, wanted at most a bilateral meeting but preferred first to stage in late 1962 and early 1963 a series of five European Communist congresses which culminated in the Chinese delegate being hissed and booed down in East Berlin in January 1963, an incident which, as Peking soon made clear, it would neither forgive nor forget. But attempts at mediation continued, and not only from such relative neutrals as Ho Chi Minh and Castro, who had much to lose and little to gain by an open split; the pro-Soviet rightists, like Gomulka and Togliatti, and quite possibly Kádár as well (although not Tito—he had the most of all to gain from a split) feared that an open break would limit their new-found and utilised manoeuvrability *vis-à-vis* the Soviet Union, which particularly needed them against the Chinese. Such archaic Stalinists as the French Communists were significant as premature indicators of what Soviet positions actually were; *i.e.*, they, but not Moscow declared that dogmatism was now a greater danger than revisionism— just the contrary of the 1960 Moscow Declaration, and Moscow immediately quietly reprinted it. Rumania, whose régime could hardly be called reformist, profited perhaps the most of all; only within the context of the Sino-Soviet dispute, where even Bucharest was essential in the Soviet sponsored anti-Chinese ranks, could the Rumanians dare continually, and to date successfully, to refuse to submit to Soviet pressure for complete economic integration of Eastern Europe and the consequent abandonment of Bucharest's own extensive industrialisation programme in favour of continued Rumanian specialisation in raw material production.

These attempts at mediation, plus the mutual Soviet and Chinese interest in avoiding the blame for an open rupture, finally resulted in early July 1963 in a Sino-Soviet party meeting. It was clear before it convened, however, that the increasingly hostile exchange of letters between Peking and Moscow which had preceded it had already made it most unlikely that Sino-Soviet relations would improve; Khrushchev's expressed willingness to sign a partial atomic test ban treaty with the West made its failure more certain. The meeting was accompanied by a series of violent Sino-Soviet polemics and deterioration of state relations as well as by the successful conclusion of the test ban negotiations with Washington and London; and its publicly inconclusive end could not conceal, as immediately subsequent events proved, that it had, as the Chinese said, brought Sino-Soviet relations " to the verge of an open split." The Chinese thereafter proceeded to charge the Russians openly with attempts at splitting and overthrowing the Chinese leadership, reneging on their promise to give atomic weapons to China, enticing Chinese citizens from Sinkiang into the Soviet Union and open alliance with Kennedy to prevent China's obtaining atomic weapons; the Russians replied in an equally violent fashion, denouncing the Chinese as atomic warmongers, violators of the Soviet border, neo-Trotskyites, and splitters. In early October 1963 it even seemed that Moscow was seriously considering the excommunication of the Chinese at an international Communist meeting. But the opposition of the pro-Soviet moderate parties to this Draconian measure was too great, and by November Moscow was reportedly again negotiating with Peking with a view toward resuming the bilateral Sino-Soviet discussion which had broken off in July.

Conclusions

How have the events of 1962 and 1963 changed one's general picture of the origins, course, and prospects of the Sino-Soviet dispute? In the first place, as the dispute has become a rift and all but an open break, and particularly since the Chinese and the Russians have publicly raised the Sino-Soviet border issue and that of Chinese atomic weapons, one becomes increasingly aware of how, particularly in the atomic age, the interests of any strong Chinese state and any strong Russian state must and do conflict. Their common boundaries are too long, their historic hostility has been too ancient and too great, and the Chinese have over the last three hundred years lost too much territory to Russia and to Outer Mongolia for Sino-Soviet comity to be natural or permanent. Within a generation the Soviet Union has become one of the two atomic super-powers; and within fifteen years China, for a century prostrate before internal disunity and external intervention, has again become the most powerful state in Asia. Need one wonder that Sino-Soviet relations have deteriorated?

Furthermore, the Soviet attitudes toward the United States and toward India are unacceptable to any strong Chinese régime: the former because China, unlike the Soviet Union, has an irredenta, Formosa, and an area of ambition, Asia, which Washington prevents it from conquering; and the Soviet Union because not only the whole Soviet strategy toward underdeveloped areas but also its fear of total Chinese predominance in Asia impel it to maintain good relations with India. Finally, the increase in Soviet power together with Khrushchev's flexible and aggressive foreign policy has made Moscow seek to expand its influence in underdeveloped areas, while its vulnerability to superior American strategic power has required it to substitute economic aid for military risk in seeking this goal. The amount of economic aid required to give China anywhere near what she needs is in any case out of the question for the Soviet Union; but Khrushchev's economic aid programme to underdeveloped countries has made Soviet aid to China even less than it could have been.

For Moscow as for Washington the operation and the power base of its alliance system have been outmoded by changed reality. Neither China nor Western Europe was either as powerful or as ambitious when the Sino-Soviet alliance and NATO were established as they are now. Thus in East and West economic and military reality are ahead of alliance structure and doctrine. Furthermore the nature of atomic weapons and the difficulty of their control by an alliance make this problem still worse: for Mao (like de Gaulle) does not feel that Khrushchev (Johnson) should be allowed to determine Chinese (French) fate.

Communist ideology intensifies the clash of Sino-Soviet national interests. Marxist-Leninist ideology can cope neither with nationalism, the most potent force of our times, nor with the racist xenophobia of much of the coloured majority of the world's population. It cannot cope with an economically developed country as the Soviet Union to a large extent now is. A messianic, pre-nationalist creed applicable at best, and attractive to a traditional society in the initial stages of rapid industrialisation and modernisation, it is quite incapable of encompassing present Soviet and Chinese—to say nothing of Italian and Albanian—reality. Furthermore, it requires a " principled " (*i.e.*, a totally explained) treatment of every difference, thus making pragmatic compromise the more difficult. Finally, while Khrushchev has tried (with indifferent success) to revitalise Communist ideology at home, his own pragmatism abroad has forced him first in 1960 to abandon the Soviet " leading role " in favour of only Soviet ideological leadership, and then in 1962 to relativise even this (and inevitably thus eventually to erode it) in order to contain within his Soviet " socialist commonwealth " such deviant parties as the Yugoslav and Polish. On the other hand, the enormous increase in Soviet power has brought with it an élite and popular Soviet chauvinism which makes Soviet imperial forbearance in practice the more difficult, while growing Chinese power plus Peking's resentment over the level of Soviet economic and atomic aid has made Peking determined to challenge Moscow's control of the international Communist movement. What Marx would have called the base of Sino-Soviet relations is now far removed from its superstructure and a true Marxist can only consider the Sino-Soviet rift a qualitative leap backward.

The more one reviews the developments of the past eighteen months and the more one reflects on the Soviet cancellation of atomic aid to China in June 1959 and the circumstances of the removal of Marshal P'eng Teh-huai at the Lushan Plenum in August of the same year, the more one thinks that the Sino-Soviet dispute was probably already then irreparable. The total failure of Soviet attempts to influence or subvert the Chinese leadership, so stubbornly pursued despite Moscow's previous unsuccessful attempts with Hebrang and Žujović in 1948 in Belgrade and with Belishova and Tashko in Tirana in 1960, could hardly have been soon forgiven by Mao or permanently accepted by Khrushchev. In all three instances, as Richard Lowenthal has pointed out, Moscow failed primarily because the Chinese, Yugoslav, and Albanian party leaderships had never been completely controlled by the Soviet Union, and their leaders, Mao, Tito, and Hoxha, had been able not only to maintain their own personal power but must have been determined if necessary to defy Moscow for some time before they made the final decision to do so.

By 1960, therefore, the Chinese were probably determined not to come to any agreement with the Soviet Union as long as Khrushchev was at its head. But Khrushchev probably equally feels that there can be no agreement as long as the present Chinese leadership is in control; and in any case have not the fundamental state interests of the Soviet Union and of China diverged so much that no lasting agreement is by now likely—the more so since the Chinese have now repudiated

Moscow's ideological leadership (*i.e.*, denied its legitimate claim to lead world Communism) and staked out this claim for the leadership themselves.

Be that as it may, and remembering the rapid change in Soviet-Yugoslav relations as soon as Stalin died, it would probably be correct to conclude that the two most important factors in Sino-Soviet relations in the near future will be the passing from the scene of Khrushchev and Mao. The other great unknowns are, first, how long China can go without Soviet (or other) aid in such crucial areas as spare parts for tanks, jet fighters, and the other instruments of modern war; and, second, when China will acquire at least a nominal atomic capacity, and what the effect of that will be on Moscow, Washington, and the already fearful Asian states.

Yet even so one should still beware of predicting an inevitable, total and above all a permanent Sino-Soviet break. Marxist-Leninist ideology has already shown itself remarkably able to preserve ritualistic unity amid actual schism; and the acquisition of a Chinese atomic capacity would even more deter the Soviet Union, as Soviet atomic capacity does China, from any military sanctions to change the situation. Furthermore, in the near future both Moscow and Peking still have common and powerful enemies: the United States and its Western allies. Yet these factors have existed since at least 1949, and only in 1960 were most specialists on Communism prepared to admit that Sino-Soviet relations were anywhere nearly as bad as we now know they were for some years before.

There is almost always one vital element missing in the public record of Communist developments: human personality. Yet in regard to those rare moments about which we know something near to the whole picture (the Polish October, the Hungarian Revolution, the Moscow meeting in November 1960 of the 81 Parties), it becomes clear, as it should always have been assumed, that the personalities of Communist leaders, like the accidents of history, play a major and often a decisive role. It would be probably prudent, therefore, when reflecting on Sino-Soviet relations, to remember Edward Gibbon's verdict on the schism between Rome and Constantinople:

> . . . Bigotry and national aversion are powerful magnifiers of every object of dispute; but the immediate cause of the schism of the Greeks may be traced in the emulation of the leading prelates, who maintained the supremacy of the old metropolis, superior to all, and of the reigning capital, inferior to none, in the Christian world . . .[18]

[18] *Decline and Fall of the Roman Empire*, Chap. LX.

Part II

RUSSIA AND CHINA TO THE BRINK

1. Public Lull and Esoteric Controversy: February–August 1962

IN the analysis of a prolonged and largely esoteric controversy like the Sino-Soviet dispute proper periodisation is very important. The Soviet counter-attack against the Chinese challenge, beginning with the June 1960 Peking and Bucharest confrontations, culminated in the November 1960 Moscow meeting. It was succeeded in early and middle 1961 by an apparent lull, which concealed a continuing deterioration in Soviet-Albanian and, therefore, in Sino-Soviet relations and culminated at the October 1961 Twenty-Second CPSU Congress. The Sino-Soviet dispute then continued to worsen until March 1962; thereafter another apparent lull set in.[1]

The immediate post-Twenty-Second Congress escalation of the Sino-Soviet dispute proceeded on three levels: intensified but still esoteric, or veiled, Sino-Soviet polemics, more outspoken " surrogate " polemics (the Soviets attacking the Albanians and the Chinese attacking the Yugoslav " modern revisionists "; the Soviets reprinting anti-Chinese comments by " fraternal parties " and the Chinese reprinting the Albanian diatribes against the CPSU),[2] and direct public ideological controversy in international Communist front organisations.

Since this was a period still dominated by the Soviet counter-attack against the Chinese, the major intensification of esoteric and surrogate polemics was from Moscow. The Soviet pronouncements,[3] always more extreme when directed against the Albanians than in their esoteric anti-Chinese versions, ran the gamut of the themes of the dispute:

---

[1] Zagoria, *op. cit.*, pp. 288–383; Griffith, *Albania*, pp. 35–150; Dallin, *Diversity in International Communism*, pp. 1–258.

[2] For the late 1961 Sino-Soviet reprinting of direct attacks on each other by fraternal parties, see Griffith, *Albania*, pp. 112–118 and the detailed summary in Dallin, *op. cit.*, p. 212, n. 3, and pp. 220–222, nn. 4, 5. This practice ceased in January 1962, to be resumed in the late autumn.

[3] Cited in Griffith, *Albania*, p. 115 *et seq.* and documented in Dallin, *op. cit.*, pp. 605–647.

peaceful co-existence as the general line of the world Communist movement until the final victory of socialism (Khrushchev's Twenty-First Congress thesis), world-wide economic competition between socialism and capitalism as a form of intensification of the international class struggle, the necessity of Soviet aid for the transition to socialism and communism, the observance by all parties of decisions determined jointly rather than unanimously, *i.e.*, the November 1960 Soviet position on factionalism,[4] the international significance of CPSU pronouncements, notably the Twentieth Congress and the new Party Programme (with particular reference to the concept of the all-people's party and state), the importance of neutrals and neutralism, and the bourgeois nationalist origin of dogmatism, *i.e.*, the nationalist nature of the Chinese deviation.

The Chinese replies, since they were made primarily through their predictably violent Albanian mouthpieces, reiterated Peking's 1960 ideological and policy positions and added the Albanian " exposé " of Moscow's behaviour in party and state relations with Tirana.[5] However, in another indication of Peking's defensive posture and concentration on the procedural issue (opposition to public unilateral censure of any fraternal party,[6] the most favourable posture for it to assume) China also reprinted, but less extensively, Soviet and pro-Soviet attacks on Albania.

The December 1961 international Communist meetings of the World Federation of Trade Unions (WFTU) and World Peace Council (WPC) witnessed a direct Sino-Soviet confrontation.[7] These meetings also included a largely unsuccessful attempt by the Italian Communists (and Nenni Socialists) to widen the extent of international affiliation and internal autonomy of national trade union peace council units, a policy which the Italians continued to pursue thereafter. At the Stockholm WPC meeting the Chinese and their allies unprecedentedly voted against the final resolution, on the issue of the relative priority of disarmament over national liberation.[8] They were supported by some African and

4 Griffith, " The November 1960 Moscow Meeting: A Preliminary Reconstruction," *op. cit.*
5 The Chinese reprinted *inter alia* the complete text of Hoxha's November 7, 1961, speech on November 16, 1961, in *People's Daily*. See also " Holding Aloft the Marxist-Leninist Revolutionary Banner of the Moscow Statement," *People's Daily*, December 1, 1961 (*Peking Review*, IV, 49 [December 8, 1961], and Dallin, *op. cit.*, pp. 212–220) and " New Year's Greeting," *People's Daily*, January 1, 1961 (*Survey of China Mainland Press* [SCMP] [Hong Kong: U.S. Consulate-General] 2653, January 8, 1962, pp. 1–6, and Dallin, *op. cit.*, Doc. 33, pp. 243–248).
6 This was the explicit objection expressed by Chou En-lai in his speech to the Soviet Twenty-Second Party Congress following Khrushchev's denunciation of Albania. (*Peking Review*, IV, 43 [October 27, 1961], p. 9.)
7 Griffith, *Albania*, pp. 122–129; for documentation: Dallin, *op. cit.*, pp. 224–234.
8 For commentaries on the WPC meeting, see " Letter from the French Communist Party to the Central Committee of the Chinese Communist Party," January 24, 1962 (JPRS 17,772, February 21, 1963, pp. 28–31); " Whom Do N. Khrushchev's Views

Latin American delegates in another indication of the polycentric rather than bipolar nature of the dispute.

From early spring to September 1962, however, the trend seemed reversed: a significant détente in the Sino-Soviet dispute appeared to develop.[9] Soviet attacks against Hoxha and Shehu [10] and Albanian attacks against Khrushchev [11] by name ceased. The Chinese had previously stopped reprinting anti-Soviet Albanian attacks; the East European states renewed their trade agreements with Albania; Sino-Soviet exchanges of delegation resumed; a new, albeit far from extensive, Sino-Soviet trade agreement was signed; Sino-Soviet mutual press reports and public assertions of friendship and support became more extensive; esoteric polemics, at least on the Soviet side, declined sharply and the Chinese Ambassador to the Soviet Union returned to Moscow after a prolonged absence.[12] The Western press devoted much less attention to Sino-Soviet relations, and in the West the impression grew that the controversy, if not solved, had at least been successfully contained.

A cessation of polemics, as a preliminary to bilateral conversations to prepare for an international Communist meeting, was proposed in January 1962 (as only became public a year later) by the North Vietnamese Party [13] and in February by the New Zealand one.[14] Other apparently similar proposals were made by the Communist parties of Indonesia, Sweden, and Great Britain. (All five of these parties were presumably motivated in part by their fear of the disruptive effect in

and Actions Serve? " *Zëri i Popullit*, March 2, 1962 (also in Griffith, *Albania*, Document 25), and an interview with one of the Italian delegates in *L'Unità*, December 23, 1961.

[9] Griffith, *Albania*, pp. 143–145; Dallin, *op. cit.*, pp. 650–652.

[10] The last Soviet attack on Hoxha and Shehu by name was on March 16, with the exception of one Radio Moscow broadcast in English to South-East Asia, May 10, 11, 12, 1962, 1100 GMT. See also the attack on Hoxha and Shehu in George Kar, " The Socialist Revolution—Peaceful and Non-Peaceful," *World Marxist Review*, V, 5 (May 1962), pp. 28–35, at p. 34, n. 10 (passed to the press, Russian edition, April 10, 1962).

[11] The last one was " Crocodile Tears," *Zëri i Popullit*, April 13, 1962.

[12] Liu Hsiao, Chinese Ambassador to the Soviet Union, attended a meeting to celebrate the 125th anniversary of the birth of Tu Fu, China's great Tang Dynasty poet, in Moscow on April 19, 1962. NCNA in English from Moscow April 19, 1962 (SCMP 2726, April 27, 1962, pp. 42–43). See Dallin, *op. cit.*, pp. 652–653. Yet at the February 1962 Afro-Asian Writers' Conference in Cairo Sino-Soviet differences were apparently still sharp and the Chinese reportedly prevented East European observers from speaking. See Sajjad Zaheer, " Afro-Asian Writers' Movement And Its Present Problems," *New Age*, October 13, 1963.

[13] Statement of Vietnamese Workers' Party (VWP) [Lao Dong] CC, February 10, 1963, in VNA in English to Europe and Asia, February 10, 1963, 1215 GMT (BBC, *Summary of World Broadcasts*, BBC/FE/1173/C/1–3, February 12, 1963). For background on VWP, see Dallin, *op. cit.*, pp. 395–401; P. J. Honey, *Communism in North Vietnam* (Cambridge, Mass.: M.I.T., 1963); and the special issue on North Vietnam of *The China Quarterly*, No. 9, January–March 1962.

[14] " Fighting Monopoly in New Zealand and Throughout the World," *People's Voice* (Auckland), January 23, 1963; reprinted in *People's Daily*, February 16, 1963; excerpts: NCNA in English to Asia and Europe, February 16, 1963, 0310 GMT (BBC/FE/1178/C/1–2, February 18, 1963).

their ranks of a Sino-Soviet split, but the New Zealand one, a pro-Chinese extremist party, acted primarily under Chinese inspiration, the Swedish and British, both pro-Soviet moderates, primarily under Soviet, but also to avoid a total rupture and the North Vietnamese and Indonesian, then " Communist neutralists," under both.) A Soviet letter of February 22 proposed an end to polemics but demanded that the Chinese abandon their " special stand " and their support of Albania.[15] (Moscow clearly had every reason to stop the Chinese and Albanian polemics; it could afford to rely on organisational rather than ideological weapons.) Peking stated in March 1963 that on April 7, 1962, a Chinese Central Committee letter to the Soviet Central Committee " explicitly proposed " that an international Communist meeting be called and listed five points as conditions for such a meeting :

(1) All parties in the dispute should undertake " steps, however small," to " improve the atmosphere and prepare the conditions " for such a meeting.

(2) China supports the North Vietnamese proposal that " public attacks should cease."

(3) " Where needed," " certain " parties should hold " bilateral or multilateral talks to exchange opinions "—*i.e.*, Peking accepted in principle the holding of preparatory Sino-Soviet conversations, subject to negotiation regarding details, including points (2) and (4).

(4) Moscow and Tirana should " both take positive steps " to remove their differences and restore " normal relations," and, in this respect, " it seems necessary for the Soviet comrades to take the initiative "—*i.e.*, because Khrushchev first publicly attacked the Albanians, he should be the one to go to Canossa—a most difficult condition for him to accept.

(5) A revelation of a hitherto unpublished decision of the November 1957 Moscow multi-party meeting: the CPSU " is responsible " for

---

15 CCP CC to CPSU CC, March 9, 1963, *People's Daily*, March 14, 1963, *Peking Review*, VI, 12 (March 22, 1963), pp. 6–8, and CPSU CC to CCP CC, March 30, 1963, *Pravda*, April 3, 1963, and Document 1; and " The Origin and the Development of the Differences Between the Leadership of the CPSU and Ourselves," *People's Daily* and *Red Flag*, September 6, 1963, *Peking Review*, VI, 37 (September 13, 1963), pp. 6–23 (at p. 18); and Document 10. The Swedish CP proposed such a meeting, preceded by CPSU-CCP bilateral talks, in a January 10, 1962, letter to the Central Committees of the CPSU and CCP which criticised the Chinese line at the December 1961 Stockholm WCP meeting; both replied " in the affirmative." (Hilding Hagberg [Swedish CP Chairman], " The Experience and Tasks of the Communist Party of Sweden," *World Marxist Review*, VI, 10 [October 1963], pp. 17–22, at p. 21.) I have found no documentation on the contents of the Indonesian and British proposals; they are alluded to as " suggestions for a conference of fraternal parties " in the March 30, 1963, CPSU CC letter. That the New Zealand CP was not mentioned in the Soviet letter indicates clearly that its letter was far from neutral. For background, see Dallin, *op. cit.*, pp. 549–567 (Indonesia), p. 534 (Swedish), pp. 536–537 (British), and, for the episode itself and trips of Soviet delegations probably connected with it, pp. 651–652.

convening multi-party meetings, " after consultation with the fraternal parties " (*i.e.*, according to Peking's view, with the agreement of the Chinese).[16]

This April 7 Chinese letter had probably been preceded by still unpublicised Sino-Soviet discussions, which resulted in the virtual end in late March of Soviet-Albanian polemics. Moscow stated in February 1963 that it replied to this Chinese letter on May 31, 1962, again endorsing the proposals for an international conference, but by implying that, like the 1957 and 1960 ones, it should be concerned with serious changes in the international situation and " appropriate tactics " for it— *i.e.*, to revise the 1960 Declaration—they made clear their refusal to make concessions to Peking on any of the substantive or organisational issues. In any case, the subsequent intensification of the Soviet rapprochement with Yugoslavia and the reorganisation of the Council for Mutual Economic Aid (CMEA) indicate that the Russians agreed only to mutual cessation of open polemics and refused to go to any Albanian Canossa. Peking declared in September 1963 that the Russians demanded in the letter that " the Albanian comrades abandon their own stand " as a precondition for the convocation of an international meeting.[17]

Thus the dispute had neither been settled nor contained; the contestants had only decided that it be carried on less publicly. In January and February both had given exhaustive coverage in five areas to the ideological and policy issues in dispute, and thereafter the Soviet Union made clear on occasion its continued rejection of Peking's theses.[18] Being the stronger and ideologically the more moderate participant in the dispute, Moscow had the advantage in organisational rather than ideological moves: Soviet superior power made the former easy, while the Soviet ideological position, like that of all " reformists " in doctrinaire movements, was much less favourable. Moscow's objectives were twofold: to force Peking to bow to its will and to abandon its organisational and ideological challenge to Soviet leadership of the camp; and to unseat Hoxha, whose régime would then collapse, thus providing to the Communist world a visible symbol of Soviet victory. Success in the first

16 CCP CC letter to CPSU CC, March 9, 1963; *People's Daily*, March 14, 1963, and *Peking Review*, No. 12 (March 22, 1963), pp. 6–8.
17 The May 31 Soviet letter is mentioned in the letter of the central committee of the Soviet Communist Party to the central committee of the Chinese Communist Party, February 21, 1963, in *Peking Review*, No. 12 (March 22, 1963), pp. 8–10; for its contents see letter of the central committee of the Soviet Communist Party to the central committee of the Chinese Communist Party.
18 F. Burlatsky, " Soviet All Peoples' State," *Pravda*, April 5, 1962, and S. Titarenko, " The Unity of Socialist Patriotism and Proletarian Internationalism," *Politicheskoe Samoobrazovanie*, March 1962, pp. 17–27.

required increased political and economic pressure; this the Soviets presumably exerted—without success. The overthrow of Hoxha, internal subversion having failed in 1960, could certainly be aimed toward, and Moscow's general policy furthered, by intensifying the Soviet rapprochement with Yugoslavia.

These Soviet organisational moves were not notably expressed in ideological terms; indeed, they were clearly contrary to previous Soviet ideological commitments. The Soviet rapprochement with Yugoslavia, ostensibly only on the state level, had clear implications for party rapprochement as well and was thus in direct contradiction to the 1960 Moscow Declaration. The tacit exclusion of Albania from the Warsaw Pact and CMEA coincided with the reorganisation of CMEA to include Outer Mongolia and presumably to consider restoring Yugoslavia's observer status. These moves, only in part publicly acknowledged and not at all ideologically justified,[19] in reality represented the Soviet military and economic adjustment to the actual political relationships. Indeed, the CMEA membership changes marked the creation on the economic level of a Soviet, as opposed to a Sino-Soviet, group of parties in power, and therefore were a major new step in the intensification of the Sino-Soviet dispute.

China responded to this intensified Soviet counter-attack primarily with esoteric ideological polemics in which China was strong. The Chinese support of Albania also continued and, along with Hoxha's and Shehu's determination, prevented Moscow from undermining the leadership of its defiant Balkan ex-satellite. However, the Chinese (and Albanian) propaganda response to the Soviet moves about CMEA and Yugoslavia was curiously limited in length and intensity.

The same cannot be said for the Chinese ideological polemics, which from February through May were longer, more comprehensive, and more esoteric than ever. With the exception of a retort to the Yugoslav ideologist Edvard Kardelj for his anti-Chinese pamphlet *Socialism and War*, they were cast in the framework of historical essays on the sins of previous revisionists: Bernstein, Kautsky, and the Economists (pre-

---

[19] Communiqué of the Conference of Representatives of the Communist and Workers' Parties of Countries Participating in the Council for Mutual Economic Aid, *Pravda*, June 9, 1962, and Warsaw Pact Declaration, *ibid.*, June 10, 1962. The non-participation of Albania in both organisations had been indicated months earlier (D. I. Medvedev, " From Dogmatism in Theory to Adventurism in Politics," *Izvestiya*, February 4, 1962). According to the Soviet view Albania officially broke off participation in CMEA after the Twenty-Second Soviet Communist Party Congress held in October 1961. See statement of Nikolai Fadeyev, secretary-general of CMEA, at a press conference in Bucharest, *The Times* (London), December 24, 1962. Albania, however, protested vigorously against its exclusion from the June 1962, Moscow meetings of CMEA and the Warsaw Pact (*Zëri i Popullit*, June 6, 1962, and Griffith, *Albania*, p. 146, and Documents 28 and 29 therein).

1917 Russian opponents of Lenin).[20] (One cannot help being impressed by the extensively detailed and documented, albeit personalised, historical research that went into them.) Although they represented a new apogee in Sino-Soviet polemics, at first they went almost unnoticed outside the Communist world, largely because, unlike the 1960 articles on the 90th anniversary of Lenin's birth " Long Live Leninism! " and others), they were not transmitted abroad by the Chinese in Western languages. (Their publication in Chinese alone was probably also a part of the previous minimal Sino-Soviet agreement.)

These articles were of great substantive importance. They reiterated the Chinese views on foreign policy expressed in " Long Live Leninism! " and went beyond them to charge the Soviet leadership, by implication, with outright and total ideological revisionism. The first article [21] attacked the founder of modern ideological revisionism, Edward Bernstein, as a surrogate apparently for both Tito and Khrushchev. The second article, against Kardelj,[22] although it did not cast him as a surrogate for Khrushchev, had direct ideological implications for Moscow. The third [23] was directed against the orthodox German Social Democratic ideologist Karl Kautsky as a surrogate for Khrushchev (Bernstein this time being Tito). The fourth one,[24] against the Economists, was clearly aimed at Khrushchev, and for the first time on the organisational as well as the ideological plane. In this article Lenin, a surrogate for Mao, was portrayed as combating the spontaneous reformist tendencies of the Economists, as unmasking their deceptive concept of " lending the economic struggle itself a political character," and as raising trade union politics to the level of proletarian revolution. The article concluded with the explicit observation that Mao and the CCP are applying Lenin's example to Chinese conditions.

[20] They were thus similar in format to the Soviet article by Pospelov in *Pravda*, January 18, 1962, which praised the 1912 Prague Conference of Bolsheviks for its resolute opposition not only toward the Mensheviks but also toward the " left-wing liquidators . . . and sectarians . . . who failed to understand the necessity for making skilful use, under party leadership, of even limited legal possibilities." Since long and excellently chosen excerpts from these four (but no detailed analysis of them) may be found in Dallin, *op. cit.*, Documents 37–38, 40–41, pp. 258–271, 277–296, none of their texts is reproduced here.

[21] Hsiao Shu and Ma Ch'un-ping, " on Bernsteinian Revisionism," *Red Flag*, No. 3–4, February 10, 1962 (SCMP 303, March 5, 1962, pp. 19–28; excerpts: Dallin, *op. cit.*, Doc. 37, pp. 258–268).

[22] Wu Chiang, " Our Age and Edvard Kardelj's ' Dialectics,' " *Red Flag*, No. 5, March 1, 1962 (SCMP 306, March 26, 1962, pp. 14–36; excerpts: Dallin, *op. cit.*, Doc. 38, pp. 269–271).

[23] Li Fu, Li Ssu-wen and Wang Fu-ho, " On Kautskyism," *Red Flag*, No. 8–9, April 25, 1962 (SCMP 314, May 21, 1962, pp. 33–47; and JPRS 13,615, May 1, 1962, pp. 32–64; excerpts: Dallin, *op. cit.*, Doc. 40, pp. 277–289).

[24] Pien Chung-yin, " The Revolutionary Tradition of Political Parties of the Proletariat," *Red Flag*, No. 10, May 16, 1962 (SCMP 317, June 12, 1962; excerpts: Dallin, *op. cit.*, Doc. 41, pp. 289–296).

With regard to specific foreign policy views, Kardelj [Khrushchev] was accused of advocating peaceful co-existence to the exclusion of class struggle on the basis of the anti-Marxist-Leninist thesis of a radical change in the inherently aggressive nature of imperialism, of joining Kennedy in opposition to wars and therefore becoming a " defender of imperialist wars and an opponent of revolution," of not believing in revolution in underdeveloped areas [including China], especially because of their lack of productive capacity [including opposition to the Chinese people's communes], and of foolishly placing his trust in the disarmament of imperialist countries and the growth of greater foreign trade with them [Khrushchev's thesis of international economic competition as part of peaceful co-existence].

Turning to a more sweeping indictment, the articles declared that revisionism originates in bourgeois rightist opportunism [*i.e.*, not in nationalism, of which the Soviets implicitly accused the Chinese]. Its philosophical characteristics are gradualism, relativism and eclecticism. It rejects the dictatorship of the proletariat and stresses the adaptability of capitalism. It establishes the priority of economics, and in particular of satisfying people's needs [Khrushchev's stress on material incentives and a rising standard of living], over politics, political struggle and particularly the theory and practice of revolution. Because of its super-class concept of the state, it advocates only a flexible, peaceful, legal and parliamentary rather than a violent, revolutionary transition to socialism through armed struggle and the smashing of the state machine, alleging that progress in military techniques [atomic and thermonuclear weapons] has made war absolutely unacceptable and its prevention an overriding imperative. Once socialism is reached, revisionism abandons the dictatorship of the proletariat for the " all-peoples' state." By advocating pragmatism and experience in opposition to so-called dogmatism and utopianism it embraces the pretence of orthodoxy and the reality of deviation. Finally, its total and exact parallels with " modern revisionism," particularly as expressed by Tito, make essential the study of its history.

Although the sharpest organisational conclusions concerning the struggle against revisionism were not drawn until the mid-May Chinese article against the Economists, they were clearly implied in the April attack on the Khrushchev-surrogate Kautsky. Kautsky [Khrushchev] had initially played a positive role and had been intimate with Engels [Stalin]; but he had displayed a weak attitude toward Bernstein [Tito], had then become the head of a " middle faction " [the CPSU] which accepted the thesis of a change in the nature of imperialism, and finally after 1917 [1956] played an entirely revisionist role. Indeed, the whole

Second International [the present international Communist movement] had played an initially positive but later a negative role, and Lenin [Mao (?)] had correctly demanded its splitting. Kautsky [Khrushchev] had been conciliationist, had deceived the masses and had turned chauvinist, and others [other pro-Soviet Communist parties] had underestimated the revisionist danger, while only Lenin [Mao] remained adamant against revisionism, as Engels [Stalin] had before him.

The attack against the Economists [the CPSU] made the organisational implications even clearer:

> . . . The Economists [the CPSU] . . . confined the working-class movement and the tasks of the party to economic struggle and political support for bourgeois liberalism. They neglected and disparaged the function of revolutionary theories . . . and slandered the Marxists [the CCP] as " dogmatists " while they themselves became intoxicated with fashionable propaganda in favour of opportunism. They justified the confusion, disunity, and vacillation of the working-class movement at the time. . . . These stands . . . were virtually tantamount to disarming the working class in the face of the pressing revolutionary tasks and the powerful enemy. It was the greatest danger to the Russian working-class movement at that time. In order to put an end to the confusion and vacillation and build a really revolutionary political party based on Marxism, it was necessary, first of all, to combat this opportunist clique, criticise their erroneous views and ideology, and " draw a line of demarcation clearly " against them. . . .

The challenge to Khrushchev—that Peking would "draw a line of demarcation clearly" against him—was obvious. Furthermore, the Chinese plainly indicated their refusal to imitate the Soviet pattern in practice or theory:

> . . . Although the German Party [the CPSU] was the most experienced in the international working-class movement at that time, and while its experience was undoubtedly a valuable asset common to the international working class; yet Lenin [Mao] opposed cramming of German [Soviet] things into the Russian [Chinese] masses in doctrinaire and dogmatist ways (just like Karl Marx and F. Engels opposed cramming of West European experience into the American masses); in particular, he opposed copying of the opportunist dogmas that had already been criticised [25] within the German Party [the CPSU] and opposed transformation of such an integral revolutionary theory as scientific socialism into a "hodge-podge 'freely' diluted with the contents of every new German [Soviet] textbook [Kuusinen's 1959 *Foundations of Marxism-Leninism*] that appeared." . . .

In retrospect it thus seems that in March or April 1962 there was a minimal and provisional Sino-Soviet agreement to diminish the intensity and public nature of their polemics, motivated by the continuing desire

[25] By Molotov?—W. E. G.

41

of both to avoid a total break, by the hope that a partial détente might lead to a more substantive agreement, and, finally, by the mutual realisation that such open polemics could only profit the "imperialists." However, ideological and surrogate organisational moves continued; and on the most acute public issue, the Albanian one, it seems that no agreement was reached beyond the minor one of discontinuing personalised Soviet-Albanian polemics.

2. The Soviet-Yugoslav Rapprochement

SINCE the Second World War Moscow's relations with Belgrade have been a consistent indicator of Soviet policy toward East Europe and, since 1957, toward China as well.

Stalin, intent on the total Sovietisation of East Europe, refused to tolerate Yugoslav autonomy at home and ambitions in the Balkans; but he could neither intimidate nor overthrow Tito's partisan-forged régime. Faced with no other alternative, after the 1948 break Tito shifted reluctantly to liberalisation at home and, abroad, to the West for aid and to the non-aligned neutralists for allies. But Tito has always been a convinced and internationalist Communist, and when Khrushchev's 1954–56 overtures to Yugoslavia offered him the chance to rejoin a looser socialist camp and to regain and expand Yugoslav influence in East Europe, he readily took up the Soviet offer, and the rapprochement proceeded apace.

Although the Polish and Hungarian events of 1956 dealt a serious blow to the already far advanced Soviet-Yugoslav rapprochement, Khrushchev and Tito tried once more in 1957 to complete it. Khrushchev's need to reconsolidate his weakened control over East Europe and Tito's insistence (in the Ljubljana *Programme* of 1958) on continuing the international propagation of his deviant ideology would most likely have doomed this attempt anyway; a new element, the anti-Yugoslav policy of Peking, guaranteed its collapse. Like Khrushchev, Mao felt that the 1956 events required reconsolidation of the bloc; but Mao also felt that the 1957 Soviet scientific and military achievements made possible a more forward strategy against the West, while his domestic Hundred Flowers experience had greatly heightened his hostility to revisionism. Mao therefore seized upon relations with Yugoslavia as a means to push Khrushchev farther toward hostility to Yugoslavia (and to the West) than the Soviet leader was prepared to go—and much farther than Tito would accept; and although a second Soviet-Yugoslav break

43

occurred, it was Peking, not Moscow, which led the outcry against "Yugoslav revisionism."[1]

Khrushchev was slower and less extreme in his attacks on Belgrade and clearly wanted to leave open the possibility of a renewed rapprochement. As the Sino-Soviet dispute deepened and Khrushchev intensified his de-Stalinisation policy at home and wooing of neutralists abroad, he saw increasingly less reason to concern himself about Chinese opposition to the Yugoslavs. Moreover, after 1958 Tito again intensified his relations with the neutralists and thus became a more attractive ally for Khrushchev. At the November 1960 81-party Moscow meeting Khrushchev took a considerably less anti-Yugoslav position than the Chinese,[2] and thereafter he increased his overtures to Tito for a new rapprochement.

Meanwhile the Yugoslav internal situation was worsening. By early 1962 the Yugoslav economy, which in 1959–60 had appeared flourishing, was again in a major crisis. The very high industrial growth rate (15 per cent. in 1960) had fallen to 7 per cent. in 1961 and 1962.[3] The 1961 liberalisation of foreign trade and further decentralisation of industry led to a rush to import from abroad, particularly consumer goods, and thus to a great increase in the foreign trade deficit.[4] The slackening of central control over the factories produced a rapid rise in wage fund expenditures, far exceeding the increase in labour productivity. Bad harvests in 1960, 1961, and 1962 [5] further intensified the crisis, while the régime's political restrictions on the private peasantry kept agricultural productivity stagnant. Finally, the success of the European Common Market, its 1962 extension to agriculture and the resultant threat to Yugoslav agricultural exports, as well as the increasing integration of the Soviet camp in CMEA threatened Yugoslavia with economic isolation.

The régime's increased emphasis on economics rather than politics prior to 1962 had lowered the political morale of many of the Yugoslav party cadres. In the leadership the permanent feud between the Serb Rankovic and the Slovene Kardelj reached new heights. Elite demoralisation below and leadership conflict above also lessened the régime's

[1] Zagoria, *op. cit.*, pp. 145–151.
[2] Griffith, " The November 1960 Moscow Meeting: A Preliminary Reconstruction."
[3] John C. Campbell, " Jugoslavia: Crisis and Choice," *Foreign Affairs*, XLI, 2 (January 1963), p. 386; *Commercial News of Yugoslavia*, IX, 3 (February 1, 1963).
[4] William E. Griffith, " The Special Yugoslav Role," in Zbigniew Brzezinski, ed., *Africa and the Communist World* (Stanford: Stanford University Press, 1963), Table VI.
[5] As compared to the excellent 1959 one. See *Commercial News of Yugoslavia*, IX, 3 (February 1, 1963).

ability to keep suppressed one of Yugoslavia's continuing major problems: the traditional ethnic hostility between the Roman Catholic, Westernised Croats and Slovenes and the more eastern Orthodox Serbs, Montenegrins and Macedonians. The declining memory of the fratricidal slaughter during the Second World War was counteracted by the increasing economic gap between the two groups. The régime's large politically-motivated investments in the southern and eastern areas did not overcome this gap and further infuriated the Croats and Slovenes, from whose relative prosperity the funds came. Nationalities tension was thus further accentuated. All in all, by early 1962 the economy and even the politics of Yugoslavia were threatening to escape from the régime's control.[6]

The internal crisis facing the Belgrade régime thus intensified Tito's desire to respond to Khrushchev's wish, increased by the steadily worsening Sino-Soviet dispute, for a rapprochement.

For Khrushchev, a Soviet-Yugoslav rapprochement was a permanent objective not only for strategic reasons (Yugoslavia's position in the Balkans and on the Mediterranean, including its proximity to Albania), but also as a means of gaining more influence among Yugoslavia's fellow neutralists, as a weapon against the Chinese, and as a demonstration (like de-Stalinisation) that intra-camp relations were being placed on a new basis. However, Khrushchev's " socialist commonwealth," originally intended to stabilise endangered Soviet influence in China and East Europe, became even looser as a result of Sino-Soviet competition for power and influence within all parties in the international Communist movement. The " socialist commonwealth " to which Khrushchev wished Tito to return was therefore a far cry from Stalin's " camp of socialism."

For Tito and even more for Rankovic and his more dogmatic Serb Communist associates, the Sino-Soviet dispute and Khrushchev's renewed desire for a rapprochement with Belgrade offered a possibility of rejoining the " socialist commonwealth " on terms which would not seriously interfere with their independence in internal affairs. Rapprochement would at least partially offset, through increased Soviet trade and aid, the losses suffered as a result of the Yugoslav internal economic crisis and the threat of the EEC. It would provide the more orthodox Yugoslav Communist *apparatchiki* with a renewed sense of ideological assurance and " fraternal solidarity," and Rankovic and the Serb Communists with a perhaps necessary source of support to counter the probable increase in Croat and Slovene hostility toward Serb Communist hegemony after Tito's death.[7] Furthermore, Tito and his associates

---

[6] See Viktor Meier's chapter on Yugoslav communism in William E. Griffith, ed., *Communism in Europe*, I (Cambridge, Mass: M.I.T., 1964).

[7] Slobodan Stankovic, " Die Frage der Nachfolge Titos," *Neue Zürcher Zeitung*, December 12, 1961.

viewed the Sino-Soviet dispute as a great opportunity for Yugoslavia to renew and expand its influence within the Communist world while at the same time maintaining its activity in non-aligned areas. Thus from Tito's viewpoint both pressure from within and opportunities without could best be met by renewed political and economic controls at home and by rapid and extensive rapprochement with Khrushchev abroad.

By spring 1962 Tito was turning away from liberalisation at home and moving rapidly toward a reconciliation with Moscow. His May 1962 speech at Split first signalised a significant increase in political and economic centralisation, a more anti-Western cultural and political attitude, and a major attempt to revitalise the party as the prime directing element in national affairs. This and subsequent speeches also revealed a degree of concern over the problem of ethnic hostility within Yugoslavia which indicates the seriousness of that situation.[8]

The Soviet-Yugoslav rapprochement intensified steadily throughout 1962. In April Soviet Foreign Minister Gromyko visited Belgrade (returning Popovic's 1961 visit to Moscow) and declared that Soviet and Yugoslav attitudes on foreign policy were identical or close.[9] Shortly before Gromyko arrived, Djilas was rearrested,[10] a move intended at least in part to appeal to Moscow. In May Khrushchev declared in Bulgaria that Soviet-Yugoslav relations were now no longer " strained " but " normal," even " good," and that political, economic, and cultural relations should be intensified to help Yugoslavia consolidate its " socialist positions " [11]—i.e., that Yugoslavia is a socialist country and therefore not, as Peking and Tirana regularly continued to reiterate, an *agentura* of the imperialists. For the first time since 1948 the Belgrade May Day parade included Soviet-made tanks.

At the same time, almost unnoticed in the West, Moscow and Belgrade began readjusting their ideological positions in each other's favour. An article by the leading Soviet ideologist Rumyantsev in the April 1962 *Problems of Peace and Socialism* appeared to condemn the " Yugoslav revisionists " violently—and in many respects did so.[12] (Perhaps it was also a last Soviet attempt thus to gain a point *vis-à-vis* the Chinese.)

---

[8] LCY CC Executive Committee meeting, March 14–16, 1962, and letter, April 3, 1962 (*Komunist*, June 14, 1962); Tito's speech at Split (*Borba*, May 7, 1962), and in Belgrade (*ibid*. June 22, 1962); speech by Rankovic to Executive Board of SAWPY (*ibid*., May 23, 1962); speech by Kardelj to Federal National Assembly (*ibid*., May 29, 1962).

[9] *Pravda*, April 25, 1962. See also the communiqué on Gromyko's visit to Yugoslavia, April 21, 1962, *Borba*, April 22, 1962.

[10] *New York Times*, April 8, 1962.

[11] Khrushchev's speech at Varna, *Pravda*, May 17, 1962.

[12] A. Rumyantsev, " Under Cover of Devotion to Principle," *World Marxist Review*, V, 4 (April 1962), pp. 88–89 (passed to press, Russian edition, March 12, 1962).

However, it carefully ascribed their deviations, as it did those of the Albanians, to " nationalistic positions "; *i.e.*, it repeated the charge of the 1948 Cominform Resolution, one which the Chinese had refused to have included in the November 1960 Moscow Declaration (presumably lest it be used against them), and one for which they had substituted, implicitly if not explicitly, the accusation of the 1949 Cominform Resolution that the Yugoslavs were a " direct *agentura* of imperialism." [13] Rumyantsev also stated:

> ... It is untrue, furthermore, that Yugoslavia is criticised for seeking new forms of participation by the working people in economic management. (That each party may have its own opinion on these forms is another matter.) ...

In other words, the Russians were willing to cease criticising Yugoslav workers' self-management if the Yugoslavs would cease criticising them for not having the same institution.[14]

A carefully expressed and lengthy article by one of Tito's leading ideologists, Punisa Perovic,[15] repeated the familiar Yugoslav position, expressed in the Ljubljana *Programme* and elsewhere, of opposition to any guided, or directing, centre in international Communism. However, the article took a relatively positive view of the CPSU Twenty-Second Congress and even more so of declarations by the Italian, Hungarian and Belgian Communist parties (the " reformist " current in international Communism). Moreover, in one carefully phrased section at the end, presumably reflecting the already mutually agreed Soviet-Yugoslav basis for the rapprochement, it declared that one must reckon with " contradictions " and " differences " among Communist parties. One must, however, " keep working to reduce them," co-operate on the basis of " elements which are held in common," avoid " anathematising of those who do not abide by . . . declarations adopted." Finally, " if there is any need for declarations," it should concern only questions " on which they are in full accord." (This was a clear forerunner of the position Tito and Khrushchev made public at the end of the year.)

13 " Communist Party of Yugoslavia in the Power of Murderers and Spies," *For a Lasting Peace, for a People's Democracy!* No. 28 (55), November 29, 1949, p. 2. For the Chinese refusal, see Thorez's report to the December 15, 1960, PCF CC plenum in *Problèmes du mouvement communiste international* (Paris: PCF, January 1963), pp. 49–54, at pp. 51, 53 (JPRS 17,772, February 21, 1963, pp. 9–14, at pp. 11, 13).
14 *Cf.* Ernst Halperin in *Die Tat* (Zürich), May 24, 1962.
15 Punisa Perovic, " Problems of Leadership and Relationships in the International Workers' Movement," *Nasa Stvarnost*, XVI, 3 (March 1962), pp. 251–292 (JPRS 14, 573, July 24, 1962 [a very bad translation]). Belgrade's English-language version of the article (" Discussion on ' Polycentrism,' " *Review of International Affairs* [Belgrade], April 20, 1962; excerpts: Dallin, *op. cit.*, Doc. 95, pp. 599–604) omits these significant passages (deliberately, it would seem).

As usual theory reflected and justified action. Yugoslav-Soviet trade agreements were sharply revised upwards.[16] Exchanges of delegations also increased; the speeches on both sides further indicated that an ideological truce, with " agreement to disagree " on outstanding points of difference, was probably already in effect. Belgrade announced that Khrushchev had invited Tito to " spend his vacation " in the Soviet Union.[17] The Albanians retorted that the " Tito clique " was the " bridge between the revisionists and the imperialists," both of whom now wanted to restore " the red colouring to the faded mask of the Tito clique." [18] Thus in the spring and summer of 1962 the Soviet-Yugoslav rapprochement was clearly intensifying.

---

[16] Griffith, *Albania*, p. 149. The first trade agreement in 1962, signed on February 15 (Vujica Cajinovic, " Economic Co-operation with the Soviet Union," *Review of International Affairs*, XIII, 296–297 [August 5–20, 1962], p. 19) envisaged roughly $120 million (yearly average) turnover for the 1963–65 period. This raised the amount of the already existing agreement (until 1965) by approximately one-third. The first expansion occurred during the Mikoyan-Todorovic negotiation conducted in Moscow, from 3 to 6 July of the same year (*Komunist*, July 11, 1962). The extent of the increase, however, was only described as " considerable."

[17] *New York Times*, May 24, 1962.

[18] " The Rumpus over Tito's ' Reversal ' and the Undeniable Truth," " by the editorial collegium," *Zëri i Popullit*, June 30, 1962, and Griffith, *Albania*, Document 30.

3. The Reintensification of Sino-Soviet Polemics

ESOTERIC and surrogate Chinese and direct Albanian anti-Soviet polemics broke out again in mid-September 1962. One can assume that the violently anti-Soviet Albanians had ceased attacking Khrushchev by name the previous April not on their own initiative but on the instigation of the Chinese. The Soviet exclusion of Albania from CMEA and the Warsaw Pact and even more the intensifying Soviet-Yugoslav rapprochement gave Hoxha and Shehu strong incentives to resume and intensify their personalised anti-Soviet polemics. Thus Shehu attacked Khrushchev directly in a speech on July 16, and several other brief but hostile Albanian personal references to Khrushchev also occurred in July and August, presumably with the approval of the Chinese. Meanwhile, at the Moscow World Peace Congress in early July neither the Chinese nor the Russians altered their opposed positions on the priority of disarmament over national liberation, and in late July Chinese Foreign Minister Marshal Ch'en Yi indirectly but clearly indicated the persistence of serious Sino-Soviet differences. In August Khrushchev rejected unnamed (but in fact Chinese) criticism of the Economists and endorsed further CMEA integration, without Albania but with Mongolia.[1] During the same period Peking ordered the closing of all Soviet consulates in China. Sino-Soviet tension increased in international Communist front organisations. Finally, in mid-September Chinese anti-Yugoslav and Albanian anti-Soviet attacks reached a level of intensity and vehemence exceeding even that of the previous spring.[2] Clearly the minimal and precarious reduction of Sino-Soviet tension

---

[1] N. S. Khrushchev, " Vital Questions of Development of the World Socialist System," *World Marxist Review*, V, 9 (September 1962), pp. 2–18 (passed for the press, August 18, 1962). Also Frantisek Havlicek, " Perspectives of Socialist Society in Czechoslovakia," *ibid.*, pp. 34, 42.

[2] Griffith, *Albania*, p. 150 *et seq.* For Sino-Soviet polemics at the 7th IUS Congress in Leningrad, August 18–28, 1962, see the report of the National Federation of Canadian University Students observer, F. J. Griffiths, " Sino-Soviet Conflict at the 7th IUS Congress " (Ottawa, mimeographed., n.d. [August 1963]).

which had became apparent in April did not last beyond mid-July, when an accelerating process of reintensification took its place. Why, then, did the attempt at détente fail?

While both sides probably wanted some détente, neither was prepared to make any substantive ideological, economic, military or organisational concessions to bring it about, and neither expected— any more than in November 1960—that it would be successful. Indeed, close study of this period leads to the conclusion that the chances of any genuine reconciliation during Khrushchev's and Mao's lifetime were minimal after 1959, that the Chinese ideological and organisational onslaught in the spring and early summer of 1960 represented the first public indication of this fact, and that Sino-Soviet relations since that time have been primarily dominated by jockeying for position within the context of ideological struggle, by canvassing for supporters among other Communist parties, and by preparing ideological and organisational positions for a possible or perhaps even probable future break.

Periodisation of the more recent phases of the Sino-Soviet conflict is difficult enough; to venture an opinion as to which side was on the offensive and which on the defensive is not only extremely hazardous but probably unwise as long as the full course of secret Sino-Soviet negotiations in the spring and early summer of 1962 remains unknown. If with Lenin one accepts the primacy of the " organisational weapon," then Moscow's consolidation of a pro-Soviet " socialist camp," including the rapprochement with Yugoslavia, was a far more effective offensive than were the *Red Flag* ideological articles. Furthermore, in view of the overwhelming relative power on Moscow's side (a disproportion made still more drastic by the Chinese economic crisis), it was only natural for the Russians to take advantage of their peculiarly favourable situation.

On the surface the Sino-Albanian reintensification of anti-Soviet polemics was a response to the most recent symbol of the Soviet rapprochement with Yugoslavia: Soviet head of state Brezhnev's arrival in Belgrade on September 24. In reality, however, it was a reaction to the more extensive Soviet organisational offensive, involving *inter alia* CMEA. Improved Soviet relations with the Italian Communists as well as hints of a more flexible Soviet approach toward the European Common Market [3] were part of the same process. On August 25 (the Chinese stated in September 1963) Moscow secretly informed Peking that it had replied affirmatively to an American proposal to halt the proliferation

[3] N. S. Khrushchev, " Vital Questions of Development of the World Socialist System," *op. cit.*, and " Theses on Imperialist ' Integration ' in Western Europe," *Pravda*, August 26, 1962, and *CDSP*, XIV, 34 (September 19, 1962), pp. 9–16. See also Marshall D. Shulman, " The Communist States and Western Integration," *International Organization*, XVII, 3 (Summer 1963), pp. 649–662, also in *Problems of Communism*, XII, 5 (September–October 1963), pp. 47–54.

of nuclear weapons by banning the transfer of nuclear information to non-nuclear countries and by the latter agreeing to remain non-nuclear. In a secret reply of September 3 the Chinese demanded that Moscow not agree to such a treaty and threatened to denounce it publicly.[4] The co-ordination of Soviet and Chinese policies toward India had probably already proved so impossible that the Russians could have been anticipating, as the Chinese must have been planning, the October 20 Chinese attack on the Indian northern frontier. The concurrent Soviet emplacement of missiles in Cuba, of which the Chinese may have been informed—not by Moscow but by Havana—might appear to be a case of Sino-Soviet synchronisation contradicting this general trend, but in view of subsequent developments the contrary was probably the case.

The Brezhnev visit was in all probability an opportunity for further narrowing differences with Belgrade as well as one result of a preceding Soviet-Yugoslav agreement—indeed, in view of subsequent Soviet-Yugoslav developments, an agreement in principle on the resumption of full party relations in spite of the lack of total ideological agreement. The Chinese and Albanian attacks thus represented a reaction to a new and higher level of Soviet-Yugoslav accord. Yet the relationship was certainly complex: the renewed Chinese and Albanian attacks can equally well be interpreted as a preparatory ideological barrage for the month-later Chinese armed attack on the Indian northern frontier. In view of past examples of the simultaneity of ideological and politico-economic-military moves, all were part of the same syndrome of sharply increased Sino-Soviet tension.

The violence of the Chinese attacks on Yugoslavia, surpassing any since the early spring of 1960, surely indicated that their ostensible target, Tito, was more than ever a surrogate for Khrushchev and that the Brezhnev visit to Belgrade was part of a major over-all turning-point in Sino-Soviet relations. It probably also marked the final defeat of Moscow's attempts to prevent the Chinese incursion into India and Peking's defiance of Moscow on the atomic issue, and it certainly marked the end of the short-lived spring and summer attempt at a Sino-Soviet détente.

The upsurge of Chinese attacks against Yugoslavia began in early August with a *People's Daily* commentary on the Tito régime's recent measures against its economic difficulties.[5] An article in the September 1

---

4 See the CPR governmental statement, *People's Daily*, August 15, 1963 and *Peking Review*, VI, 33 (August 16, 1963), pp. 7–15, at p. 14. No Soviet, U.S., or U.K. published material is available on this point, but the U.S.-U.K. proposal for a partial nuclear test ban treaty was tabled in Geneva on September 27, 1962.

5 Liao Ching, " Yugoslavia's Economic Troubles," *People's Daily*, August 4, 1962, and *Peking Review*, V, 33 (August 17, 1962), pp. 11–13.

issue of *Red Flag* further elaborated on economic deterioration in Yugoslavia, explicitly charged the régime with " sinking deeper and deeper in the quagmire of capitalism along the revisionist line," and termed the Yugoslav workers' councils " an important step in the transformation of Yugoslavia towards capitalism."[6] A few days later a *People's Daily* article directed ostensibly against the nineteenth-century Bavarian revisionist Social Democratic leader Georg von Vollmar[7] repeated many of the themes of the esoteric *Red Flag* articles of the previous spring. In particular it stressed, even more strongly than did the May attack on the Economists, the priority of the struggle against revisionism and the necessity for a break with it.

On September 17[8] and 18,[9] the *People's Daily* published two long anti-Yugoslav attacks which shifted sharply from the earlier economic emphasis to primarily political themes. Their ostensible target of attack was Tito's interview with the American correspondent Drew Pearson on August 7, 1962[10]: their real target was Khrushchev. The articles declared that the Yugoslav leadership was now clearly a " detachment of United States imperialism," whose character, Tito falsely maintained, had changed, whose activities toward the destruction of the socialist camp he was concealing, and whose policy of political and economic integration of the world (*i.e.*, the destruction of the socialist camp) he endorsed and furthered. In fact, however, the articles continued, the struggle between imperialism and socialism was becoming sharper. On September 17 Yugoslavia was charged with " peacefully evolving " toward capitalism; on September 18 " the revisionist line of the Tito group " was held responsible for " the restoration of the capitalist system in Yugoslavia." This was the most significant and extreme new Chinese assertion; previously Peking had only maintained that Yugoslavia was no longer socialist; now that it was capitalist, Khrushchev's rapprochement with it must for the Chinese be conspiracy with the enemy against his socialist Chinese ally. Absolute priority was now assigned to the necessity to " carry on the struggle against modern revisionism to the end " (*i.e.*, implying that this had priority over the unity of the

---

[6] Ch'en Maoyi, " On the Deteriorating Economic Situation of Yugoslavia," *Red Flag*, No. 17 (September 1, 1962), pp. 24–31 (SCMM 322, September 24, 1962, pp. 20–27).

[7] Li Yuan-ming, " Engels' Criticism of Georg von Vollmar and Others," *People's Daily*, September 9, 1962 (JPRS 15,829, October 22, 1962, pp. 1–19).

[8] " See to What Depths the Modern Revisionists Have Stooped!" *People's Daily*, September 17, 1962, *Peking Review*, V, 38 (September 21, 1962), pp. 12–15.

[9] Jen Ku-ping, " The Tito Group: A Detachment of U.S. Imperialism in Its ' Grand Strategy ' of Counter-Revolution," *People's Daily*, September 18, 1962, *Peking Review*, V, 41 (October 12, 1962), pp. 11–16.

[10] *Review of International Affairs* (Belgrade), XIII, 298 (September 1, 1962), pp. 30–34. The resumption in full force of Sino-Albanian polemics was accompanied by the initiation in late September of extensive North Korean attacks on Yugoslavia. (Griffith, *Albania*, p. 152, n. 110.)

international Communist movement). Finally, the articles not only made quite clear that China was following an "independent" policy in domestic and foreign affairs, but, in an oblique reference to Soviet support for India, denounced Tito for using "the propaganda language of U.S. imperialism" in making the following statement to Pearson:

> The Soviet Union is trying to exercise a pacifying influence, while China is taking various actions fairly independently in international politics and at home. The same situation arose in the Indian-Chinese border disputes where the Soviet Union is also trying to prevent further conflicts.

Chinese policy lines were re-echoed in the September 28 communiqué of the Tenth Chinese Central Committee Plenum.[11] It declared that "the general line of our country's foreign policy is entirely correct" (thus implying its independence and general applicability in a manner similar to Moscow's use of the phrase "general line"); it re-endorsed the 1959 Eighth (Lushan) Plenum's decisions against "right opportunism, *i.e.,* revisionism" (the removal of Marshal P'eng Teh-huai); and it declared that the "scheming activities, be it intrusion, provocation or aggression, or subversion within our state or party" of "the imperialists and their running-dogs in China and abroad" had been and would continue to be "resolutely smashed." The communiqué also announced the dismissal from the Secretariat of Huang K'o-ch'eng and T'an Cheng, both former associates of P'eng Teh-huai, and their replacement by Lu Ting-yi, K'ang Sheng, and Lo Jui-ch'ing, all identified with the strongest CCP anti-Soviet line. In view of the widely-known involvement of Khrushchev in P'eng's activities, the communiqué's allusion to "subversion within our . . . party" was another serious indication of the determination of the Chinese leadership to intensify its defiance of Khrushchev.

It can be assumed that the full Chinese position was even more clearly revealed in two subsequent Albanian articles. The first one appeared in two parts on September 19–20,[12] *i.e.,* immediately after the two Chinese articles; it was also couched in the format of a critique of the Tito-Pearson interview. Unlike the Chinese approach, however, the parallels between Tito and Khrushchev were directly and explicitly drawn. The Albanians declared that Tito was "the imperialist intermediary attached to the revisionist group of N. Khrushchev," who served as mediator and counsellor between Khrushchev and Kennedy, and that the modern revisionists headed by Khrushchev and Tito were now openly committed

---

[11] *People's Daily*, September 29, 1962, *Peking Review*, V, 39 (September 28, 1962), pp. 5–8. See also "The Rising People's Forces Are Invincible," *Red Flag*, No. 19, October 1, 1962, *Peking Review*, V, 40 (October 5, 1962), pp. 9–12. *Pravda* reprinted on October 1 a version of the communiqué which deleted several passages clearly objectionable to Moscow.

[12] "Modern Revisionism to the Aid of the Basic Strategy of American Imperialism," *Zëri i Popullit*, September 19–20, 1962, and Griffith, *Albania*, Document 31, p. 364.

to splitting the socialist camp and to carrying out a policy of rapprochement and fusion with imperialism by means of political and economic collaboration with imperialist countries and associations (*i.e.*, EEC). Foreshadowing the Chinese attack on India, this article for the first time publicly accused Moscow of endorsing the Indian case on the Sino-Indian border conflict and of selling arms and planes to the "Indian reactionaries."

During Brezhnev's visit to Belgrade in late September, he and Tito both publicly hailed the further intensification of Soviet-Yugoslav relations, and although party ties were not formally re-established, the protocol of the visit clearly indicated this step.[13] The final communiqué [14] completely endorsed the Soviet position on Berlin and the German question. It also provided for an increase in the exchange of official delegations as well as for the overall expansion of Soviet-Yugoslav political, cultural and, in particular, trade relations. Furthermore, both sides agreed upon the need " to inform . . . the public of both countries more widely about current events . . . and progress," thus implying that this would have priority over mutual polemics.

The Chinese did not immediately comment on the Brezhnev visit, but on October 13 the Albanians denounced it at length and without reservation.[15] For the first time they publicly called for a split in the international Communist movement: " . . . Communists . . . must . . . detach themselves from the revisionists . . ." in order to " fix once and for all the demarcation line with revisionism . . . in spite of the terrible pain this operation may cause." The article compared this necessity to that of Lenin's correct break with the Mensheviks, and declared that the struggle against modern revisionism could not be stopped, that it was in the true interests of the Soviet Union and the CPSU, and that the common Khrushchev-Tito front revealed by the Brezhnev visit would speed up the destruction of modern revisionism by unmasking its true nature—*i.e.*, that the worsening of Sino-Soviet relations was both inevitable and desirable. In view of the parallels of the Albanian article with subsequent Chinese ones, it may have reflected an unpublished decision of the Chinese September plenum or earlier.

The Soviet retort to the joint Sino-Albanian verbal assault of September and October took the form of an unsigned editorial in the November issue of the *Problems of Peace and Socialism* (passed for the

---

13 Note Tito's toast to Khrushchev as CPSU First Secretary (*Borba*, September 26, 1962). CPSU-LCY discussions reportedly took place during the visit; see C.[hristian] K.[ind], " Breschnews Besuch bei Tito," *Neue Zürcher Zeitung*, October 6, 1962.
14 *Pravda* and *Borba*, October 5, 1962. The *Pravda* version of the communiqué was textually less reserved than the *Borba* one.
15 " A Great Betrayal of Marxism-Leninism," *Zëri i Popullit*, October 13, 1962, and Griffith, *Albania*, Doc. 32.

press on October 23), pointedly entitled " The Revolutionary Platform of the International Communist Movement." [16] The first two sections, despite the absence of any concurrent mention of " dogmatism " or Albania, emphatically reaffirmed the overall Soviet position on the feasibility of the peaceful transition to socialism, the necessity of exposing the personality cult, the priority of correct economic policy among the factors promoting socialism, and the overriding importance of the international socialist division of labour, *i.e.*, of economic integration through CMEA. Direct references appeared only in the final section, which strongly implied that dogmatism would soon become the " main danger " in the international Communist movement and in which the Albanian leaders were explicitly condemned for their October 13 editorial and their call " for a split in the world Communist movement." However, the Russians welcomed the " open defection " of " Hoxha and his group " from the international Communist movement in terms similar to the Albanian denunciation of the " common revisionist front " of Tito and Khrushchev, and drew the following comparison between the Albanians and the Trotskyites:

> The open defection of the Trotskyites to the camp of the enemies of the CPSU and of the revolution spelled their defeat. Now Enver Hoxha and his group have discarded their mask. And by so doing they have simplified the struggle against modern dogmatism.

Again theory reflected and justified action. On September 5, according to a Soviet announcement,[17] the Chinese Ambassador in Moscow, Liu Hsiao, was recalled; no successor was named. On September 20 it was reliably reported in Moscow,[18] and on September 25 in Peking,[19] that the Chinese had requested the Soviet Union to close all its consulates in China (Shanghai, Dairen, Harbin, Urumchi and Ining [Kuldja]), leaving only the Soviet Embassy in the Chinese capital.

On October 20 Peking again secretly protested to Moscow against the latter's willingness to sign a partial test ban agreement with the Western Powers.[20] On the same day the Chinese Army attacked India's northern border in force.

---

[16] " The Revolutionary Platform of the International Communist Movement," *World Marxist Review*, V, 11 (November 1962), pp. 33–40.

[17] *New York Times*, September 7, 1962. It was either then or later in the year, when Liu Hsiao returned briefly to Moscow, that Khrushchev, according to an October 1963 Soviet statement, made " concrete proposals " for improving Sino-Soviet relations. See " Marxism-Lenninism Is the Basis for the Unity of the Communist Movement," *Komunist*, No. 15, October 1963 and Document 14.

[18] *New York Times*, September 21, 1962.

[19] *New York Times*, September 26, 1962. For Urumchi and Ining, see a Hong Kong dispatch in *ibid.*, November 30, 1962.

[20] " A Statement of the Spokesman of the Chinese Government," *People's Daily*, August 15, 1963, *Peking Review*, VI, 33 (August 16, 1963), pp. 7–15, at p. 15, and Document 7.

4. The Sino-Indian Border War

THE Sino-Indian clash [1] publicly split and greatly weakened the Communist Party of India (CPI).[2] Largely because of the Sino-Indian dispute, the CPI had already been sharply polarised between its revisionist, pro-Soviet right wing and the radical, pro-Chinese left wing (centred in Bengal); and the worsening of the Sino-Indian dispute had led, particularly after the death in January 1962 of the Party's secretary-general, Ajoy

[1] Mark Mancall, " What Red China Wants," *The New Republic*, CXLVII, 20 (November 17, 1962), pp. 9–12; G. F. Hudson, " Behind the Himalayan War," *The New Leader*, XLV, 23 (November 12, 1962), pp. 3–4; Norman D. Palmer, " Trans-Himalayan Confrontation," *Orbis*, VI, 4 (Winter 1963), pp. 513–527; Wilhelm von Pochhammer, *Die Auseinandersetzung um Tibets Grenzen*, Schriften des Instituts für Asienkunde in Hamburg, XIV (Frankfurt am Main and Berlin: Metzner, 1962); R.B. [Roger Bernheim], " Indiens Versagen im Himalajakrieg," *Neue Zürcher Zeitung*, September 10, 1963; Margaret W. Fisher, Leo E. Rose and Robert A. Huttenback, *Himalayan Background: Sino-Indian Rivalry in Ladakh* (New York: Praeger, 1963), and especially John Wilson Lewis, " Communist China's Invasion of the Indian Frontier: the Framework of Motivation," *Current Scene*, II, 7 (January 2, 1963). For the official CPR view, see *The Sino-Indian Boundary Question*, 2nd enlarged ed. (Peking: Foreign Language Press, 1962); for the Indian, Government of India, Ministry of External Affairs, *Notes, Memoranda and Letters Exchanged between the Governments of India and China*, White Paper, No. VIII (New Delhi, January 20, 1963) and Government of India, Ministry of Information and Broadcasting, Publications Division, *The Chinese Threat* (New Delhi, January 1963). For the Indian Communist Party (CPI), see M. Windmiller and G. Overstreet, *Communism in India* (Berkeley and Los Angeles: California, 1959), John Kautsky, *Moscow and the Communist Party of India* (New York and Cambridge: Wiley and M.I.T., 1956), and, for 1956–62 developments, Harry Gelman, " The Indian CP Between Moscow and Peking," *Problems of Communism*, XI, 6 (November–December 1962), pp. 21–30, " Indian Communism in Turmoil," *ibid*. XIII, 3 (May–June 1963), pp. 45–48, and " The Communist Party of India: Sino-Soviet Battle-ground," in A. Doak Barnett, ed., *Communist Strategies in Asia* (New York and London: Praeger, 1963), pp. 101–147.

[2] The CPI was factionalised and undisciplined even before the Sino-Soviet dispute, due to differences over revolutionary tactics, over the proper attitude towards Nehru, regional and ethnic differences, the Soviet de-Stalinisation campaign, the rising power of the CPR, and, finally, the polarisation resulting (after 1959) from the Sino-Soviet dispute. Factionalism became open in 1960–61, but even so the party maintained an indecisive but increasingly anti-Chinese official position on the Sino-Indian dispute (see the CPI resolution in *New Age*, August 26, 1962). The CPR was not openly and totally condemned until after the October 20, 1962, Chinese attack. See Gelman, " The Indian CP Between Moscow and Peking," *op. cit.*, p. 22, pp. 26–29, and also CPI resolution in *New Age*, November 4, 1962, and *Link* (New Delhi), November 4, 1962, February 10, 1963, and *Hindustani Times*, February 23, 1963.

Ghosh, to the predominance of the right. Ghosh, the Party's moderately pro-Soviet leader, had equivocated after the Twenty-First Congress on the Albanian issue and on de-Stalinisation, but had come out so strongly for Nehru and against the Chinese on the border issue that Peking had publicly denounced him, a step echoed by his leftist CPI opponents. After his death, the CPI's unstable compromise leadership was headed by the centrist Namboodiripad and the rightist S. A. Dange. In August at a national council meeting the party still remained equivocal on the Albanian issue but declared that Stalin's " excesses . . . cannot be adequately explained merely by attributing them to the cult of personality " (an echo of Togliatti's 1956 statement that the system must also have had defects) and unqualifiedly supported Nehru's position on the Sino-Indian border conflict.[3] After the October 1962 Chinese attack, the triumphant CPI right wing, led by Dange, became almost more pro-Indian and anti-Chinese than the Indian right wing,[4] and thus incurred Khrushchev's displeasure. The leaders of the left-wing pro-Chinese minority in Bengal and the Punjab were arrested (to Dange's public protests and private pleasure), but their followers continued " underground " support of the Chinese and denunciation of Nehru. Dange, for the Chinese a " self-styled Marxist-Leninist," went to Europe to gain Communist support for his cause.[5] The CPI suffered greatly in membership, in support by front organisations,[6] and in general prestige; and the Chinese seemed bent upon making the CPI, like the Albanians and the Yugoslavs, a test of orthodoxy.

[3] Gelman, *op. cit.*, pp. 24–26; August 1962 CPI resolution, quoted from *Resolutions of the National Council of the Communist Party of India, Hyderabad 14–20 August 1962* (New Delhi: CPI, September 1962), p. 17. PCI (and PZPR) influence on the CPI was indicated *inter alia* by the fact that the text of Ghosh's speech on the 22nd Congress in the CPI monthly *New Age*, X 12, and XI, 1–2 [December 1961–January–February 1962] was followed by the report of Togliatti to the subsequent PCI CC Plenum, the Plenum's resolution, and Gomulka's report to the PZRR CC Plenum. (Just to keep the balance, the next issue of *New Age*, XI, 3–4 [March–April 1962] carried the reports of Thorez and Zhivkov.) For the official (and, as he termed it, " extremely circumspect ") attitude of the CPI toward Albania, see Bhupesh Gupta, *Aid to the Study of Programme of the CPSU and Some Other Problems of International Communist Movement* (New Delhi: CPI, September 1962), Chap 3, " On the Leadership of the Albanian Party of Labour," pp. 50–64.

[4] See their parliamentary speeches, *Forward to Defense of Motherland Under the Banner of Jawaharlal Nehru!* (New Delhi: CPI, November 1962).

[5] According to the November 16, 1962, *Statesman* (New Delhi), Dange wrote a circular letter to all Communist parties alleging that China's aggression, which had " grossly violated " the November 1960 Moscow Declaration, " if not halted in time, would shatter the forces of world peace and drive the forces of democracy into the camp of imperialism." His co-chairman, the ex-Kerala premier Namboodiripad, who although essentially a centrist had begun to flirt with the left wing, was first arrested, then released, and finally in February 1963 deposed.

[6] *Thought* (New Delhi), December 22, 1962; and S. A. Dange in *New Age*, January 13, 1963.

Peking's ideological position on India [7] was clear if detached from reality: finally fighting back in self-defence after long and exemplary self-restraint, the Chinese were innocent victims of Indian aggression, which arose from the " class nature of India's big bourgeoisie and big landlords whose interests are closely connected with those of the imperialists." Nehru, an imperialist expansionist whose goal was an Asian empire, had made India economically dependent on the imperialists, with the United States now taking Britain's former monopoly role. Nehru's non-alignment

... has obviously become more and more a mere facade behind which he is actually carrying out a policy of opposing the national revolutionary movements of various countries, opposing socialism and serving imperialism. ... [8]

In this policy Nehru was aided by " some self-styled Marxist-Leninists, such as S. A. Dange." [9] Indian Communism and the socialist camp must rally to China's defence.

In October 1962 the Soviet position was agonisingly indecisive, and no wonder: the Chinese attack on India complicated the Soviet position on the eve of the Cuban crisis and called into question, as Mao undoubtedly intended it to, Khrushchev's policy toward the " zone of peace," whose most powerful state, India, had been so assiduously wooed and aided by Moscow since 1955. If Khrushchev abandoned India he would lose his gains there and much elsewhere; if he abandoned China, on the verge of the Cuban crisis and at a time when the intensification of the Sino-Soviet dispute made him more anxious than ever to influence wavering Communist parties, he risked losing influence within the international Communist movement as well as China's support (if needed) against Washington.

We now have a November 1963 Chinese [10] (but as yet no Soviet) detailed account of the then secret Moscow-Peking discussions preceding the October 20 Chinese attack. According to it, on October 8 " a Chinese leader " told the Soviet Ambassador in Peking that a " massive " Indian

7 " More on Nehru's Philosophy in the Light of the Sino-Indian Boundary Question," " by the editorial department of *People's Daily*," *People's Daily*, October 27, 1962, and *Peking Review*, V, 44 (November 2, 1962), pp. 10–12 (also in *The Sino-Indian Boundary Question*, 2nd enlarged ed., pp. 93–134); see also " Observer," " The Pretense of ' Nonalignment ' Falls Away," *People's Daily*, November 11, 1962, and *Peking Review*, V, 46 (November 16, 1962), pp. 5–7. For initial CPI refutation, see " *People's Daily* and Realities of the Indian Situation," *New Age*, XI, 11 (November 1962), pp. 11–36.
8 " More on Nehru's Philosophy in the Light of the Sino-Indian Boundary Question," *op. cit.* p. 18.
9 *Ibid.*, also " A Mirror for Revisionists," *People's Daily* (March 9, 1963), *Peking Review*, VI, 10–11 (March 15, 1963), pp. 63–66.
10 " The Truth About How the Leaders of the CPSU Have Allied Themselves With India Against China," *People's Daily*, November 2, 1963 and *Peking Review*, VI, 45 (November 8, 1963), pp. 18–27.

attack was pending and that Indian use of Soviet-manufactured planes " was making a bad impression " on the Chinese frontier guards; in reply, on October 13 and 14, Khrushchev told the Chinese Ambassador in Moscow that the Russians had similar information and that had the Soviets been in China's position " they would have taken the same measures." On October 20, quite likely without informing Moscow,[11] the Chinese launched their attack.

The initial Soviet reaction, on October 25, in the midst of the Cuban crisis, was mildly pro-Chinese [12]; but by carefully avoiding offending Delhi too much, it disappointed the Indians and angered the Chinese. After the Cuban crisis the second Soviet editorial on November 5 took an even less pro-Chinese position [13]; in spite of some indirect criticism of the super-nationalism of the Indian Communists, it marked Moscow's return to the 1959 " neutral " position. Moscow also continued to make friendly gestures toward India, including, after much hesitation, sending four MIG fighter planes.[14]

The Sino-Indian crisis thus seriously exacerbated Sino-Soviet relations. By supporting China's enemy, India, on an issue of vital Chinese national and ideological interest, Moscow further worsened its relations with Peking. By its denunciation of the Indian Communist leadership and of Nehru, whom Moscow continued to endorse, Peking made any Sino-Soviet reconciliation the more unlikely. Finally, the Indian Communist Party, hardly a serious danger in the past but always a potential one for the future, was further split and weakened.

---

[11] This was alleged by Ulbricht to the 6th SED Congress, *Neues Deutschland*, January 16, 1963.
[12] " In the Interests of the Peoples, in the Name of Universal Peace," *Pravda*, October 25, 1962 (reprinted in full in *People's Daily*, October 26, 1962).
[13] " Negotiation Is the Road to Settling the Conflict," *Pravda*, November 5, 1962 (not reprinted or quoted in *People's Daily*).
[14] Delhi correspondent to *The Times* (London), February 20, 1963; also *The Guardian* (Manchester), March 9, 1963.

5. The Cuban Crisis

THE Soviet retreat in the Cuban crisis [1] worsened Sino-Soviet relations even more rapidly and drastically than the Chinese attack on India; the interaction of the two, and especially Chinese pride at their Himalayan victory and scorn for Moscow's retreat in the Caribbean, greatly intensified Peking's anti-Soviet line and caused an equally sharp Soviet response.

The Cuban crisis initially lowered the level of the Sino-Soviet dispute. The Chinese, perhaps not without some concealed regret, firmly and totally endorsed Khrushchev's actions and words.[2] After a few days of increasingly firm response, Khrushchev began to indicate his almost frantic willingness to pull back in secret letters to Kennedy reflected in Soviet ideological pronouncements.[3] Soviet and Chinese ideological and propaganda lines thereafter began rapidly to diverge: Moscow increasingly emphasised the overriding necessity of avoiding thermonuclear war, while Peking stressed the aggressiveness of American imperialism and the absolute priority of support for Castro and of revolutionary struggle over fear of war.[4] Once the Russians pulled out

---

[1] See the detailed summary in *The New York Times*, November 3, 1962; Henry M. Pachter, *Collision Course: The Cuban Missile Crises and Coexistence* (New York: Praeger, 1963; David L. Larson, *The " Cuban Crisis " of 1962* (Boston: Houghton Mifflin, 1963).

[2] They could have hardly done otherwise; however, had the Russians won in Cuba, they would have launched an even stronger counter-attack against the then relatively discredited Chinese. See " Stop New U.S. Imperialist Adventure," *People's Daily*, October 24, 1962; Chinese governmental statement, *ibid.* October 25, 1962, *Peking Review*, V, 44 (November 2, 1962), p. 5.

[3] His retreat, which first became public in the Soviet leader's letter to Kennedy of October 28, Doc. 38, was apparently contained in his unpublished message of October 26. See an apparently authoritative account of it by Robert Donovan in the *New York Herald Tribune*, November 2, 1962; *cf.* " Reason Must Triumph! " *Pravda*, October 26, 1962. Also see Khrushchev's message to Kennedy of October 27, *The New York Times*, October 28, 1962. For the view that the October 28 Khrushchev letter was drafted after the one proposing U.S. withdrawal from Turkish bases (received on October 27), see Pachter, *Collision Course*, pp. 66–69.

[4] " Defend the Cuban Revolution! " *People's Daily*, October 31, 1962, *Peking Review*, V, 44 (November 2, 1962), p. 5; " The Heroic Cuban People Will Surely Win," *Red Flag*, November 1, 1962 (SCMP 2853, November 5, 1962, pp. 23–25); and

their missiles, this difference sharpened even more, as did those between Moscow and Havana.

The Chinese thereafter tried to delay, sabotage and prevent any Soviet-American agreement on Cuba. They directed their only available weapon, propaganda, toward Castro, who was equally opposed to the Soviet withdrawal and enraged by the humiliation of Khrushchev's disregard of his wishes. The Chinese staged enormous parades to protest American actions (and, implicitly, Soviet policy) against Cuba; they flattered and exhorted Castro to maintain his radical stance; and behind the thinnest veil of esoteric phrases they charged Khrushchev with having staged " another Munich " at the cost of Cuban independence and the international Communist and revolutionary movement.[5] Their position was supported *in toto* by the North Koreans and Albanians; it was rejected by all pro-Soviet Communist parties.

Khrushchev's withdrawal of his missiles from Cuba probably increased his popularity in the Soviet Union, the East European satellites, and among West European Communists—all areas where postwar recovery had provided sufficiently increased creature-comforts so that the threat of thermonuclear war took overriding priority. On the other hand, to the Chinese Communist leaders, as to the Albanian and North Korean, it confirmed all that they had been saying about the Soviet leader's " capitulationism." Furthermore, it damaged Soviet prestige in the eyes of the watching world—including the neutralists, whose impotence in the crisis accentuated their respect for American power and determination.

Another result of the Cuban crisis was the public revelation of Soviet-Cuban differences. Castro had always been suspicious of Khrushchev's desire for bilateral Soviet-American negotiations, his emphasis on peaceful co-existence and the threat of thermonuclear war, and his preference for the old-line Cuban Communists of the PSP (*Partido socialista popular*) over the guerrilla *Fidelistas*. Not that Castro was under Chinese control: like Tito and Mao, he is a new kind of Communist, one in whom elements of the traditional Latin American caudillo and a neo-Trotskyite totalitarianism, combined with the Latin

Kosygin's speech on the 45th anniversary of the October Revolution, *Pravda*, November 7, 1962.
[5] " The Fearless Cuban People Are the Most Powerful Strategic Weapon," *People's Daily*, November 5, 1962, *Peking Review*, V, 45 (November 9, 1962), pp. 12–13 (abridged). (" The attempt to play the Munich scheme against the Cuban people . . . is doomed to complete failure.") Also see Chinese Foreign Minister Ch'en Yi's reply to the Chargé d'Affaires of the Cuban Embassy in China, NCNA in English from Peking, November 1, 1962 (SCMP 2854, November 6, 1962, pp. 23–25); and Jen Ku-ping, " The Tito Group's Shameful Role," *Peking Review*, V, 46 (November 16, 1962), pp. 7–9. For a convenient collection of Chinese statements on Cuba, see ECMP 40, March 20, 1963.

American heritage of violence, anarchism, personal charisma, oratorical genius, and the glorification of *la revolución* have produced a new mixture.[6] Like Tito, Castro was not satisfied with dominating his own country; all of Latin America was his real objective, in the pursuit of which he was bound to collide with the old-line leaders of the major Latin American Communist parties, with their Soviet backers, and perhaps eventually even with the Chinese. For the present, however, his vehement emphasis on violence, revolution, and anti-Americanism made his policy closer to Peking's than to Moscow's; yet his total dependence on Soviet military and economic support prevented a break.

Some observers thought that the pro-Soviet old-line Cuban Communists would take over Fidel; but Castro took them over instead.[7] His first significant difference with the Russians may well have been his March 1962 purge of the old-line Communist Escalante. Soviet endorsement of it was late in coming and somewhat qualified in detail; Chinese approval was total. Castro thereafter reconstructed his leadership to make the *Fidelistas* supreme. After the October 1962 crisis he publicly stated that " differences " had existed with the Soviet Union but hastened to add that they could and would be solved; privately he apparently went considerably further.[8] His intimate associate " Che " Guevara reportedly declared that if the Cubans had kept and controlled the missiles they would have immediately fired one on New York.[9] Furthermore, under *Fidelista* influence the more radical elements in some of the Latin American Communist parties, particularly in Venezuela, launched a wave of sabotage and violence. In the Sino-Soviet dispute itself Castro publicly shifted his position from a pro-Soviet to a neutral one[10]: he reprinted Soviet and Chinese ideological attacks on each other, he

---

[6] See the brilliant characterisation by Ernst Halperin, " Castro: der permanente Rebell," *Die Zeit*, January 5, 1962, and also Boris Goldenberg, *Lateinamerika und die Kubanische Revolution* (Cologne and Berlin: Kiepenheuer & Witsch, 1963).

[7] Ernst Halperin, " Kuba zwischen Moskau und Peking," *Die Tat* (Zürich), April 2, 1962; Theodore Draper, *Castro's Revolution, Myth and Realities* (New York: Praeger, 1962), pp. 201–211.

[8] See Castro's references to Moscow-Havana differences in an interview, *Hoy* and *Revolución*, November 2, 1962. See also Tad Szulc in *The New York Times*, November 9, 1962; Theodore Draper, " Castro and Communism: A Detailed Account of the Background and Consequences of the Missiles Crisis in Cuba," *The Reporter*, XXVIII, 2 (January 17, 1963), pp. 35–48, and Pantela [pseud.], " Some Misunderstanding! A Report from Cuba on How Khrushchev's Tactics Look to Castro," *ibid.* XXVII, 10 (December 6, 1962), pp. 33–36.

[9] " Guevara Says Castro Planned to Use Soviet Missiles Against U.S.," UPI report in *The Washington Daily News*, December 10, 1962.

[10] Castro's speech to the Women of America Congress, *Revolución*, January 16, 1963, and *Red Flag*, No. 2, January 23, 1963 (JPRS 18,205, March 19, 1963, pp. 1–15). Also see Anne Philipe, " ' Che ' Guevara parle," *Le Monde*, January 2, 3, 1963; and Castro's interview with Claude Julien in *Le Monde*, March 22, 23, 1963.

refused to join the Soviet-sponsored boycott and blockade of the Albanians, with whom his relations were almost demonstratively good; and he constantly stressed the necessity of Sino-Soviet unity. Like Ho Chi Minh, Castro profited from the dispute, and dreaded the necessity, should a total public Sino-Soviet split occur, of choosing between Moscow and Peking.

6. Cuban Aftermath:
The Mid-November Sino-Soviet
Ideological Exchange

BOTH Peking and Moscow used the mid-November anniversaries of the 1957 and 1960 Moscow Declarations to restate their ideological and policy positions in the light of the Sino-Indian and Cuban crises; and although their methods remained esoteric, the import of their statements was clear.

The Chinese articles [1] appeared first and were both more extensive and more violent. In many respects they echoed the April 1960 *Red Flag* articles: revolution as the " locomotive of history," east wind over the west wind, the unchanging nature of imperialism, denunciation of modern revisionists, and the strengthening of the socialist camp and the struggle for national liberation as the necessary prerequisites for maintaining peace. Chinese attacks on the modern revisionists were stronger than before:

> . . . They substitute bourgeois pacifism for anti-imperialist struggle, reformism for proletarian revolution, bourgeois nationalism for proletarian internationalism, and humanitarianism for the Marxist-Leninist theory of class struggle. . . .

The impact of the Sino-Indian crisis was clearly evident. Peking attacked " those " [*i.e.,* Khrushchev] who " sympathise with, endorse, and give support to the reactionary actions of the reactionary nationalists " [*i.e.,* Nehru] who " collaborate with imperialism " [*i.e.,* get U.S. aid against China]. Not only was Kennedy violently denounced and total credit given to the Cubans [*i.e.,* not to Khrushchev] for the maintenance of Cuban independence, but Chinese fury at Khrushchev's Cuban compromise was clear:

---

[1] " Carrying Forward the Revolutionary Spirit of the Moscow Declaration and the Moscow Statement," *People's Daily,* November 15, 1962, and " Defend the Purity of Marxism-Leninism," *Red Flag,* No. 22, 1962, in *Peking Review,* V, 47–48 (November 30, 1962), pp. 26–30 and 30–34, respectively.

... if, in the face of imperialism, one backs down, knuckles under or even begs for peace at the expense of the revolutionary people, one only encourages imperialism to carry out more rapaciously its policies of aggression and war, thereby heightening the danger of a world war. . . .

The Soviet theory of the desirability of compromise was specifically rejected:

... Marxist-Leninists have never refused to negotiate with the enemy and make the necessary compromise under certain conditions. . . . But in any negotiation or compromise it is absolutely impermissible to barter away principles . . . [or] . . . the vital interests of the people and their revolution. . . .

Finally, the articles stressed Chinese determination to maintain their own independence and freedom of action. " Dogmatists " were defined as those " who wanted us simply to copy . . . and mechanically transplant the experiences of other countries " [*i.e.*, the Soviet Union], " thus causing exceptionally serious losses " [*i.e.*, the Shanghai rising of 1927]. Only " comradely consultations on an equal footing " [*i.e.*, no pressure such as Khrushchev was attempting to bring on the Chinese and had brought on Castro] can " guarantee internationalist unity."

The November 18 Soviet answer,[2] by the leading CPSU ideologist Boris Ponomarev, although in part a much more precise elaboration on the conclusions of the November *Problems of Peace and Socialism* editorial,[3] was primarily important as the first major post-crisis statement of the Soviet position and answer to the Chinese attacks on Soviet-Cuban policy. Ponomarev rejected the attitude of the Albanian leadership, who " preach to the whole Communist movement " on this issue but " stand in fact aloof from it " and are " carrying out provocative actions which . . . undermine the cause of peace and socialism." He listed five principal methods for the " struggle against imperialism by deeds ":

1. Peaceful economic competition
2. Peaceful co-existence as the means of safeguarding the " external political conditions " for building socialism and communism
3. Aid to all detachments of international socialism (*e.g.*, Cuba) threatened by imperialism rather than " allowing it to fall under an armed blow by imperialism " and thus involving it and the world in a " rocket-nuclear war "
4. Strengthening " the alliance of the socialist camp " with the neutralists
5. Increased support to Communist parties in capitalist countries.

[2] *Pravda*, November 18, 1962.
[3] " The Revolutionary Platform of the International Communist Movement," *World Marxist Review*, V, 11 (November 1962) (passed to press, Russian edition, October 23, 1962), pp. 31–38.

Ponomarev then gave five justifications for Khrushchev's Cuban policy during the Soviet-American confrontation, which, he declared, had saved both the peace and the " revolutionary achievements " of the Cuban people. He said that Khrushchev's policy:

1. Demonstrated that Communism saved the peace which the imperialists threatened
2. Further demonstrated the threat of U.S. imperialism
3. For the first time brought the danger of thermonuclear war home to the American people
4. Highlighted and intensified the disunity of NATO
5. Highlighted the " considerable international role " of the ex-colonial countries.

The article concluded with a fervent call for increasing the unity of the socialist camp, which was threatened by the Albanian leadership who had taken up arms against *all* the conclusions of the 1957 and 1960 Moscow Declarations and were " openly following a course aimed at . . . pushing mankind nearer toward thermonuclear war," one of " unbridled slander " against the Soviet Union; they thus " in fact join ranks with imperialist propaganda." [4]

---

[4] Ponomarev also (for the first time in any Soviet statement) by implication criticised Chinese racist tactics.

7. The European Communist Party Congresses

THE rapid worsening of the Sino-Soviet dispute, publicly apparent by September 1962 and greatly accentuated by the October Sino-Indian and Cuban crises, was further accelerated and extensively documented in November, December and January at a series of five congresses of pro-Soviet European Communist parties in Bulgaria, Hungary, Italy, Czechoslovakia and East Germany [1] (for the East German Congress, see Chapter 10). These confrontations increasingly emphasised organisational and policy, rather than ideological, issues. From the Soviet side came attacks on the Albanians, defence of the Yugoslavs, emphatic defence of Khrushchev's policy in the Cuban crisis, and a relatively neutral attitude on the Sino-India conflict; the Chinese rebuttals were notably and increasingly sharp. The major " leap forward " in escalation occurred in the interval between the Hungarian and Italian Congresses. Besides the Russians and Chinese, the host parties and other participants also played some role in the unfolding Sino-Soviet dialogue; but with the exception of the Korean party's more open public defence and support of Peking, the Cuban turn toward neutrality, and the more pro-Chinese emphasis in North Vietnamese and Indonesian Communist declarations, the line-up of parties remained stable. The issues debated at the congresses were also intermittently discussed in long ideological articles published by Moscow, Peking and other Communist party organs.

THE BULGARIAN PARTY CONGRESS

The domestic aspects of the Bulgarian Congress, although internally significant, did not play a major role in respect to Sino-Soviet relations. Bulgarian First Secretary Zhivkov, profiting from Khrushchev's endorsement, was totally victorious, as evidenced by the charges of Stalinism,

[1] *Cf.* Robert F. Lamberg, " Kommunistiche Parteikongresse im Winter 1962/63, *Osteuropa*, XIII, 2/3 (February–March 1963), pp. 158–171.

dogmatism, and " violations of socialist legality " levelled in his purge of Prime Minister Yugov, the already downgraded Georgi Tsankov, the deposed Chervenkov and others. Almost the only common denominator among the fallen was their previous association with the Bulgarian Ministry of the Interior during the Stalinist period. Chervenkov had apparently sympathised somewhat with the Chinese, particularly in 1959. However, this internal struggle in Sofia was not primarily on policy issues but rather a clash between feuding cliques of careerists and opportunists. Yugov had been purged by Chervenkov in 1950 for his " softness " toward the " Titoist " (in fact national Communist) and now totally rehabilitated Kostov. Yugov had then become Prime Minister in April 1956, during the brief and frustrated Bulgarian thaw. Zhivkov had been Chervenkov's faithful protégé and instrument until Khrushchev in 1956 threw Chervenkov out. In 1961 Zhivkov had purged such relatively genuine rightists as Terpeshev and Panov. And almost surely it was only Khrushchev's intervention which enabled Zhivkov this time to get rid of his last opponents.[2]

None of this was too surprising. Like all Balkan states long under Ottoman rule, Bulgaria has a small intelligentsia with neither a tradition of nor practice in successful political opposition. Bulgarian communism has a long tradition of pro-Soviet extremism,[3] and Bulgaria is traditionally the most pro-Russian state in the Balkans. Finally, since Chervenkov, a genuine representative of the Bulgarian Communist extremist tradition, enjoyed some popularity, the colourless Zhivkov, who owed everything to Khrushchev, had to be especially zealous in supporting Moscow and attacking Peking.

The implicit attack on the Chinese at the Sofia Congress, which began on November 5, was not made by the Russians directly (Suslov,[4] the Soviet delegate, did not even mention the Albanians or the Yugoslavs), but by Zhivkov and other pro-Soviet delegates,[5] undoubtedly under Soviet direction, thus enabling Moscow to maintain its pretence of

---

[2] *Cf.* the penetrating analyses by V.[iktor] M.[eier], " Widerspruchsvolle Entstalinisierung in Bulgarien," *Neue Zürcher Zeitung*, November 24, 1962, " Bulgariens Weg im Ostblock," *ibid.*, October 12, 13, 27, 1963, and also Norbert Bornemann, " Der Parteitag in Sofia," *Osteuropa*, XIII, 4 (April 1963), pp. 236–248. One Yugoslav report (Sofia TANJUG dispatch in *Borba*, November 8, 1962) indicates that when criticism of Zhivkov occurred at the October 31, 1962, BCP CC Plenum, the Plenum was thereupon adjourned and Zhivkov left for Moscow. Upon his return, two days later, and presumably with Khrushchev's approval, he pushed through his purge.

[3] See Joseph Rothschild, *The Communist Party of Bulgaria* (New York: Columbia, 1959).

[4] *Pravda*, November 7, 1962.

[5] *Rabotnichesko Delo*, November 6, 1962. See also Zambrowski's speech to the Congress, *Trybuna Ludu*, November 9, 1962; and the Hungarian delegate Nemes' speech, *Népszabadság*, November 9, 1962.

reticence. Their speeches ran the gamut of anti-Chinese themes: the necessity of attacking the Albanians, who out of nationalistic motives had taken the path of " schism," the position of relative neutrality between the " two fraternal peoples—the Chinese and the Indian," emphatic praise of Khrushchev for his peaceful resolution of the Cuban crisis, the importance of improving relations with Yugoslavia in spite of continuing ideological differences,[6] the absolute priority of both peaceful co-existence (which promotes, not inhibits, class struggle and national liberation) and the avoidance of thermonuclear war (a policy accepted by " sober circles " of the bourgeoisie), and finally the importance of co-ordinated economic planning under CMEA and the validity of the Soviet model for all socialist countries.

The Chinese delegate, Wu Hsiu-ch'üan, deplored the speeches " one-sidedly and groundlessly censuring " the Albanians. He called for the resolution of differences through equal consultation, demanded further unmasking of the Yugoslav revisionists in accordance with the November 1960 Moscow Declaration, and stressed that modern revisionism continued to be the main danger. He denounced the United States as " the most vicious enemy " and as the leader of imperialism (in the struggle against which the decisive factor is man), and emphasised that Castro and the Cubans (not the Russians) had defended themselves and that their sovereignty was not negotiable.[7]

Thereupon the Rumanian delegate [8] and some of the delegates of the non-ruling parties explicitly declared that they rejected the Chinese defence of the Albanians; and in his final speech Zhivkov (without mentioning the Chinese) reasserted the necessity of attacking the Albanians and declared that Georgi Dimitrov's declaration that " the main criterion of the real internationalism of each Marxist-Leninist party and each Communist " is " their attitude toward the Soviet Union and its Communist party " are words which " retain their force and validity today." [9] In another sign of the rising tension at the Congress, the pro-Soviet parties so censored Wu's speech as to pervert its true sense. Finally, the Cuban delegate, the old-line Communist Blas Roca, further signalised Castro's post-October switch to neutralism by failing to attack the Albanians.[10]

6 Although the Yugoslav press (*Borba*, November 15, 1962) reported that the Congress's final resolution declared that " the Bulgarian Communist Party is opposed to the revisionist concepts in the Programme of the League of Yugoslavia," the official published text of the resolution (*Rabotnichesko Delo*, November 16, 1962) did not contain this sentence; presumably the Yugoslavs, with Soviet support, succeeded in having it removed.
7 NCNA, English, Sofia, November 8, 1962 (SCMP 2860, November 15, 1962, pp. 25–30). According to a Yugoslav report, his speech was received in silence.
8 *Scinteia*, November 9, 1962.
9 *Rabotnichesko Delo*, November 15, 1962.
10 *Ibid.* November 10, 15, 1962.

THE HUNGARIAN PARTY CONGRESS

When the Hungarian Congress opened on November 20 the Sino-Soviet tension was already heightened in comparison with the time of the Sofia Congress by the Sino-Soviet ideological exchange of mid-month. Nevertheless, although the polemics at Budapest were certainly sharper than those in Sofia, no major change occurred.[11] In fact, at the end of the Hungarian Congress Kádár was more conciliatory toward the Chinese than Zhivkov, although Kuusinen, the Soviet delegate at Budapest, was much more violent than Suslov had been at Sofia.[12] Hungarian internal affairs [13] therefore may have played some role in Kádár's words at the Congress.

The self-rehabilitation of Quislings is a rare and difficult accomplishment, but János Kádár must be acknowledged to be a master of the art. Denounced and defamed in Hungary and abroad as Khrushchev's tool in crushing the 1956 Hungarian Revolution, he is today (far from correctly) considered by many Hungarians as a genuine patriot who accepted that unwelcome task only to prevent the Russians choosing Rákosi in his stead. Kádár has struck something of a truce with the Hungarian population and particularly the intelligentsia under the slogan, "Those who are not against us are with us." Pressure against private plots in agriculture has been eased and greater benefits given to collective farm peasants; technical competence among managers and workers is now given priority over Communist fanaticism; literary oppression has been somewhat eased; church-state relations have improved; and the remnants of the Stalinist extremists in the Hungarian party leadership have been systematically purged. Budapest today is more prosperous and in some respects freer than Warsaw; the population, its will to resist still paralysed by the crushing of the Hungarian Revolution, grudgingly accepts the régime; and an increasing number of Hungarians has been successfully deluded by Kádár into excepting him from their general dislike of their rulers.

Kádár is a patient, bureaucratic, and adept Communist tactician who, like Gomulka, is satisfied to wait a while for the triumph of communism,

11 There was no significant change until the Italian Congress in the beginning of December.
12 Hungarian domestic radio broadcasts during the congress (as reported by B.B.C. monitoring) normally omitted most of the references to Sino-Soviet affairs.
13 See three articles by C.K. [Christian Kind], " Der elastische Kurs Kadars," *Neue Zürcher Zeitung*, September 22, 1962; " Kadars Politik der Entspannung," *ibid.* April 21, 1963; and " Die Schwierigkeiten der ungarischen Landwirtschaft," *ibid.* May 5, 1963; Ernst Halperin, in *Die Presse* (Vienna), December 10, 1962; George Urban, " Hungary," in Walter Laqueur and Leopold Labedz, eds., *Polycentrism* (New York: Praeger, 1962), pp. 72–80; Paul Landy, " Hungary: Pressures from Above," *Problems of Communism*, XI, 3 (May–June 1962), pp. 27–32; Paul Detre, " Der neue innenpolitische Kurs in Ungarn vor und nach dem VIII. Parteikongress," *Osteuropa*, XIII, 2/3 (February–March 1963), pp. 175–183.

sacrificing fanaticism for efficiency and Hungarian action on the international scene to Soviet acceptance of his domestic liberalisation. Never an émigré in Moscow, always a relatively moderate centrist in policy, he has since 1957 not only killed, imprisoned, or purged the Nagyists but also gradually disposed of his opponents from the former Rákosi group as well.

The impact of the CPSU Twenty-Second Congress plus Kádár's domestic consolidation of power facilitated his carefully controlled programme of liberalisation from above. The Stalinist economic bureaucrat István Friss was quietly removed from his positions in January 1962,[14] and the priority of technical competence over party orthodoxy in industry was subsequently confirmed. The expulsion in May 1960 of Imre Dögei, Kádár's instrument in carrying out the 1959 forced collectivisation of Hungarian agriculture, for " sectarian and pseudo-leftist views and activities," was not made public until April 1962,[15] at which time it was accompanied by a less hostile attitude toward private plots. In the spring of 1962, Kádár's gradual, careful cultivation of the more conformist intelligentsia was tacitly endorsed by the great Hungarian writer László Németh in his new play *The Journey*. In August Kádár expelled Rákosi, Gerö, and some of their associates from the party and demoted the ex-Rákosist Károly Kiss; in October he purged Marosán, one of the most hated of his 1956 associates. All these actions had their effect in decreasing Kádár's unpopularity, particularly among the intelligentsia, in building the foundations for an improvement in Hungarian relations with the West, and in cementing still further his dominance over the Hungarian Party and the closeness of his relations with Khrushchev.

At the party congress in November 1962 Kádár's opening remarks [16] on Albania and Yugoslavia were substantially the same as those of Zhivkov in Sofia. However, he equated the danger of dogmatism with that of revisionism and declared that the increasing closeness of Yugoslav-Hungarian ties was possible *inter alia* because of the " similarity of fundamental social relations " (*i.e.*, Yugoslavia is a socialist country). Presumably in view of the Chinese speech at Sofia, he added an attack against " those " (*i.e.*, the Chinese) who condemn attacks on, and defend the conduct of, the Albanians. He repeated Zhivkov's declaration that a party's attitude toward the CPSU is " the criterion of internationalism," but he also declared that all parties " are now completely equal." As to domestic Hungarian affairs, Kádár's speech, as

---

[14] His official titles were dropped in the January issue of *Társadalmi Szemle*; however, he retains his membership in the Central Committee of the Party.

[15] *Pártélet*, April 1962.

[16] *Népszabadság*, November 21, 1962.

well as those of the other Hungarians, was a confirmation of tendencies toward relaxation.

Kuusinen, the chief of the Soviet delegation, echoed the line of the November 18 Ponomarev article.[17] In addition he stressed the significance of congresses, particularly those of ruling parties, for the international Communist movement, a hint of Moscow's wish to substitute the congresses for an international Communist meeting. He accused the Albanians (*i.e.*, the Chinese), themselves unable to give the Cubans any aid, of having falsely denounced (through " pseudo-revolutionary phrases and irresponsible accusations of capitulation ") the Soviet Union for their compromise on the Cuban question. He also once more condemned the Albanians for " splitting activities " and stressed disarmament and close collaboration with newly independent countries (*i.e.*, good relations with India).

Wu Hsiu-ch'üan, again the Chinese delegate, repeated the theses of the two mid-November Chinese articles and demanded that everyone support " the just struggle of the Cuban people until they win final and complete victory " (*i.e.*, without compromises). He denounced the Yugoslav " despicable renegades of the working class " more strongly than he had in Sofia, stressed the necessity of consultations on the basis of equality as the method of resolving differences of opinion between fraternal parties, and expressed " the deepest regret " over renewed " public and unilateral " attacks against the Albanians at " one's own party congress." [18] In reply to the last, Hungarian Politburo member Gyula Kállai [19] accused the Albanians of " disruption of unity, calumny and brinkmanship " and insisted that they must therefore be condemned in the interest of unity. Again some of the pro-Soviet delegates, though none from the ruling parties, condemned the Chinese by name for their support of the Albanians [20]; and the Mexican delegate [21] condemned the Chinese specifically for their rejection of the views on peaceful co-existence and peaceful transition to socialism expressed by the 1957 and 1960 Moscow Declarations and the Twentieth and Twenty-Second CPSU Congresses.

In his closing speech Kádár [22] was remarkably conciliatory toward Wu, saying that he took Wu's attitude on the Albanians into consideration and that the Chinese should do likewise for the views of the Hungarian party and " the whole " international Communist movement. He also praised the Chinese cease-fire in India and condemned the arrest

17 *Pravda*, November 22, 1962.
18 NCNA English from Budapest, November 21, 1962 (SCMP 2867, November 27, 1962, pp. 21–24). 19 *Népszabadság*, November 24, 1962.
20 *E.g.*, Guyot of the PCF (see *Népszabadság*, November 22, 1962, and *L'Humanité*, December 12, 1962). 21 J. G. Gonzales, *Népszabadság*, November 24, 1962.
22 *Népszabadság*, November 25, 1962.

of Indian Communists, but otherwise repeated his essentially neutral attitude on the Sino-Indian conflict. Thus Kádár indicated his moderate rather than extremist pro-Soviet position.

THE ITALIAN PARTY CONGRESS

The sharpness of the mid-November Sino-Soviet ideological exchange was intensified at the Congress of the Italian Communist Party (*Partito comunista Italiano—PCI*),[23] which began in Rome on December 2. Two days later the Czechoslovak Party Congress opened in Prague and Tito arrived in Moscow. On the same day, December 4, Yugoslavia was declared a capitalist country by the Chinese delegate to the Italian Party Congress,[24] while Khrushchev, welcoming Tito to Moscow, called it a socialist one.[25] These events were a collective escalation in the Sino-Soviet dispute; they are treated separately here only for clarity of presentation.

The PCI Congress marked the outbreak of direct, comprehensive polemics with China. It also saw the first public presentation and the Soviet endorsement of the revisionist PCI ideology as well as its condemnation by the Chinese. Finally, it was the first Communist Congress since 1957 attended by a Yugoslav delegation.

The Special Nature of Italian Communism. The PCI is a mass party in a large West European, Roman Catholic country. The very rapid rate of economic growth in northern Italy has produced the beginnings of " proletarian affluence " and mass migration from the underdeveloped south. The northern working class has, therefore, become economically less alienated from Italian society while the new working class of southern origin, cut off from its traditional southern social ties, has become psychologically more alienated.

Italian communism, like Italian socialism, has strong anarchist and leftist traditions. Its growth has profited from the alienation of many

---

23 For background on the Italian Communist Party see Giorgio Galli, *Storia del Partito Comunista Italiano* (Milan: Schwarz, 1958); " The Italian CP, Part II: The Road Toward a Dilemma, 1945–56," *Problems of Communism*, V, 3 (May–June 1956), pp. 41–48; " The Italian CP: Conservatism in Disguise," *ibid.* VII, 3 (May–June 1959), pp. 27–34; " Italy," *Survey*, No. 42 (June 1962), pp. 107–120 (also in Walter Laqueur and Leopold Labedz, eds., *Polycentrism* [New York: Praeger, 1962], pp. 127–141), and particularly his " Italian Communism," in William E. Griffith, ed., *Communism in Europe*, I (Cambridge, Mass.: M.I.T., 1964); Enzo Tiberti, " The Italian Ex-Communists," *Problems of Communism*, VIII, 1 (January-February, 1959), pp. 52–56; Fulvio Bellini, " The Italian CP, Part I: The Transformation of a Party, 1921–45," *ibid.* V, 1 (January–February 1956), pp. 36–42; Ernst Halperin, *Der Kommunismus in Italien* (Zürich: Verlag der *Neuen Zürcher Zeitung*, 1955)—a reprint of five articles which appeared in the newspaper in March 1955; a series of articles on the same subject by Hans E. Tütsch in *ibid.* June and July 1954.
24 *People's Daily*, December 5, 1962 (no complete text in SCMP); excerpts: " Greetings to Two Party Congresses," *Peking Review*, V, 50 (December 14, 1962), pp. 16–18.
25 *Pravda*, December 5, 1962.

Italians from the authoritarian behaviour patterns of the Italian state bureaucracy, from the long Fascist suppression of Italian democratic traditions, and, in central Italy, from the anti-clericalism of the population of the former Papal states. Its seventy-year-old leader, Palmiro Togliatti, one of the leading Comintern officials in Moscow in the twenties and thirties, is one of the most intelligent, tactically skilled, and flexible communist leaders. The older PCI leadership cadres have been moulded by Togliatti's consistent pro-Soviet opportunism and their group morale was cemented in Fascist jails, by the Spanish Civil War, and by the Second World War Italian partisan movement. Since 1945, however, their involvement in the parliamentary system, their extensive office-holding at the local and district level (where alone among West European Communist parties, the PCI is allied with a mass leftist socialist party, the PSI, led by Pietro Nenni), and their desire to win support among the peasantry and the bourgeoisie have led increasingly to bureaucratisation and moderation, at the expense of revolutionary doctrine and fervour. After 1945 Togliatti adopted a gradualist policy of gaining power by political rather than revolutionary means, one which he abandoned in 1948 only under pressure from Stalin and Zhdanov and resumed after Stalin's death. Thus by 1956 the PCI's revisionist reality contrasted with its orthodox theory except in two key areas: the authoritarian structure of the PCI and its basic subordination to Moscow's wishes.

The 1956 Polish and Hungarian events pushed the PCI, and even more the PSI, to the right. In 1957 the PSI abrogated its long-standing "unity of action" agreement with the PCI at the national level but continued to co-operate with it at the local level and in the trade union federation (CGIL). After 1960 the Christian Democratic Party, with the permission of the new Pope John XXIII, moved to the left. In early 1962 these complementary trends produced a centre-left government, the *apertura a sinistra,* supported and later participated in by the PSI. Lest he lose more workers' votes, Togliatti continued to move to the right, and the majority of the PSI drifted closer to the Christian Democrats.

In 1956, under the pressure of the PCI ferment resulting from the Twentieth CPSU Congress and Khrushchev's " secret speech," Togliatti advanced his theory of " polycentrism " and his view of Stalinism as a disease of the Soviet system,[26] but he quickly abandoned them when they were publicly condemned by Moscow. By 1960, however, a further move to the right was dictated by the internal Italian factors described

---

[26] *Nuovi Argomenti,* June 16, 1956, in *The Anti-Stalin Campaign and International Communism: A Selection of Documents Edited by the Russian Institute, Columbia University* (New York: Columbia University Press, 1956), pp. 97–141.

above and facilitated by the Sino-Soviet dispute. This was most notable on such issues as the peaceful and parliamentary transition to socialism, the domestic autonomy of individual Communist parties, the unacceptable destructiveness of thermonuclear war, and the desirability of a rapprochement with the Yugoslav Communists. At the November 1960 81-party Moscow meeting the Italians took a strongly right-wing position on all those issues.[27] The impact of the October 1961 Soviet Twenty-Second Congress further intensified the PCI's rightist tendencies and also made public a divergence of views within the Italian Communist leadership and cadres.

The Communist-dominated (but partially PSI) Italian trade union federation CGIL took a similar rightist policy line at the December 1961 WFTU Moscow meeting and thereafter, urging greater autonomy for national trade unions and a more liberal policy toward co-operation with non-affiliated regional trade union organisations (particularly in Africa) and with other national trade union organisations (Social Democratic and Catholic). In the PCI itself the centre was led by Togliatti and his deputy Luigi Longo. The rightist revisionist wing, led by Giorgio Amendola and Mario Alicata, was strong in Tuscany and Emilia, where Communist participation in local government was most extensive (in alliance with the PSI) and also in the south, where a popular front offered the only immediate prospect of access to power. The left was divided into three groups: the increasingly less significant old Stalinist *apparatchiki* typified by Scoccimarro, the young neo-Trotskyite internationalists around the PCI youth magazine *Nuova Generazione,* and the moderate left *apparatchiki* led by Pietro Ingrao.

At the November and December 1961 PCI Central Committee plenums, Amendola and his associates proposed an open confrontation of the various views at an extraordinary PCI Congress, and Togliatti initially revived his 1956 polycentrism thesis. *Nuova Generazione* even asked for public discussion of Trotsky's views on one occasion. In part reacting to Moscow pressure (and to criticism by the French, East German and Czechoslovak parties), but also determined to maintain his loyalty to Moscow and his control over a safely authoritarian party structure, Togliatti disavowed the views of both Amendola and *Nuova Generazione* and greatly watered down his theory of polycentrism.

The intensification of the Sino-Soviet dispute prior to the November 1962 PCI Congress produced demands within the Italian Party for further information about it. Although there were a few Chinese

27 For the Italian position at the meeting see *Interventi della delegazione del P.C.I. alla Conferenza degli 81 Partiti comunisti e operai* (Rome: Sezione centrale di stampa e propaganda della Direzione del PCI, January 15, 1962, and JPRS 12,461, February 14, 1962), and Griffith, " The November 1960 Moscow Meeting: A Preliminary Reconstruction."

sympathisers among the PCI Stalinists,[28] they were overshadowed by the right wing, who pressed for a more strongly anti-Chinese position.[29] This pressure coincided in November with the Soviet decision to make a more open attack on the Chinese. Togliatti therefore readily brought the case against the Chinese into the open. At the same time, cautious as ever, he did not wish a complete Sino-Soviet break if only because his and the PCI's prestige and influence profited from Moscow's need for support in its jockeying for position within the international Communist movement *vis-à-vis* Peking. He therefore carefully informed the Chinese in advance that the PCI at its Congress would take public exception to the Chinese views.

Italian Communist Revisionism. The Congress had also been preceded by the elaboration, systematisation, and publication of its *Theses* [30]—the most complete document of PCI revisionism yet available. The *Theses* centre around the concept of " structural reform " which calls for:

> ... an Italian road to socialism ... a mass struggle for positive objectives which would bring about changes in the economic institutions and in the political system, which would continue to shift the balance of power in favour of the working class and its allies, and which would promote the formation of a social and political bloc capable of implementing the socialist transformation of Italy within constitutional legality. . . .

This is possible, the *Theses* maintain, because of socialism's growing strength, technological success, and extensive support; it is necessary because of the danger of thermonuclear war, the prevention of which must be given overriding priority, because such a war would mean the " extermination of the human race and of civilisation." Unity of action in the struggle for peace requires, in spite of all ideological differences involved, co-operation and unity with the masses and the middle class, with the Social Democrats and the Catholics, with all who are for peace and against war. This is made easier because many imperialists, in particular " a political group headed by the President of the United States," also realise the catastrophic implications of thermonuclear war and the necessity of its prevention.

" Structural reform " as Togliatti said to the Congress,[31] means a " strict organic tie " between democracy and socialism, and, like the

[28] The PCI rightist position was publicly opposed by a leftist and pro-Chinese group in Padua; they were subsequently expelled. Their pamphlet *Viva il Leninismo* was reprinted in *Corrispondenza Socialista*, Rome, No. 11, November 1962, and JPRS 16, 880, December 27, 1962. Pro-Chinese elements became more active in 1963.

[29] See the contributions by Lecchini, Baracetti and Coggiola to the pre-Congress discussion in *L'Unità*, November 24, 29, and December 1, 1962 ; JPRS 16,621 (December 10, 1962), 16,801 (December 20, 1962), and 16,934 (January 3, 1962).

[30] " Tesi," *L'Unità*, September 13, 1962, pp. 1–15, JPRS 15,679, October 12, 1962.

[31] *L'Unità*, December 3, 1962, JPRS 16,620, December 10, 1962.

struggle for peace, calls for collaboration with the middle class and the intellectuals as well as for debates and joint action with the Social Democrats and the Catholics, on the domestic and international level. This " Italian road to socialism " requires a new relationship of citizens with governmental officials, more power for parliament, genuine local autonomy, and democracy in factories (*i.e.*, presumably workers' participation in management) in order to counteract the alienation of factory workers from society. The *Theses* include a qualified criticism of the pro-Nenni PSI majority coupled with the hope that they will renew co-operation with the Communists.

The PCI's foreign-policy objective is the withdrawal of Italy from all military blocs, which will, in turn, be " an effective contribution to overcoming the opposing blocs and to the creation of a new order of permanent peace." [32] (The similarity with Tito's—and with the late Imre Nagy's—foreign policy is striking.) The immediate tactical objective is the removal of NATO (*i.e.*, US bases) from Italy. The PCI's position on the European Economic Community is gradualist: the EEC is irreversible, it has stimulated economic development in West Europe, but it is under the control of the monopolists. Instead of denouncing it, one must fight within it for peace and for economic co-operation with the socialist camp.[33] The widest scope for cultural freedom is assured.

In the international Communist movement each party is " autonomous " within the framework of the 1957 and 1960 Moscow Declarations, and the actions of each party must be strictly in accord with the " concrete political situation." This is particularly true for parties in the advanced capitalist countries. Neither single nor regional centres are permissible; polycentrism is officially abandoned in favour of something which is close in theory to total independence for each party. The Albanians are fractionalists and anti-internationalists. The desirability of bilateral and multilateral party meetings, including public confrontations and the publication of documents on such meetings, is stressed. The attitude toward Yugoslavia is very favourable; one must study their experiences, some of which are very valuable, in spite of the incorrectness of some of their ideas. All deviations in the PCI are condemned: the right revisionists, the Stalinist sectarians, and the youthful left internationalists.

The revisionism inherent in the *Theses* is as always qualified by the reaffirmation of the Leninist organisational structure of the PCI and its adherence to " proletarian internationalism " (*i.e.*, support of the Soviet Union). Furthermore, this ideological revisionism was not primarily the product of Togliatti's personal views (although it was of Amendola's);

32 *Ibid.*
33 Only in the spring of 1962 did the PCI abandon its total hostility to the EEC (Galli, " Italian Communism and the Sino-Soviet Rift," *op. cit.*).

rather, it represented a tactical concession in order to gain votes. Nevertheless, the PCI's revisionism acquired some influence in the international Communist and socialist movements (notably in Japan), and, like " Yugoslav revisionism," it was seized upon by Peking as a useful club with which to bludgeon Khrushchev.

Both the Soviet and Italian Communist leaderships deliberately used the PCI Congress, and the hundreds of newspapermen who attended, to stage a major public escalation of the Sino-Soviet dispute. In his opening speech [34] Togliatti not only strongly reaffirmed the *Theses,* violently denounced the Albanians, endorsed Moscow's " honourable compromise " in the Cuban crisis, and echoed the relatively neutral Soviet position on the Sino-Indian crisis; he also directly attacked the Chinese for their opposition to the 1960 Moscow Declaration's position on peaceful co-existence, for their attack on the Soviet position on Cuba as " another Munich," and for their support of the Albanians. Kozlov, the Soviet delegate, emphatically endorsed the PCI, including the " creative Marxism " of its *Theses,* re-echoed previous Soviet positions on the Cuban and Sino-Indian crises, and denounced the " schismatic " Albanians, particularly for their warlike attitude on the Cuban crisis, but did not attack the Chinese directly.[35] Not that he needed to: all the pro-Soviet parties, with the significant exception of Poland,[36] did. The Cuban delegate, Blas Roca, as in Budapest, did not denounce even the Albanians.[37] The Chinese delegate, Chao Yi-min (Wu was in Prague), equalled Togliatti in escalation: he not only echoed Wu's Sofia and Budapest position on the Cuban and Albanian issues and surpassed Wu by calling Yugoslavia a capitalist country; he also, after deploring Togliatti's public attack on the Chinese, criticised " certain comrades " (a reference presumably to Amendola and the revisionist wing) in the PCI for their views on structural reform, Yugoslavia, Albania, and international affairs.[38]

The Yugoslav delegate, Kolishevski, was deliberately restrained in his response to Chao's attack while he warmly endorsed close co-operation with the PCI.[39] However, one of Togliatti's chief lieutenants, the right-wing leader Giancarlo Pajetta, sharply rejected Chao's attack. Defending the necessity for public discussion of the Sino-Soviet differences, which many PCI members had called for, he declared (in a remark not printed in the *L'Unità* text of his speech): " When we mean China

[34] *L'Unità*, December 3, 1962, and JPRS 16,620, December 10, 1962.
[35] *Pravda*, December 4, 1962.
[36] *Trybuna Ludu*, December 5, 1962.
[37] *L'Unità*, December 6, 1962, and *Le Monde*, December 7, 1962.
[38] *People's Daily*, December 5, 1962.
[39] *Borba*, December 7, 1962.

we have no need to say Albania." [40] He condemned Chao's criticism of " a number of Italian comrades," and specifically rejected Chinese views on " solidarity with the position of . . . peaceful co-existence of the Soviet Union," on Albania (asking " Why have some aligned themselves with it?"), and on Yugoslavia (where " our delegation that visited Yugoslavia . . . didn't find any capitalists in the factories "). He alleged that the Chinese had " specifically and heavy-handedly " carried on public discussion of Sino-Soviet differences, and intimated that literal implementation of the 1957 and 1960 Declarations was neither necessary nor desirable.[41]

In his final speech Togliatti repeated " very firmly " but in a " friendly way " Pajetta's rejection of Chao's criticism and added that " everyone knows " that the Chinese denunciation of Yugoslavia as capitalist " isn't true " and that as a result " nobody believes anything of the rest you have to say." However, demonstrating his lack of enthusiasm for a total Sino-Soviet break, Togliatti carefully qualified these words. He expressed " esteem and . . . affection " for the Chinese Communist Party, stated that he had prevented explicit denunciation of the Chinese in the Congress's final resolution, and invited Peking to send a delegation for an " exchange of ideas." [42] Thus Togliatti's moderate pro-Soviet position was clear.

Contrary to some expectations, the Congress did not result in any major debate on domestic Italian issues between the PCI right and left. This reflected not only the general desire within the PCI for unity against the Chinese attack but also the intention not to furnish its Italian political opponents with damaging material for the forthcoming Italian national election campaign.

THE CZECHOSLOVAK PARTY CONGRESS

The Czechoslovak Party Congress, which overlapped with the Italian one, reflected the same extremist pro-Soviet position as the Bulgarian Congress and the forthcoming East German one. As 1963 was to show, significant changes towards liberalisation were afoot in Czechoslovakia, many more than the congress itself seemed to observers to indicate. The pressure for liberalisation was primarily from below, and particularly from Slovak intellectuals, rather than as in Hungary and Rumania from above; and it did not result in major internal changes until the late spring and summer of 1963. But even had the changes already occurred at the time of the congress, the fact that they were toward liberalisation

---

[40] *X Congresso del partito comunista italiano, atti e risoluzioni*, (Rome: Editori Riuniti, 1963), p. 268 (not in *L'Unità*, December 6, 1962).
[41] See *L'Unità*, December 6, 1962.
[42] *L'Unità*, December 9, 1962, and JPRS 16,934, January 3, 1963, pp. 92–112.

rather than as in Poland away from it was from the policy viewpoint favourable to the Soviet trend toward intensification of the anti-Chinese campaign, while the continuing lack of splits in the traditionally extremist pro-Soviet leadership prevented the emergence of a moderate pro-Soviet position.

Nevertheless, in the larger sense the general impetus to liberalisation given by the Soviet Twenty-Second Congress and by the Soviet polemics against Chinese extremism was in Czechoslovakia (as in Hungary) one of the important factors in making the 1963 wave of liberalisation possible. Khrushchev had probably long desired some liberalisation in Prague, and he certainly did not have to fear it there as he did in East Berlin. The resistance to it by the Stalinist Czechoslovak leadership delayed it; and the history of Czechoslovakia as well did not favour either speed or intensity. Czechoslovakia was neither an historic state (it has not one but two nations); nor did it have a tradition of resistance comparable to Poland or Hungary. The Czech intelligentsia, like that in East Germany (or any industrialised mature society) was fragmented and lacked collective ethos; the Czech workers, although increasingly restless as a result of the bad economic situation, had unsuccessfully risen in 1953 at Plzen and Moravská Ostrava and were unlikely to rise again; and the intellectual and student unrest in 1956 had been easily suppressed by the régime. The situation in Slovakia was, however, quite different. Slovakia was a partially developed society in a phase of rapid industrialisation; its intelligentsia was, like the Polish, a compact, conscious representative of the nation. Slovak nationalism, although suppressed after 1948, had shown signs of breaking out in 1956 and, as the events of 1963 showed, was still strong; and the Slovak Communist intellectuals considered themselves the heirs of the strongly nationalistic communism of the executed Clementis and of the surviving Husák and Novomesky. Furthermore, although their collective responsibility for the slaughter of the Slánsky trial initially tended to make the Czechoslovak Communist leadership stick together, once the pressure became too great from below it proved an excellent weapon for their opponents to use against them.[43]

There was some factionalism in the Czechoslovak Communist Party[44] in 1956 and most likely more in 1960–61, when the significant opposition to Novotný centred around Rudolf Barák, a relatively young man not known as a Stalinist. Barák was probably not trying to replace

[43] See my " Myth and Reality in Czechoslovak History," *East Europe*, XI, 3 (March 1962), pp. 3–11, 34–36, 40–41.
[44] Pavel Tigrid, " L'ombre de Slánsky," *Preuves*, No. 142 (December 1962), pp. 58–65; Ivo Duchacek, " Czechoslovakia; The Past Reburied," *Problems of Communism*, XI, 3 (May–June 1962), pp. 22–26.

Novotný, but the latter, sensing potential danger, decided to get rid of him. In February 1962 he first jailed Barák for political, anti-party offences; then purely criminal (financial) charges were substituted,[45] only to have the first charge reinstated by Novotný at the December 1962 Congress.[46] However, in view of the removal in April 1963 of the Slovak First Secretary Bacílek and the Prague Secretariat member Kohler [47] and the May 1963 ferment in the Slovak Writers' Union,[48] one can assume that already in January Novotný was under considerable pressure from below to carry through an extensive de-Stalinisation programme, one in which he would inevitably have to include himself in order to make it complete.

Although the Czechoslovak economic situation worsened consistently during 1961 and 1962, particularly with respect to food, it did not produce any serious mass discontent. Novotný's implementation of de-Stalinisation, particularly after the CPSU Twenty-Second Congress, was reluctant, slow and almost ludicrous in its contradictions. Slánský's rehabilitation was rejected, and Gottwald, who had purged him, was further downgraded, both because they allegedly were Stalinists. Some signs of cultural de-Stalinisation appeared; but Novotný clearly intended, presumably with Khrushchev's reluctant endorsement, to keep things fully under control. Perhaps because the Czechoslovak leadership so feared and resisted any domestic de-Stalinisation, its support of Khrushchev against the Chinese was unlimited.

Although in some respects the Italian policy attacks on the Chinese had been more detailed and the Italian attitude toward revisionism in general and " Yugoslav revisionism " in particular had certainly been much more favourable, the Czechoslovak Party Congress in Prague [49] marked a still further escalation in the Sino-Soviet dispute.[50] Firstly, unlike the Italian this was a congress of a ruling Communist party. Secondly, the tone of the attacks against the Chinese, particularly against their support of the Albanians, was even stronger than that in Rome.

45 Griffith, *Albania*, p. 75; *Rudé Právo*, February 23, 1962; Novotný's speech at the KSC CC Plenum, April 12, 1962, published only in KSC, *Usnesení a Dokumenty UV KSC 1960–62* (Resolutions and Documents of the KSC CC) (Prague, 1963), II, concerning protests against Barák's arrest.
46 *Rudé Právo*, December 5, 1962.
47 At the April 3–4 KSC CC Plenum, announced only in *Rudé Právo* on May 14, 1963.
48 *Kulturny Zivot*, No. 18, May 4, 1963.
49 The best current coverage was by C.[hristian] K.[ind] from Vienna in the *Neue Zürcher Zeitung*, December 4, 8, 9, 11, 1962; see also Harry Slapnica, " Prager Parteikongress: die Entstalinisierung fand nicht statt," *Osteuropa*, XIII, 2/3 (February–March 1963), pp. 171–175. Only Communist journalists were allowed to attend the Congress and no visas were granted to Western reporters.
50 Just before the KSC Congress opened there were reports in the West European press that Prague had ordered the two top Chinese diplomats and many Chinese students to leave Prague and had sharply reduced CPR-CSSR trade. See *The Sunday Telegraph* (London), December 2, 1962, and *Il Messagero* (Rome), December 4, 1962.

Thirdly, not only did the Chinese delegate, the peripatetic Wu, repeat his previous speeches, but in a final statement to the Congress he specifically proposed an international Communist meeting and made clear that the Chinese expected the Russians to take the first step toward improving relations with the Albanians.[51]

Due probably to his continued resistance to de-Stalinisation and to the strongly pro-Soviet tradition of the Czechoslovak Party, Novotný's opening speech [52] on December 4 was comparable only to Zhivkov's and considerably exceeded both Kádár's and Togliatti's in its Byzantine subservience to Moscow. He launched an extremely violent attack on the Albanians, particularly by charging that they attempted to expand the Cuban crisis into a source of thermonuclear war—a charge on the face of it so ridiculous that only the assumption that he was using the Albanians as surrogates for the Chinese could give it any meaning. Unlike Togliatti but like Zhivkov and Kádár, however, he did not specifically refer to the Chinese in his opening speech but he insultingly listed them below the East European parties.[53] However, in a premature echo of Khrushchev's subsequent sarcastic references to Chinese complacence towards Hong Kong and Macao [54] he intimated that Peking talked with hostility but acted with complacence towards imperialism. Justifying open discussion of differences in the international Communist movement by insisting that it not only was not an obstacle but was a precondition for effective unity, Novotný was notably and relatively restrained toward the Yugoslavs (who had not been invited to send a delegation), but not surprisingly so: he has always been conspicuously unenthusiastic about improving relations with Tito.

The Soviet delegate Brezhnev, like Kozlov at Rome, extravagantly praised Soviet conduct in the Cuban crisis and Khrushchev's personal role in it, but mentioned neither the Sino-Indian crisis nor the Yugoslav issue; his strong condemnation of the Albanians concentrated on their conduct during the Cuban crisis.[55] Wu's speech was standard; he strongly, albeit implicitly, condemned Soviet, and endorsed Cuban, policy in the October Caribbean crisis, denounced the Yugoslav leaders as imperialist agents, and condemned the Congress's attacks on the Albanians.[56] The first indication of escalation was that the audience

[51] NCNA in English to Asia and Europe, December 14, 1962, 1502 GMT, in *Peking Review*, V, 51 (December 21, 1962), pp. 10–12 and SCMP 2883, December 19, 1962, pp. 29–31.
[52] *Rudé Právo*, December 5, 1962.
[53] Radio Prague, December 4, 1962, 0800 GMT.
[54] Khrushchev's speech to the Supreme Soviet, *Pravda*, December 13, 1962.
[55] *Rudé Právo*, December 5, 1962.
[56] NCNA in English to Europe, December 6, 1962, 1700 GMT, in SCMP 2877, December 11, 1962, pp. 27–31. It was reprinted in full in *Rudé Právo*, December 6, 1962.

publicly expressed its " disagreement " and the Czech presiding officer took immediate and public exception to the Chinese delegate's speech.[57]

Two Czechoslovak leaders, Prime Minister Siroký and Politburo member Koucký, rejected Wu's position in terms considerably stronger than Pajetta and Togliatti had used in Rome. Siroký flatly declared that the Chinese had given total endorsement to the " wrecking policies " of the Albanians.[58] Koucký ran the full gamut of denunciation of the Albanian leaders; they had " gone directly to the camp of anti-communism " and to " coolly calculated anti-Soviet splitting activity," and they " openly call[ed] for disruptive factions inside individual parties." He declared that " the quarrels with the Albanian leaders . . . can . . . no longer be regarded as . . . within our movement " and issued " a very grave warning to all those who tolerate, let alone support, this nefarious factional activity of the Albanian leaders whom no one of us can any longer consider Communists.[59] All the pro-Soviet delegates attacked the Albanians, and some of the pro-Soviet parties openly and directly attacked the Chinese; two even called their attitude " irresponsible, anti-Soviet, anti-Marxist." [60]

This time, however, the Chinese were not so isolated. The Cubans and the North Vietnamese were again neutral (i.e. did not attack the Albanians).[61] The delegates from Japan, Finland, Algeria, Norway and New Zealand did not attack the Albanians [62]; the Indonesian representative not only did not attack the Albanians but violently denounced the Yugoslavs for their international activities [63] and the North Korean delegate praised the Chinese and attacked the " unilateral rebuke " of them at the Congress.[64]

The full impact in Peking of the Moscow-directed intensification of anti-Chinese attacks at the Italian and Prague Congresses became apparent only when the Chinese delegation made a formal statement at the end of the Prague Congress.[65] In addition to repeating the Chinese charges made at the previous Congresses the statement charged " some

[57] Rudé Právo, December 6, 1962.
[58] Ibid. December 7, 1962.
[59] Ibid. December 8, 1962.
[60] Ezekias Papaioannou, delegate of CP of Cyprus, in Rudé Právo, December 9, 1962, and JPRS 16,888, December 28, 1962. That this was at Soviet initiative is indicated by the fact that exactly the same words were used by the Jordanian CP delegate Fuad Nasar (CTK in English to Europe, December 7, 1962, 1842 GMT).
[61] CTK in English to Europe, December 7, 1962, 1827 GMT, in BBC/EE/1122/C/19, December 11, 1962.
[62] CTK in English to Europe, December 7, 1962, 1823 GMT, in BBC/EE/1122/C/19, December 11, 1962, and December 8, 1962, 1015 GMT.
[63] Njoto, PKI Second Deputy Chairman, in Rudé Právo, December 6, 1962; Harian Rakjat, December 14, 1962; JPRS 17,596, February 12, 1963, pp. 6–12.
[64] Vice-Premier and Politburo candidate member Lee Chu-yon, Rudé Právo, December 7, 1962.
[65] Peking Review, V, 51 (December 21, 1962), pp. 10–12.

parties and some persons " with " redoubling their efforts " in " going further and further down the road toward a split." Self-righteously declaring that the " anti-China chorus coming from the imperialists, reactionaries, and revisionists " and that " the recourse to such unusual manners as shouting and hissing " only " proves that the Communist Party of China has firmly persisted in the truth and the struggle for justice," the statement said in conclusion that " the Communist Party of China and a number of other fraternal parties " have proposed an international meeting of all Communist parties, and that, as to the Soviet-Albanian crisis, " the party which first mounted attacks [*i.e.*, the Soviet Union] should take the initiative." [66] (The later Sino-Soviet exchanges of letters made clear that this was one of the conditions Peking proposed to Moscow for such a meeting to take place.)

Novotný read the Chinese letter to the Congress and in the broadcasts and printed version of his final speech made a relatively restrained reply, reiterating his previous defence of the necessity to attack the Albanians and asking the Chinese to " re-examine " their position.[67] However, a Danish Communist journalist present at the Congress reported that he also accused the Chinese of encouraging the Albanian attempts to split the international Communist movement and of reprinting Albanian attacks on Khrushchev with the deletion only of his name.[68]

---

[66] Radio Prague, December 8, 1962, 1800 GMT.
[67] *Rudé Právo*, December 9, 1962.
[68] Kjeld Oesterling from Prague in *Land og Folk* (Copenhagen), December 12, 1962.

8. Tito's Visit to the Soviet Union

THE third part of the early December Sino-Soviet confrontation was Tito's visit to the Soviet Union, ostensibly " on vacation " but actually to confirm and publicise the already extensive Soviet-Yugoslav rapprochement and to discuss with Khrushchev its future intensification. Khrushchev received the Yugoslav President with almost unprecedented party [1] as well as state honours. Tito was an honoured guest at a meeting of the Supreme Soviet,[2] where the party and state rapprochement was publicly cemented in speeches by the Soviet and Yugoslav leaders. Tito took with him Ranković, now clearly his designated successor, while he sent Moscow's *bête noir*, the Slovene Kardelj, to visit the Asian neutralists.

Yet it was Kardelj [3] who just before his departure first made public a significant change in the Yugoslav ideological attitude toward non-alignment. Yugoslavia's non-aligned policy, he said, is a specific part of its " path to socialism," and Yugoslavia is not " neutral " but stands for peace and socialism and against imperialism. Kardelj reversed Belgrade's previous criticism of Moscow's membership in a military bloc by terming it an objective and temporary result of the existence of two social systems, capitalism and socialism. On the other hand he specifically reaffirmed one of the major Yugoslav ideological innovations which had always been anathema to Moscow: the view that the transition to socialism can come by means other than the leadership of a Communist party, *i.e.*, denying the universal necessity of the dictatorship of the proletariat.

Khrushchev's Supreme Soviet speech of December 12 [4] in large part summed up and expanded on all the anti-Chinese Soviet themes of the four previous party congresses; it will thus be considered below with the December-January general Sino-Soviet exchanges. It was also, however, the most detailed and authoritative Soviet justification up to

[1] *Borba*, December 14, 1962. [2] *Ibid.*
[3] Interview with TANJUG, *Borba*, December 6, 1962.
[4] *Pravda*, December 13, 1962.

that time of Moscow's rapprochement with Belgrade. Its most important and far-reaching aspect, one which potentially went even beyond the 1955 Belgrade Declaration, was Khrushchev's recognition of various ideological roads to socialism.

After stating that " serious differences on many ideological questions . . . reflected in the *Programme* of the League of Communists of Yugoslavia " still remained, Khrushchev declared that " there cannot be a completely identical interpretation of all questions . . . in the struggle for building a new society." The important thing, he said, was the direction in which relations were moving: if both sides were trying to remove the remaining differences, one should emphasise this positive aspect more than the negative one of the remaining differences. In a passage omitted from the text of the speech printed in Yugoslavia [5] Khrushchev said that the Yugoslav leaders had " removed very much of what we considered mistaken and harmful." He reiterated that Soviet and Yugoslav views on foreign policy were substantially identical. Finally, he insisted that " it is impossible to deny " that Yugoslavia was a socialist country, thus uncompromisingly rejecting the September 1962 Chinese thesis that capitalism had been restored there. As will be seen below, in the rest of his speech he reiterated his rejection of the Chinese theses on the Cuban and Indian crises and taunted them on their neglect to retake Hong Kong and Macao. Tito could hardly have wished a more favourable Soviet setting for his triumphal return to Moscow.

Tito, in reply, expressed his total agreement with Khrushchev's views on the necessity of intensifying the rapprochement and strongly endorsed Soviet foreign policy in general and Khrushchev's Cuban policy in particular.[6]

The readjustment of Yugoslav policy away from liberalisation at home and toward the Soviet Union abroad continued apace after Tito's return to Belgrade. In Kiev, on his return trip, Tito told Yugoslav journalists [7] that they should " not dramatise " remaining differences with Moscow (*i.e.*, that they should not write about them at all), and Ranković publicly referred to " the working class of the whole world and all the progressive forces, led by the Soviet Union." [8]

The results of Tito's visit were most informatively, and quite authoritatively, summarised by the Moscow correspondent of the Italian Communist newspaper *L'Unità*:

(1) Khrushchev affirmed in a categorical fashion that, on the basis of a Marxist evaluation of the facts, " it is by now impossible to deny that Yugoslavia is a socialist country."

[5] *Borba*, December 13, 1962. [6] *Pravda* and *Borba*, December 14, 1962.
[7] *Borba*, December 22, 1962.
[8] *Ibid.*

(2) The Soviet leaders are convinced that the Yugoslav Communists have eliminated from their internal policy many of those elements which they considered prejudicial to the construction of socialism.

(3) There was admitted the possibility of the non-identity of views on certain questions without this having to be considered a motive for a break or as an obstacle to the development of fraternal relations between the two parties.

(4) Khrushchev placed the accent on the danger of dogmatism, affirming that, in the actual situation, those who slid into dogmatic extremism separated themselves much more from Marxism than did the Yugoslav leaders.

(5) The two parties declared that they would consider the polemic on the past ended and, in the future, in order to reconstruct Soviet-Yugoslav friendship, would emphasise not the disagreements which separate them but those points of agreement already reached. . . .[9]

Upon his return Tito stressed that Yugoslavia would not change its foreign policy toward any country, but he immediately added that it would now have " the closest co-operation " [10] and " the best possible friendly relations " [11] with socialist countries. (Moscow was now more equal than Washington.) Tito continued his stress on integration of nationalities within Yugoslavia, on the leading role of the League of Communists and of the working class generally [12] (as compared to intellectuals), and added two new themes: a renewed emphasis on agricultural collectivisation [13] and an attack on abstract art and Western cultural influence,[14] whose coincidence with Khrushchev's [15] similar declarations was, as Mr. Molotov would have said, " no accident."

[9] Pancaldi from Moscow in L'Unità, December 17, 1962.
[10] Tito's speech, Borba, December 23, 1962.
[11] Tito's speech at Željeznik, ibid., December 30, 1962.
[12] Ibid., and speech to Youth Congress, Borba, January 24, 1963.
[13] Tito's New Year Message, Borba, January 1–2, 1963, as well as speech to Youth Congress, ibid., January 24, 1963.
[14] Tito's speech to Youth Congress, Borba, January 24, 1963, and interview with journalists, ibid., February 14, 1963. The new Yugoslav constitution, which originally had been intended by Kardelj as an instrument to bring about a partial re-establishment of the rule of law, was now revised to bring it more in line with Tito's recent speeches. (Kardelj in Borba, August 27, 29, September 21, November 19, 1962; Bakarić in ibid. February 24–27, 1963; Tito in ibid. September 22, 1962; for analysis, C.[hristian] K.[ind], " Titos Entwurf für eine neue Verfassung," Neue Zürcher Zeitung, March 11, 1963.)
[15] For Khrushchev's comments on abstract art, see Pravda, December 2, 1962 (and Michel Tatu in Le Monde, December 4, 1962). For subsequent developments, see Max Hayward, " The Literary Purge in Retrospect," Survey, No. 49 (October 1963), pp. 54–62.

9. The December-January Sino-Soviet Ideological Exchanges

THE December-January round of Sino-Soviet polemics was more violent, detailed and prolonged than the November exchanges and further intensified the dispute in form and substance. It gave rise to the fullest exposition of both views up to that time. The major statements included Khrushchev's December 12 Supreme Soviet speech,[1] then in December and early January a series of long and extremely sharp Chinese articles,[2] and later, replies to the Chinese in an article by Zhivkov[3] and a long editorial in *Pravda*.[4]

Although the Cuban and to a lesser degree the Sino-Indian crises remained the main causes of the accelerating polemics, the latter acquired a distinct momentum of their own. Initially they were still characterised by Soviet initiative, but in mid-December the Chinese shifted to a massive ideological offensive.

The longest and hitherto most outspoken Chinese attack was overtly directed against Togliatti. However, its condemnation of the PCI theory of structural reform was one of the few charges which did not apply to Khrushchev as well. Peking's assault on the Italian Communists had been foreshadowed not only by the Chinese attitude at the Italian Congress in Rome but by a mid-November Albanian editorial blast

---

[1] *Pravda*, December 13, 1962. See also "Triumph of the Leninist Policy of Peaceful Co-existence," *Kommunist*, No. 18 (passed for the press December 26, 1962), pp. 12-19 and "A leading Soviet Diplomat," *Pravda*, December 5, 1962.

[2] "Workers of All Countries, Unite to Oppose Our Common Enemy," *People's Daily*, December 15, 1962, *Peking Review*, V. 51 (December 21, 1962), pp. 5-10; "The Differences Between Comrade Togliatti and Us," *People's Daily*, December 31, 1962, *Peking Review*, VI, 1 (January 4, 1963), pp. 9-21; "Leninism and Modern Revisionism," *Red Flag*, January 5, 1963, *Peking Review*, VI, 2 (January 11, 1963), pp. 5-10; and "Revolutionary Dialectics and How to Appraise Imperialism," *ibid*. pp. 10-16.

[3] Todor Zhivkov, "Unity of Socialist Countries is Decisive in Building Communism," *World Marxist Review*, V, 1 (January 1963), pp. 3-11.

[4] "Let Us Strengthen the Unity of the Communist Movement in the Name of the Triumph of Peace and Socialism," *Pravda*, January 7, 1963.

against the PCI which in length and scope was record-breaking even for Tirana.[5]

A major sign of continuing Soviet escalation was the reprinting in *Pravda* on December 10 of the explicit criticism of the Chinese made by Togliatti and Novotný at the Italian and Czechoslovak congresses. Khrushchev's December 12 Supreme Soviet speech, although it did not expressly attack the Chinese, strongly reaffirmed Soviet positions (including the previously summarised endorsement of Yugoslavia), sharply rejected the Chinese views on the Cuban crisis and on a whole range of other issues, and sarcastically taunted Peking for not having regained Hong Kong and Macao as India had Goa and Indonesia Dutch New Guinea. The next day, at a Plenum of the French Communist Central Committee, the PCF secretary for relations with other Communist parties, Raymond Guyot, for the first time explicitly and extensively condemned the Chinese (rather than the Albanians) on the whole range of disputed issues; and while *Pravda* did not publish his report,[6] it did publish on December 16 the open condemnation of the Chinese in the subsequent French Central Committee resolution.[7]

The previous day, December 15, had seen the publication of the first of four major Chinese documents; the second and most important (ostensibly directed against Togliatti) appeared on December 31, to be followed by two more at the beginning of January. Together they represented a major systematisation, elaboration, and sharpening of the Chinese position comparable in scope, albeit much stronger in tone, only to the April 1960 " Long Live Leninism! " series. The Soviet reply to the Chinese documents came in a detailed, systematic, strong, but not totally hostile January 7 *Pravda* editorial.

First, the escalation in form. The mid-December French Plenum documents were the first pronouncements of any major pro-Soviet Communist party which publicly, directly, and extensively analysed the whole dispute as primarily Sino-Soviet rather than Soviet-Albanian. The reprinting by *Pravda* of the explicitly anti-Chinese statements of Togliatti, Thorez, and the French Plenum resolution, plus others which followed, signalled the breaching by Moscow of one of the last barriers to a public, all-out Soviet attack against Peking. Finally, the January 7 *Pravda* editorial for the first time criticised the Chinese by name, although still only on the procedural issue of their support of the Albanians; its other anti-Chinese charges remained implicit. The Chinese still did not explicitly refer to the Soviet Union; but they systematically

5 " Concerning the Theses for the Tenth Congress of the Italian CP," *Zëri i Popullit*, November 17 and 18, 1962.
6 *L'Humanité*, December 17, 1962.
7 *L'Humanité*, December 15, 1962, and *Pravda*, December 16, 1962.

refuted Soviet positions, often by quoting, but not identifying by name, Soviet spokesmen.

Khrushchev's verbose justification of his actions in the Cuban crisis was substantially the same in content but sharper in tone than Ponomarev's in November: Moscow had installed and removed (by an honourable compromise with Washington) the missiles from Cuba in order to safeguard Cuba from invasion and to avoid thermonuclear war, a catastrophe feared by " sober " circles in the United States as much as elsewhere. Critics of Soviet Cuban policy, Khrushchev said, were now making the same error as Trotsky at Brest-Litovsk in 1917. He went on to praise Castro strongly, to support the latter's " five points," and to declare that the Soviet Union would defend Cuba against any attack. Peking replied much more precisely: China had never favoured either installing the missiles, a use of nuclear weapons for intimidation which reflected a lack of trust in popular struggle and could only be termed adventurism, or removing them, which constituted an act of capitulationism. Instead Peking reiterated its position that the imperialists should be " despised strategically and taken seriously tactically " (to which Moscow replied that strategy must not contradict tactics) and declared that adventurers and capitulationists alone could be called Trotskyites. Peking viewed the Cuban crisis as " a Munich pure and simple " not—as " those who accuse us " maintain—because China wanted " to plunge the world into a thermonuclear war " (a " most malicious and despicable . . . slander ") but because of " the sacrifice of another country's sovereignty . . . [to] a compromise with imperialism." [8]

On the Sino-Indian crisis Khrushchev reaffirmed the " neutral " stand of the November 5 *Pravda* editorial while taunting Peking about Hong Kong and Macao. The January 7 *Pravda* article reaffirmed Soviet policy on the zone of peace and the national bourgeoisie and on solving all disputes between them and socialist states through negotiation, and the Chinese denounced this attitude as one of " some self-styled Marxist-Leninists " who " have cast Marxism-Leninism to the winds." [9]

On the more general issue of the nature of imperialism and of peaceful co-existence Moscow declared that one can and should compromise with the " sober circles " of imperialism. In reply Peking repeated the themes of " Long Live Leninism! ": peace is won by unmasking the imperialists and by revolutionary struggle, particularly in the national liberation movement. One cannot separate disarmament from the latter, as do those who " place their hopes for world peace on ' mutual conciliation,' ' mutual concessions,' ' mutual accommodations,' and ' sensible

8 " The Differences Between Comrade Togliatti and Us," *loc. cit.*, p. 16.
9 " Workers of All Countries, Unite to Oppose Our Common Enemy," *loc. cit.*, p. 7.

compromises with imperialism '" (all favourite phrases of Khrushchev).[10] Nuclear weapons have not outdated the Marxist-Leninist theses on the nature of war; such a " ' logic of survival ' is the logic of slaves." [11] Overstressing the destructiveness of thermonuclear war only aids U.S. nuclear blackmail.

Defending his Cuban policy, Khrushchev had declared that if imperialism is a paper tiger it has " nuclear teeth." Replying to " other persons " [in addition to Togliatti] who assert that " today imperialism has nuclear teeth," the Chinese lengthily refuted the pro-Soviet interpretation; those who rejected it, they added, " have obviously lost every quality a revolutionary ought to have and have become as short-sighted and timid as mice," [12] are " merely chiming in with imperialism," [13] and display cowardice instead of " revolutionary optimism." To this Moscow replied that the mark of true revolutionary optimism is confidence in the policy of peaceful co-existence; the opposite view is a philosophy of suicide.

On the feasibility of peaceful transition to socialism, Moscow reiterated its previous position. In Peking's more precise and extreme reply, the Chinese asserted that since there never had been a peaceful transition to socialism, one must not concentrate on it but on revolutionary struggle. In this context Peking denounced Togliatti's concept of " structural reform " (which, it claimed, he had " unilaterally " declared valid for the whole international Communist movement) as " a new kind of social-democratic trend." [14] Furthermore

> ... the modern revisionists ... on the pretext of " democracy in general " deny the class character of democracy and strive to achieve step by step their objective of eliminating the dictatorship of the proletariat in order to facilitate the restoration of capitalism step by step in a certain form. . . .[15]

Thus the October Chinese charge that Tito had restored capitalism was implicitly extended to include Khrushchev's and Togliatti's allegiance to this goal.

The conflict on the Albanian and Yugoslav issues also sharpened further. Khrushchev violently accused the Albanians of having tried to precipitate thermonuclear war during the Cuban crisis (a charge so ludicrous that it had some meaning only if applied to the Chinese), of behaving like small boys by repeating foul words taught to them by " someone else " [i.e., the Chinese], of having broken with Marxism-Leninism, and of being Trotskyites. Zhivkov declared that the Albanians

---

10 " The Differences Between Comrade Togliatti and Us," loc. cit., p. 11.
11 " Leninism and Modern Revisionism," loc. cit., p. 8.
12 " The Differences Between Comrade Togliatti and Us," loc. cit., pp. 13, 14.
13 " Leninism and Modern Revisionism," loc. cit., p. 8.
14 " The Differences Between Comrade Togliatti and Us," loc. cit., p. 17.
15 " Leninism and Modern Revisionism," loc. cit., p. 6.

had placed themselves outside the socialist camp and the world Communist movement, and that their attitude was of major international significance; and therefore, contrary to the views of " sincere comrades " who opposed public discussion on the issue [presumably the North Vietnamese and Cuban " neutrals "], it must be criticised. The January 7 *Pravda* editorial added the charge that since 1960 the Albanians had refused to enter into the " comradely discussions " required by the November 1960 Moscow Declaration. Meanwhile, the Chinese attacked the " slanders and attacks " against the Albanians, as well as against themselves and the North Koreans for defending them, as " the very worst manifestation of splitting, sectarianism, of nationalism and bignation chauvinism," as being " amiable " to the enemy and " ruthless " toward fraternal parties.[16]

Khrushchev's views on Yugoslavia, summarised in the previous section, were reiterated in the January 7 *Pravda* editorial, which declared that anyone [*i.e.*, the Chinese] who claims that " capitalism has been restored in Yugoslavia is speaking deliberate untruth " and " fabrications." [17] The Chinese in turn called this outlook " an open, crude violation " of the 1957 and 1960 Moscow Declarations, whose denunciations of the Yugoslavs they again quoted.[18]

In their December 15 article the Chinese first publicly raised the issue of factionalism, which had dominated the November 1960 discussions,[19] and repeated essentially what Teng Hsiao-p'ing had said at that time. The [Soviet] thesis that truth is defined by the majority's view is incorrect: truth is objective and often, as in the cases of Lenin and Liebknecht, not on the side of the majority. " The sole . . . most reliable . . . majority " is " the people who decide the course of history . . . who account for more than 90 per cent. of the population of the world " [presumably the peoples of Asia, Africa, and Latin America, a theme increasingly stressed in Chinese statements]. Therefore

> . . . Their [*i.e.*, the Soviet] " majority " is only a fictitious, superficial phenomenon and in essence they are precisely in the minority, while the " minority " they have attacked is in essence precisely the majority. . . .

(One cannot help remembering Luther's defiant words at the Diet of Worms in 1520: " *Hier stehe ich. Ich kann nicht anders.*")

The contrary Soviet position was repeated by Zhivkov: " friendship and solidarity with the Soviet Union is the main criterion of the internationalism of each party and each Communist. . . ." [20] Economic

---

16 " Workers of All Countries, Unite to Oppose Our Common Enemy," *loc. cit.*, p. 8.
17 " Let Us Strengthen the Unity of the Communist Movement," *loc. cit.*, p. 10.
18 " Workers of All Countries, Unite to Oppose Our Common Enemy," *loc. cit.*, p. 9.
19 Griffith, " The November 1960 Moscow Meeting: A Preliminary Reconstruction."
20 *Op. cit.*, p. 11.

co-operation among socialist states through integration in CMEA is, he insisted, essential for the advance of socialism.

Differences sharpened not only on specific policy issues but on more general ideological ones as well. Moscow reiterated that the "fundamental nature of the present epoch" is one of "the world of socialism . . . expanding and . . . crowding out . . . the world of capitalism," and added that "the most vital problem of the day is the problem of war and peace." [21] Peking agreed that the present era is characterised by "the transition from capitalism to socialism" (the November 1957 Declaration), but added that this transition is based "on the viewpoint of proletarian revolution and proletarian dictatorship," while the modern revisionists, "shunning this viewpoint like the plague . . . regard our epoch as one of ' capitalism growing into socialism peacefully '." [22]

As to the causes of differences like the Sino-Soviet conflict, Zhivkov declared that they arise from "political regression" on the part of the leaders of a party, but not from the party itself [23]; and this phenomenon, the January 7 *Pravda* editorial added, produces "left sectarianism" which "feeds on nationalism and in turn feeds nationalism." [24] The Chinese, on the other hand (while also stating that different opinions are unavoidable) retorted that the real question in dispute is whether the 1957 and 1960 Declarations "are valid." [25]

On the question of what is now the main danger within the international Communist movement, dogmatism-sectarianism or revisionism, both sides restated and somewhat revised their positions. Moscow was in the more difficult position here, as on the Yugoslav issue, since the 1957 and 1960 Moscow Declarations had clearly termed revisionism the main danger. However, Khrushchev referred approvingly to the statement in the 1960 Declaration that dogmatism could become the main danger in certain parties, as was shown by the fact that in the Cuban crisis the Yugoslavs had taken a correct Marxist line and the dogmatists a "provocative" one, and concluded that, since the struggle against dogmatism and "left-wing opportunism" had been neglected, it had therefore developed "beyond the infant stage." Indeed, the advance of Communism in countries "with the most varied economic and social standards creates favourable conditions" for its development. Furthermore, since dogmatism is unbearable in a major party in power and dangerous when it threatens peace, it is therefore "increasingly emerging" as a serious danger and is now "no less dangerous than revisionism." The December French Plenum resolution (of which excerpts,

---

[21] "Let Us Strengthen the Unity of the Communist Movement," *loc. cit.*, pp. 3, 4.
[22] "Leninism and Modern Revisionism," *loc. cit.*, pp. 5, 6.
[23] *Op. cit.*, p. 4. [24] *Loc. cit.*, p. 8.
[25] "Workers of All Countries, Unite to Oppose Our Common Enemy," *loc. cit.*, p. 9.

including this one, were reprinted in *Pravda* and thus implicitly endorsed by Moscow) went one step further: dogmatism " lately has become the main danger to the international Communist and labour movement." [26] (Neither of these formulations, however, was repeated in the Zhivkov or the *Pravda* January 7 articles, one of the few signs that Moscow might be willing to adopt a more conciliatory policy.)

The Chinese reaffirmed the thesis of the 1960 Moscow Declaration that revisionism is the main danger. Peking added that what " those who attack the Chinese Communist Party " call " dogmatism " is " nothing but the bastion of Marxist-Leninist theory " as well as of the 1957 and 1960 Moscow Declarations, while the " anti-dogmatism " and " creativeness " of their opponents is just a " signboard " to " distort Marxism-Leninism and tamper . . . as they like " with the 1957 and 1960 Moscow Declarations, an " absolutely impermissible " attitude.[27]

Both sides used strong language to communicate the seriousness of the situation. The Chinese declared that the attacks on themselves, the Albanians, and the Koreans were " an utterly outrageous violation " of the 1957 and 1960 Declarations and " an event of the utmost gravity in the international Communist movement . . . [which took it] even further down the road towards a split." [28] However, even though the current crisis is " another serious struggle " against the " splitting activities " of the modern revisionists comparable to the two previous ones against the Second International and against the " left adventurist " Trotsky and the " right opportunist " Bukharin, it was " inevitable " and is now an " objective reality," and therefore its " public emergence enables people to see . . . and understand the harm it does " and thus hastens its defeat.[29] Chinese defiance of their opponents was total:

> . . . we only submit to truth and the fundamental interests of the people of the world; we will never obey the baton of any anti-Marxist-Leninists. No amount of name-calling and opposition by the imperialists, the reactionaries and the modern revisionists can shake our stand. . . .[30]

A " resolute struggle," " difficult and tortuous though it may be," must be waged against " modern revisionism . . . an adverse current . . . contrary to Marxism-Leninism . . . which is disrupting the unity of the international Communist movement," but it will eventually be " cast aside by the proletariat." [31]

[26] *Loc. cit.*
[27] " Workers of All Countries, Unite to Oppose Our Common Enemy," *loc. cit.*, p. 9.
[28] *Ibid.*, quoted from *loc. cit.*, p. 5.
[29] " Leninism and Modern Revisionism," *loc. cit.*, pp. 9–10. The Albanians had made this operational point in their October 13 article.
[30] " Workers of All Countries, Unite to Oppose Our Common Enemy," *loc. cit.*, p. 9.
[31] " The Differences Between Comrade Togliatti and Us," *loc. cit.*, p. 20.

Having said all this, the Chinese then repeated their Prague call for an international Communist conference. The Russians, although not taking a direct position on this, did endorse " collective discussion "[32] and thus at least left the door open for another attempt at détente.

In early January the French Communist ideologist Yves Moreau published a long and explicit series of anti-Chinese articles which, while they added nothing substantive to the dispute, were notable for their extreme verbal invective against Peking, whose position was referred to in such terms as " nefarious," " evil," " narrow-mindedness," and " contempt for reality." [33] The United States and the British Communist parties also joined the fray with explicitly anti-Chinese statements. The U.S. Party declared that it " regretfully finds it necessary to take sharp public issue with the policy of the Chinese Communist Party in respect to the Cuban crisis," which it called " pseudo-left, dogmatic and sectarian." The reference in the December 31 Chinese editorial to " a ' Munich ' pure and simple " was " an unbelievable and irresponsible slander against the CPSU . . . [which] only emphasises how the Chinese Communist leaders have . . . already departed from Marxism-Leninism." The article also repeated Khrushchev's taunt about Hong Kong and Macao.[34] The British CP statement was primarily a call to end polemics and to reduce the differences; as such it will be considered below. However, like the CPUSA pronouncement, it clearly reflected the oppositions of the British and American left-wing to Chinese " adventurism " in regard to nuclear war:

> . . . For Britain, nuclear war could well mean our national extinction. Who would be left to build socialism in the heap of radio-active ruins that would remain? . . .

Although generally much less sharp than the American one, it did declare:

> . . . Everyone knows that the phrase " modern revisionist " means the Communist parties who disagree with our Chinese comrades. Such totally irresponsible charges simply cannot be taken seriously. . . .[35]

Finally, Togliatti replied in a moderate, suave, but in one instance menacing tone to the December 31 Chinese editorial directed against him (which the PCI reprinted immediately after his article). While repeating

---

[32] *Pravda*, January 7, 1963, quoted from *loc. cit.*, p. 10.

[33] *L'Humanité*, January 5, 7, 9, 10, 11, 12, 14, 15, 16, 1963 (JPRS 17,401, January 31, 1963, quoted from pp. 2, 16). See also Charles Haroche in *France Nouvelle*, No. 800, January 16–22, 1963, pp. 11–12 and JPRS 18,210, March 19, 1963.

[34] Statement of the CPUSA, " The Cuba Crisis and the Struggle for World Peace," *The Worker* (New York), January 13, 1963.

[35] Statement of the BCP, " Restore the Unity of the International Communist Movement," *Daily Worker* (London), January 14, 1963.

his proposal made at the end of the Italian Congress that Peking send a delegation to study PCI problems and policy, he declared that the part of the November 1960 Moscow Declaration concerning Yugoslavia was " mistaken " and should be corrected—the first time that any Communist leader except the Yugoslavs themselves had publicly called for the Declaration's revision.[36]

[36] Palmiro Togliatti, " Riconduciamo la discussione ai suoi termini reali," *Rinascita*, XX, 2 (January 12, 1963), pp. 13–15, at p. 14. *Cf.* Longo in *L'Unità*, January 16, 1963, and JPRS 17,374, January 30, 1963.

10. The East German Party Congress

THIS last Congress, which opened in East Berlin on January 15, was the most completely Soviet-staged. It could hardly have been otherwise: alone among Moscow's East European satellites, the " German Democratic Republic " [1] remains neither a state nor a nation, neither democratic nor a republic, but a Soviet satellite ruled by a hated clique of rigid *apparatchiki*. Its people's nationalism and resentment of Ulbricht's economic oppression, political tyranny, and cultural philistinism deprive the East Berlin régime of any possibility of serious popular support. The June 17, 1953 risings and the 1956 intellectual ferment convinced Moscow, which on both occasions probably considered abandoning Ulbricht, that only he could make East Germany safe for Communism. By 1961 the result was so massive a flight to the West that the construction of the Berlin Wall on August 13, 1961 was Khrushchev's only alternative to the economic collapse of East Germany. Even so, the vicious circle of popular opposition and régime tyranny was eased only slightly by some economic de-Stalinisation beginning in mid-1962. By the beginning of 1963 both Khrushchev and Ulbricht must have realised more than ever that their differences in personality and policy were far overshadowed by each's need of the other in the face of the East German crisis. Even more than Gomulka's domesticism, Ulbricht's slow de-Stalinisation was purchased at the price of his total support of Moscow's foreign policy; and the Sino-Soviet conflict had by January 1963 reached such a height that Ulbricht was all the less likely to make any false step.

The East German régime, like Albania and to some extent Bulgaria, has irredentist ambitions. Ulbricht's aim is to rule a reunited but Communist Germany; and this might in theory incline him, like Hoxha

---

[1] See Melvin J. Croan, " Dependent Totalitarianism: The Political Process in East Germany " (unpub. Ph.D. diss., Harvard, 1960), W. E. Griffith, ch. on East Germany in *The East European Thaw* (Cambridge, Mass.: M.I.T., forthcoming); Evelyn Anderson, " East Germany," in Walter Laqueur and Leopold Labedz, eds., *Polycentrism* (New York: Praeger, 1962), pp. 90–106.

and Chervenkov, toward Chinese views. Thus, as in Bulgaria and Czechoslovakia, there were in 1959 a few signs of East German sympathy for the Chinese; these ceased on Moscow's orders in June 1960. Khrushchev's " honourable compromise " in the Cuban crisis must have greatly disappointed Ulbricht, not only because he and his policies thrive on international tension but also because he knew that this would mean a détente in Berlin as well—a development which soon occurred and one which Ulbricht implemented [2] unhappily but as faithfully as always.

After the Twenty-Second CPSU Congress, Ulbricht at first suppressed almost all effects of Khrushchev's renewed de-Stalinisation on East German internal policy. But he could not do this indefinitely, particularly in view of the renewed Soviet thaw in economics and (temporarily) in culture, the increasing Sino-Soviet tension, the Soviet rapprochement with Yugoslavia and the liberalisation in Hungary. The Berlin Wall had saved Ulbricht's régime from collapse but it had solved none of its other problems, which since the 1959 forced collectivisation drive had continued to worsen.[3]

In late 1962 East German endorsement of the Soviet anti-Chinese line was rapid, complete and fervent. Although, as always when the East German régime confronts difficulties, rumours circulated that Ulbricht's position was in danger (and in fact he was seventy years old), they, as usual, turned out to be groundless; Khrushchev effusively endorsed him at the SED Congress [4] and thus strengthened his power position even more. Indeed, with respect to internal affairs the Congress represented a major attack by the East Berlin régime,[5] encouraged by Khrushchev's denunciation of Soviet abstract artists the previous month,[6] against the signs of cultural thaw in East Germany.[7] As always, the master *apparatchik* Ulbricht had sensed the coming trend in Moscow; after the Congress he not only brought the cultural scene entirely back

---

[2] See his speech at Cottbus, *Neues Deutschland*, December 5, 1962, and Hermann Axen in *ibid.*, July 12, 1962.

[3] O.F. [Otto Frei], " Die wirtschaftliche Misere in der DDR," *Neue Zürcher Zeitung*, November 28, 1962.

[4] *Neues Deutschland*, January 15, 1963.

[5] See the authoritative articles by Peter Christian Ludz, " Die ' DDR ' nach dem VI. Parteitag der SED," *Hinter dem Eisernen Vorhang*, IX, 4 (April 1963), pp. 9–16, and C. St. [Carola Stern], " Küsse and Püffe," *SBZ-Archiv*, XIV, 4 (February 15–28, 1963), pp. 49–50. The best current coverage of East German affairs is by O. F. [Otto Frei] in the *Neue Zürcher Zeitung*. See also Peter Bender, " Leipziger Andeutungen," *Der Monat*, XV, 176 (May 1963), pp. 81–84, and Alois Riklin, " Das Parteiprogramm der SED," *Aus Politik und Zeitgeschichte* (Beilage zur Wochenzeitung *Das Parlament*), April 24, 1963.

[6] *Izvestiya*, December 4, 1962.

[7] O.F. [Otto Frei], " Divergierende Tendenzen in der SED," *Neue Zürcher Zeitung*, November 6, 1962, " Ulbricht's Lavieren," *ibid.* November 18, 1962, " Pankows Einschwenken auf Moskaus neuen Kurs," *ibid.* November 26, 1962, " Die Diskussion um die Kulturpolitik in der DDR," *ibid.* December 23, 1962.

under control but inaugurated a degree of cultural conformism and oppression exceptional even for East Germany.[8]

Khrushchev clearly intended the Congress,[9] the only one he attended personally, to be the stage for the culminating attack against the Chinese. His reference to it as an " international Communist forum " (i.e., as having validity for the international Communist movement) [10] further underlines his estimate of its importance. (Gomułka [11] and the Italian Communists,[12] in order to prevent a final break, had before the congress urged moderation on the Soviet leader, but Khrushchev evidently took their advice only in part.) Although he blandly proposed the suspension of public polemics in order to provide a cooling-off period before a multi-party conference, he in fact continued them on the Yugoslav and Albanian issues.

Ulbricht's opening speech [13] was notably anti-Chinese in respect to the Sino-Indian crisis: he was the first Communist leader to state publicly that the Chinese had not consulted the SED (and presumably also not the CPSU) before launching their October 20 attack.

Khrushchev's speech,[14] although it maintained the Soviet position on all the main issues in the dispute with the Chinese, was not as strong as his December 12 one. He did not repeat the Hong Kong-Macao taunt, he omitted any reference to dogmatism rather than revisionism being or becoming the main danger, he did not mention the Chinese thesis on the minority and majority, he took a somewhat harder position against non-Communist neutralist (" national bourgeois ") governments, and he was considerably less extreme on the East German and Berlin issues. In at least a potential softening of Moscow's position against Tirana, he declared that Albania as well as Yugoslavia was a socialist country and that the differences with their leaderships should and could be solved. Nevertheless, his criticism of the Albanians was much harsher than his

8 O.F. [Otto Frei], " Verstärkter Druck auf die ostdeutschen Intellektuellen," *Neue Zürcher Zeitung*, February 2, 1963, and " Widerstand gegen Ulbrichts Kulturbanausen," *ibid*. February 24, 1963; A. C., " Neostalinistische Kulturpolitik in der DDR," *ibid*. April 2, 1963, " Ulbrichts Rückkehr zum Stalinismus," *ibid*. April 6, 1963, and " ' Säuberung ' im ostdeutschen Schriftstellerverband," *ibid*. April 10, 1963.

9 The major source for the Congress' proceedings is *Neues Deutschland*, January 15–22, 1963; however, in another sign of escalation, various texts were censored. The full texts are in *Protokoll der Verhandlungen des VI Parteitages der SED* 7 Vols. ([East] Berlin, Dietz, 1963.)

10 See also the January 15, 1963, *Pravda* editorial, " Unity and Solidarity as the Guarantee of New Successes."

11 ok. [Bogdan Osadczuk-Korab], " Gomułka und Moskaus Streit mit Peking," *Neue Zürcher Zeitung*, January 19, 1963. Novotný (who was in South-East Asia), Kádár and Gheorghiu-Dej did not attend; presumably, therefore, attendance by East European leaders was optional.

12 See Longo's speech at the Congress, *infra*.

13 *Neues Deutschland*, January 16, 1963. The Chinese have since maintained they did; see p. 226, *infra*.

14 *Pravda*, January 17, 1963. For excerpts, see Dallin, *op. cit.*, pp. 746–761.

reference to " ideological disagreements " with the Yugoslavs, while he repeated (without identifying it as such) Kardelj's December 1962 distinction between blocs and social systems. However, he did not, as he had on December 12, charge Hoxha with trying to start a thermonuclear war over Cuba, nor did he say that the Yugoslav position on Cuba had been correct. Instead he declared that communism, unlike churches, should not employ excommunication, and he proposed a suspension of public polemics between all parties so that " passions could cool " and an all-party meeting thus be properly prepared. But all this, as was shown by the fact that he again demanded that the Albanian leadership publicly recant and make self-criticism, was probably more a tactic against the Chinese than a genuine expression of willingness to make concessions.

On January 17 Gomulka praised Khrushchev highly for " preventing . . . a thermonuclear catastrophe " in Cuba and frankly stated that without the Soviet Union " no socialist state could survive . . . against imperialism "—a stark admission of Polish *raison d'état*. He not only stressed the necessity of ending public Sino-Soviet polemics but also recommended only " greater modesty and moderation " on the part of the Albanians.[15]

The Cuban delegate was Armando Hart, a member of the July 26 (Castro) movement rather than, as at preceding congresses, the old-line (PSP) Cuban Communist Blas Roca. Hart stressed the impossibility of peaceful co-existence between classes (*i.e.*, of the peaceful road to socialism) in Latin America while omitting reference to the Albanians, thus again demonstrating Castro's neutral position on the dispute. He reiterated Castro's January 2 statement on the necessity of unity in the international movement.[16]

The Chinese delegate, again Wu Hsiu-ch'üan, repeated his previous position on American imperialism and on the Cuban and Indian crises as well as the substance of the Chinese statement at the end of the Czechoslovak Congress. Replying to (without identifying) Khrushchev's proposal to end public polemics, he declared it a " response to a certain degree " to the previous Chinese proposal, but added that one should not " preach the need to call a halt to attacks while . . . continuing to make attacks," a clear reference to Khrushchev's actual continuation

[15] *Trybuna Ludu* and *Neues Deutschland*, January 18, 1963, *Protokoll*, I, pp. 434–439.
[16] A partial text of Hart's speech of January 17 is in *Neues Deutschland*, January 19, 1963; the same day's *Pravda* version excised some of Hart's passages emphasising the importance of unity. The Prensa Latina version in *Hoy* and *Revolución* of January 18, 1963, was very brief but gave the key passage stressing Sino-Soviet unity, a position stressed at length in a long article in the January 18 *Hoy* by Blas Roca, " La unidad y la cohesion del campo socialista y del movimiento communista es vital para nosotros." Full text: *Protokoll*, I, pp. 559–571.

of polemics. For the first time Wu revealed in public some of the contents of the Chinese April 1962 proposal for the cessation of polemics and for a multiparty meeting, and, still without naming the CPSU, he referred to the proposal's point that Moscow should first approach Tirana.[17]

When Wu attacked the Yugoslavs, his voice was drowned out by whistles, boos, shouts and feet-stamping—an insult carefully staged, one must assume, by Khrushchev, who was ostentatiously absent when Wu spoke. The chairman that day, SED Politburo candidate member Paul Verner, declared that Wu's " provocative " remarks contradicted Communist unity, reflected an incorrect Chinese position " contradicting all the norms of the international movement " and were therefore correctly criticised by previous congresses, and that his " gross attacks " on the " fraternal party of Yugoslavia " were " resolutely rejected " by the SED and the Congress. Wu stood silent and expressionless until the demonstration ceased [18]; but Mao will hardly forget this slap in the face to him and his party. After a day's delay, *Pravda* [19] reported from Berlin that Wu's speech " defended the anti-Leninist position " of the Albanians, " expressed ideas . . . counter to the general line of the international Communist movement," " repeated attacks on fraternal parties," and spoke " in an absolutely impermissible tone " about the Yugoslav Communists.

The Italian Communist delegate, Longo, made an even more conciliatory speech than Gomułka. He reaffirmed the Soviet and also the PCI positions but stressed that he did so in brief since the congress was not the place for their full discussion; rather, they should be discussed

---

[17] The full text of Wu's speech is in NCNA English from Berlin, January 18, 1963 (SCMP 2904, January 23, 1963, pp. 21–26), and was published in *People's Daily* on January 19, excerpts: *Peking Review*, VI, 4 (January 25, 1963), pp. 7–9 (including all the key passages). The Chinese Embassy in East Berlin handed out English and German complete texts to Western correspondents; the text was distributed by the congress secretariat late and in a highly censored version in *Protokoll*, II, pp. 19–30.

[18] The most complete source for the demonstration and for Verner's rebuke of Wu is a January 18 Reuter's dispatch by their East Berlin correspondent, Jack Altman, the only non-Communist journalist present. See also *Protokoll*, II, pp. 23–24, 30–31. Much of the above comes, in addition, from the East Berlin dispatches in the July 19 *Pravda*, *L'Unità* and *Borba*, and from " Let Us Unite on the Basis of the Moscow Declaration and the Moscow Statement," *People's Daily*, January 27, 1963, and *Peking Review*, VI, 5 (February 1, 1963), pp. 5–10, at p. 5 (*q.v.* for Chinese reaction). According to the probably reliable text of an unpublished speech by Hager at the 3rd SED CC Plenum, July 29–30, 1963, Wu cried, " Stamp your feet, that is your German civilization!" See *SBZ-Archiv*, XIV, 17–18 (1.–2. Septemberheft 1963), pp. 272–283, at p. 281. It is confirmed by *Protokoll*, II, p. 24.

[19] In a Berlin dispatch from its special correspondents A. Lukovets and Vl. Kuznetsov, *Pravda*, January 19, 1963. The more complete January 21 *Pravda* version of Wu's speech omitted the attacks on Khrushchev and the references to the April 1962 CCP proposal summarised above. The January 19 *Neues Deutschland* version was so censored as to give no indication of Wu having said anything differing from the Soviet line.

frankly, fraternally and privately, so as to establish " common theses."
He repeated with emphasis Togliatti's proposal that Peking send a
delegation to Italy.[20]

The SED reply to Wu, by the SED leader Hermann Matern,
denounced the Albanians for violating their Warsaw Pact obligations
(presumably because in 1961 they forced the Russians to evacuate the
Sazan submarine base), strongly defended the Soviet line on Yugoslavia,
with whom the discussion about existing " differences of opinion "
could not be carried on with " insults and vituperations," and, unlike
Khrushchev, sharply denounced (without naming its source) the Chinese
doctrines on " majority," " minority " and " split." [21]

The Yugoslav delegate, Veljko Vlahović,[22] spoke mostly in generali-
ties; his remarks on Wu's attacks against Yugoslavia were deliberately
very restrained. Nevertheless, he praised Khrushchev for his Cuban
policy and took a position on Berlin and the German question which
was strongly anti-Bonn and pro-East German—more so, there is reason
to believe, than in the original draft of his speech.

Next to the public demonstration against the Chinese, the most
striking sign of Soviet intention to escalate the Sino-Soviet dispute at the
congress was the SED's refusal to allow any Asian delegates except the
Japanese to speak,[23] with the excuse that there was no time. Thus two
ruling parties, the North Korean and North Vietnamese, plus the largest
non-bloc party, the Indonesian, were denied the right to speak at a
congress of a ruling party—an event without precedent in post-1945
Communist history. Presumably the primary purpose of this affront was
to prevent the North Korean delegate from defending the Chinese. His
intended speech, however, was published in Pyongyang and Peking
on January 22 [24]; it stressed Chinese policy lines on unanimity through
consultations, modern revisionism as the main danger, and avoidance of
public discussion of differences; and, specifically rejecting the Soviet
" international Communist forum " thesis, it declared that, in spite
of the proposal [by Khrushchev] to end polemics, " unilateral criticism
has been made against the Chinese Communist Party," something which
is " just what our enemies want and hail."

[20] *L'Unità* and *Pravda* and, in a heavily censored version omitting most of the moderate
passages, *Neues Deutschland*, January 19, 1963, also an unsigned article in *Rinascita*,
January 26, 1963, pp. 9–10 (JPRS 17,773, February 21, 1963). Full text: *Protokoll*,
II, pp. 88–94.
[21] *Neues Deutschland*, January 19, 1963, and *Protokoll*, II, pp. 73–78.
[22] *Politika*, January 20, 1963. The text in *Neues Deutschland*, January 21, 1963, omitted
all reference to the Chinese, and *Protokoll*, II, pp. 288–296.
[23] The Japanese delegate's speech as reported in the January 22 *Neues Deutschland* was
quite colourless, but its full text (*Protokoll*, II, pp. 329–332) indicated that it was
clearly if moderately pro-Chinese. All the Asian speeches are in the *Protokoll*.
[24] *Nodong Sinmun*, NCNA in English, January 22, 1963, and *Protokoll*, II, pp. 347–355.

As usual the Burmese, Thai and Malayan greeting messages were pro-Chinese.[25] Although the Indonesian Communist Party (PKI) had immediately and publicly endorsed Khrushchev's call for a suspension of public polemics, its undelivered but published greeting to the congress was more pro-Chinese than pro-Soviet, notably in its violent denunciation of the " subversive activities " of the " modern revisionists . . . represented by the leadership of the League of Communists of Yugoslavia " in respect both to international trade union and Afro-Asian activities and to the Sino-Indian crisis.[26] The North Vietnamese greeting was carefully neutral.[27] Reportedly both the Soviets and the Chinese lobbied vigorously during the congress among the Communist delegates from underdeveloped countries.[28] Ulbricht's closing speeches expressed the hope that the Chinese would agree to Khrushchev's proposal to suspend public polemics,[29] but his tongue must have been firmly in his cheek: the congress' proceedings, as Khrushchev and Ulbricht must have known, insured the contrary.

[25] *Protokoll*, II, pp. 420–438.
[26] Telegram, Aidit to CC CPSU, in *Harian Rakjat*, January 21, 1963 (JPRS 18,383, March 27, 1963, pp. 53–54). This telegram also endorsed Khrushchev's support of a one- to two-year cooling-off period, as had a previous Aidit statement in *Harian Rakjat*, January 8, 1963 (JPRS 17,940, March 5, 1963, pp. 31–33). PKI greeting: *Harian Rakjat*, January 21, 1963 (JPRS 18,383, March 27, 1963, pp. 55–59), and *Protokoll*, II, pp. 355–356.
[27] *Nhan Dan*, January 15, 1963 (JPRS 17,735, February 19, 1963), and *Protokoll*, II, pp. 355–356.
[28] East Berlin dispatches by Jack Altman of Reuters, January 18, 19, 21, 1963.
[29] The published text (*Neues Deutschland*, January 20, 1963), and *Protokoll*, II, pp. 95–117, 329–332, omitted a repetition in the live broadcast version of Khrushchev's " international Communist forum " thesis (East German Radio domestic service, January 18, 1963, 1500 GMT, in BBC/EE/1154/C/4, January 21, 1963).

11. The February-March Exchanges of Polemics and Letters

THE East German Congress was followed by an ambivalent combination of much sharper polemics (especially from Peking) plus a gradual move toward a face-to-face Sino-Soviet confrontation, largely under the urging of other Communist parties, who feared a split above all and for whose favour both Moscow and Peking were competing.

THE POLEMICS

The initial public Soviet reaction to the SED Congress was an editorial in the February *Problems of Peace and Socialism* [1]; the Chinese reaction came in a long and violent editorial at the end of January in the *People's Daily*, [2] followed by a furious Albanian polemic. [3] Moscow replied in a February 10 *Pravda* editorial [4]; thereafter it seemed for two weeks that the Chinese were slackening their polemics. Far from it: during the last week in February, immediately after Peking's receipt of a remarkably conciliatory letter from the Soviet Central Committee, [5] the *People's Daily* published for the first time long excerpts from all the major recent anti-Chinese attacks [6] and then, at the end of the month and

---

[1] " Cementing the Unity of the Communist Movement is Our Internationalist Duty," *World Marxist Review*, VI, 2 (February 1963), pp. 3–8 (passed for the press, Russian edition, January 22, 1963).

[2] " Let Us Unite on the Basis of the Moscow Declaration and the Moscow Statement," *People's Daily*, January 27, 1963, *Peking Review*, VI, 5 (February 1963), pp. 5–10.

[3] " For Militant Unity of the Communist Movement Under the Victorious Banner of Marxism-Leninism," *Zëri i Popullit*, February 7, 1963.

[4] " For Marxist-Leninist Unity in the Communist Movement, for Solidarity of the Countries of Socialism," *Pravda*, February 10, 1963, *CDSP*, XV, 6 (March 6, 1963), pp. 3–9.

[5] Letter of the CPSU CC to the CCP CC, February 21, 1963, in *Pravda*, March 14, 1963, *Peking Review*, VI, 12 (March 22, 1963), pp. 8–10.

[6] It published the full texts of Khrushchev's December 12, 1962, speech (*People's Daily*, February 20, 1963), the January 7 *Pravda* editorial (*ibid.* February 21, 1963), Khrushchev's January 16 speech at the SED Congress (*ibid.* February 22, 1963), the February

the beginning of March, a long attack against the French Party,[7] an almost book-length programmatic manifesto against the Italian Party,[8] and briefer attacks on the United States [9] and Indian parties.[10] Altogether they were the most comprehensive statement of the Chinese case until that time.

In these articles Moscow and Peking publicly set forth much more openly and forcefully than before the true scope of the Sino-Soviet dispute. The Russians declared that there were serious differences on " cardinal issues of policy " [11] and for the first time publicly described (still without identifying their origin) the full charges made by the Chinese against them, culminating with the statement that

> . . . Outright attacks were levelled against the Communist Party of the Soviet Union. Its leaders were accused of revisionism, and cries were raised for their removal. . . .[12]

Thus for the first time one of Peking's main objectives was publicly identified as the removal of Khrushchev. (There has been much press speculation that the Chinese actually calculate on a pro-Chinese or at least an anti-Khrushchev faction in the Soviet leadership; whether or not this be true, there is in my view no adequate evidence for the existence of such a faction.)

The Chinese took an equally serious view of the situation. " The international Communist movement," they declared, " is at a critical juncture " and " in more and more serious danger of a split "; the 1957 and 1960 Moscow Declarations " are in great danger of being publicly torn up," and therefore " it is time to rein in on the brink of the precipice." [13] They made public the treatment meted out to them at the SED Congress and their fury at such a " deliberately planned "

10 *Pravda* editorial (*ibid.* February 23, 1963), plus, on February 24, long excerpts from PCF and PCI statements, including those at the Italian Congress and the *Tesi* (the *Tesi* were also published as a pamphlet by the Peking World Knowledge Publishing House on February 23), and on February 26 the full text of the February 7 *Zëri i Popullit* editorial (including all its attacks on Khrushchev by name).

7 " Whence the Differences?—A reply to Thorez and Other Comrades," *People's Daily*, February 27, 1963, *Peking Review*, VI, 9 (March 1, 1963), pp. 7–16.

8 " More on the Differences Between Comrade Togliatti and Us—Some Important Problems of Leninism in the Contemporary World," " by the Editorial Department of *Hongqi*," *Red Flag*, Nos. 3–4, March 4, 1963, *Peking Review*, VI, 10–11 (March 15, 1963), pp. 8–58.

9 " A Comment on the Statement of the Communist Party of the U.S.A.," *People's Daily*, March 8, 1963, *Peking Review*, VI, 10–11 (March 16, 1963), pp. 58–62 (with it were published several CPUSA documents).

10 " A Mirror for Revisionists," *People's Daily*, March 9, 1963, *Peking Review*, VI, 10–11 (March 15, 1963), pp. 63–66.

11 " Cementing the Unity of the Communist Movement is Our Internationalist Duty," *op. cit.*, p. 3.

12 *Ibid.* p. 4.

13 " Let Us Unite on the Basis of the Moscow Declaration and the Moscow Statement," *op. cit.*, pp. 6–9; " Whence the Differences?" *op. cit.*, p. 14.

exhibition of " extreme rudeness," a " disgusting . . . new high " in " double-dealing," a " strange and almost incredible . . . phenomenon . . . in the international Communist movement." [14]

In reply to the Soviet proposal to discontinue polemics the Chinese reiterated Wu's sarcastic reference to this in East Berlin: although " certain people " [Khrushchev] " have suddenly begun to strike up the tune of ' unity,' " this really

> . . . consists of giving themselves permission to abuse others, while not allowing the others to reason with them. By " calling a halt to open polemics," they mean permission for themselves to attack others as they please, while the others are forbidden to make whatever reply is called for. . . .[15]

Moscow replied that although the Chinese endorsed in principle all steps toward unity, they had nevertheless attacked various speeches delivered at the East German Congress as well as the Yugoslav Communists; even so, " we should like to believe that this is not . . . an effort to continue the polemics." [16]

The Chinese concentrated their assault against Moscow on the Yugoslav issue. On no other point could they cite the 1960 Moscow Declaration with such telling effect; on no other point had Khrushchev so openly, consistently and increasingly defied both them and the Declaration, most recently by the presence of Yugoslav party delegations at the Italian and East German congresses and by Tito's visit to Moscow. The " attitude toward Yugoslav revisionism," the Chinese declared, " is not a minor but a major question "; it does not concern " just one detail or another " or " how to interpret the 1960 Moscow Statement," and " what attitude to take toward a fraternal party "; it is not " a question of helping comrades rectify the mistakes they have made," but rather it is a question

> . . . that . . . concerns the whole . . . of whether to adhere to Marxism-Leninism or to wallow in the mire with the Yugoslav revisionists . . . of what attitude to take toward traitors toward the Communist cause . . . of unmasking and denouncing enemies of Marxism-Leninism . . . whether genuinely to strengthen unity or merely to pay lip-service to unity while in fact creating a split. In the final analysis it is a question of whether to adhere strictly to the Moscow Declaration and the Moscow Statement or to tear them up. . . .

---

[14] " Let Us Unite on the Basis of the Moscow Declaration and the Moscow Statement," *op. cit.*, p. 5 ; " Whence the Differences?" *op. cit.*, p. 14 ; " More on the Differences Between Comrade Togliatti and Us," *op. cit.*, p. 50.

[15] " More on the Differences Between Comrade Togliatti and Us," *op. cit.*, p. 56.

[16] " For Marxist-Leninist Unity of the Communist Movement, for Solidarity of the Countries of Socialism," *op. cit.*, p. 5 (the reference is to the January 27 *People's Daily* editorial, " Let Us Unite on the Basis of the Moscow Statement and the Moscow Declaration ")

The Chinese attacked "certain people" for having termed the Moscow Declarations a "stereotyped formula," specifically Togliatti for having called them "incorrect" on Yugoslavia. The origin of "the current great debate," the Chinese declared, was "the open betrayal of Marxism-Leninism . . . by the Tito clique of Yugoslavia. . . ." The Chinese then quoted at length Khrushchev's 1957–59 anti-Yugoslav statements and stated that "they [Khrushchev] are trying to install the Tito clique as their ideological centre." No one party or parties, Peking declared, could "correct" such unanimously reached decisions. Those trying to "reverse the verdict on the Tito clique" are trying to "tear . . . up completely" the 1957 and 1960 Declarations, to replace "the revolutionary line of Marxism-Leninism" by "the capitulationist line of revisionism," and thus to stage "a deliberate attempt to create a split" in the international Communist movement.

> . . . Were this to happen, what possible common basis would there be for unity? . . . The Chinese Communist Party will never allow the common agreement of the fraternal parties to be either doctored or scrapped, will never allow traitors to be pulled into our ranks. . . .[17]

Moscow agreed that "the question of relations with Yugoslavia is a serious question of principle" (although certainly not "the main, decisive result" of the SED Congress, as the Chinese implied) but defined it as one of "mutual relations among the Communist parties of socialist countries," not, as the Chinese did, as one of relations between Communists and traitors. Elaborating upon Khrushchev's December 12 speech, *Pravda* declared on February 10 that the November 1960 Moscow Declaration "proceeded from an appraisal of Yugoslavia as a socialist country" (since otherwise it would not have referred to the possibility of its "revolutionary gains" being "jeopardised") and that therefore

> . . . the international Communist movement has set the goal of aiding Yugoslavia and its leaders to correct the existing errors and to return to the path of unity with the world socialist system. . . .

Furthermore for the first time *Pravda* mentioned "fourteen socialist countries," thus including Albania, Yugoslavia and Cuba.[18] *Pravda* cited specific Yugoslav Communist speeches and resolutions which confirmed the fact that

> . . . mistakes and shortcomings . . . have been subjected to criticism and practical measures for their correction . . . outlined . . . [in such areas as]

---

17 " Let Us Unite on the Basis of the Moscow Declaration and the Moscow Statement," *op. cit.*, pp. 6–8; " More on the Differences Between Comrade Togliatti and Us," *op. cit.*, pp. 9, 50.
18 This was reiterated in A. Lukovets, " The Triumphant Achievement of Socialism," *Pravda*, February 20, 1963.

> the leading role of the party . . . the planned basis of the economy . . . reorganising agriculture on socialist lines . . . and emphasis . . . on the general laws governing the building of socialism. . . .

Just to give tit for tat, *Pravda* then quoted several 1957 pro-Yugoslav Chinese statements. The article mentioned only Tito and Ranković favourably by name, while condemning " the attempts of some LCY leaders to identify the commonwealth of socialist countries with a military bloc and in effect to equate it with NATO," a clear slap at Kardelj, and one which was not reprinted in Belgrade. The article emphasised in conclusion, as had Khrushchev on December 12, that " a policy of severing and alienating its supporters from communism is not a Leninist policy." [19]

On the related issue of Albania the Chinese strengthened their previous position. They quoted (without identifying specifically its author) Khrushchev's statement in his closing Twenty-Second Congress speech that no one could do more than the Chinese Communists to help settle the Albanian problem, and pointed out that

> . . . these comrades broke off the Soviet Union's diplomatic relations with . . . Albania without any scruples.
>
> Did this not convincingly demonstrate that they had not the slightest desire to improve relations between the Soviet Union and Albania? [20]

In a furious article of February 7 (reprinted later that month in *People's Daily*) the Albanians themselves declared that

> . . . the question of Soviet-Albanian relations is an important question of principle . . . a case of open attempts to impose on other parties, by entirely inadmissible methods and dangerous actions . . . a line and point of view in contradiction with . . . the Moscow Declarations. . . . The anti-Marxist attitude of the N. Khrushchev group toward the Albanian Party of Labour and the Albanian People's Republic is not an isolated and fortuitous action but the logical consequence of its whole line and activity. . . .

and proposed that Moscow and Tirana should jointly publish all the documents in the Soviet-Albanian dispute.[21]

Moscow repeated its previous position: it was prepared to re-establish fraternal party relations with the Albanians if the latter would " renounce their erroneous views " and " revert to the path of unity and close co-operation within the fraternal family " [*i.e.*, if Hoxha would surrender to Khrushchev].[22]

---

[19] " For Marxist-Leninist Unity of the Communist Movement, For Solidarity of the Countries of Socialism," *op. cit.*, p. 8.

[20] " Whence the Differences?" *op. cit.*, p. 12.

[21] " For Militant Unity in the Communist Movement Under the Victorious Banner of Marxism-Leninism," *op. cit.*

[22] " For Marxist-Leninist Unity of the Communist Movement, For Solidarity of the Countries of Socialism," *op. cit.*, p. 8.

Somewhat less was said about the Cuban and Sino-Indian crises. Reiterating their previous position on Cuba, the Chinese denied [Khrushchev's] " most absurd " analogy between their conduct and Trotsky's attitude toward the Brest-Litovsk Treaty and denounced the " particularly vicious slandering " by the U.S. Communist Party on this issue. They further charged the CPUSA [Khrushchev] with

> . . . bringing up the question of Hong Kong and Macao [as] . . . merely a fig-leaf to hide your disgraceful performance in the Caribbean crisis. . . . While you ostensibly speak for China, you are actually stabbing her in the back. . . .[23]

Moscow kept silent on Cuba [24] as well as on the Sino-Indian border dispute—a possible indication of ideological embarrassment.

Not so the Chinese. Although they had for some months been relatively silent on the Indian CP, Peking on March 9—perhaps in response to a strong February 12 CPI attack on the Chinese " violation " of the 1957 and 1960 Declarations [25]—denounced the majority CPI leadership headed by S. A. Dange as one which has

> . . . embarked on the road of national chauvinism and class capitulationism. . . . Their intention is to turn the Indian Communist Party into an appendage of India's big bourgeoisie and big landlords and a lackey of the Nehru government [and to] . . . serve the purposes of U.S. imperialism which is prompting neo-colonialism in India. . . .

Dange, the Chinese declared, has

> wholly turned himself into an instrument of the ruling class for repressing the working class . . . and split the party wide apart. . . .

Finally, in a passage which indicated that Dange was, like Tito, becoming for Peking a litmus test of " revolutionary Marxist " orthodoxy, the Chinese declared that

> . . . The Dange clique provides another mirror [besides the Tito clique]. It reveals how the leaders of a Communist party in a capitalist country take the road of revisionism, slide down it, and end up as the servants and the tail of the bourgeoisie. . . .[26]

23 " More on the Differences Between Comrade Togliatti and Us," op. cit., p. 55; " A Comment on the Statement of the Communist Party of the U.S.A.," op. cit., pp. 58, 62.
24 The Russians did, however, react on the esoteric level to Peking's refutation of their Brest-Litovsk analogy. On March 7 Pravda published an historical essay defending at length Lenin's policy towards the 1918 Brest-Litovsk peace treaty, in opposition to the views of both Trotsky and Bukharin, and warning in conclusion that " the experience of this struggle . . . is extraordinarily important and relevant under present-day conditions as well " (V. Zaitsev, " The Historic Victory of the Theory and Tactics of Leninism," Pravda, March 7, 1963).
25 CPI National Council Resolution, " On Certain Ideological Questions Affecting the Unity of the International Communist Movement," New Age, February 17, 1963.
26 " A Mirror for Revisionists," op. cit., pp. 63–64, 66.

On the issue of factionalism (or, in the phraseology of the Chinese, of the " real " versus the " arithmetical " majority and minority) both sides stood firm. Denouncing this " utterly groundless " [Chinese] concept, the Russians for the first time used the formulation, " the parties adhering to creative Marxism," as their counterpart to the Chinese category, " modern revisionists," and equated their version with the " overwhelming majority " of parties whose " strategy and tactics . . . are the fruit of the experience of decades." [27]

The Chinese developed three themes: (1) Soviet domination of other Communist parties (by " the baton "), (2) the overriding priority of the revolutionary movement in Asia, Africa and Latin America and, implicitly, the claim for Chinese leadership of it, and (3) the Sino-Soviet boundary issue.

Never before had the Chinese so openly and bitterly denounced Soviet domination of international communism. A large part of Peking's denunciation of Thorez consisted of bitterly sarcastic documented references to the PCF's " complete turns of 180 degrees in response to . . . masters wielding batons over the heads of servants." [28]

Nor had the Chinese ever before made so explicit their desire for concentration on and predominance in the underdeveloped (and coloured) areas of Asia, Africa and Latin America. These, they declared, form the " focus of world contradictions " and of the struggle against imperialism; for their people this struggle is " the cardinal and most urgent task "; the support of these " revolutionary struggles [is] . . . decisive for the cause of the international proletariat " and is therefore a " fundamental task of the international Communist movement." Communist parties, particularly in the " metropolitan imperialist countries," must no longer " flaunt their seniority," " put on lordly airs," " carp and cavil," and, like " some people " [Khrushchev], view such support as " a one-sided ' burden.' " On the contrary, " without a correct stand, line, and policy " on this struggle, Communist parties in the " metropolitan imperialist countries " [and presumably elsewhere as well] cannot have a correct line on their own struggle. Wars of national liberation are inevitable; " it is impossible for anybody to prevent " them,

> even if certain self-styled Marxist-Leninists [Khrushchev] only worry lest the " sparks " of resistance by the oppressed nations and people . . . might lead to disaster and disturb their own tranquillity . . .[29]

---

[27] " Cementing the Unity of the Communist Movement is Our Internationalist Duty," *op. cit.*, pp. 4, 7; " Let Us Unite on the Basis of the Moscow Declaration and the Moscow Statement," *op. cit.*, p. 9.

[28] " Whence the Differences?" *op. cit.*, p. 15; " More on the Differences Between Comrade Togliatti and Us," *op. cit.*, p. 8.

[29] " More on the Differences Between Comrade Togliatti and Us," *op. cit.*, pp. 16–17, 19–20, 24.

Finally, Peking produced its delayed but much more violent answer to Khrushchev's taunt on Hong Kong and Macao. In the course of their March 8 editorial attack on the CPUSA, the Chinese, in listing all the " unequal treaties " imposed upon the Chinese Empire by the imperialists, referred specifically to those by which the Russian Tsars annexed from China the territory which now forms the Soviet Maritime Provinces and part of Soviet Central Asia. First they carefully pointed out that Peking, in dealing with this question, differentiates between socialist and imperialist countries, and even with the latter strives for a peaceful settlement. The Chinese then turned on " those " [Khrushchev] who had " picked up . . . this filthy stone . . . from a cesspool ":

> . . . In raising questions of this kind, do you intend to raise all the questions of unequal treaties and have a general settlement? Has it ever entered your heads what the consequences would be? Can you seriously believe that this will do any good? . . .
>
> Anyone with a discerning eye can see at once that your sole intention is to prove that the Chinese are cowards. . . .[30]

The most violent Chinese language to date was employed in ridiculing Moscow for its failure to republish (as Peking had been doing since mid-December) the attacks against it made by other parties:

> . . . they [the Russians] are mortally afraid of the Albanian comrades' replies; they dare not publish them and are afraid of others doing so. . . .
> . . . Comrade Thorez and other comrades! We have already published your statements accusing us. Will you do the same? Do you have that kind of statesmanship? Do you have that kind of courage? . . .[31]
>
> The doughty warriors who claim to possess the totality of Marxist-Leninist truth are mortally afraid of the articles written in reply to their attacks by the so-called dogmatists, sectarians, splitters, nationalists and Trotskyites whom they have so vigorously condemned. They dare not publish these articles in their own newspapers and journals. As cowardly as mice, they are scared to death.
>
> Dear friends and comrades who claim to possess the whole truth! Since you are quite definite that our articles are wrong, why don't you publish all these erroneous articles and then refute them point by point so as to inculcate hatred among your people against the " heresies " you call dogmatism, sectarianism and anti-Marxism-Leninism? You are divorced from the masses. That is why you fear the truth and carry your fear to such absurd lengths. . . . Friends, comrades! If you are men enough, step forward! Let each side in the debate publish all the articles in which it is criticised by the other side, and let the people in our own countries and the whole world think over and judge who is right and who is wrong. This is what we are doing, and we hope you will follow our example. We are not afraid to publish everything of yours in full. We publish all the " masterpieces " in which you rail at us. Then in reply

---

30 " A Comment on the Statement of the Communist Party of the U.S.A.," *op. cit.*, p. 61.
31 " Whence the Differences?" *op. cit.*, pp. 14–15.

we either refute them point by point or refute their main points. Some-times we publish your articles without a word in answer, leaving the readers to judge for themselves. Isn't that fair and reasonable? You, modern revisionist masters, do you dare to do the same? If you are men enough, you will. But having a guilty conscience and an unjust case, being fierce of visage but faint of heart, outwardly as tough as bulls but inwardly as timid as mice, you will not dare. We are sure you will not dare. Isn't that so? Please answer! [32]

On more general ideological issues both sides, and particularly the Chinese, repeated and somewhat expanded their previous views. On the question of the origin of the differences between them Moscow declared that among socialist states and Communist parties the identity of interests, of ultimate aims, and of ideology leads objectively to unity but, because of differing conditions in various countries, there arise divergent ways of applying the " general principles of Marxism-Leninism " [*i.e.*, differences of tactics]. But there cannot be differing interpretations of the basic principles or differences in strategy, particularly when these develop into " a theoretical and political platform hostile to Marxism-Leninism " which is then " universalised," and when " organisational steps " against unity are taken; after all, " there can be only one international Communist movement, and one Communist party in each country, just as there can be only one truth." [33]

The Chinese reiterated their most extreme view that the origin of " modern revisionism " [the Soviet position] is " anti-Marxist-Leninist . . . bourgeois ideology," a product of the " labour aristocracy " at home and " of the policies of imperialism " abroad. Therefore the struggle against it on the part of " genuine proletarian ideology, that is, revo-lutionary Marxism-Leninism," is a conflict between " right and wrong." While the first great struggle between " Marxists on the one hand and revisionists and opportunists on the other " was carried on by Lenin against Kautsky, Bernstein and the Second International, and the second by " Stalin against Trotsky, Bukharin and other ' Left ' adventurers and Right opportunists," the " third great debate is now in progress." Thus the Chinese sharply underscored their view of the significance of the dispute and of their own intransigent position in it.

The Chinese also further elaborated their own version of the history of the controversy. Denying Thorez's charge that they had refused to

---

[32] " More on the Differences Between Comrade Togliatti and Us," *op. cit.*, pp. 56–57.
[33] " Cementing the Unity of the Communist Movement Is Our Internationalist Duty," *op. cit.*, pp. 4–5 ; " For Marxist-Leninist Unity of the Communist Movement, For Solidarity of the Countries of Socialism," *op. cit.*, p. 8. Although these pro-Soviet articles did not refer to the question of whether revisionism or dogmatism is the " main danger," a *Pravda* article (A. Lukovets, " Triumphant Achievement of Socialism," *Pravda*, February 20, 1963) quoted a statement by Raymond Guyot (*L'Humanité*, February 15, 1963) that " sectarianism and dogmatism . . . have become the main danger," a thesis to which the CCP could only take the most violent exception.

accept the theses of the Twentieth Congress, they declared that " no one has the right to demand that all fraternal parties should accept the thesis of any one party." Indeed, they " held different views all along " about the negative aspects of the Congress which, however, they did not intend to discuss " in the present article." The differences arose, the Chinese continued, because " certain comrades of a fraternal party " [the Russians] violated the 1957 Moscow Declaration. " Around the time of the Camp David talks in September 1959," " they " [the Russians] acted contrary to its provisions on the nature of imperialism. They relied on " summit meetings " instead of " joint struggle," lauded the U.S. imperialists, interpreted peaceful co-existence as " nothing but ideological struggle and economic competition," proclaimed that through disarmament imperialism could aid underdeveloped countries, counterposed the national liberation struggle to the struggle for peace, and laid " one-sided stress " on the peaceful transition to socialism.[34] " They " [the Russians] first publicly exposed these differences in their statement of September 9, 1959, on the Sino-Indian border situation,[35] which " made no distinction between right and wrong " and was

> . . . the first instance in history in which a socialist country instead of condemning the armed provocation of the reactionaries of a capitalist country, condemned another fraternal socialist country when it was confronted with such armed provocation. . . .

After Camp David " certain comrades [the Russians] became more and more intemperate " in their attacks on Chinese foreign and domestic policies, on " its general line of socialist construction, its big leap forward and its people's communes," and " spread the slander " that the Chinese state policy was " adventurist." Then at the June 1960 Peking WFTU meeting these " certain comrades " spread many erroneous views and opposed the " correct views " of the Chinese. Several weeks later at Bucharest " someone [Khrushchev] went so far as to wave his baton and launch an all-out and converging surprise attack on the Chinese Communist Party." Not only did " they [the Russians] employ all kinds of base devices against . . . the Albanian comrades " but they

> . . . lost no time in taking a series of grave steps to apply economic and political pressure, even to the extent of perfidiously and unilaterally tearing up agreements and contracts . . . not in twos or threes or in scores, but in hundreds. . . .[36]

The Chinese did not add any new information on the November 1960 81-party meeting; they merely stated that " we intend to give the true picture and clarify right from wrong at the proper time and place."

---

[34] " For Marxist-Leninist Unity," *op. cit.*, p. 9.
[35] *Pravda*, September 10, 1959.   [36] " Whence the Differences?" *op. cit.*, pp. 8–13.

They declared, however, that they had "many times" advised the Russians to take the initiative in settling their differences with Albania or at least to exercise patience, apparently once in early 1961 and again just before the Twenty-Second Congress. On Cuba they repeated their previous positions; on India they added the charge (first lodged publicly by the Albanians in September 1962) that Moscow had furnished "war material" to Nehru.

In the most detailed Chinese ideological refutation of the Soviet positions, the long March 4 article against Togliatti, the only attack directed solely against the PCI was on the policy of "structural reform," which they termed "a most serious challenge to the theory of Marxism-Leninism and an attempt to overthrow it completely," even worse than Kautsky's and one which could be summed up as the development of "pre-monopoly-bourgeois socialism into monopoly-bourgeois-socialism." [37] (The strong anti-PCI Chinese attitude may have been partially caused by an article by Longo in the February *Problems of Peace and Socialism* which was much sharper than Togliatti's previous remarks; Longo referred to the Chinese "distortion of our standpoint" as "incomprehensible," "preposterous," and one which could only be made by "blind sectarians.") [38]

THE EXCHANGES OF LETTERS

The February-March exchanges of letters between Moscow and Peking did not improve Sino-Soviet relations; probably they were not intended or expected to do so. On the contrary, they were part of the Sino-Soviet manoeuvres to win support among other Communist parties and to shift the odium for worsening relations to the other side.

The Soviets sent a letter to the Chinese dated February 21 [39]; the Chinese reply was dated March 9 (these first two were both published simultaneously in Moscow and Peking on March 14) [40]; the Soviet rejoinder was dated March 30. [41] Of the three only the first Soviet letter bears any mark of a genuine attempt to reduce tension. (It was also the only one not published immediately after its transmittal.) It expressed "serious concern" over the "serious damage" caused by the "open, ever aggravating polemics" and declared that "future generations will

[37] "More on the Differences Between Comrade Togliatti and Us," *op. cit.*, pp. 11, 31, 41.
[38] Luigi Longo, "The Struggle for Structural Reforms and Its Revolutionary Significance," *World Marxist Review*, VI, 2 (February 1963), pp. 15–21, at pp. 18, 21.
[39] CPSU CC to CCP CC, *Pravda*, March 14, 1963, and *CDSP*, XV, 11 (April 10, 1963), pp. 3–6.
[40] CCP CC to CPSU CC, *People's Daily*, March 14, 1963, and *Peking Review*, VI, 12 (March 22, 1963), pp. 6–8.
[41] CPSU CC to CCP CC, *Pravda*, April 3, 1963, *CDSP*, XV, 14 (May 1, 1963), pp. 3–9. and Document 1 (published in *People's Daily*, April 4, 1963).

never forgive us " if " we should fail to find in ourselves the courage and strength . . . to surmount the existing differences." It emphasised the necessity of taking " immediate concrete practical steps " to improve the atmosphere. It even appeared to move the Soviet position closer to the Chinese on the issue of aid to national liberation movements by declaring that Moscow was ready to furnish them with arms, and on the issue of factionalism by advocating the resolution of differences through " joint comradely consultations," a formulation which avoided specific endorsement either of the previous Soviet stand on the binding nature of simple majority decisions or of the Chinese insistence on unanimity. Finally, the letter specifically proposed an immediate bilateral Sino-Soviet meeting " at a high level " in order to bring Sino-Soviet positions closer and, " by creating a favourable climate," to move towards an all-party meeting.

Yet on closer study of its timing the Soviet letter appears much less conciliatory. It was dated one day after the *People's Daily* reprinted Khrushchev's December 12 speech, thereby signalling the imminence of another major round of Chinese polemics. It must have been delivered almost immediately since on February 23 Mao gave to Chervonenko, the Soviet Ambassador to Peking, an " estimation " of the contents of the letter.[42] It must therefore have been intended in part to forestall further polemics from Peking, *i.e.*, to leave the Soviets the last word (the February 10 *Pravda* editorial). Little wonder that the Chinese refused to fall into this trap!

As has been outlined above, the Chinese polemics of February 27 and March 4, 8 and 9, all published after Peking's receipt of the first Soviet letter, were much sharper than the preceding Soviet statements and clearly indicated that Peking had no intention of making any concessions to Moscow. Chinese intransigence was confirmed by the uncompromising tone and content of the March 9 Chinese reply, and by the fact that it was almost immediately published in the Chinese (and Soviet) press.

The Chinese letter must be read against the background of the above-mentioned Chinese articles, of which the last appeared on the same day the letter was dated. While it began by " welcoming " the Soviet note and formally accepted the Soviet proposal for a bilateral meeting, the letter was in fact a highly polemical document, harsh, unyielding and blandly sarcastic. While granting the existence of " serious differences in the international Communist movement on a series of important questions of principle " which " have to be settled," it declared that their primary cause was not the differing conditions of the various parties, as

42 CCP March 9 letter, p. 6.

115

Moscow alleged, but the basic attitudes towards Marxism-Leninism and the 1957 and 1960 Moscow Declarations—*i.e.*, towards " right and wrong." The differences, stated the letter, should be settled by " consultation on an equal footing "—*i.e.*, by unanimous agreement either between Peking and Moscow or among all Communist parties—and those " which cannot be settled immediately may be laid aside, pending later settlement." This was, in effect, a claim for a Chinese veto over any international Communist decision and for the continued propagation of Chinese views unacceptable to Moscow. The letter blamed the Russians for carrying on public polemics, *inter alia* through " the convening of party congresses " (a clear allusion to the five in Europe).

While accepting the Soviet proposal of a general bilateral Sino-Soviet meeting, the Chinese presented their own agenda in the form of a summary of the key points of the 1957 and 1960 Declarations as well as a listing of specific points for discussion, whose order and content clearly indicated that Peking remained adamant on all key points at issue. For the first time this letter made public a summary of the April 7, 1962, Chinese letter, which indicated (as Wu had hinted in East Berlin) that one of Peking's conditions was a Soviet approach to Tirana for a Soviet-Albanian settlement. Furthermore, the Chinese description of the contents of the 1957 and 1960 Declarations, as had all such Chinese references since late 1962, included a. specific citation from them on the necessity of " continuing the struggle against Yugoslav revisionism, which has betrayed Marxism-Leninism," which, along with their repeated demand that Khrushchev go to an Albanian Canossa, sufficiently indicated their intransigence.

In closing, the letter blandly indicated that Khrushchev might if he wished come to Peking, but that Mao would not go to Moscow. On February 23 Mao had " expressed the hope " to Chervonenko that Khrushchev would stop off in Peking for talks " while making his visit to Cambodia "; if he did not, a Soviet delegation could be sent to Peking or a Chinese delegation could be sent to Moscow. Furthermore (as the Chinese stated publicly in mid-June only),[43] Mao also " clearly stated the reason why he was not prepared to visit the Soviet Union at the present time." (Unfortunately, Peking has not yet said what the reason was; one wonders if it was not in fact largely his personal antipathy to Khrushchev.) In other words, unless Khrushchev was willing to bow to Mao's prestige by coming to Peking, the discussions would be only on a secondary level and therefore necessarily inconclusive. The one concession in the letter was the statement that the Chinese would

---

[43] CCP CC letter to CPSU CC, June 14, 1963, in *People's Daily*, June 17, 1963, *Peking Review*, VI, 25 (June 21, 1963), pp. 6-22, at p. 22, and Document 2.

" temporarily suspend " polemics (as well they could afford to after their immediately preceding massive outpouring of them!), but they insisted that a joint Sino-Soviet agreement must be reached as the basis for their permanent suspension.

Although the Chinese did halt overt polemics as of March 9, the next few weeks saw the publication in the *People's Daily* of excerpts from over fifteen major Communist party attacks on the CCP,[44] a clear indication that Peking's suspension of polemics was indeed only temporary. Furthermore, as during the previous spring, the Chinese continued to publish polemics on the esoteric level.[45]

During this period there also occurred the still obscure episode of the Soviet approach to the Albanians. According to the second Soviet letter to the Chinese of March 30, Moscow " at the end of February " had sent a letter to the Albanians proposing a bilateral Soviet-Albanian meeting, which the Albanians initially " did not see fit to accept," but to which the Albanians " presumably on second thought," later replied, " staging a number of reservations and conditions " but nonetheless speaking of such a meeting. Thus according to this version the Russians had fulfilled this one of the Chinese April 1962 conditions *prior* to its reiteration in the Chinese reply of March 9.

The more detailed Albanian version, however, gives a quite different date for the Soviet letter to Albania: March 11, *following* the Chinese reply. On that date, according to an Albanian article of April 18,[46] the Czechoslovak Chargé d'Affaires in Tirana delivered to the Albanian Central Committee a letter from the CPSU Central Committee which transmitted an information copy of " a " Soviet letter (presumably the one of February 21) to the Chinese, and " in only a few lines " proposed " in passing " bilateral Soviet-Albanian party talks. In their letter to the

---

44 The articles and dates of publication are listed in *Peking Review*, VI, 13 (March 29, 1963), pp. 3–4; for citations of an earlier series of Chinese reprints of anti-CCP statements (from February 20 to February 24, 1963), see JPRS 18,255, March 21, 1963, pp. 1–3.

45 Following the initial exchange of letters, both Moscow and Peking reverted to the method of esoteric polemics which had characterised the Sino-Soviet dispute prior to late 1962. For implicit Soviet refutations of the Chinese attacks on the PCF and the PCI, see " The Traditions of the Paris Commune Are Immortal," *Pravda*, March 18, 1963; and " A Half Century of Struggle for Socialism " in honour of " The 70th Year of Comrade Palmiro Togliatti, General Secretary of the Italian Communist Party," *Pravda*, March 26, 1963. For the Chinese reiteration of their views on policy and theory, see Fan Cheng-hsiang, " The Development of Imperialist Contradictions," *Peking Review*, VI, 13 and 14 (March 29 and April 5, 1963), pp. 7–12 and 7–14; and Hsü Cheng-fan, Tseng Man-hsi and Kuo Yung-hsien, " Without Class Struggle, Socialism Will Be Empty Talk: Study Notes on the Works of the Three Great Utopian Socialists," *People's Daily*, March 16, 1963, and SCMP 2951, April 2, 1963, pp. 1–6.

46 " Khrushchev Again in the Role of Demagogue, Slanderer and Divider," *Zëri i Popullit*, April 18, 1963 (which contains the text of the Albanian March 13 reply).

117

CPSU of March 13, the Albanians declared that this was "unacceptable" since it treated the Albanian party as one "depending" on the Chinese and was clearly only a "false pretext" to prove that the Albanians rejected such talks; however, the Albanians were quite willing to have such talks when Moscow "creates all conditions for total equality." (As of this writing [November 1963] the Soviets have not denied this Albanian version.) It seems likely that some Soviet letter was in fact sent to the Albanians on March 11, after the receipt of the hostile March 9 Chinese reply, when Moscow could hardly have anticipated any genuine agreement or relaxation of tension with Peking. The Soviet approach to the Albanians was therefore probably only tactical rather than a serious effort at détente.

The Soviet rejoinder of March 30, like the Chinese reply of March 9, was clearly a polemic document intended primarily for public effect; and it was published almost immediately after its delivery. It was also polite in form, noting "with satisfaction" the "positive" Chinese reply, but in content it was a strong albeit veiled restatement of the whole Soviet position, which permitted neither "compromise" nor "reconsideration." It agreed to a mid-May meeting in Moscow but declared that this could be only a preliminary to an all-party meeting [*i.e.*, no joint Sino-Soviet directorate of the international Communist movement could be established]. It also referred to the "groundless attacks contained in the recent articles" of the Chinese press, which the Russians did not "now" intend to answer. As for Khrushchev's visit to Peking during his trip to Cambodia, the letter pointed out that not Khrushchev but Brezhnev was to make that journey as had been decided on February 12 "and announced in the press" [*i.e.*, the Chinese knew this full well but pretended otherwise in their letter for polemical advantage]. While agreeing to the Chinese agenda, the letter, in the form of a restatement of principles reiterated the [unidentified] Twenty-First Congress theses on the possibility of avoiding war before the final victory of socialism, the existence of a "radical qualitative change" brought about by thermonuclear war, the compatibility between this and the national liberation struggle, and the desirability of a peaceful transition to socialism if judged feasible by the party concerned.

As described above, the letter also stated that the Soviets had in late February approached the Albanians, who at first "did not see fit to accept our letter and later did so, and a joint meeting, only with a number of reservations and conditions." On Yugoslavia the letter repeated the thesis of Khrushchev's December 12 speech and the February 10 *Pravda* editorial, but with a somewhat less pro-Yugoslav tinge: the "serious differences" now lay with the LCY and not—as the *Pravda* editorial had said—with " some comrades " within it. Nevertheless the letter maintained that Yugoslavia was socialist, that the members of the LCY were " comrades," and that one should not allow " the lopping off " of any party from the international Communist movement; furthermore, by stating that an all-party conference should consider

> . . . the new features with which the line of the world Communist movement embodied in the Declaration and the Statement had been enriched in recent years. . . .

it indicated that the Russians intended to revise the 1960 formulation at least on Yugoslavia.

The letter equivocated on the relative dangers of revisionism and dogmatism, stating both that revisionism was the " principal " danger and that " right and left opportunism . . . is today no less dangerous than revisionism " [*i.e.*, China is as bad as Yugoslavia]. It rejected the reactionary " threadbare lie " about " the hand of Moscow " [*i.e.*, the Chinese charge about Khrushchev's " baton "] commanding fraternal parties. Finally, it denounced all efforts to rally the masses on the basis of " nationality, colour of skin, or geography . . . solely along continental lines—according to whether they are Africans, Asians, Latin Americans or Europeans "—one of the major themes in current Chinese propaganda.

Weeks passed before there was any specific announcement regarding a bilateral Sino-Soviet encounter, although the Soviet March 30 letter had proposed a meeting of representatives of the CPSU and the CCP in Moscow on approximately May 15. Finally, on May 9 Peking suggested changing the date to mid-June and named as heads of their delegation the two leading Chinese Communists most publicly identified with Sino-Soviet clashes—Teng Hsiao-p'ing (the major Chinese spokesman at the 1960 Moscow meeting) and P'eng Ch'en (the Chinese delegate to Bucharest in June 1960).[47] On May 11 Moscow proposed holding the meeting on July 5 because of the number of events already scheduled for June, " including some of an international nature." On May 14 Peking announced that this date was acceptable,[48] and two days later *Pravda* described the above steps by which the agreement had been reached and declared that the Soviet delegation would be headed by M. A. Suslov, and would also include Yu. B. Andropov, L. F. Ilichev and B. N. Ponomarev as well as the Soviet Ambassador to China, S. B. Chervonenko.[49]

[47] *People's Daily*, May 10, 1963
[48] *Ibid*. May 15, 1963.
[49] *Pravda*, May 16, 1963.

12. Attempts at Mediation by Smaller Parties

As Sino-Soviet polemics intensified during and after the five European Communist congresses, some of the smaller parties, threatened with internal strife at the prospect of a total public break, began to urge Moscow and Peking to make another attempt at détente. Others, acting wholly or partially under the influence of one or the other side, made proposals ostensibly aimed at mediation but which in fact served only the polemical interests of the side concerned. All this discussion centred increasingly on the question of the form of direct inter-party confrontation.

It is important to make clear the precise nature of the Chinese and Soviet positions on bilateral, multilateral and all-party meetings. Both ostensibly favoured an international Communist conference preceded by preparatory bilateral and multilateral talks. In fact, however, the Chinese were primarily interested in the immediate convocation either of an all-party meeting or of a multi-party gathering which would officially serve as a preparatory commission for the former (as in September-October 1960). In either case the Chinese would not be isolated; Albania, North Korea, in all probability the Indonesian Party, and perhaps the North Vietnamese—one or more of whom was bound to be on such a preparatory committee—would be on their side, and Peking could thus insist, as in November 1960, on unanimity, *i.e.*, on the postponement of all key issues until the all-party meeting and, in fact, indefinitely; *i.e.*, they could remain in the movement and conduct factional activity aimed at taking it over. The Russians, on the other hand, did not want an all-party meeting. Presumably they feared sizeable support for China and many-sided pressure for concessions in order to avert an open split, and, above all, the impossibility in such a meeting (as the November 1960 one had showed) of forcing the Chinese to abandon their factional activity. Moreover, in a preparatory committee the Chinese could effectively use the November 1960 Moscow Declaration to prevent the admission of Yugoslavia to the all-party meeting. Therefore Moscow at first attempted to use the European party congresses as a platform for anti-Chinese manoeuvres and then insisted on a bilateral Sino-Soviet meeting, where the Chinese would have no supporters and where the absence of both Albania and Yugoslavia would be automatic, thus perhaps easing discussion about them.[1] It was only at the East German Congress that Khrushchev accepted in principle the idea of an international conference after a cooling-off period.

In December 1962 the New Zealand [2] and Indian [3] Communist parties called for an all-party meeting. The former was a pro-Chinese extremist party; the latter a moderate pro-Soviet one; nevertheless, minorities are serious problems in both, and their leaders were probably acting under pressure from their members for mediation as well as under the instigation of their respective ideological " centres." On January 14 the British Communist Party, a pro-Soviet moderate, also proposed an international conference, partly in response to pressure from its pro-Chinese minority, albeit within the context of a pro-Soviet policy statement.[4] It advanced the following requisites for such a meeting: (1) the replacing of the " present public polemic . . . by serious internal preparation " and (2) " completely adequate time. . . . Only the preparation itself will show how much time we need." A similar position had been previously indicated by the pro-Soviet moderate Danes and the briefly " neutralist " Norwegians.[5] It became the expressed Soviet view only on January 16 at the SED Congress.

On January 16 Fidel Castro, a " Communist neutralist," called for the resolution of differences within the international Communist movement.[6] On February 10 the North Vietnamese Politburo, still " Communist neutralist," issued a cautiously neutral statement which

[1] See " Whence the Differences?" *op. cit.*; " More on the Differences Between Comrade Togliatti and Us," *op. cit.*; and the Longo interview reprinted in *Pravda*, February 25, 1963.
[2] " Communist Party of New Zealand Calls for World Meeting," *People's Voice* (Auckland), December 19, 1962, summarised in NCNA in English to Asia and Europe, January 11, 1963, 1331 GMT.
[3] Referred to in the CPI resolution of February 12, 1963, in *New Age*, February 17, 1963.
[4] *Daily Worker* (London), January 14, 1963. Significantly, the item concerning it in the January 15, 1963, *Pravda* omitted the BCP's call for an end for public polemics.
[5] *Land og Folk* (Copenhagen), December 30, 1962; *Friheten* (Oslo), January 8, 1963; and, for a January 1963 (pro-Soviet) Portuguese CP resolution criticising the Chinese and calling for an end to public polemics, a report by its Secretary-General Alvaro Cunhal to an August 1963 Portuguese CP CC Plenum, in Radio Free Portugal (clandestine), September 18, 1963, 2330 GMT (BBC/EE/1358/A3/3–4, September 21, 1963). The Norwegian CP briefly flirted with the Chinese but later returned to a pro-Soviet line, only in October 1963 to become neutralist. See p. 181, *infra*.
[6] Speech to the Inter-American Women's Congress, *Revolución*, January 23, 1963.

specifically advocated the end of open polemics and other actions aggravating differences as well as " careful " (as Moscow proposed) but " speedy " (as Peking proposed) preparations for an all-party meeting, in which differences discussed should be settled " unanimously " (the Chinese view). It added that the CPSU and the CCP " have the greatest share of responsibility in preparing all the necessary conditions " for a successful meeting.[7] In essence, this Vietnamese statement was a continuation of Hanoi's previous neutral line; but the Chinese were soon to put successful pressure on Hanoi to move it more in Peking's direction. A similar statement made by the " Communist neutralist " Japanese Communist Party on February 15 spoke of Sino-Soviet unity as the " nucleus " of international solidarity, but its criticism of public attacks on fraternal parties indicated continuing sympathy for China in the JCP's leadership.[8]

A more clearly pro-Chinese position indicating his shift from the " Communist neutralist " to the pro-Chinese moderate was taken by Aidit in his February 10 report to a PKI Central Committee Plenum.[9] He reiterated the December 15, 1961, PKI criticism of inter-party public attacks and refusal to criticise Albania at the Twenty-second CPSU Congress, strongly criticised the " impression of rift and dissension " left by the recent five European congresses, and declared that those in Rome and East Berlin " were misused by the Yugoslav revisionists to split the international Communist movement." (He also implied that the Russians had criticised the PKI for these attitudes.) He emphasised the PKI's determination to fight " modern revisionism " as " the main danger," and he repeated the Chinese definition of " modern dogmatism " as " the lack of an objective critical attitude towards the experiences, conclusions, and programmes of the parties

---

[7] VNA, February 10, 1963, 1215 GMT, in BBC/FE/1173/C1/1-3, February 12, 1963. The statement was not reprinted or broadcast in Peking (indicating Chinese displeasure about its neutral attitude) but was printed in full in *Pravda* (on February 12, 1963), with one significant alteration: " unanimous view " was translated as " one " or " single " view, thus omitting the statement's specific endorsement of the Chinese position on factionalism. For authoritative and detailed analyses of the statement and subsequent developments on which the above is largely based, see P. J. Honey, " North Vietnam: New Developments in the Sino-Soviet Dispute," *China News Analysis* (Hong Kong), No. 472, June 14, 1963, and his *Communism in North Vietnam* (Cambridge, Mass.: M.I.T., 1963), pp. 144–151.

[8] Resolution of the JCP CC 5th Plenum, " Communist and Workers Parties of the World, Firmly Unite," February 15, 1963, in *Akahata*, February 19, 1963.

[9] Aidit report to 1st Plenum of PKI CC, *Harian Rakjat*, February 11, 1963 (JPRS 19, 310, May 21, 1963). A much-censored version of this report, omitting the pro-Chinese and anti-Yugoslav passages, was published as D. N. Aidit, " Indonesian Communists March Forward for Full Independence," *World Marxist Review*, VI, 6 (June 1963), pp. 11–18. For other anti-Yugoslav PKI statements, see Njoto, " Develop the Manipol Offensive in the Press!", *Harian Rakjat*, February 8, 1963 (JPRS 18,774, April 17, 1963, pp. 12–25) (also in *People's Daily*, February 10, 1963); and another speech by Njoto in *Harlan Rakjat*, March 5, 1963, excerpts in *Kung-jen Jih-pao* (Peking), February 12, 1963 (JPRS 18,135, March 14, 1963, pp. 8–14).

of our comrades in other countries," which was clearly intended to refer to Soviet control of other Communist parties. Finally, he denounced "so-called 'non-committed' countries like Yugoslavia and India" for trying to wreck Afro-Asian solidarity, and Yugoslavia particularly for trying to wreck the Colombo Conference, and completely took the Chinese position on the Sino-Indian border conflict. In view of the foregoing, the fact that Aidit also called for an all-party conference can hardly be interpreted as other than support for Chinese policy on this issue as well. It is not surprising that *People's Daily* reprinted the Aidit report on February 14, while *Pravda* on the same day gave it only three lines. Following the subsequent exchange of letters between Moscow and Peking, Aidit wrote a letter to both on March 19 endorsing their agreement to hold bilateral talks, but his use of the Chinese phrase "the imperialists and their running dogs, including the modern revisionists" indicated that the PKI's pro-Chinese rather than "neutralist" orientation continued.[10]

---

[10] In *People's Daily*, March 26, 1963 (SCMP 2949, March 29, 1963). For a discussion of the reasons behind this PKI stand, see pp. 194–196, *infra*.

13. Polycentrism Gathers Momentum

THE CHINESE ORGANISATIONAL DRIVE

DEVELOPMENTS during the spring and summer of 1963 in the international Communist front organisations, particularly in the Afro-Asian Solidarity groups, provided some of the clearest signs that the Sino-Soviet exchange of letters and agreement on a bilateral conference did little more than paper over and render esoteric the deep and probably irreconcilable differences between Moscow and Peking on strategy and tactics. It will be remembered that in December 1961 the Chinese had carried on a sharp offensive at meetings of the WFTU and World Peace Council, while by spring 1962 the dispute in this realm was once again muted within the context of the general return to esoteric polemics. After the Cuban and Sino-Indian crises such organisational clashes broke out again, primarily because the Chinese were increasingly attempting to take over control of the various Afro-Asian Solidarity organisations, to promote Latin-American membership in them, and thus to extract the national liberation struggle from Soviet influence.

The Moshi Afro-Asian Solidarity Conference [1]

Open conflict erupted at the Third Afro-Asian Solidarity Conference, held from February 4 to 11 in Moshi, Tanganyika. The Chinese initially attempted, during preliminary negotiations in Cairo, to exclude observers

---

[1] The best running coverage of the conference was in *Le Monde*, February 2, 6–9, 12, 1963; see also *The New York Times* (Western Edition), February 6, 15, 1963. For the speech by the Chinese delegate, Liu Ning-yi, on February 4, and excerpts from a February 13 *People's Daily* editorial on it, see *Peking Review*, VI, 7 (February 15, 1963), pp. 5–9; for NCNA coverage from Moshi, see NCNA in English to Asia and Europe, February 5, 1963 (SCMP 2916, February 11, 1963, pp. 20–21); *ibid*. February 12, 1963 (SCMP 2920, February 15, 1963, p. 12). The best analysis of the meeting is by Richard Lowenthal, in Brzezinski, *Africa and the Communist World*, pp. 196–199 (with excellent bibliography); see also the eyewitness report and analysis by Fritz Schatten, " Die III. Afro-Asiatische Solidaritätskonferenz," *Ost-Probleme*, XV, 11 (May 31, 1963), pp. 332–337, and also *The Economist*, February 16, 1963. For

(*i.e.*, pro-Soviet representatives from East Europe and elsewhere). At Moshi the Chinese and Soviet delegations continually lobbied for support among uncommitted delegates, to the point where many African delegates became suspicious of both, and President Nyerere of Tanganyika warned that it was not only the capitalists [but also, by implication, the Communists] who might endanger full African independence. The Russians privately appealed to the Chinese not to engage in polemics but the Chinese refused; as a result, although the Chinese and Soviet delegates did not explicitly and overtly clash, the Chinese reportedly said that as whites the Soviets would never support the anti-imperialist struggle. Furthermore, the Chinese succeeded in barring as delegates all WPC delegates not from African and Asian countries, including the exiled Turkish Communist poet Nazim Hikmet, who had long lived in the Soviet Union. The Indian delegation denounced the Chinese invasion of India and left the conference in protest, returning only at the end when a meaningless compromise resolution on the subject was adopted. Finally, the Chinese secured the acceptance by the delegates of a Cuban invitation to hold an Afro-Asian-Latin American Conference in Havana. After the conference most observers concluded that the Chinese rather than the Russians had played the major role, the first time that this had occurred at such a gathering, and an indication that the more revolutionary Chinese line has increasingly wide support among radical anti-colonialists.

The Djakarta Afro-Asian Journalists' Conference

Soviet representatives attended the Moshi Conference as delegates; but during its preparations the Chinese had been clearly anxious to scale down the pro-Soviet representation from Europe and the Middle East. Chinese strategy first became clear at a preparatory meeting for the Afro-Asian Journalists' Conference, held in Djakarta from February 10 to 15—still within the period prior to the Sino-Soviet agreement to suspend open polemics. A UAR resolution proposing Soviet participation was defeated as a result of Chinese and Indonesian pressure (presumably although not explicitly on the racial issue), and the final decision on this question was then postponed to the meeting itself, while the Russians were guaranteed only the status of observers.[2]

Soviet resentment of " anti-white " sentiment at Moshi (without explicitly identifying its source as Chinese) see V. Kudryavtsev, " Problems of Afro-Asian Solidarity," *International Affairs* (Moscow), No. 5, 1963, pp. 51–56 (which first indicated publicly some Soviet disillusionment with the way the AAPSO was going); for its specific identification as Chinese, see " The Great Force of Proletarian Internationalism," *World Marxist Review*, VI, 9 (September 1963), pp. 3–10, at p. 7 and " Marxism-Leninism, the Basis of the Unity of the Communist Movement," *Kommunist*, No. 15, October 1963 and Document 14.

2 AFP dispatch from Djakarta, February 23, 1963.

The meeting opened in Djakarta on April 24. A resolution to admit the Russians as delegates instead of observers, proposed and strongly pushed by Outer Mongolia, was crushingly defeated; only eight of the forty-nine countries at the conference voted for it. The Russians protested sharply, declaring that the refusal was " incomprehensible and undemocratic," but to no avail. The conference resolutions in Djakarta, as in Moshi, inclined towards the Chinese rather than the Soviet line.[3]

Thus for the first time Moscow's representatives were specifically treated as " second-class members " of Afro-Asian front organisations— a major tactical victory in China's drive towards the assumption of the leadership of communism and the national liberation movement in Asia, Africa and Latin America.

The WFTU [4]

Although the World Federation of Trade Unions (WFTU) had been a major Sino-Soviet battlefield in June 1960, when controversy broke out again in this organisation, first in December 1961 and then in late 1962 and early 1963, both the key issues and the chief participants had changed. The critical issue had become the attitude to be taken towards the Common Market, of which the major protagonists were the Italians, who insisted upon recognising its success and working from within it (and who were cautiously supported by the Poles [5] and Yugoslavs), while almost all the other members wished to continue the old tactics of total opposition to West European integration.

In late summer 1962, as has already been pointed out, Moscow had begun to modify its position on this subject. However, when at the end of the year the Italians insistently raised the question of setting up a WFTU representation in Brussels to deal directly with the EEC Commission, this was strongly opposed by the still rigid French, and it went too far even for the Russians. The Italian Communists, while taking a more flexible approach to the EEC, were at the same time under constant pressure from the socialist minority in the CGIL to take a position stronger than the PCI itself probably favoured.[6] The Chinese and Albanians could thus watch with pleasure and attempt to exacerbate a controversy among their opponents.

[3] Dennis Bloodworth from Singapore in *The Observer* (London), May 5, 1963; " Soviet Uneasiness Over Split," *The Times* (London), May 3, 1963; AFP Djakarta dispatch, May 1, 1963; " Politics of Nemesis," *Hindustan Times*, May 3, 1963; and Boris Burkov, " International Solidarity of Journalists," *Sovetskaya Pechat*, No. 8, August 1963, pp. 51–55.

[4] My colleague Professor D. L. M. Blackmer is preparing a study of the World Federation of Trade Unions.

[5] Olsen from Warsaw in *The New York Times*, October 27, 1962.

[6] See Galli, " Italian Communism," in Griffith, *Communism in Europe, I.*

The first severe clash occurred at the postponed [7] meeting of the WFTU Executive Committee held in Leipzig in mid-December 1962 [8] after the Italians had made clear their position [9] (including even a threat to withdraw from the WFTU); the delegates were unable to agree on any firm course. The issue was raised again at another WFTU meeting at the end of January 1963 in Prague, where the CGIL made clear its intention to set up the Brussels office itself if necessary and abstained on the final vote on the resolution.[10] Finally, at a meeting in Brussels on March 4–6, the Communist parties from the other Common Market countries made no formal objection to the CGIL setting up such an office, which it then proceeded to do.

The Chinese denounced the EEC *in toto* [11] and termed Khrushchev's modified attitude towards it a concession to the traitorous theory of " world integration." They and their supporters also violently denounced all Yugoslav international trade union activities, particularly the Belgrade proposal for an international trade union meeting, toward which Moscow remained equivocal.

The Chinese and Dissident Communist Parties

Late 1962 and early 1963 saw a great upswing in Chinese propaganda activities throughout the world, and particularly in areas such as Latin America where Soviet control of Communist parties was not as firm as in Western Europe. In the Communist Party of Brazil, as yet an isolated but not necessarily an insignificant case, the left extremist elements were expelled after the CPSU Twenty-Second Congress as an " anti-party group " and formed a new party, the Brazilian Communist

7 O.F. [Otto Frei] in *Neue Zürcher Zeitung*, November 16, 1962.
8 See Diamante Limita from Leipzig in *L'Unità*, December 18, 1962, and an excellent retrospective analysis by him in *Rinascita*, December 29, 1962 (JPRS 17,246, January 23, 1963). For the Chinese speech by Liu Shan-chang, see NCNA in English to Asia and Europe, December 19, 1962, 2003 GMT, published in *People's Daily*, December 20, 1962, as " The Formation of the European Common Market Has Sharpened the Contradictions Among Imperialist Powers. The Struggle Against the Common Market Is Inseparable from the General Struggle Against the Imperialist Groups Headed by the United States " (for a summary see SCMP 2887, December 28, 1962, pp. 36–37).
9 Luciano Lama to the CGIL Executive Committee, in *L'Unità*, October 14, 1962 (JPRS 15,986, November 1, 1962); " Precisazioni della CGIL sui problemi del MEC," *L'Unità* and *Avanti!*, September 29, 1962. For PSI pressure, see an editorial in *Avanti!*, September 28, 1962, and Foa (PSI) at the Fifth Polish TU Conference, *L'Unità*, November 29, 1962; for CGIL threat to withdraw, Novella in *ibid.* November 18, 1962.
10 Declaration of Lama and Didò, in *L'Unità*, February 3, 1963, and " Ufficio presso la CEE istituto della CGIL," *ibid.* March 15, 1963. For the Chinese speech by Liu Chang-sheng, see NCNA English, Prague, February 1, 1963 (SCMP 2913, February 6, 1963, pp. 28–30).
11 Fan Cheng-hsiang, " The Development of Imperialist Contradition," *Peking Review*, VI, 13 and 14 (March 29 and April 5, 1963), pp. 7–12 and 7–14.

Party.[12] Thereafter their publications were strongly pro-Castro and pro-Chinese.[13] On March 31, 1963, after the suspension of direct Sino-Soviet polemics, a delegation of this dissident party arrived in Peking [14] and was received by Mao on April 19.[15] Luis Carlos Prestes, the head of the pro-Soviet Communist Party of Brazil, had been received by Khrushchev in Moscow on February 23.[16] This was one of the first examples of an intention on the part of Peking to create or to support new pro-Chinese, anti-Soviet parties formed from splinter groups in areas where communism has been under traditional but not entrenched Soviet domination. True, the Soviet Union has tolerated splits in Latin American Communist parties much more frequently than elsewhere, but this was the first time that Peking thus officially recognised an overtly anti-Soviet splinter party.

Liu Shao-ch'i's Visit to North Vietnam

One of the most remarkable signs of the rise in Chinese Communist influence over Asian Communism occurred in mid-May during Chinese Chief of State Liu Shao-ch'i's state visit to North Vietnam, after he had paid state visits to Indonesia, Burma and Cambodia. Up until that time, in spite of an occasional inclination towards one side or the other, North Vietnam had appeared to maintain a neutral position between Moscow and Peking; for whatever reason, the Liu visit marked a significant shift in Ho Chi Minh's policy in favour of Peking (from a "Communist neutralist" to a pro-Chinese moderate) and a further worsening in Sino-Soviet relations.[17]

It will be remembered that the North Vietnamese February 10 declaration was carefully neutral, except for its reiteration of the Chinese view on "unanimity" as the method for arriving at binding inter-party declarations.[18] On March 13 Le Duan, a major North Vietnamese

12 Dallin, *Diversity*, p. 581, and especially Louis L. Wiznitzer in *The New Republic*, December 1, 1962, and BBC/CRU "Brazilian Communist Crisis," Background Note No. 1,780, January 16, 1963. For the pro-Soviet CPB view, see *Novos Rumos* (Rio de Janeiro), No. 152, January 5, 1963, and an article by Giocondo Dias in *ibid*. December 22–28, 1961, p. 4 (JPRS 12,080, January 24, 1962). Neither the Brazilian Communist Party nor CPB should be confused with the pro-Castro leader Juliao's peasant league.
13 See, *e.g.*, articles in their publication *A Classe Operaria* (Rio de Janeiro), February 1–15, 1963 (JPRS 18,399, March 27, 1963, pp. 93–104).
14 NCNA English, March 31, 1963 (SCMP 2953, April 4, 1963).
15 NCNA English, April 19, 1963 (SCMP 2965, April 24, 1963).
16 *Pravda*, February 24, 1963.
17 My treatment of the Liu visit owes much to Honey, *Communism in North Vietnam*, pp. 154–167.
18 This neutrality was also echoed in "Reinforce the Solidarity and Unity of the International Communist Movement and the Socialist Camp," *Hoc Tap*, No. 3, March 1963 (JPRS 18,691, April 15, 1963, and 19,056, May 6, 1963).

Communist, gave a speech, published only in early April,[19] which came considerably closer to Chinese views, particularly on the revolutionary transition to socialism and on the " Yugoslav revisionists." His speech was published in full in *People's Daily*.[20] Another article, which like Le Duan's appeared in the April issue of the North Vietnamese theoretical journal (which was presumably passed for the press in late March), not only took a strongly anti-Yugoslav stand but also, while not denying the possibility of peaceful transition to socialism, asserted that it " is not applicable to all or most countries." [21] Presumably Hanoi's decision to shift to a more pro-Chinese cause was taken some time in late March or early April,[22] and probably not without dissension in the party leadership.[23]

Liu's most significant statement during the visit was his May 15 speech to the North Vietnamese party school. One of his assertions seemed almost openly directed against the hitherto neutral policy of Ho Chi Minh:

> . . . We cannot act as lookers-on or follow a middle course . . . the militant task of all Marxist-Leninists is not to evade the challenge of modern revisionism, but to unite to smash its attack completely in defence of the purity of Marxism-Leninism. . . .

Furthermore, Liu declared that to combat modern revisionism one should " first of all seek instructions from Marx, Engels, Lenin and Stalin "— one of the few references which the Chinese have recently made to Stalin, and a sure indicator that Sino-Soviet relations were again deteriorating.[24] Finally, he made quite clear that the forthcoming meeting with the Russians would reach no solution, nor did Peking expect one in the near future: " the present struggle will be a protracted and complicated one with twists and turns."

The final joint communiqué, signed by Liu and Ho Chi Minh, although not totally pro-Chinese (it made explicit reference to Ho's

19 Le Duan, " Let Us Hold High the Revolutionary Banner of Creative Marxism," *Hoc Tap*, No. 4, April 1963 (JPRS 19,246, May 17, 1963); see Honey, *Communism in North Vietnam*, pp. 155–156.
20 *People's Daily*, April 16, 1963 (SCMP 2963, April 22, 1963, p. 14).
21 " Let Us Develop the Revolutionary Spirit of Lenin," *Hoc Tap*, No. 4, 1963 (JPRS 19,532, June 3, 1963, at p. 11).
22 An editorial in the March 13 *Nhan Dan*, " The Name and Work of Karl Marx Live Forever " (JPRS 18,630, April 9, 1963) spoke of 13 socialist countries, *i.e.*, with Albania and Cuba but without Yugoslavia—the Chinese thesis.
23 See the statement in " To Reinforce the Solidarity and Unity of the International Communist Movement and the Socialist Camp," *Hoc Tap*, No. 3, March 1963: " The divergence of views on a number of concrete problems may exist not only among communist and workers' parties but also among a number of comrades in the same party."
24 NCNA in English to Asia and Europe, May 15, 1963, 2010 GMT, in *Peking Review*, VI, 21 (May 27, 1963), pp. 9–10. The text of the speech was also carried by VNA in English, May 18, 1963, 1336 GMT.

reiteration of the previous North Vietnamese view that Moscow and Peking bear the greatest responsibility for Communist unity),[25] was certainly much more so than the February 10 Vietnamese statement or any other previous Vietnamese declarations, unilateral or joint. In addition to the reiteration of the Chinese formula of " unanimity through consultation," revisionism was again labelled the main danger, the Chinese view of dogmatism (insufficient attention to concrete practice of the revolution in each country) was restated, Chinese attainment of nuclear capacity was implicitly endorsed, as was Chinese policy towards India and, most important, the " Yugoslav revisionist clique " was declared to have " betrayed Marxism-Leninism " and to be " engaged in sabotage within the socialist camp and the world Communist movement," " further exposure " of which " remains essential." True, it did not call them a " special detachment of U.S. imperialism," nor did it state that " capitalism has been restored in Yugoslavia " (the two most extreme Sino-Albanian formulae), but nevertheless the shift in Hanoi's position towards China was definite and significant.[26]

Other Chinese and Albanian Actions

The Chinese were not satisfied merely to renew the esoteric polemics of spring 1962. They continued their violent polemics against Nehru [27] (to which the CPI replied extensively in late April),[28] they used the mid-April National Conference of the pro-Chinese New Zealand Communist Party and the mid-May visit to Peking of its General Secretary, V. G. Wilcox, to spread their own views [29] as well as those of their New Zealand supporters,[30] and they extensively reprinted pro-Chinese articles appearing in North Korean, Indonesian, North Vietnamese and Japanese Communist publications. Most significantly, they kept up a barrage of anti-Yugoslav denunciations and on May 10 the *People's Daily* declared that

25 In addition, Hanoi as usual hastened to publish an article a few days later praising Soviet-Vietnamese friendship. See Ton Duc Thang, " Vietnamese-Soviet Friendship To Last Forever," *Nhan Dan*, May 23, 1963 (JPRS 19,972, July 1, 1963) and Honey, *Communism in North Vietnam*, pp. 166–167.

26 NCNA in English to Asia and Europe, May 16, 1963, 1230 GMT, *People's Daily*, May 17, 1963, and *Peking Review*, VI, 21 (May 24, 1963), pp. 10–14.

27 " What Is the ' Socialism ' Advocated by Nehru?" *Red Flag*, No. 6, April 1, 1963, pp. 1–9 (JPRS 19,024, April 30, 1963, pp. 1–30).

28 S. A. Dange, " Neither Revisionism Nor Dogmatism Is Our Guide," supplement to *New Age*, April 21, 1963. This 14-page article was a summary of the CPI anti-Chinese position but added little or nothing new to the CCP-CPI controversy.

29 Speech by Liu Ning-yi and CCP greeting message, *People's Daily*, April 16, 1963 and *Peking Review*, VI, 16 (April 9, 1963), pp. 16–18.

30 Report of NZCP General Secretary V. G. Wilcox, " Out of the People; On to the Offensive Against Monopoly," April 12, 1963, in *Peking Review*, VI, 19 (May 10, 1963), pp. 15–21; speech by Wilcox to the CCP Higher Party School, May 25, 1963, in *Peking Review*, VI, 22 (May 31, 1963), pp. 17–18; CCP-NZCP joint statement, May 25, 1963, in *ibid*. pp. 15–17. See an Auckland dispatch in the *New York Times*, June 2, 1963.

the new Yugoslav constitution was " a constitution to protect the restoration of capitalism "[31] while the following day *Izvestiya* declared that it demonstrated the " socialist " character of the country.[32]

The Albanians, meanwhile, persisted in their periodic outbursts against Moscow. On April 17 *Zëri i Popullit* published the text of the March 30 Soviet letter to the Chinese (it had not published the first Soviet letter of February 21). The next day an editorial appeared attacking the Soviet Union for its alleged initiative in arranging a bilateral meeting between the Soviet and Albanian parties.[33] It insisted that the " so-called Albanian question " was by no means of secondary importance but was " a question concerning the general line of the international Communist movement," and it denounced Khrushchev's attempt to force the acceptance of Yugoslavia as a socialist country in return for Soviet recognition of Albania as a socialist country. Furthermore, it flatly stated that " . . . the most hideous amongst the erroneous and harmful acts of N. Khrushchev . . . was undoubtedly his attitude in the Cuban crisis and in the Chinese-Indian frontier conflict."

On May 7 the organ of the Albanian Writers' and Artists' Union, in a lengthy diatribe against contemporary Soviet literature and art, denounced Khrushchev's recent campaign against the liberal Soviet intellectuals as merely a smokescreen to conceal the fact that " the true source of the evil " lay in Khrushchev's own revisionist orientation.[34] On May 12 *Zëri i Popullit* described the brief visit of U.S. Secretary of State Dean Rusk to Belgrade on May 4 as " the legal form for the maintenance of contacts between boss and lackey." It further declared that " all doors have been opened to . . . [the Tito clique] . . . in the Soviet Union and certain people's democracies in Europe " and that Tito's *agentura* was thereby conducting its U.S. directed espionage activity against the Soviet Union with " the complete knowledge and with the blessings and tolerance of N. Khrushchev. . . ."[35]

THE YUGOSLAV PLENUM: MAY 1963

By mid-May Tito was ready to launch a major Yugoslav initiative in the Sino-Soviet conflict. His domestic situation was somewhat improved.[36] His efforts to prevent the Soviet-Yugoslav rapprochement from

---

[31] " Commentator," " A Comment on the New Yugoslav Constitution," *People's Daily*, May 10, 1963, and *Peking Review*, VI, 20 (May 17, 1963), pp. 11–13.
[32] *Izvestiya*, May 11, 1963.
[33] *Zëri i Popullit*, April 18, 1963.
[34] " The Source of Evil Is Revisionism," *Drita*, III, 18 (May 7, 1963).
[35] " The ' Trojan Horse ' Continues Its Activity in the Service of American Imperialism," *Zëri i Popullit*, May 12, 1963.
[36] He has sanctioned some slight relaxation in the previous retreat from liberalisation, for example in regard to private artisans; see his speech to a meeting of artisans on

causing further deterioration in his relations with Washington were marked by considerable success,[37] as the state visit of U.S. Secretary of State Dean Rusk to Belgrade in early May demonstrated.[38] Thus, with his Western flank secure, he could now turn to his life-long dream of playing a major role in the international Communist movement.[39]

The Yugoslav Central Committee Plenum, where this initiative occurred, met for only four and one-half hours on Saturday morning, May 18, 1963, to hear a long report by Tito [40] and eight other brief speeches. No Croat and only one Slovene (the low-ranking Dušan Kveder) addressed the meeting; all the other speakers (with the exception of one obscure Montenegrin) were Serbs—a clear indication of the victory of the Rankovic Serbian group. The following summary and analysis concentrates primarily on Tito's speech, since the other speakers and especially Ranković,[41] Vlahović,[42] Todorović [43] and Vukmanović-Tempo [44] only elaborated and made more organisationally precise his " grand design." Tito's new initiative was presumably announced with Khrushchev's knowledge; but the fact that almost all of the sharpest anti-Chinese passages in Tito's speech were deleted in the version published in *Pravda* on May 26 indicates that it went considerably farther than what the Soviet First Secretary was prepared publicly to identify himself with.

Tito's speech was by far the most violent direct attack against the Chinese made by any Communist leader to date. The Chinese position on war and peace, he said, was " Trotskyite." Peking attacked Yugoslavia because of the latter's " great prestige " in the non-aligned countries of Asia and Africa, her " unselfish and principled support " to them, and her " peaceful policy." The Chinese were cultivating " nationalism of the worst kind " in their attempt to place the peoples of Asia, Africa and Latin America in opposition to those of Europe and the other developed countries, and in their attempt to set up a new, eastward centre of revolution in China.[45] Tito further charged that Peking's support of Albania and distribution of propaganda literature constituted

---

April 6, in *Ekonomska Politika*, April 20, 1963 (excerpts: *Borba* and *Politika*, April 21, 1963).

[37] He sent a private letter to President Kennedy on April 18 (*New York Times*, April 20. 1963).

[38] Joint U.S.-Yugoslav communiqué, *Borba*, May 5, 1963; analysis: C.K. [Christian Kind], " Zwischenhalt Dean Rusks in Belgrad," *Neue Zürcher Zeitung*, May 6, 1963.

[39] The course of the May 19 LCY CC Plenum was presumably fixed at the April 23 meeting of the LCY Executive Committee (*Borba*, April 25, 1963). For an authoritative Belgrade régime analysis of it, see Punisa Perovic in *Medjunarodna Politika*, XIV, 316 (June 1, 1963), pp. 22–23.

[40] *Borba*, May 19, 1963.   [41] *Ibid*. May 21, 1963.

[42] *Ibid*. May 20, 1963.   [43] *Ibid*.

[44] *Ibid*. May 21, 1963.

[45] Vlahović charged that the Chinese attack on India was " expansionist nationalist," not socialist.

a form of Chinese factional activity towards this end which, especially among the Asian Communist parties, was " achieving a certain degree of temporary success." Finally, he called Chinese dogmatism the greatest current danger to the international Communist movement. Vukmanović-Tempo declared that the Chinese wanted to revise the Stalinist ideological monopoly and Vlahovic said they had adopted the policy of

> pressure, bureaucratic methods, and forcible, barracks-like and blind discipline . . . adventurousness and Bonapartism in foreign policy and bureaucracy and militarism in internal policy. . . .[46]

Turning to relations among socialist states and Communist parties (which the Chinese, he said, were determined to distort and monopolise), Tito repeated his praise of the Soviet Union [47] and Khrushchev personally and declared that Soviet-Yugoslav state and party relations had greatly improved,[48] that the 1960 Moscow Declaration's condemnation of Yugoslavia was now " a thing of the past," and that new, equal and better forms of inter-party relations, with no centre of control, should be sought.[49] On the other hand, in a possible indication of fear that Khrushchev might compromise with Mao at Yugoslavia's expense, he condemned " any compromise or unprincipled agreements at the expense of anyone."

Tito justified at length Yugoslavia's renewed activity in the international Communist movement. " We are a part of that movement and not something outside of it," he declared; " there can be no differing points of view " in the LCY on Yugoslav policy within it. It is the duty of all Communist parties, including the Yugoslav, to work for " the most progressive relations of equality and comradeship " with each other [50]; and it is the LCY's specific duty to struggle against " all those [*i.e.* the Chinese] . . . deliberately trying to disunite the international workers movement," and to participate " most actively in a principled way in clearing up disagreements among Communist parties." (Actually, Tito is probably the Communist leader who most desires a Sino-Soviet split.)

It was clear that there had been considerable resistance within the LCY to Tito's policy of rapprochement with the Soviet Union (mostly

---

[46] Both Vlahović (*Borba*, May 20, 1963) and Dobrivoje Vidić (*ibid.* May 21, 1963) denounced the Chinese in great detail.

[47] Vukmanović-Tempo praised in detail the latest developments in Soviet industry and agriculture.

[48] Tito also referred favourably to Yugoslav relations with the Hungarian, Bulgarian, Italian, East German and French Communist parties, but made no mention of the Czechoslovak, Rumanian or Polish parties.

[49] Vlahović added that there is " a greater responsibility of individual countries and parties."

[50] Tito emphasised that Yugoslav Communists should not preach the virtues of the Yugoslav model.

in Croatia and Slovenia and among the younger party members, one may well conjecture). He lamented the lack of interest shown by the LCY in international developments, particularly those in the Communist world. He declared openly that

> . . . there are people in the ranks of the LCY who do not grasp the tremendous positive significance of establishing not only normal but good relations between our country and the Soviet Union and other socialist countries. . . .

He stated that the " youngest generation of LCY members, which grew up during a time when our relations with the socialist countries were abnormal," must now learn more about the achievements of the socialist countries and must carry on the tradition of " sympathy and solidarity with the progressive and revolutionary struggle of other peoples " ingrained in " our party, later the League of Communists " (*i.e.*, the internationalist tradition of the old Yugoslav Communist Party and of Tito himself).

Rankovic was even clearer, to the point of making open threats:

> . . . we have always been imbued with the awareness that we are but a part of the working class and working people of the world, and that we are an inseparable part of the international Communist and, in general, progressive movement. . . .

He attacked " some comrades in the institutions . . . charged with the study of the possibility of developing co-operation with socialist countries " for not having understood this well; he declared that the LCY must play a much greater role in the training and guidance of Yugoslavs engaged in the conduct of foreign affairs at home and abroad; and he announced, in scarcely veiled words, that all those who supported the Soviet-Yugoslav rapprochement would be favoured in LCY cadre policy (and presumably, those opposed would be penalised):

> . . . The leading bodies of the League of Communists and other social organisations should pay particular attention to . . . comrades, including also younger ones, who are studying with more interest, knowledge and competence the stirrings in the international workers movement and in international relations . . . [and] work plans in our organisations. . . .

Todorović made clear that while Yugoslavia was still not willing to join CMEA Belgrade was searching for new bilateral and multilateral methods of intensifying trade with socialist countries. Ranković criticised those who gave precedence to economic relations with Europe, " particularly to those European countries which . . . have the greatest economic significance for us " (*i.e.*, Italy and Germany, precisely the countries with which Slovenia and Croatia have far closer ties than Serbia does) over economic relations with non-aligned countries (*i.e.*, Yugoslav economic aid to them, which comes primarily out of Slovene and Croat pockets).

SOVIET MOVES

The Changes in the Soviet May Day Slogan on Yugoslavia

Once again the Russians were also not idle; like the Chinese, their " suspension of public polemics " was more nominal than real. Furthermore, in a remarkable parallel to the situation exactly one year earlier, their continued intransigence *vis-à-vis* the Chinese demands was manifested primarily on the Yugoslav issue. This time, however, it was expressed in a curious and not entirely explicable fashion—in the post-publication correction of the Soviet May Day slogan on Yugoslavia. The initial slogan, published in *Pravda* on April 8, referred to the " Federal People's Republic " of Yugoslavia (not, as proclaimed in the new constitution, the " Socialist Federal Republic "), and it did not contain the phrase " who are building socialism " (unlike the slogans for all the other socialist countries, including Albania and Cuba). The next day, April 9, the list of May Day slogans appeared in *Izvestiya* (only *Pravda* was published on Monday, April 8); this version read " Socialist Federal Republic of Yugoslavia." [51] What was much more surprising, indeed unprecedented, was the appearance two days later, in *Pravda* of April 11, of a third version, printed on the front page as a specific correction, which added the phrase " who are building socialism," thus making the slogan identical with those of all the other socialist countries.

It seems safe to assume that Khrushchev, who was on vacation in the Crimea at the time (Kozlov was presumably in charge in Moscow),[52] ordered the second correction. However, it hardly seems likely that the original version was only a mistake; Soviet ideologists do not make such mistakes and survive in their jobs. Two possible hypotheses may be mentioned. The first would be that there was some opposition in the Soviet Party *apparat* to the final version, *i.e.*, to Khrushchev's insistence that Yugoslavia was also building socialism. However, if there was such opposition its members were probably less pro-Chinese than simply reluctant to exacerbate the Sino-Soviet controversy just when a bilateral meeting had been agreed upon in principle through the exchange of letters. The second explanation would be that the initial version of the slogan, identical with that of the previous year, was automatically repeated. However, precisely at this time, in some manner still not

[51] This change could be explained by the fact that on the afternoon of the 7th the Yugoslav Skupština finally approved (*Borba*, April 8, 1963) the new Yugoslav constitution, which formally changed " People's " to " Socialist " in the state's name.

[52] Kozlov was last seen in public on the day of the final change in the Yugoslav slogan, April 10 (*Pravda*, April 11, 1963); he was not present at the April 12 cosmonaut celebration (*ibid.* April 13, 1963), the celebration on April 13 of the 80th anniversary of the birth of Khrushchev's favourite balladist Demyan Bedny (*ibid.* April 14, 1963), or the Lenin birthday celebration on April 22 (*ibid.* April 23, 1963).

publicly known, Sino-Soviet relations became much worse, and Khrushchev therefore had the slogan changed. In any case it seems likely that the Yugoslavs immediately protested, a factor which probably had some influence on Khrushchev's decision. The second hypothesis seems more likely, but in any case the Scottish verdict of " not proven " is the appropriate one.[53]

The Castro Visit

The one encouraging development for Moscow during this period was Castro's long visit to the Soviet Union and the evidently far-reaching Soviet-Cuban understanding achieved at that time. The final joint communiqué[54] reflected more of the Soviet than of the Chinese line. It endorsed without qualification Soviet policy during the October 1962 Cuban crisis. It warmly praised Soviet military and economic aid to Cuba (including a new, Soviet-initiated rise in the price of sugar purchased from Cuba). It seemed to uphold the Soviet line on war and peaceful co-existence: the absolute necessity of the prevention of war, the consequent necessity of the policy of peaceful co-existence, and the specific rejection of the Chinese thesis that peaceful co-existence means weakening the national liberation struggle. It also intimated the possibility of a less anti-American Cuban policy. On the other hand, the communiqué for the first time established full party relations between Moscow and Havana and formally recognised the Cuban PURS (United Party of the Socialist Revolution) as a fraternal Marxist-Leninist party. Furthermore it declared Castro's two Declarations of Havana to be " of historic significance for the national liberation struggle of the peoples of Latin America "—something close to a very general endorsement of Castro's example for the Latin American revolution. However, on the issue of the peaceful transition to socialism, the only point on which Castro had publicly differed with Khrushchev, the communiqué took an intermediate position by stating that this question would be settled " by the fighting peoples themselves." Finally, it did not mention the Chinese, Albanians or Yugoslavs, thus indicating that Castro did not intend to sever his ties with the Chinese. Even so, the communiqué and Castro's subsequent resounding praise of Khrushchev upon his return[55] indicated that Khrushchev had scored a substantial success in restoring Soviet-Cuban amity, which the October 1962 crisis had severely strained, and that for the time being Castro was again leaning towards Moscow. However,

---

[53] Cf. Carl Gustaf Ströhm, " Chruschtschow rappelt sich hoch," *Christ und Welt*, XVI, 17 (April 26, 1963), p. 5.

[54] *Pravda*, May 25, 1963; reprinted in full in *People's Daily*, May 31, 1963.

[55] *Hoy* and *Revolución*, June 5, 1963; reprinted in *Pravda*, June 6 and 7, 1963, but not reprinted in *People's Daily*.

Castro was hardly a constant friend, and his messianic ambitions in Latin America, the most serious potential source of conflict with Moscow, certainly remained unchanged. (The subsequent failure of Castro to sign the test ban treaty confirmed the incompleteness of the Soviet-Cuban rapprochement; Castro had only temporarily shifted from a " Communist neutralist " to a pro-Soviet moderate position.)

Again Polemics

Several other signs during the period from the second Soviet letter (March 30) to the second Chinese one (June 14) indicated continued Soviet hostility to China. Both Ponomarev [56] and Khrushchev [57] sharply rejected (without identifying its Chinese source) the theory of a racist Afro-Asian-Latin American Communist movement. *Kommunist* conveniently discovered and reprinted a 1920 Lenin speech supporting the granting to the United States of economic concessions and even a military base in Kamchatka which, it noted, retained " tremendous theoretical and political importance, since it expressed the principles of peaceful co-existence of states with opposed social systems," [58] *i.e.*, Khrushchev's right to negotiate with Kennedy. A chapter of a new biography of Lenin, published under the direction of Pospelov, Ilichev and other senior Soviet ideologists, re-affirmed the whole range of Soviet theses on foreign policy.[59] Khrushchev commented quite favourably on Kennedy's June 10 American University speech.[60] In mid-May *Pravda* again reprinted a passage from a French Communist Central Committee resolution repeating the PCF thesis that dogmatism has become the main danger.[61]

RUMANIA AND CMEA

One other development, the opposition of Rumania to Khrushchev's accelerated economic integration of East Europe through CMEA, was peripherally connected with the Sino-Soviet rift and the Soviet-Yugoslav rapprochement, without both of which it probably would not have taken place at all.

Three points about it are important. First of all, it largely resulted from Rumania's nationalism and increasing prosperity and from the

---

[56] In a speech on the anniversary of Lenin's birthday, *Pravda*, April 23, 1963. For the Castro visit, see Theodore Draper, " Castro, Khrushchev, and Mao," *The Reporter*, XXIX, 3 (August 15, 1963), pp. 27–31.

[57] In his speech at the Moscow Soviet-Cuban friendship rally, *Pravda*, May 24, 1963.

[58] " New V. I. Lenin Document," *Kommunist*, No. 6, April 1963, pp. 3–10, quoted from *CDSP*, XV, 16 (May 15, 1963), pp. 10–13, at p. 10.

[59] Reprinted in *Pravda*, April 19, 1963.

[60] *Ibid.* June 15, 1963.

[61] " . . . dogmatism and sectarianism . . . have become the main danger in the international Communist movement. . . ." (*L'Humanité*, May 11, 1963 [JPRS 19,467. May 29, 1963], reprinted in *Pravda*, May 19, 1963.)

Soviet move towards a policy of economic integration, *i.e.*, it was a problem in the Soviet alliance system arising from the increasing power of its junior members. Secondly, it does not seem similar to the Albanian case. Thirdly, Rumania does not appear to be revolting against Soviet influence *per se* or trying to defect either to the Chinese or Western sphere; on the contrary, it is attempting to utilise the Sino-Soviet rift for Rumanian nationalistic purposes [62]; *i.e.*, although (or, more correctly, in part because) it is Stalinist in domestic policy, the Rumanian Party leadership is pro-Soviet moderate, not extremist.

Although the Rumanian First Secretary Gheorghiu-Dej is not a liberal but a neo-Stalinist, he does have some things in common with Gomułka, Togliatti and Tito. He is one of the small group of Rumanian Communists of ethnic Rumanian origin, who were not in Moscow in exile before and during the Second World War, whose opponents have all been purged, and who although still probably detested in the country have at least some of the prerequisites of eventually attaining some popularity. Secondly, the fundamental motive in his action is nationalism. From the viewpoint of economic rationality, if one treats the Soviet Union and East Europe as one economic area, it is quite logical to develop further the industrial base that already exists in the Soviet Union, Czechoslovakia and East Germany, and to encourage the primary raw material producers (Rumania, Bulgaria and in part Poland and Hungary) to expand further this aspect of their economy. But this is not logical from the point of view of nationalistic economic autarky. Gheorghiu-Dej and his associates are opposed to Khrushchev's plan of increased " joint " (as opposed to the looser " co-ordinated ") planning in CMEA (decided upon at the June 1962 First Secretaries meeting in Moscow) because this would prevent Rumania from becoming a fully industrialised country. And like Kádár and Gomułka, he can always gain popularity by resisting Moscow; Rumanians have always been anti-Russian, even more so since 1945 because of their irredentist feelings arising from the loss of Bessarabia to the Soviet Union.

With Bulgaria this new policy of Khrushchev's has apparently encountered little difficulty; but Rumania is quite different. It is potentially one of the richest countries in Europe; its post-war rate of economic growth and of industrialisation has been among the highest in East Europe; its industrialisation, particularly its development and utilisation of its extensive oil deposits, gives it the potential base for becoming a

---

62 The best analyses of this matter are the excellent and balanced dispatches from Bucharest by its Vienna correspondent [Dessa Bourne] in *The Times* (London), May 10, 1963, and by C.K. [Christian Kind], " Schwierigkeiten der Wirtschaftskoordination in Ostblock : Rumäniens Drang nach einem ' eigenen Weg,' " *Neue Zürcher Zeitung*, May 12, 1963, and the article by J. F. Brown, " Rumania Steps Out of Line," *Survey*, No. 49 (October 1963), pp. 19–34.

significant industrial power.[63] The Rumanian government (and probably most of the Rumanian intelligentsia in spite of their hatred of their Communist régime) are determined for nationalistic reasons to carry a programme of industrialisation through to fruition.

This programme was threatened by Khrushchev's intensified CMEA integration. Over the last years several small signs [64] have indicated that the Rumanians not only were quietly refusing to go along with any joint economic planning which would impede their own industrialisation programme but were also intensifying their economic contacts with West Europe. At the February 1963 CMEA Executive Committee meeting the Rumanian resistance became clear,[65] a Rumanian Central Committee Plenum in early March almost ostentatiously endorsed the attitude of the Rumanian CMEA representative, of

. . . successfully developing and deepening the socialist international division of labour and coordination of the national economic plans in the spirit of the principles proclaimed by the 1960 Moscow Statement, of observance of national independence of sovereignty, of full equality of rights, comradely mutual aid and mutual benefit. . . .[66]

and Rumanian Party cadres were confidentially briefed on the nature and extent of the differences with Moscow.[67] Subsequent Rumanian

[63] J. M. Montias, " Unbalanced Growth in Rumania," *American Economic Review*, LIII, 2 (May 1963), pp. 562–571.

[64] See an article in the Annals of the Historical Institute of the Central Committee of the Rumanian Workers' Party (summarised in a Bucharest dispatch in *Politika*, December 17, 1962) criticising a 1961 book on Nazi foreign policy by the Soviet party historian V. A. Ushakov for allegedly neglecting the role of Rumanian Communists (as opposed to the Red Army) in liberating Rumania. This Soviet claim was withdrawn in E. D. Karpeshchenko, " The Victory of Socialism in the Rumanian People's Republic," *Novaya i Noveshchaya Istoria*, No. 2, 1963. Compare Khrushchev on June 24 during his visit to Bucharest just after the June 1962 CMEA First Secretaries meeting in Moscow: " The international division of labour and the specialisation of production not only do not harm the development of the industry of the countries of the socialist camp, but on the contrary create the best conditions for the development of each of them " (*Pravda*, June 25, 1962), with Ion Gheorghe Maurer on June 21, 1962, during the same visit: " . . . the Conference . . . showed the great progress attained in the . . . realisation of the international socialist division of labour and facilitated the strengthening of co-operation among these countries, based on respect for independence and sovereignty, on complete equality and mutual benefit " (*ibid.* June 22, 1962). See also the somewhat equivocal article by the Soviet economist I. P. Oleinik, " The Equalisation of the Economic Development Level of the Socialist Countries," *Probleme Economice* (Bucharest), No. 4, April 1962 (not entirely accurately summarised in a dispatch by the Bucharest TANJUG correspondent Djurica in *Politika*, June 16, 1962) and a speech in Rumania by DDR planning chief Leuschner (*Neues Deutschland*, September, 18, 1963) which may be interpreted as criticising the Rumanian position. For possible earlier signs in 1960–61, see Brown, *op. cit.*, pp. 21–23, and for the role of the Galati steel works, *ibid.*, p. 24.

[65] *Cf.* a denial by Jaroszewicz that CMEA tends to stratify its members so as to stress the agricultural production of some countries at the expense of their industrial development, *Trybuna Ludu*, January 18, 1963.

[66] *Scînteia*, March 8, 1963. See a dispatch by Božidar Djurica, the Bucharest TANJUG correspondent, in *Politika*, March 21, 1963.

[67] TANJUG dispatch from Bucharest in *Politika*, April 9, 1963.

declarations [68] made clear that the Rumanians really meant that the primary purpose of international co-ordinated (not joint) planning must be, not economic rationality and the maximisation of over-all economic productivity, but " the equalisation of the level of development of the socialist countries . . . an indispensable condition for building a Communist society," [69] *i.e.* to assist the less developed countries to catch up with the more developed ones—a primarily political, nationalistic objective. Rumania also was increasing its trade with the West,[70] and even in May 1963 publicly criticised the slowness and lack of quality of Czechoslovak deliveries.[71]

CMEA Executive Committee sessions in April and mid-May 1963 were equally frustrated by Rumanian opposition [72] (all CMEA decisions must be unanimous). The immediately following visit to Bucharest by a high-powered Soviet delegation headed by Ukrainian First Secretary Podgorny also produced no complete meeting of minds.[73]

For our purposes, however, the main interest of this Rumanian economic opposition is its relevance to Sino-Soviet relations.[74] For the last two years Rumania has been relatively reticent in denouncing China and Albania and in praising Yugoslavia, and its régime has been slow in de-Stalinisation.[75] By late March 1963 it was becoming clear that Bucharest was making gestures of relative comity towards Peking and Tirana—ones immediately reciprocated by these two capitals—as a means of putting pressure on Moscow to bring about a more conciliatory attitude and also of signalling to Moscow and Peking the increased Rumanian limits of manoeuvre as a result of the Sino-Soviet rift. In late March the Rumanian Ambassador returned to Tirana, from where he had long been absent, a short time after an increased foreign trade agreement had been signed with the Albanians [76]; in early April Rumania signed a trade agreement with China which provided for a 10 per cent.

---

[68] Editorial in *Romania Libera*, April 21, 1963; Joja at the Lenin Birthday celebration, *Scînteia*, April 24, 1963.
[69] Rumanian Politburo member Nicolae Ceausescu at Brašov, *Scînteia*, May 30, 1963. *Cf.* Ceausescu in *Pravda*, February 4, 1963: " . . . gradually equalising the level of economic development in order to realise the transition to communism within the same historical epoch, . . ." and a similar formulation by Gheorghe Apostol in *Romania Libera*, February 3, 1963.   [70] Brown, *op. cit.*, pp. 26–27.
[71] *Scînteia*, May 24, 1963; " The Good Name of Our Workmanship," *Pravda* (Bratislava), July 12, 1963.   [72] Brown, *op. cit.*, p. 27.
[73] Ceausescu at Brašov, *Scînteia*, May 30, 1963; Gheorghiu-Dej in *ibid.* June 5, 1963. See Topping from Moscow in *The New York Times*, June 6, 1963, and *cf.* Brown, *op. cit.*, pp. 28–29.   [74] *Cf.* Brown, *op. cit.*, pp. 30–34.
[75] See Mirko Ostrojic (from Bucharest), " Ten Days All Around Rumania," *Oslobodjenje* (Sarajevo), April 21, 1963.
[76] *Zëri i Popullit*, March 29, 1963. There had been no official announcement of his withdrawal, which had, however, occurred (interview with the Rumanian Minister in Paris in *Le Monde*, December 21, 1962). On March 7, 1963, the increased Rumanian-Albanian foreign trade agreement had been signed in Bucharest at a ceremony attended by the Rumanian Minister of Foreign Trade (*Zëri i Popullit* and *Scînteia*, March 9, 1963).

increase over the 1962 volume [77]; in mid-April the Albanian press twice favourably referred to Rumania [78]; in late April, after a delay of seven weeks, the Peking *People's Daily* suddenly reprinted long excerpts from the early March Rumanian Central Committee communiqué mentioned above endorsing Rumanian obstinacy in CMEA.[79] In early June the Albanians published an article which, although ostensibly criticising the Yugoslavs for their pre-1948 exploitation of Albania, was probably an esoteric reference to Soviet pressure on Rumania.[80] The Chinese letter to Moscow of June 14 referred clearly to the same subject; and, by far the most significant of all, the Rumanian press was the only one in East Europe to print even a summary of it,[81] which, as is elaborated upon below, the Soviets officially stated they would not publish because of its anti-Soviet character. In late June Rumania stopped jamming Western radio broadcasts.[82] Furthermore, Gheorghiu-Dej did not attend the June 30 meeting of East European First Secretaries with Khrushchev in East Berlin.[83]

Not until September 1963 did it become clear that in the spring and summer of 1962 there had been a serious renewal of Sino-Soviet friction in Sinkiang and along the Amur river. In retrospect then, the border issue must be seen as one of the most important reasons for the renewed deterioration of Sino-Soviet relations in the summer and early autumn of that year.

According to 1963 Soviet accounts [84] and Western government sources [85] an anti-Chinese rebellion broke out in the Ili valley in western

[77] *Scînteia*, April 9, 1963 and NCNA English Bucharest, April 8, 1963 (SCMP 2959, April 16, 1963, p. 21).
[78] *Zëri i Popullit*, April 12, 14, 1963. The only other references of this sort to any East European countries during January–April 1963 were in *ibid.* January 15 and February 15.
[79] *People's Daily*, April 28, 1963, from *Scînteia*, March 9, 1963 (SCMP 2970, May 2, 1963, p. 23).
[80] " How the Yugoslav Modern Revisionists Understand Economic Co-operation with Socialist Countries," *Zëri i Popullit*, June 6, 1963. See Vienna dispatches in *The Times* (London), June 11, 1963, and in the *Neue Zürcher Zeitung*, June 12, 1963.
[81] Agerpress Peking dispatch (giving a short NCNA summary of the CCP letter) in *Scînteia*, June 20, 1963. The summary was very brief and only in a minority of points clearly reflected Chinese disagreement with Soviet theses. Nevertheless, even its listing of the titles of the 25 points would clearly indicate to any Rumanian Communist activist the extent of the Chinese letter's challenge to Moscow. The same issue of *Scînteia* also published the CPSU CC statement refusing to publish the CCP letter; thus Rumania, as Cuba and North Vietnam had done previously, was indicating its dissatisfaction with both sides (but its continued leaning towards Moscow) by publishing more of both sides of the controversy than either Moscow or Peking would like.
[82] Bourne from Bucharest in *The Christian Science Monitor*, October 10, 1963.
[83] *Pravda*, July 1, 1963.
[84] See especially Zunan Taipov (a former Chinese Major General), in *Kazakhstanskaya Pravda*, September 29, 1963.
[85] See especially Szulc from Washington in *The New York Times*, September 7, 1963 (giving " United States officials " as source) and Robert Guillain in *Le Monde*, September 8, 1963. The Chinese statement that in April and May 1962 the Soviets

Sinkiang in April 1962 and continued until the summer. At Ining Kuldja, the capital of the Ili-Kazakh province, the Soviet consulate was besieged by the rebels asking for Soviet aid; and a Soviet report by a Kazakh refugee [86] states that in May demonstrators before the Chinese Party committee in the same city were dispersed by machine-gun fire. Whether or not the Russians directly aided the rebellion, they clearly did give asylum to some tens of thousands [87] of Kazakh and Uighur refugees who fled across the Soviet border once the Chinese repression of the rebellion convinced them of its hopelessness. The Soviet consulates at Urumchi and Ining were ordered closed by the Chinese shortly thereafter.[88]

As the Russians declared in September 1963,[89] the Chinese Government allegedly encouraged Chinese fishermen to occupy and refuse to leave disputed islands in the Amur river.

Finally, as refugee interrogation in Hong Kong has now revealed, there was under way throughout China an extensive, systematic private briefing of both elite and mass audiences by the party leadership on the sins of Khrushchev. Beginning after Chou En-lai's November 1961 return from Moscow, it became intensive in the spring of 1962 and has continued so until this day. In addition to the published Chinese line, it stressed Khrushchev's personal responsibility for betraying Marxism-Leninism, for trying to overthrow the Chinese leadership, and for being responsible for the Chinese food shortage; and it implied that there is serious opposition to him in the Soviet Union. All these themes emerged in published Chinese material only after the signature of the test ban treaty in July 1963.[90]

---

used their consulates in Sinkiang " to carry out large-scale subversive activities in the Ili region and enticed and coerced several tens of thousands of Chinese citizens into going to the Soviet Union " is probably a distorted version of the same incident. See " The Origin and Development of the Differences Between the Leadership of the CPSU and Ourselves," *People's Daily* and *Red Flag*, September 6, 1963, *Peking Review*, VI, 37 (September 13, 1963), pp. 6–23, at p. 18, and Document 10.

[86] Taipov, *op. cit.*

[87] Szulc, *op. cit.*, quoting " U.S. officials," gives 50,000 to 70,000.

[88] Hong Kong dispatch in *The New York Times*, November 30, 1962.

[89] Soviet governmental statement, September 21, 1963, *Pravda*, September 21 and 22, 1963, and Document 12.

[90] The only systematic treatment of this subject I have found is Jerrold L. Schechter, " Khrushchev's Image inside China," *The China Quarterly*, No. **14** (April–June 1963), pp. 212–217.

14. The Chinese Letter of June 14

On June 15, 1963, the Central Committee of the CCP delivered in Moscow a letter dated June 14 [1] in reply to the letter of the Central Committee of the CPSU of March 30. It was a cold, brittle and totally uncompromising document. The developments of April and May had clearly indicated that Peking was intensifying its pressure on Moscow following the February–March exchange of letters, that the Russians were replying in kind, and that Sino-Soviet relations were thereby further deteriorating prior to the scheduled July 5 bilateral meeting in Moscow. Nevertheless the intransigence of the Chinese letter was unexpected. (Only in August did the Chinese announce that on June 6 they had for the third time protested to Moscow against the latter's agreement to sign a partial test ban treaty with the Western Powers. It may be assumed that this protest marked the final failure of whatever Sino-Soviet negotiations preceding the July meeting had been under way.)

The introduction and conclusion to the letter contained bland assurances of Peking's good will and desire to restore the unity of the international Communist movement. Its bulk, however, consisted of a 25-point " proposal on the general line of the international Communist movement and on some related questions of principle " which could only further wreck what little of that unity was still left. Where previously the Chinese views had been vague or esoteric, they were now spelled out with unmistakable clarity; where they had been explicit, they were now reiterated with careful precision. The Peking statement considerably deepened the Sino-Soviet rift in two respects: the Chinese

---

[1] The full text was published in Peking in *People's Daily*, June 17, 1963, *Peking Review*, VI, 25 (June 21, 1963), pp. 6–22 and Document 2. For other analyses of the June 14 Chinese letter, see Kx. [Ernst Kux], " Pekings Anklageschrift gegen Chruschtschew : Ein Gegenprogram für den internationalen Kommunismus," *Neue Zürcher Zeitung*, June 25, 1963, and Wolfgang Leonhard, " Das rote Konzil im Kreml," *Die Zeit*, July 12, 1963. For the Chinese August announcement, see " A Statement by the Spokesman of the Chinese Government," *People's Daily*, August 15, 1963, *Peking Review*, VI, 33 (August 16, 1963), pp. 7–15, at p. 15, and Document 7.

challenge to Soviet organisational predominance over Communist parties (particularly over non-ruling parties in underdeveloped areas), and Chinese denunciation of Soviet domestic policies. In short, although presumably Peking had long voiced the same arguments in closed discussions with the Russians, it represented the most significant Chinese pronouncement to date.

Constant reference was made in the letter to the " revolutionary Marxist-Leninist general line," violations of which were defined as anything that one-sidedly reduces Communist policy to " peaceful co-existence," " peaceful competition " and " peaceful transition." [2] The letter claimed that this " general line " had been formulated at the 1957 and 1960 Moscow Conferences on the basis of " unanimity through consultations " [3] (thus reiterating Peking's procedural position). It further declared that whatever the particular stage or conditions in various countries, they cannot transcend the general law of history, which requires the " resolute revolutionary struggle of carrying the proletarian world revolution through to the end," [4] i.e., differences in specific national conditions cannot justify abandoning revolutionary struggle.

With the increase in the number of socialist countries from one to thirteen (including Albania and Cuba but not Yugoslavia), loyalty to the " whole of the socialist camp " (rather than loyalty to the Soviet Union) was declared to have become " the touchstone of proletarian internationalism." Indeed,

> If anybody [Khrushchev] . . . does not defend the unity of the socialist camp but on the contrary creates tension and splits within it. or even follows the policies of the Yugoslav revisionists, tries to liquidate the socialist camp or helps capitalist countries to attack fraternal socialist countries, then he is betraying . . . [Communism]. . . .

Furthermore,

> If anybody [Khrushchev's allies] following in the footsteps of others defends the erroneous opportunist line and policies pursued by a certain socialist country . . . then he is departing from Marxism-Leninism and proletarian internationalism. [5]

In this context " a certain socialist country " could only mean the Soviet Union; and Peking's intention openly to challenge Moscow's ideological leadership of the international Communist movement could hardly be more clearly stated.

The letter went on to term the attitude towards the revolutionary struggle in Asia, Africa and Latin America " an important criterion " for distinguishing between those who support revolution and defend world peace and those who do not. [6] Those who deny the significance of

---

[2] *Ibid.* point 3, p. 7.
[3] *Ibid.* point 1, p. 6.
[5] *Ibid.* point 6, pp. 8–9.

[4] *Ibid.* point 3, p. 7.
[6] *Ibid.* point 8, pp. 9–10.

this struggle " on the pretext of breaking down the barriers of nationality, colour and geographical location " were charged with seeking in fact to maintain the rule of the " superior nations " over the oppressed nations. While opposing " reactionary nationalism," the statement sanctioned unity with all elements of the " patriotic national bourgeoisie," including even kings [*e.g.*, Norodom Sihanouk of Cambodia].[7] There followed a passage which must be interpreted as a barely concealed call for the deposition of pro-Soviet leaderships in parties not in power, an implicit sanction of the path taken by the " bourgeois revolutionary " Castro *vis-à-vis* the " reformist " old-line Cuban Communist Party (PSP), and an implied call for Khrushchev's removal:

> . . . If the leading group in any party adopt a non-revolutionary line and convert it into a reformist party, then Marxist-Leninists inside and outside the party will replace them and lead the people in making revolution. In another kind of situation the bourgeois revolutionaries will come forward to lead the revolution, and the party of the proletariat will forfeit its leadership of the revolution. . . .[8]

This appeal to replace the leadership of a Communist party with non-party Marxist-Leninists and even bourgeois revolutionaries was unprecedented and totally contrary to Marxist-Leninist orthodoxy; more than any other sign to date it indicated that the Chinese were actively preparing for an open split in the international Communist movement.

The letter's definition of peaceful co-existence was the most explicit Chinese one yet. It was described as a policy correctly practised by Lenin, Stalin and China but recently distorted by " certain persons " (the Russians) who " suddenly claimed Lenin's policy of peaceful co-existence as their own ' great discovery.' " Khrushchev's interpretation was abruptly rejected: " It is wrong to make peaceful co-existence the general line of the foreign policy of the socialist countries." Rather, the letter stressed that peaceful co-existence applies only to relations between socialist and capitalist states, while relations among socialist states must be conducted according to proletarian internationalism, and relations with oppressed peoples must be based upon support for their revolutionary struggles. Therefore, peaceful co-existence should " never be described as the main content of the transition from capitalism to socialism; still less should it be asserted that peaceful co-existence is mankind's road to socialism." [9]

The letter reiterated Peking's view that the peaceful transition to socialism is highly unlikely in practice and totally unacceptable as a

---

[7] *Ibid.* point 9, pp. 10–11.
[8] *Ibid.* point 12, p. 12.
[9] *Ibid.* point 16, pp. 15–16. As Leonhard pointed out, the fact that " certain persons " now for the first time replaced the previous Chinese formula " certain comrades " was in itself a significant sign of Chinese escalation.

new world-wide strategic principle [10]; that national liberation wars are desirable and indiscriminate opposition to war is bourgeois pacifism; that only the world victory of socialism can eliminate the threat of war [11]; and that nuclear weapons cannot alter the law of revolutionary class struggle or the nature of imperialism.[12]

The letter then for the first time openly and totally rejected the theory of the " all-peoples' state "—the outstanding theoretical innovation of the 1961 Soviet Party *Programme* and the ideological justification of de-Stalinisation and indeed of all the liberalisation measures of the Khrushchev era.[13] The letter declared that the class struggle and thus the necessity of the proletarian dictatorship would continue until the attainment of full communism and that the all-people's state made " any transition to communism out of the question." Indeed, it asked,

> . . . In calling a socialist state the " state of the whole people," is one trying to replace the Marxist-Leninist theory of the state by the bourgeois theory of the state . . . and the dictatorship of the proletariat by a state of a different character?

Peking's rhetorical reply implied a direct challenge to the Soviet leadership's domestic policies and pre-eminence:

> . . . This is not a question about the internal affairs of any particular country but a fundamental problem involving the universal truth of Marxism-Leninism . . . ,[14]

i.e. it must be judged by the entire international Communist movement. Furthermore, in a challenge to Khrushchev's efforts to impose Soviet domestic policies on the international Communist movement, the letter expressed the desire to have " a frank exchange of opinion " on " the criticism of Stalin " [15] and on " some important questions of principle regarding the international Communist movement . . . raised at the 20th and 22nd Congresses of the CPSU." The frequently reiterated Chinese denial of the validity of individual Communist party congresses for the whole international Communist movement was thereby concretely articulated.[16]

---

[10] *Ibid.* points 10–11, pp. 11–12, at point 11, p. 11
[11] *Ibid.* point 14, pp. 13–14.
[12] *Ibid.* point 15, pp. 14–15.
[13] See the new Soviet Party *Programme*, in Herbert Ritvo, ed., *The New Soviet Society* (New York: New Leader Paperback, 1962), pp. 166–167, and Khrushchev's report on the new *Programme* to the CPSU 22nd Congress, in Charlotte Saikowski and Leo Gruliow, eds., *Current Soviet Policies*, IV (New York: Columbia, 1962), pp. 101–102.
[14] CCP June 14 letter, point 18, pp. 16–17. For analysis, see Meissner, " Der Zweifrontenkampf der KPdSU," pp. 601–604.
[15] In a March 5 speech in Tirana commemorating the tenth anniversary of Stalin's death, Albanian Politburo member Ramiz Alia had declared that " the attitude towards J. V. Stalin and his work is a line of demarcation between the true Marxist-Leninists and the modern revisionists " (*Zëri i Popullit*, March 6, 1963).
[16] In the concluding remarks, CCP June 14 letter, p. 22.

Turning to relations among socialist states, the letter unequivocally proclaimed Peking's commitment to economic self-sufficiency:

> . . . To observe the principle of mainly relying on oneself in construction is to apply proletarian internationalism concretely.

It declared that " ' international division of labour ' and ' specialisation ' " [*i.e.*, Khrushchev's CMEA policy] and " putting economic pressure on other fraternal countries " [*e.g.*, Rumania] was " great-power chauvinism," and concluded that mutual economic assistance, co-operation and exchange among socialist states, " whether more developed or less developed economically," must be based on " complete equality " and " mutual benefit." [17]

The letter welcomed Moscow's statement in its March 30 letter that there are no " superior " or " subordinate " parties, but it caustically added that the observance of proletarian internationalism was more important in deeds than in words and that this precluded the imposition of the programme, resolutions or line of one's own [the Soviet Party Congresses and *Programme*] as the " common programme " of the international Communist movement. It reiterated Peking's insistence on the socialist norms of unanimity through consultations, abstention from public polemics and non-extension of ideological differences to state relations. Regarding adherence to these principles, it referred to Soviet-Albanian relations as an " outstanding " question at present which " must on no account be placed on a par " with the question of how to treat the " Yugoslav revisionist clique of traitors to Marxism-Leninism." The letter openly placed the responsibility for the state of Soviet-Albanian relations on the Soviet leaders and once again expressed the hope that they would " take the initiative in seeking an effective way to improve Soviet-Albanian relations." As for Sino-Soviet relations, while cautioning that the CCP had " exercised the greatest restraint " in the face of the " grave incidents " and " many difficulties and losses " imposed upon them, the letter pointedly declared that " here we do not desire to go back and enumerate the many unpleasant events that have occurred in the past " [18]—a clear intimation of Peking's readiness in the future to launch an exposé of Soviet violations of proletarian internationalism similar to the Albanian outpouring in late 1961 and early 1962.

The letter concluded, as had previous Chinese polemics, with a renewed call to the Russians to publish Peking's replies to " some of the articles and speeches in which fraternal Parties have attacked us " while the Chinese expressly stated that " we have not yet replied to others. For example, . . . to the many articles and speeches of the comrades of the CPSU." [19]

---

[17] *Ibid.* point 21, p. 18. Note the similarity to the Rumanian phraseology quoted above.
[18] *Ibid.* point 22, pp. 18–19.　　　　　　　　[19] *Ibid.* point 25, pp. 21–22.

The Chinese June 14 letter was thus a programmatic ideological manifesto which could well serve, if needed, as the basis for an open and total Sino-Soviet split. Its essence was a declaration by the Chinese Communist Party that it no longer recognised the ideological primacy of the Soviet Party, since its leadership had committed treason to Marxism-Leninism, and that therefore the Chinese Party must and would now assume the leadership of " revolutionary Marxism-Leninism " in order to pursue the protracted struggle required to defeat Khrushchev and his allies and to carry through the world-wide revolutionary struggle to final victory.

Suiting practice to theory, on June 16 (according to a subsequent Soviet charge) the Chinese began mass distribution of a Russian-language text of the letter in Moscow and elsewhere in the Soviet Union; they even allegedly

> scattered [them] from the car windows . . . of the Moscow-Peking train . . . [and] read [them] over the public-address systems during train stops. . . .[20]

---

20 Soviet Foreign Ministry Statement, *Izvestiya*, July 5, 1963, quoted from *CDSP*, XV, 27 (July 31, 1963), pp. 10–11.

15. Diplomatic Hostilities

As might have been expected in view of the unparalleled hostility of the June 14 Chinese letter and of its extensive distribution by the Chinese in the Soviet Union, Moscow reacted with at least equal, albeit verbally briefer, sharpness. On June 17 the Soviet Foreign Ministry orally protested to the Chinese Embassy against this " unheard-of " distribution of the Chinese letter.[1] On June 18, a formal Soviet Central Committee statement declared that the Chinese letter gave an " arbitrary interpretation " to the 1957 and 1960 Moscow Declarations, distorted their " major theses," and contained unwarranted attacks on the CPSU and other fraternal parties; therefore, in order to prevent public polemics from continuing, the letter would not be published in the Soviet press.[2] (As has been pointed out above, only the Rumanians among the pro-Soviet parties published a brief summary of it.) The immediately following Soviet Central Committee plenum, which had been scheduled to discuss internal ideological problems and the literary crisis, was apparently instead largely devoted to Sino-Soviet relations, and Khrushchev and other speakers at it made clear their contemptuous rejection of what his son-in-law Adzhubei called " sorry theoreticians." [3] (Furthermore, the plenum's attitude towards the liberal Soviet writers was far from totally hostile.) The plenum's final resolution, however, was sharper still; it marked the first time that any Soviet document, to say nothing of a formal Central Committee resolution, had so publicly, directly and totally denounced the Chinese. After " completely and unanimously " endorsing all Khrushchev's " political activity " concerning Sino-Soviet relations, and " instructing " the Presidium to be guided by the Twentieth, Twenty-first and Twenty-second Congresses and the 1957 and 1960 Moscow Declarations in the forthcoming July 5 meeting with the Chinese, the resolution flatly declared that

---

[1] Soviet Foreign Ministry statement, July 5, 1963, quoted from *CDSP*, XV, 27 (July 31, 1963), p. 10.
[2] *Pravda*, June 19, 1963.
[3] *Ibid.*, June 20, 1963; Khrushchev's speech in *ibid.*, June 29, 1963.

. . . The CPSU Central Committee categorically rejects as groundless and slanderous the attacks of the CCP Central Committee on our party and other Communist parties, on the decisions of the Twentieth, Twenty-First and Twenty-Second Congresses, and on the CPSU Programme . . . which have been unanimously approved by all Soviet people and by the international Communist movement. . . .[4]

In the meantime, a joint Chinese-North Korean communiqué indicated that Peking was fully maintaining the adamant position of its June 14 letter.[5] This new Sino-Soviet crisis had immediate repercussions in the international Communist front organisations. The Women's Congress, which was meeting in Moscow at this time, saw scenes of Sino-Soviet hostility far more striking than the December 1961 WFTU and WPC meetings. When the Chinese delegate attacked the Americans, the Italian delegation walked out and the other pro-Soviet delegates protested violently. Thereupon the Chinese delegate cried: " Do you want to come to terms with Mrs. Kennedy?", to which that old reliable Soviet spokesman La Pasionaria replied

. . . We want to come to terms with Mrs. Kennedy too if she is ready to defend her children from the danger of nuclear war. . . .

The Chinese delegate unsuccessfully tried to get the floor to reply but was prevented from speaking by the hostile cries of the audience and the chair-woman's bell. The Chinese and Albanian delegates thereupon voted against the final, relatively moderately phrased resolution (the North Korean delegate abstained) amid shouts from the audience of " Shame on you! " and the Chinese delegate, Yang Yuan-yu, in a speech explaining her negative vote, called the resolution " empty words " and declared amid shouts and boos from the other delegates that the congress sponsor had been guilty of

. . . anti-Chinese manoeuvres, manipulating the debate and violating democratic principles, and maliciously spreading all kinds of slanderous stories about the Chinese delegation. . . .[6]

---

[4] *Ibid.*, June 22, 1963 (*JPRS* 20, 194, July 16, 1963, pp. 24–34), republished in *People's Daily*, June 26, 1963 (SCMP 3010, July 2, 1962, p. 16).

[5] *People's Daily*, June 24, 1963.

[6] See the coverage from Moscow in *The New York Times*, June 28–30, 1963, and especially Tatu from Moscow in *Le Monde*, July 2, 1963, for Yang Yuan-yu's speech, and the Chinese delegation's statements, see *Peking Review*, VI, 27 (July 5, 1963), pp. 10–14, and for her subsequent detailed version of the proceedings, *People's Daily*, July 19, 1963, and *Peking Review*, VI, 30 (July 26, 1963), pp. 49–59. See also Wang Hsi (a member of the Chinese delegation), " The World Congress of Women. It Sets a Disgraceful Precedent for an International Conference," *Peking Review*, VI, 29 (July 19, 1963), pp. 13–16. For a pro-Soviet account which, however, gave no indication of the Sino-Soviet clash, see Helena Berg and Valentina Zakharova, " Unity for the Sake of Peace," *World Marxist Review*, VI, 8 (August 1963), pp. 77–79.

The Chinese later attacked the Russians for their alleged " manipulations " which resulted in the adoption of resolutions " which in effect serve imperialism." [7]

On June 24 the Soviet Foreign Ministry again protested against the Chinese distribution of the June 14 letter in the Soviet Union.[8] Allegedly in retaliation to this, but also in further response to the letter itself, the Soviet Union in a diplomatic note to Peking on June 29 requested the recall of three Chinese diplomats from its Moscow Embassy and two Chinese students in Moscow. The Russians did not at first publicly announce these expulsions, but the Chinese immediately replied to them on June 30, on the eve of the CPSU-CCP Moscow meeting, in a statement of the Peking Foreign Ministry.[9] The statement declared that Soviet diplomats and other personnel in Peking had always been allowed to distribute similar Soviet documents, that the Soviet " demand " was therefore " unreasonable " and its " excuse untenable," that Moscow's expulsion of the Chinese diplomats was " unprecedented " in Sino-Soviet relations, and that, particularly on the eve of the July 5 Sino-Soviet meeting, the question now arose as to whether Moscow was

> . . . deliberately trying to undermine Sino-Soviet unity, vitiate the relations between the two states, and create obstacles to the talks between the Chinese and Soviet parties. . . .

Despite this " unreasonable and unfriendly action," the statement blandly and self-righteously continued, the Chinese would not retaliate in kind (*i.e.*, by implication they did not fear anything the Russians would distribute in China, while the Russians, like the " mice " they were, did not dare allow Chinese declarations to be distributed in the Soviet Union). (This whole episode bears a remarkable resemblance to the prelude to the Soviet-Albanian break in diplomatic relations; then, too, Moscow gave as a justification the Albanians' distribution of their literature in the Soviet Union.) [10] A statement of the Chinese Central Committee on July 1 and a diplomatic note to the Soviet Embassy in Peking on July 4 declared that the recent Soviet actions were

> . . . a serious step in further worsening Sino-Soviet relations and in manufacturing a split in the international Communist movement. . . .

and represented the extension of ideological differences to state relations but added that in spite of this the Chinese delegation would go to Moscow

[7] Wang Hsi, *op. cit.*
[8] Soviet Foreign Ministry statement, July 5, *loc. cit.* The July 4 Chinese reply to the Soviet protest (*People's Daily*, July 5, 1963, and SCMP 3015, July 10, 1963, pp. 27–28) gave the date of the (hitherto unpublished) Soviet protest as June 27.
[9] *People's Daily*, June 30, 1963, and *Peking Review*, VI, 27 (July 5, 1963), p. 8.
[10] Griffith, *Albania*, pp. 113–121.

as scheduled and that in view of these talks Peking would not immediately reply to the Soviet actions.[11] On July 3 Chou En-lai received and congratulated the Chinese expelled from Moscow and on July 7 a large and well-publicised meeting was held in Peking in their honour.[12] Peking also announced that four Soviet citizens had smashed the glass in a display case in front of the Chinese Embassy in Moscow, and added:

... It is really extraordinarily astonishing that such a flagrant provocative incident disrupting Sino-Soviet friendship should have happened in the capital of the Soviet Union. . . .[13]

On July 2, in a speech in East Berlin,[14] Khrushchev made the first public announcement that Moscow was prepared to sign a limited test ban agreement with the United States and Great Britain; and although he coupled this with a renewed proposal of an East-West non-aggression pact, the latter did not appear to be an indispensable precondition for the former.

On July 4 the Chinese Foreign Ministry, in a reply [15] to the second Soviet protest (at the end of June) at the distribution of the June 14 Chinese letter in Moscow, declared that such distribution was " normal," that the Soviet Union had done the same thing in China, and that it should have published the Chinese letter itself. On the following day a Chinese Central Committee statement,[16] in reply to the Soviet Central Committee's statement of the previous day, said that its delegation in Moscow would " make the necessary answers at the talks . . . to [Soviet] distortions, accusations, and attacks."

Moscow hastened to reply in kind. A July 4 Soviet Central Committee statement [17] " decisively repudiated " the Chinese statement as a

---

[11] Statement of CCP CC, *People's Daily*, July 1, 1963, and of CPR Ministry of Foreign Affairs, *ibid.*, July 4, in *Peking Review*, VI, 27 (July 5, 1963), pp. 5–6.

[12] *Peking Review*, VI, 28 (July 12, 1963), pp. 3–5.

[13] *People's Daily*, July 1, 1963 (SCMP 3013, July 8, 1963, p. 21). Moscow subsequently announced that this had been done on June 27 by a drunken student, who had been arrested, and that on July 28 the Soviet Foreign Ministry had expressed its regrets over the incident to the Chinese Embassy. See *Trud*, July 4, 1963, which, however, accused NCNA of having " entirely distorted " and " excessively exaggerated " it.

[14] *Pravda*, July 3, 1963. Khrushchev's speech had been preceded on June 10 by President Kennedy's conciliatory speech and by the Soviet leader's indication to Harold Wilson that he would no longer accept three on-site inspections but also the intimation that a partial test ban treaty might be possible. Other signs of an approaching Moscow-Washington détente also occurred. In May Soviet jamming of Western broadcasts diminished and ceased entirely after Kennedy's June 10 speech; the Soviet representative to the International Atomic Energy Authority signed an agreement on supervision of agency-provided reactors on June 19; and the " hot line " (direct tele-typewriter communication) agreement between Moscow and Washington was signed on June 20. See Shulman, " Artificial Tensions and the Test Ban," *op. cit.*

[15] Note, CPR Ministry of Foreign Affairs to Soviet Embassy in Peking, July 4, 1963, in *People's Daily*, July 5, 1963, and *Peking Review*, VI, 27 (July 5, 1963), pp. 7–8.

[16] CCP CC Statement, *People's Daily*, July 5, 1963, and *Peking Review*, VI, 27 (July 5, 1963), p. 6.

[17] CPSU CC Statement, *Pravda*, July 4, 1963, quoted from *CDSP*, XV, 27 (July 31, 1963), p. 10.

" slander " and declared that because of it the CPSU would (contrary to its earlier intention) answer the June 14 Chinese letter " in due time." On the following day, as the Sino-Soviet Moscow meeting opened, a Soviet Foreign Ministry statement [18] gave a detailed version (outlined above) of the Chinese distribution of their June 14 letter and the subsequent expulsion of the Chinese from Moscow, and denounced these Chinese " illegal activities " as well as the " unseemly [and] distorted . . . fantasies " of the Chinese statement concerning them.

[18] Soviet Foreign Ministry Statement, *Izvestiya*, July 5, 1963, quoted from *CDSP*, XV, 27 (July 31, 1963), pp. 10–11.

16. The Sino-Soviet Moscow Meeting and the Test Ban Treaty

THE Sino-Soviet meeting opened in Moscow on July 5, after Khrushchev's well-publicised departure for Kiev, and continued until July 20, when the discussions were " suspended " upon the motion of the Chinese delegation. As yet (November 1963) they have not been resumed. The Anglo-American-Soviet test ban negotiations opened in Moscow on July 15 and were successfully concluded on July 25. Thus the Soviet leadership was for several days host to both their Chinese " comrades " and their " Western imperialist enemies," after which these roles, at least as far as the test ban treaty was concerned, appeared reversed.

The die had long since been cast in Sino-Soviet relations (probably as early as 1959). The Chinese have since stated [1] (and the Russians have so far not denied) that Moscow notified them in August 1962, eleven months before the July meeting, that it intended to sign a treaty with Washington to avoid the proliferation of atomic weapons. Indeed, since 1957 the issue of Soviet aid for China's desired atomic capacity, and therefore of any international agreement which would preclude this, has been one of the major causes of and factors in the whole dispute—a phase to which the test ban negotiations furnish one of the best available indicators. Furthermore the course of the Sino-Soviet Moscow meeting was and still (November 1963) remains secret; one must therefore make deductions from published Soviet and Chinese material.

However, this is not too difficult. The Chinese letter of June 14, their subsequent distribution of it in Moscow, the resultant Soviet expulsion of the Chinese diplomats and students, and the subsequent

---

[1] " Statement by the Spokesman of the Chinese Government," *People's Daily*, August 15, 1963 and *Peking Review*, VI, 33 (August 16, 1963), pp. 7–15.

bitter Sino-Soviet exchange of notes and statements (all summarised above), plus Khrushchev's announcement of his willingness to sign a partial test ban treaty, had already made clear that the July 5 Sino-Soviet meeting in Moscow, probably always intended by both sides as a manoeuvre from which each hoped to profit by fixing the blame for its prospective failure on the other, and which had in any case been agreed to largely as a result of pressure from other Communist parties, was almost certainly doomed to failure in advance.

Signs indicating this continued throughout the meeting. On July 7, two days after it began, a mass rally was held in Peking to welcome home the Chinese " unreasonably " expelled from the Soviet Union.[2] On July 9 a Soviet Central Committee statement [3] retorted that this demonstration was intended to bring about the " serious exacerbation " of Sino-Soviet relations. The next day a Chinese Central Committee statement [4] repeated Peking's previous protest against the " preposterous " expulsion, taunted Moscow about its refusal to publish the Chinese June 14 letter, and declared that the Russians were " whipping up a campaign " against the Chinese party.

The failure of the Sino-Soviet Moscow discussions became even clearer with a series of Chinese editorials, of which the first and most important appeared on July 13.[5] They reiterated all the well-known previous Chinese positions, particularly the attack on Moscow for not publishing the Chinese declarations. They attacked the United States,[6] Yugoslavia,[7] and India [8] for attempting to sabotage the Sino-Soviet negotiations (*i.e.,* they attacked Khrushchev for his favourable policies toward these three countries); they accused the CPSU of " conducting a campaign " against the CCP and " inflaming feeling against China,"

2 *People's Daily,* July 8, 1963, quoted from *Peking Review,* VI, 28 (July 12, 1963), pp. 3–5, at p. 3.

3 *Pravda,* July 9, 1963, quoted from *CDSP,* XV, 27 (July 31, 1963), p. 11; reprinted in *Peking Review,* VI, 28 (July 12, 1963), p. 8.

4 *People's Daily,* July 10, quoted from *Peking Review,* VI, 28 (July 12, 1963), pp. 7–8. See also speech by Kuo Mo-jo, NCNA English Peking, July 11, 1963 (SCMP 3019, July 16, 1963, pp. 27–28).

5 " We Want Unity, Not a Split," *People's Daily,* July 13, 1963 and *Peking Review,* VI, 29 (July 19, 1963), pp. 7–9. A probably reliable text of the unpublished speech by Hager to the Third SED CC Plenum, July 29–30, 1963 states that at the meeting the Chinese refused to agree to a mutual cessation of polemics, stating that " one could agree upon that between the two meetings or at the next one." See *SBZ-Archiv,* XIV, 17–18 (1.-2. Septemberheft 1963), pp. 272–283, at p. 283.

6 " Observer," " No Meddling in Sino-Soviet Differences by U.S. Imperialism," *People's Daily,* July 14, 1963 and *Peking Review,* VI, 29 (July 19, 1963), pp. 9–10.

7 " Observer," " A Demarcation Line Must Be Drawn With the Renegade Tito Group," *People's Daily,* July 15, 1963 and *Peking Review,* VI, 29 (July 19, 1963), pp. 10–11. Note the similarity in phraseology to " A Great Betrayal of Marxism-Leninism," *Zëri i Popullit,* October 13, 1962, for which see Griffith, *Albania,* pp. 156–157 and Document 32, pp. 387–399.

8 " Observer," " Indian Reactionaries in the Anti-China Chorus," *People's Daily,* July 16, 1963 and *Peking Review,* VI, 29 (July 19, 1963), pp. 12–14.

a fact which justified " people . . . in worrying whether the Central Committee of the CPSU wants to push Sino-Soviet relations to the brink of rupture " (*i.e.*, they accused Moscow of intending to bring about a split and asserted that the Chinese were unalterably opposed to it); and they finally declared that:

> . . . If the differences cannot be resolved today, they can wait until tomorrow. If they cannot be resolved this year, they can wait until next year . . . Differences that cannot be settled immediately may be laid aside, pending later settlement. If we cannot finish our discussions in one session, several can be held, and our parties can hold future bilateral talks . . .

This was a clear intimation that the Chinese were proposing (as the final communiqué indicated) an indefinite adjournment of the talks. This was not surprising; it is always in the interest of the less powerful, more orthodox partner in a Communist dispute to maintain the semblance of unity. Within such a context it can more easily propagate its views while awaiting their eventual victory; conversely, the majority party, especially if it is less orthodox, must attempt to restore ideological and organisational conformity even at the risk of a formal split.

THE JULY 14 SOVIET OPEN LETTER

The publication on July 14 of the " Open Letter " of the CPSU Central Committee " to All Party Organisations and All Communists of the Soviet Union " [9] made the failure of the Moscow Sino-Soviet talks obvious to all.

The very fact that the letter was addressed not to the Chinese Central Committee but to all members of the CPSU (and, by its immediate publication, to the whole Soviet people) alone indicated that the dialogue previously carried on between the parties through the exchange of letters had been terminated for the present by this Soviet action. Party relations were *de facto* suspended. The wording of this attack was sharper than ever, accusing the Chinese of " arbitrary," " distorted," " groundless," " slanderous," " hostile actions," " unworthy fabrications." Like the Chinese, the Russians of course presented themselves as patiently working for reconciliation, while the Chinese were allegedly continuing to worsen the atmosphere of the Moscow negotiations.

[9] *Pravda*, July 14, 1963 and Document *3*, republished in *People's Daily*, July 20, 1963 and *Peking Review*, VI, 30 (July 26, 1963), pp. 28–46. *Pravda* simultaneously published in full the June 14 Chinese letter. For other analyses, see Robert Guillain in *Le Monde*, July 17, 1963 and Kx. [Ernst Kux], " Moskaus Antwort auf die Anklage Pekings," *Neue Zürcher Zeitung*, July 21, 1963. Curiously, the August 1963 *Problems of Peace and Socialism* (passed for the press, Russian edition, July 8, 1963) did not include any overtly anti-Chinese polemics.

The Open Letter rehearsed the Soviet charges against the Chinese distribution of the June 14 letter and the warm reception given the Chinese expelled for this " illegal " activity; but it then went on to far more serious charges by giving the first extensive Soviet " history " of the dispute. The very fact that Moscow now gave its own lengthy version of the dispute represented a step in its escalation. For the first time Communists in the Soviet Union and the satellite countries received a detailed account from their own press. The Chinese countered with their first comprehensive statement, an exhaustive discussion of " The Origin and Development of the Differences Between the Leadership of the CPSU and Ourselves " only in early September.

This anti-Chinese Soviet " history " may be summarised as follows: (1) The Chinese began the dispute ideologically in April 1960 with the publication of " Long Live Leninism " and organisationally in June 1960 at the WFTU Peking Congress and at the Bucharest Congress, and at Moscow in November 1960. (2) They stubbornly resisted patient efforts by the CPSU and the " absolute majority " of other parties to make them see the errors of their ways, and their signature of the 1960 Moscow Declaration was only " manoeuvring." (3) Immediately thereafter they continued their opposition, through their Albanian " mouthpiece," whom they " openly pushed . . . on to the road of open struggle " against the Soviet Union and the other Communist parties. (4) Within this context they " launched a campaign against the CPSU Central Committee and the Soviet Government " (i.e., their goal was to overthrow the Soviet leadership—an interpretation further strengthened by the Open Letter's warm endorsement of Khrushchev). (5) Thereafter, ignoring all Soviet efforts at conciliation, the Chinese first carried the ideological differences into the field of state relations by cutting off trade with the Soviet Union. (6) They carried over these differences into the activities of international front organisations, specifically the meetings at Stockholm, Moshi and Jakarta. At the latter two, the Open Letter implied that the Chinese employed clearly racist tactics. (7) Most seriously of all (next to the implied charge that Mao was trying to remove Khrushchev), the Chinese were charged with " organising and supporting various anti-party groups of renegades " against the United States, Brazilian, Italian, Belgian, Australian and Indian parties, glorifying these groups, reprinting their " slanderous articles," and in Ceylon of even being in contact with a Trotskyite group.[10]

[10] Note that the New Zealand CP, which since 1960 has been under predominant Chinese influence, was not mentioned. Its April 1963 national conference was also favourably reported in the Soviet-controlled *World Marxist Review*, VI, 7 (July 1963), pp. 45–46. See Daniel Tretiak, " Kiwi Communists Join Peking," *Far Eastern Economic Review*, XL, 12 (June 20, 1963), pp. 647–649.

Turning to substantive issues, the Soviet Open Letter concentrated its fire on a most promising target: the alleged warlike nature of Chinese policy:

> . . . in questions of war and peace the CCP leadership has cardinal differences, based on principle, with us and with the world Communist movement. The essence of these differences lies in a diametrically opposite approach to such vital problems as the possibility of averting thermonuclear world war, peaceful coexistence between states with different social systems, and the interconnection between the struggle for peace and the development of the world revolutionary movement . . . These " incorrect views " could only be caused either by Chinese lack of understanding or by the fact that " behind the [Chinese] rumpus about the ' world revolution ' . . . there are other [Chinese] goals which have nothing in common with revolution " [*i.e.*, either the desire to precipitate a thermonuclear war, on the ruins of which China could dominate the world, or to replace the Soviet Union as the head of the international Communist movement]:

In turn, the letter provided a new and more extreme ideological formulation of the Soviet view that " the nuclear bomb does not adhere to the class principle "; *i.e.*, the formal postulation of an exception to the fundamental Marxist principle of looking at the world from the standpoint of the class struggle, an example of how both the course of events (the discovery and spread of thermonuclear weapons) and the Sino-Soviet dispute can begin to erode Marxist-Leninist ideology.[11]

The letter systematically refuted the other substantive aspects of the Chinese June 14 letter without adding anything very new to the exchange with the exception of the accusation that the Chinese were attempting " to undermine the unity of the socialist commonwealth " by trying to " impose . . . on other socialist countries " (presumably North Korea, North Vietnam, and to some extent Rumania) their concept of " self-sufficient national economies."

It was, as Mr. Molotov would have said, no accident that the next day, July 15, a smiling and joking Khrushchev personally opened the test ban negotiations with Averell Harriman and Lord Hailsham.[12]

The July 14 Soviet Open Letter was followed by a flood of Soviet anti-Chinese polemics. The strongest of these was a slashing attack on the " racism " of the " modern schismatics " in Peking. Turning their own charges against them, it declared that the Chinese priority for the peoples of Asia, Africa, and Latin America would inevitably lead to alliance with bourgeois nationalists from their countries, and that

---

11 *Cf.* Raymond Aron, " Coexistence and the Class Struggle," *The New Republic*, CXLIX, 13 (September 28, 1963), pp. 10–11.
12 *Pravda* and *The New York Times*, July 16, 1963.

. . . It is only one step from this to a call for a split in the world Communist movement and to the creation of a new international Communist centre. . . .[13]

THE FAILURE OF THE SINO-SOVIET MEETINGS AND THE CONCLUSION OF THE TEST BAN TREATY

Thereafter Western newspaper reports continued to report excellent progress in the test ban negotiations, and on July 19 Khrushchev publicly [14] indicated a further softening in the Soviet attitude. After attacking (but not naming) the Chinese on the issues of peace and de-Stalinisation (popular among the Soviet people), and implying that Peking was trying to overthrow the Soviet leadership, he not only reiterated the Soviet willingness to sign a partial test ban treaty but also made a series of other proposals: a freezing, or better, a decrease in military budgets, the establishment of control posts against surprise attack in the Soviet Union and in other countries or in West and East Germany and the mutual reduction of troops in the two German states. He also modified the Soviet attitude on an East-West non-aggression treaty, declaring that the Soviet Union " hoped also " (*i.e.*, did not necessarily insist upon) for its signature along with the test ban treaty and that the " form " of such a treaty could be settled " without particular difficulty " (*i.e.*, the Soviet Union was prepared to find some form which would settle the issue of East German participation without involving Western recognition of the Ulbricht régime).

On the same day, July 19, in the first detailed statement of its views on the test ban treaty, Peking declared [15] that the American purpose in the partial test ban treaty, as Averell Harriman had said, was " ' to prevent China from getting a nuclear capacity '," that the American proposal (to which Khrushchev had already indicated his agreement) was " an out-and-out fraud," a " trap . . . to manacle the socialist countries " which would " increase greatly " the danger of war. It solicitously hoped that the Soviet Union " will not fall into this trap." A simultaneous and blandly sarcastic statement by " a spokesman " of the Chinese Central Committee,[16] intended as a preliminary comment

---

[13] G. Mirsky, " Socialism, Imperialism, and Afro-Asian Solidarity," *Izvestiya*, July 16, 1963, quoted from *CDSP*, XV, 29 (August 14, 1963), pp. 11–13, at p. 12. See also Nikolai Tikhonov, Alexander Korneichuk, and Yury Zhukov, " The Rallying of All Peace-Loving Forces is the Primary Task in the Struggle to Avert a World War," *Pravda*, July 15, 1963, and L. Stepanov, " Important Component of the World Revolutionary Process," *ibid.*, July 18, 1963. Meetings were also held throughout the Soviet Union on the subject.

[14] *Pravda*, July 20, 1963, quoted from *CDSP*, XV, 29 (August 14, 1963), pp. 3–7, at p. 7.

[15] " U.S. Nuclear Fraud Exposed," *People's Daily*, July 19, 1963, and *Peking Review*, VI, 30 (July 26, 1963), pp. 47–49.

[16] *People's Daily*, July 19, 1963 and *Peking Review*, VI, 30 (July 26, 1963), p. 9.

on the Soviet July 14 Open Letter, praised final publication of the Chinese June 14 statement by the Russians, while terming the open letter " not up to the mark and not convincing, but indeed, superlative material for learning by negative example."

On July 20 the Sino-Soviet Moscow meeting was formally adjourned " until some later time " (i.e., indefinitely); the communiqué [17] stated only that " both sides expounded their own views " (i.e., no agreements were reached). Presumably they did the same at the final banquet given by the CPSU Presidium for the Chinese delegation; but whether it proceeded, as Tass declared,[18] " in a friendly atmosphere " seems somewhat doubtful.

On the same day, July 20, People's Daily published the full text of the Soviet July 14 Open Letter (plus the text of the Chinese June 14 letter), preceded by an " editor's note " [19] which gave a preliminary and partial refutation of the Soviet letter, which described as a " distortion of facts " and a " reversal of right and wrong." It charged Moscow with slandering Mao by declaring that he was in favour of war and paraphrased Mao's November 18, 1957, speech at the Moscow 12-party meeting as proof to the contrary. It further declared that Peking had never agreed with the Soviet Twentieth Congress (as the July 14 Soviet Open Letter had charged) and that Mao had remonstrated with Moscow four times on this matter between April and November 1956. Peking, the note continued, had equally disagreed with Moscow's line on peaceful transition to socialism and in November 1957 had presented a comprehensive memorandum on the subject to Moscow. In conclusion it declared that there were " no less than 70 to 80 " other such instances, which Peking would cover later (i.e., the Chinese would soon answer the Soviet July 14 letter by providing their own detailed history of the dispute). The next day the returning Chinese delegation was greeted at the airport by the whole CCP leadership, headed (a rare honour) by Mao Tse-tung in person,[20] and Peking declared that the CPSU Central Committee:

> . . . in a new wave of opposition to the Communist Party of China, has set in motion all its propaganda media to launch unbridled slanders and vilifications against the CCP . . . statements flagrantly attempting to incite the Chinese people and the members of the Chinese Communist Party against the beloved leadership of the CCP. . . .[21]

---

[17] Pravda and People's Daily, July 22, 1963; CDSP, XV, 29 (August 14, 1963), p. 10; Peking Review, VI, 30 (July 26, 1963), p. 6.
[18] Pravda, July 21, 1963 and Peking Review, VI, 30 (July 26, 1963), p. 8.
[19] People's Daily, July 20, 1963 and Peking Review, VI, 30 July 26, 1963), pp. 27–28.
[20] People's Daily, July 22, 1963 and Peking Review, VI, 30 (July 26, 1963), pp. 6–8.
[21] People's Daily, July 20–23, 1963 and SCMP 3026, July 25, 1963, pp. 30–32 and SCMP 3027, July 26, 1963, pp. 23–24. On July 22 the Czechoslovak government ordered the closing of the NCNA office in Prague, after, on July 18, ordering its two correspondents to leave the country within 48 hours. See Rudé Právo, July 23,

while a leading Soviet Far Eastern expert declared that:

> ... the Chinese dogmatists deform Marxist-Leninist theory, in particular concerning the role and place of the Far Eastern countries in the development of the world. In practice they substitute for Marxist-Leninist historical science their own chauvinist, nationalist, and even racist concepts. . . .[22]

On July 25 Gromyko, Harriman, and Hailsham initialed the test ban treaty[23] in Moscow amid signs of a considerable improvement in the climate of East-West relations. Khrushchev warmly endorsed it and repeated his previous proposals for further East-West agreements to facilitate the relaxation of tension.[24] A conference of the first secretaries and heads of government of the Warsaw Pact countries, which had convened in Moscow on July 24 (with Gheorghiu-Dej of Rumania present this time) also endorsed the treaty.[25] On the same day, July 25, Peking announced that Mao had received E. F. Hill, a former member of the Politburo and Secretariat of the Australian Communist Party and one of the leaders of its pro-Chinese faction (who had been expelled in 1962 when the pro-Soviet faction had recovered control of the party),[26] a clear sign that the Chinese leader was pursuing his aim of obtaining control over, or splitting, Communist parties throughout the world.

1963 and *People's Daily*, July 25 and 26, 1963 (JPRS 21,141, September 19, 1963) and (for their return of the rest of the NCNA Prague Personnel to Peking), *People's Daily*, September 18–19, 1963 (SCMP 3066, September 24, 1963), pp. 16–20.

[22] In an interview with B. G. Gafurov, Director of the Institute of the Peoples of Asia in the Soviet Academy of Sciences, *Krasnaya Zvezda*, July 21, 1963.

[23] *Pravda* and *The New York Times*, July 26, 1963.

[24] In an interview with *Pravda* and *Izvestiya*, July 27, 1963.

[25] *Pravda*, July 27, 1963.

[26] *People's Daily*, July 25, 1963 (SCMP 3029, July 30, p. 21). For Hill's expulsion, see Günther Nollau, *Zerfall des Weltkommunismus* (Cologne and Berlin: Kiepenheuer and Witsch, 1963), pp. 86–88.

17. The Aftermath of the Test Ban Treaty

THE CHINESE REACTION

THE immediate Chinese reaction to the signature of the test ban treaty,[1] although strong, was no more so than previous Chinese statements. On July 31, however, a violent Chinese Government statement against the treaty [2] made clear that the failure of the Moscow talks and its signature had much worsened Sino-Soviet relations. Peking now opened an overt and all-out attack on Moscow: the Sino-Soviet schism had now clearly occurred. Dropping all pretence about " modern revisionists," the Chinese statement named names in a tone worthy of the most frenetic Albanian foamings. The Soviet signature of the test ban treaty was a " dirty fake," and " fraud," and a " sell-out," which " the Chinese Government regards . . . as its unshirkable and sacred duty to thoroughly expose." The treaty's central purpose was " to prevent all the threatened peace-loving countries, including China, from increasing their defence capability " (*i.e.*, to prevent China from obtaining atomic weapons). Its signature by Moscow demonstrated that:

> . . . the policy pursued by the Soviet Government is one of allying with the forces of war to oppose the forces of peace, allying with imperialism to oppose socialism, allying with the United States to oppose China, and allying with the reactionaries of all countries to oppose the people of the world. . . .

The statement concluded with a Chinese proposal for the complete prohibition of nuclear weapons throughout the world.

A flood of subsequent Chinese propaganda declarations underlined and expanded on all these themes. They declared that the Soviet signature of the treaty was " a concentrated manifestation of capitulationism "

---

[1] Speech by Kuo Mo-jo, *People's Daily*, July 27, 1963 (SCMP 3030, July 31, 1963, pp. 31–32), and editorial note preceding publication of Khrushchev's July 19 speech, *ibid.*, July 29, 1963 (SCMP 3031, August 1, 1963, pp. 28–29).
[2] *People's Daily*, July 31, 1963 and *Peking Review*, VI, 31 (August 2, 1963), pp. 7–8.

and "a U.S.-Soviet alliance against China pure and simple," caused by the Soviet leaders having "embraced the U.S. imperialists in joyous abandon." In a clear indication that Mao now regarded Khrushchev as having betrayed Marxism-Leninism and having thereby forfeited any claim to be the legitimate Soviet ruler, one Chinese article declared:

> . . . He who claims to be the legitimate heir of Lenin now joins hands with the chieftain of imperialism. . . .[3]

THE SOVIET REJOINDER

Moscow in turn charged that Peking was "entering into a bloc" with Goldwater, Teller, de Gaulle, and Adenauer [4] and accused the Chinese of following a Trotskyite foreign policy, the "basic aim" of which was "shifting the centre of the world revolution to the zone of the national-liberation movement"—a "dangerous, schismatic course" intended

> . . . to disparage the role of the Soviet Union, to discredit the socialist camp . . . by regarding it (and particularly the industrially developed socialist countries) merely as an instrument of the national-liberation movement and a source of aid to the young national states rather than as the main force of the revolutionary transformation of *all* human society. . . .[5]

The probably reliable complete text of an unpublished speech by Kurt Hager, the chief SED ideologist, at the Third SED CC Plenum on July 29–30, 1963 [6] gives some interesting indications of what was

[3] "This is Betrayal of the Soviet People!", *People's Daily*, August 3, 1963 and *Peking Review*, VI, 32 (August 9, 1963), pp. 10–11. See also "People of the World Unite! Strive for the Complete Prohibition and Thorough Destruction of Nuclear Weapons!", *People's Daily*, August 2, 1963 and *Peking Review*, VI, 32 (August 9, 1963), pp. 8–10 (which also has seven anti-Khrushchev anti-test ban treaty statements), and Mao's August 8 anti-American statement (his first public pronouncement since 1957) *People's Daily*, August 9, 1963 and *Peking Review*, VI, 33, 1963 and Document 5. At a Peking meeting on August 1 two Russian correspondents walked out after Kuo Mo-jo attacked the treaty. (Reuter's from Peking, *The Times* (London), August 2, 1963.) For Chinese reprinting of alleged Soviet anti-Khrushchev letters, see CB 713, September 10, 1963.

[4] N. Polyanov, "In Strange Company," *Izvestiya*, July 30, 1963, quoted from *CDSP*, XV, 30 (August 21, 1963), pp. 5–6; see also Yury Zhukov, "Who Is For, Who Is Against?", *Pravda*, July 29, 1963 (which discussed in a remarkably frank manner the dangers of nuclear proliferation); F. Burlatsky, "Concrete Analysis Is a Major Requirement of Leninism" and I. Lemin, "Revolutionary Theory: A Guide to Action," both in *Pravda*, July 25, 1963; N. Inozemtsev, "Peaceful Co-existence and the World Revolutionary Process," *ibid.*, July 28, 1963; P. Pospelov, "Historical Significance of Second Congress of Russian Social-Democratic Labor Party," *ibid.*, July 30, 1963; and a letter in the same issue by a group of old Bolsheviks.

[5] A. Chernyayev, "Socialism Is the Main Force of World Revolutionary Development," *Pravda*, August 3, 1963, quoted from excerpts in *CDSP*, XV, 31 (August 28, 1963), pp. 8–11, at p. 9 (full translation: JPRS 20, 930, September 5, 1963, pp. 1–9). See also the more esoteric "The World Revolutionary Process and Unity of the Communist Movement," *World Marxist Review*, VI, 8 (August 1963), pp. 3–11.

[6] *SBZ-Archiv*, XIV, 17–18 (1.-2. Septemberheft 1963), pp. 272–283.

then and probably remains the complete anti-Chinese Soviet position. As of this writing the following aspects of it have not yet appeared (many did in the July-November period) in published Communist material: (1) at the July 1963 CPSU-CCP Moscow meeting the Chinese refused to agree to an end to polemics; (2) the CCP has always suffered from too much traditional, peasant and petit-bourgeois influence; (3) Mao's works are not a further development of Marxism-Leninism but rather essentially " a simplified and in part already incorrect version " of it; and (4) the overcoming of the incorrect Chinese views will be a long and wearying process, but there are no objective reasons for Sino-Soviet differences and therefore they will be overcome.

A Soviet Government statement of August 3 [7] presented a systematic refutation of the July 31 Chinese statement. Its tone was quite as sharp: the Chinese declaration was full of " hopelessness and pessimism " and of " unprecedented . . . profoundly regrettable . . . fabrications "; in fact, " it is impossible to imagine anything more absurd." The Chinese proposal for a worldwide conference on total disarmament was dismissed as a " cloak " to conceal Peking's refusal to sign the test ban treaty. This refusal allied China with the U.S. " madmen " and the French and West German " extremists "—a step which in fact increased tension and was thus " tantamount to actual connivance with those who stand for thermonuclear war." [8]

At the beginning of August a more comprehensive attack on the totality of Chinese ideological positions and political moves appeared in the leading editorial of the CPSU ideological journal *Kommunist*.[9] Its tone was unremittingly violent: the " inadmissible tone " of the Chinese " combines hypocrisy . . . and unprecedented presumption . . . with arrogance and coarseness which transcend all bounds. . . . The present deviation of the CCP's leadership from the general line of the Marxist-Leninist parties " has resulted in their " schismatic actions . . . striving to impose their erroneous views . . . [and] their special platform . . . on the world Communist movement. . . .

The article, although in large part repetitive, did add some material to the July 14 Soviet version of the history of the dispute. The Chinese

---

[7] *Pravda*, August 4, 1963, quoted from *CDSP*, XV, 31 (August 28, 1963), pp. 4–7.
[8] *Pravda* and *The New York Times*, August 6, 1963.
[9] " For Triumph of Creative Marxism-Leninism, Against Revising Course of World Communist Movement," *Kommunist*, No. 11, July 1963 (passed for the press, July 31, 1963), pp. 3–36, quoted from *CDSP*, XV, 35 (September 25, 1963), pp. 10–24. See also three articles in the next issue: " The CPSU Is Creatively Developing Marxist-Leninist Theory," *Kommunist*, No. 12, 1963 (passed for the press August 19, 1963), pp. 3–11; N. Lomakin, " The Party of All the People," *ibid.*, pp. 12–22; and Yu. Zhukov, " The National Liberation Movement in a New Stage," *ibid.*, pp. 23–32. On August 23, 1963 *Pravda* declared that dogmatism has become " the main danger "; previously Soviet newspapers had only quoted foreign communist declarations to this effect.

published " Long Live Leninism! " because " the Soviet Union and the other countries of socialism unequivocally declined " to support the Chinese against India in the summer and autumn of 1959. The long series of Chinese articles from December 1962 to early March 1963 were a " reconsideration " (*i.e.*, a revision) of the 1957 and 1960 Moscow Declarations and " a previously thought-out, deliberately intensified attack " (rather than, as before, an opposition only on " individual questions ") to the " general line of the Marxist-Leninist parties." They also involved the beginning of shifting from ideological to political differences and to an " anti-Soviet . . . propaganda campaign in China." This in turn led, in the June 14 Chinese letter, to a " full-scale platform " against " the line of the Communist movement." All this, the article continued, was " linked " with " erroneous " internal Chinese policies, from whose real causes " the leaders of the CCP are attempting to distract the attention of the masses."

Repeating the Soviet July 14 charges of Chinese " subversive work " against other Communist parties, the article declared that:

> . . . Not since the time of the Trotskyites' struggle against the Comintern . . . has there been such unbridled factional activity in the ranks of the revolutionary workers' movement. . . .

The Chinese leaders, the article continued:

> . . . are attempting to subordinate many fraternal parties to their ideological influence and are forming opposition groups within them. In this they do not disdain to use Trotskyites, renegades, and other scum. In its articles the Chinese press has gone so far as to appeal for the establishment of factions within the Communist and workers' parties. . . .

The Chinese, the article continued, incorrectly declared the " intermediate zone " of Africa, Asia, and Latin America and its national liberation movements (instead of the world socialist system) to be the " epicentre of the world revolutionary process." This is a " petty-bourgeois approach," whereby " the national bourgeoisie . . . must have hegemony over the world struggle against imperialism," a Chinese gamble in order to bring the national liberation movement under Peking's " hegemony . . . [and] isolate it from the international working class and the world socialist system (*i.e.*, the Soviet Union). China's policy of " relying on one's own forces . . . reeks quite obviously of a nationalist spirit." Peking's " slanderous accusations " against the Soviet Party *Programme*, comparable to those of the Trotskyites, the right-wing Social Democrats, and " the ideologists of imperialism and the preachers of anti-Communism," conceal the Chinese " denial of the need for the development of democracy in the transition from socialism to communism." Only thanks to Chinese encouragement do the " Albanian schismatics " continue their anti-Soviet campaign.

An editorial appearing shortly thereafter in *Problems of Peace and Socialism*,[10] the first time that this Soviet-controlled international Communist organ had published explicit anti-Chinese polemics, attacked the Chinese for splitting the international Communist organisations and for supporting "disruptive elements" in the Belgian, United States, Italian, Brazilian and Australian Communist Parties. It further explicitly accused them of racism because of their attacks on whites at the Moshi Conference and because of their republishing without comment a racist statement by a non-Communist Japanese leader.

KHRUSHCHEV'S VISIT TO YUGOSLAVIA

The fact itself that Khrushchev chose late August—from August 20 through September 3—to visit Yugoslavia [11] was another public Soviet slap at the Chinese. The visit's final communiqué emphasised Soviet-Yugoslav" co-operation . . . in aid to the developing countries," *i.e.*, Tito's use of Yugoslavia's influence in the underdeveloped countries to aid Soviet policy and combat Chinese activity in those areas.[12] Both Khrushchev and Tito, the latter more forcefully but both without specifically identifying the Chinese, frequently attacked Chinese ideological positions in their speeches; however, the communiqué contained no reference to Peking. The communiqué stated that Khrushchev and Tito "exchanged views" (*i.e.*, did not completely agree) on "urgent problems of the international workers' movement" (*i.e.*, presumably on Sino-Soviet problems) and on "strengthening the unity of the socialist and other progressive forces" (*i.e.*, Tito would not rejoin the bloc formally but remain non-aligned along with the "other progressive forces").[13] The meeting did not therefore bring a formal "readmission" of Yugoslavia to the Communist camp; Tito was opposed to it [14] because it would limit his relations with the West and the non-aligned

---

10 "The Great Force of Proletarian Internationalism," *World Marxist Review*, VI, 9 (September 1963) (passed for the press, Russian edition, August 16, 1963), pp. 3–9. See also the article by Jacques Duclos, "Vanguard of Mankind," *ibid.*, pp. 10–15.

11 For official coverage, see *Borba* and *Pravda*, August 21–September 3, 1963. The best Western coverage was in *The Times* (London) [by Dessa Bourne] and C. K. [Christian Kind] in the *Neue Zürcher Zeitung*; for analysis, see particularly the latter's "Ergebnisse der Gespräche Chruschtschews mit Tito," *Neue Zürcher Zeitung*, September 4, 1963 and "Nach Chruschtschews Jugoslawienbesuch," *ibid.*, September 6, 1963.

12 See Tedeschi from Pula in *L'Unità*, August 28, 1963.

13 Communiqué, *Pravda* and *Borba*, August 28, 1963, quoted from CDSP, XV, 35 (September 25, 1963), p. 3. See C. K. [Christian Kind], "Abschluss der Gespräche auf Brioni," *Neue Zürcher Zeitung*, August 29, 1963. One report indicated that Khrushchev had agreed in principle to Tito's attending the next international Communist meeting. See C.K. [Christian Kind], "Nach Chruschtschews Jugoslawienbesuch," *Neue Zürcher Zeitung*, September 6, 1963.

14 *Borba*, August 23, 1963.

countries (from which Khrushchev also hoped to profit), and Khrushchev probably did not want to give Tito so much freedom of movement in East Europe. Khrushchev specifically endorsed Kardelj's December 1962 formula [15] that blocs are a temporary phenomenon and that adherence to a common ideology is the essential unifying factor [16] (i.e., he implicitly endorsed Yugoslavia's officially non-aligned policy). He added that there could be no fundamental differences between the Soviet Union and Yugoslavia since both are socialist countries.[17] Furthermore, he never referred to the " camp " but only to the " socialist system." His visit was a party as well as a governmental one, but neither the speeches nor the communiqué made clear what if any specific further progress in improvement in party relations had occurred, and the latter implied that differences still remained; Tito said that there was no question of either side making " concessions " and specifically of Yugoslavia joining the bloc.[18]

The themes of Tito's visit to Moscow [19] were all again reiterated: agreement in principle, remaining points of difference played down, and co-ordination of foreign policy. Khrushchev's emphasis on the pan-Slavist ties between Moscow and Belgrade [20] further enraged China's embattled European ally Albania.[21] Nevertheless, the visit marked a further step in the extension and stabilisation of the Soviet-Yugoslav rapprochement. It was soon followed by visits of the Yugoslav Foreign Minister Popović to Warsaw, of the Hungarian leader Kádár to Belgrade, and of Yugoslav Defence Minister Gosnjak to Moscow, all further indications of continuing improvement in Soviet-Yugoslav and East European-Yugoslav relations.

Tito carefully registered his continuing ideological autonomy: " divergent views on individual questions . . . are possible; . . . therefore the need for frank and comradely exchanges of views and experiences. . . ." [22] In one instance he came close to claiming universal validity for Yugoslav " social management," which he referred to as " at

---

15 See p. 85, *supra*.
16 *Borba*, August 29, 1963 (not reprinted in *Pravda*); Yankovitch from Belgrade in *Le Monde*, September 4, 1963 and C.K. [Christian Kind] from Trieste in *Neue Zürcher Zeitung*, August 30, 1963. Khrushchev's continued sensitivity on this point was indicated by his hardly delicate remark to a Yugoslav journalist on this point: " Are you searching for the nauseous odors of the human backside?" (Yankovitch from Belgrade in *Le Monde*, August 30, 1963).
17 Khrushchev at Velenje, *Pravda*, September 1, 1963.
18 Tito's toast at a dinner, *Borba*, August 23, 1963.
19 See pp. 85–87, *supra*.
20 Khrushchev at Rakovice, *Pravda*, August 22, 1963.
21 See " N. Khrushchev Has Openly Unfurled the Banner of Division and Treason," *Zëri i Popullit*, October 4, 1963.
22 Airport farewell speech, *Borba*, September 4, 1963.

the basis of the ideas of Marx, Engels and Lenin." [23] He was presumably encouraged to do this by Khrushchev's only public ideological concession to the Yugoslavs—his favourable reference to workers' councils as a " specific and interesting " aspect of " specific Yugoslav development." [24] In any case, Yugoslavia's economic situation had already considerably improved as compared to 1962,[25] so Tito could afford to be somewhat more self-assertive.

INTENSIFIED CHINESE ATTACKS

A new major Chinese barrage began with the publication on September 6 in *People's Daily* and *Red Flag* of a long article by the editorial staffs of both publications,[26] announced as the first of a series commenting on the Soviet July 14 Open Letter. The first article gave a long and detailed Chinese version of the history of Sino-Soviet relations; it was followed on September 13 by another on Stalin [27] and on September 26 by a third on Yugoslavia [28]; two others followed in October and November.[29]

The first three together were the most violent, detailed, and comprehensive Chinese attack against the Russians until that time, although

---

23 Speech at Velenje, *Borba*, August 31, 1963, reprinted in *Pravda*, September 1, 1963. In his speech at Velenje the same day Khrushchev, according to the Soviet version, explicitly endorsed only Tito's foreign policy remarks (*Pravda*, September 1, 1963) while, according to the Yugoslav one his endorsement referred to everything Tito said (*Borba*, August 31, 1963). (The translation " public " found in *CDSP*, XV, 35 [September 25, 1963], p. 4 of the Russian *obshchestvennoe* is incorrect.)

24 Khrushchev's remarks at Rakovice, *Borba*, August 22, 1963. However, this was strongly qualified by Khrushchev's immediately following reference to reconciling them with *yedinonachalie* and the remark was not reproduced in the *Pravda* account on August 23, 1963, presumably because Khrushchev was not yet ready to allow discussion of it in the Soviet Union. See particularly a Belgrade dispatch (by Dessa Bourne) in *The Times* (London), August 22, 1963, which gives a detailed account of how sceptical Khrushchev's attitude remained. There were some subsequent signs there, however, of more Soviet interest in the idea: see " Workers' Assembly," *Izvestiya*, August 31, 1963 and Popov in *Pravda*, September 17, 1963.

25 See an authoritative analysis by S. W. in the *Neue Zürcher Zeitung*, October 22, 1963.

26 " The Origin and Development of the Differences Between the Leadership of the CPSU and Ourselves—Comment on the Open Letter of the Central Committee of the CPSU," " by the Editorial Departments of *People's Daily* and *Red Flag*," *People's Daily* and *Red Flag*, September 6, 1963, *Peking Review*, VI, 37 (September 13, 1963), pp. 6–23 and Document 10 (hereafter cited " Origin ").

27 " On the Question of Stalin—Comments on the Open Letter of the Central Committee of the CPSU (2)," " by the Editorial Departments of *People's Daily* and *Red Flag*," *People's Daily* and *Red Flag*, September 13, 1963, *Peking Review*, VI, 38 (September 20, 1963), pp. 8–15 and Document 11 (hereafter cited " Stalin "). On the Chinese attitude Toward Stalin, see Stuart R. Schram, " Mao Tse-tung, Stalin and Khrushchev," *Current Scene*, II, 23 (November 1, 1963).

28 " Is Yugoslavia a Socialist Country?—Comment on the Open Letter of the Central Committee of the CPSU (3)," " by the Editorial Departments of *People's Daily* and *Red Flag*," *People's Daily* and *Red Flag*, September 26, 1963, *Peking Review*, VI, 39 (September 27, 1963), pp. 14–27 and Document 13 (hereafter cited " Yugoslavia "). For the Yugoslav reply, see Bogdan Osolnik, " Yugoslav Reality and Chinese Politics," *Komunist*, November 7, 1963.   29 See pp. 224–229, *infra*.

the fourth and fifth were to exceed them. They were particularly notable for the violence of their personal attack on Khrushchev and for the first explicit Chinese accusations that the Russians were conspiring against the boundaries of China and subverting Chinese citizens within them. The first article set their tone at once: the Russians

... have pushed Sino-Soviet relations to the brink of a split and . . . to a new stage of unprecedented gravity. . . .

The purpose of the articles was to declare and prove that the leadership of the CPSU had forfeited all legitimate claim to leadership of the international Communist movement and of the Soviet Communist Party itself. Toward this end, the Chinese now made their catalogue of Soviet sins explicit and complete:

... the leadership of the CPSU has departed from Marxism-Leninism and the revolutionary principles of the 1957 Declaration and the 1960 Statement and pursued a revisionist and splitting line in the international Communist movement . . .
... the present differences . . . are differences between the line of adhering to Marxism-Leninism and the line of clinging to revisionism, between the revolutionary line and the non-revolutionary and counter-revolutionary line, between the anti-imperialist line and the line of capitulation to imperialism. They are differences between proletarian internationalism and great-power chauvinism, sectarianism and splittism. . . .
The leadership of the CPSU has allied itself with U.S. imperialism, the Indian reactionaries and the renegade Tito clique against socialist China and against all Marxist-Leninist parties, in open betrayal of Marxism-Leninism and proletarian internationalism, in brazen repudiation of the 1957 Declaration and the 1960 Statement and in flagrant violation of the Sino-Soviet Treaty of Friendship, Alliance and Mutual Assistance. . . . It is you, and not we, who are really anti-Soviet and who are defaming and discrediting the CPSU and the Soviet Union . . . you have committed innumerable foul deeds. Not all the water in the Volga can wash away the great shame you have brought upon the CPSU and upon the Soviet Union. . . .[30]

Furthermore, the Chinese now attacked Khrushchev overtly and violently for having " actively supported and firmly executed " Stalin's policies (they also reproduced some of Khrushchev's choicer words of praise for Stalin) and for now shifting " the blame for all errors on to Stalin alone, while altogether whitewashing himself." They also declared that in order to carry out their revisionist line Khrushchev and his associates had burned Stalin's body in 1962.[31] As for the Chinese position on Stalin, the September 3 article pointedly declared that " while defending Stalin, we do not defend his mistakes." Indeed, Chinese Communists have " first-hand experience " of Stalin's mistakes.

[30] " Origin," pp. 6, 19, 20.   [31] " Stalin," pp. 12–13.

Of the erroneous " Left " and Right opportunist lines which emerged in the Chinese Communist Party at one time or another, some arose under the influence of certain mistakes of Stalin's, insofar as their international sources were concerned. In the late twenties, the thirties, and the early and middle forties, the Chinese Marxist-Leninists represented by Comrades Mao Tse-tung and Liu Shao-ch'i resisted the influence of Stalin's mistakes; they gradually overcame the erroneous lines of " Left " and Right opportunism and finally led the Chinese revolution to victory.[32]

The reference to Liu Shao-ch'i in addition to Mao indicated that he had maintained his number two position in the Chinese hierarchy.

Most of the first article was given up to a detailed historical reconstruction of the dispute. Since it was still incomplete and since the Soviet reconstruction (primarily in their July 14 Open Letter) was even more so, it is covered briefly in this volume in the " Brief, Revised History " with which the introduction begins [33] and throughout the text. Within the present context, however, several points may be made with respect to the political significance of this historical reconstruction. It was the most detailed reconstruction either side had published until that time, particularly for the 1956–60 period. It quoted extensively from previously unpublished Chinese documents and reproduced the complete or partial text of three of them, one from 1957 and two from 1960. It stressed the Sino-Soviet differences on the issue of the peaceful (parliamentary) road to socialism (the issue on which the Russians could count on the least support in underdeveloped areas) and on Soviet predominance in the international Communist movement, presumably in order to overcome the Soviet advantage on the issue of thermonuclear war.

The Chinese article on Yugoslavia, in addition to reiterating in the most violent form all the previous Chinese accusations against the Titoist régime, for the first time gave a detailed ideological justification for the Chinese thesis that capitalism had been restored in that country:

> The degeneration of the state power in Yugoslavia occurred not through the overthrow of the original state power by violence and the establishment of a new state power but through " peaceful evolution." In appearance the same people remain in power, but in essence these people no longer represent the interests of the workers, peasants and the working people but those of imperialism and the old and new bourgeoisie of Yugoslavia.
>
> Utilising state power and controlling the economic life of the country, the Tito clique exploited the Yugoslav working people to the utmost extent and brought into being a bureaucrat capitalist class. Being dependent on U.S. imperialism, this class is strongly comprador in character and is also a comprador capitalist class. The state power

---

[32] *Ibid.*, p. 10.
[33] See pp. 16–20, *supra*.

controlled by the Tito clique is that of the dictatorship of the bureaucrat-comprador bourgeoisie. . . .[34]

Two points may be made about this thesis: first, its resemblance to those of Trotsky and Djilas is striking, and second, it probably foreshadows the final public (and already existing secret) Chinese thesis on Khrushchev and the CPSU leadership.

Soviet and Soviet-controlled organs simultaneously continued their escalation of charges, in tone and content, against the Chinese; in so doing they raised some new issues which were only developed and systematised in the more extensive Soviet polemics of early October. In early September two articles in the Soviet ideological organ *Kommunist* declared that Chinese " left opportunism corresponds exactly to the requirements of the petit bourgeois, peasant type of socialism," and that the " ever more overt nationalism and chauvinism of the Chinese leaders, . . . their chauvinistic passion [against the socialist camp], and their actual complicity with the forces opposing the easing of international tensions " have produced the " expanded splitting activities of the Chinese leaders . . . an expanded war, not only ideological but political as well, against the general line of the international Communist movement." [35]

Two articles in the October *Problems of Peace and Socialism* (passed for the press in mid-September) by extremist pro-Soviet leaders, Papaioannou of the Cypriot and Sharkey of the Australian Communist Parties,[36] expanded upon these themes. The Chinese are working for a split, Papaioannou declared: " left opportunism, dogmatism and sectarianism " are now the " main danger "; " public discussion of controversial issues . . . in a calm, comradely atmosphere " (*i.e.*, by the CPSU and pro-Soviet parties) " deepens and develops . . . Marxist theory," but the Chinese " actions in violation of the agreement to end the polemic . . . in no way promote the unity and solidarity of the Communist movement." Sharkey was even stronger:

> Engendered by nationalism, petty-bourgeois intolerance and the desire to occupy the dominant positions in the fraternal community of equal parties, the views of the CCP leadership on all important issues verge with Trotskyism. . . .

[34] " Yugoslavia," p. 24.
[35] A. Butenko, " The Soviet All-National State " and T. Timofeyev, " The Leninist Course of the World Communist Movement and Its Adversaries," *Kommunist*, No. 13, 1963 (passed for the press September 6, 1963), pp. 22–32 and 33–42, quoted from JPRS 21, 536, October 22, 1963, pp. 16–17, 29–30, 38.
[36] Ezekias Papaioannou, " Unity Is the Guarantee of Success for the Communist Movement " and L. Sharkey, " Creative Marxism Is the Basis for Revolutionary Practice," *World Marxist Review*, VI, 10 (October 1963) (passed for the press, Russian edition, September 14, 1963), pp. 3–9 and 10–16.

The Sino-Soviet Border Issue

The most important section of the Chinese September 6 article was the one concerning the Sino-Soviet border.[37] The Chinese stated that:

> ... In April and May 1962 the leaders of the CPSU used their organs and personnel in Sinkiang, China, to carry out large-scale subversive activities in the Ili region and enticed and coerced several tens of thousands of Chinese citizens into going to the Soviet Union. The Chinese Government lodged repeated protests ... but the Soviet Government refused to repatriate these Chinese citizens on the pretext of the " sense of Soviet legality " and " humanitarianism."

This " astounding [and] unheard of event," the Chinese added, " remains unsettled." It thus became clear that the March 1963 Chinese hints about the Sino-Soviet border [38] were more than just hints, and that the border issue had for some time been a serious factor in the deterioration of Sino-Soviet relations.

A Soviet Government statement of September 21 [39] gave the first Soviet version of the border problem. Although it neither specifically referred nor replied to the September 6 Chinese charge, it was clearly intended to counter it. Taking a much harder tone, the Soviet statement declared that since 1960 the Chinese had been " systematically violating the Soviet frontier "; that in 1962 alone " more than 5,000 " such violations had occurred; and that the Chinese were trying illegally to annex certain disputed territory, specifically the islands in the Amur and Ussuri rivers. Indeed, they had issued instructions to Chinese fishermen, from which the Soviet statement quoted passages, to refuse to leave the islands when ordered to do so by the Soviet border guards. Peking, the Soviet statement continued, had consistently refused to discuss the question, a fact which " cannot but make us wary," since Chinese propaganda (*i.e.,* the March 8 Chinese article)

> ... is giving clear hints alleging that there has been unjust demarcation of some sections of the Soviet-Chinese border in the past. ...

This, the Russians added, was " a very dangerous path," a significant addition to an earlier article [40] hinting that further Chinese aggressiveness on the Soviet border would be met by military retaliation if necessary.

---

[37] " Origins," p. 18.

[38] See p. 111, *supra.*

[39] *Pravda*, September 21 and 22, 1963 and Document 12. This statement was nominally and probably originally drafted as a reply to the Chinese September 1 government statement but was probably amended to answer some of the September 6 Chinese charges as well

[40] The article was primarily devoted to the Sino-Indian border issue, but the following excerpts make clear what was really meant:
> ... As for the Soviet Union, it treats with respect the countries bordering on it. It understands that good-neighbourliness is possible only if the frontiers existing between states are respected. ... When soldiers of two neighbouring

INCREASING SOVIET BITTERNESS

The September 21 Soviet statement was harsher and more defiant in all other respects than any previous Moscow pronouncement. It made clearer than the statement of August 21 that Moscow was unwilling to tolerate the Chinese attacks on the test ban treaty and implied that if the Chinese did not retreat steps would be taken toward expelling them from the international Communist movement.

Not only was the Soviet September 21 statement more violent than before (the Chinese were guilty of " slander," of having " falsified . . . documents," of " complete apostasy, . . . treachery, and hypocrisy ") but it stated more clearly and precisely than previously that Moscow now considered Peking to have abandoned the course of

> comradely discussion [for that of] pursuing their own great power [and] special vanguardist aims which cannot be supported by the military force of the socialist camp . . .

[*i.e.*, Moscow will not support Peking militarily in such aims . . . and the Sino-Soviet alliance is therefore no longer totally in force]

> . . . [and of] open political struggle against the CPSU and the other Marxist-Leninist parties . . . of splitting the Communist movement and undermining the unity of the anti-imperialist forces [and of] openly hostile acts against the Soviet Union . . . [by] making a breach in the . . . friendship and co-operation between the U.S.S.R. and other countries of socialism and the national liberation movement, [a course] tantamount to a betrayal of world socialism, the working class, and the national liberation movement, to treason to the cause of world revolution. . . .

The Chinese did this, the statement continued, in order to pursue their " special aims " of obtaining nuclear weapons at all costs, increasing their influence in Asia, Africa, and Latin America, creating " a ' position of strength ' on disputed international issues," and " increasing international tension."

The article added a few new details concerning the history of the Sino-Soviet dispute. Khrushchev was credited with privately attempting to dissuade the Chinese from the " great leap forward " in the people's communes during the summer of 1958. According to the Russians, he had advocated in October 1959 not a two-China policy (as the Chinese had alleged in their September 6 statement) but a " peaceful " solution of the Taiwan question. Furthermore, the Chinese had deliberately attacked the Indians in 1959, in spite of Soviet efforts to dissuade them, in

> states stand with rifles levelled at each other, especially if fierce fighting had taken place between them earlier, there is naturally the danger that bloodshed may be started by an accidental rifle shot. . . .

("A Serious Source of Tension in Asia," *Pravda*, September 19, 1963).

order to sabotage Khrushchev's attempt to bring about a détente with the United States. The article also quoted two Chinese officials as having said that Czechoslovakia and Italy would be obliterated in a thermonuclear war but that " ' imperialism will be destroyed ' " and " ' the small countries would have to subordinate their interests to the common interests of the camp as a whole. . . .' " It gave another version of Mao's November 1957 speech, quoting him as having said:

> In China construction has not got under way in earnest. If the imperialists impose a war on us, we shall be prepared to terminate the construction; let us first have a trial of strength, and then return to construction. . . .

It again accused China of having disclosed " confidential correspondence " to the imperialists. The statement also declared (quite correctly) that the overwhelming majority of the underdeveloped countries were in favour of and had signed the test ban treaty and that the Chinese propaganda against it " had no success."

Finally, the September 21 statement again proposed an end to open polemics; but it ominously added that the Chinese apparently did not intend to resume the interrupted Sino-Soviet conversations and that if they continued their " hostile actions [and] slandering . . . [and] factional activities " they must expect to receive " the most vigorous rebuff " from Moscow—*i.e.*, to be faced with excommunication from the international Communist movement.[41]

THEORY AND PRACTICE: THE NAUSHKI STATION INCIDENT

The Soviet Siberian railway border station of Naushki was the scene on September 12 of an incident which reflected the violence of current Sino-Soviet polemics. The Soviet [42] and Chinese [43] accounts of it are almost completely contradictory; the following is an attempt [44] to summarise both and deduce something of what actually happened.

On September 7, in the course of Soviet customs inspection at Naushki of Chinese passengers and crew of the Peking-Moscow Express, Soviet customs officials confiscated several copies of the Chinese September 1 statement in Russian. Thereafter, according to the

---

[41] For the continuation of the sharpening of the Soviet ideological line, see pp. 210 *et seq., infra.*

[42] The text of the Soviet protest note is in *Pravda*, September 10, 1963 and *Soviet News*, No. 4892, September 11, 1963; see also accounts by eyewitnesses in *Pravda*, *Komsomolskaya Pravda*, and *Gudok*, September 11, 1963 and *Izvestiya*, September 16, 1963.

[43] See NCNA English Peking, September 13, 1963 (SCMP 3062, September 18, 1963, pp. 34–36), September 15, 1963 (SCMP 3063, September 19, 1963, pp. 38–44), and September 16, 1963 (SCMP 3064, September 20, 1963, pp. 37–40).

[44] *Cf.* Kx. [Ernst Kux], " Die sowjetisch-chinesischen Grenzzwischenfälle," *Neue Zürcher Zeitung*, September 18, 1963.

Russians, the Chinese surrounded and locked up the customs officials, refused to allow the train to continue, and

> . . . holding hands, and having tied themselves to each other with belts . . . these unrestrained rowdies went to such extremes of cynicism, in front of the indignant passengers, as provocatively violating elementary sanitary and hygienic norms in the station buildings. . . .[45]

As an outraged female Soviet railway employee later described the incident in what may be termed a rather low-level Soviet radio broadcast to errant Albania:

> . . . I saw with my own eyes and would like to tell the details. The vagabonds from the CPR violated the most elementary sanitary and hygienic practices in the railway station. As a woman, I find it difficult to describe what I saw. They unbuttoned their trousers and started to urinate. We were surprised. Only animals could behave in such a way. This is how low they sank. Shame on them. . . .[46]

According to the Chinese, the Russians " forcibly seized " the Chinese literature, tore some of it up, seized the passports of the crew,

> . . . abused Chinese students, who were reasoning with them, as " hooligans " and " brazen-faced," and even used filthy and vulgar language against Chinese girl students. . . .

The next morning the Russians first made the Chinese stand for two hours, then threw them out of the station office. They denied the Chinese students food and water for more than 20 hours, " besieged " them, " twisted their arms," and " attacked them with elbows," as a result of which some " fell ill," whereupon the Russians refused to give them medicine. Finally, at 1.00 a.m. on September 10 armed Soviet frontier guards forced them and the train back over the Chinese border.[47]

Moscow sent Peking a formal note of protest on September 9, which the Chinese rejected in a violent answer of September 16, declaring that:

> . . . the Soviet Government is seizing every opportunity to fan up an anti-China hysteria to further worsen the relations between the two countries. . . .[48]

The returning students and train crew were ceremoniously welcomed in Peking, and Chou En-lai and Ch'en Yi " praised them for . . . persevering in principles and standing firm in struggle. . . ." [49]

[45] Soviet Foreign Ministry note to Chinese Embassy, September 8, quoted from *Soviet News*, No. 4892, September 11, 1963.
[46] Radio Moscow in Albanian to Albania, September 11, 1963, 1700 GMT.
[47] Quoted from NCNA English Peking, September 15, 1963 (SCMP 3063, September 19, 1963, pp. 38–40).
[48] Text: NCNA English Peking, September 16, 1963 (SCMP 3064, September 20, 1963, pp. 37–39).
[49] *Ibid.* p. 40.

On balance it seems probable that Moscow had ordered the intensified searches of Chinese for anti-Soviet literature and that the Chinese, aware of this, decided to dramatise the matter by a public incident.

Nor was the Naushki train incident the only incident during the late summer and autumn; at the end of August the Russians complained about the bad treatment of their sailors in Chinese ports.[50] On September 9 five Chinese military cadets were deported from the Soviet Union [51]; at the end of September Moscow declared that the Chinese were deliberately framing basketball games so that the Soviet teams would lose [52]; and in October there were Western press reports of two Chinese diplomats defecting to the Soviet Union.[53]

---

[50] TASS English to Europe, August 31, 1963, 0706 GMT.
[51] *Ibid.*
[52] " How They Met Us in Peking," *Krasnaya Zvezda*, September 25, 1963.
[53] *Le Monde,* October 5, 1963 ; *Japan Times,* October 9, 1963.

18. The International Communist Movement after the Test Ban Treaty

THUS by the end of September the Sino-Soviet rift had reached new heights of bitterness. This book has already treated lesser peaks—after the Twenty-Second Congress at the end of 1961, and the beginning of 1963. Both of those peaks of tension generated attempts by the pro-Soviet and the pro-Chinese moderate parties to prevent an open rupture, attempts which led in turn to a lessening of Sino-Soviet tension, and, in the second instance, to a Sino-Soviet bilateral meeting. Yet both attempts at détente failed and thereafter new crises arose which were more acute than the previous ones. Certainly the sequel to the test ban treaty was a Sino-Soviet crisis far worse than ever before. The rift had in fact occurred. Yet because this time the danger of total, public rupture was so imminent, in particular, as will be seen, because the Russians appeared to be working to bring it about, the moderates were more energetic in their efforts to prevent it. The obstacles they had to overcome, the fury of the Russians and the stubborn fanaticism of the Chinese, were greater than ever before; but the course and increasing depth of the rift had produced such a slackening of effective Soviet discipline in the international Communist movement that the Russians, although themselves adopting a more extreme attitude and exerting more pressure than before, had in spite of this—and, paradoxically, in part because of it—a much more difficult job in gaining sufficient support among their more moderate associates.

In short, the potential power of the other Communist parties and their determination to use it (particularly the pro-Soviet moderates) had increased. Furthermore the international Communist scene had become one of far greater diversity. In order to understand the role of the other Communist parties in the October 1963 crisis, therefore, as well as to see the effect of the rift upon them—*i.e.*, to view them both as subjects and objects in the Sino-Soviet picture, one must survey the worldwide Communist picture in some detail. In what follows the emphasis will be upon the position and role of each party in the rift, the causes for that position, and the changes, if any, during the 1962–63 period.

COMMUNISM IN EUROPE [1]

THE division of European Communist parties (except for the totally pro-Chinese extremist Albanian party) into pro-Soviet moderates and pro-Soviet extremists continued during 1962 and 1963; the only significant change was Rumania's partial and successful defiance of Moscow while remaining pro-Soviet in policy orientation. Rumania's moves demonstrated that a party can be (1) pro-Soviet moderate in the Sino-Soviet context, *i.e.,* opposed to an open rupture, while (2) remaining proto-Stalinist in domestic policy, indeed, in part in order so to remain, since (3) the fundamental common factor among the pro-Soviet moderates is nationalism, *i.e.,* the desire for greater autonomy from, although not a break with, Moscow, without which either pro-Soviet moderation in the dispute or extreme liberalisation (or neo-Stalinism) is impossible.

The main European moderate pro-Soviet parties are the Poles, Rumanians, Hungarians, and Italians; the minor ones are the British, Belgian, and Scandinavian. The extremist pro-Soviet parties are the French, Czechoslovak, East German, the illegal ones (Spanish, Portuguese, Greek), and on some occasions the Yugoslavs. My assertion that Belgrade belongs in this group may cause eyebrows to lift, notably in Belgrade; but the fact is the Yugoslav Communists fear a Sino-Soviet reconciliation more than any Communist party in Europe (except the Albanians), since it alone would be an insuperable obstacle to their re-entering and thus increasing their influence in the " socialist commonwealth." They prefer a rupture to it, but most of all they favour increased polycentrism. The Albanians are pro-Chinese extremist because only a total Sino-Soviet rupture will guarantee them against Peking's abandoning them (and thus leaving them to the far from tender mercies of the Yugoslavs) in a Sino-Soviet rapprochement. The Czechoslovak, East German, and Bulgarian parties are extremist because of long Stalinist and pro-Soviet traditions and because both need Soviet support against potential or actual popular opposition; the French for the same reasons and also recently because they incline to Soviet policy, being opposed to de Gaulle, on the issue of atomic weapons and a popular front.

The smaller West European parties also remain pro-Soviet because of tradition and the need for Soviet ideological and financial support; but most of them are moderates because they fear the results in their

---

[1] This is in part based on my " European Communism and the Sino-Soviet Schism," *The Annals,* CCCIL (September 1963), of which a revised version will appear in my *Communism in Europe I.*

own parties of a Sino-Soviet rupture. The illegal parties, however, are totally pro-Soviet because of their dependence upon Moscow, although some of their members (e.g., in West Germany) may be pro-Chinese. The Italian Communists are moderate because they fear an open rupture and its effects both upon their members and upon the party's powers of manoeuvre and also because Togliatti (and Italy) prefers compromise to heresy-hunting. The same is true of the Poles and Hungarians. As to Gheorghiu-Dej and the Rumanians, the Rumanians' motives are almost entirely nationalistic; they want to retain the power of manoeuvre that has enabled them to prevent Moscow from forcing them into total integration into CMEA.

WESTERN EUROPE AND NORTH AMERICA

The West European Communist parties inevitably reflected the intensification of Sino-Soviet polemics following the signing of the test ban treaty, and by November 1963 there were increasing signs that the small pro-Chinese groups within them were increasingly in touch with each other and with Peking; but alignments among and within them did not substantially change because of it.

The moderate pro-Soviet Italian Communist Party remained largely faithful to the Soviet line but it showed renewed signs (not to unmixed Soviet pleasure) of at least professing a degree of autonomy. In October 1963 (along with the Poles and Rumanians) it took a clear stand against an all-party meeting to excommunicate the Chinese, thus opposing what appears to have been initially a Soviet project and contributing to Moscow's at least temporary abandonment of it. Khrushchev's summer relaxation of pressure on Soviet intellectuals removed one previous, albeit minor, cause of friction between him and the PCI. The pro-Chinese group outside the PCI issued more publications and held more meetings, but its increased activity did not and likely will not (any more than the much more influential right-wing) pose any serious threat to the PCI leadership.[2]

---

[2] See the report by Giancarlo Pajetta to a PCI CC Plenum, with subsequent discussion, *L'Unità*, July 26–27, 1963 and especially " Noi e il Compagni Cinesi," a supplement to *L'Unità*, September 29, 1963; also Rome dispatches to *The Times* (London), July 5, 1963 and to *Die Zeit*, July 12, 1963; PCI CC resolution, *L'Unità*, October 26, 1963 and *Pravda*, October 28, 1963. For the pro-Chinese groups, see *Corrispondenza Socialista* (Rome), IV, 4 (April 1963), p. 195 (JPRS 19,588, June 6, 1963); Leone Iraci, " I communisti ' di sinistra ' e il PC cinese," *ibid.*, IV, 8–9 (August-September 1963), pp. 445–460; and Gino Bianco and Nello Finocchiaro, " Rapporto sui ' cinesi ' italiani " *Critica Sociale*, July 20, 1963; their Rome publication *Ritorniamo a Lenin*; and, for indications of renewed professed stirrings of autonomist sentiment in the PCI leadership, Mario Alicata, " Lettere sulla Cina," *L'Unità*, August 11, 1963, who apparently deliberately distorted a passage from the July 14 Soviet Open Letter (*Pravda*, July 14, 1963) so as to imply criticism of the CPSU for its anti-Albanian policy, and which in turn was excerpted in *Pravda*, July 14, 1963, in such a deliberately incomplete fashion as to make clear Moscow's disapproval of Alicata's position. See also an editorial on the Sino-Soviet dispute in the PCI monthly

The French Communist Party continued its traditional course of unconditional loyalty to the Soviet line. Spurred on by the desire to form an anti-Gaullist alliance with all the other French parties except the UNR and opposed to French (and Chinese) atomic armament, its allegiance to an extremist pro-Soviet position became increasingly easier. However, the PCF had continuing troubles with its rebellious and pro-Soviet moderate university student wing, and increased Chinese agitation in Paris, notably through the appearance in September of a new pro-Chinese journal *Révolution*, edited by non-whites and clearly directed toward the French-speaking territories in the underdeveloped areas.[3]

Only in the Belgian Communist Party did the Chinese succeed in detaching a significant part of the organisation from the control of the pro-Soviet leadership. As early as 1962 the Brussels Federation of the PCB, under the leadership of Jacques Grippa, openly supported the Chinese position. By mid-1963 this segment of the party was completely under Chinese influence and openly defying the Belgian Communist Party and the Soviet Union. Its leaders travelled regularly to Peking and Tirana. Its publications were reprinted regularly in Peking, and it presumably received ample Chinese financial support. Nevertheless, it seemed unlikely that the dissident group could gain control of the Belgian party itself.[4]

More recently a small group also split off from the Swiss Communist Party which has been increasingly under Italian Communist influence, and formed a new "Swiss Communist Party." However, this development has not as yet been exploited in Chinese propaganda.[5]

Critica Marxista, I, 4 (July–August 1963), pp. 1–18 (JPRS 21,150, October 18, 1963), pp. 41–52.

3 For the PCF-UEC quarrel, see *Le Monde*, September 25, 1963 and particularly an article by its editor, Pierre Kahn, " Les Héritiers de Staline," in the UEC monthly *Clarté*, November 1963 ; for *Révolution* and other pro-Chinese French publications, see an interview with its editor Jacques Vergès, in *France-Observateur*, September 5, 1963, an article by Henri Cazals in *Corrispondenza Socialista*, IV, 5 (May 1963), pp. 279–282; " Le cas de M. Jacques Vergès," *Est & Ouest*, XV (N.S.), 307 (October 16–31, 1963), pp. 6–9; and Raymond Barrillon, " Comment le ' matériel idéologique ' chinois est-il diffusé en France," *Le Monde*, November 3–4, 1963; for the PCE's continuing anti-Chinese role, a CC Plenum and subsequent speeches by Thorez and Waldeck-Rochet in *L'Humanité*, October 7, 8, 10, 17, 23, 1963.

4 *Cf.* p. 127, *supra*; Nicolas Lang, " Vers la creation d'un mouvement communiste dissident en Belgique?", *Est et Ouest*, XV (N.S.), 302 (June 16–30, 1963), pp. 4–7. On October 15, 1963, Grippa began to publish a bi-weekly, *Le Voix du Peuple*. For the official position, see reports by Burnelle in *Le Drapeau Rouge*, April 16, 1963 (JPRS 19,588, June 6, 1963) and September 16, 1963 (JPRS 21,386, October 9, 1963).

5 Jeane-René de Ziegler, " Die PdA und das Schisma im Kommunismus," *Neue Zürcher Zeitung*, February 16, 1963; AFP dispatch from Vevey in *Le Monde*, September 18, 1963; *Vorwärts* (Swiss CP weekly), September 20, 1963 and *Voix Ouvrière* (Swiss CP daily), September 18, 1963 (the latter two are in JPRS 21,592, October 24, 1963, pp. 52–66).

The British Communist Party continued on the moderately pro-Soviet line, in large part because the existence of a relatively small group of Chinese sympathisers within the party made its attitude somewhat less anti-Chinese than that of the PCF.[6]

The Austrian Communist Party likewise remained officially loyal to the Soviet line, but within its ranks a small pro-Chinese (and a larger pro-PCI reformist) current emerged.[7]

The Dutch Party showed no significant changes from its pro-Soviet position. The illegal West German KPD remained under SED control at the top, officially pro-Soviet. There was, however, considerable evidence of sympathies for Peking among some of its frustrated and harried membership.[8]

In Scandinavia, the Swedish Party, although harassed by the dissident pro-Chinese Swedish Communist Workers' Federation (SKAF),[9] remained loyal to the moderate pro-Soviet course and committed to the peaceful road to socialism. The Danish Party was still primarily preoccupied by the revisionism of its pre–1956 leader, Axel Larsen, now the head of the Socialist People's Party.[10] After a 1962 flirtation with the Chinese the Norwegian Communist Party returned to a moderately pro-Soviet position, only to attempt to disassociate itself from the dispute in October 1963 and return to a neutralist position.[11] The Finnish Party, as ever, kept its completely pro-Soviet stance.[12]

[6] See the CPGB resolution and Gollan speech, *Daily Worker* (London), September 17–18, 1963. For a manifesto of the pro-Chinese group, see " An Appeal to All Communists," see *The Sunday Telegraph* (London), November 10, 1963 and *The Guardian* (Manchester), November 11, 1963, and *The Daily Worker* (London), November 13, 1963.

[7] For the official line, see *Volksstimme* (Vienna), July 20, 1963; for the dissidents, an analysis by Manfred von Conta in *Süddeutsche Zeitung* (Munich), July 20, 1963, and Franz Marek in *Weg und Ziel* (Vienna), No. 6, June 1963, pp. 413–415 (JPRS 20,548, August 8, 1963, pp. 61–68). The first issue of a pro-Chinese Austrian publication, *Die rote Fahne*, appeared in October 1963 (*Die Presse* [Vienna], October 14, 1963).

[8] KPD CC resolution, *Neues Deutschland*, July 21, 1963; *Ostspiegel* (Bonn: SPD: Ostburo), July 23, 1963.

[9] See Hilding Hagberg (the chairman) in *Pravda*, September 16, 1963 and an article by him, " The Experience and Tasks of the Communist Party of Sweden," *World Marxist Review*, VI, 10 (October 1963), pp. 17–22. For dissidence in the Swedish CP, see articles in the Stockholm newspapers *Dagens Nyheter*, *Expressen*, and *Aftonbladet*, May 31, 1963 (all in JPRS 19,760, June 20, 1963). In mid-November Hagberg reportedly resigned under pressure of younger, less pro-Soviet elements (*Aftonbladet*, November 13, 1963).

[10] See a Danish CP resolution in *Land og Folk* (Copenhagen), August 28, 1963 (JPRS 21,131, September 18, 1963) and *Pravda*, September 3, 1963; and Ib Noerlund, " Revisionism Must Be Fought," *World Marxist Review*, VI, 7 (July 1963), pp. 9–17.

[11] Norwegian CP CC statements, *Friheten* (Oslo), January 8, and October 7, 1963, an editorial in *ibid.*, July 5, 1963 (JPRS 20,387, July 29, 1963); Hans Kleven, " The Communist Party of Norway on the Paths to Peace and Socialism," *World Marxist Review*, VI, 9 (September 1963), pp. 23–28, and an article by him in *Friheten*, February 11, 1963 (JPRS 18,063, March 11, 1963).

[12] See a pro-test ban editorial by Armas Aikia in the CP newspaper *Kansan Uutiset* (Helsinki), August 8, 1963 (JPRS 21,045, September 12, 1963).

In North America the Canadian and United States Parties remained pro-Soviet extremist. However, as in France, some small extremist groups outside the latter became pro-Chinese, notably the minute pro-Chinese *Hammer and Steel* group in Boston [13] and the pro-Castro *Monthly Review* and the Progressive Labour group in New York.[14]

EASTERN EUROPE

Except in Czechoslovakia, the summer and early autumn of 1963 saw no major changes in the East European régimes or in their posture toward the Sino-Soviet rift.

To begin with the two parties most involved in the rift itself: Albania [15] and Yugoslavia. Sino-Albanian relations remained excellent and Albania remained pro-Chinese extremist. China continued to supply Albania with Canadian and Australian wheat,[16] while Tirana became a point of pilgrimage for pro-Chinese Belgian and other dissident Communists from western Europe.[17] Albanian fury at Moscow increased—if possible—with Khrushchev's visit to Yugoslavia and the test ban treaty.[18] Moscow, in turn, stepped up its propaganda warfare against Tirana toward the end of August.[19] Given this situation, it is not surprising that Albania, not the Soviet Union, introduced the resolution for Communist Chinese entry into the United Nations at the September 1963 General Assembly in New York.[20]

As for Yugoslavia, Khrushchev's August visit further cemented Soviet-Yugoslav relations, and Yugoslav relations with East Europe also

[13] See their mimeographed monthly newsletter of the same name. That Marxist and *Fidelista* Communist splinter groups are no less fanatically sectarian than were their predecessors in the 1930s was indicated by the October 1963 *Hammer and Steel Newsletter's* attack on the *Fidelista* Progressive Labour group in New York.

[14] This monthly, edited by Paul Sweezy and Leo Huberman, formally proclaimed its pro-Chinese position in its May 1963 issue. See " The Split in the Socialist World," *Monthly Review*, XV, 1 (May 1963), pp. 1–20 and also " What Do the Chinese Want?", *ibid.*, V, 6 (October 1963), pp. 289–304.

[15] *Cf.* Kx. [Ernst Kux], " Der sowjetisch-albanische Gegensatz," *Neue Zürcher Zeitung*, September 21, 1963.

[16] See, *e.g.*, a Reuter's dispatch from Perth (Australia) in *The Times* (London), September 27, 1963.   [17] See p. 180, *supra*.

[18] See, *e.g.*, " The Revisionist Khrushchev in the Role of the Panslavist," *Zëri i Popullit*, August 29, 1963; " Ignoring Public Opinion Cannot Conceal the Plots of the Tito-Khrushchev Group," *ibid.*, September 1, 1963; " The Revolutionary Communists of the Entire World Rise Determinedly Against the Modern Revisionists, in Defense of Marxism-Leninism," *ibid.*, September 6, 1963. A long editorial in *ibid.*, October 4, 1963, was Tirana's main answer to the Soviet July 14 Open Letter. It contained only two items of interest : Iraq was specifically identified as one of the areas where Communists were suffering " terrible death " as the result of Khrushchev's " revisionist and treacherous " course, and Moscow was accused of having ceased jamming Western broadcasts and instead jamming Radio Tirana and Radio Peking.

[19] *e.g.*, Radio Moscow in Albanian, August 30, 1963, 1700 GMT (BBC/SU/1341/A2/1-2) and October 8, 1963, 1800 GMT (BBC/SU/1375/A2/1).

[20] See the September 16 letter by Albanian Foreign Minister Shtylla to U.N. Secretary-General U Thant, *Zëri i Popullit*, September 18, 1963.

continued to improve. Tito's trip to Latin America and the United States, while it did not bring any major or immediate results, served to repair his image as a nonaligned neutralist, an image somewhat tarnished in the eyes of the non-Communist world by his embraces with Khrushchev.[21] A close reading of Tito's October 22 speech to the United Nations General Assembly, however, reveals a sharpening of Kardelj's December 1962 redefinition of the Yugoslav concept of nonalignment [22] so as to make it even less offensive to the Soviet Union:

> The Moscow [test ban] agreement and the other steps . . . recently . . . taken are vivid evidence of the existing trends toward the overcoming of the division which has hitherto split the world into military and political groupings. . . .
> . . . we have . . . always considered that such a division . . . is neither unavoidable nor permanent . . . precisely therein . . . lay the vast historical significance of the policy of nonalignment. . . .
> Under the new conditions their [the nonaligned nations'] activity acquires a broader basis and an increased significance.
> In this new phase in the evolution of international relations the conditions under which the policy of nonalignment had come into being are also changing.
> It may be said that the term nonalignment has in a way been superseded by the new and positive evolution of international relations.
> The question of nonalignment is posed today in a far broader sense. . . .
> The polarisation of the forces of peace, on the one hand, and of the forces of cold war on the other, is taking place at an accelerated pace. . . .
> Nonalignment is thus changing, both in quantitative and in qualitative terms, and is transforming itself into a general movement for peace and for the finding of peaceful and constructive means for settlement of various problems among nations. . . .[23]

In other words, the neutralist countries, Yugoslavia, and—on the basis of this definition—the Soviet Union and pro-Soviet Communist countries, are for peace and therefore, so to say, neo-nonaligned. The " imperialists " (but presumably not all of them) and Communist China are for the cold war. Khrushchev could hardly object to such a formulation. Furthermore, the continued signs of Yugoslav apprehension at the November signs of a renewed Sino-Soviet lessening of tension [24] again demonstrated Yugoslavia's fear of a Sino-Soviet rapprochement and its consequent pro-Soviet position.

Of the other East European countries, Bulgaria continued to

---

[21] For Tito's trip, see especially C. K. [Christian Kind], " Titos Reise in die Neue Welt," *Neue Zürcher Zeitung*, October 30, 1963; for East Europe, *cf.* " Tito and the Satellites," *East Europe*, XII, 10 (October 1963), pp. 2–11; for texts of joint communiqués, see *Review of International Affairs* (Belgrade), XIV, 324 (October 5, 1963), pp. 12–13 and XIV, 325 (October 20, 1963), pp. 17–19.

[22] See p. 85, *supra*.   [23] *The New York Times*, October 23, 1963.

[24] See a Vienna dispatch [by Dessa Bourne] in *The Times* (London), November 15, 1963.

combine political and economic subservience to the extremist Soviet position (although with some contradictory indications of possible future internal change) with denunciation of the Chinese.[25] As for East Germany, the Chinese constantly accused Khrushchev of sacrificing DDR interests,[26] but Ulbricht, totally dependent on Soviet support and allowed by Khrushchev to liberalise his domestic course only slowly, could not but acquiesce in Moscow's extremist anti-Chinese line.[27] He also probably hoped to raise his international status and possibly get some Western concessions on Berlin; but in view of Washington's increasing interest in preserving good relations with Bonn,[28] Ulbricht's attempt to gain some advantage from the Soviet-American détente did not succeed.[29]

In Poland, after the signature of the test ban treaty and the resulting intensification of Sino-Soviet polemics, Gomulka was less able effectively to play a moderating role, although he continued to try,[30] and reportedly again had some success in October, when he apparently opposed the calling of an international Communist meeting. In general the Polish party strongly supported the Soviet position, particularly with respect to Yugoslavia, but it still devoted less attention to the dispute than did the East German or Czechoslovak parties, and it continued to try to present an open rupture.[31] Poland remained the most exceptional country of any in East Europe. While the general tendency, with Soviet support, was toward liberalisation, Gomulka continued his careful and partial " retreat from October," particularly on the cultural front. Yet the predominance of privately cultivated land in agriculture continued; the cultural retrogression was partial and hardly penetrated below the surface; and

25 See especially V. M. [Viktor Meier] from Sofia in the *Neue Zürcher Zeitung*, October 13, 27, November 3, 14, 1963.
26 See, *e.g.*, Chinese government statement of August 15, 1963, in *People's Daily*, August 15, 1963, *Peking Review*, VI, 33 (August 16, 1963), pp. 7–15, and Document 7, reprinted in *Neues Deutschland*, August 22, 1963, and replied to in *ibid.*, August 25; DDR governmental statement in *ibid.*, August 29, 1963.
27 See especially O. F. [Otto Frei], " Die SED im sowjetisch-chinesichen Konflikt," *Neue Zürcher Zeitung*, November 1, 1963 and " Aemterkumulation in der Hand Ulbrichts," *ibid.*, November 17, 1963. The 4th SED CC Plenum (*Neues Deutschland*, November 2–6, 1963) again confirmed Ulbricht's position.
28 W. W. Rostow, " The Third Round," *Foreign Affairs*, XLII, 1 (October 1963), pp. 1–10, and speech at Dayton, Ohio, September 18, 1963 (Department of State Press Release No. 475, September 17, 1963).
29 SED CC resolution, *Neues Deutschland*, July 31, 1963; O. F. [Otto Frei], " Flexiblere Berlinpolitik Pankows," *Neue Zürcher Zeitung*, July 28, 1963, " Unbehagen in Pankow," *ibid.*, August 27, 1963, and Bö., " Hoffnungen Pankows auf die Entspannungspolitik," *ibid.*, September 12, 1963.
30 See Underwood from Warsaw in *The New York Times*, November 2, 1963, and ok. [Bogdan Osadczuk-Korab], " Polens Vermittlungsversuch im Ideologiekonflikt," *Neue Zürcher Zeitung*, November 11, 1963.
31 For general background and current coverage see the chapter on Poland by Hansjakob Stehle in William E. Griffith, ed., *Communism in Europe*, I (Cambridge, Mass.: M.I.T., 1964); for Gomulka's speech at the 13th PZPR CC Plenum, *Trybuna Ludu*, July 6, 1963; for the resignation of the anti-partisan Zambrowski, *ibid.*, July 4, 1963, and of Matwin and Werfel, Underwood from Warsaw in *The New York Times*, November 10, 1963, and ok. [Bogdan Osadczuk-Korab], " Fraktionskämpfe unter

although the power of the internal party forces pressing for retrogression, the " partisans," [32] increased and some of their opponents fell, Gomulka kept them safely under his control. Hungary, on the other hand, continued both the trend toward liberalisation which has characterised the country since the CPSU Twenty-second Congress and its total, indeed enthusiastic, support of Moscow against Peking.[33]

It will be remembered that Rumanian First Secretary Gheorghiu-Dej did not participate in the gathering of Khrushchev and East European leaders ostensibly to celebrate Ulbricht's 70th birthday in East Berlin at the end of June, thus indicating that Soviet-Rumanian relations had dropped to a new low. Then, probably because he realised that, given his problems with China, he could not afford unrest on his western flank, Khrushchev apparently decided to suspend, at least temporarily, his pressure on Bucharest. As a result Rumania attended the CMEA summit meeting in Moscow in late July, where Khrushchev seems to have stopped pushing for the extensive integration of the Rumanian economy with that of the other CMEA countries and to have bowed to Bucharest's continued demand that multilateral economic coordination within the Council be preceded by bilateral coordination.[34] Thereafter

den polnischen Kommunisten," *Neue Zürcher Zeitung*, October 31, 1963; for the more strongly anti-Chinese line, Golde in *ibid.*, August 15, 1963, Krasucki in *ibid.*, August 17, 1963, and especially " On the Divergencies Between the CCP Leadership and the International Communist Movement," *Nowe Drogi*, No. 9, September 1963. For the Polish-East German rapprochement during this period, see ok. [Bogdan Osadczuk-Korab], " Gomulkas Kurs in der Deutschlandfrage," *Neue Zürcher Zeitung*, July 4, 1963.

[32] Relatively anti-Soviet but equally anti-liberalisation elements from the wartime Communist underground, like Strzelecki, Moczar and Szlachcic.

[33] See speeches by Kádár welcoming U Thant, *Népszabadság*, July 3, 1963, and in Moscow, *Pravda*, and *Népszabadság*, July 20, 1963. See also " Hungary in the Shallows," *The Economist*, September 28, 1963, " New Deal for Hungary," *The Times* (London), September 25 and 26, 1963; and Peter Bender, " Ungarn 1963," *Die Zeit*, November 8, 1963.

[34] Communiqué, *Pravda*, July 28, 1963. The only source of any detailed information on this meeting is a summary of the unpublished speech by Ulbricht at the 3rd SED CC Plenum, issued by *Informationsbüro West* (IWE), a West Berlin news agency, on August 20, 1963, No. 157/1963; this document, in my opinion a reliable one, indicates that the Rumanians at the July CMEA summit meeting insisted on only bilateral relationships and that the Soviets agreed. The successful Rumanian insistence on bilateral agreement as a precondition to multilateral co-ordination was further confirmed by a speech delivered in Moscow by Birladeanu on October 22, 1963 (*Scînteia*, October 25, 1963), and by an interview with him, " The Economic Links among the Fraternal Countries are Becoming Stronger," *Pravda*, October 25, 1963. See also a Rumanian-East German discussion (about the Rumanian thesis): Gerhard Huber in *Wirtschaftswissenschaft* No. 4, 1963; C. Murgescu, " Pseudo-theories which Attempt to Disparage Industrialization," *Viata Economica*, No. 1, August 1963 (against Huber); Karl Morgenstern in *Die Wirtschaft*, October 7, 1963 (pro-Rumanian), reprinted in *Viata Economica*, No. 9, October 18, 1963. This kind of indicator appeared as early as 1961, when the March 1961 *Probleme Economice* reprinted an article by Gertrud Gräbig in *Die Wirtschaft* criticising those who objected to heavy industry development in all socialist countries. See also ok. [Bogdan Osadczuk-Korab], " Das Comecon-Gipfeltreffen in Moskau," *Neue Zürcher Zeitung*, July 25, 1963, and " Das Ergebnis der Comecon-Tagung," *ibid.*, July 30,

Rumania signed the test ban treaty. In late August, however, a Rumanian leader condemned Chinese attacks on the Soviet signature of the treaty without specifying their source and in such a way [35] as to leave no doubt that Rumania intended to maintain its own interests against Soviet pressure.

Rumania's continuing nonconformist attitude was reiterated in early November by its Premier, Ion Gheorghiu Maurer. In an article published in *Problems of Peace and Socialism* as well as in *Lupta de Clase* (and therefore presumably having Soviet approval) he not only aligned the Rumanian party with the Polish and Italian Communists on the pro-Soviet moderate position, *i.e.*, against any immediate international Communist meeting, but also reiterated the successful Rumanian position on CMEA and even added that " all " socialist countries (*i.e.*, including China) should join it. " International specialisation " must be combined with

> the complex multi-branch development of the economy of each socialist country, the liquidation of the historic differences between their economic levels, primarily by the industrialisation of countries with a relatively low standard of economic development . . .

i.e., Rumania must be brought up to the industrial level of the other socialist countries and Bucharest would like China in CMEA so that the Rumanians would have more opportunity for manoeuvre within it.[36]

CHANGES IN CZECHOSLOVAKIA

By far the most significant internal changes occurred in Czechoslovakia; but as has been indicated above,[37] although the Sino-Soviet rift furthered

1963, an AFP dispatch from Moscow in *Le Monde*, September 26, 1963 (reporting that the Rumanians had been authorised another steel mill), and Harry Schwartz in *The New York Times*, August 18, 1963.

35 Speech by Nicolae Ceausescu, Radio Bucharest, August 22, 1963, 1900/GMT (BBC/EE/1335/C/2–3). See also the Warsaw Pact meeting communiqué (*Pravda*, July 27, 1963), where the reference to the " consistent peace-loving foreign policy course of the Soviet Union and *all* socialist courses " [my italics—W.E.G.] seems likely to have been a Rumanian formula; *cf.* its omission in the July 29 *Pravda* editorial and the July 27 Khrushchev interview in *Izvestiya* but its inclusion in a *Scinteia* editorial reprinted in *Pravda*, July 29, in a Rumanian CP CC letter to the CPSU CC, *Pravda*, August 1, and in a Gheorghiu-Dej *Pravda* article of August 1.

36 *Scinteia*, November 4, 1963, *Lupta de Clasa*, November 11, 1963, and *World Marxist Review*, VI, 11 (November 1963), pp. 12–21. For its remarks on the Sino-Soviet rift, see p. 222, *infra*.

37 See pp. 79–81, *supra*; C. K. [Christian Kind] from Prague, " Etappen der Entstalinisierung in der Tschechoslowakei," *Neue Zürcher Zeitung*, August 13, 1963, and, from Bratislava, " Slowakische Wandlungen," *ibid.*, November 17, 18, 1963; " Prague's Political Crisis," *East Europe*, XII, 7 (July 1963), pp. 24, 39–41; Zdenek Suda, " La révision des procès politiques en Tchecoslovaquie," *Est & Ouest*, XV (N.S.), 308 (November 1–15, 1963), pp. 11–13; Arnulf Baring from Prague, " ' In der DDR verdächtig . . .'," *Die Zeit*, November 22, 1963; and for the rapidly intensifying Czechoslovak-Yugoslav rapprochement, an interview with Jovan Veselinov upon his return from heading a SAWPY delegation to Prague, *Komunist*, November 7, 1963.

the process by diminishing Soviet interference with KSC affairs, liberalisation in Czechoslovakia occurred primarily for domestic reasons. Furthermore, the liberalisation did not moderate the traditionally extremist pro-Soviet Czechoslovak position. In order to see why not, a brief sketch of the causes and course of the Czechoslovak changes must be given.

The December 1962 Czechoslovak Party Congress had at first seemed to reflect comparative domestic stagnation, but its final resolution [38] did call on the Central Committee to " conclude within four months all the remaining cases of political trials from the period of the cult of the personality "—i.e., to dispose completely of the 1952 Slánský trial and other related purges. Upon its receipt of the resultant unpublished report, an April 1963 KSC Central Committee Plenum, as was not made public until a month later,[39] juridically but only partially politically rehabilitated the Slovak " bourgeois nationalist " Communists Clementis, Husák and Novomeský and repudiated the whole Slánský trial; it also removed Karol Bacílek and Bruno Kohler, two old Stalinists, from the KSC Presidium and Secretariat. But this minor and partial sacrifice, far from reinforcing the dam holding back de-Stalinisation, was only the first breach in it.

These concessions signalled the beginnings of an offensive by Slovak Communist intellectuals against the Prague leadership, a partial renewal of the 1956 thaw in Slovakia and, to a lesser degree, in Prague [40] as well. The Slovak Communist writers used the December 1962 KSC Congress resolution and the incrimination of the Czechoslovak leadership, particularly that of Prime Minister Siroký,[41] a Slovak, and also, more importantly, Slovak Communist nationalist opposition to Prague's centralism, as weapons against the Bratislava and Prague party leaderships. In spite of attempts by Novotný [42] and others [43] to suppress their campaign,[44] their initial purpose to force the formal and complete rehabilitation of the whole Slovak " bourgeois nationalist " group of Communists in the late forties—Clementis, Husák and Novomeský [45]—was almost but not quite achieved.[46] The Slovak Communist cultural monthly

---

[38] *Rudé Právo*, December 9, 1963.
[39] *Rudé Právo*, May 14 and August 22, 1963; *Rolnické Noviny* (Bratislava), May 28, 1963.
[40] See *Kultúrny Zivot* and *Pravda* (Bratislava) and *Literarní Noviny* (Prague), *passim*.
[41] See particularly the speech by Miro Hysko at the Slovak Writers' Congress, *Pravda* (Bratislava), June 3, 1963; for excerpts and replies, see *East Europe*, XII, 8 (August 1963), pp. 22–28.   [42] Speech at Košice, *Rudé Právo*, June 13, 1963.
[43] *e.g.*, a speech by Hendrych, *ibid.*, June 29, 1963.
[44] See C. K. [Christian Kind], " Novotnys Kritik an der slowakischen Intelligenz," *Neue Zürcher Zeitung*, July 23, 1963.
[45] See, *e.g.*, Novomeský's speech at the April 22, 1963, Slovak Writers' Conference, *Kultúrny Zivot*, May 4, 1963.
[46] Their removal from the KSC and KSS CCs remained effective.

Kultúrny Zivot and the Slovak party daily *Pravda* had partially escaped the control of the Bratislava party leadership, thus giving the dissident segment a channel of communication, one of the key factors in the spread of any Communist thaw. Attempts of the party leadership to regain control of these publications were not immediately successful. Many of the themes of the 1956 Czechoslovak thaw and of the 1962–63 developments in Hungary (which certainly exercised great influence in Czechoslovakia) reappeared: the leading role of the intellectuals in the party, the importance of supra-class humanism, the necessity of economic reform, the rehabilitation of the 1918 revolution and the 1944 Slovak rising (including their non-Communist aspects), and the freeing of education from politics. Discontent also arose among the workers, resulting not only from the bad economic situation but also from CMEA integration plans.[47] Furthermore, the Slovak intellectuals enjoyed support among Czech intellectuals as well, as the Czechoslovak Writers' Congress on May 22–24, followed by a similar Slovak Congress on May 27–28, demonstrated.

The main political effect of this surge came on September 20, when a KSC Central Committee Plenum replaced Premier Siroký by a 40-year-old Slovak, Jozef Lenárt, and also removed such old Stalinists as Jaromír Dolanský, Ludmila Jankovcová, and Juliús D'uris.[48] However, many of the inner circle around Novotny, particularly Jiří Hendrych and Vladimír Koucký, still remained, and although Novomeský became a member of the newly-established party ideological commission, Koucký became its head, while the entry into this commission of Nový and Reiman, purged during the Slánský trial period, was counterbalanced by that of the Stalinist Ladislav Stoll.

Perhaps the most significant element of these sweeping changes was the youth of the eight newly appointed ministers: they were on average only 43. The party *apparat* was (with Khrushchev's approval) being rejuvenated and the old Stalinists gradually replaced. Life in Czechoslovakia changed considerably: the pall of fear and terror was partially lifted, the influence of the West became more evident, and Czechoslovakia by the end of 1963 seemed on the way toward achieving a degree of liberalisation which might become comparable to Poland and Hungary. By November 1963 it seemed likely that Novotný himself would be sidetracked if not removed within the coming year, but unlikely that the

---

[47] See J. Svoboda, " Urgent and Without Reservations," *Rudé Právo*, August 11, 1963 and C. K. [Christian Kind] from Prague, " Die tschechische Wirtschaft im Rahmen des Ostblocks," *Neue Zürcher Zeitung*, August 17, 1963.
[48] *Rudé Právo*, September 21, 1963; see C. K. [Christian Kind], " Sturz Sirokys in Prague," *Neue Zürcher Zeitung*, September 23, 1963 and " Verjüngung der Regierung in Prag," *ibid.*, September 27, 1963; " Czechs Rattle the Lock," *The Economist*, September 28, 1963.

ferment would escape the control—it had only partially and temporarily —of an increasingly young, flexible, post-Stalinist and still united Czechoslovak party leadership.[49] And because the leadership neither split nor lost control, it could and did maintain its pro-Soviet extremist line on the Sino-Soviet rift.

ASIAN SUPPORT FOR THE SOVIET UNION [50]

The only three major Asian Communist parties which remained pro-Soviet, the Outer Mongolian, Indian, and Ceylonese, did so primarily for reasons of history and nationalism. All had been under primary and until recently exclusive Soviet influence during their whole history, and all were in countries whose traditional national interests are threatened by China. Outer Mongolia was a part of the Chinese Empire until the Soviet Union acquired effective control over it after the First World War, and India's threat from China became clear to all in October 1962. Yet the very nearness to China, and in India the strong pro-Chinese Communist minority, made them moderately rather than extremely pro-Soviet.

Mongolia. Until the Second World War Mongolia was the Soviet Union's only satellite, and Soviet influence has remained predominant there. Historically the Chinese rather than the Russians were the main threat to Mongol nationalism, and China's continued possession and Sinification of Inner Mongolia (Ulan Bator's irredenta) further increases anti-Chinese Mongol sentiment. It is natural therefore that Mongolian factional struggles have regularly resulted in victory of the pro-Soviet group and that Outer Mongolia has become increasingly integrated with the pro-Soviet group of Communist countries, notably in June 1962 by becoming a full member of CMEA. On the other hand, in spite of the fact that Outer Mongolia's public declarations have been consistently pro-Soviet, Mongolian nationalism has also increased, a development which Moscow and the pro-Soviet Ulan Bator leadership has successfully kept in check. As the only pro-Soviet ruling party in Asia (or indeed outside Europe), Outer Mongolia's importance to Moscow has certainly increased, a fact from which Ulan Bator will probably continue to profit.[51]

49 See, *e.g.*, an article by one of them, Cestmir Cisar, " The Clean Shield of Communism," *Nova Mysl*, No. 4, April 1963.
50 For excellent general background, see Barnett, *Communist Strategies in Asia*, Robert A. Scalapino, " Moscow, Peking and the Communist Parties of Asia," *Foreign Affairs*, XLI, 2 (January 1963), pp. 323–343, A. M. Halpern, " The Emergence of an Asian Communist Bloc," *The Annals*, CCCIL (September 1963), pp. 117–129.
51 See Robert A. Rupen, " The Mongolian People's Republic and Sino-Soviet Competition," in Barnett, *Communist Strategies in Asia*, pp. 262–292, particularly his discussion of the Tömör-Ochir case, and C. R. Bawden, " Mongolian People's Republic," *China News Analysis*, No. 493, November 15, 1963.

Ceylonese Communism. The Ceylonese Communist Party has remained consistently pro-Soviet throughout the Sino-Soviet dispute. Like the CPI, the Ceylonese party was primarily European rather than Far Eastern in origin. Furthermore, Ceylon is one of the two countries in the world (the other is Bolivia) where there is a significant Trotskyite movement, which is the main competitor on the left to the Ceylonese Communist Party. It is not surprising therefore that the newly-discovered affinity between Trotskyism and Maoism should further cement the Ceylonese Communist Party's allegiance to Moscow. Nevertheless, Ceylon's government has recently taken a less anti-Chinese position, the Chinese victory over India having reminded Southeast Asia of Peking's increased power, and Peking has been very active in Ceylon in bribing, persuading, and organising support for its activities. Perhaps in part because of this, in late October 1963 a pro-Chinese group including two Politburo members was expelled from the Ceylonese CP.[52]

Indian Communism. While Dange managed to retain the leadership of the CPI, to draw closer to such Congress left-wing figures as Krishna Menon and Malaviya, and to continue his anti-Chinese agitation, in 1963 the CPI's pro-Chinese elements became more active and influential. At a CPI national council meeting in mid-October 1963 Dange reportedly did not gain a clear victory; he failed to censure A. K. Gopalan, the CPI parliamentary leader, for co-operation with the pro-Chinese leftists in West Bengal and Andhra Pradesh, while the powerful Kerala organisation also still inclines toward the pro-Chinese left. Why the pro-Chinese CPI elements have gained in strength is more difficult to determine. One may hazard the hypothesis that it has been caused primarily by the move of Nehru and the Congress leadership toward more military co-operation with the West.[53]

ASIAN SUPPORT FOR CHINA

The summer and early autumn of 1963 saw an intensification of the drift toward the Chinese position which had been characteristic of the North Korean, North Vietnamese, Japanese, and Indonesian Communist Parties since the dispute began.

---

[52] Scalapino, " The Communist Parties of Asia," *op. cit.*, p. 325. See NCNA (English) Peking Radio, November 20, 1963, 1700 GMT, 1853 GMT, 1931 GMT.

[53] Sabavala from New Delhi in *The Christian Science Monitor*, November 2, 1963; " Peking's Pull," *The Economist*, October 26, 1963; *Link* (New Delhi), June 30, July 7, September 15, October 13, 20, 1963. For official declarations of the pro-Soviet Dange CPI leadership, see a July 20, 1963, CPI Secretariat statement in favour of the July 14 CPSU Open Letter, *New Age*, July 28, 1963; a July 27 one in favour of the test ban treaty, *ibid.*, August 4, 1963; and a CPI national council resolution, *ibid.*, October 27, 1963; and a criticism of Gopalan, *ibid.*, November 3, 1963. I am grateful to my colleague Professor Myron Weiner for assistance on CPI developments.

The term "Communist neutralist"[54] can no longer accurately describe their position *vis-à-vis* the Sino-Soviet rift. They have not aligned themselves completely with the extreme Chinese position, as have the much smaller Malayan, Thai, and Burmese Communist parties[55]; on the contrary, certain small, subtler signs of differentiation still exist; they may now, therefore, best be considered pro-Chinese moderates. Nevertheless, the great intensification of the Sino-Soviet rift which occurred during the summer and autumn of 1963, and particularly the issue of the test ban treaty, made "Communist neutralism" no longer tenable, least of all for the ruling North Korean and North Vietnamese parties. Even so like the Japanese and Indonesian Communist leaderships, as of this writing (November 1963) the former "Communist neutralists" still refrain from direct explicit criticism of the Russians (the euphemism "modern revisionists" is used instead, with Tito and the Yugoslavs explicitly attacked); but the test ban treaty is opposed, on the major issues of the dispute the Chinese position is in general taken, and the priority of combating "modern revisionism" has become greater than that of maintaining the unity of the international Communist movement.

Why this has occurred differs from case to case, but certain common factors can be isolated. These parties share with China a common strong hostility to the United States, and they cannot therefore support Khrushchev's Soviet-American détente. The North Korean and North Vietnamese Communists rule divided countries the other parts of which are American allies, and in Vietnam a guerilla war continues to rage. All these are underdeveloped countries for whom Chinese domestic extremism is attractive. They are all within the traditional area of Chinese cultural influence (and find Soviet ways, because European, foreign) and within the contemporary reach of Chinese power. Finally, they share with China a desire to limit Soviet domination of international communism; but, unlike the Chinese, most of them probably do not wish to end it entirely, nor do they wish to exchange it for total subordination to Peking.

North Korea. North Korea steadily drifted toward China in the Sino-Soviet dispute, particularly after its intensification in 1962 and 1963; by November 1963 it was Peking's most reliable major Asian ally. The North Korean Communist movement has historically been rent by factionalism, purge, and slaughter. From its beginning the Russians and to a lesser degree the Chinese have influenced and fought

---

[54] For its definition, see Scalapino, "The Communist Parties of Asia," *op. cit.*, pp. 330–331, and his "The Foreign Policy of North Korea," *The China Quarterly*, No. 14 (April–June 1963), pp. 30–50, at pp. 43–44.

[55] For them, see Scalapino, "The Communist Parties of Asia," *op. cit.*, pp. 332–334, and, for the Malayan, "The Three-Power Nuclear Treaty and World Peace," *Malayan Monitor* (London), XVI, 8 (August 31, 1963), pp. 1–6.

over it. Its present unchallenged head, Kim Il-song (of guerilla background, like Ho, Tito, and Hoxha), successfully eliminated his pro-Soviet, pro-Chinese, and " native " competitors for power, and, although initially pro-Soviet, has by now decided (as has Ho Chi Minh) that his country's interests can best be served by alliance with, although not domination by, Communist China. Unlike Ho, however, Kim did not wait until decision was inevitable to make his choice; he had made it already in 1961.

In addition to the general factors outlined above, Kim's decision was also influenced by (1) his own Stalinist predilections: the régime remains repressive and tyrannical and he therefore naturally opposes Khrushchev's de-Stalinisation while (2) China, not the Soviet Union, played the decisive role in aiding Pyongyang during the Korean War.

Even so, having due regard to its borders with the Soviet Union as well as with China, Pyongyang has not yet denounced Khrushchev or the Soviet Union by name; and formal Soviet-Korean state and party relations remain " correct " (but hardly more), Pyongyang thus maintaining, if only by a thread, a moderate rather than an extremist pro-Chinese position.[56]

North Vietnam. Like North Korea, in 1963 North Vietnam had to choose between Moscow and Peking, but unlike Kim Il-song, Ho Chi Minh delayed as long as possible, and has at least as yet remained more moderate (*i.e.*, less clearly anti-Soviet) than Kim. The May 1963 visit of Liu Shao-ch'i to Hanoi [57] marked the ascendancy of a pro-Chinese course in North Vietnam, and the further worsening of Sino-Soviet relations in summer and autumn 1963 further intensified

[56] See especially the special number of *The China Quarterly* on North Korea, No. 14 (April–June 1963), and within it especially Robert A. Scalapino, " The Foreign Policy of North Korea," pp. 30–50; also Chong-Sik Lee's " Politics in North Korea: Pre-Korean War Stage," pp. 3–16, and Glenn D. Paige and Dong Jun Lee, " The Post-War Politics of Communist Korea," pp. 17–29; see also Glenn D. Paige, " North Korea and the Emulation of Russian and Chinese Behavior," in Barnett, *Communist Strategies in Asia*, pp. 228–261, and (for pre-1945 Korean Communism) Robert A. Scalapino and Chong-Sik Lee, " The Origins of the Korean Communist Movement," *Journal of Asian Studies*, XX, 1 (November 1960), pp. 9–31, and XX, 2 (February 1961), pp. 149–167; Chong-Sik Lee, " Korean Communists and Yenan," *The China Quarterly*, No. 9 (January–March 1962), pp. 182–192; and Glenn D. Paige, " Korea and the Comintern, 1919–35," *Bulletin of the Korean Research Center*, No. 13 (December 1960), pp. 1–25. See also John Bradbury, " Sino-Soviet Competition in North Korea," *The China Quarterly*, No. 6 (April–June 1961), pp. 15–28. For the pro-CCP North Korean position, see the June 23, 1963, joint communiqué of North Korean President Choi Yong Kun and Liu Shao-ch'i, *Peking Review*, VI, 26 (June 28, 1963), pp. 8–12; " Self-Reliance and Independent National Economic Construction," *Nodong Sinmun*, June 12, 1963, and *Peking Review*, VI, 28 (July 12, 1963), pp. 9–12; " We Must Fight Against U.S. Imperialism's Nuclear War Provocations and for the Destruction of Nuclear Weapons," *Nodong Sinmun*, August 4, 1963, and *Peking Review*, VI, 32 (August 9, 1963), pp. 17–18 (against the test ban treaty); speech by Liu Shao-ch'i in Pyongyang, September 18, 1963, in *Peking Review*, VI, 39 (September 27, 1963), pp. 8–14. [57] See pp. 128–130, *supra*.

Hanoi's pro-Peking position. Specifically, North Vietnam publicly refused to sign the test ban treaty,[58] denounced Yugoslavia furiously, and took the pro-Chinese line on all major policy issues of the Sino-Soviet dispute.[59] (Like North Korea, however, North Vietnam did not explicitly denounce the Soviet Union or Khrushchev by name; the euphemism " modern revisionists " continued to be employed.) Reports indicated that Moscow-Hanoi relations had reached a new low, and Ho Chi Minh was faced with the prospect of the withdrawal of Soviet and East European aid and technicians.

Why did Ho choose Peking? In the first place, some choice was practically inevitable; a state either does or does not sign the test ban treaty, for example. Secondly, with the intensification of guerilla warfare in South Vietnam, the prospect of Ngo Dinh Diem's government falling, and the increased American military efforts in support of Saigon, and faced with a Moscow-Washington détente which did not involve American departure from Saigon, Ho's policy inevitably became more anti-American and therefore pro-Chinese.

Japanese Communism. The Japanese Communist Party (JCP) is unique in Asian Communism. It alone exists in a modernised, industrialised, developed society, where foreign domination (even post-1945 American influence) has never been a major factor toward radicalisation, where a conservative party is in power, and where the minute Japanese CP (which gets between 2 and 4 per cent. of the vote) faces a mass-based, radical, Marxist Socialist party.

The Japanese Communist Party can therefore best be compared to one in a West European country. Japanese nationalism and the JCP's foreign ties, both with Moscow and Peking, have prevented it from achieving a mass base, and it is dominated by intellectuals even more alienated and dogmatic than the average Japanese intellectual. The JCP has never been able to combine Communism and nationalism, like other Asian CPs, nor has it had the kind of influence that the Italian Communists have. Indeed, its still extremist majority leadership has been menaced by a reformist splinter faction under largely PCI ideological influence and on the left by the fanatical neo-Trotskyite

58 " Ceaselessly Heighten Vigilance; Unite and Struggle to Smash the Imperialists' Plots to Prepare a Nuclear War," *Nhan Dan*, August 9, 1963, excerpts in *Peking Review*, VI, 33 (August 16, 1963), pp. 34–35.

59 " The True Colours of the Yugoslav Revisionist Group as Provocateurs and Saboteurs of the International Communist Movement Have Been Exposed," *Nhan Dan*, May 22, 1963, " and " The Tito Group's New Constitution: It Can't Cover Up Their True Colours," *Hoc Tap*, No. 6, June 1963, both in *Peking Review*, No. 27 (July 5, 1963), pp. 15–17; " Renegade Tito Again Spews Venom of Revisionism," *Hoc Tap*, No. 7, July 1963 (JPRS 20, 364, July 29, 1963), and particularly " Let Us Resolutely Defend the Revolutionary Principles of the Two Moscow Statements," *Hoc Tap*, No. 11, November 1963, in VNA Hanoi English, November 16, 1963, 1200 GMT.

Zengakuren, for whom even Mao is a bourgeois nationalist and Khrushchev a traitor and American agent.

There have been no sharply defined pro-Soviet or pro-Chinese factions in the JCP, but its leadership, many of whom before 1945 preferred Yenan to Moscow, have gradually drifted toward the Chinese, under the pressure of the natural extremism of alienated, dogmatic intellectuals, of the threat of the Zengakuren students, and in reaction to the pro-Soviet reformism and to Khrushchev's rapprochement with the United States, the *bête noire* of the JCP. Yet the JCP's pro-Peking drift has been less pronounced than that of the North Koreans or even perhaps of the Indonesian Communists, with both of which the JCP retains close ties. In spite of the JCP's leadership's desire to suppress or play down Sino-Soviet differences and of their hopes of acting as mediators, the 1963 intensification of the Sino-Soviet rift caused them to take a definitely pro-Chinese stand on such issues as the test ban treaty. Even so, they must still be considered only moderately rather than extremely pro-Chinese.[60]

Indonesia. We have already seen that in February 1963 Aidit and other members of the PKI leadership, in the course of urging a CPSU-CCP meeting, seemed to take a quite clearly pro-Chinese line on the major issues in dispute between Peking and Moscow. In the summer of 1963 Aidit undertook an extensive world tour, including stops at Moscow, Havana, and finally Peking; it may be assumed that he was trying to mediate between Khrushchev and Mao. Nevertheless, the PKI's published position on the Sino-Indian, Cuban, and test ban treaty[61] issues was very close to the Chinese and far removed from that of the Russians, and Aidit's September 1963 proposal for a resumption of Sino-Soviet conversations, as will be seen below, was closer to the Chinese than the Soviet position. It did, however, strongly stress the importance of the autonomy of each Communist party, a fact which indicated the PKI leadership's desire to profit from the Sino-Soviet dispute by increasing its own freedom of action while working to prevent a complete Sino-Soviet rupture.

[60] Paul F. Langer, "Independence or Subordination: The Japanese Communist Party Between Moscow and Peking," in Barnett, *Communist Strategies in Asia*, pp. 63–100. For examples of the JCP's pro-Chinese stand, see Sanza Nosaka, "On the Importance of Educational Work and Institution of the Educational System," *Akahata*, June 14, 1963, and *Peking Review*, VI, 27 (July 5, 1963), pp. 17–18; "Strive for Genuine Unity and Development of the International Communist Movement," *Akahata*, November 10, 1962 (reprinted in full in *People's Daily*, November 12, 1963, summarised in NCNA English Peking, November 12, 1963, 1552 GMT) and an anonymous question-and-answer article, *ibid.*; for its very partial and qualified opposition to the test ban treaty, "On the Partial Nuclear Weapons Test Ban," *Akahata*, July 29, 1963, excerpts in *Peking Review*, VI, 32 (August 9, 1963), pp. 20–21.
[61] See *Harian Rakjat*, August 10, 1963, and *Peking Review*, VI, 34 (August 23, 1963), p. 15.

Yet its freedom of action has always been great; there is no reason to believe that the PKI is or was a mere satellite of either Moscow or Peking; and it is clearly only moderately rather than extremely pro-Chinese. Claiming a membership of over 2 million, it is the largest Communist party not in power and a major factor in Indonesian politics. Although its strength is almost entirely in Java, and although it has never succeeded in getting serious support among the bureaucracy or the army, it has control over a major trade union federation, SOBSI, has extensive influence over the peasantry, and is considered a legitimate element of Indonesian life (*i.e.*, not a foreign body in it). Furthermore, after the disastrous failure of its 1948 attempt at a rising, the new and younger leadership (Aidit, Lukman, Njoto, and Sudisman) made remarkable progress in using the parliamentary system to increase the PKI's power; today it is the only powerful political party in the country. But the very framework within which its successes were so striking, the parliamentary régime, itself practically collapsed after the unsuccessful 1958 rising in the outer islands, to be replaced by an authoritarian rule by President Sukarno and the army, and the PKI had to rely upon Sukarno's support to save it from suppression by the anti-Communist military. Sukarno's death would thus face the PKI with an almost insoluble dilemma.

To maintain its power in the present situation, therefore, the PKI must both endorse the " peaceful road to socialism " and cooperate with Sukarno and ostensibly with the army; thus internal political imperatives require it to follow a domestic policy which puts it far closer to Moscow than to Peking. Yet its constant competition both with the army and with Sukarno and his advisors, all committed to a vague kind of radical national collectivism, make it impossible to take a favourable attitude toward Tito's " national Communist " régime which it in fact now attacks violently [62]; while its foreign policy, one of attempting to outbid Sukarno and the army in anti-colonialism, anti-Westernism, and particularly anti-Americanism and anti-Malaysianism, tends to push it in the direction of Chinese anti-Americanism rather than Soviet rapprochement with the West. Finally, and this is perhaps the key element in its present position, its size and strength, plus its

---

[62] See, *e.g.*, " Yugoslavia's *Komunist* and *Harian Rakjat's* Reply," *Harian Rakjat*, April 19, 1963, and *Peking Review*, VI, 20 (May 17, 1963), pp. 13–15. For favourable Chinese comment on the PKI's anti-Yugoslav attitude, see Hsiung Fu, " The Indonesian People's Revolutionary Struggle and the Indonesian Communist Party," *Red Flag*, Nos. 10–11, May 20, 1963, and *Peking Review*, VI, 23 (June 7, 1963), pp. 7–13. See also Njoto, " Safeguarding the Unity of the International Communist Movement," *Peking Review*, VI, 29 (July 19, 1963), pp. 21–22.

geographical distance from both Moscow and Peking and its necessity to preserve its domestic image of being a nationalistic party, push it in the direction of obtaining as much autonomous freedom of action as possible. As Aidit has said, the PKI has an " independent attitude," it works toward " ' Indonesianising ' Marxism-Leninism," [63] and it " rejects the baton of any other Communist Party." [64] Here also China rather than the Soviet Union, particularly on the Albanian issue, presents a position which the PKI is inclined to support.[65]

Australasian Communism. The minuscule New Zealand Communist Party remained safely in the extremist Peking camp and was used by the Chinese as an intermediary with Moscow and as an instrument in its anti-Soviet campaign.[66] The Australian Communist Party continued on its post-1961 pro-Soviet course, but one of its former leaders, E. F. Hill, who had been expelled in 1961 when the party returned to a pro-Soviet position after a brief flirtation with Peking, with Chinese encouragement and support organised a dissident pro-Chinese group in Melbourne.[67]

AFRICA

The Sino-Soviet struggle in Africa during 1962–1963 [68] saw first China and then the Soviet Union gain ground in the Afro-Asian Peoples' Solidarity Organisation (AAPSO), the main forum of Chinese influence on the continent. At Moshi in February 1963 the Chinese clearly scored a victory,[69] and an even greater one at the foundation of the Afro-Asian Journalists' Organisation at Djakarta in May [70]; but at the AAPSO Executive Committee meeting at Nicosia in September the Russians were again in the lead, this time on the issue of the test ban treaty.[71]

---

[63] See a speech by Aidit to the CCP CC Higher Party School on September 2, 1963 (excerpts in *Peking Review*, VI, 37 (September 13, 1963) pp. 26–35, at p. 35), and his speech at Canton, NCNA English Canton, September 25, 1963 (SCMP 3070, September 30, 1963, pp. 19–26).

[64] See a speech by Aidit in Djakarta, September 30, 1963, in *Harian Rakjat*, October 4, 5, 1963; tr. excerpts, *Peking Review*, VI, 41 (October 11, 1963), pp. 17–18.

[65] This discussion of the PKI is primarily based on Ruth T. McVey, " Indonesian Communism and the Transition to Guided Democracy," in Barnett, *Communist Strategies in Asia*, pp. 148–198. I am grateful to my colleague Dr. McVey, whose forthcoming book on the PKI and the Sino-Soviet rift will be published in this series, for advice on PKI problems. *Cf.* Herbert Feith, " The Dynamics of Guided Democracy," in Ruth T. McVey, ed., *Indonesia* (New Haven, Conn.: HRAF Press, 1963), pp. 309–409.

[66] See pp. 35–36, 130, *supra*, p. 209, *infra*.

[67] See the text of three resolutions adopted at the Melbourne meeting in *People's Daily*, September 25, 1963, and *Peking Review*, VI, 40 (October 4, 1963), pp. 25–27.

[68] See Zbignieu Brzezinski, ed., *Africa and the Communist World* (Stanford, Cal.: Stanford University Press, 1963), especially the chapter by Richard Lowenthal, " China," pp. 142–203. I have also drawn on my own two trips to Africa in 1962 and 1963 and on Fritz Schatten's *Afrika Schwarz oder Rot?* (Munich: Piper, 1962).

[69] See p. 124, *supra*.

[70] See p. 125, *supra*.

[71] See p. 203, *infra*.

Furthermore, although the Chinese increased their contacts with and aid to Somaliland,[72] it was to Moscow rather than to Peking that Mogadiscio turned for arms,[73] and while the apparently initially significant Chinese influence in the Zanzibar Nationalist Party (ZNP),[74] centring in the party's secretary-general Babu, seemed to vanish when the Arab conservative majority in the party's leadership manoeuvred Babu out of the party in 1963, Peking's efforts there will continue.

Nevertheless, China's activities in Africa—in radio broadcasts, distribution of propaganda literature, student scholarships, exchange of delegations, and financing of some extremist elements—continued to increase sharply during these two years.

Peking obviously hoped that its increasingly racist tone would appeal to the Africans, but on balance this seems doubtful. External political and cultural influence in Africa, including Communist, remains primarily European; the British and French Communist parties, the parents of the African Communist movement, remain pro-Soviet; the Chinese are almost as opposed to pan-Africanism as are the Russians; and the African leaders, radical and otherwise, are as aware of Chinese as they are of Soviet chauvinism; while the disarray that the Sino-Soviet rift is bringing to world communism will only increase the African radical view that Moscow and Peking can be helpful but that one certainly need not remain faithful to them.

For Peking as for Moscow the time for rapid growth of influence in Africa has for the present passed, except for the southern part of the continent, where the defiance of the whites and the hesitation of the West may well give both Communist powers a chance to attach strings to and gain influence from the aid the African states will probably require to overrun the white redoubt, and which probably only the major Communist powers can and will give them. But this time is not yet, and fundamentally the tide of communism and of Soviet (and Chinese) influence in Africa, never very strong, is still receding before the advancing pan-Africanist wave. For Peking, as for Moscow, Africa remains, contrary to their hopes and the West's fears, a difficult field for their endeavours until the struggle for the white redoubt begins in earnest.

[72] See I. M. Lewis, " Pan-Africanism and Pan-Somalism," *Journal of Modern African Studies*, I, 2 (June 1963), pp. 147–162 and Saadia Touval, *Somali Nationalism* (Cambridge, Mass.: Harvard, 1963); and August 11, 1963, *People's Daily*, greeting the arrival in Peking of the Somali Prime Minister (SCMP 3040, August 15, 1963, pp. 20–21).

[73] *The New York Times*, November 13, 1963.

[74] Michael Lofchie, " Party Conflict in Zanzibar," *Journal of Modern African Studies*, I, 2 (June 1963), pp. 185–208.

CUBA AND LATIN AMERICAN COMMUNISM

It will be remembered that Castro's May 1963 visit to the Soviet Union and his speeches upon his return to Havana had appeared to indicate an almost complete Soviet-Cuban rapprochement after the previous tension arising from Khrushchev's withdrawal of his missiles from Cuba.[75] But the Moscow-Havana love feast, like Castro's moods, was very short-lived: the successful conclusion of the test ban negotiations in July again seriously worsened Soviet-Cuban relations; thus, having shifted from a neutral to a moderately pro-Soviet position, Cuba again resumed its neutral stance. Nor was this surprising. Having seen Moscow sacrifice what he considered Cuban interests to an accord with the United States in October 1962, and having seen a new high in Soviet-American rapprochement in July 1963, Castro naturally felt himself again in danger of being sacrificed by Khrushchev for the latter's larger goal of a world-wide Soviet-American rapprochement.

The Cuban press and radio did not at first even discuss the test ban treaty question, except for one brief mention by the old-line PSP Rector of the University of Havana, Juan Marinello; the Chinese stepped up their praise of Castro; and, at the beginning of August " Che " Guevara publicly returned Cuba to a position of complete neutralism on Sino-Soviet differences:

> For us the Sino-Soviet dispute is one of the saddest events. We do not participate in this dispute. We are trying to mediate. But as it is a fact, we inform the people about it and it is discussed by the party. Our party's attitude is not to analyse who is in the right and who is not. We have our own position, and as they say in the American movies, any resemblance is purely coincidental.[76]

Furthermore, although the joint Soviet-Cuban communiqué had been non-committal on the desirability of armed revolution rather than peaceful transition in Latin America, at the end of July the Cuban President Dorticos again reported Castro's previous formulation.

> In our judgment, the objective conditions of the majority of the Latin American countries are unfortunately not favourable to the peaceful road. But, naturally, the matter depends on the decision of each people. . . .[77]

Although Castro adopted a less hostile attitude toward the Western diplomats in Havana,[78] and declared that agriculture would now be

---

[75] See pp. 136–137, *supra.*
[76] In an interview with U.S. students, *Revolución*, August 2, 1963.
[77] In a press conference with foreign journalists, of which the stenographic transcript was published in *Rinascita*, July 27, 1963, pp. 17–21, at p. 19.
[78] *Le Monde*, July 18, 1963.

given preference over industry [79] (which would imply that less foreign aid would be necessary). Guevara again fully endorsed violent revolution in Latin America:

> On this continent in general there exist objective conditions which impel the masses to violent actions against the bourgeois and landowner governments. . . .

He also clearly rejected for Latin America the Soviet thesis of the possibility of collaboration with the national bourgeoisie:

> . . . Most of the national bourgeoisie have joined North American imperialism and must suffer the same fate as the latter in each country. Even in the cases where there are pacts or identity of contradictions between the national bourgeoisie and other imperialisms with the North American, this happens in the framework of a fundamental struggle which necessarily, in the course of its development, will include all the exploited and all the exploiters. . . .[80]

Castro broke his silence on the test ban treaty on September 29 by publicly declaring that Cuba would not sign it. He attempted to justify this decision by the special United States hostility toward Cuba, and he made clear his hostility to a Soviet-American détente.

> . . . an ironclad blockade exists and the imperialists are trying to bring more and more pressure to bear. It is even true that while tension is being relaxed in other parts of the world, while tension is lessening in other parts of the world, the Yankee imperialists are trying to tighten the siege of Cuba and are trying to make their blockade of Cuba still more implacable. And it is even clear that during the past few months they have accentuated that policy. . . . And so imperialism tries to tighten its noose around Cuba, even when pressure elsewhere in the world is slackening. And of course this situation determines our conduct!
>
> Naturally, we will not calmly accept a situation in which tensions decrease elsewhere while they increase for us. It is not that we want tensions in the world. No. We are glad when tensions relax. But we cannot consider ourselves at peace with the imperialists; we cannot consider ourselves at peace with an imperialism that tries to strangle us more and more. And this situation will determine our international conduct. This is not a policy that favours war; this policy stands for peace. (applause) But we are not to blame for the war waged on us. We are not to blame for the strong blockade established against us, as a small country, attacked, blockaded, against which a policy of undeclared war is being followed, a policy of piratical attacks, infiltration of saboteurs, introduction of arms and explosives, establishment of bases to attack and kill. No one can expect from us a beatific smile toward those imperialist enemies. (applause)
>
> They are our enemies and we will be theirs. This situation will determine our policy in the international arena, in the United Nations,

[79] *The New York Times*, August 18, 1963.
[80] From an article by " Che " Guevara in *Cuba Socialista*, September 1963.

and everywhere. It will determine our stand on the nuclear pact, and toward the proposals on denuclearisation. (applause) We will resist, for we have enough self-respect, dignity, courage, heroism, and spirit of sacrifice. (long applause, chanting) The imperialists try to intrigue in connection with Cuba's stand, and Cuba's stand is defined above all by anti-imperialism. What is our stand? The stand of anti-imperialism, the stand of basically Yankee anti-imperialism. That is, we are in a concrete situation. The enemy is 90 miles from us, harassing us, blockading us, threatening us, trying to destroy us. . . .

Castro's position was repeated a few days later by the Cuban delegate in the United Nations General Assembly.[81] Yet the Cuban daily *Hoy* (the former PSP organ) made clear that Castro still hoped to maintain ties with both Moscow and Peking:

. . . Cuba wishes to maintain fraternal ties with the entire socialist world and will not allow itself to be separated from this or that country which is a part of it or from this or that country which accords it solidarity and support. . . .[82]

By November 1963 this ostensibly neutral position promised to be increasingly more difficult for Castro to maintain. Although Soviet-American relations did not remain untroubled (as the frequent stoppages of American convoys on the Berlin Autobahn demonstrated), Moscow appeared to be cutting its military commitments in Cuba: by November Washington reports indicated that only about 5,000 Soviet combat troops were left on the island.[83] The destructive autumn hurricane sharply worsened the already critical Cuban economic crisis, and although Moscow finally promised to send more economic aid, China and Albania were suspiciously more rapid and generous in their response. Some reports even indicated that Moscow and the East European Communist states were proposing to cut economic aid to Cuba, in part because of the Communist agricultural crisis but also, one may assume, for political reasons, but these remain unconfirmed.[84] One may well wonder, indeed, now that the test ban treaty has become such a key issue in Sino-Soviet competition within the international Communist

[81] *Revolućión*, September 30, 1963 ; *The New York Times*, October 8, 1963.

[82] *Hoy*, October 2, 1963, quoted from an AFP Havana dispatch in *Le Monde*, October 4, 1963.

[83] *The New York Times*, August 20, September 23, November 10, 1963.

[84] *e.g.*, Lederer from London in *The Washington Post*, October 27, 1963. This report was denied in *Izvestiya* on November 12 but similar ones persisted. The pro-Soviet Havana University Rector, Juan Marinello, was removed (Radio Havana, November 9, 1963, 2300 GMT) and one report (*New York Times*, November 11, 1963), indicated that the old-line PSP leader Carlos Rafael Rodriguez's position was in danger. See also some enthusiastically pro-Albanian statements made by Cuban students departing from that country (*Bashkimi*, October 25, 1963). For East European denials of Soviet aid cuts, see Raymont from Washington in *The New York Times*, November 18, 1963. In mid-November Havana announced the establishment of a Cuban diplomatic mission in Albania. See *Revolućión*, November 15, 1963.

movement, if Khrushchev can indefinitely tolerate Castro's refusal to sign it and still give him such extensive economic aid; but Castro's prestige in underdeveloped areas makes it most difficult for Khrushchev to break with him.

Castro's ambitions and his conflicts with Khrushchev involve much more than Cuba. That Caribbean island is much too small for Castro's political goal; which is no less than the communising of all Latin America, by immediate guerilla revolution, under his leadership. A strikingly charismatic leader, Castro is obsessed with *la revolución*; for him " permanent revolution " is an imperative which carries almost more Hitlerian than Trotskyite overtones. A rootless half-intellectual of bourgeois origin, emotional rather than doctrinaire (the Chinese ideological mandarins can hardly ever capture his allegiance), Castro like Hitler is a man with whom any permanent compromise is probably impossible. In any case, his ambitions throughout Latin America and his insistence upon armed guerilla risings bring him into direct conflict with the old-line pro-Soviet bureaucratic leaders of the long-established Latin American Communist leaders, particularly Prestes in Brazil, Codovilla in Argentina, and Corvalán in Chile, who must therefore oppose him, in spite of the damage the struggle does to their parties. (This reluctance makes them moderately rather than extremely pro-Soviet in the dispute.) Khrushchev is therefore faced with either turning the leadership of Latin American Communism over to Castro or allowing the present leadership to combat Castro's influence in Latin America.

Castroism, far more than Chinese Communism, is a force among radical Communist intellectuals and students throughout Latin America —indeed more among what Robert Alexander has called the " Jacobin left " (non-Communist revolutionary radicals)—than within the old-line Communist parties themselves. At first Castro's chances of success seemed good, but his troubles at home, his inability to capture the leadership of any Latin American Communist party (except in Venezuela), and Khrushchev's sacrifice of Cuban interests have of late made Castro lose influence in Latin American Communist and other radical circles. Moreover it does not seem that the attempts of the Venezuelan *Fidelistas* at armed rising are likely to succeed; and their failure would be a body-blow to Castro's Latin American ambitions.

The Chinese themselves have increased their activity in Latin America to the best of their ability. They flood the continent, especially the universities, with their propaganda; they are organising student exchanges and mutual visits by delegations; they are organising and supporting dissident groups in Latin American Communist parties. This is perhaps most strikingly the case in Brazil [85] and Chile [86]; in the latter country the influence of Peking is greater on the extremist members of the Socialist Party than on the Communists themselves. It is much easier for the Chinese than for the Russians to ride the *Fidelista* bandwagon, and this is substantially what the Chinese have been trying to do; but it would probably be more accurate to say that Castro has been riding theirs. The primary conflict in Latin American communism is between Moscow and Havana, not between Moscow and Peking.[87]

INTERNATIONAL COMMUNIST FRONT ORGANISATIONS

One of the best indications of the effects of the post-test ban intensification of Sino-Soviet polemics and the reactions of Communist parties to them was their reverberations in the fora provided constantly by the international Communist front organisations.[88] Although the overt polemics within them centred on the test ban treaty, the Sino-Soviet struggle in their ranks centered upon the intensified Chinese attempt, in process since late 1962, to set up a series of competing Afro-Asian (and if possible Afro-Asian-Latin American) international organisations while maintaining Chinese membership and agitation within the existing Soviet-controlled ones. Both of these tendencies were particularly evident at the Hiroshima anti-atom congress in August and the Nicosia Afro-Asian solidarity meeting in September, but they were also present in all the other front organisations.

Hiroshima. The Ninth World Conference Against Atomic and Hydrogen Bombs opened at Hiroshima on August 5,[89] the day the test ban treaty

---

[85] See pp. 127–128, *supra*.

[86] My colleague Dr. Ernst Halperin is preparing a book on Latin American communism.

[87] For the above, see, in addition to the material cited on p. 62, footnotes 6–10, *supra*, the following: Boris Goldenberg, " The Cuban Revolution: An Analysis," *Problems of Communism*, XII, 5 (September–October 1963), pp. 1–8; Ernst Halperin, " Castroism—Challenge to the Latin American Communists," *ibid.*, pp. 9–17; Andrés Suárez, " Castro Between Moscow and Peking," *ibid.*, pp. 18–26; Ernst Halperin, " The Sino-Cuban and the Chilean Communist Road to Power: Latin American Debate," and " Castro and Latin American Communism " (M.I.T., Center for International Studies, mimeo., February and May 1963, respectively), and " Castro's Cuba: August 1963 " (M.I.T., Center for International Studies, mimeo., September 1963, *Encounter*, February 1964); Daniel Tretiak, " Sino-Soviet Rivalry in Latin America," *Problems of Communism*, XII, 1 (January–February 1963), pp. 26–33.

[88] For the Soviet case against the Chinese, see the Soviet Open Letter, *Pravda*, July 14, 1963, and Document 3, and Nikolai Tikhonov, Aleksandr Korneichuk, and Yury Zhukov, " The Unity of All Peace-Loving Forces Is an Object of Paramount Importance in the Struggle for the Prevention of World War," *Pravda*, July 15, 1963. For analysis, see John Boynton, " The Sino-Soviet Dispute and International Congresses," *The World Today*, IX, 8 (August 1963), pp. 323–326.

[89] The best coverage of the congress was in the dispatches from Hiroshima in *The Times* (London), August 2, 5 and 6, 1963; the best analysis is Kx. [Ernst Kux], " Die Differenzen zwischen Moskau und Peking. Neue Zusammenstösse auf dem Hiroshima-Kongress," *Neue Zürcher Zeitung*, September 5, 1963. For the Chinese

was signed in Moscow. It clearly demonstrated that the post-test ban intensification of the Sino-Soviet rift had rendered impossible the efficient functioning of international Communist front organisations and made much more difficult any effective cooperation with other left-wing organisations. The conference marked at least the temporary end of cooperation between the Japanese Socialist and Communist Parties and the split of the once powerful Japanese anti-atomic movement, Gensukyo, from which the Socialists and the Japanese trade union federation SOHYO withdrew in the aftermath of the Hiroshima Conference.

The previous year the Japanese Socialists and SOHYO had denounced the Communists' unwillingness to protest against Soviet as well as Western atomic explosions. This year they withdrew from the demonstration before it began and staged their own. Neo-Trotskyite Zengakuren students also demonstrated during the congress; the Soviets and the Chinese denounced each other furiously; the result was disorder and near chaos. The Chinese and Soviet polemics repeated, with equal violence, the August positions outlined previously. They were accompanied by such gestures as the Soviets turning their backs on the Chinese when the latter were speaking and the Chinese retorting, " This is Japan and not America; you had better go home! " As before, the Chinese were supported by the East Asian and some African delegates, the Soviets by the others. The final compromise resolution omitted any mention of the test ban treaty. The real result of the gathering was that Moscow and Peking demonstrated to the world their willingness to sacrifice common propaganda aims to their fierce struggle.

The Afro-Asian Solidarity Organisation (Nicosia). It will be remembered that at the Moshi meeting in February 1963 [90] the Chinese made considerable gains in the Afro-Asian Solidarity Organisation and that at the Jakarta meeting in May [91] they had set up a new Afro-Asian Journalists' Organisation from which they managed to exclude the Soviets. Thereafter they developed plans for setting up a series of Afro-Asian organisations, if possible with Latin American participation. The purpose clearly was to split the international Communist front organisations by providing Chinese-dominated substitutes limited to the

version, see NCNA English from Peking, August 6–10, 1963 (SCMP 3037, August 12, 1963, pp. 33–42, SCMP 3038, August 13, 1963, pp. 29–30, and SCMP 3039, August 14, 1963, pp. 40–42); for the Soviet, *Pravda* and *Izvestiya*, August 1–10, 1963.
90 See pp. 124–126, *supra*.
91 See p. 126, *supra*.

under-developed areas.[92] However, Castro's renewed rapprochement with Moscow [93] forced postponement of the proposed Havana Afro-Asian-Latin American meeting.[94]

The test ban treaty not only polarised Sino-Soviet conflict in the various Afro-Asian Solidarity organisations but also gave the Soviets an issue—peace and anti-atom testing—with which they could hope to combat Chinese influence in most of the underdeveloped areas. This was first demonstrated when the executive committee of the Afro-Asian Solidarity Organisation met at Nicosia, the capital of Cyprus, from September 10 to 12, 1963.[95] The Chinese tried without success to prevent the meeting from passing a resolution in favour of the test ban treaty, but they were so isolated in their opposition to the resolution that they abstained from voting against it. Furthermore, the meeting passed a resolution banning any Afro-Asian meetings of subsidiary organisations not authorised by the central Afro-Asian Solidarity Organisation.

Sino-Soviet polemics at the Nicosia meeting were as violent as ever. The Chinese accused the Soviets of "collaboration with imperialism" and of "deliberate treason to the peoples of the world." Each accused the other of packing the meeting with unaccredited, unrepresentative, and bribed delegates,[96] and the Chinese finally declared that the resolutions were illegally passed and therefore invalid.

Trade Union Activities.[97] Using the Communist-controlled Indonesian trade union federation SOBSI as its main instrument, the Chinese began as early as October 1962 to organise an Afro-Asian trade union conference, originally scheduled for May 1963 and then postponed

---

[92] For an account of a Sino-Soviet encounter in July see a speech by the Chinese delegate Yang Shuo at a meeting in Bali (Indonesia) of the Executive Committee of the Afro-Asian Writers' Conference, NCNA English Bali, July 18, 1963 (SCMP 3026, July 25, 1963, pp. 26–28); for the Soviet version of it see an article by three Soviet delegates to the meeting in *Liternaturnaya Gazeta*, September 10, 1963, another article in *Sovetskaya Kultura*, September 12, 1963, and Sajjad Zaheer, "Afro-Asian Writers' Movement and its Present Problems," *New Age*, October 13, 1963.

[93] See p. 136, *supra*.

[94] I have seen no further mention of this meeting.

[95] See dispatches from Nicosia in *Le Monde*, September 12, 13, 1963, and in *The Times* (London), September 12, 1963. For the Soviet version, see Radio Moscow in Serbo-Croat to Yugoslavia, September 14, 1963, 1530 GMT, and in Spanish to Cuba, September 17, 1963; Sukhachev from Nicosia in *Izvestiya*, September 17, 1963, 2300 GMT; Mirzo Tursun-Zade, head of the Soviet delegation, in *Literaturnaya Gazeta*, September 21, 1963, and *Izvestiya*, October 6, 1963; B. Homola from Nicosia in *Rudé Právo*, September 17, 1963; and "The Splitters Found Themselves in Isolation," *Pravda*, September 19, 1963; for the Chinese, NCNA English Nicosia, September 10 and 11, 1963 (SCMP 3060, September 16, 1963, pp. 22–23, and SCMP 3062, September 18, 1963, pp. 21–22), and *People's Daily* and NCNA English Peking, September 24, 1963 (SCMP 3069, September 27, 1963, pp. 15–19).

[96] See also "Peking Accused of Bribing African Delegate," *The Times* (London), September 13, 1963.

[97] I am much indebted to my colleague, Professor D. L. M. Blackmer, who is doing research on this subject, for his assistance concerning this section.

until the fall. Neither the WFTU nor the Soviet trade unions were invited to participate in the conference preparations, which raised protests from S. A. Dange, leader of the Indian Communist trade union federation as well as of the CPI, and from the Japanese trade union federation SOHYO. The Jakarta conference was also opposed by the Yugoslavs, who had for some years been attempting themselves to organise an international conference of trade unions, primarily from neutralist Asian and African states.[98] The Soviet Union maintained silence about the Chinese effort until October 1963, when it came out in favour of convening "The Afro-Asian Trade Union Conference" on a truly representative basis and condemned the Chinese for their efforts to disrupt working-class unity.[99] At this writing (November 1963) it is difficult to determine whether this move represents in some sense an endorsement of the original Yugoslav initiative (which the Soviets had previously attacked) in order to counter the Chinese move or a more direct attack on the Chinese proposal, i.e., an effort either to win control of the Chinese-sponsored conference or to set up a rival conference with the same name but under direct Soviet control. The Jakarta meeting finally took place from October 28 through November 3, but as of this writing (November 27, 1963) it was unclear whether or not the Soviets participated or would do so in the Conference itself, rescheduled for mid-1964. The meeting was in any case clearly under Chinese and Indonesian Communist control.[100] It should be added, however, that neither the aims of the moderately pro-Chinese PKI, which controls SOBSI, nor even those of the Sukarno government, which was also supporting the project, coincided with Peking's; as Nasser in past years had demonstrated to Moscow, this new Afro-Asian organisation would be far from a total tool of Peking.

Other International Communist Organisations. During the summer and autumn all other international Communist organisations were to a greater or lesser degree factionalised by the Sino-Soviet rift. The Chinese voted against WPC resolutions; they refused to participate in and denounced the summer Mediterranean cruise meeting of the International Organisation of Journalists (held on a ship in part to

[98] *International Communist Front Organizations*, Nos. 149–151, July–September 1963: *Asian Analyst*, July 1963, pp. 14–15; Boynton, *op. cit.*, pp. 324–325; Arnold Beichman, " China and Indonesia Plan ' Labour Bandung,' " *Forum Service*, August 10, 1963 ; *Rad* (Belgrade), July 20, 1963 ; *New Age*, March 24, 1963 ; Milos Marinović, " Background and Meaning of a Campaign," *Review of International Affairs*, XIV, 324 (October 1, 1963), pp. 9–10.

[99] Grishin to a Soviet trade union conference, *Pravda*, October 30, 1963. Vukmanović-Tempo to the same, in TANJUG in English to Europe, October 30, 1963, 1641 GMT.

[100] See Radio Jakarta, October 28–November 3, 1963 (which stated that a Soviet delegation attended). Neither *Pravda* nor *Trud* mentioned the meeting at all during this period.

avoid Chinese disruption); they staged an uproar at the 19th General Assembly of the international Communist Telecommunications Organisation; they founded a " Peking Centre " of the World Federation of Scientific Workers for activities in Asia, Africa and Latin America, they began preparations for an Afro-Asian-Latin American Students' Conference to meet in Bandung in April 1964; and in many other ways they pursued their efforts to form separate Afro-Asian-Latin American organisations to combat the existing Soviet-controlled international ones, from which, however, they neither resigned nor were expelled.[101]

---

[101] For the summer IOJ Mediterranean cruise, see a witty report by a Western journalist who went along, Ronald Payne, in *The Sunday Telegraph* (London), October 6, 1963.

19. Towards an International Communist Meeting?

It will be remembered that the July 1963 Sino-Soviet meeting in Moscow was preceded by a series of proposals for an international Communist meeting by smaller Communist parties. Some of these proposals were Soviet-inspired, some of Chinese origin, and some (specifically, one may assume, the pro-Chinese moderate North Vietnamese and Indonesians and the [then] pro-Soviet moderate Cubans) were motivated by a genuine desire on the part of these moderates to prevent a total Sino-Soviet rupture.[1] A new series of proposals for either bilateral or multilateral meetings began in September and October 1963. By this time, however, they reflected more clearly than their predecessors the influence of the moderates, and, more importantly, the then intended but thereafter at least temporarily abandoned Soviet intent to condemn and if possible expel the Chinese. The category of " Communist neutrals " had, with the exception of Cuba, largely disappeared.

By September 1963 Soviet and Chinese positions on such a meeting were reversed. Previously the Chinese had wanted an all-party or at least a multi-party meeting as a preparation for an all-party conference, while the Soviets had first tried to use the European Communist congresses as a substitute and finally agreed to an international meeting only when the Chinese agreed to bilateral and ostensibly preparatory Sino-Soviet talks. By September the Russians appeared to be seriously considering an international meeting while the Chinese pushed for the resumption of the Sino-Soviet bilateral discussion. Two points may be made as to the causes of the reversal. First, the Russians probably felt they could use the test ban issue to rally more easily the support of other Communist parties. Secondly, and more importantly, it seems likely that by early October 1963 Moscow considered that Sino-Soviet relations were at such a bad stage and Chinese factionalism throughout the world so

[1] See pp. 35–36, *supra.*

207

active and dangerous that nothing less than the formal excommunication of the Chinese from the international Communist movement and the consequent crushing of neutralist tendencies would adequately protect Soviet prestige and influence. In any case, in September and early October 1963 it was the Russians, not the Chinese, who were clearly in favour of calling an international meeting, with the maximum objective either to force the Chinese to capitulate or to excommunicate them. The pro-Soviet extremists as usual supported Moscow; the pro-Soviet moderates opposed the convocation of such a meeting and were in large part responsible for Moscow's late October abandonment—at least temporarily—of the project.

The Chinese, on the other hand, were of course opposed to any such international meeting; they still preferred to remain formally a member of the movement while carrying on factional activities within it. In order to prevent the Russians from calling such an international meeting, and, if Moscow called it, to prevent their formal excommunication, the Chinese had two weapons, ideological and organisational, and three categories of potential allies: (1) the reliably pro-Chinese extremists (the Albanians, the Burmese, Thais, and Malayans); (2) the pro-Chinese moderates (the North Vietnamese, Indonesians, and Japanese, and to a lesser extent the North Koreans) who did not want an open rupture and would therefore support the Chinese in trying to prevent the Russians from succeeding in bringing it about; and (3) the pro-Soviet moderates, who also did not want an open rupture and might therefore be brought to serve the Chinese aim. Thus as to the first group, the Chinese had no worries; as to the second and third, their strategy combined persuasion and threat: persuasion, particularly with the second group, that there was mutual interest in avoiding the split (this was evidenced by the formally correct Chinese gestures toward Moscow, particularly in mid-October); threats, with the third group more effective than persuasion, that the Chinese would remain so adamant that if the Russians insisted on excommunication they would obtain it—thus convincing both pro-Chinese and pro-Soviet moderates that only effective pressure on Moscow could prevent an open rupture. (This the Chinese did by continuing the publication of their violently anti-Soviet ideological articles and by indicating that they still demanded that Khrushchev capitulate to the Albanians.)

By late September, after the publication of the first three of the long Chinese articles, signs began to indicate that the Russians had probably become convinced that excommunication of the Chinese was necessary. The Chinese presumably were aware of this Soviet stance, but so were the moderates, both those like Gomułka, Ho Chi Minh, and Aidit, who had previously tried to contain and mediate the dispute, and those like

Gheorghiu-Dej who had strong nationalistic reasons for trying to avoid a break. One must assume that they intensified their private efforts to forestall and if possible reverse the Soviet decision to force an excommunication of Peking and to persuade Peking to moderate its position.

THE EXTREME CHINESE VIEW OF A MEETING

The extreme Chinese view was mirrored in a statement in late October by Peking's faithful satellite the New Zealand Communist Party, which declared that there was indeed need for a world meeting but that this must be preceded by " comprehensive preparations, including adequate bilateral discussions between various parties." Specifically, the bilateral talks between the CPSU and the Chinese and between the CPSU and the New Zealand party should be resumed, and in addition

> . . . there also exists the need for the initiating of bilateral discussions between the leaderships of other parties. This applies with particular force to discussions between the leaderships of the Soviet and Albanian parties. . . .

i.e., Peking's early 1962 and early 1963 Albanian precondition still remained in force.[2] If these were not initiated, the New Zealand statement continued,

> . . . a world meeting would be premature and . . . almost certainly . . . largely abortive . . . [but] . . . initiating and finalising of bilateral talks between parties, plus the circulation of their viewpoints to others of the world parties, would lay the basis for an over-all assessment of ideas. . . .[3]

THE MODERATE PRO-CHINESE VIEW OF A MEETING

At the end of September, Aidit outlined one moderately pro-Chinese view. Although closer to Peking's than to Moscow's, unlike the New Zealand one it was not totally pro-Chinese. After attempting to put as good a face as possible on the drastic deterioration of Sino-Soviet relations, Aidit emphasised that the PKI had urged the CPSU and the CCP to resume their bilateral meetings and that the next meeting, on the rotation principle, should be in Peking. (Presumably also a Chinese condition, this would appeal to the PKI and other moderate parties as well.) He also made clear the PKI's opposition to a split. Finally, he strongly emphasised the " independent " and " self-reliant " attitude of the PKI, the necessity of " Indonesianising " Marxism-Leninism, and the PKI's rejection of " the baton " of any other Communist party. All this the Chinese republished, thus indicating their (probably

2 See pp. 36, 116, *supra*.
3 Statement by M. H. Williams, Chairman of the National Committee of the NZCP, on behalf of the party's National Secretariat, in *Peking Review*, VI, 44 (November 1, 1963), p. 19.

reluctant) approval of this moderate PKI position. Yet they did not republish (perhaps because they felt it still tactically unwise) other, more significant excerpts of the September 29 Aidit speech: his stronger praise for North Korea than for China, his violent denunciation of the pro-Soviet Indian Communists, and, most important, his fourfold classification of Communist parties: (1) entirely Marxist-Leninist, (2) revisionist leadership but Marxist-Leninist opposition within, (3) revisionist leadership and expelled Marxist-Leninists beginning to organise, and (4) two Communist parties, the old one revisionist and the new one Marxist-Leninist. Aidit's operational conclusions drawn from these categories, somewhat more moderate than the CCP's, were: Marxist-Leninist struggle against revisionists should be within rather than without parties, unless the former are expelled by the latter; then the Marxist-Leninists must be supported by all parties. Yet the PKI, Aidit concluded, will maintain relations with anti-imperialist ` " old " (*i.e.*, revisionist Communist parties, presumably including the CPSU) as well as " new " (Marxist-Leninist) ones.[4]

A Japanese CP editorial of November 10 also took, although less clearly, the moderately pro-Chinese position of opposition to an international meeting such as Moscow originally had in mind in order to excommunicate Peking:

> If the proposal . . . is promoted by a desire to hold the international conference hurriedly and to decide matters by a majority vote, our party cannot endorse this proposal. Such practice can only make the disunity within the international Communist movement and the socialist camp an irretrievable thing. What is more, it is against the policy laid down in the Moscow Statement. . . .

The Japanese editorial declared that not only Sino-Soviet meetings but also ones by other parties were necessary to prepare such an international gathering; *i.e.*, the Japanese position was somewhere between the extremist pro-Chinese New Zealand and the moderately pro-Chinese Indonesian one.[5]

THE EXTREME SOVIET VIEW OF A MEETING

The extremist and moderately pro-Chinese positions during this period were probably primarily in response to the Soviet offensive for an international meeting to excommunicate the Chinese. Whether it was doubtful if such a project would succeed and therefore preferred not to commit its prestige prematurely, or because it wanted to smoke out reactions in

4 *Harian Rakjat*, October 4, 5, 1963; tr. excerpts, *Peking Review*, VI, 41 (October 11, 1963), pp. 17–18.
5 " Strive for Genuine Unity and Development of the International Communist Movement," *Akahata*, November 10, 1962, in NCNA English Peking, November 12, 1963, 1552 GMT (SCMP 3102, November 18, 1963, p. 31).

advance, Moscow used the time-tested Soviet technique of reprinting documents of other Communist parties advocating the course which it had either decided to adopt or on which it at least wanted to test the response. Yet to a far greater extent than on the two previous occasions, in early 1962 and early 1963, the reaction of the other parties was varying, so much so that in mid-course Moscow reversed course and at least temporarily abandoned this tactic.

The first sign of how extreme the Soviet position had become came when a condensed and clearly excerpted version of the first such resolution, adopted by the Executive Committee of the moderately pro-Soviet British Communist Party (CPGB) on September 14,[6] appeared in *Pravda* on September 17. The moderate CPGB resolution had declared that " a new and dangerous stage " had been reached, stated that British Communists " refused to accept that a split . . . is inevitable," and called for the resumption of the Sino-Soviet bilateral negotiations or at least for a cessation of polemics. As it had in January 1963, *Pravda* omitted all these parts of the resolution; it reprinted only the anti-Chinese statements and the call to all Communist parties " to study the question of the necessity of beginning to prepare for an international conference." The qualification that such talks should be " sometime within the next year " was also omitted. Thus Soviet censorship of the CPGB resolution reflected Moscow's current desire to have an international conference soon.

The Soviet Government's statement of September 21, it will be remembered, again called for a cessation of Sino-Soviet polemics but intimated that the resumption of bilateral Sino-Soviet talks was dependent upon Peking's ceasing its " openly hostile campaign " against Moscow.

Moscow's next step was *Pravda's* publication on September 24 of a resolution of the Portuguese Communist Party Central Committee. The Portuguese CP is illegal and its leadership is largely dependent on Soviet support. Not surprisingly therefore its strongly anti-Chinese resolution accused Peking of factionalism and referred to " the socialist system on a world scale headed by the great and mighty Soviet Union." It then called for an international Communist conference " in the very near future," one which, even if it did not overcome all

> . . . ideological disagreements . . . would nevertheless be useful if it culminated in unanimous agreement to stop polemics and to forbid any party unilaterally to criticize any other party, to intervene in its internal affairs, or to maintain political links with Communists who are members of the party of another country without the permission of, or instructions to that effect from, the leaders of the party concerned . . .

6 Excerpts: *Daily Worker* (London), September 17, 1963; text: *New Age* (New Delhi), October 6, 1963.

i.e., the resolution called for the Chinese to accept the Soviet ban against factionalism proposed by Moscow in the November 1960 meetings—a proposal which Peking was certain to reject. The resolution declared that there should be formed " immediately . . . a commission composed of several representatives of Communist and workers' parties "—*i.e.*, a preparatory commission such as met in September and October 1960. It also declared that " at the present time dogmatism is the main danger " and that

> . . . basically the struggle against dogmatism . . . amounts at present to the fight against the conceptions and concrete policies of the leaders of the Chinese party and against their influence on the Communist and national liberation movements . . .

i.e., the international meeting should declare ideological and political war on the Chinese. Finally, it declared that the Yugoslav Communists' influence " has greatly declined," they have been " defeated ideologically," and they " are attempting to adopt the positions of the international Communist movement "; *i.e.*, it implied that they should participate in such a meeting.[7]

Less than a week later, on September 30, *Pravda* published a resolution by the Paraguayan Communist Party, which like the Portuguese is illegal, led by emigrés, and also dependent upon the Soviet Union. The Paraguayan resolution went considerably beyond the Portuguese one in setting forth the maximum Soviet objectives against the Chinese. Although it did not specifically call for an international conference, it not only forcefully stated (for the first time in any such document) that " the dogmatic deviation of Comrade Mao Tse-tung has become the main danger within the international Communist movement " but also declared :

> In this particular case the Declaration of 1960 no longer reflects the situation which has now occurred. Therefore it would be correct to amend this item, possibly by adopting an additional declaration . . .

i.e., the Chinese, not the Yugoslavs, are now the main danger and the 1960 Declaration should be amended accordingly.[8] The resolution flatly demanded the " political isolation " of the Chinese and (again for the first time in any such document) the abandonment of any position but an

---

[7] For the 1960 Soviet draft resolution on factionalism, see Griffith, " The November 1960 Moscow Meeting: A Preliminary Reconstruction." It is even questionable whether this *Pravda* version of this Portuguese CP resolution was an accurate reproduction of the original. The speech to the Portuguese CP CC August plenum by its secretary-general Alvaro Cunhal (according to a late September version given in clandestine Portuguese Communist radio broadcasts) contained neither a mention of dogmatism being the main danger, nor anything about an international Communist meeting. See Radio Free Portugal (Clandestine), September 18, 1963, 2330 GMT (BBC/11/1358/A3/3–4, September 21, 1963), and September 19 and 20, 1963, 2330 GMT (BBC/EE/1360/A3/1–5, September 24, 1963).

[8] *Cf.* the article in *Kommunist*, No. 15, 1963, p. 466, *infra*.

212

extremist pro-Soviet one:

> . . . there can be no justification for any vacillation or hesitation in the principled struggle, any " neutralist " position or any position of passive contemplation.
>
> Certain honest comrades maintain that because they do not want to take the high seat of a judge they cannot " take a stand in favour of one group or the other." But it is precisely by refusing to take a definite stand in this principled struggle that one elevates oneself above the international Communist movement. We are not judges—all of us are soldiers of this noble movement. But a soldier is obliged to take a definite position. Consequently to talk about " two groups " means to assist those who are trying to split our movement into two groups. The ideological struggle is a struggle of the Communist movement as a whole against the mistaken and factionalist position of the CCP leadership. A position like the one which advocates the " maintenance of good relations with everybody," even if it is prompted by a healthy desire for unity and fraternity, does not help the defense of the unity of the Communist movement. On the contrary, it can weaken the collective defense of unity. . . .
>
> The good intentions of all those who have played a role of mediator in this principled struggle have misfired in the face of the intransigence of the splitters. In connection with this objective situation, the way of political isolation of the splitters remains the only way for the preservation of unity. It is essential that everywhere a resolute rebuff be given to their attempts at creating confusion and split. Only by means of a struggle of views and a clear-cut demarcation of positions on all basic questions, as Lenin demanded, can one stop the aggressive activity of the Chinese leaders and force them to weigh all the aspects of the case.
>
> Present experience confirms the truth that on main, fundamental questions an eclectic position, a position of " sitting on the fence," is objectively impossible. It is not a principled position. Therefore it is not characteristic of Marxist-Leninists. Therefore Lenin contemptuously described it as a " quagmire." Now more than ever before there is the possibility and necessity of strengthening the unity of action and collaboration of all Marxist-Leninist forces by means of adopting collective measures envisaged in the Statement of 1960. . . .

In other words, all parties must either come down completely on the extreme Soviet side or be excommunicated from the international Communist movement along with the Chinese and their supporters. Furthermore, although the reference to the " collective measures " of the 1960 Statement was highly misleading (the latter had referred only to " collective efforts " toward " enriching . . . Marxist-Leninist theory and . . . working out joint positions "), it forecast the method of action being considered by Khrushchev: an excommunication of the Chinese by an international meeting.

The impression given by *Pravda*'s publication of the Portuguese and Paraguayan resolutions, that Moscow was steering toward an international meeting to excommunicate the Chinese, was deepened when a long article in the Soviet ideological monthly *Kommunist*, approved for publication on September 30,[9] declared that after first breaking with Moscow " on a number of contemporary questions," the Chinese had then " carried out an all-out action against the whole general line of the international movement " and now have " embarked upon a new phase of schismatic and undermining activity," have " developed a front against the fraternal socialist states, the Marxist-Leninist parties," and have " surpassed their own unworthy and base methods." The article then repeated the Portuguese resolution's version of what the 1957 and 1960 Moscow Declarations allegedly had " formulated with full clarity " (but in fact had not) about factionalism in the international Communist movement:

> The basic conditions for international discipline in the Communist movement have been formulated with full clarity in the [1957] Declaration banning the creation of factions and groupings within the ranks of Communist parties and the [1960] Statement which made the Communist parties duty-bound not to permit any actions that could undermine the unity of the international Communist movement. . . .[10]

Yet this *Kommunist* article practically ended there; it did not propose any specific measures or even indicate paths of action against the Chinese. Moscow was still not tying its own prestige irrevocably to the excommunication of the Chinese.

Moscow's continued adherence to its extremist line and its disapproval of the moderate view, however, was indicated by its treatment of an October 2 joint communiqué of the Dutch and Italian Communist parties,[11] which after condemning Chinese factionalism, declared that both parties

> . . . emphasised the necessity of conducting the discussion on the differences of opinion in such a manner that they lead to renewed international unity on the basis of complete respect for the autonomy of each party. . . .

As it had with the British party's resolution, and as it was to do later with the Italian's, *Pravda's* October 3 version omitted this statement.[12]

On October 10 the Norwegian Communist Central Committee returned [13] to its previous neutral position between Moscow and Peking.

9 " For a General Line of the World Communist Movement, Against Leftist Opportunism, Nationalism, and Adventurism," *Kommunist*, No. 14, 1963 (passed for the press, September 30, 1963), pp. 3–38. This article for the first time stated that the Soviet Union would henceforth give economic aid to the " revolutionary struggle of the working class in capitalist countries "—*i.e.*, to West European Communist parties. It also gave a long defence of the CPSU *Programme's* " all-peoples' state."

10 *Ibid*. p. 36. What this passage did not mention was that the 1957 Declaration's phrasing related only to factionalism within individual parties and the Soviet attempt in 1960 to extend this to the international movement was blocked by the Chinese. See Griffith, " The November 1960 Moscow Meeting: A Preliminary Reconstruction," *op. cit.*

11 *De Waarheid* (Amsterdam) (JPRS 21,637, October 29, 1963) and *L'Unità*, October 2, 1963.   12 *Pravda*, October 3, 1963.

13 Norwegian CP CC Resolution, *Friheten* (Oslo), October 10, 1963.

Declaring that " it is possible in a friendly manner to explain and discuss the differences," the Norwegian CP Central Committee proclaimed that

> . . . we will not participate in the discussion in a manner which may result in a further sharpening and deterioration of the situation, but instead we shall try to give our contribution in such a manner that the friendly norms for the relations and discussions between fraternal Communist parties are restored.

The [Norwegian] Central Committee will therefore appeal to all Communist parties that they end all further public polemics and at least see to it that the discussion is carried on in a spirit of comradeship and in a proper political manner. Furthermore the Central Committee will repeat its proposal from January, that one or more committees are appointed with representatives from several parties in order to discuss the questions. The unity of the World Communist Movement is a question which does not concern only the largest Communist parties, the Communist Party of the Soviet Union and the Communist Party of China. It is a question which concerns all Communist parties, small and large, and for which all parties are co-responsible.

The Central Committee furthermore instructed the Secretariat:

1. to send the statement to the Communist Party of the Soviet Union and to the Communist Party of China together with a letter which further explains the view of the Norwegian Communist Party; and

2. to compose information to be sent to the local groups with a more detailed explanation of the attitude of the Central Committee and of what the differences of opinion in the World Communist Movement are about.

Not surprisingly, *Pravda* did not even mention this Norwegian resolution; but the Chinese [14] and the Italian Communists [15] later sent cordial greeting messages on the occasion of the Norwegian Communist Party's fortieth anniversary and Peking reprinted an article by a Norwegian CP leader.[16] Nor, as was indicated by an October 21 joint Soviet-Norwegian CP communiqué, did Moscow succeed at once in bringing the erring Norwegians back into line.[17]

On October 13 *Pravda* reprinted excerpts from an October 10 speech by Maurice Thorez,[18] as it had on October 9 from the same day's French

14 On November 1, 1963; see *Peking Review*, VI, 45 (November 8, 1963), p. 4.

15 *L'Unità*, November 4, 1963. The PCI message stressed the importance of struggling against dogmatism and sectarianism and of " more intense contacts " among the West European Communist parties.

16 " Long Live Proletarian Internationalism," by Just Lippe, in *People's Daily*, November 4, 1963; see *Peking Review, loc. cit.*, and excerpts in SCMP 3097, November 8, 1963, pp. 37–39.

17 *Pravda*, October 21, 1963. The communiqué favourably mentioned the 20th CPSU Congress, but the Norwegian CP was in any case committed to the peaceful transition to socialism. Its reference to the importance of " observing the standards of relations between the Communist parties defined by the 1960 Statement," however, was equivocal; Peking has used this formulation more frequently than Moscow.

18 *L'Humanité*, October 10, 1963; *Pravda*, October 13, 1963.

Central Committee Plenum resolution.[19] *Pravda* omitted the passage
from the PCF CC resolution which called for the convocation

> ... with the least possible delay [*dans les meilleurs délais*] of a conference
> of all the Communist and workers' parties of the world in order to
> reaffirm—taking into account the changes which have occurred—the
> general line of the international Communist movement and to take all
> the decisions capable of assuring the defense of its unity. . . .[20]

—*i.e.*, to amend the 1960 Declaration and formally to condemn if not
indeed to excommunicate the Chinese.[21] But when, in addition to long
and sharp attacks against the Chinese, Thorez declared that the PCF is
" resolutely in favour of the impending [*prochain, predstoyashchii*]
convocation of an international conference," [22] *Pravda* on October 13
reprinted the latter passage. Apparently Moscow was uncertain just how
rapidly the international meeting could and should be convened. On the
same day that *Pravda* reprinted the Thorez speech, October 13, *Izvestiya*
carried the only Soviet-originated (as opposed to reprinted) statement
echoing the Paraguayan theme that " Communist neutralism " was no
longer possible. An article by the 86-year-old Elena Stasova, a Communist party member since 1898 and the only surviving member of the
1918–1919 Soviet Communist Central Committee [23] (therefore able to
speak of Lenin from personal experience), declared:

> I firmly believe that all members of the Communist parties will give
> a worthy rebuff to the Chinese revisionists who violate what is most
> holy in the contemporary stage, the unity of the world Communist
> and workers' movement. All Communists must consistently struggle
> against the Chinese splitters who try to aggravate the international
> situation and push the world into the abyss of an atomic catastrophe.
> . . . This struggle must be carried on with irreconcilability . . . and
> consistency exactly as it was carried on by V. I. Lenin and our entire
> party in the period of struggle against Trotskyism. I am convinced
> that the Communists of all countries, that the peoples of the whole
> world will not allow themselves to be allured by the clamorous appeals
> of the Chinese revisionists. The difference between Leninist revolu-
> tionary Marxism and their empty, demagogic verbiage is too great.

Shortly after *Pravda* reprinted Thorez's call for an international
conference it began to reprint articles and statements which made no

---

[19] *L'Humanité*, October 9, 1963 ; *Pravda*, October 9, 1963.

[20] *L'Humanité*, October 9, 1963.

[21] *Pravda*, October 9, 1963. *Pravda* also did not report Waldeck Rochet's identical
statement in *L'Humanité*, October 8, 1963, nor the report by Raymond Guyot, *ibid.*
October 7, 1963.   [22] *Pravda*, October 13, 1963.

[23] But her apostolic succession from Lenin had been, to say the least, interrupted. She
ceased to be a CC member in 1920 (*i.e.*, while Lenin was still alive) and returned to
a significant position, member of the Comintern Central Commission, in 1935 (just
before the great Comintern purges). See B. L. [Branko Lazitch], " Un nouveau plan
d'attaque de Moscou: Mao=Trotsky," *Est & Ouest*, XV (N.S.), 308 (November
1–15, 1963), pp. 18–19.

mention of such a meeting, thus indicating that the Russians might not now be so committed to its convocation.[24] However, on October 17 the Soviet October Revolution slogans,[25] while seeming to emphasise Sino-Soviet unity even more than those of the previous year, referred only to the unity of the Soviet and Chinese " peoples " (*i.e.*, not of the parties) on the basis of the 1957 and 1960 Moscow Declarations (*i.e.*, the Soviet, not the Chinese interpretation of them); furthermore, the word " unbreakable " in the 1962 passage about Sino-Soviet unity did not reappear in the 1963 slogans.

The peak of the Soviet offensive was reached by a long editorial in the October *Kommunist*, approved for publication on October 18.[26]

It was by far the strongest, most bitter, and most complete condemnation of the Peking leadership which had yet appeared. The Chinese, it said, have mobilised all their state as well as party organs " to carry on a campaign of unprecedented scope against the fraternal parties." They conduct " increasingly overtly a splitting activity " within them, justifying it by the " utterly anti-Leninist ' theory ' " of the " temporary majority " and the " temporary minority," thus completely revising the 1960 Moscow Declaration's " strict prohibition of factionalist activities within the Communist movement " [27] and establishing " nothing but an anti-Leninist faction in the international Communist movement."

The Chinese, the article continued, are attempting the renaissance of the ideology and practice of the " cult of the individual "; " the internal policy of the Chinese leaders . . . is based on [the cult] " which is " an appeal to support the idolisation of Mao Tse-tung. . . . The Communist movement has been confronted with attempts to substitute ' Mao Tse-tungism ' for Leninism." (This marked the first time that Moscow had retaliated against the violent Chinese anti-Khrushchev campaign with an

[24] A Uruguayan CP declaration appearing before Thorez's speech (*Pravda*, October 12, 1963) expressed confidence that common sense will see that unity is restored at the next international meeting, without specifically calling for such a meeting. The issue of an international CP conference was not mentioned in the resolution of the Ceylonese CP (*ibid*. October 14, 1963); the decision of the CP of Turkey (*ibid*. October 15, 1963); statements by the First Secretary of the CP of Costa Rica (*ibid*. October 17, 1963); by the Australian CP (*ibid*. October 20, 1963); by a leading Argentine Communist (*ibid*. October 25, 1963); by a leading Belgian Communist (*ibid*. October 26, 1963); and a joint PCI-AKEL (Progressive Party of Working People of Cyprus) declaration (*ibid*. October 26, 1963).

[25] *Pravda*, October 17, 1963.

[26] " Marxism-Leninism, the Basis of the Unity of the Communist Movement," *Kommunist*, No. 15, 1963 (passed for the press, October 18, 1963), pp. 13–47, and Document 14, quoted from *CDSP*, XV, 43 (November 20, 1963), pp. 3–14. Three other articles in the same issue, by Morris, Evdokimov and Korionov, add nothing of significance to the editorial. Khrushchev also continued his efforts to improve his relations with the Social Democrats, a policy to which Peking is sharply opposed. See particularly the joint CPSU-SFIO communiqué (" in spite of important divergencies in the area of ideology "), *Le Monde*, November 6, 1963, and the report by Norden to the 4th SED CC Plenum, *Neues Deutschland*, November 4, 1963.

[27] For the inaccuracy of this statement, see p. 19, *supra*.

attack against Mao—another sure sign that the breaking-point had been reached.) Making this accusation more specific, the Soviet article declared that the Chinese

> . . . are trying to replace the general international nature of Leninism with a so-called national, or " nationalised," " Sinified " Marxism . . .

[a move which is]

> an attempt against the very foundations of Marxism-Leninism such as has not appeared since the times of Trotsky. . . .

However (and this was the first time that such a number was given),

> up to the present time 65 Communist parties have condemned the views and actions of the Chinese schismatics. . . .

The article gave a detailed, schematised analysis of the alleged Chinese departure from Marxism-Leninism: in theory that departure is subjectivism, specifically, " Sinification " of Marxism; domestically it is the personality cult; in foreign policy it is

> . . . an orientation toward maintaining international tension, which is [regarded as a favourable atmosphere] for implementing hegemonistic plans, masked in the slogan of " world revolution." . . . A world thermonuclear war . . . it would seem . . . is not a hindrance but . . . a good thing for the revolution. . . .

In the area of relations with socialist countries it is " many-sided co-operation of the socialist countries." Since none of these views can find support in the socialist camp, the Chinese are trying to " assume the position of leader in the . . . national liberation movement "; hence the " racist notes in the Chinese propaganda."

Turning to Chinese methods, the article made the single most serious accusation against the Chinese until that date:

> In order to achieve their ends the Chinese leaders have, to judge by their actions, decided to tear down the international Communist movement and create some kind of new movement under their aegis. They see the shortest route to this in discrediting the CPSU. . . .

The article denounced at length the hostile Chinese attitude towards Communist parties in capitalist countries, specifically their attacks on the peaceful parliamentary transition to socialism. As for the national liberation movement,

> When people [i.e., the Chinese] try to split the world-wide anti-imperialist forces by inciting national and race hostility, and when these people call themselves Marxists and wave the " revolutionary " banner, this is sometimes even more dangerous for the revolutionary liberation movement than even the intrigues of the imperialists. . . .

Specifically,

> Peking's position in the Indian-Chinese conflict was of direct assistance to the imperialists' schemes to drag India into the aggressive blocs. . . .

Finally, the article came much closer than Moscow ever had before to labelling the Chinese as Trotskyites. After quoting many passages from Trotskyite declarations to prove the similarity of aims with Peking, the article concluded:

> The solidarity and the frequently almost literal concurrence of the statements of Chinese theoreticians with those of the Trotskyites fully expose Peking's peculiar " general line " as a rupture with Leninism. . . .

Yet, all this having been said, the article's recommendations for action were once more curiously general and vague, thus again reflecting the tactical uncertainty and hesitation of Soviet leadership. The article did not declare that the Chinese " petty-bourgeois nationalist revolutionary attitude, leftist phrasemongering, and leftist opportunism " was more dangerous than revisionism, but only " no less a danger." It concluded merely that the " Marxist-Leninists " must " launch a struggle—as they previously did in the case of revisionism," designed to cure, not destroy the Chinese, " to have them return to the positions of Marxism-Leninism." It neither called for an international Communist meeting nor specifically denounced " Communist neutralism." Yet implicitly it condemned the latter:

> . . . every Communist, in whatever country he may live and under whatever conditions he may be struggling for his ideals, is duty-bound to fulfil his international obligations: to do everything he can to stop the development of events in the direction desired by Peking. . . .

All these developments led to many articles in the Western press by Moscow correspondents predicting that such an international meeting would convene in Moscow in early November at the anniversary celebrations of the October Revolution.[28]

THE SOVIET RETREAT

The lack of operational conclusions in the *Kommunist* article might only have indicated Soviet hesitation. In fact, however, either shortly before or after its publication Khrushchev must have decided to abandon at least for the present his projected international meeting to excommunicate the Chinese. On October 25 he personally called for an end to Sino-Soviet polemics and said that time would show who was the most correct [29]; *i.e.*, no immediate Soviet excommunication of the Chinese was likely.

The first public sign of why he had decided to retreat came with the publication in *L'Unità* of October 26 and republication of excerpts in

---

[28] See, *e.g.*, an AFP Moscow dispatch in *Le Monde*, October 10, 1963, which reported that Kádár had told Westerners that he had participated at a secret inter-party meeting in Moscow at the end of September to discuss this matter.
[29] *Pravda*, October 27, 1963.

Pravda of October 28 of a long resolution by the Italian Communist Central Committee which explicitly opposed the immediate calling of such an international meeting. Although the pro-Soviet moderates publicly emerged only at this point, their pressure on Khrushchev must have been a major factor in his retreat.

Pravda reprinted the following passage from the Italian resolution:

> Our party considers it, however, necessary to express its reservations regarding the advisability of calling in the near future a new international conference of the Communist and workers' parties regarding the situation which exists at present in the Communist movement. . . .

However, presumably because Moscow disapproved of the PCI's relatively moderate position on this issue, *Pravda* failed to reprint the following:

> An essential element in the calling of such conferences is, however, the examination of the true possibilities which they offer with regard to developing the analysis of the situation and the elaboration of common orientations, with regard to arriving at precise conclusions, and with regard to achieving progress toward unity of the movement. Important conditions for their usefulness and efficiency are therefore the time at which these conferences take place, their adequate preparation, and a clear and realistic grasp of the subjects that are to be tackled and of the objectives that can and must be reached. . . .
>
> Today such a conference could in fact find itself before two alternative solutions both of which would be prejudicial to the Communist movement: either a further exacerbation of present divergences and even a break, or a completely formal and unsatisfactory compromise. It would almost certainly be impossible to tackle in an objective way those new problems of analysis and of elaboration which present themselves today and thereby to arrive at even a partial, but effective, step toward a more solid political and ideological unity of our movement. It is, however, toward this objective that we must work today. But this necessitates that there be created certain conditions and possibilities which do not seem to exist as yet, and it necessitates complex preparatory work.
>
> For progress in this way, and, more generally, for all the developments of the debate between the Communist parties, it is also of particular importance that the method and the tone of the discussion be such as not to exacerbate the divergencies, such as not to push toward breaches and ruptures, but such as to favour the true and objective confrontation of the positions.
>
> Today it would certainly be completely utopian if one did not see that in the present conditions the debate on the divergencies in actions and the struggle for the correct political line cannot but assume also aspects of a lively polemic. Another thing, however, and one that is absolutely to be condemned, are the insults, the curses, and the accusations of betrayal which the Chinese have been the first to launch with regard to other Communist parties and with regard to the Communist Party of the Soviet Union, which has made, and is making, the

major contribution to the cause of the socialist revolution, of peace, of the liberation of the peoples. Another thing is the appeals, the schismatic action, the inadmissible factionalist activities to which the Chinese comrades have recourse; another thing, and equally to be condemned, is the opportunistic deformation of the theses and of the line of other parties which seems to have become a constant method in the polemic of the Chinese comrades, who have had recourse exactly to this method in order to attack and to calumniate our party. A reason for serious preoccupation is finally the fact that the exacerbation of the polemic went so far that also certain state relations between the socialist countries have been attacked and harmed. . . .

Furthermore, as has been outlined above,[30] the Italian Communists were tending towards at least the appearance, and perhaps even gradually more than that, of autonomy from Moscow; this PCI resolution also reiterated this line in words which also were not reprinted in *Pravda*.[31] There was also one report that Togliatti had sent Pajetta and Alicata to Moscow to try to influence Khrushchev toward moderation.[32]

The general position of a second pro-Soviet moderate, Gomułka, had already been expressed, although not explicitly on the question of an international meeting, in early October. In a speech which strongly but not polemically criticised the Chinese he centred his objections, as did the Italians later, on their anti-Soviet post-test ban treaty polemics whose volume and bitterness he contrasted unfavourably with the brief French statement. Finally, he supported the call in the Soviet September 21 statement for an end to polemics, but the whole context of his remarks made clear that he did so genuinely, rather than, as had Moscow, in part for tactical reasons.[33]

The third major pro-Soviet moderate party, the Rumanians, in early November publicly indicated its opposition to a Sino-Soviet rupture and its preference for a carefully prepared international meeting. An

30 See pp. 73–79, *supra*.
31 An article by Otto Kuusinen, " How Lenin Cured the Infantile Disorder ' Leftism ' in the Cominform," *Pravda*, November 6, 1963, appears to contain esoteric criticism of the PCI position. An article by Luigo Longo, " The Historical Role and Significance of the Struggle of the Communist Party of the Soviet Union," *World Marxist Review*, VI, 11 (November 1963) (passed for the press, Russian edition, October 19, 1963), pp. 3–11, took a strong anti-Chinese and pro-Soviet stand, but omitted any mention of an international meeting or of the possibility of " Communist neutralism."
32 Tanner from Moscow in *The New York Times*, November 20, 1963.
33 *Trybuna Ludu*, October 1, 1963. The speech was on the occasion of a state visit by Ulbricht, whose speech the same day (*Neues Deutschland*, October 1, 1963) characteristically did not mention the Sino-Soviet issue at all. The joint communiqué (*Trybuna Ludu* and *Neues Deutschland*, October 2, 1963) echoed Gomułka's views. A series of anti-Chinese polemics in *Polityka* ceased after October 12, as did such polemics in other PZPR organs. See in general Underwood from Warsaw in the *New York Times*, November 2, 1963; ok. [Bogdan Osadczuk-Korab], " Sondierungen polnischer Kommunisten im Ausland," *Neue Zürcher Zeitung*, November 3, 1963, and " Polens Vermittlungsversuch im Ideologiekonflikt," *ibid*. November 11, 1963. See also the Polish greeting message to Peking on the occasion of the Chinese National Day, NCNA English Peking, October 1, 1963 (CB 719, October 17, 1963, pp. 12–13).

article by Rumanian Premier Ion Gheorghe Maurer, which appeared in early November not only in the Rumanian press [34] but also in the Soviet-controlled *Problems of Peace and Socialism* and thus must have had previous Soviet approval, referred approvingly to the British CP proposal to end polemics and resume bilateral CPSU/CCP talks

> . . . [in order] that all parties should consider the necessity to start preparations for a world conference next year. . . .[35]

Although Maurer clearly albeit not explicitly criticised the tone and content of the Chinese polemics, and supported the Soviet policy positions, he stressed the independence and increasing "diversity" of all parties and repeated the Rumanian position on CMEA.[36]

These statements by pro-Soviet moderate parties were accompanied by Soviet or directly Soviet-inspired moves which made increasingly probable that Moscow was considering the abandonment of its original intent to hold an international meeting in the near future to excommunicate the Chinese. *Pravda's* November 2 account of a joint French-Dutch Communist Party communiqué [37] altered a sentence which repeated practically word for word the passage in the PCF resolution on the timing of an international conference (which *Pravda* had omitted on October 9); *Pravda* translated "*dans les meilleurs délais*" ("with the least possible delay") as "*naibolee podkhodyashchii moment*" ("the most appropriate moment")—a significant difference. On the same day, November 2, the SED leader Albert Norden echoed Khrushchev's call for an end to public polemics.[38]

On November 3 *Pravda* published a long article by Alvaro Cunhal, Secretary-General of the Portuguese Communist Party, which, contrary to the September 24 Portuguese CP resolution, made no mention of the need for calling an international conference, of a ban against factionalism, of dogmatism being the main danger, or of Yugoslavia. Cunhal's criticism of the Chinese was an expression more of regret than defiance, and he expressed confidence that the Sino-Soviet differences would be

---

[34] *Scinteia*, November 4, 1963, and *Lupta de Clasa*, No. 10, October 1963.

[35] *World Marxist Review*, VI, 11, November 1963 (passed for the press, Russian edition, October 19, 1963), pp. 12–21, at p. 21. See also C. K. [Christian Kind], " Rumänien zwischen Moskau und Peking," *Neue Zürcher Zeitung*, November 9, 1963. One cannot argue (from the October 19 passed for the press date) that Moscow had abandoned its extremist position as of that date since the same issue (*World Marxist Review, op. cit.*, pp. 58–60) included the key passages of the Portuguese and Paraguayan resolutions. In November 1963 Rumania was the only Communist state which voted in favour of instead of abstaining on a Latin American proposal in the UN General Assembly for a nuclear-free zone in Latin America. For differing views of its motivation, see Philippe Ben from New York in *Le Monde*, November 22, 1963, and M. B. [Max Beer] from New York in *Neue Zürcher Zeitung*, November 21, 1963.

[36] For his position on CMEA see pp. 185–186, *supra*.

[37] *L'Humanité*, October 30, 1963.

[38] Norden to the 4th SED CC Plenum, *Neues Deutschland*, November 2, 1963.

overcome.[39] Subsequently, informed Communist journalists in Moscow began to report that there would be no international meeting at the November 7 celebration of the October Revolution anniversary after all.[40] Attacks against China in the Soviet press declined in length and fierceness.[41] The November 7 celebrations not only failed to result in an international meeting [42] but also were characterised by a less hostile Soviet line towards Peking. Podgorny, the main speaker, said that there were no objective reasons preventing a Sino-Soviet reconciliation and reiterated the Soviet proposal that polemics be ended. Although he did declare that the Chinese were using " impermissible " methods against the Soviets, he did not mention Albania or Yugoslavia; and Khrushchev declared that he was sure that Sino-Soviet agreement would come " sooner or later." [43]

Finally, on November 15 the head of the Swedish Communist Party publicly declared upon his return from Moscow that there would be no international conference in the near future because careful preparation for it was required.[44]

In retrospect, it seems likely that Khrushchev must have concluded in mid-October that an international meeting of the type he had envisaged would not produce a sufficiently large majority for his purposes. (There is no evidence that he encountered any internal Soviet opposition to this.) One of the major factors in his conclusion was the opposition of the pro-Soviet moderates to such a meeting.[45]

THE CHINESE RESPONSE

Beginning in mid-October Peking began to make some relatively conciliatory gestures toward Moscow, presumably in order to demonstrate its own organisationally correct position and thus to encourage the moderates to put pressure on Moscow. A new Sino-Soviet rail agreement was signed,[46] presumably making incidents like the Naushki one more unlikely. In a long interview with Reuter's, Chou En-lai said that the Sino-Soviet differences were between parties and would not result in

39 Alvaro Cunhal, " The USSR—the Main Bulwark of World Revolution," *Pravda*, November 3, 1963.
40 Rsto Bajalski from Moscow in *Borba*, October 21, 1963; Giuseppe Boffa from Moscow in *L'Unità*, November 2, 1963.
41 Note particularly the difference between *Agitator*, No. 20, October 1963, and No. 21, November 1963 (passed for the press October 29, 1963).
42 No foreign Communist leaders were listed in *Pravda*, November 8, 1963, as having been present at the November 7 parade and demonstration in Red Square.
43 *Pravda*, November 7, 1963 (his remarks indicated that the CPSU had formally proposed the ending of polemics to the CCP); Khrushchev at the Kremlin banquet, *ibid.* November 8, 1963, where he had a public and cordial conversation with the Chinese ambassador (Boffa from Moscow in *L'Unità*, November 8, 1963).
44 AFP dispatch from Stockholm in *Le Monde*, November 16, 1963.
45 *Cf.* Tanner from Moscow in *The New York Times*, November 20, 1963.
46 *The New York Times*, October 15, 1963.

breaking off party or state relations. As to the 1962 Sinkiang border incidents, he said that " the situation has recently become better." [47] The Chinese speaker at the November 6 anniversary meeting of the October Revolution stressed the unity of the Soviet and Chinese peoples. However, the Chinese indicators were contradictory. The November 7 Chinese speaker reiterated the familiar Chinese ideological theses, as did the outwardly cordial Chinese message of greeting to Moscow, and the attending Chinese dignitaries at the ceremonies were second-rank.[48] Albanian articles [49] and Chinese reprinting of Albanian and Malayan Communist articles and of anti-Chinese Soviet attacks [50] also indicated that Peking's softening was formal rather than real.

The true Chinese response to the early October Soviet offensive was much more clearly shown by Peking's publication on October 21, after a pause of several weeks, of the fourth in the series of long articles replying to the Soviet July 14 Open Letter, entitled " Apologists of Neo-Colonialism." [51]

This fourth article gave the most extreme ideological version to date of the Chinese attack against the Russians on the national liberation issue :

> . . . the leaders of the CPSU dare not completely discard the slogans of support for the national liberation movement, and at times, for the sake of their own interests, they even take certain measures which create the appearance of support. But if we probe to the essence and consider their views and policies over a number of years, we see clearly

47 Reuter's from Peking, The Times (London), October 14, 1963.
48 Peking Review, VI, 45 (November 8, 1963), pp. 5–7, and SCMP 3098, November 12, 1963, pp. 34–35. Note the speaker's (Wu Yu-chang) reference to 13 socialist countries, i.e., not including Yugoslavia. See also Shih Tung-hsiang, " Lenin and Stalin on the Road of the October Revolution," Red Flag, No. 21, November 7, 1963, and Peking Review, VI, 45 (November 8, 1963), pp. 7–15, and " Long Live the Great October Revolution!" People's Daily, November 7, 1963 (SCMP 3099, November 13, 1963, pp. 28–31).
49 Speech by Balluku, Zëri i Popullit, November 5, 1963; Çarçani at the November 7 Tirana October Revolution celebration, ibid., November 8, 1963; " New Deeds of Treason of the Renegade Tito," ibid. November 9, 1963; Ndreçi Plasari, " Historic Turning Point in the History of Our Party and Country," ibid. November 10, 1963, and reportage on the pro-Chinese Belgian weekly La Voix du Peuple, ibid. November 4, 12, 1963, and the pro-Chinese Brazilian one, A Classe Operaria, ibid. November 17, 1963.
50 On October 28, 1963, People's Daily reprinted the October 4 Albanian editorial devoted to the July 14 Soviet Open Letter, " N. Khrushchev Has Openly Raised the Banner of Split and Betrayal " (SCMP 3091, October 31, 1963, p. 22); " Anti-China Outbursts in the Soviet Press Become More Nasty and Fantastic," People's Daily, October 31 and November 1, 1963 (SCMP 3094, November 5, 1963, pp. 37–38, and SCMP 3095, November 6, 1963, pp. 43–44, including lists of the Soviet articles reprinted); " 46th Anniversary of the Great October Socialist Revolution," Malayan Monitor, XVI, 10 (October 31, 1963), pp. 6–11, reprinted in People's Daily, November 14, 1963 (SCMP 3103, November 19, 1963, p. 21).
51 " Apologists of Neo-Colonialism," Comment on the Open Letter of the Central Committee of the CPSU (4), " by the Editorial Departments of People's Daily and Red Flag," People's Daily and Red Flag, October 21, 1963, Peking Review, VI, 43 (October 25, 1963), pp. 6–15, and Document 15.

that their attitude towards the liberation struggles of the oppressed nations of Asia, Africa, and Latin America is a passive or scornful or negative one, and that they serve as apologists for neo-colonialism. . . .

Attacking Khrushchev personally, it indicated that he wished " to step into the shoes of William II . . . in propagating the ' theory of the Yellow Peril.' " Turning to the Congo question, it declared that the

> . . . leaders of the CPSU . . . not only . . . refused to give active support to the Congolese armed struggle against colonialism, but they were anxious to co-operate with U.S. imperialism in putting out the spark in the Congo. . . .
>
> In 1961 the leaders of the CPSU persuaded Gizenga to attend the Congolese parliament. . . .
>
> Clearly these wrong policies of the leadership of the CPSU rendered U.S. imperlialism a great service in its aggression against the Congo. Lumumba was murdered, Gizenga was imprisoned, many other patriots were persecuted, and the Congolese struggle for national independence suffered a setback. Does the leadership of the CPSU feel no responsibility for this?

The article concluded with a call to the national liberation movement to line up with Peking against Moscow and to eradicate Soviet influence over it:

> . . . if the national liberation movement is to achieve complete victory it must form a solid alliance with the revolutionary working-class movement, draw a clear line of demarcation between itself and the revisionists who serve the imperialists and colonialists, and firmly eradicate their influence. . . .

Furthermore, in a phrase ominously reminiscent of the 1949 Cominform Resolution, the article for the first time extended an anathema the Chinese had previously applied only to the Yugoslavs to include, implicitly, Khrushchev: " The revisionists are agents of imperialism who have hidden themselves among the ranks of the international working class movement."

This fourth article was particularly violent on the question of Soviet aid to India:

> . . . here their [the Soviet] ulterior motives are especially clear. India tops the list of newly independent countries to which the Soviet Union gives economic aid. This aid is obviously intended to encourage the Nehru government in its policies directed against communism, against the people, and against socialist countries. . . .

On November 1 Peking continued its attack against Soviet policy toward India under the expressive title, " The Truth About How the Leaders of the CPSU Have Allied Themselves with India Against China." [52] Ostensibly analysing but in fact distorting a Soviet article of

[52] *People's Daily*, November 2, 1963, and *Peking Review*, VI, 45 (November 8, 1963), pp. 18–27. For analysis, see Kx. [Ernst Kux], " Polemik Pekings gegen die sowjetische Haltung im Himalajakrieg," *Neue Zürcher Zeitung*, November 10, 1963.

225

September 19 which had attacked Chinese policy toward India, reiterated the Soviet support of " a peaceful solution," and declared that the Sino-Indian conflict had only helped " reactionary forces in India," [53] and taking another step in the ideological escalation of Sino-Soviet controversy on the Indian issue, the November 2 Chinese article declared :

> The Soviet leaders have long allied themselves with the Indian reactionaries to oppose socialist China. This article [the September 21 one] marks their advance from their previous attitude of feigning neutrality while actually favouring the Indian reactionaries to alignment with U.S. imperialism in openly supporting them. . . .

It gave a detailed chronological Chinese version of this aspect of the Sino-Soviet dispute. Its most significant feature was its assertion that Khrushchev had on October 13 and 14, 1963, one week before the Sino-Indian conflict broke out, told the Chinese Ambassador in Moscow that China's information on an impending Indian attack was correct. The article added (probably correctly) that the Soviets

> . . . during the Caribbean crisis . . . spoke a few seemingly fair words out of considerations of expediency, but when the crisis was over, they went back on their words. . . .

It went on to declare that the Russians had published the September 19 article

> . . . because they want to exploit the Sino-Indian boundary question to sow dissension between China and other Asian-African countries, divert the people in Asia and Africa from the struggle against imperialism, and cover up the U.S. imperialists' aggressive and warlike activities. . . .

Finally, the article drew a general conclusion from Soviet policy toward India :

> The stand and policy of the Soviet leaders on the Sino-Indian boundary question amply prove that they have betrayed the Chinese people, the Soviet people, the people of all the countries in the socialist camp, the Indian people, and all the oppressed peoples and nations. It is becoming clearer and clearer that the Soviet leaders no longer consider the imperialists headed by the United States and the reactionaries of all countries to be their enemy. It is the Marxist-Leninists, the revolutionary people, and China in particular who are their enemy.
>
> We would like to advise the Soviet leaders not to rejoice too soon. Revolutionary China can never be isolated. The more brazenly you collaborate with all imperialists and reactionaries, the more you isolate yourselves. China cannot be discredited because the truth is on China's side. . . .

Luther could not have been more defiant.

---

[53] " A Serious Hotbed of Tension in Asia," *Pravda*, September 19, 1963, quoted from *CDSP*, XV, 38 (October 16, 1963), pp. 18–19.

A little more than two weeks after the November 2 Chinese article, on November 19, Peking published the fifth in the series of long Chinese ideological answers to the Soviet July 14 Open Letter. Entitled "Two Different Lines on the Question of War and Peace," this article [54] dealt with perhaps the most important element of conflict in the whole Sino-Soviet dispute: the question of thermonuclear weapons and world-wide Communist strategy. Its defensiveness against the Soviet charge that China wanted nuclear war demonstrated how effective the accusation had been. Its implicit appeal to the Red Army against Khrushchev showed Peking's continuing fury. The tone and content of the article was as violent, if not more so, than any of its predecessors. Indeed, in some respects the substantive attack against Khrushchev reached new heights of vilification. Take, for example, perhaps the most insulting passage:

> . . . the U.S. imperialists have not become beautiful angels in spite of Khrushchev's Bible-reading and psalm-singing; they have not turned into compassionate Buddhas in spite of Khrushchev's prayers and incense-burning. However hard Khrushchev tries to serve the U.S. imperialists, they show not the slightest appreciation. They continue to expose their own peace camouflage by fresh and numerous activities of aggression and war, and thus they continue to slap Khrushchev in the face and reveal the bankruptcy of his ridiculous theories prettifying imperialism. The lot of the willing apologists of U.S. imperialism is indeed a sorry one. . . .

Coming eighteen months after the Chinese esoteric articles [55] identifying Khrushchev's policies with those of Kautsky and Bernstein this article devoted much space, replete with appropriate quotations and footnotes, to elaborating these charges. Its only contribution to illuminating the history of Sino-Soviet relations, or at least the polemics about them, was its accusation that " some comrades " (*i.e.*, Khrushchev) were unwilling to support Mao sufficiently against Chiang Kai-shek because they feared the latter's American support.

The main part of the article, however, was devoted to by far the most explicit, extreme, and logically consistent exposition yet published of the Chinese position on thermonuclear war. Of course this does not mean that it was entirely an accurate statement: the article's charge that not Peking but Moscow favours thermonuclear risk-taking might be somewhat difficult to document. Even so, the Chinese arguments should not be entirely discounted because of their highly polemic nature.

54 " Two Different Lines on the Question of War and Peace," " by the Editorial Departments of *People's Daily* and *Red Flag*," *People's Daily* and *Red Flag*, November 19, 1963 and *Peking Review*, VI, 47 (November 22, 1963), pp. 6–16.
55 See pp. 38–41, *supra*.

"Lenin and Stalin are right and Khrushchev is wrong," the Chinese argument began. Wars of national liberation are inevitable (Khrushchev had said the same in January 1961).[56]

"The revisionist line," the article continued, "serves to increase the danger of a new war." In explaining this thesis that Khrushchev, not Mao, is a danger to world peace the article emphasised more than ever before the importance of the thermonuclear issue in Mao's opposition to Khrushchev:

> . . . Nuclear fetishism and nuclear blackmail are the theoretical basis and guiding policy of modern revisionism. . . . The heart of the theory of the leaders of the CPSU on war and peace is their thesis that the emergence of nuclear weapons has changed everything and has changed the laws of class struggle. . . .

This Soviet thesis means, the article went on, that

> . . . with the emergence of nuclear weapons, the contradictions between the socialist and the imperialist camps . . . between the proletariat and the bourgeoisie in the capitalist countries, and . . . between the oppressed nations and imperialism have all disappeared. The world no longer has any class contradictions. They regard the contradictions in the contemporary world as boiling down to a single contradiction; that is, their fictitious contradiction between the so-called common survival of imperialism and the oppressed classes and nations on the one hand and their total destruction on the other. . . .
>
> This is the philosophy of out-and-out renegades. It is a shameless statement, to be found only in the confessions of renegades. . . .

In other words, the Soviet Union, an industrialised country with atomic weapons, whose revolution had been successful more than forty years before, is much more fearful of atomic war with the superior thermonuclear power of the United States than is the non-industrialised, agrarian China, whose revolution is less than fifteeen years old.

Clearly China was trying to recover the peace issue and thus deprive the Soviet Union of what had proven a most useful cudgel with which to belabour Peking after the signature of the nuclear test ban treaty. This was Peking's answer:

> . . . the oppressed peoples and nations can achieve liberation only by their own resolute revolutionary struggle, and . . . no one else can do it for them . . . socialist countries must not use nuclear weapons to support the people's wars of national liberation and revolutionary civil wars and have no need to do so. . . .
> . . . in the hands of a socialist country nuclear weapons must always be defensive weapons for resisting imperialist nuclear threats. A socialist

[56] N. S. Khrushchev, "For New Victories of the World Communist Movement," *Kommunist*, No. 1, January 1961, pp. 3–37, and *World Marxist Review*, IV, 1 (January 1961).

> country absolutely must not be the first to use nuclear weapons, nor
> should it in any circumstances play with them or engage in nuclear
> blackmail and nuclear gambling. . . .

Easy to say, one might think, when one has no nuclear weapons to use.
The Chinese adduced as a specific example of their forbearance China's
fighting " side by side " with the North Koreans " so that the Soviet
Union might stay in the second line."

The article made a clear albeit implicit appeal to Soviet military
leaders, particularly of the Red Army ground forces. " Khrushchev's
military ideas based on nuclear fetishism and nuclear blackmail are
entirely wrong. He maintains that ' the air force and the navy have
lost their former importance,' and of course those units and men having
combat duties on the ground are even less significant." His " whole set
of military theories," which " run completely counter to Marxist-Leninist
teachings on war and the army," would mean " disintegrating the army
and disarming oneself morally." On the contrary, the article continued,
as Mao said in 1938, " ' political power grows out of the barrel of a gun,' "
and now as well as before " the army is the chief component of state
power." Of course one must negotiate with imperialists, but not by
capitulation :

> . . . The more Khrushchev retreats before the imperialists and the more
> he begs, the more the appetite of the imperialists will grow. Khrushchev
> . . . is always an unrequited lover and too oft a laughing stock. . . .

How much more insulting could the Chinese be?

SOME TENTATIVE CONCLUSIONS

The escalation of the Sino-Soviet dispute continued in its previous
cyclical fashion during 1962 and 1963. In 1963 when the Sino-Indian
border fighting, the Cuban crisis, and the partial test ban treaty all
sharply intensified Sino-Soviet differences, the dispute developed from
esoteric and ideological polemics to overt and political-military conflict.
The Chinese, their weakened military potential counterbalanced by the
thermonuclear stalemate, concentrated with considerable success on the
national liberation struggle and on factional activity within the international Communist movement. They began actively supporting pro-
Chinese factions within Communist parties and helping to establish new ones when possible. Undoubtedly, by the end of 1963 the
Chinese were continuing to win support; the Russians continued to
lose support. The Chinese also began to set up new Afro-Asian international front organisations while continuing to disrupt the old ones.
The Soviet Union entered into a post-Cuban crisis strategic pause
vis-à-vis the United States and combined it with the test ban treaty

to prevent the proliferation of nuclear arms to the Chinese. Moscow was certainly no more anxious to see Peking gain nuclear weapons than Washington was to give nuclear weapons to Paris, with whom Peking was showing signs of improved relations. Both the Russians and the Chinese demonstrated that they were prepared to deal with " imperialist " powers (as the Americans and the French were to deal with Communist ones) against each other. The postwar bipolar world was making way for a differentiated multi-power structure.

Faced with Chinese gains, the Russians appeared to resort to their most obvious weapon—the precipitation by Moscow of an open, public, total rupture with Peking. Yet in the course of their losing struggle with China, the Russians had felt compelled to allow some of their less unconditional allies (specifically the Polish, Rumanian, and Italian parties) a degree of autonomy which in September-October 1963 these parties (not wishing to endanger their newly acquired manoeuvrability) used to block, at least temporarily, the first apparent move by Moscow towards total rupture. Thus the Soviet dilemma became more clearly apparent and less likely to be solved.

Marxism-Leninism has been one of the last and greatest products of nineteenth-century Promethean optimism. None of its Promethean dreams was more daring or, it now appears, more rapidly doomed to collapse than " proletarian internationalism." Stalin replaced it by Soviet nationalism, and China has now forced its abandonment. This was not surprising, since ours is an age of nationalism. The successful revolt of China and the consequent end of Soviet hegemony over the international Communist movement marks the beginning of decolonisation in the one area of the world where it seemed still to maintain itself successfully—within the Communist states and parties. Nor will the Communist world now be divided only into spheres of Soviet and Chinese hegemony; on the contrary, the rift has now attained a dynamic of its own out of which only polycentrism can result. In desperation Goethe's *Sorcerer's Apprentice* cried out: " The spirits that I summoned I cannot now rid myself of again! " Nor can Khrushchev.

APPENDIX

SINO-SOVIET ECONOMIC RELATIONS

Economic considerations have by now lost some of their earlier significance as an indicator of and a factor in Sino-Soviet relations; the political aspects are both more publicised and, as the dispute has intensified, more important. The Chinese have always been exceptionally reluctant to publish meaningful data on any aspect of their economic situation, and in foreign trade Moscow and Peking continue to conceal the nature and full extent of their economic ties. Foreign trade or loan statistics do not give adequate evidence concerning China's over-all trade deficit with the Soviet Union. Even so, the basic trend seems sufficiently clear.

From the very beginning Sino-Soviet economic relations were characterised by features unknown in Moscow's dealings with other Communist states. Stalin reportedly negotiated directly with the Manchurian leader Kao Kang in July 1949 concerning the restoration of Soviet-dismantled industries in Manchuria,[1] but the final treaty of April 1950 [2] designated the contracting parties as China and the Soviet Union. Thus the Chinese were temporarily forced to assume the obligations which Manchuria incurred as a result of her relatively weaker bargaining position.

From then on Soviet machines, equipment, and other industrial goods were exchanged for industrial and agricultural raw materials from China. Sino-Soviet trade was more closely geared to Chinese than to Soviet requirements. Some of the Soviet deliveries, however, were simply transfers of captured Chinese assets and reparations or of military aid consigned from stocks stored during the Korean War. These items reportedly took the form of loans to be settled by shipment of Chinese goods.[3]

[1] Chin Szu-k'ai, *Communist China's Relations with the Soviet Union, 1949–1957*, Communist China Problem Research Series No. 26 (unpublished) (Hong Kong: Union Research Institute, 1961), p. 4.

[2] In April 1950, the U.S.S.R. and China signed the first trade agreement, which was preceded by a $300 million loan granted in February of the same year for the procurement of construction materials. " Outlook on Sino-Soviet Economic Co-operation," *Ajia Kenkyu (Data for Asia Research)* (Tokyo) No. 315, pp. 2–10 and JPRS 14,351 July 2, 1962, p. 6. For details of the agreements, *Vneshnaya Torgovlya* (Moscow), October 1959, p. 6 and September 1961, p. 5, quoted by Marshall I. Goldman in " Sino-Soviet Trade: A Barometer," *Problems of Communism*, XI, 6 (November–December 1962), p. 47.

[3] " Outlook on Sino-Soviet . . .," *op. cit.*, p. 9.

Similar terms were also envisaged for the compensation of the Soviet economic interests in China relinquished between 1952–1954. Yet these arrangements already bore the signs of an uneasy relationship and did not seem to stem from a long-term co-ordinated programme. Legal claims remained unsettled, values were never properly estimated by mutual agreement, and the whole procedure reflected temporising, particularly on the part of China.

Khrushchev's visit to China in the autumn of 1954, probably his first major effort to improve Sino-Soviet relations, produced a series of Soviet concessions to China's insistence on formal [4] emancipation from Soviet technical tutelage, the liquidation of Sino-Soviet joint enterprises, and so on. Those demands in themselves were not unique but given the complete economic dependence of China on the Soviet Union they must have appeared at least irritating for the latter. Thus the temporary satisfaction of one party became the source of resentment for the other and only aggravated rather than eliminated the frictions.

Table I

SOVIET-CHINESE TRADE

(in million U.S. dollars)

Year	Soviet Exports to China	Soviet Imports from China	Turnover	Balance Soviet	China
(1)	(2)	(3)	(4)	(5)	(6)
1950	388·25	188·25	576·50	200·00	
1951	476·25	332·00	808·25	144·25	
1952	554·25	413·75	968·00	140·50	
1953	697·50	474·75	1172·25	222·75	
1954	759·25	578·25	1337·50	181·00	
1955	742·50	643·50	1386·00	99·00	
1956	733·00	764·25	1497·25		31·25
1957	544·00	738·25	1282·25		194·25
1958	633·90	881·20	1515·10		247·30
1959	954·45	1100·25	2054·70		145·80
1960	817·00	848·00	1665·00		31·00
1961	367·33	551·44	918·77		184·11
1962	233·21	515·82	749·03		282·61

Total surpluses..987·50   1,116·32

Sources:

1950-1960: " Zu den chinesisch-sowjetischen Wirtschaftsbeziehungen," *Der Ostblock und die Entwicklungsländer* (Hannover: Verlag für Literatur und Zeitgeschehen GmbH), No. 7, April 1962, p. 47.

1961: *Vneshnaya Torgovlya SSSR za 1961 god* (Moscow, 1962), pp. 179, 185.

1962: *Vneshnaya Torgovlya SSSR za 1962 god* (Moscow, 1963), pp. 182 and 187.

---

[4] Khrushchev's visit produced the first formal agreement on scientific and technical co-operation. Until that time, the *ad hoc* Soviet assistance was *de jure* unilateral

While Khrushchev felt it politic to make these concessions, he may well, considering Soviet industrial and financial capacity in the early fifties, have considered Soviet generosity toward China a unique and heavy sacrifice. Without Soviet industrial and technical assistance China's First Five-Year Plan could never have been launched. One only has to contrast Soviet aid to China at this time with Moscow's economic exploitation of East Europe to see what a relatively privileged position Peking enjoyed. No doubt Moscow's compliance with China's demands was rightly recognised by the latter both as a result of the predicament in which the Soviet leadership temporarily found itself during the first years following Stalin's death and the dubious benefit, with all its consequences, of enforced generosity.

The exact nature of Soviet-Chinese economic relations during the fifties is still a matter for conjecture. Soviet foreign trade statistics and the officially announced Soviet loans do not reveal the full picture.

A constant Soviet delivery surplus, $987.5 million by 1955 (according to published Soviet foreign trade statistics), characterised Sino-Soviet trade through 1955. (We know little or nothing of prices.)

From 1955 to 1956 the Chinese began to repay their debts by substantially increasing their deliveries, whereas the Soviets reduced their exports. For that reason these two years are generally regarded as the watershed of present Sino-Soviet trade relations. Even if we assume, however, that the above data cover the full extent of both goods exchange and financial transactions (which we cannot),[5] the fallacy of such an arbitrary, mechanical explanation is clear. To view this period as a dividing line in Soviet-Chinese trade relations one must assume that the pre-1956 situation was basically harmonious and unilaterally advantageous for Peking because of her constant import surplus. The truth is, however, that the Chinese were bitterly disappointed at the economic treatment they received during and after the Korean War; and the decline in Soviet deliveries, just when China was suffering from the dislocations of agricultural collectivisation, only aggravated their disenchantment even though the significance of the drop in trade was largely symbolic. This was particularly so since given China's size, a $100 million-odd alteration in her trade balance can hardly be regarded as a major change. Furthermore during the same period the Soviet Union launched a massive aid programme to the neutralist countries (mainly Egypt, Indonesia, and India) thereby significantly re-allocating its foreign aid resources, a step which must have infuriated the Chinese leadership and further worsened Sino-Soviet relations.

5 These figures, although undoubtedly some of the more reliable ones, should be treated with reservation. By the end of 1960 China's cumulative trade deficit was $338 million, which was re-financed through a Soviet loan of $320 million granted in April 1961 (*Vneshnaya Torgovlya*, Moscow, May 17, 1961). The pro-Chinese Japanese *Ajia Kenkyu*, after mentioning the above credit as well as the $40 million value of 500,000 tons of sugar delivered to China, sums up the total Chinese indebtedness by the end of 1960 as "about $900 million" ("Sino-Soviet Economic Relations during the Second Five-Year Plan," *Ajia Kenkyu*, No. 316, April 1962 and JPRS 14,351, July 2, 1962, p. 21). A third source referring only to industrial equipment gives a $2,152 million Chinese indebtedness by 1957 as the amount acknowledged by the Chinese Communists, while referring to industrial equipment alone ("The China Market: 1962," *Current Scene* (Hong Kong), II, 14 (June 1, 1963), p. 3); this would leave approximately $1,500 million at the end of 1960. The discrepancies ($338, $900, $1,500 millions, all referring to 1960) are much too broad to be acceptable for an analysis of China's indebtedness. Furthermore, the statistics give a Chinese surplus since 1962 which can only be explained by assuming a pre-1950 Soviet excess in deliveries.

In the case of Moscow's policy and gestures toward India,[6] which the Chinese were watching with utmost sensitivity, a brief chronological comparison of Sino-Soviet and Soviet-Indian trade relations seems appropriate, even though the magnitude of India's exchange of goods with the Soviet Union was until recently not in the same digital category.

Table II

DEVELOPMENT OF SOVIET-INDIAN TRADE COMPARED WITH SOVIET EXPORTS TO CHINA

(in million U.S. dollars)

		Soviet-Indian Trade		Soviet-Chinese Trade
Year	Turnover	Soviet Imports	Soviet Exports	Soviet Exports
(1)	(2)	(3)	(4)	(5)
1955	11·6	5·2	6·4	742·5
1956	57·8	26·4	31·4	733·0
1957	84·5	36·8	47·7	544·0
1958	94·8	49·0	45·8	633·9
1959	101·0	63·2	37·7	954·5
1960	91·0	63·0	28·0	817·0
1961	119·0	65·5	53·5	367·3
1962	168·0	83·0	85·0	233·2
1963	210·0	—	—	—

Sources:

For China: same as Table I.

India:

1955-58: *Records and Statistics: Quarterly Bulletin of Eastern Economist* (New Delhi: Asia Press), X, 4 (August 1959), p. 220

1959-60: *Ibid.*, XII, 4 (August 1961), p. 216

1961: *Ibid.*, XIII, 3 (May 1962), p. 149

1962: Government of India, Department of Statistics, New Delhi, *Monthly Abstract of Statistics*, XVI, 2 (February 1963), p. 36, table 22, column 21, and p. 37, table 23, column 21.

1963: *Baltimore Sun*, October 11, 1962 (estimated).

Soviet exports to China thus declined markedly from 1956 through 1958, while Soviet-Indian trade jumped more than 500 per cent in 1956 and nearly doubled again by 1958. Similarly, the temporary upsurge of Soviet exports to China during 1959 and 1960 again coincided with a simultaneous slump in exports to India. The third and present phase comprised a more than 50 per cent decline in Soviet exports to China during 1961 paralleled by a near doubling of exports to India; the same trend continued during 1962. All this was made much more unfavourable to China within the context of her domestic economic crisis.

[6] Between 1955 and 1962, the Soviet Union granted loans to India amounting to $800 million (*New Age*, September 23, 1962), an amount close to the excess of Soviet deliveries over imports from China prior to 1955.

Peking's gradual post-1957 realisation that no meaningful Soviet economic support [7] could be counted upon resulted in its search for indigenous resources to continue its previous high rate of growth. Together with the drastic organisational measures promulgated in the " great leap " period, it was announced that China would accelerate her economic expansion. There was a clear ideological connotation that China had found a short cut to build communism. However, the economic policy of the " great leap " period, when reduced to its essence, signalled only the first open attempt by Peking to mitigate its dependency upon the Soviet Union rather than the much advertised rapid acceleration in economic growth.

By this time the international situation began to develop more favourably for China. After 1957 the sanctioning effect of the Western embargo on Communist China began to fade away while the spirit of Bandung was still alive.

Trade with the West and the rest of Asia was also rapidly expanding by 1958, and Peking probably hoped to import from the West those items not available from the Communist bloc.

Thus the three main economic features of the " great leap forward " were:
1. Substitution of labour-intensive for capital-intensive construction.
2. Emphasis on small units and native methods of production, thus reducing the need of Soviet deliveries and technical assistance.
3. Substitution of intensified political and ideological agitation for material incentives in an effort to improve the country's foreign trade capacity by curtailing the amount of domestically consumed agricultural products.

Clearly these measures can hardly be considered the instruments of a large-scale economic offensive even if one attributes complete incompetence to the Chinese leadership. For this reason the 1958-60 period should be interpreted rather as a transparent and desperate attempt to make a virtue out of necessity. This is not to imply that the evaporation of the Soviet export surplus or the later contraction of deliveries by one to two hundred million dollars is the sole explanation for the launching of the " great leap forward." Obviously, given the size of China, these factors were less than decisive. Nevertheless, they were instrumental inasmuch as they indicated: (1) that the Soviet Union and her satellites were unwilling to extend assistance which would thwart their own pace of development and/or could provide a rate of growth faster than theirs; and (2) that unless China was capable of accelerating the increase of her potential, her capacity might improve in absolute terms, but her relative position and weight was likely to stagnate if not deteriorate, within and without the bloc. It is therefore conceivable that the proper aim of the " great leap " programme was to attain a faster rate of growth than the bloc was prepared to allocate to China.

Had the Chinese " great leap forward " and the people's communes had a less ideologically disturbing and militant connotation to Moscow, the temporarily increased Soviet exports during 1959-60 might have been coupled

---

[7] The economic negotiations between Moscow and Peking (in August 1958, *i.e., after* the second Chinese FYP with its sharply increased targets had already got under way) resulted in an agreement for the construction of only 47 new enterprises (" Sino-Soviet Economic Relations during the Second Five-Year Plan," *op. cit.,* p. 15). During the first Chinese FYP some 156 enterprises had been promised by the Soviet Union but only 61 were (partially or totally) completed (Chin Szu-k'ai, *op. cit.,* pp. 22-24).

with financial support as well. (The Soviet Twenty-First Congress in January 1959 saw a significant effort at Sino-Soviet détente.) But the Chinese continued stubbornly to insist upon the principle of economic self-sufficiency, while Moscow emphasised " increased productivity through international division of labour "—*i.e.,* bloc integration through CMEA. Consequently every attempt to lessen dependence upon Moscow became anathema, obsolete, dogmatist. The Chinese, however, remained adamant throughout the fifties in their commitment to autarky and were unwilling to develop their economy in a manner which would permanently tie them to the bloc and ultimately make them dependent upon the Soviet Union. Also, the Chinese ideological claims irritated Moscow and corroded her prestige, in return for which she subsequently reacted to China's economic difficulties with a dispassionate indifference.[8]

As the two opposing standpoints became more rigid, prospects for compromise faded away and by August 1959 the possibility of China's economic isolation became an impending reality.

However, the Soviet Union did not cease to be the main supplier of investment goods to China nor did it terminate its technical assistance at once. The latter occurred only in the late summer of 1960,[9] while the former took place in the following year.[10] The Soviet Union, on the other hand, in committing itself increasingly to the policy of peaceful co-existence, *i.e.,* economic competition with capitalism, was compelled to concentrate its resources on continuous domestic economic expansion as well as to allocate resources to the underdeveloped countries where they had some likelihood of falling on fertile ground. In the case of China, however, where the same amount would only strengthen a disturbing ally both on the international scene and in inter-bloc relations, no justification could be found for economically detrimental co-operation.

Consequently, the last two years have brought significant changes in China's trade pattern and economic development programme. First, her previous reliance upon the Soviet Union and East Europe as major trading partners has sharply decreased, and it seems unlikely that Sino-Soviet trade will be above the limit necessary to amortise outstanding debts. In this context the question of the exact amount is negligible compared to the fact that China at the moment is still apparently anxious to repay her debts.

---

8 Except for the re-financing of the Chinese trade deficit of $320 million which was irrecoverable anyway at that time; see footnote 5. In this context, it is worthwhile to point out that the temporary increase in Soviet exports to China during 1959–60 can only be interpreted as Soviet support of China if we disregard the simultaneous increase of Soviet imports from China. This is particularly true in view of the difficult circumstances in which China was making her deliveries.

9 TANJUG report from Peking, August 12, 1960, 1830 GMT. See F. Schatten's comments on withdrawal of Soviet experts, in *Neue Zürcher Zeitung,* August 19, 1960.

10 The proportion of machines and equipment in the total Soviet export dropped from 62–63 per cent in 1959–60 to 29·5 per cent in 1961. *Vneshnaya Torgovlya SSSR za 1960 god* (Moscow, 1961), p. 162, and *Vneshnaya Torgovlya SSSR za 1961 god* (Moscow, 1962), p. 179, and *Vneshnaya Torgovlya SSSR za 1962 god* (Moscow, 1963), p. 182. In the case of equally crucial oil deliveries, however, the contraction of Soviet exports did not commence until 1962.

Soviet exports (in thousand tons)	1959	1960	1961	1962
Crude oil	636	568	—	—
Oil products	2,412	2,395	2,928	1,856

1959–61: *Petroleum Press Service,* London, XXIX, 11 (November 1962), p. 408.
1962: *Vneshnaya Torgovlya SSSR za 1962 god* (Moscow, 1963), p. 184.

Table III

DEGREE OF CHINA'S DEPENDENCE ON TRADE
WITH THE SOVIET UNION AND OTHER COMMUNIST COUNTRIES

(in percentages)

Year	Soviet Union	Other Communist Countries	Non Communist Countries
(1)	(2)	(3)	(4)
1960	42·0	22·0	36·0
1961	34·5	14·0	51·5
1962	27·0	12·0	61·0

Sources:
Compiled and calculated from " The China Market: 1962," *op. cit.*, pp. 1 and 6, and Takashi Oka in *The Christian Science Monitor*, February 6, 1963.

Secondly, since the beginning of 1961, in order to cope with repeated crop failures, the Chinese have been buying various surplus grains from the major Western producers, especially Canada and Australia (excluding the United States). Its estimated purchase of approximately 12 million tons during 1961-62 committed Peking to the payment of approximately $588 million,[11] while for 1963, 4·3 million tons have already been contracted for.[12] The allocation of this large amount of foreign exchange to food imports finally compelled China to alter radically the composition of its foreign trade. During 1961-62 delivery of investment goods from CMEA countries was reduced from approximately 65 per cent to 25 per cent,[13] and from the West from 48·4 per cent to 17·8 per cent.[14] Peking is undoubtedly aware of the long-term consequences of a continuous shortage in capital goods, and recent Chinese soundings of Western markets suggest that the composition of Chinese foreign trade may be altered in its favour. Lastly, China's foreign trade is likely to be determined in the near future more by commercial motives such as the search for foreign exchange and better credit terms, standards of quality, effectiveness, etc., than by politics.

Correspondingly, in domestic production emphasis has recently shifted from quantity to quality, and there has been a partial return to material incentives as a means of increasing labour productivity.[15] Priority in national planning is now given to agriculture, light industry, and heavy industry in that order, and in the latter emphasis is put upon production and maintenance over new construction.[16] Under these circumstances the increasingly frequent Chinese references in spring 1962 to the desirability of an " independent, complete and modernised " national economy which is

---

[11] *Sunday Telegraph* (London), September 16, 1962.
[12] " The China Market: 1962," *op. cit.*, pp. 6-7.
[13] See note 10.
[14] " The China Market: 1962," *op. cit.*, p. 7.
[15] A. A. Cohen and C. F. Steffens, " Disillusionment within the Ranks," *Problems of Communism*, XII, 3 (May-June 1963), pp. 11-16.
[16] Ryuzo Yamashita, " The Characteristics and Problems of the Economic Adjustment Period," *Chugoku Kenkyu Geppo* (China Research Monthly) (Tokyo: China Research Institute), No. 168 (April 10, 1962), pp. 1-28 and JPRS 14,887, August 17, 1962, p. 4. In this respect, of course, the procurement of spare parts, blueprints for repairs, etc., from the bloc is a thorny problem for the Chinese planners.

self-sufficient and not dependent upon foreign aid,[17] *i.e.*, Peking's implicit announcement of her economic independence from Moscow, only spelled out a foregone conclusion if not an accomplished fact.

But accomplished facts are not necessarily irreversible. In the present state of Sino-Soviet economic relations the final word, oddly enough, is not likely to come either from Moscow or from Peking but from China's rather unexpected difficulties with Southeast Asia.[18] The traditionally strong economic position of Chinese minorities there is challenged by both the population and the governments. These Chinese have constituted a major source of foreign exchange for China, flowing through the two main entry points of Singapore and Hong Kong.[19] Defiance of Moscow, though damaging, is still possible while these sources of income remain open. But should they be blocked and Soviet aid remain as low as it is at present, Peking's economic situation would be even more serious. In any case, the growth of Chinese hostility towards the Soviet Union has not been significantly limited by its desire for Soviet economic aid. On the contrary, the decline in Soviet aid to China has only intensified Peking's anti-Soviet attitude, the primary causes of which, however, have been political rather than economic.

[17] Ch'eng Ou-yang, " On the Establishment of an Independent, Complete and Modernized System of National Economy," *Ta Kung Pao* (Peking), June 27, 1962; and JPRS. 15,445, September 24, 1962, pp. 1–11.
[18] *New York Times*, June 10, 1963.
[19] " The China Market : 1962," *op cit.*, pp. 6–8.

Part III

THE DISPUTE IN DOCUMENTS

DOCUMENT 1

Letter from the Central Committee of the Communist Party of the Soviet Union to the Central Committee of the Communist Party of China, March 30, 1963

The Central Committee of the
Communist Party of China

Dear Comrades,

The Central Committee of the Communist Party of the Soviet Union notes with satisfaction that our proposals on measures aimed at strengthening unity and solidarity in the ranks of the communist movement have met with a favourable response on the part of the Central Committee of the Communist Party of China. We welcome your agreement to the holding of a meeting between representatives of the CPSU and CPC. This meeting is called upon to play an important part in creating a favourable atmosphere in relations between the fraternal Parties and in smoothing out the differences which have arisen in recent times in the world communist movement. We would like to hope that as a result of this meeting it will be possible to carry out a number of constructive measures to surmount existing difficulties.

In its letter the CPC Central Committee invites Comrade N. S. Khrushchov to visit Peking en route to Cambodia. The CPSU Central Committee and Comrade N. S. Khrushchov express gratitude for this invitation. Comrade N. S. Khrushchov would with great pleasure visit the People's Republic of China, and meet the leadership of the Communist Party of China to exchange views on urgent questions of the international situation and of the communist movement with the object of achieving a common understanding of our tasks and strengthening solidarity between our Parties. However, it is not in fact planned that Comrade N. S. Khrushchov will make a tour of Cambodia as you mention in your letter. As we all know, in conformity with a decision passed by our leading bodies on February 12, 1963, Comrade L. I. Brezhnev, President of the Presidium of the U.S.S.R. Supreme Soviet, will travel to Cambodia, as the Cambodian Government has already been notified and as has been announced in the press. Comrade N. S. Khrushchov, who has already visited the People's Republic of China three times, does not lose hope of availing himself of your kind invitation in the future to visit China and meet the Chinese comrades.

We remember that during his stay in Moscow in 1957 Comrade Mao Tse-tung said that he had only been in the U.S.S.R. twice and had only visited Moscow and Leningrad. He expressed the desire to visit the Soviet Union again to become better acquainted with our country. He said then that he would like to travel from the Far Eastern borders of our country to the western borders and from the northern to the southern borders. We welcomed this desire of Comrade Mao Tse-tung.

The CPSU Central Committee sent a letter to Comrade Mao Tse-tung on May 12, 1960, inviting him to come and spend a holiday in the USSR and familiarize himself with the life of the Soviet people. Unfortunately, Comrade

Mao Tse-tung could not at that time avail himself of our invitation. The CPSU Central Committee would welcome a visit by Comrade Mao Tse-tung. The best time for such a visit would be the approaching spring or summer, which are the good seasons of the year in our country. We are also ready at any other time to give a worthy reception to Comrade Mao Tse-tung as a representative of a fraternal Party and of the fraternal Chinese people. In this tour of our country, Comrade Mao Tse-tung would not, of course, be alone. Comrades from the leadership of our Party would go with him, and it would be a fine opportunity for an exchange of opinion on different questions. Comrade Mao Tse-tung would be able to see how the Soviet people are working, and what successes they have scored in the construction of communism and in the implementation of the Programme of our Party.

If a visit by Comrade Mao Tse-tung to Moscow cannot take place at present, we are ready to accept your ideas about a top-level meeting between representatives of the CPSU and CPC in Moscow. We believe that a meeting of this kind could take place around May 15, 1963, if this date is acceptable to you.

We are very pleased that the Chinese comrades, like ourselves, regard the forthcoming meeting of representatives of the CPC and the CPSU as a " necessary step in preparing for the meeting of representatives of Communist and Workers' Parties of all countries." Indeed, without violating the principle of equality and without infringing upon the interests of other fraternal Parties, this meeting must facilitate the better preparation and holding of the meeting. Without such a meeting, and without the ending of open polemics in the press and of criticism within the Party of other fraternal Parties, preparation for the meeting and the achievement of its main aim—the strengthening of the unity of the international communist movement—would be difficult. Precisely for this reason the Central Committee of the CPSU, while agreeing with the proposals made by the Vietnamese, Indonesian, British, Swedish and other comrades at the beginning of 1962 regarding the convocation of a meeting of fraternal Parties of all countries, at the same time stressed the need for taking such measures as would create a favourable atmosphere for the work of the world communist forum.

In its letter of February 22, 1962, the Central Committee of the CPSU urged that " unnecessary arguments be stopped regarding questions on which we have different opinions, that public statements capable of aggravating rather than smoothing out our differences be given up." In the letter to the Central Committee of the CPC of May 31, 1962, we wrote : " As you are well aware, our Party has always come out and still comes out for collective discussion of vital problems of the world communist movement. The Central Committee of the CPSU was the initiator of the Meetings of Fraternal Parties in 1957 and 1960. In both cases these meetings were connected with serious changes in the international situation and the need for working out corresponding tactics in the communist movement. Now too we fully support the proposal for the convocation of a meeting of all the fraternal Parties."

We considered it would be useful in the preparations for such a meeting that the fraternal Parties could thoroughly and profoundly analyse the new phenomena in international affairs and their own activity in carrying out the collective decisions of our movement. The Central Committee of the CPSU displayed concern, perfectly understandable to all Communists, that the meeting should not aggravate the differences but do as much as possible to overcome them.

In their pronouncements many of the leaders of fraternal Parties have recently been justly expressing the same point of view on the necessity of taking, before the meeting, a number of steps to create a normal situation in the communist movement and to place conflicts of opinions within the permissible bounds of a comradely Party discussion. Now you also agree with this, as is seen from your letter, and it can be said that certain progress has been made in the preparation of the forthcoming meeting.

It goes without saying that when our two Parties are discussing questions concerning all fraternal Parties, the discussion can only be of a preliminary nature. The 1957 and 1960 Meetings have shown that the elaboration of the policy of the international communist movement can be successful only if all fraternal Parties collectively take part in it and if due consideration is given to the extensive experience of all its component detachments.

We have attentively studied your views concerning the range of questions which could be discussed at the meeting of representatives of the Communist Party of the Soviet Union and the Communist Party of China. These are important questions, and we are ready to discuss them.

In our turn, we would like to dwell in this letter on some questions of principle, which, in our opinion, are the centre of attention of the fraternal Parties and their struggle for our common cause. We do not mean, of course, an exhaustive statement of our views on these questions. We only wish to note that which is of paramount importance, by which we are guided in our policy in the international arena and in our relations with fraternal Parties.

We hope that this statement of our views will help to define the range of questions requiring an exchange of opinions at a bilateral meeting and will contribute to overcoming the existing differences. We are doing this so as to stress once again our determination to uphold firmly and consistently the ideological standpoint of the entire world communist movement, its general line as expressed in the Declaration and the Statement.

During the time that has passed since the adoption of the Statement, experience has not only not invalidated any of its main conclusions, but has, on the contrary, fully confirmed the correctness of the course taken by the world communist movement, as worked out jointly through generalization of present-day experience and the creative development of Marxism-Leninism.

The Communist Party of the Soviet Union proceeds from the basis that our epoch, whose main content is the transition from capitalism to socialism, initiated by the Great October Socialist Revolution, is an epoch of struggle between two opposed social systems, an epoch of socialist revolutions and national-liberation revolutions, an epoch of the collapse of imperialism, of the abolition of the colonial system, an epoch of transition to socialism by ever more nations, of the triumph of socialism and communism on a world scale.

The situation that has developed in the world and the changes in the development of the class forces in the international arena which opened up new opportunities for our movement demanded that a general line be worked out for the world communist movement, a general line in conformity with its basic tasks at the present stage.

After the Second World War a number of countries in Europe took the road of socialism, a socialist revolution triumphed in China and other Asian countries, and a world socialist system was formed. The new system grew strong in the countries of People's Democracy and was able to ensure a rapid rate of economic, political and cultural development in the countries following the road of socialism. The socialist community was closely united politically and militarily. Thanks to the achievements of the Soviet Union and other fraternal countries the correlation of forces in the world changed substantially in favour of socialism, and to the detriment of imperialism. An important part in this respect was played by the ending of America's monopoly of atomic and hydrogen weapons and by the creation of a mighty war potential by the Soviet Union.

The formation of the world socialist system is a historic achievement of the international working class and of all the working people. This achievement is the incarnation of mankind's dreams of a new society. The growth of production and the vast achievements of science and engineering in the socialist countries have helped to provide the socialist community with an economic and military might that reliably defends the gains of socialism and also serves as a mighty mainstay of peace and security for the peoples of the world.

The radical change in the correlation of forces is also connected with a further intensification of the general crisis of capitalism, the intensification of all its contradictions. After the end of the Second World War a change occurred in the distribution of forces within the imperialist camp. Following the economic centre, the political and military centres of imperialism also shifted from Europe to the United States of America. The monopolist bourgeoisie of the U.S.A. has become the main citadel of international reaction, and has assumed the role of the saviour of capitalism. The American imperialists are now performing the functions of an international gendarme. Using the policy of military blocs, the American imperialists endeavour to subordinate to their rule other capitalist states. This evokes opposition to the United States on the part of France, West Germany, Japan and other major capitalist states. The recovery of the economy of the capitalist countries which had suffered in the world war, and their rate of development, more rapid than in the United States, intensify the desire of a number of European countries to free themselves from the American diktat. All this leads to the aggravation of existing centres of imperialist competition and conflicts, and the appearance of new ones and weakens the capitalist system on the whole.

The anti-popular and rapacious nature of imperialism has not changed, but with the formation of the world socialist system and the growth of its economic and military might the ability of imperialism to influence the course of historical development has been noticeably narrowed, while the forms and methods of its struggle against the socialist countries and the world revolutionary and national-liberation movement have changed. The imperialists are frightened by the tempestuous growth of the forces of socialism and the national-liberation movement, they unite their forces, make feverish efforts to continue the struggle for their exploiting aims, and everywhere strive to undermine the positions of the socialist countries and the national-liberation movement, and to weaken their influence.

It is perfectly obvious that in our age the main content and the chief trends of the historical development of human society are no longer determined by imperialism but by the world socialist system, by all the progressive forces struggling against imperialism for the reorganization of society along socialist lines. The contradiction between capitalism and socialism is the chief contradiction of our epoch. On the outcome of the struggle of the two world systems the destinies of peace, democracy and socialism depend to a decisive extent. And the correlation of forces in the world arena is changing all the time in favour of socialism.

The struggle of the peoples of Asia, Africa and Latin America for their national and social liberation, and the successes already achieved in this field, the growing struggle of the working class, of all the working people of the capitalist countries against the monopolies and against exploitation, in the interests of social progress, are of the greatest importance for the destinies of the historical development of mankind. Socialist revolutions, national-liberation anti-imperialist and anti-colonial revolutions, people's democratic revolutions, extensive peasant movements, the struggle of the masses for the overthrow of fascist and other tyrannical regimes, general democratic movements against national oppression—in our time all these merge into a single world revolutionary stream undermining and destroying capitalism.

Working out its policy in conformity with the new conditions, the world communist movement could not fail to take into account quite seriously also such an important factor as the radical qualitative change in the military-technical means of waging war resulting from the emergence and stockpiling of thermonuclear weapons possessing unprecedented destructive force. Until disarmament is effected the socialist community must always maintain superiority over the imperialists in their armed forces. We shall never allow the imperialists to forget that should they unleash a war with the aim of deciding by force of arms whether mankind must develop along the road of capitalism or of socialism, it will be the last war, the one in which imperialism will be finally routed.

Under present-day conditions it is the duty of all champions of peace and socialism to use to the utmost the existing favourable opportunities for the victory of socialism, and not to allow imperialism to unleash a world war.

The correct analysis of the alignment of class forces in the world arena, and the correct Marxist-Leninist policy elaborated at the Moscow Meetings, made it possible for the fraternal Parties to gain major successes in developing the world socialist system, and facilitated the growth of the class revolutionary struggle in the capitalist countries and of the national-liberation movement.

The socialist system is exerting an ever-growing influence on the course of world development. The entire world revolutionary process is today developing under the direct influence of the great example provided by the new life in the countries of socialism. The more successfully the ideas of communism make their way to the minds and hearts of the general masses, the greater and more significant are our achievements in the building of socialism and communism. It is, therefore, clear that he who wants to bring closer the victory of socialism throughout the entire world should, in the first place, show concern for strengthening the great socialist community and its economic might, should seek to raise the standard of living of its peoples, develop science, engineering and culture, consolidate its unity and solidarity and the growth of its international authority. The Statement of the Moscow Meeting places the responsibility to the international working-class movement for the successful building of socialism and communism on the Marxist-Leninist parties and the peoples of the socialist countries.

Tirelessly strengthening the world socialist system, the fraternal Parties and peoples of our countries make their contribution to the great cause of the struggle of the international working class, of all the working people, of the entire liberation movement for solving the basic problems of the day in the interests of peace, democracy and socialism.

The present correlation of forces in the world arena gave the socialist countries, together with all peace-loving forces, the opportunity of envisaging as an entirely feasible task for the first time in history that of averting a new world war and of ensuring peace and security of the peoples.

The years that have passed since the adoption of this Statement have fully corroborated the correctness of this thesis. The failure of the aggressive forces to push mankind over the abyss of a destructive thermonuclear war is a highly important result of the strengthening of the might of the socialist countries, of the peace-loving foreign policy which they unswervingly pursue and which is increasingly winning recognition and support among hundreds of millions of people and gaining the upper hand over the imperialist policy of aggression and war.

No Marxist doubts that imperialism, losing one position after another, is trying by every means to preserve its domination over peoples and to regain its lost positions. At present the greatest conspiracy ever of the international imperialists is taking place against the countries of socialism and the world movement of liberation. Of course, there is no guarantee that the imperialists will not try to unleash a world war. The Communists should clearly see this danger.

But the position of the aggressor under present-day conditions radically differs from his position before the Second World War and, even more, before the First World War. In the past, wars usually ended with some capitalist countries defeating others, but the vanquished continued to live, regained their strength after a time, and even proved able to start renewed aggression, as is shown, in particular, by the example of Germany. A thermonuclear war does not offer such a prospect to any aggressor, and the imperialists are compelled to reckon with this. Fear of a retaliatory blow, fear of retribution, keeps them from letting loose a world war. The socialist community has become so strong that imperialism can no longer impose its conditions on the peoples and dictate its will as before. This is a historic gain by the international working class and the peoples of all countries.

By virtue of its predatory nature imperialism cannot get rid of the desire to solve contradictions in the international arena by means of war. But on the other hand it cannot unleash a world thermonuclear war without realizing that it will thereby place itself in danger of being destroyed.

A world war, such as imperialism threatens mankind with, is not fatally inevitable. With the balance of forces increasingly tipping in favour of socialism and against imperialism, and with the forces of peace increasingly gaining weight over the forces of war, it will become really possible to rule out the possibility of world war from the life of society even before socialism fully triumphs on earth, with capitalism still existing in a part of the world.

Of course, to prevent such a war it is necessary to continue strengthening the socialist system to the utmost and to rally all the forces of the international working-class and the national-liberation movement, to rally all democratic forces. Those who prize the interests of socialism and the interests of peace must do everything to frustrate the criminal designs of world reaction and to prevent it from unleashing a thermonuclear war and dragging hundreds of millions of people down into the grave with it. A sober appraisal of the inevitable consequences that a thermonuclear war would have for the whole of mankind and for the cause of socialism sets before Marxist-Leninists the need to do everything in our power to prevent a new world conflict.

The CPSU Central Committee firmly abides by the thesis of the 1960 Statement that " In a world divided into two systems, the only correct and reasonable principle of international relations is the principle of peaceful coexistence of states with different social systems advanced by V. I. Lenin and further elaborated in the Moscow Declaration and Peace Manifesto of 1957, in the decisions of the 20th and 21st Congresses of the CPSU, and in the documents of other Communist and Workers' Parties."

Our Party, which the great Lenin educated in the spirit of relentless struggle against imperialism, keeps in mind Lenin's warning that moribund capitalism is still able to cause humanity untold calamities. The Soviet Union is doing everything to boost its economy and to improve its defences on this basis; it is building up its armed might and maintaining its armed forces in a state of constant readiness. However, we have employed and will continue to employ our country's increasing might not to threaten anyone or to fan war passions, but to consolidate peace, prevent another world war, and defend our own country and the other socialist countries.

The policy of peaceful coexistence accords with the vital interests of all the peoples; it serves to strengthen the positions of socialism, to help the international influence of the socialist countries, and to increase the authority and influence of the Communists.

Peaceful coexistence does not imply conciliation between socialist and bourgeois ideologies. That policy would spell abandonment of Marxism-Leninism and obstruction of the building of socialism. Bourgeois ideology is a sort of Trojan horse, which imperialism is trying to sneak into the ranks of the communist and working-class movement. The peaceful coexistence of states with different social systems presupposes an unremitting ideological, political and economic struggle between the two social systems, and the class struggle of the working people inside the countries of the capitalist system, including armed struggle when the peoples find that necessary, and the steady advance of the national-liberation movement among the peoples of the colonial and dependent countries.

The facts go to show that efforts to prevent a world war in no way weaken the forces of the world communist and national-liberation movements but on the contrary rally the broadest masses to the Communists. It was precisely in conditions of peaceful coexistence between states with different social systems that the socialist revolution triumphed in Cuba, that the Algerian people gained national independence, that more than 40 countries won national independence, that the fraternal Parties grew in number and strength, and that the influence of the world communist movement increased.

Availing themselves of the conditions of peaceful coexistence, the socialist countries are scoring more and more victories in the economic competition with capitalism. Our adversaries realize that it is difficult for them to count on winning the competition against us. They are unable to keep up with the rapid economic advance of the socialist countries; they are powerless in the face of the appeal that the example of the socialist countries makes to the peoples under capitalism's yoke.

As the economy of the socialist commonwealth advances, the advantages and superiority of socialism, and the greater opportunities of the working people to obtain material and spiritual riches, as compared to capitalism, will display themselves more and more vividly. The rising standards of living in the socialist countries are a great magnet for the working class of all the capitalist countries. The achievements of the socialist commonwealth will constitute a kind of catalyst, a revolutionizing factor in broadening the class struggle in the capitalist countries and enabling the working class to triumph over capitalism.

The peoples embarking on socialism inherit from the past economies and cultures at different levels. Regardless of this, however, socialism awakens mighty productive forces—as exemplified by the Soviet Union and the People's Democracies. The Soviet Union has already outpaced the leading capitalist countries of Europe in economic development and has taken second place in the world; the time is not far off when it will take first place in the world. The other socialist countries have likewise gained great successes. The socialist system is so progressive by nature that it enables the peoples to swiftly eliminate their backwardness, to catch up with the more highly developed countries, and, marching in one rank with them, to fight for the building of communism.

All this inspires the peoples, giving them the conviction that they can embark upon the road of socialism and score achievements, regardless of their present level of historical development. The advance of the peoples to a new life is facilitated by their opportunity to select the best from the world's experience in building socialism, taking into account both the merits and the shortcomings in the practices of socialist construction.

The faster the productive forces of the socialist countries develop, the higher their economic potential will rise, and the stronger the influence of the socialist community will become on the rate and trend of the whole of historical development in the interests of peace and of the complete triumph of socialism.

Our Party proceeds from the thesis that there are favourable international and internal conditions in the present epoch for more and more countries to go over to socialism. This is true of the developed capitalist countries as well as of the countries which have recently achieved national independence.

The world revolutionary process is developing on an ever larger scale, embracing all continents. The struggle of the working class in the developed capitalist countries and the national-liberation movement are closely linked, and help one another. The course of social development has led to a situation in which the revolutionary struggle, in whichever country it takes place, is directed against the main common enemy, imperialism and the monopoly bourgeoisie.

The Marxist-Leninist parties throughout the world have a common ultimate aim, to mobilize all forces in the struggle for the winning of power by the workers and the labouring peasantry, and to build socialism and communism. In drawing up the tactical policy for their struggle, every Communist Party must take into account the experience of the entire world communist movement, must take into consideration those interests, aims and tasks set by our movement as a whole, its general line at the present time.

But at the same time, the working out of forms and methods of fighting for socialism in each separate country is the internal affair of the working class of that country and of its communist vanguard. No other fraternal Party, whatever its membership, experience and authority, can lay down the tactics, forms and methods of the revolutionary struggle in other countries. Revolution is the cause of the masses themselves. An accurate analysis of the actual situation and a correct estimation of the correlation of forces are among the most important conditions of a revolution. The enthusiasm of the revolutionary masses in the struggle for the victory of a socialist revolution cannot be kept back when objective and subjective conditions are ripe. It would be tantamount to death. But a revolution cannot be artificially instigated if conditions for it are not yet ripe. A premature uprising, as the experience of the revolutionary class struggle teaches, is doomed to failure. Communists rally the working people under the red banner in order to win in the struggle for a better life on earth, and not to perish, even though heroically. Heroism and self-sacrifice, necessary in revolutionary battles, are of no use by themselves, but only for the victory of the great ideas of socialism.

The CPSU has always hailed and will continue to hail the revolutionary working class and the working people of any country who, headed by their communist vanguard, make skilful use of the revolutionary situation to inflict a crushing blow against the class enemy and to establish a new social system.

The tactics and policy of the Communist Parties in the capitalist countries have in common substantial features connected with the present stage of the general crisis of capitalism and the correlation of forces that has developed in the international arena. The development of state-monopoly capitalism has, besides aggravating the contradictions of the capitalist society which appeared before, also given birth to new contradictions. State-monopoly capitalism has led to a still greater narrowing of the social base of imperialism within a country, and to the concentration of power in the hands of a small group of the strongest monopolists. This gives rise, on the other hand, to a joint anti-monopoly movement embracing the working class, the peasants, the petty bourgeoisie, the working intellectuals and certain other sections of capitalist society interested in freeing themselves from the sway of the monopolies and from exploitation, and interested in changing over to socialism.

Our time is characterized by a sharp growth in the significance of democratic movements—the struggle for world peace, for the prevention of a world thermonuclear catastrophe, for the preservation of national sovereignty; movements in defence of democracy, against the onslaught of fascism, for the introduction of agrarian transformations, the humanistic movement in defence of culture, and others.

Our Party fully adheres to Leninist principles and to the principles expressed in the Statement, in saying that socialist revolution is not necessarily connected with war. If world wars bring about triumphant revolutions, revolutions are nevertheless quite possible without wars.

If Communists were to start tying up the victory of the socialist revolution with world war, this would not evoke any sympathy for socialism, but would drive the masses away from it. With modern means of warfare having such terrible destructive consequences, an appeal like this would only play into the hands of our enemies.

The working class and its vanguard, the Marxist-Leninist parties, endeavour to carry out socialist revolutions in a peaceful way without civil war. The realization of such a possibility is in keeping with the interests of the working class and all the people, and with the national interests of the country. At the same time the choice of the means of developing the revolution depends not only on the working class. If the exploiting classes resort to violence against the people, the working class will be forced to use non-peaceful means of seizing power. Everything depends on the particular conditions and on the distribution of class forces within the country and in the world arena.

Naturally, no matter what means are used for the transition from capitalism to socialism, such a transition is possible only by means of a socialist revolution and of the dictatorship of the proletariat in various forms. Appreciating highly the selfless struggle of the working class headed by the Communists in the capitalist countries, the CPSU considers it its duty to render them every kind of aid and support.

Our Party regards the national-liberation movement as an integral part of the world revolutionary process, as a mighty force destroying the front of imperialism. The peoples of the former colonies are today rising to full stature as independent creators of history, and are seeking ways to promote their national economy and culture. The growth of the forces of the socialist system actively helps the liberation of the oppressed peoples, their achievement of economic independence, the further development and expansion of the national-liberation movement, and the peoples' struggle against all forms of old and new colonialism.

The national-liberation movement has entered the final stage of the abolition of colonial regimes. The time is not far off when all the peoples as yet living under the yoke of the colonialists will win freedom and independence. The freed peoples are now faced with the problem of consolidating political independence, overcoming economic and cultural backwardness and putting an end to all forms of dependence upon imperialism.

The countries that have thrown off the colonial yoke carry out the vital tasks of national resurgence successfully only in vigorous struggle against imperialism and the remnants of feudalism, by uniting all the patriotic forces of the nation in a single national front—the working class, the peasantry, the national bourgeoisie and the democratic intellectuals.

The peoples who are fighting for their national liberation and have already won political independence have ceased, or are ceasing, to serve as a reserve for imperialism; with the support of the socialist states and of all progressive forces they are more and more frequently inflicting defeats upon the imperialist powers and coalitions.

The young national states are developing at a time when there is competition between the two world social systems. This circumstance has the strongest influence upon their political and economic development, upon the choice of the roads they will follow in the future. The states that have recently achieved their national liberation belong neither to the system of socialist states nor to the system of capitalist states, but the overwhelming majority of them have not yet broken away from the orbit of the world capitalist economy, although they hold a special place there. This part of the world is still exploited by the capitalist monopolies.

Now when political independence has been won, the struggle of the young sovereign states against imperialism, for their ultimate national revival, for economic independence comes to the forefront. The achievement of complete independence by the developing countries would mean a further serious weakening of imperialism, for then the entire present system of the predatory, unequal international division of labour would be destroyed, and the foundation of the economic exploitation of the " world countryside " by the capitalist monopolies would be undermined. The development of independent national economies in the developing countries relying upon the effective assistance of the socialist system will deal a further heavy blow against imperialism.

In the struggle for the attainment and consolidation of independence it is necessary to muster the whole of a nation's forces in readiness to fight against imperialism. In an endeavour to strengthen its dominant position after the attainment of independence, the Right-wing national bourgeoisie sometimes succeeds in establishing reactionary political regimes for a time, and starts persecuting Communists and other democrats. However, such regimes are short-lived for the simple reason that they obstruct progress and the solution of vital national problems—primarily the attainment of economic independence and the development of productive forces. That is why, in spite of the active support of the imperialists, these regimes will be overthrown as a result of the struggle of the masses.

The CPSU regards fraternal alliance with the peoples who have shaken off the colonial yoke and with the peoples of semi-colonial states as one of the cornerstones of its international policy. Our Party considers it its international duty to help the peoples who have taken the road of winning and consolidating national independence, all the peoples fighting for the complete abolition of the colonial system. The Soviet Union has always supported the sacred wars of the peoples for freedom, and given every kind of moral, economic, military and political support to the national-liberation movement.

The Soviet people gave great support to the Algerian people when they fought against the French colonialists. When the Yemeni people rose up in revolt against slavery in their country, we were the first to offer them a helping hand. We rendered various kinds of aid to the Indonesian people in their struggle for the liberation of West Irian, against the Dutch imperialists who got their support from the U.S. imperialists. We hail the struggle of the Indonesian people for the liberation of Northern Kalimantan.

Colonialists, both old and new, are busy weaving intrigues and plots against the liberation movement of the peoples of Southeast Asia. Our sympathies and support are invariably with those who fight for national freedom and independence. We are deeply convinced that, in spite of all the efforts of the American imperialists and their puppets, the peoples of south Viet Nam and south Korea will be victorious in their struggle and will achieve the reunification of their native lands.

While being against the export of revolution, our Party has always done everything to prevent the export of counter-revolution. We are firmly convinced that the interconnection and unity of action of the three great revolutionary forces of our time—the peoples building socialism and communism, the international revolutionary working-class movement, and the national-liberation movement—are the foundation of the peoples' struggle against imperialism, and a guarantee of their victory.

The entire course of world development in recent years has fully confirmed the correctness of the policy of the communist movement, which has yielded remarkable practical results. Thanks to the realization of this policy, the forces fighting against imperialism, for peace, national independence and socialism, have scored new successes. The CPSU considers it its duty consistently and steadfastly to carry out this policy.

We are firmly convinced that there are no grounds for a revision of this policy.

Besides this, the CPSU Central Committee is of the opinion that it would be beneficial during the preparations for the meeting, as well as at the meeting of representatives of Communist and Workers' Parties, to exchange opinions on the new aspects with which life has in recent years enriched the

251

policy of the world communist movement as laid down in the Declaration and Statement.

In your letter, dear comrades, you justly note that the guarantee of all our achievements is the strengthening of the unity of the communist movement and the solidarity of the socialist countries. In recent time the CPSU has at its congresses and at international communist meetings time and again expressed its conception of the principles concerning the relations between Marxist-Leninist parties. We emphasised, for the whole world to see, that in the communist movement, just as in the socialist community, all Communist and Workers' Parties, of all socialist countries have always been completely equal. In the communist movement there are no " higher ranking " and " subordinate " Parties. And it could not be so. The domination of any Party, or the manifestation of any hegemony whatsoever, does not benefit the international communist and workers' movement; on the contrary, it can only do it harm. All Communist Parties are independent and equal. All bear responsibility for the destiny of the communist movement, for its victories and setbacks, all must build their relations on the basis of proletarian internationalism and mutual assistance.

We also proceed from the basis that proletarian internationalism places equal demands on all Parties, big and small, but makes no exceptions for any one. All fraternal Parties must show equal concern that their activities be based on Marxist-Leninist principles, in accordance with the interests of strengthening the unity of the socialist countries and of the entire world communist and workers' movement.

The formation and development of the world socialist system gives special significance to the question of correct relations between Marxist-Leninist parties. Communist and Workers' Parties in the countries of socialism are ruling parties. They bear responsibility for the destiny of the states, for the destiny of their peoples. Under these conditions the violation of Marxist-Leninist principles in the relations between Parties can affect not only Party interests but the interests of the wide masses of the people.

Guided by the supreme interests of our cause, the CPSU has eliminated the consequences of the Stalin personality cult, and done everything to restore in full the Leninist principles of equality in the relations between the fraternal Parties and respect for the sovereignty of socialist countries. This has played a large and positive role in strengthening the unity of the entire socialist community. A favourable situation has been created for the strengthening of our friendship on the basis of equality, respect for the sovereignty of each state, mutual assistance and comradely cooperation, voluntary fulfilment of international duty by each country. At the same time, we should like to emphasize that socialist equality not only means having equal rights to take part in working out collectively the common policy but also entails equal responsibilities for the fraternal Parties of socialist countries for the destinies of the entire community.

The Statement of the Moscow Meeting of the Fraternal Parties stressed the need for the closest alliance between countries breaking away from capitalism, for the pooling of their efforts in the building of socialism and communism. National interests and the interests of the socialist system as a whole combine harmoniously. Life has proved convincingly that every country can best solve its national tasks only through the closest co-operation with the other socialist countries on the basis of genuine equality and mutual aid.

Our unity, our well-concerted actions, do not arise spontaneously. They are dictated by objective necessity, they are the result of conscious activities, of the purposeful internationalist policy of the Marxist-Leninist parties and their tireless concern for the uniting of our ranks.

We do not close our eyes to the fact that different interpretations of certain questions of internal construction and the international communist movement, different interpretations of the forms and methods of our co-operation may occur in the relations between socialist countries. This is possible, for the countries making up the world socialist system are at different stages in the construction of a new society, and their experience in developing relations with the outside world is not the same in all respects. One should not exclude the possibility, either, that differences may result from different approaches to the solution of some questions of Marxism-Leninism in individual fraternal Parties. To exaggerate the role of national, specific, features may lead to a departure from Marxism-Leninism. To ignore national features may lead to a breaking away from life and from the masses, and do harm to the cause of socialism.

All this necessitates constant efforts to find ways and means to enable us to settle the differences arising, from positions of principle and with the least damage to our common cause.

We Communists can argue between ourselves. But in all circumstances our sacred duty remains the education of the peoples of our countries in the spirit of deep solidarity with all the peoples of the socialist community. Communists must inculcate in the peoples not only love for their own country, but also love for the whole of the socialist community, for all peoples; they must foster in each man and woman living in any socialist country an understanding of their fraternal duty towards the working people of the world. Failure to do this means failure to follow the first rule of Communists, which requires the uniting of the Marxist-Leninist parties and the peoples building socialism, the cherishing of our unity above all else.

Ideological and tactical differences must in no circumstances be used to incite nationalist feelings and prejudices, mistrust and dissension between the socialist peoples. We declare with full responsibility that the Communist Party of the Soviet Union has never taken and will never take a single step that could sow hostility among the peoples of our country towards the fraternal Chinese people or other peoples. On the contrary, in all circumstances our Party has steadily and consistently propagated the ideas of internationalism and warm friendship with the peoples of the socialist countries, and with all peoples of the world. We consider it important to stress this, and we hope that the Central Committee of the Communist Party of China shares this view.

In the international communist, working-class and liberation movements it is necessary to unite all efforts, mobilizing the peoples for struggle against imperialism. The militant call " Workers of all countries, unite ! " formulated by Marx and Engels means that at the basis of this unity lies anti-imperialist class solidarity, and not any principle of nationality, colour or geographical location. The uniting of the masses in the struggle against imperialism solely on the basis of their belonging to a particular continent—whether Africa, Asia, Latin America or Europe—can be detrimental to the fighting peoples. This would be not uniting but in fact splitting the forces of the united anti-imperialist front.

The strength of the world communist movement lies in its faithfulness to Marxism-Leninism and to proletarian internationalism. The Communist

Party of the Soviet Union has fought and will continue to fight any departure from Marxism-Leninism and any opportunism. We firmly adhere to the principles of the Statement of 1960 indicating the necessity for a struggle on two fronts—against Right and " Left " opportunism. The Statement rightly says that the main danger in the world communist movement is revisionism, and at the same time points out the necessity for a resolute struggle against sectarianism and dogmatism, which can become the main danger at any stage in the development of separate Parties if not consistently combated.

Motivated by the desire to consolidate the unity of the world communist movement on the basis of the principles of Marxism-Leninism, our Party will continue to fight resolutely against both Right-wing and Left-wing opportunism, which are today every bit as dangerous as revisionism. But while being implacable as regards fundamental questions of principle in the theory and tactics of the communist movement, while struggling against revisionism and sectarianism, we shall spare no effort to elucidate, by painstaking comradely discussion, questions on which there are different interpretations, so as to clear away all extraneous obstacles interfering with our unity. In so doing, we proceed from the premise that when criticizing any mistake relating to questions of the principles of Marxism-Leninism, the fraternal Parties, and also international conferences of the communist movement, should set themselves the objective of pointing out the danger of such mistakes and of helping to remedy them, and not of harping on these mistakes for all time. We are striving to facilitate the complete uniting of revolutionary forces, and not their disintegration or the amputation of one or another section in our movement. Naturally, Communists cannot allow concessions on points of principle in Marxist-Leninist theory.

As an internationalist Party, the CPSU carefully studies the experience accumulated in the struggles of the Marxist-Leninist parties in all countries. We greatly prize the struggle being waged by the working class and its revolutionary vanguard of Communist Parties in France, Italy, the U.S.A., Britain, the other capitalist countries, as well as the heroic struggle which the Communist Parties of Asian, African and Latin American countries are carrying on for national and social emancipation from the domination of the imperialist monopolies, colonialism and neo-colonialism.

The Communist Parties have developed into influential national forces, into advanced detachments of fighters for the happiness of their peoples. No wonder the reactionaries are striking blow after blow at the Communists in their efforts to break their will. In their fight against the communist movement the reactionaries bring out the shop-soiled lie about the " hand of Moscow," claiming that the Communist Parties are not a national force but a vehicle for the policy of another country, the tool of another country. The imperialists are doing this with evil intent, in order to counter the mounting influence of the Communist Parties, in order to make the masses suspect them, in order to justify police persecution of the Communists.

However, all honest-minded men and women know that the Communist Parties are the true upholders and champions of national interests, that they are staunch patriots who combine love for their country and proletarian internationalism in their struggle for the happiness of the people. The CPSU considers it its obligation to give every support to its brothers in the heroic struggle they are waging in the capitalist countries, to strengthen international solidarity with them.

These, in general outline, are some of our ideas on important contemporary questions of principle, on the strategy and tactics of the international communist movement, which we thought it necessary to touch upon in this letter.

Being firmly convinced that the present policy of the international communist movement, which found its expression in the Declaration and Statement of the fraternal Parties, is the only correct one, we believe that at the forthcoming meeting between the representatives of the CPSU and CPC it would be expedient to discuss the following most urgent problems :

(a) Questions concerning the struggle for the further strengthening of the might of the world socialist system and its transformation into the decisive factor in the development of human society, which is the main distinguishing feature of our era. We could jointly discuss how faster and better to secure a victory for the socialist countries in peaceful economic competition with capitalism;

(b) Questions concerning the struggle for peace and peaceful coexistence. The need to pool the efforts of all peace-loving forces for the struggle to prevent a world thermonuclear war. The creation and the strengthening of the broadest united front of peace supporters. The exposure of the reactionary essence of imperialism, the heightening of vigilance and the mobilization of the broad masses to fight against the preparations being made by the imperialists for a new world war, frustrate their aggressive schemes and isolate the forces of reaction and war. Assertion in international relations of the Leninist principle of peaceful coexistence between states with different social systems. The struggle for general and complete disarmament and for the elimination of the traces of the Second World War;

(c) Questions concerning the struggle against imperialism headed by the U.S. The use, in the interests of our cause, of the weakening positions of capitalism and the growing instability of the entire capitalist system of world economy, the aggravation of contradictions of capitalism, and above all contradictions between labour and capital, and the severe crisis in bourgeois ideology and politics. Support of the revolutionary and class struggle of the working people in capitalist countries against the monopolies, for their social liberation, for the abolition of the exploitation of man by man, for the extension of the democratic rights and freedoms of the peoples;

(d) Questions concerning the national-liberation movement. The support and utmost development of the national-liberation movement of the peoples. The struggle for the complete and final ending of colonialism and neo-colonialism in all its forms. The rendering of support to peoples fighting against colonialism, and also to countries which have achieved their national liberation. The development of economic and cultural co-operation with these countries;

(e) Questions concerning the consolidation of the unity and cohesion of the socialist community and of the ranks of the communist movement. The need for consolidating in every way the international communist movement, the most influential political force of our times, particularly in conditions where the imperialist reactionaries have joined forces in the fight against communism. The prevention of any actions which could undermine this unity, the firm adherence by each fraternal Party to the assessments and conclusions worked out jointly. The continuation of the struggle against revisionism and dogmatism, as an indispensable condition for the defence of Marxism-Leninism in its pure form, and of its creative development, and for the further successes of the communist movement. The development of relations among the fraternal Parties on the basis of the principles of proletarian internationalism and mutual aid and support. The working out of joint measures to intensify the ideological and political struggle against imperialism and reaction.

During the talks it will be possible to discuss all the questions mentioned in your letter, questions of common interest stemming from the tasks in the struggle to implement the decisions of the Moscow Meetings. An important role could be played by the discussion of the questions connected with the consolidation of unity between the U.S.S.R. and the People's Republic of China.

In your letter you raise the Albanian and Yugoslav questions. We have already written to you that these questions, though of a basic nature, cannot and should not eclipse the main problems of our times which call for discussion at our meeting.

Our Party, having condemned the splitting activities of the Albanian leaders, has at the same time taken a number of steps towards normalizing the relations between the Albanian Party of Labour and the CPSU and other fraternal Parties. In spite of the fact that the leaders of the Albanian Party of Labour have recently been coming out with slanderous attacks on our Party and the Soviet people, we, being guided by supreme interests, do not relinquish the hope that the relations between the CPSU and the Albanian Party of Labour may be improved. At the end of February this year the CPSU Central Committee once again took the initiative and suggested to the Central Committee of the Albanian Party of Labour that a bilateral meeting be held between representatives of our two Parties. However, this comradely step on our part did not meet with due response on the part of the Albanian leadership. The leaders of the Albanian Party of Labour did not even deem it necessary to acknowledge our letter containing the CPSU Central Committee's proposal about the bilateral meetings. Having obviously later come to their senses, the Albanian leaders sent us a letter in which, after some reservations and stipulations, they speak of such a meeting. If real desire is in fact shown, we are ready to have a meeting.

As far as Yugoslavia is concerned, we maintain, proceeding from an analysis and assessment of the objective economic and political conditions in that country, that it is a socialist country, and in our relations with it we strive to establish closer relations between the Federative People's Republic of Yugoslavia and the socialist commonwealth, in accordance with the policy pursued by the fraternal Parties for the cementing together of all the anti-imperialist forces of the world. We also take into consideration the definite positive tendencies shown of late in Yugoslavia's economic and socio-political life. Meanwhile the CPSU is aware of the serious differences that exist with the League of Communists of Yugoslavia on several ideological questions and considers it necessary to tell the Yugoslav comrades so frankly, criticizing those views of theirs which it finds wrong.

In its letter of March 9, 1963, the Central Committee of the Communist Party of China agrees with us in saying that today the world communist movement faces a crucial time. It depends on us, on our Parties, on the correctness of our policy, whether we continue to advance together in one rank or allow ourselves to be involved in a struggle harmful to the working class, to our peoples and to all working people, a struggle that can only result in mutual estrangement, weaken the forces of socialism, and undermine the unity of the world communist movement.

Naturally, being large, strong Parties, the Communist Party of the Soviet Union and the Communist Party of China would emerge from this situation with smaller losses; but as far as the other fraternal Parties, especially those working in complex conditions, are concerned, they would be faced with great and moreover unnecessary complications, which, of course, is not our aim.

Everything depends on how we act in this serious and complex situation. Are we to continue engaging in polemics, to fall prey to our passions and to turn arguments into recriminations and unproved accusations and sallies against the fraternal Parties? Or are we, aware of the great responsibility that we bear for the destinies of our great cause, to direct developments along a different channel, and show enough courage to rise above all that divides us today, cease uncomradely polemics, and concentrate on a search for ways of consolidating militant Soviet-Chinese co-operation, of consolidating the friendship of all the fraternal Parties?

We realize that any movement, including the communist movement, is unthinkable without controversy. However, no differences, no displeasure at the behaviour of a particular Party, can justify methods of struggle detrimental to the interests of the international communist movement. The deeper and broader our understanding of the aims and tasks of the international working class, the greater the vigour with which we should strive to analyse our differences, however serious they may seem today, quietly and relevantly, and prevent them from interfering with our positive work, from disorganizing the revolutionary activities of the international working class.

Let us struggle together for consistent adherence to the Marxist-Leninist course in the international communist movement, against revisionism and dogmatism, for closer unity in the ranks of the international communist movement, for respect for collectively worked out policies, and against any violations or arbitrary interpretations of these.

Our Party does not succumb to the heat of the polemic struggle but, aware of our common responsibility to the world communist movement, wishes to stop the dangerous process of sliding into a new series of discussions. It is obvious to everyone that we could have found much to say in defence of the Leninist policy of the CPSU, in defence of the common line of the international communist movement, in reply to groundless attacks made in articles recently carried by the Chinese press. And if we are not doing it now it is only because we do not want to gladden the foes of the communist movement. We hope that the harm caused by the sharpening polemics will be realized, and the interests of the unity of the socialist system and the international communist movement will be placed above all else. Therefore we suggest a meeting to you, not in order to aggravate the dispute but in order to reach a mutual understanding on major problems that have arisen in the international communist movement.

We know that such a meeting is being looked forward to by our friends in all the countries of the world, and that they pin great hopes on it. It depends on us, on our will and reason, whether results gladdening to our friends and upsetting to the enemies of communism will be achieved at the

257

meeting. This will be our common contribution to the cause of the struggle for the liberation of all oppressed people, for the victory of peace and socialism on earth, for the triumph of the great revolutionary doctrine of Marxism-Leninism.

With communist greetings,

The Central Committee of the Communist Party of the Soviet Union

[*Pravda*, April 14, 1963, *Peking Review*, VI, 25 (June 21, 1963), pp. 23–32.]

Full title: The Letter from the Central Committee of the CPSU to the Central Committee of the CCP, March 30, 1963 (complete text).

DOCUMENT 2

The CCP's Proposal Concerning the General Line of the International Communist Movement, June 14, 1963.

June 14, 1963

The Central Committee of the Communist
Party of the Soviet Union

Dear Comrades,

The Central Committee of the Communist Party of China has studied the letter of the Central Committee of the Communist Party of the Soviet Union of March 30, 1963.

All who have the unity of the socialist camp and the international communist movement at heart are deeply concerned about the talks between the Chinese and Soviet Parties and hope that our talks will help to eliminate differences, strengthen unity and create favourable conditions for convening a meeting of representatives of all the Communist and Workers' Parties.

It is the common and sacred duty of the Communist and Workers' Parties of all countries to uphold and strengthen the unity of the international communist movement. The Chinese and Soviet Parties bear a heavier responsibility for the unity of the entire socialist camp and international communist movement and should of course make commensurately greater efforts.

A number of major differences of principle now exist in the international communist movement. But however serious these differences, we should exercise sufficient patience and find ways to eliminate them so that we can unite our forces and strengthen the struggle against our common enemy.

It is with this sincere desire that the Central Committee of the Communist Party of China approaches the forthcoming talks between the Chinese and Soviet Parties.

In its letter of March 30, the Central Committee of the CPSU systematically presents its views on questions that need to be discussed in the talks between the Chinese and Soviet Parties, and in particular raises the question of the general line of the international communist movement. In this letter we too would like to express our views, which constitute our proposal on the general line of the international communist movement and on some related questions of principle.

We hope that this exposition of views will be conducive to mutual understanding by our two Parties and to a detailed, point-by-point discussion in the talks.

We also hope that this will be conducive to the understanding of our views by the fraternal Parties and to a full exchange of ideas at an international meeting of fraternal Parties.

(1) The general line of the international communist movement must take as its guiding principle the Marxist-Leninist revolutionary theory

concerning the historical mission of the proletariat and must not depart from it.

The Moscow Meetings of 1957 and 1960 adopted the Declaration and the Statement respectively after a full exchange of views and in accordance with the principle of reaching unanimity through consultation. The two documents point out the characteristics of our epoch and the common laws of socialist revolution and socialist construction, and lay down the common line of all the Communist and Workers' Parties. They are the common programme of the international communist movement.

It is true that for several years there have been differences within the international communist movement in the understanding of, and the attitude towards, the Declaration of 1957 and the Statement of 1960. The central issue here is whether or not to accept the revolutionary principles of the Declaration and the Statement. In the last analysis, it is a question of whether or not to accept the universal truth of Marxism-Leninism, whether or not to recognise the universal significance of the road of the October Revolution, whether or not to accept the fact that the people still living under the imperialist and capitalist system, who comprise two-thirds of the world's population, need to make revolution, and whether or not to accept the fact that the people already on the socialist road, who comprise one-third of the world's population, need to carry their revolution forward to the end.

It has become an urgent and vital task of the international communist movement resolutely to defend the revolutionary principles of the 1957 Declaration and the 1960 Statement.

Only by strictly following the revolutionary teachings of Marxism-Leninism and the general road of the October Revolution is it possible to have a correct understanding of the revolutionary principles of the Declaration and the Statement and a correct attitude towards them.

(2) What are the revolutionary principles of the Declaration and the Statement? They may be summarised as follows:

Workers of all countries, unite; workers of the world, unite with the oppressed peoples and oppressed nations; oppose imperialism and reaction in all countries; strive for world peace, national liberation, people's democracy and socialism; consolidate and expand the socialist camp; bring the proletarian world revolution step by step to complete victory; and establish a new world without imperialism, without capitalism and without the exploitation of man by man.

This, in our view, is the general line of the international communist movement at the present stage.

(3) This general line proceeds from the actual world situation taken as a whole and from a class analysis of the fundamental contradictions in the contemporary world, and is directed against the counter-revolutionary global strategy of U.S. imperialism.

This general line is one of forming a broad united front, with the socialist camp and the international proletariat as its nucleus, to oppose the imperialists and reactionaries headed by the United States; it is a line of boldly arousing the masses, expanding the revolutionary forces, winning over the middle forces and isolating the reactionary forces.

This general line is one of resolute revolutionary struggle by the people of all countries and of carrying the proletarian world revolution forward to the end; it is the line that most effectively combats imperialism and defends world peace.

If the general line of the international communist movement is one-sidedly reduced to " peaceful coexistence," " peaceful competition " and " peaceful transition," this is to violate the revolutionary principles of the 1957 Declaration and the 1960 Statement, to discard the historical mission of proletarian world revolution, and to depart from the revolutionary teachings of Marxism-Leninism.

The general line of the international communist movement should reflect the general law of development of world history. The revolutionary struggles of the proletariat and the people in various countries go through different stages and they all have their own characteristics, but they will not transcend the general law of development of world history. The general line should point out the basic direction for the revolutionary struggles of the proletariat and people of all countries.

While working out its specific line and policies, it is most important for each Communist or Workers' party to adhere to the principle of integrating the universal truth of Marxism-Leninism with the concrete practice of revolution and construction in its own country.

(4) In defining the general line of the international communist movement, the starting point is the concrete class analysis of world politics and economics as a whole and of actual world conditions, that is to say, of the fundamental contradictions in the contemporary world.

If one avoids a concrete class analysis, seizes at random on certain superficial phenomena, and draws subjective and groundless conclusions, one cannot possibly reach correct conclusions with regard to the general line of the international communist movement but will inevitably slide on to a track entirely different from that of Marxism-Leninism.

What are the fundamental contradictions in the contemporary world? Marxist-Leninists consistently hold that they are:

the contradiction between the socialist camp and the imperialist camp;

the contradiction between the proletariat and the bourgeoisie in the capitalist countries;

the contradiction between the oppressed nations and imperialism; and

the contradictions among imperialist countries and among monopoly capitalist groups.

The contradiction between the socialist camp and the imperialist camp is a contradiction between two fundamentally different social systems, socialism and capitalism. It is undoubtedly very sharp. But Marxist-Leninists must not regard the contradictions in the world as consisting solely and simply of the contradiction between the socialist camp and the imperialist camp.

The international balance of forces has changed and has become increasingly favourable to socialism and to all the oppressed peoples and nations of the world, and most unfavourable to imperialism and the reactionaries of all countries. Nevertheless, the contradictions enumerated above still objectively exist.

These contradictions and the struggles to which they give rise are inter-related and influence each other. Nobody can obliterate any of these fundamental contradictions or subjectively substitute one for all the rest. It is inevitable that these contradictions will give rise to popular revolutions, which alone can resolve them.

(5) The following erroneous views should be repudiated on the question of the fundamental contradictions in the contemporary world:

(a) the view which blots out the class content of the contradiction between the socialist and the imperialist camps and fails to see this contradiction as one between states under the dictatorship of the proletariat and states under the dictatorship of the monopoly capitalists;

(b) the view which recognizes only the contradiction between the socialist and the imperialist camps while neglecting or underestimating the contradictions between the proletariat and the bourgeoisie in the capitalist world, between the oppressed nations and imperialism, among the imperialist countries and among the monopoly capitalist groups, and the struggles to which these contradictions give rise;

(c) the view which maintains with regard to the capitalist world that the contradiction between the proletariat and the bourgeoisie can be resolved without a proletarian revolution in each country and that the contradiction between the oppressed nations and imperialism can be resolved without revolution by the oppressed nations;

(d) the view which denies that the development of the inherent contradictions in the contemporary capitalist world inevitably leads to a new situation in which the imperialist countries are locked in an intense struggle, and asserts that the contradictions among the imperialist countries can be reconciled, or even eliminated, by " international agreements among the big monopolies "; and

(e) the view which maintains that the contradiction between the two world systems of socialism and capitalism will automatically disappear in the course of " economic competition," that the other fundamental world contradictions will automatically do so with the disappearance of the contradiction between the two systems, and that a " world without wars," a new world of " all-round co-operation," will appear.

It is obvious that these erroneous views inevitably lead to erroneous and harmful policies and hence to setbacks and losses of one kind or another to the cause of the people and of socialism.

(6) The balance of forces between imperialism and socialism has under-gone a fundamental change since World War II. The main indication of this change is that the world now has not just one socialist country but a number of socialist countries forming the mighty socialist camp, and that the people who have taken the socialist road now number not two hundred million but a thousand million, or a third of the world's population.

The socialist camp is the outcome of the struggles of the international proletariat and working people. It belongs to the international proletariat and working people as well as to the people of the socialist countries.

The main common demands of the people of the countries in the socialist camp and the international proletariat and working people are that all the Communist and Workers' Parties in the socialist camp should:

262

Adhere to the Marxist-Leninist line and pursue correct Marxist-Leninist domestic and foreign policies;

Consolidate the dictatorship of the proletariat and the worker-peasant alliance led by the proletariat and carry the socialist revolution forward to the end of the economic, political and ideological fronts;

Promote the initiative and creativeness of the broad masses, carry out socialist construction in a planned way, develop production, improve the people's livelihood and strengthen national defence;

Strengthen the unity of the socialist camp on the basis of Marxism-Leninism, and support other socialist countries on the basis of proletarian internationalism;

Oppose the imperialist policies of aggression and war, and defend world peace;

Oppose the anti-communist, anti-popular and counter-revolutionary policies of the reactionaries of all countries; and

Help the revolutionary struggles of the oppressed classes and nations of the world.

All Communist and Workers' Parties in the socialist camp owe it to their own people and to the international proletariat and working people to fulfil these demands.

By fulfilling these demands the socialist camp will exert a decisive influence on the course of human history.

For this very reason, the imperialists and reactionaries invariably try in a thousand and one ways to influence the domestic and foreign policies of the countries in the socialist camp, to undermine the camp and break up the unity of the socialist countries and particularly the unity of China and the Soviet Union. They invariably try to infiltrate and subvert the socialist countries and even entertain the extravagant hope of destroying the socialist camp.

The question of what is the correct attitude towards the socialist camp is a most important question of principle confronting all Communist and Workers' Parties.

It is under new historical conditions that the Communist and Workers' Parties are now carrying on the task of proletarian internationalist unity and struggle. When only one socialist country existed and when this country was faced with hostility and jeopardized by all the imperialists and reactionaries because it firmly pursued the correct Marxist-Leninist line and policies, the touchstone of proletarian internationalism for every Communist Party was whether or not it resolutely defended the only socialist country. Now there is a socialist camp consisting of thirteen countries, Albania, Bulgaria, China, Cuba, Czechoslovakia, the German Democratic Republic, Hungary, the Democratic People's Republic of Korea, Mongolia, Poland, Rumania, the Soviet Union and the Democratic Republic of Viet Nam. Under these circumstances, the touchstone of proletarian internationalism for every Communist Party is whether or not it resolutely defends the whole of the socialist camp, whether or not it defends the unity of all the countries in the camp on the basis of Marxism-Leninism and whether or not it defends the Marxist-Leninist line and policies which the socialist countries ought to pursue.

If anybody does not pursue the correct Marxist-Leninist line and policies, does not defend the unity of the socialist camp but on the contrary creates tension and splits within it, or even follows the policies of the Yugoslav revisionists, tries to liquidate the socialist camp or helps capitalist countries to attack fraternal socialist countries, then he is betraying the interests of the entire international proletariat and the people of the world.

If anybody, following in the footsteps of others, defends the erroneous opportunist line and policies pursued by a certain socialist country] instead of upholding the correct Marxist-Leninist line and policies which the socialist countries ought to pursue, defends the policy of split instead of upholding the policy of unity, then he is departing from Marxism-Leninism and proletarian internationalism.

(7) Taking advantage of the situation after World War II, the U.S. imperialists stepped into the shoes of the German, Italian and Japanese fascists, and have been trying to erect a huge world empire such as has never been known before. The strategic objectives of U.S. imperialism have been to grab and dominate the intermediate zone lying between the United States and the socialist camp, put down the revolutions of the oppressed peoples and nations, proceed to destroy the socialist countries, and thus to subject all the peoples and countries of the world, including its allies, to domination and enslavement by U.S. monopoly capital.

Ever since World War II, the U.S. imperialists have been conducting propaganda for war against the Soviet Union and the socialist camp. There are two aspects to this propaganda. While the U.S. imperialists are actually preparing such a war, they also use this propaganda as a smokescreen for their oppression of the American people and for the extension of their aggression against the rest of the capitalist world.

The 1960 Statement points out:

" U.S. imperialism has become the biggest international exploiter."

" The United States is the mainstay of colonialism today."

" U.S. imperialism is the main force of aggression and war."

" International developments in recent years have furnished many new proofs of the fact that U.S. imperialism is the chief bulwark of world reaction and an international gendarme, that it has become an enemy of the peoples of the whole world."

U.S. imperialism is pressing its policies of aggression and war all over the world, but the outcome is bound to be the opposite of that intended—it will only be to hasten the awakening of the people in all countries and to hasten their revolutions.

The U.S. imperialists have thus placed themselves in opposition to the people of the whole world and have become encircled by them. The international proletariat must and can unite all the forces that can be united, make use of the internal contradictions in the enemy camp and establish the broadest united front against the U.S. imperialists and their lackeys.

The realistic and correct course is to entrust the fate of the people and of mankind to the unity and struggle of the world proletariat and to the unity and struggle of the people in all countries.

Conversely, to make no distinction between enemies, friends and ourselves and to entrust the fate of the people and of mankind to collaboration with U.S. imperialism is to lead people astray. The events of the last few years have exploded this illusion.

(8) The various types of contradictions in the contemporary world are concentrated in the vast areas of Asia, Africa and Latin America; these are

the most vulnerable areas under imperialist rule and the storm-centres of world revolution dealing direct blows at imperialism.

The national democratic revolutionary movement in these areas and the international socialist revolutionary movement are the two great historical currents of our time.

The national democratic revolution in these areas is an important component of the contemporary proletarian world revolution.

The anti-imperialist revolutionary struggles of the people in Asia, Africa and Latin America are pounding and undermining the foundations of the rule of imperialism and colonialism, old and new, and are now a mighty force in defence of world peace.

In a sense, therefore, the whole cause of the international proletarian revolution hinges on the outcome of the revolutionary struggles of the people of these areas, who constitute the overwhelming majority of the world's population.

Therefore, the anti-imperialist revolutionary struggle of the people in Asia, Africa and Latin America is definitely not merely a matter of regional significance but one of overall importance for the whole cause of proletarian world revolution.

Certain persons now go so far as to deny the great international significance of the anti-imperialist revolutionary struggles of the Asian, African and Latin American peoples and, on the pretext of breaking down the barriers of nationality, colour and geographical location, are trying their best to efface the line of demarcation between oppressed and oppressor nations and between oppressed and oppressor countries and to hold down the revolutionary struggles of the peoples in these areas. In fact, they cater to the needs of imperialism and create a new " theory " to justify the rule of imperialism in these areas and the promotion of its policies of old and new colonialism. Actually, this " theory " seeks not to break down the barriers of nationality, colour and geographical location but to maintain the rule of the " superior nations " over the oppressed nations. It is only natural that this fraudulent " theory " is rejected by the people in these areas.

The working class in every socialist country and in every capitalist country must truly put into effect the fighting slogans, " Workers of all countries, unite ! " and " Workers and oppressed nations of the world, unite ! "; it must study the revolutionary experience of the peoples of Asia, Africa and Latin America, firmly support their revolutionary actions and regard the cause of their liberation as a most dependable support for itself and as directly in accord with its own interests. This is the only effective way to break down the barriers of nationality, colour and geographical location and this is the only genuine proletarian internationalism.

It is impossible for the working class in the European and American capitalist countries to liberate itself unless it unites with the oppressed nations and unless those nations are liberated. Lenin rightly said,

> The revolutionary movement in the advanced countries would actually be a sheer fraud if, in their struggle against capital, the workers of Europe and America were not closely and completely united with the hundreds upon hundreds of millions of " colonial " slaves who are oppressed by capital.[1]

[1] Lenin, " The Second Congress of the Communist International," *Selected Works*, Foreign Languages Publishing House, Moscow, 1952, Vol. II, Part 2, pp. 472–473.

Certain persons in the international communist movement are now taking a passive or scornful or negative attitude towards the struggles of the oppressed nations for liberation. They are in fact protecting the interests of monopoly capital, betraying those of the proletariat, and degenerating into social democrats.

The attitude taken towards the revolutionary struggles of the people in the Asian, African and Latin American countries is an important criterion for differentiating those who want revolution from those who do not and those who are truly defending world peace from those who are abetting the forces of aggression and war.

(9) The oppressed nations and peoples of Asia, Africa and Latin America are faced with the urgent task of fighting imperialism and its lackeys.

History has entrusted to the proletarian parties in these areas the glorious mission of holding high the banner of struggle against imperialism, against old and new colonialism and for national independence and people's democracy, of standing in the forefront of the national democratic revolutionary movement and striving for a socialist future.

In these areas, extremely broad sections of the population refuse to be slaves of imperialism. They include not only the workers, peasants, intellectuals and petty bourgeoisie, but also the patriotic national bourgeoisie and even certain kings, princes and aristocrats who are patriotic.

The proletariat and its party must have confidence in the strength of the masses and, above all, must unite with the peasants and establish a solid worker-peasant alliance. It is of primary importance for advanced members of the proletariat to work in the rural areas, help the peasants to get organized, and raise their class consciousness and their national self-respect and self-confidence.

On the basis of the worker-peasant alliance the proletariat and its party must unite all the strata that can be united and organize a broad united front against imperialism and its lackeys. In order to consolidate and expand this united front it is necessary that the proletarian party should maintain its ideological, political and organizational independence and insist on the leadership of the revolution.

The proletarian party and the revolutionary people must learn to master all forms of struggle, including armed struggle. They must defeat counter-revolutionary armed force with revolutionary armed force whenever imperialism and its lackeys resort to armed suppression.

The nationalist countries which have recently won political independence are still confronted with the arduous tasks of consolidating it, liquidating the forces of imperialism and domestic reaction, carrying out agrarian and other social reforms and developing their national economy and culture. It is of practical and vital importance for these countries to guard and fight against the neo-colonialist policies which the old colonialists adopt to preserve their interests, and especially against the neo-colonialism of U.S. imperialism.

In some of these countries, the patriotic national bourgeoisie continue to stand with the masses in the struggle against imperialism and colonialism and introduce certain measures of social progress. This requires the proletarian party to make a full appraisal of the progressive role of the patriotic national bourgeoisie and strengthen unity with them.

As the internal social contradictions and the international class struggle sharpen, the bourgeoisie, and particularly the big bourgeoisie, in some newly independent countries increasingly tend to become retainers of imperialism and to pursue anti-popular, anti-communist and counter-revolutionary policies. It is necessary for the proletarian party resolutely to oppose these reactionary policies.

Generally speaking, the bourgeoisie in these countries have a dual character. When a united front is formed with the bourgeoisie, the policy of the proletarian party should be one of both unity and struggle. The policy should be to unite with the bourgeoisie, in so far as they tend to be progressive, anti-imperialist and anti-feudal, but to struggle against their reactionary tendencies to compromise and collaborate with imperialism and the forces of feudalism.

On the national question the world outlook of the proletarian party is internationalism, and not nationalism. In the revolutionary struggle it supports progressive nationalism and opposes reactionary nationalism. It must always draw a clear line of demarcation between itself and bourgeois nationalism, to which it must never fall captive.

The 1960 Statement says,

> Communists expose attempts by the reactionary section of the bourgeoisie to represent its selfish, narrow class interests as those of the entire nation; they expose the demagogic use by bourgeois politicians of socialist slogans for the same purpose. . . .

If the proletariat becomes the tail of the landlords and bourgeoisie in the revolution, no real or thorough victory in the national democratic revolution is possible, and even if victory of a kind is gained, it will be impossible to consolidate it.

In the course of the revolutionary struggles of the oppressed nations and peoples, the proletarian party must put forward a programme of its own which is thoroughly against imperialism and domestic reaction and for national independence and people's democracy, and it must work independently among the masses, constantly expand the progressive forces, win over the middle forces and isolate the reactionary forces; only thus can it carry the national democratic revolution through to the end and guide the revolution on to the road of socialism.

(10) In the imperialist and the capitalist countries, the proletarian revolution and the dictatorship of the proletariat are essential for the thorough resolution of the contradictions of capitalist society.

In striving to accomplish this task the proletarian party must under the present circumstances actively lead the working class and the working people in struggles to oppose monopoly capital, to defend democratic rights, to oppose the menace of fascism, to improve living conditions, to oppose imperialist arms expansion and war preparations, to defend world peace and actively to support the revolutionary struggles of the oppressed nations.

In the capitalist countries which U.S. imperialism controls or is trying to control, the working class and the people should direct their attacks mainly against U.S. imperialism, but also against their own monopoly capitalists and other reactionary forces who are betraying the national interests.

Large-scale mass struggles in the capitalist countries in recent years have shown that the working class and working people are experiencing a new awakening. Their struggles, which are dealing blows at monopoly capital and reaction, have opened bright prospects for the revolutionary cause in their own countries and are also a powerful support for the revolutionary struggles of the Asian, African and Latin American peoples and for the countries of the socialist camp.

The proletarian parties in imperialist or capitalist countries must maintain their own ideological, political and organizational independence in leading revolutionary struggles. At the same time, they must unite all the forces that can be united and build a broad united front against monopoly capital and against the imperialist policies of aggression and war.

While actively leading immediate struggles, Communists in the capitalist countries should link them with the struggle for long-range and general interests, educate the masses in a Marxist-Leninist revolutionary spirit, ceaselessly raise their political consciousness and undertake the historical task of the proletarian revolution. If they fail to do so, if they regard the immediate movement as everything, determine their conduct from case to case, adapt themselves to the events of the day and sacrifice the basic interests of the proletariat, that is out-and-out social democracy.

Social democracy is a bourgeois ideological trend. Lenin pointed out long ago that the social democratic parties are political detachments of the bourgeoisie, its agents in the working-class movement and its principal social prop. Communists must at all times draw a clear line of demarcation between themselves and social democratic parties on the basic question of the proletarian revolution and the dictatorship of the proletariat and liquidate the ideological influence of social democracy in the international working-class movement and among the working people. Beyond any shadow of doubt, Communists must win over the masses under the influence of the social democratic parties and must win over those Left and middle elements in the social democratic parties who are willing to oppose domestic monopoly capital and domination by foreign imperialism, and must unite with them in extensive joint action in the day-to-day struggle of the working-class movement and in the struggle to defend world peace.

In order to lead the proletariat and working people in revolution, Marxist-Leninist parties must master all forms of struggle and be able to substitute one form for another quickly as the conditions of struggle change. The vanguard of the proletariat will remain unconquerable in all circumstances only if it masters all forms of struggle—peaceful and armed, open and secret, legal and illegal, parliamentary struggle and mass struggle, etc. It is wrong to refuse to use parliamentary and other legal forms of struggle when they can and should be used. However, if a Marxist-Leninist party falls into legalism or parliamentary cretinism, confining the struggle within the limits permitted by the bourgeoisie, this will inevitably lead to renouncing the proletarian revolution and the dictatorship of the proletariat.

(11) On the question of transition from capitalism to socialism, the proletarian party must proceed from the stand of class struggle and revolution and base itself on the Marxist-Leninist teachings concerning the proletarian revolution and the dictatorship of the proletariat.

Communists would always prefer to bring about the transition to socialism by peaceful means. But can peaceful transition be made into a new worldwide strategic principle for the international communist movement? Absolutely not.

Marxism-Leninism consistently holds that the fundamental question in all revolutions is that of state power. The 1957 Declaration and the 1960

Statement both clearly point out, " Leninism teaches, and experience confirms, that the ruling classes never relinquish power voluntarily." The old government never topples even in a period of crisis, unless it is pushed. This is a universal law of class struggle.

In specific historical conditions, Marx and Lenin did raise the possibility that revolution may develop peacefully. But, as Lenin pointed out, the peaceful development of revolution is an opportunity " very seldom to be met with in the history of revolution."

As a matter of fact, there is no historical precedent for peaceful transition from capitalism to socialism.

Certain persons say there was no precedent when Marx foretold that socialism would inevitably replace capitalism. Then why can we not predict a peaceful transition from capitalism to socialism despite the absence of a precedent?

This parallel is absurd. Employing dialectical and historical materialism, Marx analysed the contradictions of capitalism, discovered the objective laws of development of human society and arrived at a scientific conclusion, whereas the prophets who pin all their hopes on " peaceful transition " proceed from historical idealism, ignore the most fundamental contradictions of capitalism, repudiate the Marxist-Leninist teachings on class struggle, and arrive at a subjective and groundless conclusion. How can people who repudiate Marxism get any help from Marx?

It is plain to everyone that the capitalist countries are strengthening their state machinery—and especially their military apparatus—the primary purpose of which is to suppress the people in their own countries.

The proletarian party must never base its thinking, its policies for revolution and its entire work on the assumption that the imperialists and reactionaries will accept peaceful transformation.

The proletarian party must prepare itself for two eventualities — while preparing for a peaceful development of the revolution, it must also fully prepare for a non-peaceful development. It should concentrate on the painstaking work of accumulating revolutionary strength, so that it will be ready to seize victory when the conditions for revolution are ripe or to strike powerful blows at the imperialists and the reactionaries when they launch surprise attacks and armed assaults.

If it fails to make such preparations, the proletarian party will paralyse the revolutionary will of the proletariat, disarm itself ideologically and sink into a totally passive state of unpreparedness both politically and organis-ationally, and the result will be to bury the proletarian revolutionary cause.

(12) All social revolutions in the various stages of the history of mankind are historically inevitable and are governed by objective laws independent of man's will. Moreover, history shows that there never was a revolution which was able to achieve victory without zigzags and sacrifices.

With Marxist-Leninist theory as the basis, the task of the proletarian party is to analyse the concrete historical conditions, put forward the correct strategy and tactics, and guide the masses in bypassing hidden reefs, avoiding unnecessary sacrifices and reaching the goal step by step. Is it possible to avoid sacrifices altogether ? Such is not the case with the slave revolutions, the serf revolutions, the bourgeois revolutions, or the national revolutions; nor is it the case with proletarian revolutions. Even if the guiding line of the revolution is correct, it is impossible to have a sure guarantee against setbacks and sacrifices in the course of the revolution. So long as a correct line is adhered to, the revolution is bound to triumph in the end. To abandon revolution on the pretext of avoiding sacrifices is in reality to demand that the people should for ever remain slaves and endure infinite pain and sacrifice.

Elementary knowledge of Marxism-Leninism tells us that the birth-pangs of a revolution are far less painful than the chronic agony of the old society. Lenin rightly said that " even with the most peaceful course of events, the present [capitalist] system always and inevitably exacts countless sacrifices from the working class." [2]

Whoever considers a revolution can be made only if everything is plain sailing, only if there is an advance guarantee against sacrifices and failure, is certainly no revolutionary.

However difficult the conditions and whatever sacrifices and defeats the revolution may suffer, proletarian revolutionaries should educate the masses in the spirit of revolution and hold aloft the banner of revolution and not abandon it.

It would be " Left " adventurism if the proletarian party should rashly launch a revolution before the objective conditions are ripe. But it would be Right opportunism if the proletarian party should not dare to lead a revolution and to seize state power when the objective conditions are ripe.

Even in ordinary times, when it is leading the masses in the day-to-day struggle, the proletarian party should ideologically, politically and organisationally prepare its own ranks and the masses for revolution and promote revolutionary struggles, so that it will not miss the opportunity to overthrow the reactionary regime and establish a new state power when the conditions for revolution are ripe. Otherwise, when the objective conditions are ripe, the proletarian party will simply throw away the opportunity of seizing victory.

The proletarian party must be flexible as well as highly principled, and on occasion it must make such compromises as are necessary in the interests of the revolution. But it must never abandon principled policies and the goal of revolution on the pretext of flexibility and of necessary compromises.

The proletarian party must lead the masses in waging struggles against the enemies, and it must know how to utilise the contradictions among those enemies. But the purpose of using these contradictions is to make it easier to attain the goal of the people's revolutionary struggles and not to liquidate these struggles.

Countless facts have proved that, wherever the dark rule of imperialism and reaction exists, the people who form over 90 per cent. of the population will sooner or later rise in revolution.

If Communists isolate themselves from the revolutionary demands of the masses, they are bound to lose the confidence of the masses and will be tossed to the rear by the revolutionary current.

If the leading group in any Party adopt a non-revolutionary line and convert it into a reformist party, then Marxist-Leninists inside and outside the Party will replace them and lead the people in making revolution. In another kind of situation, the bourgeois revolutionaries will come forward

[2] Lenin, " Another Massacre," Collected Works, F.L.P.H., Moscow, 1961, Vol. V, p. 25.

to lead the revolution and the party of the proletariat will forfeit its leadership of the revolution. When the reactionary bourgeoisie betray the revolution and suppress the people, an opportunist line will cause tragic and unnecessary losses to the Communists and the revolutionary masses.

If Communists slide down the path of opportunism, they will degenerate into bourgeois nationalists and become appendages of the imperialists and the reactionary bourgeoisie.

There are certain persons who assert that they have made the greatest creative contributions to revolutionary theory since Lenin and that they alone are correct. But it is very dubious whether they have ever really given consideration to the extensive experience of the entire world communist movement, whether they have ever really considered the interests, the goal and tasks of the international proletarian movement as a whole, and whether they really have a general line for the international communist movement which conforms with Marxism-Leninism.

In the last few years the international communist movement and the national-liberation movement have had many experiences and many lessons. There are experiences which people should praise and there are experiences which make people grieve. Communists and revolutionaries in all countries should ponder and seriously study these experiences of success and failure, so as to draw correct conclusions and useful lessons from them.

(13) The socialist countries and the revolutionary struggles of the oppressed peoples and nations support and assist each other.

The national-liberation movements of Asia, Africa and Latin America and the revolutionary movements of the people in the capitalist countries are a strong support to the socialist countries. It is completely wrong to deny this.

The only attitude for the socialist countries to adopt towards the revolutionary struggles of the oppressed peoples and nations is one of warm sympathy and active support; they must not adopt a perfunctory attitude, or one of national selfishness or of great-power chauvinism.

Lenin said, " Alliance with the revolutionaries of the advanced countries and with all the oppressed peoples against any and all the imperialists—such is the external policy of the proletariat." [3] Whoever fails to understand this point and considers that the support and aid given by the socialist countries to the oppressed peoples and nations are a burden or charity is going counter to Marxism-Leninism and proletarian internationalism.

The superiority of the socialist system and the achievements of the socialist countries in construction play an exemplary role and are an inspiration to the oppressed peoples and the oppressed nations.

But this exemplary role and inspiration can never replace the revolutionary struggles of the oppressed peoples and nations. No oppressed people or nation can win liberation except through its own staunch revolutionary struggle.

Certain persons have one-sidedly exaggerated the role of peaceful competition between socialist and imperialist countries in their attempt to substitute peaceful competition for the revolutionary struggles of the oppressed peoples and nations. According to their preaching, it would

[3] Lenin, " The External Policy of the Russian Revolution," *Collected Works*, 4th Russian edition, State Publishing House for Political Literature, Moscow, 1949, Vol. XXV, p. 69.

seem that imperialism will automatically collapse in the course of this peaceful competition and that the only thing the oppressed peoples and nations have to do is to wait quietly for the advent of this day. What does this have in common with Marxist-Leninist views?

Moreover, certain persons have concocted the strange tale that China and some other socialist countries want " to unleash wars " and to spread socialism by " wars between states." As the Statement of 1960 points out, such tales are nothing but imperialist and reactionary slanders. To put it bluntly, the purpose of those who repeat these slanders is to hide the fact that they are opposed to revolutions by the oppressed peoples and nations of the world and opposed to others supporting such revolutions.

(14) In the last few years much—in fact a great deal—has been said on the question of war and peace. Our views and policies on this question are known to the world, and no one can distort them.

It is a pity that although certain persons in the international communist movement talk about how much they love peace and hate war, they are unwilling to acquire even a faint understanding of the simple truth on war pointed out by Lenin.

Lenin said,

> It seems to me that the main thing that is usually forgotten on the question of war, which receives inadequate attention, the main reason why there is so much controversy, and, I would say, futile, hopeless and aimless controversy, is that people forget the fundamental question of the class character of the war; why the war broke out; the classes that are waging it; the historico-economic conditions that gave rise to it.[4]

As Marxist-Leninists see it, war is the continuation of politics by other means, and every war is inseparable from the political system and the political struggles which give rise to it. If one departs from this scientific Marxist-Leninist proposition which has been confirmed by the entire history of class struggle, one will never be able to understand either the question of war or the question of peace.

There are different types of peace and different types of war. Marxist-Leninists must be clear about what type of peace or what type of war is in question. Lumping just wars and unjust wars together and opposing all of them undiscriminatingly is a bourgeois pacifist and not a Marxist-Leninist approach.

Certain persons say that revolutions are entirely possible without war. Now which type of war are they referring to—is it a war of national liberation or a revolutionary civil war, or is it a world war?

If they are referring to a war of national liberation or a revolutionary civil war, then this formulation is, in effect, opposed to revolutionary wars and to revolution.

If they are referring to a world war, then they are shooting at a non-existent target. Although Marxist-Leninists have pointed out, on the basis of the history of the two world wars, that world wars inevitably lead to revolution, no Marxist-Leninist ever has held or ever will hold that revolution must be made through world war.

---

4 Lenin, " War and Revolution," *Collected Works*, 4th Russian edition, S.P.H.P.L., Moscow, 1949, Vol. XXIV, p. 362.

Marxist-Leninists take the abolition of war as their ideal and believe that war can be abolished.

But how can war be abolished?

This is how Lenin viewed it:

> . . . our object is to achieve the socialist system of society, which, by abolishing the division of mankind into classes, by abolishing all exploitation of man by man, and of one nation by other nations, will inevitably abolish all possibility of war.[5]

The Statement of 1960 also puts it very clearly, " The victory of socialism all over the world will completely remove the social and national causes of all wars."

However, certain persons now actually hold that it is possible to bring about " a world without weapons, without armed forces and without wars " through " general and complete disarmament " while the system of imperialism and of the exploitation of man by man still exists. This is sheer illusion.

An elementary knowledge of Marxism-Leninism tells us that the armed forces are the principal part of the state machine and that a so-called world without weapons and without armed forces can only be a world without states. Lenin said:

> Only *after* the proletariat has disarmed the bourgeoisie will it be able, without betraying its world-historical mission, to throw all armaments on the scrap heap; and the proletariat will undoubtedly do this, but *only when this condition has been fulfilled, certainly not before.*[6]

What are the facts in the world today? Is there a shadow of evidence that the imperialist countries headed by the United States are ready to carry out general and complete disarmament? Are they not each and all engaged in general and complete arms expansion?

We have always maintained that, in order to expose and combat the imperialists' arms expansion and war preparations, it is necessary to put forward the proposal for general disarmament. Furthermore, it is possible to compel imperialism to accept some kind of agreement on disarmament through the combined struggle of the socialist countries and the people of the whole world.

If one regards general and complete disarmament as the fundamental road to world peace, spreads the illusion that imperialism will automatically lay down its arms and tries to liquidate the revolutionary struggles of the oppressed peoples and nations on the pretext of disarmament, then this is deliberately to deceive the people of the world and help the imperialists in their policies of aggression and war.

In order to overcome the present ideological confusion in the international working-class movement on the question of war and peace, we consider that Lenin's thesis, which has been discarded by the modern revisionists, must be restored in the interest of combating the imperialist policies of aggression and war and defending world peace.

The people of the world universally demand the prevention of a new world war. And it is possible to prevent a new world war.

---

[5] *Ibid.* p. 363.
[6] Lenin, " The War Program of the Proletarian Revolution," *Selected Works*, F.L.P.H., Moscow, 1952, Vol. I, Part 2, p. 574.

The question then is, what is the way to secure world peace? According to the Leninist viewpoint, world peace can be won only by the struggles of the people in all countries and not by begging the imperialists for it. World peace can only be effectively defended by relying on the development of the forces of the socialist camp, on the revolutionary struggles of the proletariat and working people of all countries, on the liberation struggles of the oppressed nations and on the struggles of all peaceloving people and countries.

Such is the Leninist policy. Any policy to the contrary definitely will not lead to world peace but will only encourage the ambitions of the imperialists and increase the danger of world war.

In recent years, certain persons have been spreading the argument that a single spark from a war of national liberation or from a revolutionary people's war will lead to a world conflagration destroying the whole of mankind. What are the facts? Contrary to what these persons say, the wars of national liberation and the revolutionary people's wars that have occurred since World War II have not led to world war. The victory of these revolutionary wars has directly weakened the forces of imperialism and greatly strengthened the forces which prevent the imperialists from launching a world war and which defend world peace. Do not the facts demonstrate the absurdity of this argument?

(15) The complete banning and destruction of nuclear weapons is an important task in the struggle to defend world peace. We must do our utmost to this end.

Nuclear weapons are unprecedentedly destructive, which is why for more than a decade now the U.S. imperialists have been pursuing their policy of nuclear blackmail in order to realise their ambition of enslaving the people of all countries and dominating the world.

But when the imperialists threaten other countries with nuclear weapons, they subject the people in their own country to the same threat, thus arousing them against nuclear weapons and against the imperialist policies of aggression and war. At the same time, in their vain hope of destroying their opponents with nuclear weapons, the imperialists are in fact subjecting themselves to the danger of being destroyed.

The possibility of banning nuclear weapons does indeed exist. However, if the imperialists are forced to accept an agreement to ban nuclear weapons it decidedly will not be because of their " love for humanity " but because of the pressure of the people of all countries and for the sake of their own vital interests.

In contrast to the imperialists, socialist countries rely upon the righteous strength of the people and on their own correct policies, and have no need whatever to gamble with nuclear weapons in the world arena. Socialist countries have nuclear weapons solely in order to defend themselves and to prevent imperialism from launching a nuclear war.

In the view of Marxist-Leninists, the people are the makers of history. In the present, as in the past, man is the decisive factor. Marxist-Leninists attach importance to the role of technological change, but it is wrong to belittle the role of man and exaggerate the role of technology.

The emergence of nuclear weapons can neither arrest the progress of human history nor save the imperialist system from its doom, any more than the emergence of new techniques could save the old systems from their doom in the past.

The emergence of nuclear weapons does not and cannot resolve the fundamental contradictions in the contemporary world, does not and cannot alter the law of class struggle, and does not and cannot change the nature of imperialism and reaction.

It cannot, therefore, be said that with the emergence of nuclear weapons the possibility and the necessity of social and national revolutions have disappeared, or the basic principles of Marxism-Leninism, and especially the theories of proletarian revolution and the dictatorship of the proletariat and of war and peace, have become outmoded and changed into stale "dogmas."

(16) It was Lenin who advanced the thesis that it is possible for the socialist countries to practise peaceful co-existence with the capitalist countries. It is well known that after the great Soviet people had repulsed foreign armed intervention the Communist Party of the Soviet Union and the Soviet Government, led first by Lenin and then by Stalin, consistently pursued the policy of peaceful co-existence and that they were forced to wage a war of self-defence only when attacked by the German imperialists.

Since its founding, the People's Republic of China too has consistently pursued the policy of peaceful co-existence with countries having different social systems, and it is China which initiated the Five Principles of Peaceful Co-existence.

However, a few years ago certain persons suddenly claimed Lenin's policy of peaceful co-existence as their own " great discovery." They maintain that they have a monopoly on the interpretation of this policy. They treat " peaceful co-existence " as if it were an all-inclusive, mystical book from heaven and attribute to it every success the people of the world achieve by struggle. What is more, they label all who disagree with their distortions of Lenin's views as opponents of peaceful co-existence, as people completely ignorant of Lenin and Leninism, and as heretics deserving to be burnt at the stake.

How can the Chinese Communists agree with this view and practice ? They cannot, it is impossible.

Lenin's principle of peaceful co-existence is very clear and readily comprehensible by ordinary people. Peaceful co-existence designates a relationship between countries with different social systems, and must not be interpreted as one pleases. It should never be extended to apply to the relations between oppressed and oppressor nations, between oppressed and oppressor countries or between oppressed and oppressor classes, and never be described as the main content of the transition from capitalism to socialism, still less should it be asserted that peaceful co-existence is mankind's road to socialism. The reason is that it is one thing to practise peaceful co-existence between countries with different social systems. It is absolutely impermissible and impossible for countries practising peaceful co-existence to touch even a hair of each other's social system. The class struggle, the struggle for national liberation and the transition from capitalism to socialism in various countries are quite another thing. They are all bitter, life-and-death revolutionary struggles which aim at changing the social system. Peaceful co-existence cannot replace the revolutionary struggles of the people. The transition from capitalism to socialism in any country can only be brought about through the proletarian revolution and the dictatorship of the proletariat in that country.

In the application of the policy of peaceful co-existence, struggles between the socialist and imperialist countries are unavoidable in the political, economic and ideological spheres, and it is absolutely impossible to have " all-round-co-operation."

It is necessary for the socialist countries to engage in negotiations of one kind or another with the imperialist countries. It is possible to reach certain agreements through negotiation by relying on the correct policies of the socialist countries and on the pressure of the people of all countries. But necessary compromises between socialist countries and the imperialist countries do not require the oppressed peoples and nations to follow suit and compromise with imperialism and its lackeys. No one should ever demand in the name of peaceful co-existence that the oppressed peoples and nations should give up their revolutionary struggles.

The application of the policy of peaceful co-existence by the socialist countries is advantageous for achieving a peaceful international environment for socialist construction, for exposing the imperialist policies of aggression and war and for isolating the imperialist forces of aggression and war. But if the general line of the foreign policy of the socialist countries is confined to peaceful co-existence, then it is impossible to handle correctly either the relations between socialist countries or those between the socialist countries and the oppressed peoples and nations. Therefore it is wrong to make peaceful co-existence the general line of the foreign policy of the socialist countries.

In our view, the general line of the foreign policy of the socialist countries should have the following content: to develop relations of friendship, mutual assistance and co-operation among the countries in the socialist camp in accordance with the principle of proletarian internationalism; to strive for peaceful co-existence on the basis of the Five Principles with countries having different social systems and oppose the imperialist policies of aggression and war; and to support and assist the revolutionary struggles of all the oppressed peoples and nations. These three aspects are interrelated and indivisible, and not a single one can be omitted.

(17) For a very long historical period after the proletariat takes power, class struggle continues as an objective law independent of man's will, differing only in form from what it was before the taking of power.

After the October Revolution, Lenin pointed out a number of times that:

(a) The overthrown exploiters always try in a thousand and one ways to recover the " paradise " they have been deprived of.

(b) New elements of capitalism are constantly and spontaneously generated in the petty-bourgeois atmosphere.

(c) Political degenerates and new bourgeois elements may emerge in the ranks of the working class and among government functionaries as a result of bourgeois influence and the pervasive, corrupting atmosphere of the petty bourgeoisie.

(d) The external conditions for the continuance of class struggle within a socialist country are encirclement by international capitalism, the imperialists' threat of armed intervention and their subversive activities to accomplish peaceful disintegration.

Life has confirmed these conclusions of Lenin's.

For decades or even longer periods after socialist industrialisation and agricultural collectivisation, it will be impossible to say that any socialist country will be free from those elements which Lenin repeatedly denounced, such as bourgeois hangers-on, parasites, speculators, swindlers, idlers, hooligans and embezzlers of state funds; or to say that a socialist country will no longer need to perform or be able to relinquish the task laid down by Lenin of conquering " this contagion, this plague, this ulcer that socialism has inherited from capitalism."

In a socialist country, it takes a very long historical period gradually to settle the question of who will win—socialism or capitalism. The struggle between the road of socialism and the road of capitalism runs through this whole historical period. This struggle rises and falls in a wave-like manner, at times becoming very fierce, and the forms of the struggle are many and varied.

The 1957 Declaration rightly states that "the conquest of power by the working class is only the beginning of the revolution, not its conclusion."

To deny the existence of class struggle in the period of the dictatorship of the proletariat and the necessity of thoroughly completing the socialist revolution on the economic, political and ideological fronts is wrong, does not correspond to objective reality and violates Marxism-Leninism.

(18) Both Marx and Lenin maintained that the entire period before the advent of the higher stage of communist society is the period of transition from capitalism to communism, the period of the dictatorship of the proletariat. In this transition period, the dictatorship of the proletariat, that is to say, the proletarian state, goes through the dialectical process of establishment, consolidation, strengthening and withering away.

In the *Critique of the Gotha Program*, Marx posed the question as follows:

> Between capitalist and communist society lies the period of the revolutionary transformation of the one into the other. There corresponds to this also a political transition period in which the state can be nothing but *the revolutionary dictatorship of the proletariat.*[7]

Lenin frequently emphasised Marx's great theory of the dictatorship of the proletariat and analysed the development of this theory, particularly in his outstanding work, *The State and Revolution*, where he wrote:

> . . . the transition from capitalist society—which is developing towards communism—to a communist society is impossible without a " political transition period," and the state in this period can only be the revolutionary dictatorship of the proletariat.[8]

He further said:

> The essence of Marx's teaching on the state has been mastered only by those who understand that the dictatorship of a *single* class is necessary not only for every class society in general, not only for the *proletariat* which has overthrown the bourgeoisie, but also for the entire *historical*

---

[7] Marx and Engels, *Selected Works*, F.L.P.H., Moscow, 1955, Vol. II, pp. 32–33.
[8] Lenin, *Selected Works*, F.L.P.H., Moscow, 1952, Vol. II, Part 1, p. 289.

period which separates capitalism from " classless society," from communism.[9]

As stated above, the fundamental thesis of Marx and Lenin is that the dictatorship of the proletariat will inevitably continue for the entire historical period of the transition from capitalism to communism, that is, for the entire period up to the abolition of all class differences and the entry into a classless society, the higher stage of communist society.

What will happen if it is announced, halfway through, that the dictatorship of the proletariat is no longer necessary?

Does this not fundamentally conflict with the teachings of Marx and Lenin on the state of the dictatorship of the proletariat?

Does this not license the development of " this contagion, this plague, this ulcer that socialism has inherited from capitalism "?

In other words, this would lead to extremely grave consequences and make any transition to communism out of the question.

Can there be a " state of the whole people "? Is it possible to replace the state of the dictatorship of the proletariat by a " state of the whole people "?

This is not a question about the internal affairs of any particular country but a fundamental problem involving the universal truth of Marxism-Leninism.

In the view of Marxist-Leninists, there is no such thing as a non-class or supra-class state. So long as the state remains a state, it must bear a class character; so long as the state exists, it cannot be a state of the " whole people." As soon as society becomes classless, there will no longer be a state.

Then what sort of thing would a " state of the whole people " be?

Anyone with an elementary knowledge of Marxism-Leninism can understand that the so-called state of the whole people is nothing new. Representative bourgeois figures have always called the bourgeois state a " state of all the people," or a " state in which power belongs to all the people."

Certain persons may say that their society is already one without classes. We answer: No, there are classes and class struggles in all socialist countries without exception.

Since remnants of the old exploiting classes who are trying to stage a comeback still exist there, since new capitalist elements are constantly being generated there, and since there are still parasites, speculators, idlers, hooligans, embezzlers of state funds, etc., how can it be said that classes or class struggles no longer exist? How can it be said that the dictatorship of the proletariat is no longer necessary?

Marxism-Leninism tells us that in addition to the suppression of the hostile classes, the historical tasks of the dictatorship of the proletariat in the course of building socialism necessarily include the correct handling of relations between the working class and peasantry, the consolidation of their political and economic alliance and the creation of conditions for the gradual elimination of the class difference between worker and peasant.

When we look at the economic base of any socialist society, we find that the difference between ownership by the whole people and collective ownership exists in all socialist countries without exception, and that there is individual ownership too. Ownership by the whole people and collective

9 *Ibid*. p. 234.

ownership are two kinds of ownership and two kinds of relations of production in socialist society. The workers in enterprises owned by the whole people and the peasants on farms owned collectively belong to two different categories of labourers in socialist society. Therefore, the class difference between worker and peasant exists in all socialist countries without exception. This difference will not disappear until the transition to the higher stage of communism is achieved. In their present level of economic development all socialist countries are still far, far removed from the higher stage of communism in which " from each according to his ability, to each according to his needs " is put into practice. Therefore, it will take a long, long time to eliminate the class difference between worker and peasant. And until this difference is eliminated, it is impossible to say that society is classless or that there is no longer any need for the dictatorship of the proletariat.

In calling a socialist state the " state of the whole people," is one trying to replace the Marxist-Leninist theory of the state by the bourgeois theory of the state? Is one trying to replace the state of the dictatorship of the proletariat by a state of a different character?

If that is the case, it is nothing but a great historical retrogression. The degeneration of the social system in Yugoslavia is a grave lesson.

(19) Leninism holds that the proletarian party must exist together with the dictatorship of the proletariat in socialist countries. The party of the proletariat is indispensable for the entire historical period of the dictatorship of the proletariat. The reason is that the dictatorship of the proletariat has to struggle against the enemies of the proletariat and of the people, remould the peasants and other small producers, constantly consolidate the proletarian ranks, build socialism and effect the transition to communism; none of these things can be done without the leadership of the party of the proletariat.

Can there be a " party of the entire people "? Is it possible to replace the Party which is the vanguard of the proletariat by a " party of the entire people "?

This, too, is not a question about the internal affairs of any particular Party, but a fundamental problem involving the universal truth of Marxism-Leninism.

In the view of Marxist-Leninists, there is no such thing as a non-class or supra-class political party. All political parties have a class character. Party spirit is the concentrated expression of class character.

The party of the proletariat is the only party able to represent the interests of the whole people. It can do so precisely because it represents the interests of the proletariat, whose ideas and will it concentrates. It can lead the whole people because the proletariat can finally emancipate itself only with the emancipation of all mankind, because the very nature of the proletariat enables its party to approach problems in terms of its present and future interests, because the party is boundlessly loyal to the people and has the spirit of self-sacrifice; hence its democratic centralism and iron discipline. Without such a party, it is impossible to maintain the dictatorshp of the proletariat and to represent the interests of the whole people.

What will happen if it is announced halfway before entering the higher stage of communist society that the party of the proletariat has become a " party of the entire people " and if its proletarian class character is repudiated?

Does this not fundamentally conflict with the teachings of Marx and Lenin on the party of the proletariat?

Does this not disarm the proletariat and all the working people, organizationally and ideologically, and is it not tantamount to helping restore capitalism?

Is it not " going south by driving the chariot north " to talk about any transition to communist society in such circumstances?

(20) Over the past few years, certain persons have violated Lenin's integral teachings about the interrelationship of leaders, party, class and masses, and raised the issue of " combating the cult of the individual "; this is erroneous and harmful.

The theory propounded by Lenin is as follows:

(a) The masses are divided into classes;

(b) Classes are usually led by political parties;

(c) Political parties, as a general rule, are directed by more or less stable groups composed of the most authoritative, influential and experienced members, who are elected to the most responsible positions and are called leaders.

Lenin said, " All this is elementary."

The party of the proletariat is the headquarters of the proletariat in revolution and struggle. Every proletarian party must practise centralism based on democracy and establish a strong Marxist-Leninist leadership before it can become an organized and battle-worthy vanguard. To raise the question of " combating the cult of the individual " is actually to counterpose the leaders to the masses, undermine the Party's unified leadership which is based on democratic centralism, dissipate its fighting strength and disintegrate its ranks.

Lenin criticized the erroneous views which counterpose the leaders to the masses. He called them " ridiculously absurd and stupid."

The Communist Party of China has always disapproved of exaggerating the role of the individual, has advocated and persistently practised democratic centralism within the Party and advocated the linking of the leadership with the masses, maintaining that correct leadership must know how to concentrate the views of the masses.

While loudly combating the so-called cult of the individual, certain persons are in reality doing their best to defame the proletarian party and the dictatorship of the proletariat. At the same time, they are enormously exaggerating the role of certain individuals, shifting all errors on to others and claiming all credit for themselves.

What is more serious is that, under the pretext of " combating the cult of the individual," certain persons are crudely interfering in the internal affairs of other fraternal Parties and fraternal countries and forcing other fraternal Parties to change their leadership in order to impose their own wrong line on these Parties. What is all this if not great-power chauvinism, sectarianism and splittism? What is all this if not subversion?

It is high time to propagate seriously and comprehensively Lenin's integral teachings on the interrelationship of leaders, party, class and masses.

(21) Relations between socialist countries are international relations of a new type. Relations between socialist countries, whether large or small, and whether more developed or less developed economically, must be based on the principles of complete equality, respect for territorial integrity, sovereignty and independence, and non-interference in each other's internal affairs, and must also be based on the principles of mutual support and mutual assistance in accordance with proletarian internationalism.

Every socialist country must rely mainly on itself for its construction. In accordance with its own concrete conditions, every socialist country must rely first of all on the diligent labour and talents of its own people, utilize all its available resources fully and in a planned way, and bring all its potential into play in socialist construction. Only thus can it build socialism effectively and develop its economy speedily.

This is the only way for each socialist country to strengthen the might of the entire socialist camp and enhance its capacity to assist the revolutionary cause of the international proletariat. Therefore, to observe the principle of mainly relying on oneself in construction is to apply proletarian internationalism concretely.

If, proceeding only from its own partial interests, any socialist country unilaterally demands that other fraternal countries submit to its needs, and uses the pretext of opposing what they call " going it alone " and " nationalism " to prevent other fraternal countries from applying the principle of relying mainly on their own efforts in their construction and from developing their economies on the basis of independence, or even goes to the length of putting economic pressure on other fraternal countries—then these are pure manifestations of national egoism.

It is absolutely necessary for socialist countries to practise mutual economic assistance and co-operation and exchange. Such economic co-operation must be based on the principles of complete equality, mutual benefit and comradely mutual assistance.

It would be great-power chauvinism to deny these basic principles and, in the name of " international division of labour " or " specialization," to impose one's own will on others, infringe on the independence and sovereignty of fraternal countries or harm the interests of their people.

In relations among socialist countries it would be preposterous to follow the practice of gaining profit for oneself at the expense of others, a practice characteristic of relations among capitalist countries, or go so far as to take the " economic integration " and the " common market," which monopoly capitalist groups have instituted for the purpose of seizing markets and grabbing profits, as examples which socialist countries ought to follow in their economic co-operation and mutual assistance.

(22) The 1957 Declaration and the 1960 Statement lay down the principles guiding relations among fraternal Parties. These are the principle of solidarity, the principle of mutual support and mutual assistance, the principle of independence and equality and the principle of reaching unanimity through consultation—all on the basis of Marxism-Leninism and proletarian internationalism.

We note that in its letter of March 30 the Central Committee of the CPSU says that there are no " superior " and " subordinate " Parties in the communist movement, that all Communist Parties are independent and equal, and that they should all build their relations on the basis of proletarian internationalism and mutual assistance.

It is a fine quality of Communists that their deeds are consistent with their words. The only correct way to safeguard and strengthen unity among the fraternal Parties is genuinely to adhere to, and not to violate, the principle of proletarian internationalism and genuinely to observe, and not to undermine, the principles guiding relations among fraternal Parties—and to do so not only in words but, much more important, in deeds.

If the principle of independence and equality is accepted in relations among fraternal Parties, then it is impermissible for any Party to place itself above others, to interfere in their internal affairs, and to adopt patriarchal ways in relations with them.

If it is accepted that there are no " superiors " and " subordinates " in relations among fraternal Parties, then it is impermissible to impose the programme, resolutions and line of one's own Party on other fraternal Parties as the " common programme " of the international communist movement.

If the principle of reaching unanimity through consultation is accepted in relations among fraternal Parties, then one should not emphasize " who is in the majority " or " who is in the minority " and bank on a so-called majority in order to force through one's own erroneous line and carry out sectarian and splitting policies.

If it is agreed that differences between fraternal Parties should be settled through inter-Party consultation, then other fraternal Parties should not be attacked publicly and by name at one's own congress or at other Party congresses, in speeches by Party leaders, resolutions, statements, etc.; and still less should the ideological differences among fraternal Parties be extended into the sphere of state relations.

We hold that in the present circumstances, when there are differences in the international communist movement, it is particularly important to stress strict adherence to the principles guiding relations among fraternal Parties as laid down in the Declaration and the Statement.

In the sphere of relations among fraternal Parties and countries, the question of Soviet-Albanian relations is an outstanding one at present. Here the question is what is the correct way to treat a fraternal Party and country and whether the principles guiding relations among fraternal Parties and countries stipulated in the Declaration and the Statement are to be adhered to. The correct solution of this question is an important matter of principle in safeguarding the unity of the socialist camp and the international communist movement.

How to treat the Marxist-Leninist fraternal Albanian Party of Labour is one question. How to treat the Yugoslav revisionist clique of traitors to Marxism-Leninism is quite another question. These two essentially different questions must on no account be placed on a par.

Your letter says that you " do not relinquish the hope that the relations between the CPSU and the Albanian Party of Labour may be improved," but at the same time you continue to attack the Albanian comrades for what you call " splitting activities." Clearly this is self-contradictory and in no way contributes to resolving the problem of Soviet-Albanian relations.

Who is it that has taken splitting actions in Soviet-Albanian relations?

Who is it that has extended the ideological differences between the Soviet and Albanian Parties to state relations?

Who is it that has brought the divergences between the Soviet and Albanian Parties and between the two countries into the open before the enemy?

Who is it that has openly called for a change in the Albanian Party and state leadership?

All this is plain and clear to the whole world.

Is it possible that the leading comrades of the CPSU do not really feel their responsibility for the fact that Soviet-Albanian relations have so seriously deteriorated?

We once again express our sincere hope that the leading comrades of the CPSU will observe the principles guiding relations among fraternal Parties and countries and take the initiative in seeking an effective way to improve Soviet-Albanian relations.

In short, the question of how to handle relations with fraternal Parties and countries must be taken seriously. Strict adherence to the principles guiding relations among fraternal Parties and countries is the only way forcefully to rebuff slanders such as those spread by the imperialists and reactionaries about the " hand of Moscow."

Proletarian internationalism is demanded of all Parties without exception, whether large or small, and whether in power or not. However, the larger Parties and the Parties in power bear a particularly heavy responsibility in this respect. The series of distressing developments which have occurred in the socialist camp in the past period have harmed the interests not only of the fraternal Parties concerned but also of the masses of the people in their countries. This convincingly demonstrates that the larger countries and Parties need to keep in mind Lenin's behest never to commit the error of great-power chauvinism.

The comrades of the CPSU state in their letter that " the Communist Party of the Soviet Union has never taken and will never take a single step that could sow hostility among the peoples of our country towards the fraternal Chinese people or other peoples." Here we do not desire to go back and enumerate the many unpleasant events that have occurred in the past, and we only wish that the comrades of the CPSU will strictly abide by this statement in their future actions.

During the past few years, our Party members and our people have exercised the greatest restraint in the face ᴏɪ a series of grave incidents which were in violation of the principles guiding relations among fraternal Parties and countries and despite the many difficulties and losses which have been imposed on us. The spirit of proletarian internationalism of the Chinese Communists and the Chinese people has stood a severe test.

The Communist Party of China is unswervingly loyal to proletarian internationalism, upholds and defends the principles of the 1957 Declaration and the 1960 Statement guiding relations among fraternal Parties and countries, and safeguards and strengthens the unity of the socialist camp and the international communist movement.

(23) In order to carry out the common programme of the international communist movement unanimously agreed upon by the fraternal Parties, an uncompromising struggle must be waged against all forms of opportunism, which is a deviation from Marxism-Leninism.

The Declaration and the Statement point out that revisionism, or, in other words, Right opportunism, is the main danger in the international communist movement. Yugoslav revisionism typifies modern revisionism.

The Statement points out particularly:

> The Communist Parties have unanimously condemned the Yugoslav variety of international opportunism, a variety of modern revisionist " theories " in concentrated form.

It goes on to say:

> After betraying Marxism-Leninism, which they termed obsolete, the leaders of the League of Communists of Yugoslavia opposed their anti-Leninist revisionist programme to the Declaration of 1957; they set the

League of Communists of Yugoslavia against the international communist movement as a whole, severed their country from the socialist camp, made it dependent on so-called " aid " from U.S. and other imperialists. . . .

The Statement says further:

> The Yugoslav revisionists carry on subversive work against the socialist camp and the world communist movement. Under the pretext of an extra-bloc policy, they engage in activities which prejudice the unity of all the peace-loving forces and countries.

Therefore, it draws the following conclusion:

> Further exposure of the leaders of Yugoslav revisionists and active struggle to safeguard the communist movement and the working-class movement from the anti-Leninist ideas of the Yugoslav revisionists, remains an essential task of the Marxist-Leninist parties.

The question raised here is an important one of principle for the international communist movement.

Only recently the Tito clique have publicly stated that they are persisting in their revisionist programme and anti-Marxist-Leninist stand in opposition to the Declaration and the Statement.

U.S. imperialism and its NATO partners have spent several thousand millions of U.S. dollars nursing the Tito clique for a long time. Cloaked as " Marxist-Leninists " and flaunting the banner of a " socialist country," the Tito clique has been undermining the international communist movement and the revolutionary cause of the peace of the world, serving as a special detachment of U.S. imperialism.

It is completely groundless and out of keeping with the facts to assert that Yugoslavia is showing " definite positive tendencies," that it is a " socialist country," and that the Tito clique is an " anti-imperialist force."

Certain persons are now attempting to introduce the Yugoslav revisionist clique into the socialist community and the international communist ranks. This is openly to tear up the agreement unanimously reached at the 1960 meeting of the fraternal Parties and is absolutely impermissible.

Over the past few years, the revisionist trend flooding the international working-class movement and the many experiences and lessons of the international communist movement have fully confirmed the correctness of the conclusion in the Declaration and the Statement that revisionism is the main danger in the international communist movement at present.

However, certain persons are openly saying that dogmatism and not revisionism is the main danger, or that dogmatism is no less dangerous than revisionism, etc. What sort of principle underlies all this?

Firm Marxist-Leninists and genuine Marxist-Leninist parties must put principles first. They must not barter away principles, approving one thing today and another tomorrow, advocating one thing today and another tomorrow.

Together with all Marxist-Leninists, the Chinese Communists will continue to wage an uncompromising struggle against modern revisionism in order to defend the purity of Marxism-Leninism and the principled stand of the Declaration and the Statement.

While combating revisionism, which is the main danger in the international communist movement, Communists must also combat dogmatism.

As stated in the 1957 Declaration, proletarian parties " should firmly adhere to the principle of combining . . . universal Marxist-Leninist truth with the specific practice of revolution and construction in their countries." That is to say:

On the one hand, it is necessary at all times to adhere to the universal truth of Marxism-Leninism. Failure to do so will lead to Right opportunist or revisionist errors.

On the other hand, it is always necessary to proceed from reality, maintain close contact with the masses, constantly sum up the experience of mass struggles, and independently work out and apply policies and tactics suited to the conditions of one's own country. Errors of dogmatism will be committed if one fails to do so, if one mechanically copies the policies and tactics of another Communist Party, submits blindly to the will of others or accepts without analysis the programme and resolutions of another Communist Party as one's own line.

Some people are now violating this basic principle, which was long ago affirmed in the Declaration. On the pretext of " creatively developing Marxism-Leninism," they cast aside the universal truth of Marxism-Leninism. Moreover, they describe as " universal Marxist-Leninist truths " their own prescriptions which are based on nothing but subjective conjecture and are divorced from reality and from the masses, and they force others to accept these prescriptions unconditionally.

That is why many grave phenomena have come to pass in the international communist movement.

(24) A most important lesson from the experience of the international communist movement is that the development and victory of a revolution depend on the existence of a revolutionary proletarian party.

There must be a revolutionary party.

There must be a revolutionary party built according to the revolutionary theory and revolutionary style of Marxism-Leninism.

There must be a revolutionary party able to integrate the universal truth of Marxism-Leninism with the concrete practice of the revolution in its own country.

There must be a revolutionary party able to link the leadership closely with the broad masses of the people.

There must be a revolutionary party that perseveres in the truth, corrects its errors and knows how to conduct criticism and self-criticism.

Only such a revolutionary party can lead the proletariat and the broad masses of the people in defeating imperialism and its lackeys, winning a thorough victory in the national democratic revolution and winning the socialist revolution.

If a party is not a proletarian revolutionary party but a bourgeois reformist party;

If it is not a Marxist-Leninist party but a revisionist party;

If it is not a vanguard party of the proletariat but a party tailing after the bourgeoisie;

If it is not a party representing the interests of the proletariat and all the working people but a party representing the interests of the labour aristocracy;

If it not an internationalist party but a nationalist party;

If it is not a party that can use its brains to think for itself and acquire an accurate knowledge of the trends of the different classes in its own country through serious investigation and study, and knows how to apply the universal truth of Marxism-Leninism and integrate it with the concrete practice of its own country, but instead is a party that parrots the words of others, copies foreign experience without analysis, runs hither and thither in response to the baton of certain persons abroad, and has become a hodgepodge of revisionism, dogmatism and everything but Marxist-Leninist principle;

Then such a party is absolutely incapable of leading the proletariat and the masses in revolutionary struggle, absolutely incapable of winning the revolution and absolutely incapable of fulfilling the great historical mission of the proletariat.

This is a question all Marxist-Leninists, all class-conscious workers and all progressive people everywhere need to ponder deeply.

(25) It is the duty of Marxist-Leninists to distinguish between truth and falsehood with respect to the differences that have arisen in the international communist movement. In the common interest of the unity for struggle against the enemy, we have always advocated solving problems through inter-Party consultations and opposed bringing differences into the open before the enemy.

As the comrades of the CPSU know, the public polemics in the international communist movement have been provoked by certain fraternal Party leaders and forced on us.

Since a public debate has been provoked, it ought to be conducted on the basis of equality among fraternal Parties and of democracy, and by presenting the facts and reasoning things out.

Since certain Party leaders have publicly attacked other fraternal Parties and provoked a public debate, it is our opinion that they have no reason or right to forbid the fraternal Parties attacked to make public replies.

Since certain Party leaders have published innumerable articles attacking other fraternal Parties, why do they not publish in their own press the articles those Parties have written in reply?

Latterly, the Communist Party of China has been subjected to preposterous attacks. The attackers have raised a great hue and cry and, disregarding the facts, have fabricated many charges against us. We have published these articles and speeches attacking us in our own press.

We have also published in full in our press the Soviet leaders' report at the meeting of the Supreme Soviet on December 12, 1962, the *Pravda* editorial board's article of January 7, 1963, the speech of the head of the CPSU delegation at the Sixth Congress of the Socialist Unity Party of Germany on January 16, 1963 and the *Pravda* editorial board's article of February 10, 1963.

We have also published the full texts of the two letters from the Central Committee of the CPSU dated February 21 and March 30, 1963.

We have replied to some of the articles and speeches in which fraternal Parties have attacked us, but have not yet replied to others. For example, we have not directly replied to the many articles and speeches of the comrades of the CPSU.

Between December 15, 1962, and March 8, 1963, we wrote seven articles in reply to our attackers. These articles are entitled:

"Workers of All Countries, Unite, Oppose Our Common Enemy!",

"The Differences Between Comrade Togliatti and Us,"

"Leninism and Modern Revisionism,"

"Let Us Unite on the Basis of the Moscow Declaration and the Moscow Statement,"

"Whence the Differences?—A Reply to Thorez and Other Comrades,"

"More on the Differences Between Comrade Togliatti and Us—Some Important Problems of Leninism in the Contemporary World,"

"A Comment on the Statement of the Communist Party of the U.S.A."

Presumably, you are referring to these articles when towards the end of your letter of March 30 you accuse the Chinese press of making "groundless attacks" on the CPSU. It is turning things upside down to describe articles replying to our attackers as "attacks."

Since you describe our articles as "groundless" and as so very bad, why do you not publish all seven of these "groundless attacks," in the same way as we have published your articles, and let all the Soviet comrades and Soviet people think for themselves and judge who is right and who wrong? You are of course entitled to make a point-by-point refutation of these articles you consider "groundless attacks."

Although you call our articles "groundless" and our arguments wrong, you do not tell the Soviet people what our arguments actually are. This practice can hardly be described as showing a serious attitude towards the discussion of problems by fraternal Parties, towards the truth or towards the masses.

We hope that the public debate among fraternal Parties can be stopped. This is a problem that has to be dealt with in accordance with the principles of independence, of equality and of reaching unanimity through consultation among fraternal Parties. In the international communist movement, no one has the right to launch attacks whenever he wants, or to order the "ending of open polemics" whenever he wants to prevent the other side from replying.

It is known to the comrades of the CPSU that, in order to create a favourable atmosphere for convening the meeting of the fraternal Parties, we have decided temporarily to suspend, as from March 9, 1963, public replies to the public attacks directed by name against us by comrades of fraternal Parties. We reserve the right of public reply.

In our letter of March 9, we said that on the question of suspending public debate "it is necessary that our two Parties and the fraternal Parties concerned should have some discussion and reach an agreement that is fair and acceptable to all."

* * *

The foregoing are our views regarding the general line of the international communist movement and some related questions of principle. We hope, as we indicated at the beginning of this letter, that the frank presentation of our views will be conducive to mutual understanding. Of course, comrades may agree or disagree with these views. But in our opinion, the questions we discuss here are the crucial questions calling for attention and solution by the international communist movement. We hope that all these questions and also those raised in your letter will be fully discussed in the talks between our two Parties and at the meeting of representatives of all the fraternal Parties.

In addition, there are other questions of common concern, such as the criticism of Stalin and some important matters of principle regarding the international communist movement which were raised at the 20th and 22nd Congresses of the CPSU, and we hope that on these questions, too, there will be a frank exchange of opinion in the talks.

With regard to the talks between our two Parties, in our letter of March 9 we proposed that Comrade Khrushchov come to Peking; if this was not convenient, we proposed that another responsible comrade of the Central Committee of the CPSU lead a delegation to Peking or that we send a delegation to Moscow.

Since you have stated in your letter of March 30 that Comrade Khrushchov cannot come to China, and since you have not expressed a desire to send a delegation to China, the Central Committee of the Communist Party of China has decided to send a delegation to Moscow.

In your letter of March 30, you invited Comrade Mao Tse-tung to visit the Soviet Union. As early as February 23, Comrade Mao Tse-tung in his conversation with the Soviet Ambassador to China clearly stated the reason why he was not prepared to visit the Soviet Union at the present time. You were well aware of this.

When a responsible comrade of the Central Committee of the Communist Party of China received the Soviet Ambassador to China on May 9, he informed you that we would send a delegation to Moscow in the middle of June. Later, in compliance with the request of the Central Committee of the CPSU, we agreed to postpone the talks between our two Parties to July 5.

We sincerely hope that the talks between the Chinese and Soviet Parties will yield positive results and contribute to the preparations for convening the meeting of all Communist and Workers' Parties.

It is now more than ever necessary for all Communists to unite on the basis of Marxism-Leninism and proletarian internationalism and of the Declaration and the Statement unanimously agreed upon by the fraternal Parties.

Together with Marxist-Leninist parties and revolutionary people the world over, the Communist Party of China will continue its unremitting efforts to uphold the interests of the socialist camp and the international communist movement, the cause of the emancipation of the oppressed peoples and nations, and the struggle against imperialism and for world peace.

We hope that events which grieve those near and dear to us and only gladden the enemy will not recur in the international communist movement in the future.

The Chinese Communists firmly believe that the Marxist-Leninists, the proletariat and the revolutionary people everywhere will unite more closely, overcome all difficulties and obstacles and win still greater victories in the struggle against imperialism and for world peace, and in the fight for the revolutionary cause of the people of the world and the cause of international communism.

Workers of all countries, unite! Workers and oppressed peoples and nations of the world, unite! Oppose our common enemy!

With communist greetings,

The Central Committee of the Communist Party of China

[*People's Daily*, June 17, 1963; *Peking Review*, VI, 25 (June 21, 1963), pp. 6–22.]

Full title: A Proposal Concerning the General Line of the International Communist Movement—The Letter from the Central Committee of the Communist Party of China in Reply to the Letter from the Central Committee of the Communist Party of the Soviet Union of March 30, 1963—June 14, 1963 (complete text).

DOCUMENT 3

The Soviet " Open Letter," July 14, 1963

Dear comrades,

The central committee of the CPSU considers it necessary to address this Open Letter to you in order to set out our position on the fundamental questions of the international communist movement in connection with the letter of the central committee of the Communist Party of China of June 14, 1963.

The Soviet people are well aware that our party and government, expressing as they do the will of the whole Soviet people, spare no effort to strengthen fraternal friendship with the peoples of all socialist countries, with the Chinese people. We are united by a common struggle for the victory of communism; we have the same aim, the same aspirations and hopes.

For many years relations between our parties were good. But, some time ago, serious differences came to light between the CPC on the one hand and the CPSU and other fraternal parties on the other. At the present time the central committee of the CPSU feels increasingly concerned over statements and actions by the leadership of the Communist Party of China which undermine the cohesion of our parties and the friendship of our peoples.

The CPSU central committee, for its part, did everything possible to overcome the differences which came to light and, during January this year, proposed that the open polemics in the Communist movement should stop in order that the disputed issues should be discussed calmly and in a businesslike manner and that they should be solved on a principled Marxist-Leninist basis. This proposal from the CPSU met with warm support on the part of all fraternal parties. Subsequently, agreement was reached to hold a meeting between representatives of the CPSU and the CPC, and this is taking place in Moscow at present.

The CPSU central committee hoped that the Chinese comrades, too, would display goodwill and would contribute to the success of the meeting in the interest of our peoples and in the interest of strengthening the unity of the communist movement. To our regret, when agreement had already been reached on a meeting of representatives of the CPSU and CPC in Moscow, when the delegations had been appointed and the date of the meeting set, the Chinese comrades, instead of submitting the existing differences for discussion at the meeting, unexpectedly found it possible not only to set out the old differences openly, before the whole world, but also to make new charges against the CPSU and other Communist Parties.

This found expression in the publication of the letter from the CPC central committee of June 14 of this year, which gave an arbitrary interpretation of the Declaration and Statement of the Moscow meetings of representatives of the Communist and Workers' Parties and distorted the principal propositions of these historic documents. The letter of the CPC central committee contained groundless, slanderous attacks on our party and on other Communist Parties, on the decisions of the 20th, 21st and 22nd Congresses and on the Programme of the CPSU.

As you know from the statement by the CPSU central committee published in *Pravda* on June 19 of this year, the presidium of the CPSU central committee, having studied the letter of the CPC central committee of June 14, arrived at the conclusion that its publication in the Soviet press at that time would have been inadvisable. Its publication would naturally have required a public reply on our part, which would have led to a further sharpening of the polemics and would have inflamed passions and thereby worsened relations between our parties. Publication of the letter of the CPC central committee would have been the more untimely in that a meeting was to be held between representatives of the CPSU and the CPC with the purpose, in our opinion, of contributing, through consideration of the existing differences in a comradely spirit, to better mutual understanding between our two parties on the principal questions of world development today and to the establishment of a favourable atmosphere for the preparation and holding of a meeting of representatives of all Communist and Workers' Parties.

At the same time, the presidium of the central committee of the CPSU found it necessary to acquaint the members of the CPSU central committee and all those taking part in the plenary meeting with the letter from the CPC central committee, and it also informed them of the substance of the differences between the CPC leadership and the CPSU and other Marxist-Leninist parties.

In its unanimously adopted decision, the plenary meeting of the central committee fully approved the political work of the presidium of the CPSU central committee and of Comrade Nikita Khrushchov, the first secretary of the CPSU central committee and Chairman of the U.S.S.R. Council of Ministers, in further rallying the forces of the world communist movement, and also all the specific actions and measures taken by the presidium of the CPSU central committee in its relations with the central committee of the Communist Party of China.

The plenary meeting of the CPSU central committee instructed the presidium of the central committee, at the meeting with the representatives of the CPC, to follow unswervingly the line of the 20th, 21st and 22nd Congresses of our party, the line which was approved at the meetings of the representatives of the Communist Parties and set out in the Declaration and Statement, the line which was fully vindicated by life and by the course of international developments.

Emphatically rejecting as groundless and slanderous the attacks of the central committee of the Communist Party of China on our party and other Communist Parties, on the decisions of the 20th, 21st and 22nd Congresses and on the Programme of the CPSU, the plenary meeting of the central committee, expressing the will of the whole party, declared its readiness and determination consistently to pursue the course of rallying the fraternal parties and of overcoming the existing differences.

The plenary meeting declared that our party would continue to strive to strengthen unity on the basis of the principles of Marxism-Leninism and socialist internationalism and of fraternal friendship between the CPSU and the CPC in the interest of the struggle for our common cause.

Unfortunately, the events of the past period have shown that the Chinese comrades interpret our restraint in their own way. They depict our sincere striving to avoid a sharpening of polemics in the communist movement as all but an intention to hide the views of the Chinese leaders from the communists and from the Soviet people.

Mistaking our restraint for weakness, the Chinese comrades, contrary to the standards of friendly relations between fraternal socialist countries, began, with increasing importunity and persistence, to spread illegally in Moscow and other Soviet cities the letter of the CPC central committee of June 14, which was brought out in Russian in a mass printing. Not content with this, the Chinese comrades began sedulously to propagandise and spread this letter and other documents directed against our party throughout the world, not scrupling to use imperialist publishing houses and agencies for their distribution.

Matters were further aggravated by the fact that when the U.S.S.R. Ministry of Foreign Affairs called the attention of the Chinese Ambassador in the Soviet Union to the impermissibility of such actions, which crudely violate the sovereignty of our state, the Chinese representatives, far from halting them, declared in a demonstrative way that they considered it their right to continue to circulate the letter in the U.S.S.R.

On July 7, when the meeting in Moscow had already begun, a mass meeting was held in Peking at which officials gave a heroes' reception to the Chinese expelled from the Soviet Union for unlawfully distributing materials containing attacks on our party and on the Soviet government. Whipping up sentiments and feelings of hostility to the U.S.S.R. among the fraternal Chinese people, Chinese officials at the meeting sought again and again to prove their right to violate the sovereignty of our state and the standards of international relations. On July 10, the CPC central committee issued another statement in which it sought to justify these actions and, in effect, tried to arrogate to itself the right to interfere in the internal affairs of the Soviet Union, which the Soviet government, naturally, will never allow. Such actions, inevitably, only tend to aggravate relations, and can do nothing but harm.

In its leading article on July 13, the newspaper *People's Daily* again attacked our party and twisted the fact that the Soviet press had not published the letter of the CPC central committee of June 14.

The frankly hostile actions of the CPC leaders, their persistent striving to sharpen polemics in the international communist movement, the deliberate distortion of the position of our party and the incorrect interpretation of the motives for which we refrained temporarily from publishing the letter, impel us to publish the letter of the CPC central committee of June 14, 1963, and to give our appraisal of this document.

All who read the letter of the CPC central committee will see, behind the bombastic phrases about unity and cohesion, unfriendly and slanderous attacks on our party and the Soviet country and a striving to play down the historic significance of our people's struggle for the victory of communism in the U.S.S.R. and for the triumph of peace and socialism throughout the world. The document is crammed with charges—overt and covert— against the CPSU and the Soviet Union. The authors of the letter permit themselves unworthy fabrications—insulting to communists— about " the betrayal of the interests of the whole international proletariat and all the peoples of the world," about "a departure from Marxism-Leninism and proletarian internationalism "; they hint at "cowardice in face of the imperialists," at "a step back in the course of historic development," and even at "the organisational and moral disarming of the proletariat and all working people," which is tantamount "to helping to restore capitalism" in our country.

How can they say such things about the party of the great Lenin, about the motherland of socialism, about the people who first in the world carried out a social revolution, upheld its great gains in violent battles against international imperialism and domestic counter-revolution, and who are displaying miracles of heroism and dedication in the struggle for the building of communism, and are honestly fulfilling their internationalist duty to the working people of the world!

1

For nearly half a century the Soviet country, under the leadership of the Communist Party, has been leading the struggle for the triumph of the ideas of Marxism-Leninism, in the interest of the freedom and happiness of the working people of the whole world. From the very first days of the existence of the Soviet state, when the great Lenin stood at the helm of our country, to the present day, our people have rendered and are rendering an enormous and disinterested aid to all peoples fighting for their liberation from the yoke of imperialism and colonialism and for building a new life.

World history has known no example of one country rendering such extensive aid to other countries in developing their economy, science and technology.

The working people of China and the Chinese communists felt in full measure the fraternal solidarity of the Soviet people and of our party both in the period of their revolutionary struggle for the liberation of their homeland and in the years of the construction of socialism. Immediately after the forming of the Chinese People's Republic, the Soviet government signed with the government of People's China a Treaty of Friendship, Alliance and Mutual Assistance, which is a mighty means of rebuffing the encroachments of imperialism, and is a factor consolidating peace in the Far East and in the whole world.

The Soviet people generously shared with its Chinese brothers all its many years' long experience in socialist construction and its achievements in the field of science and technology. Our country has rendered and is rendering substantial aid to the development of the economy of People's China. With the active assistance of the Soviet Union, People's China built 198 industrial enterprises, shops and other projects equipped with the up-to-date machinery.

With the assistance of our country such new branches of industry as automobile, tractor, aircraft manufacturing, and others, were created in China. The Soviet Union handed over to the People's Republic of China over 21,000 sets of scientific-technical documentation, including more than 1,400 blueprints of big enterprises. We have unswervingly assisted China in consolidating the defence of the country and the creation of a modern defence industry. Thousands of Chinese specialists and workers were trained in Soviet establishments of higher education and at our enterprises. Now, too, the Soviet Union continues to render technical assistance to the

Chinese People's Republic in the construction of 88 industrial enterprises and projects.

We speak about all this not to boast, but only because the leaders of the CPC have recently sought to belittle the significance of Soviet aid, and we do not forget that the Soviet Union, in its turn, received the goods it needed from the People's Republic of China.

Only a short time ago, the Chinese leaders spoke much and justly about the friendship of the peoples of China and the Soviet Union, about the unity of the CPSU and the CPC, expressed great appreciation for Soviet aid, and urged the people to learn from the experience of the Soviet Union.

Comrade Mao Tse-tung said in 1957:

" In the course of struggle for national liberation, the Chinese people enjoyed the fraternal sympathy and support of the Soviet people. After the victory of the Chinese Revolution, the Soviet Union is also rendering tremendous all-round assistance to the cause of the construction of socialism in China. The Chinese people will never forget all this."

One can only regret that the Chinese leaders have begun to forget it.

Our party and all Soviet people rejoiced at the successes of the great Chinese people in the building of a new life, and took pride in them. Speaking at a reception in Peking on the occasion of the tenth anniversary of the Chinese People's Republic, Nikita Khrushchov said:

" Under the leadership of its glorious Communist Party, the heroic and hard-working people of China have demonstrated what a people is capable of when it takes power into its own hands. . . .

" Now everybody admits the successes of the Chinese people and of the Communist Party of China. The peoples of Asia and Africa see how and under which system the talents and the creative forces of the peoples can be fully developed, and in which a people can demonstrate in both width and depth its mighty creative force."

This was how matters stood until the Chinese leaders began to retreat from the general line of the world communist movement.

In April 1960 the Chinese comrades openly revealed their differences with the world communist movement by publishing a collection of articles called *Long Live Leninism!* This collection, based on distortions, truncated and incorrectly interpreted theses from well-known works of Lenin, contained propositions in fact directed against the fundamentals of the Declaration of the Moscow Meeting of 1957, which was signed on behalf of the CPC by Comrade Mao Tse-tung, against the policy of peaceful co-existence between states with different social systems, against the possibility of preventing a world war in the present-day epoch and against the use both of the peaceful and non-peaceful road of the development of socialist revolutions.

The leaders of the CPC began to impose their views on all the fraternal parties. In June 1960, during the session of the general council of the World Federation of Trade Unions, which took place in Peking, without the knowledge of the leaderships of fraternal parties, the Chinese leaders gathered a meeting of representatives of several parties, which were then in Peking, and started openly to criticise the positions of the CPSU and other Marxist-Leninist parties and the Declaration adopted by the Moscow meeting of 1957. Furthermore, the Chinese comrades made their differences with the CPSU and other fraternal parties a subject of open discussion in a non-party organisation.

These steps by the leadership of the CPC aroused serious concern among the fraternal parties, and, in view of this, an attempt was made at the Bucharest meeting of Communist Parties in 1960 to discuss the differences which had arisen with the leaders of the CPC. Representatives of 50 Communist and Workers' Parties subjected the views and actions of the Chinese leaders to comradely criticism and urged them to return to the road of unity and co-operation with the international communist movement in conformity with the principles of the Moscow Declaration. Unfortunately, the CPC leadership ignored this comradely assistance and continued to pursue its erroneous course and to deepen its differences with the fraternal parties.

Seeking to prevent such a development of events, the CPSU central committee came out with a proposal to hold talks with the central committee of the Communist Party of China. These negotiations took place in Moscow in September 1960. But, even then, it was impossible to overcome the differences that had arisen due to the stubborn unwillingness of the CPC delegation to heed the opinion of the fraternal party. At the meeting of representatives of 81 Communist and Workers' Parties, which took place in November 1960, the absolute majority of the fraternal parties rejected the incorrect views and concepts of the CPC leadership. The Chinese delegation at this meeting stubbornly upheld its own particular views, and signed the Statement only when the danger arose of its complete isolation.

Today it has become absolutely obvious that the CPC leaders were only manoeuvring when they affixed their signatures to the Statement of 1960. Shortly after the meeting they resumed propaganda for their course, using the leadership of the Albanian Party of Labour as a mouthpiece. Behind the back of our party, they launched a campaign against the CPSU central committee and the Soviet government.

In October 1961, the CPSU central committee undertook new attempts to normalise relations with the CPC. Comrades Nikita Khrushchov, Frol Kozlov and Anastas Mikoyan had talks with comrades Chou En-lai, Peng Chen and other leading officials, who arrived for the 22nd Congress of the CPSU. Comrade Nikita Khrushchov set out in detail to the Chinese delegation the position of the CPSU central committee on the questions of principle, which were discussed at the 22nd Congress and declared our unswerving desire to strengthen friendship and co-operation with the Communist Party of China.

In its letters of February 22 and May 31, 1962, the CPSU central committee drew the attention of the CPC central committee to the dangerous consequences for our common cause which could be brought about by the weakening of the unity of the communist movement. We then offered to the Chinese comrades to take steps in order not to give the imperialists an opportunity to use in their interests the difficulties which had arisen in Soviet-Chinese mutual relations. The CPSU central committee also proposed that more effective measures should be taken on such questions as the exchange of internal political information and the co-ordination of the positions of fraternal parties in the international democratic organisations and in other spheres.

However, these letters and the other practical steps aimed at improving relations with the CPC and the People's Republic of China in all directions, did not find a response in Peking.

In the autumn of last year, before the departure from Moscow of the former Chinese Ambassador in the Soviet Union, Comrade Liu Hsiao, the presidium of the CPSU central committee had a long discussion with him. In the course of this conversation the members of the presidium of the central committee once again displayed initiative in the matter of strengthening Chinese-Soviet friendship. Comrade Nikita Khrushchov asked Comrade Liu Hsiao to forward to Comrade Mao Tse-tung our proposal: " to put aside all disputes and differences, not to try and establish who is right and who is wrong, not to rake up the past, but to start our relations with a clear page." But we have not even received an answer to this sincere call.

Deepening their ideological differences with the fraternal parties, the leaders of the CPC began to carry them over to international relations. The Chinese organs began to curtail the economic and trade relations of the People's Republic of China with the Soviet Union and other socialist countries. On the initiative of the government of the People's Republic of China the volume of China's trade with the Soviet Union has been cut almost 67 per cent. in the past three years, and deliveries of industrial plant have dropped to a fortieth. This reduction has taken place on the initiative of the Chinese leaders. We regret that the leadership of the People's Republic of China has embarked on such a course. We have always believed, and believe now, that it is necessary to go on developing Soviet-Chinese relations and to develop co-operation. This would have been mutually beneficial for both sides, and above all to People's China, which had received great assistance from the Soviet Union and other socialist countries. The Soviet Union developed extensive relations with China before, and, today, it also stands for their expansion and not their curtailment. It would seem that the CPC leadership should have displayed primary concern for the development of economic relations with the socialist countries. However, it began acting in the opposite direction, disregarding the damage caused by such actions to the economy of the People's Republic of China.

The Chinese leaders did not tell their people truthfully whose fault it was that these relations were curtailed. Extensive propaganda was started among the Chinese communists and even among the people aimed at discrediting the foreign and domestic policy of the CPSU and at stirring up anti-Soviet sentiments.

The CPSU central committee called the attention of the Chinese comrades to these incorrect actions. We told the Chinese comrades that the people should not be prompted to praise or anathematise this or that party on the basis of disputes or differences which arise. It is clear to every Communist that disagreements among fraternal parties are nothing more than temporary episodes, whereas relations between the peoples of the socialist countries are now being established for all time to come.

Every time, however, the Chinese leaders ignored the comradely warnings of the CPSU and further exacerbated Chinese-Soviet relations.

From the end of 1961 the Chinese representatives in international democratic organisations began openly to impose their erroneous views. In

December 1961, at the Stockholm session of the World Peace Council, the Chinese delegation opposed the convocation of the World Congress for Peace and Disarmament. In the course of 1962, the activities of the World Federation of Trade Unions, the World Peace Movement, the Afro-Asian Solidarity Movement, the World Federation of Democratic Youth, the Women's International Democratic Federation and many other organisations were endangered as a result of the splitting activities of the Chinese representatives. They came out against the participation at the Third Solidarity Conference of the Peoples of Asian and African countries in Moshi of representatives of the Afro-Asian Solidarity Committees of the European socialist countries.

The leader of the Chinese delegation told the Soviet representatives that "the Whites have nothing to do here." At the journalists' conference in Jakarta the Chinese representatives took the line of preventing Soviet journalists from participating as full delegates on the plea that the Soviet Union . . . is not an Asian country!

It is strange and surprising that the Chinese comrades accused the overwhelming majority at the recent World Congress of Women of splitting activities and of a wrong political line, while at the adoption of the Appeal to the women of all continents the representatives of only two countries— China and Albania—out of the 110 countries represented at the congress, voted against it. So the whole multi-millioned army of freedom-loving women is marching out of step and only two are marching in step, keeping in line!

Such is in brief the history of the differences of the Chinese leadership with the CPSU and other fraternal parties. It shows that the CPC leaders counterpose their own special line to the general course of the communist movement, and try to impose their own dictate and their deeply erroneous views on the key problems of our time on it.

2

What is the gist of the differences between the CPC on the one hand and the CPSU and the international communist movement on the other? This question is no doubt asked by everyone who studies the letter from the CPC central committee of June 14.

At a first glance many theses in the letter may seem puzzling: whom are the Chinese comrades actually arguing with? Are there communists who, for instance, object to socialist revolution or who do not regard it as their duty to fight against imperialism and to support the national-liberation movement? Why does the CPC leadership set out these theses with such obsession?

The question may also arise why it is impossible to agree with the positions of the Chinese comrades set forth in their letter on many important problems? Take, for instance, such cardinal problems as war and peace. In its letter the CPC central committee speaks of peace and peaceful co-existence.

The essence of the matter is that having started an offensive against the positions of the Marxist-Leninist parties on cardinal problems of today, the Chinese comrades first ascribe to the CPSU and other Marxist-Leninist parties views which they have never expressed and which are alien to them; secondly, by paying lip service to formulae and positions borrowed from the documents of the communist movement, they try to camouflage their erroneous views and incorrect positions. To come out openly against the people's struggle for peace and for peaceful co-existence between states with different social systems, against disarmament, etc., would mean to expose their positions in the eyes of the communists of the whole world and all peaceloving peoples and to repulse them. Therefore the further the polemics develop and the clearer the weakness of the positions of the CPC leadership becomes, the more zealously it resorts to such camouflage.

If this method of the Chinese comrades is not taken into consideration, it may even seem from outside that the dispute has acquired a scholastic nature, that separate formulae far removed from vital problems are the points at issue.

In point of fact, however, the questions which bear on vital interests of the peoples are in the centre of the dispute.

These are the questions of war and peace, the question of the role and development of the world socialist system, these are the questions of the struggle against the ideology and practice of the " cult of the individual," these are the questions of the strategy and tactics of the world labour movement and the national liberation struggle.

These questions have been brought forward by life itself, by the deep-going changes which have occurred in the socialist countries and throughout the world, the changes in the balance of forces in recent years between socialism and imperialism and the new possibilities for our movement.

The communist movement had to give and did give answers to these questions by outlining the general course applicable to the conditions and demands of the present stage of world development.

The unanimous opinion of the Communist Parties is that a tremendous role in this respect was played by the 20th Congress of the CPSU which ushered in a new stage in the development of the entire communist movement. This appraisal was recorded in the 1957 Declaration and in the 1960 Statement, the documents of the Communist Parties worked out collectively and formulating the general political course of the communist movement in our epoch.

The CPC leaders, however, have now advanced a different course in opposition to it, and their positions diverge more and more from the joint line of the communist movement on basic issues.

This first of all refers to the question of war and peace.

In the appraisal of the problems of war and peace and in the approach to their solution, there can be no uncertainties or reservations, for this involves the destinies of peoples, the future of all mankind.

The CPSU central committee believes it to be its duty to tell the party and the people with all frankness that in questions of war and peace the CPC leadership has cardinal differences, based on principle, with us and with the world communist movement. The essence of these differences lies in a diametrically opposite approach to such vital problems as the possibility of averting thermonuclear world war, peaceful co-existence between states with different social systems and the interconnection between the struggle for peace and the development of the world revolutionary movement.

Our party, in the decisions of the 20th and 22nd Congresses, and the world communist movement, in the Declaration and Statement, set before communists as a task of extreme importance the task of struggling for peace and for averting a thermonuclear world catastrophe. We appraise the balance of forces in the world realistically, and from this draw the conclusion that, though the nature of imperialism has not changed, and the danger of the outbreak of war has not been averted, in modern conditions the forces of peace, of which the mighty community of socialist states is the main bulwark, can, by their joint efforts, avert a new world war.

We also soberly appraise the radical, qualitative change in the means of waging war and, consequently, its possible aftermaths. The nuclear rocket weapons which have been created in the middle of our century change the old notions about war. These weapons possess an unprecedented devastating force. Suffice it to say that the explosion of only one powerful thermonuclear bomb surpasses the explosive force of all the ammunition used during all previous wars, including the First and Second World Wars. And many thousands such bombs have been accumulated!

Do communists have the right to ignore this danger? Do we have to tell the people all the truth about the consequences of thermonuclear war? We believe that, without question, we must. This cannot have a " paralysing " effect on the masses, as the Chinese comrades assert. On the contrary, the truth about modern war will mobilise the will and energy of the masses in the struggle for peace and against imperialism—the source of military danger.

The historic task of communists is to organise and lead the struggle of the peoples to avert a thermonuclear world war.

To prevent a new world war is a real and quite feasible task. The 20th Congress of our party came to the extremely important conclusion that in our times there is no fatal inevitability of war between states. This conclusion is not the fruit of good intentions, but the result of a realistic, strictly scientific analysis of the balance of class forces on the world arena; it is based on the gigantic might of world socialism. Our views on this question are shared by the entire world communist movement. " World war can be averted "; " A real possibility to exclude world war from the life of society will appear even before the complete victory of socialism on earth, while capitalism still remains in part of the world," the Statement declares.

This statement also bears the signature of the Chinese comrades.

And what is the position of the CPC leadership? What do the theses that they propagate mean : an end cannot be put to wars so long as imperialism exists; peaceful co-existence is an illusion; it is not the general principle of the foreign policy of socialist countries; the peace struggle hinders the revolutionary struggle?

These theses mean that the Chinese comrades are acting contrary to the general course of the world communist movement in questions of war and peace. They do not believe in the possibility of preventing a new world war; they underestimate the forces of peace and socialism and overestimate the forces of imperialism; in fact they ignore the mobilisation of the masses for the struggle with the war danger.

It emerges that the Chinese comrades do not believe in the ability of the peoples of the socialist countries, of the international working class, and of all democratic and peace-loving forces to frustrate the plans of the warmongers and to achieve peace for our and future generations. What stands behind the loud revolutionary phrases of the Chinese comrades? Lack of faith in the forces of the working class and its revolutionary capabilities, lack of faith both in the possibility of peaceful co-existence and in the victory of the proletariat in class struggle. All peaceloving forces unite in the struggle to avert war. They differ as to their class composition and their class interests. But they can be united by the struggle for peace and to avert war, because the nuclear bomb does not adhere to the class principle—it destroys everybody within the range of its devastating force.

To adopt the course proposed by the Chinese comrades means to alienate the masses of the people from the Communist Parties which have won the sympathies of the peoples by their insistent and courageous struggle for peace.

Socialism and peace are now inseparable in the minds of the broad masses!

The Chinese comrades obviously underestimate the whole danger of thermonuclear war. " The atomic bomb is a paper tiger "; " it is not terrible at all," they contend.

The main thing, don't you see, is to put an end to imperialism as quickly as possible, but how, with what losses this will be achieved seems to be a secondary question. To whom, it is right to ask, is it secondary? To the hundreds of millions of people who are doomed to death in the event of the unleashing of a thermonuclear war? To the states that will be erased from the face of the earth in the very first hours of such a war?

No one, and this also includes big states, has the right to play with the destinies of millions of people. Those who do not want to make an effort to exclude world war from the life of the peoples, to avert a mass annihilation of people and the destruction of the values of human civilisation, deserve condemnation.

The letter of the CPC central committee of June 14 says much about " inevitable sacrifices," allegedly in the name of the revolution. Some responsible Chinese leaders have also declared that it is possible to sacrifice hundreds of millions of people in war. " On the ruins of destroyed imperialism the victorious peoples "—asserts the collection *Long live Leninism!* which was approved by the CPC central committee, " will create with tremendous speed a civilisation a thousand times higher than under the capitalist system and will build their really bright future."

It is permissible to ask the Chinese comrades if they realise what sort of " ruins " a nuclear rocket world war would leave behind?

The CPSU central committee, and we are convinced that all our party and the whole Soviet people unanimously support us in this, cannot share the views of the Chinese leadership about the creation " of a thousand times higher civilisation " on the corpses of hundreds of millions of people. Such views are in crying contradiction with the ideas of Marxism-Leninism.

It is permissible to ask the Chinese comrades: what means do they propose for the destruction of imperialism? We fully stand for the destruction of imperialism and capitalism. We not only believe in the inevitable destruction of capitalism but also are doing everything for this to be accomplished by way of class struggle and as soon as possible. Who must decide this historic question? First of all the working class led by its vanguard, the Marxist-Leninist party, the working people of each country.

The Chinese comrades propose another thing. They straightforwardly say: " On the ruins of a destroyed imperialism "—in other words, as a result of the unleashing of war—" a bright future will be built." If we agree to this, then, indeed, there is no need for the principle of peaceful co-existence and for the struggle for the strengthening of peace. We cannot agree to such an adventurist course: it contradicts the nature of Marxism-Leninism.

It is generally known that under present conditions a world war would be a thermonuclear war. The imperialists will never agree to withdraw from the scene voluntarily, to lie in the coffin of their own free will, without having used the extreme means they have at their disposal.

Apparently the people who refer to the thermonuclear weapon as a " paper tiger " are not fully aware of the destructive force of this weapon. We soberly consider this. We ourselves produce the thermonuclear weapon and have manufactured it in sufficient quantity. We know its destructive force full well. And if imperialism starts a war against us we shall not hesitate to use this formidable weapon against the aggressor; but if we are not attacked, we shall not be the first to use this weapon.

Marxist-Leninists strive to ensure an enduring peace not by begging for it from imperialism but by rallying the revolutionary Marxist-Leninist parties, by rallying the working class of all countries, by rallying the peoples fighting for their freedom and national independence, and by relying on the economic and defensive might of the socialist states.

We would like to ask the Chinese comrades who suggest building a bright future on the ruins of the old world destroyed by a thermonuclear war whether they have consulted the working class of the countries where imperialism dominates? The working class of the capitalist countries would certainly tell them: are we asking you to trigger off a war and destroy our countries while annihilating the imperialists? Is it not a fact that the monopolists, the imperialists, are only a comparatively small group, while the bulk of the population of the capitalist countries consists of the working class, working peasantry and working intelligentsia?

The nuclear bomb does not distinguish between the imperialists and working people, it hits great areas, and therefore millions of workers would be destroyed for one monopolist. The working class, the working people, will ask such " revolutionaries ": what right have you to decide for us the questions of our existence and our class struggle? We also are in favour of socialism; but we want to gain it through the class struggle and not by unleashing a thermonuclear world war.

The posing of the question in this way by the Chinese comrades may give rise to the well justified suspicion that this is no longer a class approach in the struggle for the abolition of capitalism, but has some entirely different aims. If both the exploiters and the exploited are buried under the ruins of the old world, who will build the " bright future "?

In this connection it is impossible not to note the fact that instead of the internationalist class approach expressed in the call " workers of all countries, unite ! " the Chinese comrades stubbornly propagate the slogan which is devoid of any class meaning: " The wind from the East prevails over the wind from the West."

In the question of the Socialist revolution, our party firmly adheres to the Marxist-Leninist class positions, believing that revolutions in every country are carried out by the working class and the working people, without military interference from outside.

There is no doubt, of course, that if the imperialist madmen do unleash a war, the peoples will wipe out and bury capitalism. But the communists, representing the peoples, the true advocates of socialist humanism, must do everything they can to prevent another world war in which hundreds of millions of people would perish.

No party which truly cherishes the interests of the people can fail to realise its responsibility in the struggle to avert another world war and to ensure peaceful co-existence between states with different social systems.

Expressing the line of our party, Comrade Nikita Khrushchov said: " There will be wars of liberation as long as imperialism exists, as long as colonialism exists. These are revolutionary wars. Such wars are not only permissible but even unavoidable, since the colonialists do not grant independence to people voluntarily. Therefore it is only through struggle, including armed struggle, that the peoples can win their freedom and independence."

The Soviet Union is rendering the broadest support to the national liberation movement. Everybody is familiar with the practical assistance our country rendered the peoples of Vietnam, Egypt, Iraq, Algeria, Yemen, Cuba and other peoples.

The Communist Party of the Soviet Union proclaimed the Leninist principles of peaceful co-existence as the general line of Soviet foreign policy and is following it unswervingly. Since 1953, and particularly after the 20th CPSU Congress, there was a sharp increase in the activity of our peace policy, and its influence on the whole course of international relations grew in the interests of masses of the people.

The Chinese comrades allege that we proceed from the premise that the concept of " peaceful co-existence " covers all the principles of our relations, not only with the imperialist countries, but also with the socialist countries and the countries that have recently got rid of the colonial yoke. They know very well that this is not so, that we were the first to proclaim the principle of friendship and comradely mutual assistance as the most important principle in the relations between the countries of socialism and we adhere to it firmly and consistently, that we render all-round and many sided assistance to the liberated peoples. And yet, for some motives, they find it advantageous for themselves to present all this in an entirely distorted light.

The Soviet Union's persistent struggle for peace and international security, for general and complete disarmament, for the elimination of the vestiges of the Second World War, for a negotiated settlement of all controversial international issues has yielded fruit. The prestige of our country throughout the world stands higher than ever, our international position is more solid than ever. We owe this to the steadily growing economic and military might of the Soviet Union and of other socialist countries, and to their peaceful foreign policy.

The CPSU central committee declares that we have been, are and will continue to pursue the Leninist policy of peaceful co-existence between states with different social systems. In this our party sees its duty both to the Soviet people and the peoples of all other countries. To ensure peace means to contribute most effectively to the consolidation of the socialist system, and, consequently, to the growth of its influence on the entire course of the liberation struggle and the world revolutionary process.

The deep difference between the views of the CPSU and other Marxist-Leninist parties on the one hand and the CPC leaders on the other, on the questions of war, peace and peaceful co-existence was demonstrated with particular clarity during the 1962 crisis in the Caribbean Sea. It was a sharp international crisis: never before did mankind come so close to the brink of a thermonuclear war as it did in October last year.

The Chinese comrades allege that in the period of the Caribbean crisis we made an "adventurist" mistake by introducing rockets into Cuba and then "capitulated" to American imperialism when we removed the rockets from Cuba.*

Such assertions utterly contradict the facts.

What was the actual state of affairs? The CPSU central committee and the Soviet government possessed trustworthy information that an armed aggression by United States imperialism against Cuba was about to take place. We realised with sufficient clarity that the most resolute steps were needed to rebuff the aggression and to defend the Cuban revolution effectively. Curses and warnings—even if they are called "serious warnings" and repeated two and a half hundred times over—have no effect on the imperialists.

Proceeding from the need to defend the Cuban revolution, the Soviet government and the government of Cuba reached agreement on the delivery of missiles to Cuba, because this was the only effective way of preventing aggression on the part of American imperialism. The delivery of missiles to Cuba meant that an attack on her would meet with a resolute rebuff and the use of rocket weapons against the organisers of the aggression. Such a resolute step on the part of the Soviet Union and Cuba was a shock to the American imperialists, who felt for the first time in their history that if they were to undertake an armed invasion of Cuba, a shattering retaliatory blow would be dealt against their own territory.

Inasmuch as the point in question was not simply a conflict between the United States and Cuba, but a clash between the two major nuclear powers, the crisis in the Caribbean Sea area would have turned from a local into a world one. A real danger of thermonuclear world war arose.

There was one alternative in the prevailing situation: either to follow in the wake of the "madmen" (this is how the most aggressive and reactionary representatives of American imperialism are dubbed) and embark upon a course of unleashing a world thermonuclear war or, profiting from the opportunities offered by the delivery of missiles, to take all steps to reach an agreement on a peaceful solution of the crisis and to prevent aggression against the Republic of Cuba.

As is known, we chose the second path and are convinced that we did the right thing. We are confident that all our people are unanimous on this score. The Soviet people have proved more than once that they know how to stand up for themselves, how to defend the cause of the revolution and the cause of socialism. And nobody knows better than they do how much sorrow and suffering a war brings, what difficulties and sacrifices it costs the peoples.

Agreement to remove the missile weapons in return for the United States government's commitment not to invade Cuba and to keep its allies from doing so, the heroic struggle of the Cuban people and the support rendered to them by the peaceloving nations, made it possible to frustrate the plans of the extreme adventurist circles of American imperialism, which were ready to go the whole hog. As a result it was possible to defend revolutionary Cuba and to save peace.

* These allegations were made in the leading article in *People's Daily* on March 8, 1963, "On the Statement of the Communist Party of the U.S.A."

The Chinese comrades regard our statement that the Kennedy government also displayed a certain reasonableness and a realistic approach in the course of the crisis around Cuba as "embellishing imperialism." Do they really think that all bourgeois governments lack all reason in everything they do? Thanks to the courageous and farsighted position of the U.S.S.R. and the staunchness and restraint of the heroic Cuban people and their government, the forces of socialism and peace have proved that they are able to curb the aggressive forces of imperialism and to impose peace on the advocates of war. This was a major victory for the policy of reason and for the forces of peace and socialism; this was a defeat for the forces of imperialism and for the policy of military ventures.

As a result of this, revolutionary Cuba is living in peace and building socialism under the guidance of its United Party of the Socialist Revolution and the leader of the Cuban people, Comrade Fidel Castro Ruz.

When agreement was reached with the President of the United States of America and a start was thereby made towards eliminating the crisis in the Caribbean Sea area, the Chinese comrades did their best in insulting and attacking the Soviet Union, trying to prove that the word of the imperialists cannot be trusted in anything.

We are living in an epoch when there are two worlds, two systems: socialism and imperialism. It would be absurd to think that all the questions which inevitably arise in relations between the countries of these two systems must be solved only by force of arms, ruling out all talks and agreements. Wars would never end then. We are against such an approach.

The Chinese comrades argue that the imperialists cannot be trusted in anything, that they are bound to cheat; but this is not a case of faith, but rather a case of sober calculation. Eight months have passed since the elimination of the crisis in the Caribbean Sea area, and the United States government is keeping its word—there is no invasion of Cuba. We also assumed a commitment to remove our missiles from Cuba, and we have fulfilled it.

It should not, however, be forgotten that we have also given a commitment to the Cuban people: if the United States imperialists do not keep their promise but invade Cuba, we shall come to the assistance of the Cuban people. Every reasonable person realises full well that, in the event of aggression by the American imperialists, we shall come to the assistance of the Cuban people from Soviet territory, just as we would have helped them from Cuban territory, too. True, in this case the rockets would be in flight slightly longer, but their precision will not be impaired.

Why then do the Chinese comrades stubbornly ignore the assessment which the leaders of the Cuban revolution themselves give to the policy of the government of the Soviet Union, which they call a policy of fraternal solidarity and genuine internationalism? What are the Chinese leaders dissatisfied with? Is it, perhaps, the fact that it was possible to prevent the invasion of Cuba and the unleashing of a world war?

And what was the line of behaviour of the CPC leadership during the Caribbean crisis? At this critical moment the Chinese comrades opposed the realistic and firm stand of the Soviet government with their own particular position. Guided by some sort of peculiar concepts of their own, they concentrated the fire of their criticism not so much on the aggressive imperialism of the United States, but rather on the CPSU and the Soviet Union.

The CPC leadership, which, prior to that, argued that imperialism might unleash a world war at any time, assumed the stand of a critic, not of a militant ally and comrade at the most responsible moment. Nobody heard any statements from the Chinese leaders during those days about their practical actions in defence of the Cuban revolution. Instead of this, the Chinese leaders obviously tried to aggravate the situation in the Caribbean Sea area, which was tense even without this, and added fuel to the smouldering fire of the conflict.

The true position of the CPC leadership is demonstrated very clearly in the questions of war and peace, in its complete underestimation, and what is more, deliberate ignoring, of the struggle for disarmament. The Chinese communists object even to the very raising of this question by communists, permitting themselves to make references to Marxism-Leninism and going out of their way to prove that disarmament is " not feasible " on the one hand, and that there is no need for it, on the other. Juggling with quotations, they try to prove that general disarmament is possible only when socialism triumphs all over the world.

Must the Marxists sit on their hands, waiting for the victory of socialism all over the world, while mankind suffocates in the clutches of the arms race, while the imperialists, stockpiling nuclear arms, threaten to plunge mankind into the abyss of a world war?

No, this would be criminal inaction in face of the imperative call of the time.

This truth has long ago been understood by all true Marxists-Leninists, who realise their responsibility to the peoples and who have already been waging for a number of years—and will go on waging—a stubborn and persistent struggle for general and complete disarmament, for the ending of tests and the banning of nuclear weapons.

In fighting for peace and in advancing the slogan of universal disarmament, we proceed from the vital interests of the peoples, take the actual situation into account and do not shut our eyes to the difficulties. The imperialists are naturally doing everything to delay and wreck agreement on disarmament—they stand to gain by this. They use the arms race to enrich themselves and to hold the masses of the people in the capitalist countries in fear. But must we go with the current, must we follow in the wake of imperialism and refuse to mobilise all forces to struggle for peace and for disarmament?

No. To do this would be to capitulate to the aggressive forces, to the militarists and imperialists. We hold that the working class, the working people of all countries, can force the imperialist governments to consent to disarmament and can prevent war. For this, they must above all realise their strength and unite.

Against the forces of imperialism and war it is necessary to oppose the organised might of the world working class, which now has the advantage of being supported by the material power and the defensive might of the socialist countries opposed to imperialism. The time has gone when imperialism held undivided sway. The situation has also changed radically compared with the first decades after the October Revolution, when our country was alone and much weaker than today. In our time the balance of forces in the world has become entirely different. This is why to hold now that war is inevitable is to show lack of faith in the forces of socialism and to surrender to the mood of hopelessness and defeatism.

One can repeat *ad infinitum* that war is inevitable, claiming that such a viewpoint is evidence of one's "revolutionary spirit." In fact, this approach merely indicates lack of faith in one's strength and fear of imperialism.

There are still powerful forces opposed to disarmament in the imperialist camp; but it is precisely to compel these forces to retreat that we must arouse the anger of the people against them and force them to comply with the will of the peoples.

The peoples want disarmament and believe that it is the communists who are the vanguard and organisers of the peoples' struggle to achieve this aim.

Our struggle for disarmament is not a tactical expedient. We sincerely want disarmament. And here, too, we stand four-square on the positions of Marxism-Leninism. As early as the end of the last century Engels pointed out that disarmament was possible, and he called it a "guarantee of peace." In our time the slogan of disarmament was first advanced as a practical task by Lenin, and the first Soviet proposals for complete or partial disarmament were submitted as early as 1922, at the Genoa conference. This was in Lenin's lifetime, and the disarmament proposals were formulated by him.

The struggle for disarmament is a most important factor for averting war. It is an effective struggle against imperialism. In this struggle the socialist camp has on its side the absolute majority of mankind.

The Chinese comrades have advanced the slogan of "spearpoint against spearpoint," opposing it to the policy of the other socialist countries which aims at relaxing the international situation and ending the cold war. In actual fact, this slogan adds grist to the imperialist policy of brinkmanship, and helps the champions of the arms race. The impression is given that the leaders of the CPC regard as advantageous the preservation and intensification of international tension, especially in relations between the U.S.S.R. and the United States. They apparently hold that the Soviet Union should reply to provocations by provocations, fall into the traps set by the "wild men" from the imperialist camp, and accept the challenge of the imperialists to a competition in adventurism and aggressiveness, that is competition not for ensuring peace but for unleashing war.

To take this path would be to jeopardise peace and the security of peoples. Communists, who cherish the interests of the peoples, will never follow this road.

The struggle for peace and to implement the principles of the peaceful co-existence between states with different social systems is one of the most important forms of the peoples' struggle against imperialism, against new wars prepared by it, against the aggressive actions of the imperialists in colonial countries, against the military bases of imperialists on foreign territories, against the arms race, etc. The struggle is in the interest of the working class and of all the working people, and in this sense it is class struggle.

Our party and all the fraternal parties remember, and are guided, in all their activities, by the conclusion in the Statement that struggle against the danger of a new world war should be developed without waiting for the first atom and hydrogen bombs to begin to fall; this struggle should be waged now and be intensified daily. The main thing is to curb the aggressors in time, to prevent war and not to allow it to flare up. To fight for peace today means to maintain the greatest vigilance, tirelessly to expose the policy of imperialism, vigilantly to follow the manoeuvrings and machinations of the war incendiaries, to arouse the holy anger of the peoples against those who aim at war, to enhance the organisation of all the forces of peace, continually to step up the actions of the masses in defence of peace, and to strengthen co-operation with all the states which are not interested in new wars.

The struggle for peace and peaceful co-existence weakens the front of imperialism, isolates its more aggressive circles from the masses of the people, and helps the working class in its revolutionary struggle and the peoples in the struggle for national liberation.

The struggle for peace and for peaceful co-existence is bound up organically with the revolutionary struggle against imperialism. The 81 Communist Parties wrote in their statement that: " In conditions of peaceful co-existence, favourable opportunities are created for the development of the class struggle in the capitalist countries and of the national liberation movement of the peoples of the colonial and dependent countries. In turn, the successes of the revolutionary class and national liberation struggle help to strengthen peaceful co-existence."

In conditions of peaceful co-existence, new and important victories have been scored in recent years in the class struggle of the proletariat and the struggle of the peoples for national freedom. The world revolutionary process is developing successfully.

This is why to separate the struggle for peaceful co-existence between states with different social systems from the revolutionary struggle against imperialism, against colonialism, for independence and socialism, to set one against the other, as the Chinese comrades are doing, is to reduce the principle of peaceful co-existence to an empty phrase, to emasculate it, to ignore in practice the need for a resolute struggle against imperialism and for peace and peaceful co-existence—which would only be to the benefit of the imperialists.

In its letter of June 14, the CPC central committee accuses the Communist Parties of extending peaceful co-existence between states with different social systems to relations between the exploiters and the exploited, between the oppressed and the oppressing classes, between the working masses and the imperialists. This is a truly monstrous fabrication and a slander on the fraternal parties which lead the proletariat in its class battles against capital and which always support the revolutionary struggle and the just wars of liberation against imperialism.

The arguments of the CPC leaders in the struggle against the CPSU and other fraternal parties are so weak that they have to resort to all sorts of ruses. They begin by ascribing to us views which are absolutely without foundation, of their own invention, and then they accuse us and fight us by exposing these views. This is precisely the case with their absurd allegations that the CPSU and other fraternal parties renounce revolution and substitute peaceful co-existence for the class struggle. In all political study groups in our country it is well known that when we speak of peaceful co-existence we mean the inter-state relations of the socialist countries with the countries of capitalism. The principle of peaceful co-existence, naturally, can in no way be applied to relations between the antagonistic classes inside the capitalist states; it is impermissible to apply it to the struggle of the working class for its class interests against the bourgeoisie and to the struggle of the oppressed peoples against the colonialists. The CPSU resolutely opposes peaceful co-existence in the ideological sphere. This is a simple truth which all who regard themselves as Marxist-Leninists should have mastered long ago.

3

There are serious differences between the CPC and the CPSU and other Marxist-Leninist parties on the question of **the struggle against the consequences of the Stalin personality cult.**

The CPC leaders have taken on themselves the role of defenders of the cult of the individual, propagators of Stalin's wrong ideas. They are trying to thrust upon other parties the practices, the ideology and ethics, and the forms and methods of leadership which flourished in the period of the cult of the individual. We must say outright that this is an unenviable role which will bring them neither honour nor glory. No one will succeed in luring Marxist-Leninists and progressive people onto the path of defending the cult of the individual!

The Soviet people and the world communist movement appreciated at their proper worth the courage and boldness, the truly Leninist firmness of principle, demonstrated in the struggle against the consequences of the cult of the individual by our party and by its central committee headed by Comrade Nikita Khrushchov.

Everybody knows that our party did so in order to remove the heavy burden which fettered the powerful forces of the working people and thus to speed up the development of Soviet society. Our party did so in order to free the ideals of socialism bequeathed to us by the great Lenin from the stigma of abuses of personal power and arbitrary rule. Our party did so in order to prevent recurrence of the tragic events which accompanied the cult of the individual and to make all the fighters for socialism draw the lessons from our experience.

The whole communist movement correctly understood and supported the struggle against the cult of the individual which was alien to Marxism-Leninism and against its harmful consequences. At one time it was approved by the Chinese leaders, too. They spoke about the tremendous international significance of the 20th Congress of the CPSU.

Opening the Eighth Congress of the Communist Party of China in September of 1956, Comrade Mao Tse-tung said:

" The Soviet comrades and the Soviet people acted in accordance with Lenin's instructions. Within a short space of time they have achieved brilliant successes. The recent 20th Congress of the CPSU also worked out many correct political principles and denounced the shortcomings in the party. It can be said with confidence that in the future their work will result in exceptionally great developments."

In the political report of the CPC central committee made at the congress by Comrade Liu Shao-chi this appraisal was developed further:

" The 20th Congress of the Communist Party of the Soviet Union, held in February this year, is a most important political event of world-wide significance. Not only did the Congress outline the magnificent sixth Five-Year Plan and a number of most important political propositions directed towards the further development of the cause of socialism, and condemned the cult of the individual which had led to serious consequences inside the party, but it also advanced proposals for further promoting peaceful co-existence and international co-operation and made an outstanding contribution to the cause of easing international tension."

Comrade Teng Hsiao-ping, in his report on the changes in the party rules at the same Eighth Congress of the Communist Party of China, said:

" Leninism demands that decisions on all important questions should be taken in the party by an appropriate collective, and not individually. The 20th Congress of the CPSU provided a convincing explanation of the most important significance of the unswerving observance of the principle of collective leadership and the struggle against the cult of the individual. This explanation had a tremendous influence, not only on the CPSU but also on other Communist Parties in all countries of the world."

In the well-known editorial in the newspaper *People's Daily*, " Once more about the Historical Experience of the Dictatorship of the Proletariat " (December 1956) Chinese comrades wrote:

" The 20th Congress of the Communist Party of the Soviet Union showed tremendous determination and courage in eliminating the Stalin cult, in exposing Stalin's serious mistakes and in removing the consequences of Stalin's mistakes. Throughout the world the Marxist-Leninists and persons sympathising with the cause of communism support the efforts of the Communist Party of the Soviet Union directed towards correcting mistakes and wish the efforts of the Soviet comrades to be crowned with complete success."

And that is really so.

Any unbiased person who compares these pronouncements of the Chinese leaders with what is said in the letter of the CPC central committee of June 14 will become convinced that they have made a 180° turn in evaluating the 20th Congress of our party.

But are any vacillations and waverings permissible on such questions of principle? Of course they are not permissible. Either the Chinese leaders then had no differences with the CPSU central committee on these questions of principle, or all these statements were false.

It is well known that practice is the best measure of truth.

It is precisely practice that convincingly proves the wonderful results in our country's life brought about by implementing the line of the 20th, 21st and 22nd Congresses of the CPSU. In the course of the ten years that have gone by since the time when our party made a sharp turn towards the restoration of the Leninist principles and standards in party life, Soviet society has achieved truly magnificent results in developing the economy and promoting the advance of culture and science, in improving the people's well-being and strengthening the defence potential, and in the successes of foreign policy.

The atmosphere of fear, suspicion and uncertainty which poisoned the life of the people in the period of the cult of the individual has gone, never to return. It is impossible to deny the fact that the Soviet people now live better and enjoy the benefits of socialism. Ask the worker who has received a new flat (and there are millions of them!), ask the pensioner who is well provided for in his old age, the collective farmer who is now well-to-do, ask the thousands upon thousands of people who undeservedly suffered from reprisals in the period of the cult of the individual and to whom freedom and good repute have been restored, and you will realise what the victory of the Leninist course of the 22nd Congress of the CPSU means in practice for the Soviet people.

Ask the people whose fathers and mothers were victims of the reprisals in the period of the cult of the individual what it means for them to obtain recognition that their fathers, mothers and brothers were honest people and that they themselves are not outcasts in our society, but worthy, fully-fledged sons and daughters of the Soviet motherland.

Industry, agriculture, culture, science, art — no matter where we turn our eyes, everywhere we see rapid progress. Our spaceships are flying through the expanses of the universe, and this, too, provides brilliant confirmation of the correctness of the path along which our party is leading the Soviet people.

Of course, we do not consider that everything possible has already been done for Soviet men and women, to improve their lives. Soviet people realise that the implementation of this principle does not depend only on our wishes. We have to build a communist society and create an abundance of material benefits. That is why our people are stubbornly working in order to create material and spiritual values more rapidly and bring the victory of communism nearer. Everyone can see that we are following a correct course, that we clearly see the prospects of our development.

The CPSU Programme maps out a concrete plan for building communism. The implementation of that plan will ensure for the Soviet people the highest living standards and will mean the beginning of a gradual transition to the cherished communist principle: " From each according to his ability, to each according to his needs."

Soviet people find it strange and outrageous that the Chinese comrades should be trying to smear the CPSU Programme—that magnificent plan for creating a communist society.

Alluding to the fact that our party proclaims as its task the struggle for a better life for the people, the CPC leaders hint at some sort of " bourgeois-ification " and " degeneration " of Soviet society. To follow their line of thinking, it transpires that if a people walks in rope sandals and eats watery soup out of a common bowl—that is communism, and if a working man lives well and wants to live even better tomorrow—that is almost tantamount to the restoration of capitalism!

And they want to present this philosophy to us as the latest revelation in Marxism-Leninism! This completely exposes the authors of such " theories " as people who do not believe in the strength and capabilities of the working class, which has taken power into its own hands and created its own, socialist state.

If we turn to the history of our country, to the CPSU Programme, we shall easily see from what we began, when under the leadership of Lenin we took power into our hands, and what summits the Soviet people have achieved. Our country has become a great socialist power. As regards the volume of industrial output the Soviet Union is first in Europe and second in the world, and will soon surpass the United States and move to first place. The Soviet working class, the Soviet collective-farm peasantry and the Soviet intelligentsia are the creators of all our victories.

We are convinced that not only the Soviet people, but also the peoples of other socialist countries, are capable of great feats of labour—it is only necessary that correct guidance of the working class and peasantry be ensured; it is necessary that the people giving this guidance should reason in a realistic way and take decisions that will make it possible to channel the strength and energy of the working people along the correct course.

In an attempt to justify the cult of the individual, the Chinese leaders have filled their letter with a lot of talk about class struggle in the U.S.S.R. and about the allegedly erroneous theses of the CPSU Programme on the state of the whole people and the party of the whole people—which are "remote from Marxism."

We do not intend in this letter to analyse all their arguments in detail. Anyone who reads the letter of the CPC central committee of June 14, will undoubtedly pay attention to the utter inadequacy and the lack of knowledge about the life of the Soviet people shown in the outpourings contained in the letter of the CPC central committee.

We are being taught that hostile classes still remain in Soviet society and therefore, you see, the need for the dictatorship of the proletariat remains. What then are these classes?

It can be seen from the letter of the CPC central committee that these are " bourgeois hangers-on, parasites, black-marketeers, swindlers, idlers, hooligans, embezzlers of public property." It must be conceded that this is quite an original notion on the part of the Chinese comrades about classes and class struggle. Since when have these parasitical elements been considered a class? And what class? A class of idlers, or a class of hooligans? A class of embezzlers of public property, or a class of parasites? In no society have criminals comprised a particular class. Every schoolboy knows this. Of course, in socialist society, too, these elements do not comprise a class. These are manifestations of the vestiges of capitalism.

The dictatorship of the proletariat is not necessary for the struggle against such people. The state of the whole people can cope, and is coping, with this task. We know from our own experience that the higher the level of educational work in party, trade union and other public organisations, the greater the role of the public and the better the work of the Soviet militia, the more effective is the struggle against crime.

It is impossible to refute the fact that the present Soviet society is made up of two main classes—the workers and the peasants, as well as the intelligentsia—and that not a single class in Soviet society occupies a position permitting it to exploit other classes. Dictatorship is a class concept. Over whom do the Chinese comrades propose to effect a dictatorship of the proletariat in the Soviet Union? Over the collective-farm peasantry, or over the people's intelligentsia? One cannot ignore the fact that in socialist society the class of workers and the class of peasants have undergone considerable changes, and the differences and distinctions between them are disappearing more and more.

After the complete and final victory of socialism, the working class exercises its leading role, but no longer through the dictatorship of the proletariat. The working class remains the front-ranking class in society in the conditions of the full-scale construction of communism as well. Its front-ranking role is determined both by its economic position—it is directly connected with the highest form of socialist ownership—and the fact that it is the most tried and tempered class as a result of decades of class struggle and revolutionary experience.

The Chinese comrades refer to the pronouncement of Karl Marx that the content of the transitional period from capitalism to communism cannot be anything but a dictatorship of the proletariat. But in stating this, Marx was speaking of communism as a whole, as a single social and economic formation (of which socialism is the first stage), the transition to which would be impossible without a socialist revolution and the dictatorship of the proletariat. There are a number of pronouncements of Lenin which stress with absolute clarity that the dictatorship of the proletariat is needed precisely in order to overcome the resistance of the exploiting classes, to organise socialist construction, to ensure the victory of socialism—the first phase of communism. It is clear from this that the need for the dictatorship of the proletariat disappears after the victory of socialism, when only working people, friendly classes, the nature of which has entirely changed, remain in society, and there is no longer anyone to supress.

If one is to extract the real content of all this mass of pseudo-theoretical talk contained in the letter of the CPC central committee on these questions, it boils down to the following: The Chinese comrades come out against the line of the CPSU aimed at developing socialist democracy, which was proclaimed with such force in the decisions of the 20th, 21st and 22nd Congresses of our party and in the CPSU Programme. It is not by chance that nowhere in their long letter have they found room for even a mere mention of the development of democracy in the conditions of socialism, in the conditions of building communism.

It is difficult to pass judgment in full measure on the motives by which the Chinese comrades are guided when they uphold the cult of the individual. Actually, for the first time in the history of the international communist movement we encounter an open glorification of the cult of the individual. It must be said that even during the period when the cult of the individual was flourishing in our country, Stalin himself was forced, at least in words, to refuse to have anything to do with this petty bourgeois theory and said that it came from the Social Revolutionaries.

The attempts to use Marx and Lenin to defend the ideology of the cult of the individual arouses nothing but surprise. Can it really be true that the Chinese comrades do not know that Lenin, as long ago as the time when our party was being born, waged a gigantic struggle against the narodniks' theories about heroes and masses, that under Lenin genuinely collective methods of leadership were implemented in the central committee of our party and the Soviet state, that Lenin was extremely modest and lashed out mercilessly against the slightest manifestations of toadying and servility towards himself personally?

Of course, the struggle against the cult of the individual was never regarded by our party, or the other Marxist-Leninist parties, as the negation of the authority of party and government leaders. The CPSU has stressed time and time again—including the 20th and 22nd Congresses—that the party cherishes the authority of its leadership and that in dethroning the cult of the individual and fighting against its consequences, the party has a high estimation of leaders who really express the interests of the people and give all their strength to the struggle for the victory of communism, and for this reason enjoy well-deserved prestige.

4

The next important question on which we differ is that of the ways and methods of the revolutionary struggle of the working class in the capitalist countries, the struggle for national liberation, the paths of the transition of all mankind to socialism.

As depicted by the Chinese comrades, the differences on this question appear as follows: one side—they themselves—stands for the world revolution, while the other—the CPSU, the Marxist-Leninist parties—have forgotten the revolution and even " fear " it, and, instead of revolutionary struggle, are concerned with things " unworthy " of a real revolutionary, such as peace, the economic development of the socialist countries and the improvement of the living standards of their peoples, things such as the struggle for the democratic rights and vital interests of the working people of the capitalist countries.

In actual fact, the dividing line between the views of the CPC and the views of the international communist movement lies on an entirely different plane: some—namely, the leaders of the CPC—talk about the world revolution in and out of place, throw about " revolutionary " phrases on any and every occasion, and sometimes without any occasion, while others— precisely those whom the Chinese comrades are criticising—approach the question of the revolution with the utmost seriousness and, instead of indulging in phrase-mongering, work hard, seeking to find the best ways to the victory of socialism—the ways which are most in keeping with the present conditions—and fight hard for national independence, democracy and socialism.

Let us consider the main views of the Chinese comrades on questions concerning the revolutionary movement today.

Is the thesis of ceasing, in the name of the " world revolution," to fight for peace, renouncing the policy of peaceful co-existence and peaceful economic competition, and abandoning the struggle for the vital interests of the workers and for democratic reforms in the capitalist countries, conducive to the transition of countries and peoples to socialism? Is it true that in coming out for peace and pursuing the policy of peaceful co-existence, the communists of the socialist countries are thinking only of themselves and have forgotten about their class brothers in the capitalist countries?

Everyone who has pondered over the significance of the present struggle for peace and against thermonuclear war realises that by their policy of peace the Soviet communists and the fraternal parties of the other socialist countries are giving inestimable aid to the working class, the working people of the capitalist countries. And this is not only because preventing nuclear war means saving the working class, the peoples of entire countries and even continents from death—although this alone is sufficient to justify our entire policy.

The other reason is that this policy is the best way to help the international revolutionary working-class movement to achieve its principal class aims. And is it not a tremendous contribution to the struggle of the working class, when the countries of socialism, in the conditions of peace which they themselves have won, achieved magnificent successes in developing the economy, win ever new victories in science and technology, constantly improve the living and working conditions of the people, and develop and improve socialist democracy?

Looking at these successes and victories, every worker in a capitalist country will say: "Socialism is proving by deeds that it is superior to capitalism. This system is worth fighting for." In the present conditions, socialism is winning the hearts and minds of the people, not only through books, but primarily by its deeds, by its living example.

The Statement of 1960 sees the main feature of our time in the fact that the world socialist system is becoming the decisive factor in the development of human society. All the Communist Parties which took part in the meeting arrived at the common conclusion that at the heart of our epoch there stands the international working class and its creation—the world system of socialism.

The carrying out of all the other tasks of the revolutionary movement depends to a tremendous extent on the consolidation of the world system of socialism. That is why the Communist and Workers' Parties have pledged themselves " tirelessly to strengthen the great socialist community of peoples whose international role and influence on the course of world development is growing year by year." Our party regards the fulfilment of this overriding task as its supreme international duty.

Lenin taught that " We exert our main influence on the international revolution by our economic policy. . . . In this field the struggle has been transferred to a worldwide scale. If we accomplish this task, we shall win on the international scale, for certain and forever." (*Collected works, vol. 32, page 413, Russian edition.*)

This behest of the great Lenin has been firmly learned by Soviet communists. It is followed by the communists of other socialist countries. But now it turns out that there are comrades who have decided that Lenin was wrong.

What is this—lack of faith in the ability of the socialist countries to defeat capitalism in economic competition? Or is it the attitude of persons who, on meeting with difficulties in building socialism, have become disappointed and do not see the possibility of exerting the main influence on the international revolutionary movement by their economic successes, by the example of the successful building of socialism in their countries? They want to achieve the revolution sooner, by other, and what seem to them to be shorter, ways. But the victorious revolution can consolidate its successes and prove the superiority of socialism over capitalism by the work, and only by the work, of the people.

It is true that this is not easy, especially if the revolutions are accomplished in countries which have inherited an underdeveloped economy. But the example of the Soviet union and many other socialist countries proves convincingly that in these conditions, too—if correct leadership is provided— it is possible to achieve great successes and demonstrate to the entire world the superiority of socialism over capitalism.

Moreover, what situation is more propitious to the revolutionary struggle of the working class in the capitalist countries—a situation of peace and peaceful co-existence, or a situation of permanent international tension and cold war?

There is no doubt as to the answer to this question. Who does not know that the ruling circles of the imperialist states exploit the situation of the cold war in order to whip up chauvinism, war hysteria and unbridled anti-communism, to put into power the most rabid reactionaries and pro-fascists, to suspend democracy and to do away with political parties, trade unions and other mass organisations of the working class?

The struggle of the communists for peace greatly strengthens their ties with the masses, their prestige and influence and, consequently, helps to build up what is called the political army of the revolution.

The struggle for peace and the peaceful co-existence of states with different social systems, far from hindering and delaying, makes it possible to develop in full measure the struggle to achieve the ultimate aims of the international working class.

It is hard to believe that the Chinese comrades, who are experienced men and who have themselves carried through a revolution, do not understand the main thing—that the world revolution today comes through the consolidation of the world system of socialism, through the revolutionary class struggle of the workers in the capitalist countries, through the struggle for national liberation, the strengthening of the political and economic independence of newly-liberated countries of Asia and Africa, and through the struggle for peace and against wars of aggression, through the struggle of the masses against the monopolies, and by many other ways which should not be set one against the other, but should be united and directed towards the same goal—the overthrow of the rule of imperialism.

The Chinese comrades, in a haughty and abusive way, accuse the Communist Parties of France, Italy, the United States and other countries of nothing less than opportunism and reformism, of " parliamentary cretinism," and even of slipping down to " bourgeois socialism." On what grounds do they do this? On the grounds that these Communist Parties do not put forward the slogan of an immediate proletarian revolution, although even the Chinese leaders must realise that this cannot be done without the existence of a revolutionary situation.

Every knowledgable Marxist-Leninist realises that to put forward the slogan of an armed uprising, when there is no revolutionary situation in the country, means condemning the working class to defeat. It is common knowledge how exceedingly serious was Lenin's approach to this question, with what political perspicacity and knowledge of the concrete situation he approached the question of choosing the time for revolutionary action. On the very eve of the October Revolution, Lenin pointed out that it would be too early to start on October 24, too late on October 26—everything might be lost—and, consequently, power had to be taken, at whatever cost, on October 25. Who determines the intensity of class contradictions, the existence of a revolutionary situation, and chooses the moment for the uprising? This can be done only by the working class of each country, by its vanguard—the Marxist-Leninist party.

The history of the international working-class movement shows that a party is bad, indeed, if, while calling itself a working-class party, it deals only with economic questions, does not bring up the working class in a revolutionary spirit, and does not prepare it for political struggle, for the seizure of power. In such a case it inevitably slips down to the positions of reformism. But equally bad is a party which sets the tasks of political struggle separately from efforts to improve the economic standards of the working class, the peasantry and all the working people. Such a party inevitably becomes divorced from the masses. Only given a correct use of all forms of class struggle, and given a skilful combination of those forms, can a party become a really revolutionary, Marxist-Leninist party, the leader of the masses, only in that case can it successfully lead the working class in storming capital, in winning power.

The Chinese leaders regard as a mortal sin of the Communist Parties of the developed capitalist states the fact that they see their direct tasks in the struggle for the economic and social interests of the working people, for democratic reforms, feasible even under capitalism and easing the living conditions of the working class, the peasantry and the petty bourgeois sections of the population, and contributing to the formation of a broad anti-monopoly front, which will serve as a basis for further struggle for the victory of the socialist revolution, that is to say, the fact that they are doing precisely what is recorded in the Moscow Statement of 1960.

Having come out against everything which the Communist Parties of the developed capitalist countries are doing, the Chinese comrades have not displayed either an elementary sense of solidarity with communists who are fighting against capital in the front line of the class struggle, or an understanding of the concrete conditions in those countries and the specific paths along which the revolutionary movement of the working class is proceeding there. In actual fact, " for the sake of revolution," they reject precisely the paths leading to revolution and try to impose a course which would place the Communist Parties in a position of isolation from the masses and would result in the working class losing its allies in the struggle against the domination of the monopolies, against capitalism.

The Chinese comrades have also disagreed with the world communist movement on the forms of the transition of different countries to socialism.

It is common knowledge that the CPSU and the other Marxist-Leninist parties, as is clearly pointed out in the documents of the Moscow meetings and in the Programme of the CPSU, proceed on the basis of the possibility both of a peaceful and a non-peaceful transition to socialism. In spite of this, the Chinese comrades stubbornly ascribe to our party and the other fraternal parties recognition of the peaceful method alone.

In its letter of March 30, 1963, the CPSU central committee has again outlined its position on this subject:

" The working class and its vanguard, the Marxist-Leninist parties, endeavour to carry out the socialist revolution in a peaceful way, without civil war. The realisation of such a possibility is in keeping with the interests of the working class and the entire people, and with the national interests of the country concerned. At the same time, the choice of the means by which the revolution is to be developed does not depend only on the working class. If the exploiting classes resort to violence against the people, the working class will be forced to use non-peaceful means of seizing power. Everything depends on the particular conditions and on the distribution of class forces within the country and in the world arena.

" Naturally, no matter what forms are used for the transition from capitalism to socialism, that transition is possible only by means of a socialist revolution and the dictatorship of the proletariat in its various forms. Greatly appreciating the selfless struggle of the working class, headed by the communists, in the capitalist countries, the Communist Party of the Soviet Union considers it its duty to render them every kind of aid and support."

We have repeatedly explained our point of view and there is no need to outline it in greater detail here.

And what is the position of the Chinese comrades on this question? It is the keynote of all their statements and of the letter of the CPC central committee of June 14.

The Chinese comrades regard as the main criterion of revolutionary spirit recognition of the armed uprising always, in everything, everywhere. The Chinese comrades are thereby in fact denying the possibility of using peaceful forms of struggle for the victory of the socialist revolution, whereas Marxism-Leninism teaches that the communists must master all forms of revolutionary class struggle—both violent and non-violent.

Yet another important question is that of the relationship between the struggle of the international working class and the national liberation movement of the peoples of Asia, Africa and Latin America.

The international revolutionary working-class movement, represented today by the world system of socialism and the Communist Parties of the capitalist countries, and the national liberation movement of the peoples of Asia, Africa and Latin America—these are the great forces of our epoch. Correct co-ordination between them constitutes one of the main prerequisites for victory over imperialism.

How do the Chinese comrades solve this problem? This is seen from their new " theory," according to which the main contradiction of our time is, you see, the contradiction, not between socialism and imperialism, but between the national liberation movement and imperialism. The decisive force in the struggle against imperialism, the Chinese comrades maintain, is not the world system of socialism, not the struggle of the international working class, but again the national liberation movement.

In this way the Chinese comrades, apparently, want to win popularity among the peoples of Asia, Africa and Latin America by the easiest possible means. But let no one be deceived by this " theory." Whether the Chinese theoreticians want it or not, this theory in essence means isolating the national liberation movement from the international working class and its creation the world system of socialism. Yet this would constitute a tremendous danger to the national liberation movement itself.

Indeed, could the many peoples of Asia have been victorious, in spite of all their heroism and selflessness, if the October Revolution, and then the formation of the world system of socialism, had not shaken imperialism to its very foundations, if they had not undermined the forces of the colonialists?

And now that the liberated peoples have entered a new stage in their struggle, concentrating their efforts on the consolidation of their political gains and economic independence, do they not see that it would be immeasurably more difficult, if not altogether impossible, to carry out these tasks without the assistance of the socialist states?

Marxist-Leninists always stress the epoch-making significance of the national liberation movement and its great future, but they regard as one of the main prerequisites for its further victories a firm alliance and co-operation with the countries of the world system of socialism as the main force in the struggle against imperialism, and a firm alliance with the working-class movement in the capitalist countries. This position was laid down in the Statement of 1960. It is based on Lenin's idea of working-class leadership (hegemony) as a prerequisite for victory in the anti-imperialist struggle. Only given such hegemony can this movement assume in the last analysis a truly socialist character, culminating in transition to the road of socialist revolution.

This idea of Lenin's has been tested by the experience of the October Revolution and by the experience of other countries, and it does not give rise to doubts in anyone's mind. However, the Chinese comrades, as has been seen, want to " amend " Lenin and prove that it is not the working class, but the petty bourgeoisie or the national bourgeoisie, or even " certain patriotically-minded kings, princes and aristocrats " who must be the leaders of the world struggle against imperialism. And after this the leadership of the Communist Party of China teaches the world communist movement that the proletarian class approach must never, in any circumstances, be abandoned!

The guarantee of the future victories, both of the international working class and the national liberation movement, lies in their firm alliance and co-operation, in their joint struggle against imperialism, dictated by their common interests—a struggle in which the working class earns by its selflessness, by its devoted service in the interests of all peoples, recognition of its leading role and convinces its allies that its leadership is a reliable guarantee both of its own victory and of the victory of its allies, too.

Our Leninist party regards the national liberation movement as part and parcel of the world revolutionary process, as a mighty force coming out against imperialism. The great call of the founders of scientific communism, Marx and Engels: " Workers of all countries, unite! " has become the battle standard of the international working class. Vladimir Ilyich Lenin, who carried forward the cause of Marx and Engels, noted particularly in the new historical conditions which emerged after the victory of the Great October Revolution, the inseparable bonds between the socialist revolution and the national liberation movement.

The slogan " Workers of all countries, unite! " has been, and remains the main slogan in the struggle for the victory of the world revolution. In the new conditions this slogan has a broader connotation. It is common knowledge that Lenin approved of the slogan: " Workers of all countries and oppressed peoples, unite! " This slogan stresses the leading role of the proletariat and the increased significance of the national liberation movement. In all its activities our party strictly abides by this Marxist-Leninist internationalist principle.

The question arises: What is the explanation for the incorrect propositions of the CPC leadership on the basic problems of our time? It is either the complete divorcement of the Chinese comrades from actual reality, a dogmatic, bookish approach to problems of war, peace and the revolution, their lack of understanding of the concrete conditions of the present epoch, or the fact that behind the rumpus about the " world revolution," raised by the Chinese comrades, there are other goals, which have nothing in common with revolution.

All this shows the erroneous character, the disastrous nature of the course which the CPC leadership is trying to impose on the world communist movement. What the Chinese leaders propose under the guise of a " general line " is nothing but an enumeration of the most general tasks of the working class, made without due consideration for the time and the concrete correlation of class forces, without due consideration for the special features of the present stage of history. The Chinese comrades do not notice, or do not want to notice, how the tasks of our movement are changing in the conditions of the present epoch. By reducing the general line to general tasks which are valid for all stages of the transition from capitalism to socialism, they are depriving it of its concrete, purposeful and genuinely effective character.

In working out their present course, the fraternal parties have thoroughly analysed the alignment of class forces both in individual countries and on a worldwide scale, and the special features in the development of the two opposing systems and in the development of the national liberation movement at the present stage.

A thorough analysis of the changes taking place in the world situation has made it possible for the fraternal parties of the whole world to draw up a Marxist-Leninist description of the epoch: " Our epoch, the essence of which consists in the transition from capitalism to socialism, started by the Great October Socialist Revolution, is the epoch of struggle between the two counterposed social systems, the epoch of socialist revolutions and national liberation revolutions, the epoch of the collapse of imperialism, the abolition of the colonial system, the epoch of transition whenever new peoples embark upon the road of socialism, of the triumph of socialism and communism on a worldwide scale."

This definition of the present epoch served as the basis for a correct approach when drawing up the strategy and tactics of the world communist movement.

The Marxist-Leninist parties have determined their common line, the main provisions of which boil down to the following:

The nature and substance of the world revolutionary process in the present epoch is determined by the merging into one stream of the struggle against imperialism, waged by the peoples who are building socialism and communism, the revolutionary movement of the working class in the capitalist countries, the national liberation struggle of the oppressed peoples, and the democratic movements in general; in the alliance of the anti-imperialist revolutionary forces the decisive role belongs to the international working class and its main creation—the world system of socialism, which exerts the principal influence on the development of the world socialist revolution by the force of its example, by its economic construction;

Due to the prevailing objective historical conditions (the maximum growth of the aggressiveness of imperialism, the emergence of weapons of tremendous destructive power, etc.), a central place among all tasks facing the anti-imperialist forces in the present epoch is occupied by the struggle to prevent a thermonuclear war. The primary task of the Communist Parties is to rally all the peaceloving forces in defence of peace, to save mankind from a nuclear catastrophe;

The socialist revolution takes place as a result of the internal development of class struggle in every country, and its forms and ways are determined by the concrete conditions of each given country. The general regularity lies in the revolutionary overthrow of the power of capital and the establishment of a proletarian dictatorship in this or that form. It is the task of the working class and the Communist Parties to make the maximum use of the opportunities now available for the peaceful road of a socialist revolution, not involving civil war, and at the same time to be ready for the non-peaceful method, for armed suppression of the resistance of the bourgeoisie; the general democratic struggle is an indispensable part of the struggle for socialism;

The goals of the working class and the Communist Parties in the national liberation movement lie in carrying out to the end the tasks of the anti-imperialist democratic revolution, in developing and consolidating the national front, based on the alliance with the peasantry and the patriotically-minded national bourgeoisie, in preparing the conditions for setting up a national democratic state and the transition to the non-capitalist road of development;

Relations of co-operation and mutual assistance between the socialist countries, the cohesion and unity of the international communist and working-class movement, loyalty to positions and appraisals worked out jointly, to the Leninist principles of the life of the parties and the relations between them constitute the necessary conditions for the successful accomplishment of the historical tasks facing the communists.

Such, in our epoch, are the main ways of development of the world revolutionary process and such are the basic provisions of the general line of the international communist movement at the present stage. The struggle for peace, democracy, national independence and socialism—such is, in brief, the essence of this general line. The consistent implementation of this line in practice is the guarantee of the successes of the world communist movement.

All these most important principled theses of the international communist movement in present conditions, worked out collectively by the fraternal Communist and Workers' Parties in the Declaration and the Statement, have found expression in the new Programme of the CPSU, which is based entirely on the Marxist-Leninist generalisation of revolutionary experience both in our country and on an international scale.

5

The erroneous views of the CPC leaders on the paramount political and theoretical questions of our time are inseparably linked with their practical activities aimed at undermining the unity of the world socialist camp and the international communist movement.

In words Chinese comrades recognise that the unity of the U.S.S.R. and the People's Republic of China is a mainstay of the entire socialist community, but in actual fact they are undermining contacts with our party and with our country in all directions.

The CPC leadership often speaks of its loyalty to the commonwealth of socialist countries, but the attitude of the Chinese comrades to this commonwealth refutes their high-sounding declarations.

The statistics show that in the course of the past three years the People's Republic of China cut the volume of its trade with the countries of the socialist community by more than 50 per cent. Some socialist countries felt the results of this line of the Chinese comrades particularly keenly.

The actions of the Chinese leadership stand in glaring contradiction, not only with the principles governing mutual relations between socialist countries, but in many cases even with the generally-recognised rules and standards which should be observed by all states.

The flouting of agreements signed earlier did serious harm to the national economies of some socialist states. It is quite understandable that China's own economy also suffers tangibly from the curtailment of her economic contacts.

In an effort to justify its actions in the eyes of the masses of the people, the leadership of the Communist Party of China recently put forward a theory of "reliance on one's own forces." Generally speaking, building socialism in each country, relying primarily on the efforts of its own people and making the best possible use of the internal resources of the country, is the correct way of creating the material and technical basis for socialism. The building of socialism in each country is primarily a matter of concern for the people of that country, for its working class and Communist Party.

The Soviet Union, which was the first country of socialism, had to build socialism relying only on its own forces and using its own internal resources. And although there is now a system of socialist countries, this in no way means that the people of some country can sit with their arms folded and rely exclusively on the assistance of other socialist countries. The Communist Party of each socialist country regards it as its duty to mobilise all the internal reserves for successful economic development. Therefore the statement of the CPC central committee about building socialism mainly by its own forces, in its direct meaning, would give rise to no objections.

However, as is shown by the whole text of the letter of the CPC central committee and numerous statements in the Chinese press, this thesis is actually given an interpretation with which it is impossible to agree.

The formula of "building socialism mainly by our own forces" conceals the concept of creating self-sufficient national economies for which economic contacts with other countries are restricted to trade alone. The Chinese comrades are trying to impose this approach on other socialist countries, too.

The proclamation of the course of "relying on our own forces," was apparently needed by the leadership of the CPC in order to weaken the bonds of close friendship between the socialist countries. This policy, of course, has nothing in common with the principles of socialist internationalism. It cannot be regarded otherwise than as an attempt to undermine the unity of the socialist commonwealth.

Parallel with the line directed towards curtailing economic contacts, the leadership of the CPC took a number of measures aimed at worsening relations with the Soviet Union.

The Chinese leaders are undermining the unity, not only of the socialist camp, but also of the entire world communist movement, trampling underfoot the principles of proletarian internationalism and flagrantly violating the standards governing the relations between fraternal parties.

The leadership of the CPC is organising and supporting various anti-party groups of renegades who are coming out against the Communist Parties in the United States, Brazil, Italy, Belgium, Australia and India. In Belgium, for instance, the CPC is rendering support to the group of Grippa, which was expelled from the party at its last congress. In the United States support is being given to the subversive activities of the left opportunist "Hammer and Steel" group, which has set itself the main task of fighting against the Communist Party of the United States. In Brazil Chinese comrades support factional groups expelled from the Communist Party (as for instance the Amazonas-Grabois group).

In Australia the CPC central committee has tried to organise splitting activities against the Communist Party and its leadership, with the help of a former member of the leadership, E. Hill. Having visited the People's Republic of China at one time, Hill came out publicly against the Communist Party of Australia and tried to organise a group of persons of like mind. After the Communist Party of Australia had expelled Hill from the central committee of the party, he demonstratively went to Peking.

In Italy, Chinese representatives are encouraging the activity of a group of former officials of the Padua Federation of the Communist Party, who have issued leaflets with a provocative call for a " revolutionary " uprising.

Comrades of the CPC are making particular efforts to conduct subversive activities in the Communist and Workers' Parties in the countries of Asia, Africa and Latin America.

Glorifying outcasts and renegades who have found themselves outside the ranks of the communist movement, the Chinese leaders reprint in their newspapers and magazines slanderous articles from the publications of these renegade groups directed against the policy of the CPSU and against the course of the entire world communist movement.

In Ceylon Chinese representatives are maintaining close contact with the grouping of E. Semarakkodi, which is a tool of the Trotskyist " Fourth International."

The Trotskyists of the " Fourth International " are trying to use the position of the Chinese comrades for their own aims, and have even addressed an open letter to the CPC central committee in which they have openly declared:

" The Fourth International, which from the very first day of its creation has been waging . . . a struggle with ideas against which you are coming out today, is standing by your side. . . . The international secretariat of the Fourth International welcomes this discussion which you have started in the entire communist movement. It urges you to develop it."

The Chinese leaders make sharp attacks on the fraternal Communist Parties and their leaders, who do not want to retreat from the general line of the international communist movement. They have published and circulated in many languages articles disparaging the activity of the Communist Party of the United States, and the French, Italian and Indian Communist Parties. To what kind of abusive phrases do the authors of these articles not resort when writing about prominent leaders of fraternal parties! Among them are " double-dealing " and " right-wing opportunism," " revisionism," " incompatibility with the standards of communist morality," " social democratic degeneration," " faint-heartedness," " irresponsibility," " parroting," and " haughtiness and contempt for the revolutionary peoples of countries of Asia, Africa and Latin America."

The Chinese leaders accuse the Communist Parties of the United States and Western Europe of acting " at one with the most adventurist American imperialists." The leadership of the Communist Party of India is not described otherwise than as a " clique." Against the leaders of the Communist Parties of France, Italy, India and the United States is hurled the monstrous accusation of " solicitude for the fate of imperialism and all reactionaries." And in its letter of June 14 the leadership of the CPC sinks to insinuations that the CPSU too—so it alleges—" comes out in the role of a helper of imperialism." No one but Trotskyists has so far dared, in view of the obvious absurdity of this, to level such slanderous accusations against the great party of Lenin!

Should one be surprised that imperialist propaganda rejoices at such actions on the part of the Chinese comrades? It is not by chance that the bourgeois press often shouts about a " crisis " in the international communist movement and urges the imperialist governments to utilise in their own interests the differences brought about by the position of the CPC central committee.

Representatives of the CPC left the editorial board of the magazine *World Marxist Review*—the collective theoretical and information organ of the Communist and Workers' Parties, and stopped the publication of this magazine in the Chinese language, striving in that way to deprive Chinese communists of an objective source of information about the activity of the international communist movement.

The splitting activity of the Chinese leadership in the ranks of international communist movement arouses justified indignation and repudiation on the part of fraternal Marxist-Leninist parties.

The letter of the CPC central committee says that in relations with fraternal Communist Parties it is " impermissible for one party to place itself above the other fraternal parties; it is impermissible to interfere in the internal affairs of fraternal parties . . ." This is quite a good statement. But it is precisely the Chinese comrades who are resorting to such impermissible actions.

Flouting the interests of the world communist movement, they are acting contrary to the standards and principles proclaimed in the Declaration and Statement and are trying to subordinate other fraternal parties to their influence and control.

One of the clear examples of the special line of the leadership of the CPC in the socialist camp and the international communist movement is its position on the Albanian question. As is well known, in the second half of 1960 the Albanian leaders openly came out with a left opportunist platform on the main questions of our day and began to promote a hostile policy in relation to the CPSU and other fraternal parties. The Albanian leadership started an anti-Soviet campaign in the country, which led to a rupture of political, economic and cultural ties with the Soviet Union.

The overwhelming majority of Communist and Workers' Parties resolutely condemned this anti-Leninist activity of the Albanian leaders. The leaders of the CPC took an absolutely different position and did everything in their power to use the Albanian leaders as their mouthpiece. It is now known that the Chinese comrades openly pushed them on to the road of open struggle against the Soviet Union and the other socialist countries and fraternal parties.

In their attacks on the CPSU and other Marxist-Leninist parties, the leaders of the CPC assign a special place to the Yugoslav question. They try to present matters as if difficulties in the communist movement were being caused by an improvement in relations between the Soviet Union, other socialist countries and Yugoslavia. Contrary to the facts, they stubbornly allege that Yugoslavia is not a socialist country.

As is well known, in 1955 the CPSU, together with other fraternal parties, took the initiative in normalising relations with Yugoslavia so as to end a protracted conflict, the main guilt for which rests with Stalin. At that time the leaders of the CPC had no doubts as to the nature of the socialist system in Yugoslavia. Thus the newspaper *People's Daily* pointed out that "Yugoslavia has already achieved notable successes in the construction of socialism."

An objective analysis of the social and economic processes in Yugoslavia shows that the positions of socialism have been consolidated there in the years that have followed. Whereas in 1958 the socialist sector in industry amounted to 100 per cent., in agriculture to 6 per cent., and in trade to 97 per cent., now the socialist sector in industry amounts to 100 per cent., in agriculture to 15 per cent., and in trade to 100 per cent. A *rapprochement* between Yugoslavia's positions and the position of the Soviet Union and other socialist states on questions of foreign policy has taken place in the period following the beginning of the normalisation of relations.

Why, then, have the Chinese leaders so drastically changed their attitude on the Yugoslav question? It is hard to find an explanation other than that they saw in this one of the pretexts advantageous, in their opinion, for discrediting the policy of the CPSU and other Marxist-Leninist parties.

Soviet communists know that differences on a number of ideological questions of principle continue to remain between the CPSU and the League of Communists of Yugoslavia. We have openly said, and continue to say this to the Yugoslav leaders. But it would be wrong to "excommunicate" Yugoslavia from socialism on these grounds, to cut her off from socialist countries and to push her into the camp of imperialism, as the leaders of the CPC are doing. That is precisely what the imperialists want.

At the present time there are 14 socialist countries in the world. We are profoundly convinced that in the near future their number will be considerably greater. The range of questions encountered by the fraternal parties which stand at the helm of state is increasing, and besides this, each of the fraternal parties is working in different conditions.

It is not surprising that in these circumstances the fraternal parties may develop different approaches to the solution of this or that problem. How should Marxist-Leninists act in this case? Should they declare that this or that socialist country, whose leaders do not agree with them, is no longer a socialist country? That would be really arbitrary behaviour. That method has nothing in common with Marxism-Leninism.

If we were to follow the example of the Chinese leaders, then, because of our serious differences with the leaders of the Albanian Party of Labour, we should long since have proclaimed Albania to be a non-socialist country. But that would be a wrong, subjective approach. In spite of our differences with the Albanian leaders, the Soviet communists regard Albania as a socialist country and, for their part, do everything in their power to prevent Albania from being split away from the socialist community.

We see with regret how the leaders of the CPC are undermining the traditional Soviet-Chinese friendship and weakening the unity of the socialist countries.

The CPSU stands, and will continue to stand, for the unity and cohesion of the socialist community, of the entire world communist movement.

6

Let us draw some conclusions:

The period since the adoption of the Statement of 1960 has fully confirmed the correctness of the Marxist-Leninist programme of the world communist and working-class movement. The Soviet Union's successes in building communism, the successes of socialist construction in the other countries of socialism, are exerting an ever greater revolutionising influence on the minds of people throughout the world. Revolutionary Cuba has lit a beacon of socialism in the western hemisphere. Decisive blows have been struck against the colonial system, which is near to complete liquidation. New victories have been won by the working class of imperialist countries. The world revolutionary movement is developing inexorably.

All this shows that the Statement of 1960 correctly set the general line of the world communist movement. The task now is to act in accordance with this general line, to develop and specify it as applied to the conditions in which each particular Communist Party works. Therefore all attempts to impose some new general line on the world communist and working-class movement, as has been done in the letter of the CPC central committee of June 14, are bankrupt and harmful. To accept such a " general line " would be to depart from the Statement of 1960 and to agree to programmatic theses contrary to that Statement, which was adopted by 81 parties. Our party will not do this.

Throughout its history, our glorious Leninist party has waged an implacable struggle against right-wing and left-wing opportunism, Trotskyism and revisionism, dogmatism and sectarianism, nationalism and chauvinism, in all their manifestations, both within the country and in the international arena. Our party has been steeled and strengthened in this struggle for the purity of Marxism-Leninism, and fears no attacks by present-day splitters and opportunists from whatever quarter.

Life shows that the CPSU, having become a political organisation of the whole people, has strengthened its ties with the masses, has become even stronger, and has an even higher discipline. With the victory of socialism the ideology of the working class—Marxism-Leninism—has become the ideology of the entire people, of its progressive section. The aim of the working class—the building of communism—has become the aim of the entire people. Marxist-Leninists can only rejoice, of course, in this growth of the influence of communist ideology. We can say that never since Lenin's death has our party been so strong, so capable of accomplishing the most daring tasks associated with building a new world.

Now, when socialism has won finally and completely in our country, when we are raising, stone by stone, the beautiful edifice of communism, our party, the whole Soviet people, are even more convinced that the great ideas of Marxism-Leninism will triumph throughout the world.

Our confidence is shared by the peoples of the socialist countries, by all the working people of the world. They highly appreciate the great contribution made by the Soviet Union to the common cause of the struggle for peace, democracy, national freedom, independence and socialism.

The Communist Party of the Soviet Union has stood, and continues to stand, for close friendship with the Communist Party of China. There are serious differences between us and the leaders of the CPC, but we consider that the relations between the two parties, between our two peoples, should be built, proceeding from the fact that we have the same aim—the building of a new communist society, from the fact that we have the same enemy— imperialism. United, the two great powers, the Soviet Union and the People's

Republic of China, can do much for the triumph of communism. Our friends and enemies are well aware of that.

A meeting of the delegations of the CPSU and the CPC is being held in Moscow at the present time. Unfortunately the CPC representatives at the meeting are continuing to worsen the situation. In spite of this, the delegation of the CPSU are displaying the utmost patience and self-control, working for a successful outcome to the negotiations. The very near future will show whether the Chinese comrades agree to build our relations on the basis of what unites us and not what divides us, on the basis of the principles of Marxism-Leninism.

Our enemies build their calculations on deepening the contradictions between the CPC and the CPSU. They are now looking for something from which to profit. The American *Daily News* wrote recently: " Let us set Red Russia and Red China against each other so that they tear each other to pieces."* We communists should never forget those insidious plans of the imperialists.

Aware of its responsibility to the international communist movement and to the peoples of the world, our party urges the Chinese comrades to take to the road of resolving the differences and strengthening the genuine unity of our parties on the basic principles of Marxism-Leninism and proletarian internationalism.

Together with all fraternal parties, our Leninist party has fought, and is fighting, to rally the working class, all the working people, in the struggle against imperialism, for peace, democracy, national independence and socialism.

The central committee of the CPSU declares with the utmost sense of responsibility before the party and the entire Soviet people that we have done and will continue to do everything in our power to strengthen unity with the Communist Party of China, to rally the world communist movement under the banner of Lenin, to rally the countries of the world system of socialism, to provide effective aid to all peoples fighting against colonialism, to strengthen the cause of peace, and to ensure the victory of the great ideas of communism throughout the world.

All the working people of the Soviet Union will rally even more closely round their own Communist Party and its Leninist central committee and will devote all their energy to carrying out the magnificent programme for building communism.

Central Committee of Communist Party of Soviet Union

[Open Letter from CPSU CC to Party organisations and all communists of the Soviet Union, *Pravda*, July 14, *Soviet News*, No. 4872 (July 17, 1963), pp. 29–43.]

Full title: Open Letter from the CPSU Central Committee to Party Organisations and All Communists of the Soviet Union, July 14, 1963 (complete text).

---

* Retranslated from the Russian.

DOCUMENT 4

Chinese Government Statement on Test Ban Treaty, July 31, 1963

A treaty on the partial halting of nuclear tests was initialled by the representatives of the United States, Britain and the Soviet Union in Moscow on July 25.

This is a treaty signed by three nuclear powers. By this treaty they attempt to consolidate their nuclear monopoly and bind the hands of all the peace-loving countries subjected to the nuclear threat.

This treaty signed in Moscow is a big fraud to fool the people of the world. It runs diametrically counter to the wishes of the peace-loving people of the world.

The people of the world demand a genuine peace; this treaty provides them with a fake peace.

The people of the world demand general disarmament and a complete ban on nuclear weapons; this treaty completely divorces the cessation of nuclear tests from the total prohibition of nuclear weapons, legalizes the continued manufacture, stockpiling and use of nuclear weapons by the three nuclear powers, and runs counter to disarmament.

The people of the world demand the complete cessation of nuclear tests; this treaty leaves out the prohibition of underground nuclear tests, an omission which is particularly advantageous for the further development of nuclear weapons by U.S. imperialism.

The people of the world demand the defence of world peace and the elimination of the threat of nuclear war; this treaty actually strengthens the position of nuclear powers for nuclear blackmail and increases the danger of imperialism launching a nuclear war and a world war.

If this big fraud is not exposed, it can do even greater harm. It is unthinkable for the Chinese Government to be a party to this dirty fraud. The Chinese Government regards it as its unshirkable and sacred duty to thoroughly expose this fraud.

The Chinese Government is firmly opposed to this treaty which harms the interests of the people of the whole world and the cause of world peace.

Clearly, this treaty has no restraining effect on the U.S. policies of nuclear war preparation and nuclear blackmail. It in no way hinders the United States from proliferating nuclear weapons, expanding nuclear armament or making nuclear threats. The central purpose of this treaty is, through a partial ban on nuclear tests, to prevent all the threatened peace-loving countries, including China, from increasing their defence capability, so that the United States may be more unbridled in threatening and blackmailing these countries.

U.S. President Kennedy, speaking on July 26, laid bare the substance of this treaty. Kennedy pointed out that this treaty did not mean an end to the threat of nuclear war, it did not prevent but permitted continued underground nuclear tests, it would not halt the production of nuclear weapons, it would not reduce nuclear stockpiles and it would not restrict their use in time of war. He further pointed out that this treaty would not hinder the

United States from proliferating nuclear weapons among its allies and countries under its control under the name of "assistance," whereas the United States could use it to prevent non-nuclear peace-loving countries from testing and manufacturing nuclear weapons. At the same time, Kennedy formally declared that the United States remains ready to withdraw from the treaty and resume all forms of nuclear testing. This fully shows that U.S. imperialism gains everything and loses nothing by this treaty.

The treaty just signed is a reproduction of the draft treaty on a partial nuclear test ban put forward by the United States and Britain at the meeting of the Disarmament Commission in Geneva on August 27, 1962. On August 29, 1962, the Head of the Soviet Delegation, Kuznetsov, pointed out that the obvious aim of the United States and Britain in putting forward that draft was to provide the Western powers with one-sided military advantage to the detriment of the interests of the Soviet Union and other Socialist countries. He pointed out that the United States had been using underground tests to improve its nuclear weapons for many years already, and that should underground nuclear tests be legalized with a simultaneous prohibition of such tests in the atmosphere, this would mean that the United States could continue improving its nuclear weapons and increase their yield and effectivity. The Head of the Soviet Government Khrushchev also pointed out on September 9, 1961, that "the programme of developing new types of nuclear weapons which has been drawn up in the United States now requires precisely underground tests," and that "an agreement to cease only one type of testing, in the atmosphere, would be a poor service to peace; it would deceive the peoples."

But now the Soviet Government has made a 180-degree about-face, discarded the correct stand they once persisted in and accepted this reproduction of the U.S.-British draft treaty, willingly allowing U.S. imperialism to gain military superiority. Thus the interests of the Soviet people have been sold out, the interests of the people of the countries in the Socialist camp, including the people of China, have been sold out, and the interests of all peace-loving people of the world have been sold out.

The indisputable facts prove that the policy pursued by the Soviet Government is one of allying with the forces of war to oppose the forces of peace, allying with imperialism to oppose Socialism, allying with the United States to oppose China, and allying with the reactionaries of all countries to oppose the people of the world.

Why should the Soviet leaders so anxiously need such a treaty? Is this a proof of what they call victory for the policy of peaceful co-existence? No! This is by no means a victory for the policy of peaceful co-existence. It is a capitulation to U.S. imperialism.

The U.S. imperialists and their partners are with one voice advertising everywhere that the signing of a treaty on the partial halting of nuclear tests by them is the first step towards the complete prohibition of nuclear weapons. This is deceitful talk. The United States has already stockpiled large quantities of nuclear weapons, which are scattered in various parts of the world and seriously threaten the security of all peoples. If the United States really will take the first step towards the prohibition of nuclear weapons, why does it not remove its nuclear threat to other countries? Why does it not undertake to refrain from using nuclear weapons against non-nuclear countries and to respect the desire of the people of the world to establish nuclear weapon-free zones? And why does it not undertake in all circumstances to refrain from handing over to its allies its nuclear weapons and the data for their manufacture? On what grounds can the United States and its partners maintain that the United States may use nuclear threat and blackmail against others and pursue policies of aggression and war, while others may not take measures to resist such threat and blackmail and defend their own independence and freedom? To give the aggressors the right to kill while denying the victims of aggression the right to self-defence—is this not like the Chinese saying : " The magistrate may burn down houses but the ordinary people cannot even light their lamps "?

The Chinese Government is firmly opposed to nuclear war and to a world war. It always stands for general disarmament and resolutely stands for the complete prohibition and thorough destruction of nuclear weapons. The Chinese Government and people have never spared their efforts in order to realize this aim step by step. As is known to the whole world, the Chinese Government long ago proposed, and has consistently stood for, the establishment of a zone free from nuclear weapons in the Asian and Pacific region, including the United States.

The Chinese Government holds that the prohibition of nuclear weapons and the prevention of nuclear war are major questions affecting the destiny of the world, which should be discussed and decided on jointly by all the countries of the world, big and small. Manipulation of the destiny of more than one hundred non-nuclear countries by a few nuclear powers will not be tolerated.

The Chinese Government holds that on such important issues as the prohibition of nuclear weapons and the prevention of nuclear war, it is impermissible to adopt the method of deluding the people of the world. It should be affirmed unequivocally that nuclear weapons must be completely banned and thoroughly destroyed and that practical and effective measures must be taken so as to realize step by step the complete prohibition and thorough destruction of nuclear weapons, prevent nuclear war and safeguard world peace.

For these reasons, the Government of the People's Republic of China hereby proposes the following :

(1) All countries in the world, both nuclear and non-nuclear, solemnly declare that they will prohibit and destroy nuclear weapons completely, thoroughly, totally and resolutely. Concretely speaking, they will not use nuclear weapons, nor export, nor import, nor manufacture, nor test, nor stockpile them; and they will destroy all the existing nuclear weapons and their means of delivery in the world, and disband all the existing establishments for the research, testing and manufacture of nuclear weapons in the world.

(2) In order to fulfil the above undertakings step by step, the following measures shall be adopted first :

    (a) Dismantle all military bases, including nuclear bases, on foreign soil, and withdraw from abroad all nuclear weapons and their means of delivery.

    (b) Establish a nuclear weapon-free zone of the Asian and Pacific region, including the United States, the Soviet Union, China and Japan; a nuclear weapon-free zone of Central Europe; a nuclear weapon-free zone of Africa; and a nuclear weapon-free zone of Latin America. The countries possessing nuclear weapons shall undertake due obligations with regard to each of the nuclear weapon-free zones.

(c) Refrain from exporting and importing in any form nuclear weapons and technical data for their manufacture.

(d) Cease all nuclear tests, including underground nuclear tests.

(3) A conference of the government heads of all the countries of the world shall be convened to discuss the question of the complete prohibition and thorough destruction of nuclear weapons and the question of taking the above-mentioned four measures in order to realize step by step the complete prohibition and thorough destruction of nuclear weapons.

The Chinese Government and people are deeply convinced that nuclear weapons can be prohibited, nuclear war can be prevented and world peace can be preserved. We call upon the countries in the Socialist camp and all the peace-loving countries and people of the world to unite and fight unswervingly to the end for the complete, thorough, total and resolute prohibition and destruction of nuclear weapons and for the defence of world peace.

[*Peking Review*, VI, 31 (August 2, 1963), pp. 7–8.]

Full title: Statement of the Chinese Government Advocating the Complete, Thorough, Total and Resolute Prohibition and Destruction of Nuclear Weapons [and] Proposing a Conference of the Government Heads of All Countries of the World, July 31, 1963 (complete text).

DOCUMENT 5

Mao Tse-tung's Statement on Racial Discrimination, August 8, 1963

. . . The speedy development of the struggle of the American Negroes is a manifestation of the sharpening of class struggle and national struggle within the United States; it has been causing increasing anxiety to the U.S. ruling circles. The Kennedy Administration has resorted to cunning two-faced tactics. On the one hand, it continues to connive at and take part in the discrimination against and persecution of Negroes; it even sends troops to suppress them. On the other hand, it is parading as an advocate of the "defence of human rights" and "the protection of the civil rights of Negroes," is calling upon the Negro people to exercise "restraint," is proposing to Congress the so-called "civil rights legislation," in an attempt to lull the fighting will of the Negro people and deceive the masses throughout the country. However, these tactics of the Kennedy Administration are being seen through by more and more of the Negroes. The fascist atrocities committed by the U.S. imperialists against the Negro people have laid bare the true nature of the so-called democracy and freedom in the United States and revealed the inner link between the reactionary policies pursued by the U.S. Government at home and its policies of aggression abroad.

I call upon the workers, peasants, revolutionary intellectuals, enlightened elements of the bourgeoisie and other enlightened personages of all colours in the world, white, black, yellow, brown, etc., to unite to oppose the racial discrimination practised by U.S. imperialism and to support the American Negroes in their struggle against racial discrimination. In the final analysis, a national struggle is a question of class struggle. In the United States, it is only the reactionary ruling circles among the whites who are oppressing the Negro people. They can in no way represent the workers, farmers, revolutionary intellectuals and other enlightened persons who comprise the overwhelming majority of the white people. At present, it is the handful of imperialists, headed by the United States, and their supporters, the reactionaries in different countries, who are carrying out oppression, aggression and intimidation against the overwhelming majority of the nations and peoples of the world. We are in the majority and they are in the minority. At most, they make up less than 10 per cent. of the 3,000 million population of the world. I am firmly convinced that, with the support of more than 90 per cent. of the people of the world, the American Negroes will be victorious in their just struggle. The evil system of colonialism and imperialism grew up along with the enslavement of Negroes and the trade in Negroes, it will surely come to its end with the thorough emancipation of the black people.

[*Peking Review,* VI, 33 (August 16, 1963), pp. 6–7.]

Full title: Chairman Mao Tse-tung's Statement Calling Upon the People of the World to Unite to Oppose Racial Discrimination by U.S. Imperialism and Support the American Negroes in Their Struggle Against Racial Discrimination, August 8, 1963 (excerpt).

[Letter dated August 2, 1963. NCNA, August 4, 1963.]

DOCUMENT 6

Soviet Government's Reply on Test Ban Treaty, August 3, 1963

The news of the initialling in Moscow of the treaty banning nuclear weapon tests in the atmosphere, in outer space and under water was welcomed by the peoples with joy. Messages and telegrams from heads of state and leaders of government, from the most prominent political and public leaders of the world, and from ordinary people are arriving, addressed to the Soviet government and to its head, Comrade Nikita Khrushchev, in an endless stream. These messages emphasise the enormous contribution of the Soviet Union which made the proposal for ending nuclear weapon tests, the proposal which became the starting point for the Moscow talks which have ended successfully.

Those messages and telegrams express gratitude to the Soviet government for its wise and statesmanlike approach to the solution of one of the most important problems of our time. A practical step was taken, and a good beginning was made, in settling international problems in the spirit of the principles of peaceful co-existence. The governments of many states have already declared their intention of signing the treaty.

The government of the People's Republic of China made a statement on July 31 concerning the outcome of the Moscow talks on a nuclear weapon tests ban in the atmosphere, space and under water.

In this statement the PRC government announces that it is opposed to the nuclear weapons test ban treaty and refuses to accede to it. The PRC government even describes the treaty as a " fraud " which, it alleges, is " fooling " all the peoples of the world and which " contradicts the hopes of the peace-loving peoples of all countries."

In this connection the Soviet government considers it necessary to make the following statement :

The treaty banning nuclear tests is of significance in principle, from the viewpoint of continuing the search for ways of solving the outstanding issues that divide the world. The fact that states with different social systems—great powers, the contradictions between which have more than once threatened to plunge mankind into the whirlpool of world war—have been able to find a mutually acceptable solution to a momentous international problem proves the correctness and viability of the policy of peaceful co-existence.

The peoples have seen a real possibility of reducing international tension and the possibility of curbing the arms race, the grave burden of which weighs down on them.

The results of the Moscow talks provide hope that the unsettled international issues, on which the strengthening of the cause of peace on earth depends, can be settled. It is exactly this that the Soviet government is working for, having again advanced, during the Moscow three-power talks, a broad programme of action aimed at consolidating peace. The programme envisages a number of urgent measures to remove the danger of a thermo-nuclear conflict, primarily the signing of a non-aggression pact between the

NATO and the Warsaw Treaty countries. The Soviet government has once more called for the removal of the vestiges of the Second World War, for the signature of a German peace treaty, and for the normalisation of the situation in West Berlin on that basis.

The programme of struggle to strengthen peace which is advanced by the Soviet Union is in accordance with the fundamental interests of the peoples. It has met with warm support from the governments and peoples of the socialist states, from broad public circles of the countries of Asia, Africa and Latin America, from millions of working people of the capitalist countries and from all the progressive people of the world.

The collective opinion of the socialist countries on the question of ending nuclear tests is expressed in the decision of the conference of the first secretaries of central committees of Communist and Workers' Parties and heads of government of the Warsaw Treaty countries.

" The achievement of an agreement on a nuclear test ban," the communiqué says, " is the result of the steadfast peaceloving foreign policy of the Soviet Union and of all the socialist countries and is a success for the Leninist policy of peaceful co-existence between states with different social systems.

" The conference considers that the treaty will help to reduce international tension and will be a positive factor in the struggle of the peoples for peace and against the danger of a new world war."

The fraternal Marxist-Leninist parties on all continents have expressed their complete approval of the agreement. They see in it an important result of the consistent carrying ahead of the communist movement's general line of strengthening the forces of peace and progress. All who cherish peace approve the results of the Moscow talks.

In the atmosphere of this unanimous approval, you can count on the fingers of one hand those who venture openly to oppose the treaty on the prohibition of nuclear tests. And there is nothing surprising in this : those who oppose the prohibition of nuclear tests, whatever verbal contrivances they may resort to, show themselves to be opponents of peaceful co-existence and opponents of the line of easing world tension and undermining the forces of aggression and war.

The few days since the meeting of representatives of the three powers in Moscow have already clearly revealed those who find the new important success of the forces of peace unpalatable.

They are, primarily, the so-called " wild men " in the United States who are raising the bogy of " the menace of communism " and are shouting that the treaty will not give the United States the possibility of creating still more destructive weapons.

They are the extremists from the camp of the West German militarists and revenge-seekers who are still hatching plans for new military gambles.

They are the extremists from the camp of the French ruling circles who, for some unknown reason, have decided that the grandeur of France does not consist in a contribution to easing international tensions or in friendship with other nations, but in friendship with nuclear bombs, in creating a stockpile of nuclear weapons at any cost.

When such views are expressed by representatives of the most bellicose circles of imperialism, there is nothing surprising in it ; but when the treaty banning nuclear weapon tests is opposed by communists—and, what is more, by the communists standing at the head of a socialist country—this cannot but arouse well-justified amazement.

How can the leaders of a socialist country reject out of hand an international agreement which serves to strengthen peace, which is in line with the wishes of the peoples and which meets their vital interests ?

Only disregard of the vital interests of the peoples who have long been demanding an end to nuclear testing could suggest such an interpretation of the aims and significance of the treaty as those which the Chinese government seeks to give in its statement.

The government of the PRC claims in its statement that the conclusion of the treaty has the aim of " consolidating the nuclear monopoly " of the three powers, and that the Soviet Union's participation in such a treaty is " capitulation to American imperialism."

One cannot imagine a greater absurdity. In pressing for the conclusion of a treaty banning nuclear weapon tests, the Soviet Union and all peaceloving forces see in it an important step to protect mankind from the dangerous consequences of the pollution of the atmosphere, water and outer space by radioactive substances. But those who level accusations against the U.S.S.R.—bracketing a socialist power with the capitalist states—seek to present this as an attempt by the Soviet Union to achieve some sort of nuclear monopoly, and even as " capitulation."

It follows, therefore, that if nuclear weapons spread throughout the world, if the way is left open for the West German revenge-seekers to get possession of these weapons, if one series of nuclear explosions carried out by scores of states was followed by another, then that would, it appears, meet the interests of peace and would not be capitulation to imperialism !

No, it is just the other way round. That would mean playing irresponsibly with the destinies of millions upon millions of people, and everyone who shows concern for the present and future of his people, for the preservation of peace not only in words but in practical deeds, cannot but realise this.

The government of the Chinese People's Republic is trying to ignore completely the facts which are known to the whole world. The groundlessness of the attempts to cast aspersions on the Soviet Union's position on the question of nuclear weapons is proved by the fact that it was precisely the Soviet Union that, as far back as 1946, was the first to come out with a proposal for the outlawing of atomic weapons once and for all and the destruction of the stockpiles. Having the most perfect nuclear weapons and the most perfect means of delivering them in its possession, the Soviet Union has been fighting persistently and consistently for many years to secure the outlawing of atomic and hydrogen weapons, for ending this production, for the destruction of all stockpiles of these weapons, for ending their testing and for scrapping the whole military machine of states.

The head of the Soviet government, Nikita Khrushchev, speaking from the rostrum of the United Nations General Assembly in 1959, advanced a proposal for general and complete disarmament which has become the banner of the peoples in the struggle for lasting peace. The basis of the Soviet disarmament programme, its backbone, is the prohibition and complete destruction of all nuclear weapons, and of all means of delivering them to their targets. It is well known that the Soviet government is also waging a struggle for the immediate putting into effect of such measures to check the nuclear arms race as the establishment of de-nuclearised zones in various areas of the world and the dismantling of military bases on foreign territories.

Can one say that in proposing all these measures, the Soviet Union is guided solely by its own interests, and not by the interests of the whole socialist community and of all peoples ? Isn't it a fact that what the statement of the PRC government terms a nuclear monopoly—i.e., the possession by the Soviet Union of such weapons, played a definite, one may even saying the decisive, role in the fact that the socialist countries, including the PRC, have not become objects of imperialist aggression and are able to build socialism and communism successfully ?

The statement of the Chinese government further contends that the nuclear weapons test ban treaty does not entirely fulfil the task of banning all kinds of nuclear weapons, of destroying nuclear stockpiles and of ending their production. It cannot be denied that the treaty does not solve all those problems. It is, of course, plain to everyone that the wider the agreement, the better. An ideal solution would be immediately to conclude a treaty on general and complete disarmament. We call for such a treaty now, as we have done hitherto. Perhaps the Chinese leaders know the secret of how to solve this problem at one fell swoop? So far as we are concerned, we consider it better to achieve a part than to do nothing, when agreement on such a partial measure is in the interests of peace and in the interests of socialism. If, in present day conditions, it is not yet possible to solve the whole problem at once, the only reasonable way out is to solve it step by step. One must be absolutely out of touch with reality to advance the alternatives " all or nothing " in matters involving the fate of the world and the lives of millions of people.

It is not very difficult to throw out in all directions the simple and easy formula : all or nothing. In practice such a demand is devoid of any real content.

Can such an approach to international affairs be regarded as realistic ? It is the duty of communists, and above all of communists who are leaders of states, to work, let it be step by step, to save the peoples from the danger of nuclear war and annihilation. The Soviet Government is convinced that there is not a single country on earth whose people would give their seal of approval to a policy which dooms humanity to breathe radioactive air, who would approve plans for an unlimited nuclear arms race and for giving access to nuclear weapons to the most adventurous circles of the imperialist camp, including the West German revenge-seekers. No, there is no such people !

The test ban treaty can be rejected only by people who are standing aside from the struggle of the peoples against nuclear war and who cover up their lack of readiness or desire to achieve disarmament with flashy phrases about most radical disarmament measures. Only those people who view the struggle for general and complete disarmament merely as bystanders, to whom real success in the struggle for peace is of no consequence, can object. To those, on the other hand, who do wage this struggle, every step toward this great goal is important.

The Chinese leaders, by the way, had to admit themselves in their state-ment that the complete prohibition of nuclear weapons should be approached " gradually." But if they recognise the need for this approach—and there is no other possible in present conditions—why then, one may ask, is the Soviet Union being reproached with not being able to secure the solution of the whole problem at one go?

Apparently, the Chinese leaders, carried away by argument, consider that logic is not required of them in this case. For one thing, the statement by the government of the PRC contends that the treaty banning nuclear weapon tests does not give anything to the peoples since it does not provide for the complete prohibition and destruction of nuclear weapons. And for another, it says that the treaty is bad because it does not cover underground nuclear tests. Consequently, the Chinese Government, too, recognises in principle that the ending of nuclear weapon tests is a good thing, and that the peoples demand this. But, virtually a few lines later in its statement, the Chinese Government produces one contrived argument after another against this treaty, like the claim that the treaty on the prohibition of nuclear weapon tests it a " fraud " since it does not provide a complete solution to the problem of eliminating nuclear weapons.

A treaty banning nuclear tests, even if it were extended to underground tests, is, of course, only a partial measure, only a step in the direction of disarmament, providing more favourable conditions for it; but the question is in order: does this measure help or impede the solution of the cardinal task, the task of disarmament?

With the exception of the most outspoken enemies of peace in the camp of the imperialist powers, everbody admits that the reaching of agreement on ending nuclear tests creates more favourable conditions for progress on disarmament. The communists in the capitalist countries, the Communist Parties standing at the head of the socialist countries, reply to this question in the affirmative: the conclusion of the treaty banning nuclear tests helps the struggle for general and complete disarmament; but the government of the Chinese People's Republic asserts the opposite. It follows, therefore, that the whole world is in error and only the PRC Government knows the truth.

But who then is actually deceiving the peoples? Those who, having first achieved real results, call for developing further the success achieved, who call for stepping up the efforts in the struggle against the aggressive forces of imperialism and in the struggle for the solution of other important problems? Or those who treat the efforts and achievements of the fighters for peace with disdain and in this way confuse the peoples and sow disbelief in their ability to prevent war?

The whole of this concept of the PRC Government reeks of hopelessness and pessimism. Its essence could be compared with a saying that was common in our country in the past: " neck or nothing." This concept could probably be understood if it came from those who were doomed by history, from those under whose feet the ground was shaking; but it is incomprehensible how the government of a country building a socialist society can take such a stand.

Who can be inspired by such a concept of hopelessness? No, people draw energy, not from advancing nearer and nearer to the black abyss of a thermonuclear war, but from deep faith in their own ability and the possibility to restrain the forces of war and to ensure genuine peace and progress.

The government of the PRC claims that the conclusion of the treaty banning nuclear weapon tests leads to " American imperialism gaining a military advantage " while the peaceloving countries, including China, lose the " possibility of strengthening their defensive might."

Strange logic this! Even our enemies admit that it is the Soviet Union that has the most powerful nuclear weapons in the world today and the most advanced means for delivering them to any target.

This powerful rocket-nuclear shield ensures the security not only of the Soviet Union but of all the socialist countries, including the PRC, and is the bulwark of peace throughout the world.

Does the conclusion of a treaty banning tests alter the present balance of forces? No, it doesn't. The Soviet Government would never have agreed to the conclusion of such a treaty if it placed us in an unequal position, if it gave unilateral advantages to the other side. All this requires no special proof.

Lastly, if the question of who would benefit most by this treaty is to be raised, would it not be more correct to assume that, on the question of nuclear tests, the Soviet Union—as the nuclear power in the community of socialist states—is in a better position to judge whether the balance of forces will change or not, and if it does change, then in what direction. Does the government of the PRC not take too much upon itself in drawing conclusions on this question for the Soviet Government and for the Soviet Union?

No it is not concern for the defence potential of the socialist camp which has prompted the statement of the PRC government. What stands behind all this, apparently, is the desire, regardless of the position of the socialist camp and of all the peaceloving forces, to follow an individual policy on the question of what is to be done about the most destructive weapons— nuclear weapons—whether to destroy them or to open the sluice gates for them to spread, unhindered, all over the earth.

The Chinese leaders should ponder the fact that in refusing to sign the treaty to ban nuclear weapon tests, they find themselves in company with those in the imperialist bloc who oppose the treaty. No one would be able to convince the Soviet government that such a position is in the interests of any people, whether a people of Europe, America, Asia, or Africa, whether the people of a small or big state.

Apparently, the PRC government itself realises how unpopular a negative attitude to the problems of strengthening peace, on problems of disarmament, is at the present time. It is precisely for this reason that, in its statement, it tries to present matters as though it had some kind of programme of its " own " for nuclear disarmament problems—a programme even more radical than that advocated by the Soviet Union and the other socialist countries.

In the first place, however, this " programme," which is advanced in the statement of the PRC government contains nothing new. All the proposals listed in it have been put forward in the past by the Soviet Union and the other socialist countries. The PRC government has only repeated these proposals.

The whole world knows that the Soviet Union and the other socialist states, as in alliance with peaceloving forces throughout the world they have done, are continuing to conduct an active struggle for the realisation of the programme of general and complete disarmament which they have put forward—a programme including the complete destruction of nuclear weapons.

Second, the gist of the statement of the PRC government does not at all lie in the radical programme which lists proposals long since submitted by others, but in the fact that in the particular case they are trying to use this programme to cover up a refusal by the PRC government to sign a treaty banning nuclear weapons tests.

The Chinese government has not a single convincing argument in favour of its negative attitude to the test ban treaty, and, indeed, a government cannot have such arguments if it builds its policy exclusively in the interests of peace and socialism and in the interests of the peoples.

Shoulder to shoulder with the other socialist countries, the Soviet Union has fought and fights indefatigably to achieve general and complete disarmament. The Soviet government has always rejoiced in the past that the PRC was in the same ranks, making its contribution to the struggle for disarmament and to the consolidation of peace among nations.

The Soviet Union and the other socialist countries regard the statement of the PRC government as an unprecedented and most regrettable act.

All friends of peace and socialism cannot but regret that on a question involving the vital interests of all the peoples of the earth, the government of a socialist country has taken a step which completely contradicts the common line of the socialist states in the international arena and which completely contradicts the fundamental principles that guide these states in foreign policy—principles beneath which on two occasions, in 1957 and in 1960, the leaders of the People's Republic of China have affixed their signatures.

The position of the PRC government runs counter to the Leninist policy of peaceful co-existence between states with different social systems. The Chinese leaders thereby place themselves openly against the socialist commonwealth, the whole world communist movement and all the peaceloving peoples of Europe, Asia, Africa and America.

The Chinese government cannot fail to understand that, by taking such a course, it inflicts direct damage on the unity of the socialist camp and weakens the united front of the struggle against imperialism.

Such actions can bring joy only to the enemies of peace whose cherished aim is to disunite, to alienate the socialist countries, to break the great unity of the peoples of the socialist community and to weaken the world system of socialism from within.

It is impossible also not to see that the statement of the Chinese government containing attacks on our country and on the policy of the Soviet Union is further evidence that the Chinese leaders are transferring ideological differences to inter-state relations. It is impossible to explain otherwise the appearance in this document of such impudent allegations as that, by concluding the treaty banning nuclear tests, the Soviet government has " betrayed the interests of the Soviet people, betrayed the interests of the peoples of the socialist countries, including China, and betrayed the interests of the peaceloving peoples of the whole world."

It is difficult to say what predominates here—political irresponsibility or the irritation of people whose hopes have been dashed to the ground by life itself.

Who empowered the government of the PRC to speak in the name of the Soviet people and for them? Who asked it to speak for the peoples of the other socialist countries? The authors of the statement must be losing their minds if—disregarding the elementary standards of relations between states let alone the standards of relations between fraternal socialist countries—they seek, in their statement, to counterpose the Soviet people to the Soviet government.

The hopelessness of such attempts has long been realised even by the imperialists who, in the years of intervention and then in the years of the Second World War, broke their teeth on the monolithic unity of the Soviet people, the Soviet government and the glorious Communist Party. This was a vote by blood and life for the Soviet power in our country, for the policy of the Communist Party and our own Soviet government. And today, by their magnificent labour achievements in building communism, the Soviet people vote for the peaceful policy of their government and express their unlimited confidence in and support for the Communist Party of the Soviet Union and its central committee.

In whose footsteps do the Chinese leaders intend to follow? In the statement of the government of the PRC one cannot discover, even with the help of a microscope, the least trace of respect for the sovereignty of the Soviet state—though communists and the socialist countries, not only proclaim, but must consistently defend the principles of sovereignty and non-interference in internal affairs in international relations, including relations between socialist countries. In the question of national sovereignty, what can one oppose to the imperialist policy of trampling upon the sovereign rights of the peoples if the government of a socialist state flounts the principle of respect for sovereignty and goes so far as to make insulting attacks on fraternal countries and on fraternal peoples?

Only people who have fenced themselves off behind a wall of dogmatic notions from what is worrying mankind, from the concerns and hopes of working people, can either fail to see or pretend not to see the tremendous changes taking place on our planet and not believe in the reason and will of the peoples who are today capable of preventing a thermonuclear world war.

The government of the PRC is trying to find some contradictions in the position of the Soviet Union; but, while artificially selecting quotations and juggling with words, they forget the simple truth that life doesn't stand still. Science and technology are developing tempestuously, and what was unacceptable only last night proves useful, even very useful, today.

So it is, precisely, with the prohibition of nuclear weapon tests in the atmosphere, in outer space and under water. There can hardly be any doubt as to who is more competent to be the judge in this—those who possess nuclear weapons and hold their tests, or others who know about them only from reading. There can be no two opinions on this score.

As regards the proposal of the PRC government that an international conference with the participation of heads of government be called to discuss the relevant problems including the problem of disarmament, the Soviet government, of course, cannot object to it, since it is its own proposal. This is one of the suggestions repeatedly made by the Soviet government. In making this proposal we proceeded from the fact, and we stated so, that no one can assume any commitments for the People's Republic of China except its own government, and that, consequently, the question of China's commitments can be discussed only with the participation of the PRC government. The soviet government continues to adhere to that position firmly.

In this connection the question arises: Why did the PRC government find it necessary at this moment to advance the proposal for an international conference to deal with the problem of disarmament and a number of other international problems, and to claim that this is some innovation? Again, it was so as to camouflage their refusal to sign the treaty banning nuclear weapon tests.

In an effort to discredit our undeniable successes in the struggle to reduce the threat of war in the eyes of the peoples and to vilify the peaceful foreign policy of the Soviet Union, the Chinese leaders have shown the whole world that their policy leads to the sharpening of international tensions, to the further stepping up of the nuclear arms race and to the still further expansion of its scope and scale. This attitude is tantamount to actual connivance with those who advocate thermonuclear world war and who are against the settlement round the conference table of international problems in dispute. There is no doubt that this attitude cannot but meet, and does meet, with the resolute condemnation of the peoples of the socialist countries and of all peaceloving states, and all those for whom peace and progress is dear.

Expressing the will of all the Soviet people, the Soviet government rejects the fabrication about the foreign policy of the Soviet state contained in the statement of the PRC government. No fantasies or attacks can change the line of the foreign policy of the Soviet Union, which was charted by great Lenin and developed further in the decisions of the 20th and 22nd Congresses of our party, in the Programme of the CPSU, and which was unanimously approved by the whole Soviet people and by the international communist movement. Following this course, the Soviet Union will continue steadfastly to pursue a policy of peace and international friendship, to fight for general and complete disarmament, for the peaceful settlement of international issues, including those that involve the security of Europe, and for the triumph of the Leninist principles of peaceful co-existence.

The Soviet government, of course, would be sincerely happy if the foreign policy of the People's Republic of China had been based on the unity of the socialist states, whose banner is the struggle to avert the danger of a thermonuclear war, for peaceful co-existence, for the freedom of all peoples and their right to build their life as they see fit. That is what the interests of international communist solidarity, the interests of socialism and communism, and the interests of peace demand.

[*Soviet News*, No. 4881 (August 6, 1963), pp. 87–90.]

Full title: Soviet Government Answers Statement by the Chinese Government on Nuclear Weapons Testban, August 3, 1963 (complete text).

DOCUMENT 7

China Defends Her Test Ban Treaty, August 15, 1963

A COMMENT ON THE SOVIET GOVERNMENT'S STATEMENT OF AUGUST 3

On August 3 the Government of the Soviet Union issued a statement, attacking the Chinese Government's statement of July 31 on the complete prohibition and thorough destruction of nuclear weapons and defending the treaty on the partial halting of nuclear tests which was concluded by the Soviet Union with the United States and Britain. The Soviet Government of course has the right to defend its own action. However, after carefully studying this statement of the Soviet Government's, we regret to say that it is a poor defence, rambling haphazard, full of pointless talk and lacking any reasoned arguments.

I

There is a fatal weakness in the Soviet Government's statement, namely, it evades the fact that the conclusion of the treaty was a result of the abandonment of the Soviet Government's previous correct stand, the acceptance of the stand of the United States steadily upheld by two Administrations and unprincipled concessions to imperialism. The statement of the Chinese Government solemnly pointed out that the Soviet leaders made a 180 degree about-face, betrayed themselves and sold out the interests of the people of the Soviet Union and the world.

The Soviet statement is furious over the words " betrayal " and " sell-out " and asserts that there is no inconsistency in the Soviet stand, because "life does not mark time, science and technology are developing tempestuously, and what was unacceptable only yesterday may prove useful, even very useful, today." It insolently asks us who is more competent to be the judge on the question of whom the treaty benefits—" those who possess nuclear weapons and carry out tests, or those who only know about them from literature "? It appears that the Soviet leaders want to have a monopoly not only of nuclear weapons but also of the right to speak on the question of nuclear weapons.

No one can monopolize the right to speak on the question of nuclear weapons. But since the Soviet leaders regard themselves as competent to speak, let us hear what they have said in the past.

The United States put forward the proposal for the cessation of nuclear tests, excluding underground tests, for the first time on April 13, 1959. In his letter to Eisenhower of April 23 of that year, Khrushchov, Chairman of the Council of Ministers of the Soviet Union, called it a " dishonest deal."

On September 3, 1961, the United States and Britain issued a joint statement proposing the conclusion of an agreement on banning nuclear tests in the atmosphere alone. On September 9, Soviet leader Khrushchov issued a statement on the matter, saying that:

> Each line of the statement by the President of the United States and the Prime Minister of Great Britain reveals a desire, cost what it may, to ensure

for the Western powers and their allies in aggressive military blocs unilateral military advantages to the detriment of the security interests of the Soviet Union and the other socialist states.

It is a dishonest deal. Of course, the Soviet Government cannot and will not strike such a bargain.

On September 28, 1961, the Soviet Government published a memorandum on the question of nuclear weapon tests, saying that:

As to the question regarding underground and space test explosions of these weapons, it was separated from the suggested agreement and this again showed the tendency on the part of the United States and Britain to reserve for themselves the possibility of carrying out nuclear tests and to tie the hands of the Soviet Union in taking measures to improve its defence ability.

To allow such a situation to develop would be tantamount to encouraging the aggressors to carry out their designs, which are dangerous for the whole of mankind.

On August 27, 1962, the United States and Britain put forward a draft treaty on the partial halting of nuclear tests. On August 29 Kuznetsov, head of the Soviet Delegation, pointed out at a meeting of the Disarmament Commission in Geneva that this draft contained a serious danger. He said that,

The United States of America has been using underground tests to improve its nuclear weapons for many years already. . . . Should underground nuclear tests be legalized with a simultaneous prohibition of such tests in the atmosphere—this would mean that the United States could continue improving its nuclear weapons, increase their yield and effectivity, whereas the Soviet Union would have its hands bound in the question of strengthening its defence potentiality.

The Soviet Government persisted in its stand of rejecting the partial stoppage of nuclear tests. As late as June 9, 1963, it notified the Chinese Government that the Western powers' position on the halting of nuclear tests could not yet serve as a basis for agreement, and that whether negotiations could yield any results depended entirely on the Western powers.

On June 15, 1963, answering questions put by the editors-in-chief of *Pravda* and *Izvestia* on the U.S. President's speech of June 10, the Soviet leader Khrushchov said:

As far as the Soviet Union is concerned, we are ready to sign an agreement on the discontinuance of all nuclear tests today. It is up to the West now. We agreed to a meeting of the representatives of the three powers in Moscow, to try once again to reach an agreement on this question. But the success of this meeting will depend on what the United States and British representatives bring with them to our country.

On July 25, 1963, the Soviet leaders suddenly changed their above stand, accepted the refurbished version of the U.S.-British draft treaty and signed the treaty on the partial halting of nuclear tests.

The Soviet leaders says the situation has changed. When did it change? How did it change? Why is it that what was unacceptable on June 15 became acceptable on July 25, and very useful into the bargain? What changes took place within those forty days? Why did you not provide a little explanation? Why did you not give some reasons? If what you said yesterday no longer counts today, will what you say today no longer count tomorrow? You were either insincere then, or you are deliberately deceiving people now. The Soviet leaders' betrayal of the Soviet people, of the countries in the socialist camp and of the people of the whole world can by no means be denied.

II

The circumstances remain unchanged. The policy of U.S. imperialism has not changed. It is the Soviet leaders who have changed.

The conclusion of a treaty on the partial halting of nuclear tests was an object persistently pursued by the United States over a number of years. In his message to the U.S. Senate dated August 8, U.S. President Kennedy said,

> It grows out of the proposal made by President Eisenhower in 1959 and the resolution passed by the Senate in the same year. . . . Nothing has happened since then to alter its importance to our security.

The Soviet statement says that the conclusion of the tripartite treaty is the first step towards freeing mankind from the threat of nuclear war.

It does not seem so to us. On the contrary, in our view the conclusion of the tripartite treaty increases the danger of nuclear war.

On the question of nuclear weapons, don't you respect only what is said by those who possess nuclear weapons? Let us then hear what those who possess nuclear weapons have said.

In the period between July 26 and August 8, Kennedy repeatedly and outspokenly said that the tripartite treaty

—does not prohibit the United States to conduct underground nuclear tests,

—does not halt the production of nuclear weapons by the United States,

—does not reduce the U.S. nuclear stockpiles,

—does not hinder the United States from spreading nuclear weapons to its allies,

—does not restrict the use of nuclear weapons by the United States in time of war,

—does not prohibit the nuclear arms race,

—does not mean an end to the danger of nuclear war, and

—does not assure world peace.

At the ceremony of the formal signing of this treaty, Rusk said relentlessly, " It is not possible for us to guarantee now what the significance of this act will be."

The treaty was signed primarily between the Soviet Union and the United States. If the pronouncements of Kennedy and Rusk were wrong, why did not the Soviet leaders refute them? To assert that this treaty represents a so-called first step towards preventing nuclear war is a deliberate attempt to fool the people of the world.

What is more, this treaty is highly advantageous to the forces of war headed by U.S. imperialism and highly detrimental to the forces of world peace.

Kennedy said that the first advantage of this treaty to the United States is that it legalizes underground nuclear tests " in which the United Sates has more experience than any other nation," and the second advantage is that it prohibits nuclear tests in the atmosphere through which " other powers could develop all kinds of weapons more cheaply and quickly than they could underground."

It is by no means a treaty preventing war and strengthening peace, as the Soviet leaders allege; it is a treaty U.S. imperialism can use to pursue its war aims by exploiting the desire of the people of the world for peace. In no sense does the conclusion of this treaty show that U.S. imperialism has become sensible; it is the result of open capitulation by the Soviet leaders to U.S. imperialism.

III

Why did the U.S. imperialists desire such a treaty?

After dropping the first atom bomb on Hiroshima in August 1945, U.S. imperialism tried to exploit its monopoly of nuclear weapons in order to push its policies of aggression and war, to enslave the peoples and lord it over the whole world. But the U.S. policy of nuclear blackmail was unable to prevent the peoples of China, Korea, Viet Nam, Cuba and other countries from winning great victories in their revolutionary struggles. The Soviet possession of nuclear weapons smashed the nuclear monopoly of the United States and placed the U.S. imperialists in the position of courting self-destruction in case they tried to destroy others. At the same time, all the world's peace-loving countries and people unfolded increasingly powerful struggles against nuclear war and for the banning of nuclear weapons. All this rendered the U.S. imperialist policy of nuclear blackmail more and more ineffective.

In the face of this unfavourable situation, U.S. imperialism, while maintaining the means of "massive retaliation," had to adopt and stress the "strategy of flexible response," which means preparing for both nuclear war and conventional war and both continuing the development of strategic nuclear weapons as means of nuclear blackmail and threats and energetically developing tactical nuclear weapons in preparation for launching "limited nuclear wars" when necessary.

It was in pursuit of this counter-revolutionary strategy that the United States needed a treaty on halting nuclear tests which would

—divorce the cessation of nuclear tests from the general task of banning nuclear weapons and, by such a cessation, provide a screen for U.S. nuclear war preparations,

—exclude a prohibition on underground nuclear tests, so that the United States could improve its strategic nuclear weapons and develop tactical nuclear weapons,

—ensure that the United States and its allies will gain nuclear superiority over the Soviet Union and further develop it, and

—bind all the socialist countries except the Soviet Union and all countries subjected to aggression, without hindering the United States from proliferating its nuclear weapons among its allies and countries under its control.

From beginning to end, the tripartite treaty which has just been concluded satisfies these requirements of the U.S. imperialist global strategy.

IV

By completely divorcing the cessation of nuclear tests from the general task of banning nuclear weapons, the tripartite treaty creates an illusion of peace, lulls the vigilance of the people of the world and provides a screen behind which U.S. imperialism can continue to manufacture, develop and proliferate nuclear weapons, gain nuclear superiority and prepare for a nuclear war.

The authors of the Soviet Government's statement completely forget what the Soviet leaders more than once pointed out, i.e., that a treaty exclusively concerned with the halting of nuclear tests is a deal for deceiving the people. On the contrary, they boast that the tripartite treaty can protect mankind against the dangerous consequences of contamination by radioactive substances. They are cajoling support for the tripartite treaty by exploiting the peoples' natural desire to avoid contamination by radioactive substances.

It should be pointed out firstly that the United States must bear the full responsibility for the pollution of the atmosphere. It was the United States which first tested, manufactured and used atomic weapons and it is the United States which has engaged in the frenzied expansion of nuclear armaments and conducted hundreds of nuclear tests, mostly on the high seas in the Pacific. The great majority of the nuclear tests conducted on this planet have been the work of the United States. According to any principle of equity, the United States should have stopped testing long ago.

In fact, under the pressure of popular demand and world opinion and because it has obtained enough technical data, the United States has already stopped all forms of nuclear tests except underground ones. In the absence of the tripartite treaty, the United States, weighing the advantages and disadvantages, would not dare lightly to resume these forms of nuclear testing. With the tripartite treaty, however, not only is this state of affairs not fixed, but the United States is given the right to resume these forms of nuclear testing at any time. As soon as the tripartite treaty was initialled, Kennedy declared that the United States remains ready to resume nuclear tests in the atmosphere. He openly said that the tripartite treaty " does not assure the world that it will be for ever free from the fears and dangers of radioactive fallout from atmospheric tests." Unless one's purpose is to deceive the people of the world, how can one describe the treaty as a protection for mankind against contamination by radioactive substances?

Radioactive substances are indeed harmful, but the harm done by a nuclear war will be a hundred times, a thousand times more serious. The Soviet leader Khrushchov once exposed the imperialist scheme as follows:

> There is an apt saying: if the head is gone, it is no use crying over the coiffure. The imperialist gentlemen are preparing death for people in the fire of war and they chatter about people's health.

Now it is enough for us to present the Soviet leaders with the same words. It would be superfluous to add to them on this point.

V

By omitting the prohibition on underground nuclear tests, the tripartite treaty legalizes such tests and makes it easier for the United States to improve its strategic nuclear weapons, develop tactical nuclear weapons, conduct nuclear blackmail and prepare for " limited nuclear wars."

According to data published by the United States, it has carried out more than seventy underground nuclear tests since 1957, and has gained rich experience. It has set up huge, well-equipped underground testing grounds. It is already able to conduct underground medium nuclear tests with the yield of the equivalent of several hundred thousands tons of TNT. The tripartite treaty gives the United States freedom to conduct about 80 per cent of the nuclear tests it deems necessary. The reservation on underground nuclear testing is most advantageous to the United States.

The U.S. Defence Secretary McNamara said on August 13 that the United States is determined to maintain its nuclear superiority over the Soviet Union. If testing continued indefinitely without limit, the most likely ultimate result would be technical parity between the United States and the U.S.S.R. Since the United States has more experience in underground nuclear tests, to ban other forms of nuclear testing while preserving underground tests will retard Soviet progress and enhance the superiority of the United States. An underground nuclear explosion was demonstratively conducted by the United States only a week after the formal signing of the tripartite treaty.

The United States can continue to improve its strategic nuclear weapons by means of underground tests. These strategic weapons are increasingly becoming a means of political blackmail as they and their means of delivery are being developed more and more and being manufactured and stockpiled in ever greater quantities, and a nuclear stalemate has arisen as a result.

At present, the United States is eagerly seeking to develop tactical nuclear weapons. It intends to use tactical nuclear weapons in local wars in order to deal with non-nuclear socialist and other peace-loving countries and people, and in particular to deal with the Asian, African and Latin American countries and people which are subjected to oppression and aggression.

If this U.S. imperialist scheme should be allowed to succeed, and if U.S. imperialism should be permitted to win in one local war after another and so change the international balance of forces, it would in turn definitely increase the danger of a total nuclear war. This situation cannot but rouse the people's serious vigilance.

It is an indisputable fact that the tripartite treaty facilitates continued nuclear blackmail and threats by U.S. imperialism and its continued suppression of popular revolutionary movements and national-independence movements. In signing this treaty, the Soviet leaders have ignored the vital interests of the oppressed peoples and nations of the world. This is indeed to " play irresponsibly with the destiny of millions upon millions of people."

VI

The tripartite treaty can in no way prevent the United States from carrying out nuclear proliferation, and it tends to strengthen the aggressive forces of the imperialist camp.

Feigning ignorance on this point, the Soviet statement retorts:

> Thus it follows that if nuclear weapons spread throughout the world, if the way was opened for the West German revanchists to gain possession of these weapons, and if one series of nuclear explosions carried out by scores of states would succeed another, this would apparently serve the interests of peace and would not constitute a capitulation to imperialism!

Well, let us see in what way the treaty helps to prevent nuclear proliferation, and what sort of nuclear proliferation it prevents.

Can this treaty prevent U.S. imperialism from proliferating its nuclear weapons, and the technical data for their manufacture, among the West German revanchists and other allies of the United States and countries under its control?

No, absolutely not. The U.S. Government has constantly stressed that it cannot, and the Soviet leaders are aware of this, too. Please look at the facts.

On July 31, Harriman openly stated that there was nothing in the treaty to prevent the United States from disclosing nuclear secrets to its allies. And the United States has already approached France on this matter.

As the whole world knows, the so-called plan for a "multilateral nuclear force" which the United States has been promoting is one of nuclear proliferation among its allies, including the West German revanchists. The conclusion of the tripartite treaty in no way hinders the promotion of this plan. After the initialling of the tripartite treaty, the United States immediately resumed the meeting in Washington to discuss the building of a "multilateral nuclear force."

On the very day that the tripartite treaty was initialled, West German Defence Minister von Hassel serenely remarked that the tripartite treaty did not ban all nuclear tests and that it affected neither the building of a "multilateral armed force" nor the conception of NATO and the West German armed forces as a whole.

On August 12, Rusk went a step further and declared outright that the treaty would not hinder the United States from arming its allies with nuclear weapons and that therefore it would not prevent the construction of the multilateral NATO nuclear force proposed by the United States.

The facts are all here. Who will believe that this paper treaty can possibly prevent the United States from proliferating nuclear weapons and nuclear secrets among its allies and countries under its control, especially West Germany? The Soviet leaders are attempting to justify their act of capitulation by playing on the righteous feelings of the people of Europe against the revival of West German militarism. This attempt has failed in the face of iron-clad facts and will go thoroughly bankrupt in the end.

VII

The object of U.S. imperialism in advocating the prevention of nuclear proliferation is not at all to manacle itself but to manacle socialist countries other than the Soviet Union.

The United States is trying to achieve this object by consolidating the nuclear monopoly position of the United States, Britain and the Soviet Union. The Soviet leaders are fully supporting this plot and playing an active part in carrying it out.

The statement of the Soviet Government says,

> Is it not a fact that what the Statement of the PRC Government terms a nuclear monopoly, i.e. the possession by the Soviet Union of these weapons, did play a definite, one might even say the decisive, role in preventing the socialist countries, including the PRC, from becoming objects of imperialist aggression and in enabling them successfully to build socialism and communism?

We cannot agree with this view.

In fighting imperialist aggression and defending its security, every socialist country has to rely in the first place on its own defence capability, and then—and only then—on assistance from fraternal countries and the people of the world. For the Soviet statement to describe all the socialist countries as depending on the nuclear weapons of the Soviet Union for their survival is to strike an out-and-out great-power chauvinistic note and to fly in the face of the facts.

The Chinese Government has always fully appreciated the importance of the Soviet Union's possession of nuclear weapons. However, such possession must in no way be made a justification for preventing other socialist countries from increasing their own defence capabilities. The Moscow Statement of 1960 points out, " So long as there is no disarmament, the socialist countries must maintain their defence potential at an adequate level." If the Soviet Government is earnest about abiding by the Moscow Statement and really wants to fight the imperialist policies of aggression and war and to defend world peace, there is no reason why it should try so hard to obstruct other socialist countries from increasing their defence capabilities.

With regard to preventing nuclear proliferation, the Chinese Government has always maintained that the arguments of the U.S. imperialists must not be echoed, but that a class analysis must be made. Whether or not nuclear weapons help peace depends on who possesses them. It is detrimental to peace if they are in the hands of imperialist countries; it helps peace if they are in the hands of socialist countries. It must not be said undiscriminatingly that the danger of nuclear war increases along with the increase in the number of nuclear powers. Nuclear weapons were first the monopoly of the United States. Later, the Soviet Union also came to possess them. Did the danger of nuclear war become greater or less when the number of nuclear powers increased from one to two? We say it became less, not greater.

Nuclear weapons in the possession of a socialist country are always a means of defence against nuclear blackmail and nuclear war. So long as the imperialists refuse to ban nuclear weapons, the greater the number of socialist countries possessing them, the better the guarantee of world peace. A fierce class struggle is now going on in the world. In this struggle, the greater the strength on our side, the better. Does it make sense to say the less the better?

However, after attaining possession of nuclear weapons themselves, the Soviet leaders began to echo the arguments of the U.S. imperialists and to endeavour to have the monopoly of nuclear weapons among the socialist countries. This is a total repudiation of the Moscow Statement and a total repudiation of proletarian internationalism.

The Soviet leaders turn a blind eye to U.S. imperialism's proliferation of nuclear weapons to West Germany and do their utmost to prevent other socialist countries from strengthening their defence capabilities. While undermining its allies, U.S. imperialism cannot completely ignore the common interests of the bourgeoisie of different countries; the Soviet leaders, however, are bent on crushing their own class brothers, without showing an iota of proletarian internationalism.

Formerly we thought the Soviet leaders were genuinely afraid of the West German militarists coming into possession of nuclear weapons. Now we see that they trust U.S. imperialism and think it does not matter if the West German militarists possess nuclear weapons provided they are under the control of the United States. And in order to curry favour with U.S. imperialism, they would not hesitate to obliterate the international position of the German Democratic Republic. They do not really oppose the possession of nuclear weapons by the West German militarists. Nor do they take any interest in strengthening the might of the socialist camp as a whole. The real aim of the Soviet leaders is to compromise with the United States in order to seek momentary ease and to maintain a monopoly of nuclear weapons and lord it over in the socialist camp.

VIII

The Soviet statement says that one must not oppose the tripartite treaty and that whoever opposes it is opposing the relaxation of international tension. What a broad accusation!

True, Soviet-U.S. relations appear to be somewhat relaxed because the Soviet leaders, treating enemies as friends, have struck a political bargain with U.S. imperialism which is entirely to the advantage of the United States.

But at what price is this kind of relaxation achieved? It is achieved at the price of the interests of the Soviet people of the socialist camp and of the people of the whole world, and at the price of facilitating the nuclear superiority of U.S. imperialism through its manufacture, development and proliferation of nuclear weapons.

Numerous facts show that, in the strugggle against imperialism, relaxation that is won through struggle is a genuine relaxation, while relaxation bought by capitulation is a false relaxation. The so-called relaxation now appearing between the United States and the Soviet Union is only a transient and superficial phenomenon and a false relaxation. It is just what U.S. imperialism can exploit in being more unscrupulous in pushing its global strategy of enslaving the people of the whole world. The danger of war has increased. This line of action of the Soviet leaders is, as the old Chinese saying goes, "indulging in a moment's ease only to incur a century of suffering."

Can such relaxation lead to the solution of major international issues? On the contrary, to seek relaxation through surrender only leads to greater demands and more exacting conditions on the part of the imperialists and feeds their appetite, and thereby making the solution of major international issues increasingly difficult, unless further steps to surrender are taken.

Clearly, such relaxation runs counter to the wishes of the people of the world.

IX

Socialist countries do not want nuclear weapons. Nuclear weapons cannot be eaten. No one would be happier than we if nuclear weapons were thoroughly destroyed. The Chinese Government and people have always stood in the forefront of the fight to prohibit them. We maintain that a complete ban on nuclear weapons is an attainable goal and that there are ways of banning them step by step. The three-point proposal of the Chinese Government for the complete prohibition of nuclear weapons sets the general goal of completely prohibiting and thoroughly destroying nuclear weapons, puts forward four concrete measures for its attainment step by step and makes the reasonable suggestion of a conference of the government heads of all countries in the world. The Chinese proposal is firm, clear-cut and realistic.

Yet the Soviet statement attacks the Chinese attitude as one of " all or nothing " and slanders us as being out of touch with reality.

One might ask, is it unrealistic for the people of the whole world to demand the dismantling of military bases, including nuclear bases, on foreign soil?

Is it unrealistic for many countries to demand the establishment of nuclear weapon-free zones?

Is it unrealistic to demand the prohibition of the export and import of nuclear weapons and technical data for their manufacture and a genuine prohibition of nuclear proliferation?

Is it unrealistic to demand the cessation of all nuclear tests, including underground ones?

In fact, it is the concrete measures we propose that constitute the first step towards the complete prohibition of nuclear weapons. Take the proposal concerning the nuclear weapon-free zones, for instance. If only the nuclear powers undertake their due obligations, a nuclear weapon-free zone in Latin America and a nuclear weapon-free zone in Africa could be established at once. The peoples in these two areas all eagerly desire to place themselves beyond nuclear threats, so that they may successfully develop their countries. They will not menace the nuclear powers. Why cannot the nuclear powers undertake such obligations and respect these peoples' desire for the establishment of nuclear weapon-free zones?

By using the word " unrealistic," the authors of the Soviet statement try to dismiss the earnest desire of millions upon millions of people throughout the world. Clearly, in their eyes, the countries and people that do not have nuclear weapons are not worth a single glance, and the struggle waged in the interests of the people of the world is unrealistic. All they see is nuclear weapons, and in their opinion the only thing that is realistic is to divide spheres of influence with the imperialists who possess nuclear weapons.

The authors of the Soviet statement assert that there is nothing new in the Chinese proposal. It is true that what we propose now we have consistently advocated in the past. In this sense, there is indeed nothing new in our proposal. They also say that they have previously advocated everything in our present proposal. That, too, is basically true. But there is one difference. They no longer advocate it now. Occasionally, they still refer to it, but that is merely for show and for deceiving the people. Our present proposal has become a new one precisely because they have betrayed the correct position they once persistently held to.

The Soviet leaders have let fall the banner of the complete prohibition of nuclear weapons, and it is our duty to raise it still higher.

The authors of the Soviet statement assert that by not joining in their fraud, we are siding with the imperialist " madmen " and opposing the people of the world, while conversely, by collaborating with the imperialists to fool the people of the world, they have become fighters shaking the imperialist forces of aggression and become the representatives of the people of the world.

Let us then ask, who represents the imperialist forces of aggression? As the Moscow Statement points out, U.S. imperialism is the biggest international exploiter, the chief bulwark of world reaction, the mainstay of colonialism today, the international gendarme, the main force of aggression and war and the enemy of the people of the whole world.

As everybody knows, this imperialism is represented by Kennedy, Rusk, Harriman and the like. It may be asked: Is it you or is it we who call these imperialist big guns " peace fighters " and brothers and warmly embrace them?

X

The conclusion of the tripartite treaty once again shows that the Soviet leaders seek only to preserve themselves and would leave other people to sink or swim. They have repeatedly said that so long as they themselves survive and develop the people of the world will be saved. The fact is they are selling out the fundamental interests of the people of the world in order to seek their own momentary ease. All countries and peoples subjected to oppression and aggression are now engaged in earth-shaking struggles against imperialism and old and new colonialism headed by the United States and for their own independence and freedom. Yet the Soviet leaders, of one mind with U.S. imperialism, have collaborated with it in a fraud and want the people of the world to believe that the U.S. imperialists are " peace fighters," thus lulling their fighting will and undermining the cause of world peace. But the people of all countries will not likewise regard enemies as friends. Their own bitter experience will enable them to realize gradually that they can save themselves and ensure world peace only by carrying through to the end the struggle against imperialism and old and new colonialism headed by the United States.

It should be understood that the relationship between the Soviet people and the other peoples of the world is one of mutual reliance, like that between lips and teeth. The existence and development of the Soviet Union are a support to the revolutionary struggles of other peoples, while in turn these peoples' revolutionary struggles and victories support the Soviet Union. There is no reason whatsoever to think that the Soviet Union no longer needs others' support. In fact this is not the case. If the lips are gone, the teeth are exposed. If U.S. imperialism should be given a free hand to put down the revolutionary struggles of other peoples and if the Soviet leaders should ally themselves with U.S. imperialism against the fraternal countries, eventually it will not be possible for the Soviet Union itself to be preserved.

The present trend of events merits the vigilance of all peoples. Having long hoped for a ban on nuclear weapons, people understandably rejoice at hearing of a partial halting of nuclear tests. They hope it will lead to a complete cessation of nuclear tests and a complete prohibition of nuclear weapons. But the paper treaty concocted by the three nuclear powers is not to be depended on. In order to realize the complete prohibition of nuclear weapons step by step it is necessary to carry on an unswerving struggle. As a minimum, it is necessary, in the light of the proposal of the Chinese Government, first of all to compel the nuclear powers to undertake not to use, or test, or proliferate nuclear weapons and undertake to respect the nuclear weapon-free zones. Only when these undertakings are secured can we regard the situation as having advanced a step towards peace. We are convinced that, after all, a fraud is a fraud and will not be able to stand the test of time. In the end, the attempt to use the desire of the people of the world for peace to carry out speculation will fail.

XI

It is not only at present that the Soviet leaders have begun to collude with U.S. imperialism and attempt to manacle China.

As far back as June 20, 1959, when there was not yet the slightest sign of a treaty on stopping nuclear tests, the Soviet Government unilaterally tore up the agreement on new technology for national defence concluded between China and the Soviet Union on October 15, 1957, and refused to provide China with a sample of an atomic bomb and technical data concerning its manufacture. This was done as a presentation gift at the time the Soviet leader went to the United States for talks with Eisenhower in September.

On August 25, 1962, two days before the United States and Britain put forward their draft treaty on the partial halting of nuclear tests, the Soviet Government notified China that U.S. Secretary of State Rusk had proposed an agreement stipulating that, firstly, the nuclear powers should undertake to refrain from transferring nuclear weapons and technical information concerning their manufacture to non-nuclear countries, and that, secondly, the countries not in possession of nuclear weapons should undertake to refrain from manufacturing them, from seeking them from the nuclear powers or from accepting technical information concerning their manufacture. The Soviet Government gave an affirmative reply to this proposal of Rusk's.

The Chinese Government sent three memoranda to the Soviet Government, on September 3, 1962, October 20, 1962, and June 6, 1963, stating that it was a matter for the Soviet Government whether it committed itself to the United States to refrain from transferring nuclear weapons and technical information concerning their manufacture to China; but that the Chinese Government hoped the Soviet Government would not infringe on China's sovereign rights and act for China in assuming an obligation to refrain from manufacturing nuclear weapons. We solemnly stated that we would not tolerate the conclusion, in disregard of China's opposition, of any sort of treaty between the Soviet Government and the United States which aimed at depriving the Chinese people of their right to take steps to resist the nuclear threats of U.S. imperialism, and that we would issue statements to make our position known.

We hoped that after such earnest counsel from us, the Soviet leaders would rein in before reaching the precipice and would not render matters irretrievable. Unfortunately, they did not pay the slightest attention to our counsel. They finally concluded the treaty on the partial halting of nuclear tests with the United States and Britain, thereby attempting to bring pressure to bear on China and force her into commitments.

The whole course of events amounts to this: First the Soviet Government tried to subdue China and curry favour with U.S. imperialism by discontinuing assistance to China. Then it put forward all sorts of untenable arguments in an attempt to induce China to abandon its solemn stand.

Failing in all this, it has brazenly ganged up with the imperialist bandits in exerting pressure on China.

In view of all the above, China has long ceased to place any hope in the Soviet leaders in developing its own nuclear strength to resist the U.S. nuclear threats.

XII

The authors of the Soviet statement claim that since the Soviet Government put forward a proposal for the complete banning of nuclear weapons as far back as 1946 and has all along worked for a ban on nuclear weapons, it cannot possibly err on issues related to nuclear weapons. On the contrary, in our view, their error is all the more serious because they have now betrayed their past correct position.

From 1946 to 1956, the Soviet Government insisted on the complete prohibition of nuclear weapons. They were correct then and we firmly supported them. In his summary report to the 20th Congress of the Communist Party of the Soviet Union in 1956, the Soviet leader divorced the cessation of nuclear tests from the question of disarmament. Subsequently, they were wrong on certain issues and correct on others, and we supported them in all their correct views. But on July 25, 1963, they went altogether wrong, and it is quite natural that we should resolutely criticize them.

The authors of the Soviet statement charge China with disrespect for the sovereignty of the Soviet state and slander the authors of the Chinese statement as having gone out of their minds and as attempting to set the Soviet people against the Soviet Government. It pretentiously asks: Is not the Chinese Government " taking too much upon itself "? We can tell them frankly that we are not taking too much upon ourselves at all. We are Communists. According to the correct criteria they once put forward themselves, and according to Marxism-Leninism and the Moscow Declaration and the Moscow Statement, it is our proletarian internationalist duty to point out that they have now betrayed the interests of the Soviet people and the entire socialist camp. If indeed anyone has gone out of his mind, it is definitely not the Chinese people, who have consistently maintained a correct stand; it is the Soviet leaders, who have betrayed their own position midway.

If the Soviet leaders consider that betrayal of the interests of the Soviet people is within the sovereign rights of the Soviet state, then of course they are entitled to say so. But if you try to gag us on the pretext of non-interference in internal affairs, you will not succeed. To defend Marxism-Leninism, one must expose acts of betrayal of Marxism-Leninism and of proletarian internationalism. Anyone who does not expose such acts of betrayal ceases to be a Communist.

By concluding the tripartite treaty the Soviet leaders are trying to show the correctness of the so-called general line of peaceful coexistence which they have been following since the 20th Congress of the Communist Party of the Soviet Union. To glory in one's shame—this can only make people split their sides. What does the conclusion of the tripartite treaty show? It merely shows that the line followed by the Soviet leaders in foreign affairs is one of out-and-out capitulation. The imperialists are of course willing to coexist with those who surrender to them.   However, this is not peaceful coexistence but capitulationist coexistence.

The Soviet leaders have already gone far along the wrong road.   We hope they will reconsider their position and return to the road of Marxism-Leninism and proletarian internationalism, to the road of unity with the countries in the socialist camp and the people of the world.

The Soviet Government has published the July 31 statement of the Chinese Government in its press; that is not a bad thing and is in conformity with the principle of reciprocity.   We hope the Soviet leaders will carry on this good practice and publish our present statement.

[*Peking Review*, VI, 33 (August 16, 1963), pp. 7–15.]

Full title: Statement by the Spokesman of the Chinese Government—A Comment on the Soviet Government's Statement of August 3–August 15, 1963 (complete text).

DOCUMENT 8

Further Soviet Attack on China's Stand on Test Ban Treaty, August 21, 1963

Less than a month has gone by since the day when the governments of the U.S.S.R., the United States and Britain signed in Moscow the treaty banning nuclear weapon tests in the atmosphere, in outer space and under water. Yet even within this short space of time the attitude of the peoples and governments to the treaty has become clear: the day it was signed— August 5, 1963—has been impressed on the minds of all who value peace as the date when the fruits of the policy of peaceful co-existence, of the efforts to prevent a new world war, became more tangible.

For the first time in many years that have been darkened by the cold war, states of the East and the West have managed to reach agreement on a burning international issue involving the vital interests of the entire population of the Earth. For the first time the most devastating weapons that ever threatened mankind have become a zone of agreement. And for the first time an international agreement, worked out originally by three nuclear powers, has received such a mighty response and such immense support in all parts of our planet. All continents of our planet have, as it were, become the scene of a referendum and the results of that referendum are already known—the peoples of the world have come out firmly in support of the treaty.

The majority of states, differing in their political and social systems and professing at times opposing world outlooks, have proclaimed their support for, or have already signed the treaty. In spite of all the differences separating them, they have united in one thing: in their striving to put an end to the contamination of the Earth's atmosphere and at the same time to lay the foundation for further steps towards reducing international tension, towards lessening the danger of a thermonuclear war breaking out.

The peoples' universal approval of the treaty banning nuclear weapon tests has, at the same time, revealed the state of pitiable isolation in which the enemies of the treaty have found themselves. Even among those who at first got up on their hind legs at the very mention of the possibility of ending nuclear tests, governments and statesmen are now to be found who are beginning to reform their ranks as they go.

The government of the Federal Republic of Germany, for example, decided to sign this treaty and has already done so. Apparently it realised, after all, that there are limits beyond which one cannot go if one does not want to show the whole world that one's policy is pursuing a course contrary to the vital interests of the peoples. Chancellor Adenauer, who even in western countries has acquired notoriety as one of the " last of the Mohicans " of the cold war, decided, under the pressure of circumstances and of public opinion throughout the world, that it is better to stop openly opposing the nuclear test-ban treaty.

Yet the leaders of the People's Republic of China, hiding behind pseudo-revolutionary phrases, are continuing to slander this treaty which expresses the hopes of the peoples.

Already on the eve of the signing of the treaty the leaders of the People's Republic of China attempted to turn world public opinion against the signing of the treaty. On July 31, they addressed a statement to the governments of all countries of the world the essence of which, in addition to slanderous attacks on the Soviet Union and its peace-loving foreign policy, was to " prove " to all and sundry that this treaty was a " trap," a " deception," and that it was contrary to the interests of the peoples, to the interests of peace. Today the Chinese leaders can judge for themselves how this attitude of the Chinese government has been evaluated in the world. A mere glance at the list of states which have signed the treaty speaks for itself. And ever new signatures of representatives of countries of Europe, Asia, Africa and Latin America are appearing under the text of the treaty every day.

It would seem that this should give food for some hard thought; it would seem that in Peking, too, they should understand the significance of this reply of the states and the peoples to the attempts of the Chinese government to place a mine under the nuclear test-ban treaty. It goes without saying that the government of the People's Republic of China, like the government of any other country, is free to decide its own attitude, whether positive or negative, towards the treaty, whether to accede to it or not. However, if no special aims, and possibly even aims such as do not bear a direct relation to this treaty, are pursued, it would be sufficient simply to refuse to sign the treaty and let it go at that. But clearly the point is that the conclusion of the treaty banning nuclear weapon tests has not merely caused a fit of irritation and political nervousness on the part of the Chinese leaders, but they also want, by means of fabrications and low tricks, to use this major event in international life in order to impose upon other countries their adventurist platform on the fundamental issues of war and peace.

Only this can explain the fact that on August 15 there came yet another slice of slander against the nuclear test-ban treaty and against the foreign policy of the U.S.S.R., this time in the form of a statement by a government spokesman of the People's Republic of China.

Anyone who takes an objective view of the world situation will easily see that this move, which is hostile to the cause of peace and socialism, cannot drown the calm and confident voices of the peoples, expressing satisfaction with the success of the peace-loving forces which for many years have been waging an unrelenting struggle for the ending of nuclear tests, for disarmament and for peace and international friendship. If the new Chinese statement shows anything, it is simply that in its attitude to the test-ban treaty not only does the Chinese government stand shoulder to shoulder with the most aggressive circles of the imperialist powers, but it even assumes the role of someone on the extreme right flank in the ranks of the American " wild men," the West German revenge-seekers, and the French extremists.

Strictly speaking, the statement of the Chinese government spokesman in essence adds little to what had already been said by the government of the People's Republic of China in its statement of July 31, to which the Soviet government replied on August 3. Like the previous one, the new Chinese statement shows that the Chinese leadership agrees only in words with the line approved by the international communist movement at the meetings of Communist and Workers' Parties in 1957 and 1960, the line of peaceful co-existence, of reducing international tension and strengthening peace among the peoples, while in actual fact that leadership is sabotaging the efforts aimed at implementing this common line of the countries of the socialist community and of the world communist movement.

It seems that all the strong words in the Chinese language have passed over from the pages of the Chinese press, which is waging a rampant anti-Soviet campaign, to the official documents of the government of the People's Republic of China. "Shame," "plot," "treason"—what words do the Chinese leaders not use against a country to which, as they have repeatedly admitted, the Chinese people owe a great deal. It is quite natural, therefore, that because of their slanderous nature and their hostility to the Soviet Union, the two statements of the Chinese government were not accepted by the U.S.S.R. Embassy in the People's Republic of China for presentation to the Soviet government and were returned to the sender— the Chinese government.

What is difficult, or to be more accurate, impossible to detect in the statement of the spokesman of the Chinese government are serious and well-founded arguments or an objective statement of the facts.

The new Chinese statement is full of the old contentions that the nuclear test-ban treaty "is good for the forces of war and bad for the forces struggling for peace," that it is "capitulation to American imperialism" and is aimed at consolidating the "nuclear monopoly" of certain powers, etc. It goes without saying that these groundless claims do not become more convincing through endless repetition. That is why the Soviet government does not see any need to begin once again a detailed study of all those concocted assertions and absurd arguments which are being put forward by the Chinese government against this treaty. Their untenable nature has already been proved in the Soviet government's statement of August 3.

For example, the Chinese leaders are again claiming that "the danger of war has increased" as a result of the signing of the nuclear test-ban treaty. What do these assertions mean? Had they asserted that the treaty does not eliminate the danger of war, they would have been right. The Soviet government said this during the signing of the treaty and stressed that this treaty, of course, does not and cannot eliminate the danger of war, although it does open up new and more favourable opportunities for developing the struggle to strengthen peace. But the Chinese leaders are far from asserting this. They want to prove that as a result of the signing of the nuclear test-ban treaty, the danger of war has increased, has become greater than before the signing. It transpires that the whole world is wrong in appraising the significance of the nuclear test-ban treaty, and only the Chinese leaders have the key to wisdom.

One can only say that this is a very strange kind of wisdom, characteristic only of those who think that it is possible to sit on some sort of Mt. Olympus, giving utterance there to truths which have nothing in common with real life, and to abide in their actions by the belief that if life does not fit into their stillborn schemes, so much the worse for life.

But how do the Chinese leaders back up their assertion that the treaty on the banning of nuclear weapon tests increases the threat of war? According to them, the continuation and expansion of nuclear weapon tests, the creation of ever more deadly types of these weapons, the emergence of a situation in which these weapons might spread all over the world and the West German revenge-seekers might begin producing them tomorrow, while after tomorrow this might be done, perhaps, by the Chiang Kai-shek clique, and there might be people willing to assist it in that—according to them, all this would contribute to the cause of strengthening peace.

The authors of the new Chinese statement go so far as to claim: If there were no nuclear test-ban treaty, there would be no tests either, because the government of the United States, you see, would hardly dare to resume them "lightheartedly." But this is utterly absurd. Such a claim is tantamount to an attempt to persuade somebody that there would be no breaches of the law if states did not enact laws. Nor does anybody know why the Chinese leaders have taken it upon themselves to speak for the United States government about its intentions regarding the holding of nuclear tests.

Realising, apparently, that all their statements concerning the growth of the war danger as a result of the ending of nuclear tests in the atmosphere, in outer space and under water can only make the people doubt the ability of the Chinese leaders to assess the meaning of their own words, they put forward one more "argument," which, judging by everything, they consider to be a good one: The treaty, they say, does not forbid the United States of America to hold underground nuclear tests, to increase the stockpiles of nuclear weapons.

Firstly, however, the hands of the United States were not tied in this respect prior to the signing of the treaty either, so nothing new has occurred in this respect. And, secondly, the treaty does not forbid the Soviet Union either, if need be, to hold underground nuclear tests, to increase the stockpiles of its nuclear weapons and even to use these weapons against the imperialist aggressors if they unleash a war in a fit of insanity. We are on a par here, and the Chinese leaders know just as well as the leading statesmen of the United States that we, the Soviet people, are not Simple Simons either, and that having concluded a treaty banning nuclear tests, the Soviet Union does not intend to disarm unilaterally in face of imperialism.

What simpletons is it expected to persuade with the statement of the Chinese leaders about "capitulation" to American imperialism, about the "deception" which the treaty on the banning of nuclear weapon tests in the atmosphere, in outer space and under water allegedly constitutes? No such simpletons exist in our day, because the peoples have long ago learnt to distinguish truth from slander.

The leaders of the government of the People's Republic of China are striving to prove that if the Soviet government earlier abided by one stand on the question of banning nuclear weapon tests—and they magnanimously condescend to regard it as correct—and then assumed another position, that is some sort of mortal sin and little short of treason.

Yes, the position of the Soviet Union on the question of ending nuclear weapon tests did not become fossilised; it adapted itself to changes in the deployment of forces on the international scene, to the successes achieved in strengthening the defence potential of the U.S.S.R. and of all the countries of the socialist community, and took into account everything that is generally known as "the realities of the nuclear age" in their entirety.

In the first years after nuclear weapons had appeared in the arsenal of the United States, when the United States had a nuclear monopoly and when, in view of that, the security of the socialist countries was endangered, the Soviet government proceeded on the assumption that the main task was to deprive the United States of that advantage. This aim could be achieved either by completely banning nuclear weapons, which would have been tantamount to taking these weapons away from the only nuclear power at that time—the United States—or through developing our own nuclear weapons, which would help to ensure the security of all the socialist countries.

It was then that the Soviet government demanded the banning and destruction of nuclear weapons, and, when this demand was rejected by the western powers, it started to develop its own nuclear weapons, which were called upon to become a good additional guarantor of the independence and security of all the countries of the socialist community and to make the imperialists lose the taste for aggression against the socialist states. Naturally, in those years, the banning of tests of nuclear weapons without the simultaneous destruction of those weapons possessed by the United States would not have been in the interests of the socialist states: it would have brought to a halt the development of nuclear weapons in the Soviet Union and would have perpetuated the American nuclear monopoly.

But the situation did not remain unchanged. As a result of intense efforts on the part of the Soviet people, of Soviet scientists, in developing their own nuclear weapons, the American nuclear monopoly was smashed, the world socialist system received its own nuclear shield and the imperialist powers lost the material basis for pursuing a policy of nuclear blackmail, a policy " from a position of strength " with regard to the socialist countries.

This also put in a new perspective the question of banning nuclear weapon tests. Now the continuation of nuclear testing could only lead higher and higher the spiral of the nuclear arms race, in which the socialist countries, and all peaceloving states, to be sure, are not interested. At the same time, with the new balance of power, the nuclear test ban would perpetuate, not the American nuclear monopoly, but the fact of its abolition, not the unilateral advantage of the imperialist camp, but the new balance of power in the field of nuclear weapons.

Taking these circumstances into consideration and continuing to wage a stubborn struggle for disarmament and for the complete prohibition and destruction of nuclear weapons, the Soviet government put forward at the same time, in 1956, a proposal that agreement be reached on the ending of nuclear tests, without waiting for a settlement of the disarmament problem.

In the changed conditions this position was just as correct, and accorded to the same extent with the interests of the socialist states and the interests of peace, as the previous position at the previous stage.

It is also necessary to stress that the proposal for the prohibition of nuclear weapon tests put forward at that time by the Soviet government envisaged that this question should be settled precisely on the basis on which it has been settled now.

At that time nuclear tests were being held only in the atmosphere and under water—there were no tests in other environments—and the question under discussion was the banning of nuclear tests in the atmosphere and under water. A third environment, outer space, where nuclear tests were also banned, was added to this in the treaty signed on August 5. Thus the difference is that in 1956 the United States refused to accept our proposal and in 1963 it accepted it, even in a broader form—with the addition of outer space.

As for underground nuclear tests, this question arose, not in 1956—at that time no such tests were being held—but later, when the United States began holding underground nuclear tests. Naturally, from that time on, the Soviet government began to press for the prohibition of underground nuclear tests as well. However, so far it has been impossible to reach agreement on this question, because the western powers have tied up prohibition of underground nuclear tests with the setting up of so-called international control, that is to say, in actual fact, international espionage, which could involve the security interests of socialist states, and the Soviet government, naturally, has not been able to agree to this.

In view of the existing situation the Soviet Union and the world as a whole had to choose between the banning of nuclear weapon tests in the three environments and the continuation of the unbridled and unrestricted tests race. And if today we have managed to reach agreement on the banning of tests in the three media, thereby solving the most important part of the whole problem, this is a big success for the peoples, a victory for the peaceloving forces, a definite achievement of the peace policy.

These are the main landmarks of the principled and at the same time flexible and realistic policy of the Soviet Union on the question of banning nuclear weapon tests. No matter how the international situation changed, this policy met the interests, not only of the Soviet Union, but also of all the socialist, all the peaceloving peoples, just as the result of this policy— the conclusion of the treaty on the banning of nuclear weapon tests in the atmosphere, in outer space and under water—meets their most cherished interests.

Those who oppose the ending of nuclear tests, among whom the Chinese leaders have now landed, will not succeed in making political capital by seeking for contradictions of some kind in the fact that a year or two ago the Soviet government did not consider it possible to accept a partial solution to the question of ending tests, whereas now it has agreed to the conclusion of a treaty banning tests in three environments.

The Chinese leaders pretend to be especially surprised by the fact that only one, or one and a half months before the opening of the three-power talks in Moscow, the Soviet government was continuing to come out in favour of the conclusion of a treaty on the banning of all tests of nuclear weapons. But every reasonable politician or diplomat realises that each side wishes to achieve the maximum in negotiation with its partners. We strove for this maximum, that is to say, for the ending of all nuclear tests, including underground ones.

At the present stage, however, this proved to be impossible. And in these conditions the Soviet Union has agreed to an agreement on the banning of nuclear tests in three environments: in the atmosphere, in outer space and under water. This was a step meeting the expectations of public opinion throughout the world, a step dictated by concern for the health of the Soviet people and for the health of all other peoples, including the Chinese nation. It is precisely in these media, after all, that nuclear weapon tests harm the health of people and contaminate the world's animal and plant life with radioactive fall-out. Of course, the Soviet government is not giving up its efforts today either, in the struggle to ban underground nuclear weapon tests as well.

The Soviet government has already drawn the attention of the government of the People's Republic of China to the simple truth that life does not stand still, that science and technology are developing rapidly and that something which was unacceptable yesterday may turn out to be useful, and even very useful, today. Underlying this are definite material factors of great significance, connected with important and major steps of the Soviet government to strengthen the defence capacity of the U.S.S.R. and the security of all the socialist states.

These steps, which also included tests of the latest types of nuclear weapons, among them being the most powerful ones in existence in the world, have reliably ensured the security of the socialist community. We now possess all the necessary prerequisites for further maintaining our defence potential at the proper level which is or may be required by the situation.

And when we speak about this, we do so knowing the facts of the matter. The Soviet government, for 15 years or so, has had to deal with nuclear weapons and we are familiar with all aspects of the question. It is true that the Chinese leaders try to question this, clearly pretending to have opinions of their own on matters involving nuclear weapons. But when those who have only a hearsay acquaintance with nuclear weapons start to pass judgment on this, naturally they are liable, willy-nilly, to place themselves in an embarrassing position.

Incidentally this is true of the flippant pronouncements of the Chinese leaders on strategic nuclear weapons, on tactical nuclear weapons, on whether the United States needs or does not need to continue nuclear tests in the atmosphere and other similar things. To talk about this without being sufficiently well informed is rather risky. And the point is not that someone wants to monopolise the right to speak about nuclear weapons and to deny this right to others; the point is whose pronouncements on such a question can carry weight and whose sound like mere prattle.

Of course, we cannot at present divulge such things, for instance, as the concrete results of the tests of nuclear weapons we carried out in 1961–62, the data on the calibres of the nuclear warheads in our arsenal, the destination of specific nuclear combat devices, of which the Soviet Union has plenty, where these means are deployed, and so forth. That would be contrary to the security interests of the Soviet Union and of all socialist states, including the security interests of the People's Republic of China.

And if the Chinese leaders, by saying that in recent years the situation did not change, but that the U.S.S.R. policy on a test ban, so they allege, did, and in a way are thus goading the Soviet Union to demonstrate objectively the recent changes in the balance of nuclear strength and for the sake of that divulge the defence secrets of the U.S.S.R., we can tell them only one thing: While you are paying lip-service to your concern for the strengthening of the defences of the socialist countries, in point of fact you are appearing in the role of persons who do not cherish the security interests of the socialist community but are ready to play into the hands of the forces of imperialist reaction. The Chinese leaders cannot be unaware of the fact that getting the most reliable information on Soviet nuclear and rocket weapons is exactly what the military staffs of certain powers and aggressive military blocs are dreaming of.

But if, for some reason, the Chinese leaders really doubt whether the Soviet Union does possess the powerful nuclear weapons necessary for the defence of all socialist states and are not satisfied with our explanations, they could at least study the statements which highly-placed United States military leaders made only a few days ago in the American Congress, as well as the statement of the joint chiefs of staff of the United States. These statements openly acknowledge the nuclear strength that is now possessed by the Soviet Union. These statements mean a lot, especially if one takes into consideration the fact that the imperialists are forced to admit the achievements of socialist countries only when life itself compels them to do so.

Such is the Soviet government's position on the question of banning nuclear weapon tests. This is a frank and honest position, and we note with great satisfaction that it meets with the full understanding and support of the other socialist states, of all peaceloving states and peoples. The strength of our position lies in its viability, in its complete accord with the paramount interests of the peoples, in its closeness to life, in the account it takes of the changes which have occurred in recent years and are now occurring on the world scene.

It can only be regretted that the people in Peking not only fail to take into account the changes that are determining the outlook in the world today, but believe it to be the art of statesmanship tirelessly to follow ossified dogmas in politics, to set the dead letter up against the living voice of reality. This is the main flaw in the policy of the Chinese leaders, particularly on the question of banning nuclear tests.

It follows from the Chinese government's statement of August 15 that the Chinese leaders are greatly displeased with the Soviet Union for not giving China samples of atomic weapons. It looks as if annoyance with this policy of the Soviet Union and the other socialist states of not spreading nuclear weapons explains the attacks of the Chinese leaders on the U.S.S.R.'s measures in the field of foreign policy—measures which are aimed at easing international tension and strengthening peace—and especially their attacks on the nuclear test-ban treaty.

More than once the Soviet government took steps to convince the Chinese government that preventing the spread of nuclear weapons was in the interests of peace, in the interests of all socialist countries, including the interests of the People's Republic of China. As history would have it, the Soviet Union is the only socialist country that produces nuclear weapons.

By its foreign policy the Soviet Union has demonstrated that its nuclear might reliably stands guard over the interests of the world socialist community, over the interests of the peoples fighting for social and national liberation. Whether one or more socialist countries is added to the number of nuclear states—this would bring about no material change in the defence potential of the socialist camp, provided, of course, that the socialist camp is regarded as a single whole. But with each new capitalist state that gets hold of nuclear weapons, the danger of a nuclear war will increase. The possibility that the number of socialist nuclear powers may increase, while the number of nuclear states in the imperialists' camp remains unchanged, is precluded, and to build one's calculations on that means building them on sand.

It would be naive, to say the least, to assume that it is possible to conduct one policy in the West and another in the East, to fight with one hand against the arming of Western Germany with nuclear weapons, against the spreading of nuclear weapons in the world, and to supply these weapons to China with the other hand.

No, that would be an unrealistic policy, a policy divorced from life. Had the socialist countries set out on this road towards which they are being persistently pushed by the Chinese leaders, then beyond all question the western nuclear powers would have replied in kind, and it is a fact that a number of capitalist states have the economic, technical and other potentialities for the production of nuclear weapons. This entire nuclear arsenal would have gone into the common pool of the aggressive military blocs of N.A.T.O., Cento and S.E.A.T.O. and would have been set up against the nuclear arsenal of the socialist countries. Only persons blinded by their own craving to possess nuclear weapons in their own home can fail to see or realise that.

The efforts of the Soviet Union to achieve the signing of an international agreement banning the spreading of nuclear weapons meet with an extremely wide response and support throughout the world, precisely because of the fact that the Soviet Union maintains a stand on this question which is based on principle. Were it not for the consistent and resolute struggle of the Soviet Union against the spread of nuclear weapons, a struggle based on its own nuclear strength, the militarist forces in the West, and above all the West German revenge-seekers who are making an all-out effort to get hold of nuclear weapons, would be much nearer to their goal than they actually are.

We have criticised, as we do now, the policy of the United States government and other western powers inasmuch as it holds the door open for the nuclear arming of Western Germany, at least in a pool with other N.A.T.O. countries. The Soviet government has come out firmly against the plans for a " multilateral N.A.T.O. nuclear force," having unconditionally condemned these plans and having undertaken appropriate acts in the sphere of foreign policy in order to demonstrate to the peoples the danger inherent in their implementation.

This has been done by the government of the Soviet Union and not by the government of the People's Republic of China. The Soviet government has exposed and will go on exposing the false conception upheld by the N.A.T.O. powers : " It is better if Western Germany obtains access to nuclear weapons under N.A.T.O. control, within the framework of the joint nuclear forces of this military bloc, than if she develops her own nuclear weapons." The Soviet government puts the question in a different way : The nuclear arming of Western Germany must not be permitted in any form, because the provision of these weapons to a state whose foreign policy is based on revenge-seeking, on the revision of the existing national boundaries in Europe, would greatly increase the danger of a new world war. This is why the Soviet government will not relax its efforts to convince the western powers that the policy of spreading nuclear weapons, of providing for their transfer in any form to Western Germany, is a profoundly erroneous policy, fraught with great dangers to the world.

It may be thought that the Chinese leaders, having shut themselves off from the whole world by blinkers of some kind, know nothing about this and have not heard about it. After all, they claim in their statement, contrary to facts which are well known to everybody who reads the newspapers and listens to the radio, that the Soviet Union does not properly oppose the provision of nuclear weapons to the West German militarists. This can only be regarded as slander.

The position of the Chinese government, set forth in the statement of August 15, can be understood only as meaning that the Chinese leaders do not care how nuclear weapons spread among the capitalist countries so long as the leaders of the People's Republic of China get a chance to lay their hands on a nuclear bomb and see what it is like.

It must be admitted that being at a definite stage of its economic development and possessing a definite economic potential, the People's Republic of China is as yet unprepared to produce nuclear weapons in quantity. Even if the People's Republic of China were to produce two or three bombs, this would not solve the question for it either, but would bring about a great exhaustion of China's economy.

We know from our own experience what it costs for a country, for a people to produce nuclear weapons on a large scale, at a level meeting modern military techniques, modern defence requirements. But we were compelled to do this in order to stand up against the imperialist camp, which possessed such weapons, and the People's Republic of China can now rely on the means of defence which have been developed through the efforts of the Soviet people and which reliably serve the aims of defending the countries of the socialist community.

That is why the most reasonable policy for the People's Republic of China in present conditions—if, of course, its desires and its possibilities are to be made commensurate—would be to devote its efforts to the development of the national economy, science, technology and agriculture, devoting them to improving the wellbeing of the Chinese people, to meeting their vital needs. The Chinese people are experiencing many privations and that is why such a course in the policy of the Chinese leaders would be more beneficial for the Chinese people, would be more appreciated by them and would be correctly understood throughout the world.

Let us grant that by overstraining its economy the People's Republic of China may finally be able to produce a few atom bombs. Yet how many such bombs would in this case be aimed by the imperialists at the People's Republic of China? Would the Chinese leaders then feel themselves more secure, even though sitting on their own atom bomb?

If the threat of a new war were to grow in the West, and this would inevitably occur in the event of a further spread of nuclear weapons among the capitalist states, China would hardly feel herself to be in a position of greater security than she is today.

In one's imagination, and only in that way, one can erect a wall of any height and any thickness between events in the West and developments in the East. In reality there is no such wall. This was true even before the First World War; it was confirmed by the experience of both world wars, and in our own day, when distances on the Earth are shrinking increasingly due to the development of science and technology, it has become even more obvious.

If the leaders of any country, large or small, do not wish to see the international situation as it is, but proceed in their policy on the basis of a belief that only what takes place in their own house is important, and everything that happens in other areas of the world is unimportant, such a frame of mind smacks of limited provincialism and scholasticism. Such views are simply dangerous in real life owing to their adventurist nature.

The Chinese leaders abuse the Soviet Union in every way because of the fact that it possesses nuclear weapons while the People's Republic of China does not possess them. Could the Chinese leaders sincerely say that without the nuclear strength of the U.S.S.R, without the might which for all these years has served the interests of all the socialist countries, without the policy of peace and of containing the forces of aggression which the Soviet Union has pursued and is continuing to pursue, China could peacefully engage in her domestic tasks of economic and political development today?

No, the leaders of the People's Republic of China would be forced to admit that they can afford such a luxury as their statements against the treaty banning nuclear tests and their rude attacks on the Soviet Union and the C.P.S.U. only because China's external security is guaranteed by the might of the Soviet Union and the whole socialist community.

Indeed, they cannot be unaware of the real value of their claim that " in the struggle against imperialist aggression, in defending its security, any socialist state relies primarily on its own defence potential and only then on the support and help of the fraternal countries and the peoples of the whole world." It is true, of course, that every socialist country makes its contribution to the common cause of ensuring the security of the whole socialist community, and the fulfilment of its duty by each one of them in this connection deserves all respect.

Yet an attempt on the part of any socialist state to rely only on its own forces in ensuring its defences, forces which, moreover, may not be sufficient in all countries, can prove to be a fatal mistake in the age of nuclear weapons. All the socialist countries, including the People's Republic of China, no matter how much its leaders may try to prove the opposite, take into account, when organising their own defences, the nuclear might of the Soviet Union, which keeps the aggressive circles of the western powers within bounds.

The Chinese leaders allege that the Soviet Union cares only for its own welfare and, by concluding the treaty on the banning of nuclear weapon tests, " dooms the people to an age of suffering in pursuit of a minute of tranquillity."

If the government of the People's Republic of China means the absence of war when it says " tranquillity," well, we have indeed always been, are and shall be in favour of such tranquillity. We do not need war, just as the peoples of the socialist countries, all the peoples, do not need it. But if the Chinese leaders want to cast aspersions on the Soviet Union's determination to go on upholding the cause of peace to the end and safeguard the security of the nations of the socialist community—and judging by everything, that is the intention of the authors of the aforementioned statement—they will not succeed in this.

The fact cannot be erased from the memory of the peoples that at critical moments when the aggressive circles have brought the world to the brink of war, the Soviet Union, without hesitation, has thrown in all its international weight, all its military might to stay the hand raised by the aggressor over a country, large or small, geographically distant or near to us.

This was the case in the period of the Suez crisis and it was the case during the events around Syria and Iraq in 1958. This was the case when tension flared up in the Taiwan Strait—and the Chinese leaders, the Chinese people certainly remember this. It was also the case during the crisis in the Caribbean, when the Soviet Union shielded revolutionary Cuba with its nuclear rocket might. Perhaps the Chinese leaders regard all this as "minutes of tranquility." But we can say bluntly that no one will be in agreement with them on this. These steps of the Soviet government were also an expression of genuine proletarian internationalism, and not the kind on which Peking likes to expound and which is backed by nothing but noisy slogans and paper resolutions.

It is impossible to overlook one more circumstance: the government of the People's Republic of China, disregarding its duty as an ally and abusing the relations of trust existing among the socialist countries, has embarked upon the road of making public classified documents and information relating to the defences of the countries of the socialist community, and, what is more, of presenting the facts tendentiously, in a distorted light. Of course, the Soviet government will not sink so low as to set out on the road of divulging information relating to the defences of socialist states. The Soviet government is compelled to state that after these actions of the Chinese government, there is scarcely anyone who will believe the sincerity of its assurances and trust it with information of defensive importance. It is natural that the Soviet government will draw its own conclusions on this subject.

The statements of the Chinese leaders reveal a growing tendency to speak on behalf of the peoples of practically the whole world, including the Soviet people, the peoples of the other socialist countries, and also the young national states of Asia, Africa and Latin America. "Yet who has given the Chinese leaders the right," the Soviet people inquire with indignation, "to decide for us, for the Soviet government, for the Communist Party, what is in keeping, and what is not in keeping with your interests? We have not given you this right and we do not intend to give it to you."

Who has given the leaders of the People's Republic of China the right to speak on behalf of the peoples of the other socialist countries? Have they asked for the views of the Poles, Germans, Czechoslovaks, Rumanians, Bulgarians, Hungarians, Yugoslavs and Mongolians on the ending of nuclear weapon tests and are they drawing up their statements on the basis of these views? No, they have not asked for the views of the peoples of these countries. They simply maintain that they can say anything that comes into their heads, that they can make the voice of Peking pass for the voice of Warsaw, Berlin, Ulan-Bator or the capitals of the other socialist countries.

The attitude of the Chinese leaders to the real interests of the other socialist countries can be seen already from their allegation that the signing of the test-ban treaty "sacrifices" the international status of the German Democratic Republic. Perhaps the leaders of the People's Republic of China do not know that the German Democratic Republic was among the first to sign this treaty, immediately after it had been signed by the initial participants? But obviously on the question of assessing the significance of the G.D.R.'s participation in the test-ban treaty, the Chinese leaders measure everything by their own yardstick, considering that China is more versed in German affairs than the G.D.R., than the government of the German Democratic Republic.

Though the Chinese leaders do not say this openly, the content of both statements of the government of the People's Republic of China on the nuclear test-ban treaty is that not the ending, but on the contrary, the continuation of nuclear weapon tests in the atmosphere and the holding of tests in outer space and under water would be in the interests of the peoples, in the interests of peace.

However, it is permissible to ask where and when has any people announced its readiness to breathe radioactive air and eat radioactive food. We do not know of such statements. Nor have we any knowledge of the Chinese people saying: " Yes, let nuclear weapon tests continue, and we are ready for radioactive substances to poison our blood, settle in our bones and bring incurable diseases to us, our children and, through inheritance, to our posterity." We have not heard the Chinese people say anything like that.

Every communist-Leninist will feel disgust at an attitude to thermonuclear war such as this: " Never mind if a half of mankind perishes, if 300 million Chinese die, for on the other hand imperialism will be wiped from the face of the Earth and those who survive will rapidly create on the ruins of imperialism a new civilisation that will be a thousand times higher."

And it is precisely such an attitude to thermonuclear war that has been present on more than one occasion in the pronouncements of highly-placed Chinese representatives. Even if the Chinese government makes, not two, but one hundred and two statements that it is dying to achieve the prohibition and destruction of nuclear weapons and that its only concern is the interests of the peoples, it will not be able to wash off the shame of gambling on the death of hundreds of millions of people, including Chinese people, in a thermonuclear war.

By its latest statement against the nuclear test-ban treaty, however, the Chinese leadership only confirms that today, too, it is being guided in its foreign policy by this anti-Marxist, anti-Leninist, inhuman conception.

Yet who has asked those Chinese who are condemned in advance to death, if they are willing to be firewood in the furnace of a nuclear rocket war? Have they empowered the leadership of the People's Republic of China to sound their death knell for them ahead of time?

Another question also arises. If, in accordance with the forecasts of the Chinese leaders, about half of the population of such a big country as China were to perish in a thermonuclear war, then how many people would perish in countries where the size of the population is measured, not in hundreds of millions, but in tens of millions, or simply millions of people?

But it is obvious that the half of mankind which the Chinese leaders are ready to erase from among the living would include many countries and peoples in their entirety. Who has given the Chinese leaders the right to settle the fate of these peoples, to speak on their behalf?

Who has given the Chinese leaders the right to smear the ultimate goal of the international working-class movement—the victory of labour over capital—with assertions that the road to it lies through a thermonuclear world war and that it is worth while to sacrifice half the population of the world in order to build a higher civilisation on corpses and ruins? This conception has nothing in common with Marxist-Leninist teaching. We are against this savage conception.

We have waged and are continuing to wage a tireless struggle for the triumph of the ideas of Marxism-Leninism, for the liberation of the peoples from all exploitation and oppression, for the victory of labour over capital by methods worthy of the great humanist ideals of socialism and communism.

Though some people in Peking are ready to sacrifice half the population of their country, half of mankind, the central committee of the Communist Party of the Soviet Union and the Soviet government treasure the lives, not only of half the population of the Soviet Union, but also the life of every Soviet person, nor is it indifferent to the fate of the other peoples of the world. The Leninist central committee of our party and the Soviet government see their duty to the Soviet people first of all in ensuring conditions for lasting peace, for the implementation of the magnificent plans for the full-scale building of a communist society in our country. The actions of the Soviet Union in the international arena are subordinated to the task of preventing the unleashing by imperialists of a thermonuclear world war. In this we also see our international duty to the working people of the whole world.

Our people do not have to borrow courage from others. When the need arose to defend our righteous cause, the freedom and independence of our motherland and the great gains of the October Revolution, the Soviet people took up arms and routed the aggressors in a life and death struggle. No one will succeed in belittling the great exploits of our people, who in the past on more than one occasion, defending their motherland, have brought aggressors to their knees, and no one will succeed in defiling the banners of the Soviet Army, which are covered with undying glory, the banners of the liberator-army, banners which in the years of the Second World War were carried by Soviet soldiers to the heart of Europe and to the shores of the Pacific Ocean. And in the future, too, in any tests or trials, the Soviet Union will not flinch; it has everything necessary for administering a devastating rebuff to anyone who may infringe on the security of the Soviet Union or its friends and allies. But no incantations from Peking will draw the Soviet Union on to the road of madness, the road of playing irresponsibly with the lives of hundreds of millions of people.

The Chinese leaders are trying to present matters as if their statements aimed at undisguised interference in the domestic affairs of other socialist states, and in particular the Soviet Union, were motivated by a sense of "international proletarian duty." It follows from their logic that the "international duty" of a friendly state is to smear the Soviet Union and its peaceloving foreign policy, to arrogate to itself the right to speak on behalf of the peoples of the other socialist countries.

It must be said that not a single imperialist government has yet gone so far as to dare to assert that it, and not the Soviet government, represents the Soviet Union in international affairs, to speak on behalf of the Soviet people. It is not hard to realise what would happen in the world, if not only the government of the People's Republic of China but also other states, and especially big powers, were to follow the example set by the Chinese government in its statement of August 15.

Chaos and plunder would reign in international relations if any government were arbitrarily to proclaim itself, and not the government of this or that country, to be the exponent of the will of the people of that country. If in inter-governmental relations we are to follow such a criterion as the arbitrary interpretation of " international duty "—and bourgeois states could adopt such a criterion on the basis of their own understanding of that duty —then there would no longer be room either for international talks, or for respect for the sovereignty of states, or non-interference in their internal affairs.

In the statement of the Chinese government spokesman the pretentions to decide for the Soviet people what is in keeping with their interests and what is not, what ensures the security of the Soviet Union and what does not, reaches truly fantastic proportions.

What, for instance, is the worth of the idea contained in the Chinese government's statement that if the Soviet Union continues to promote in international affairs the line that has been embodied in the conclusion of the treaty banning nuclear weapon tests in the atmosphere, in outer space and under water, that is to say, if it continues further to pursue its peace-loving course in foreign policy, " then the Soviet Union itself in the last analysis will not be able to hold out." We know that the Chinese government takes its " warnings " to the United States government very seriously. Quite a number of such " warnings " have been given up to date. Perhaps the sentence that the Soviet Union " will not be able to hold out in the last analysis " is also a " warning " issued by the People's Republic of China, only to a new address?

The Chinese leaders are trying to present matters as if they were also speaking on behalf of the oppressed peoples of Asia, Africa and Latin America, as if they were some kind of mouthpiece of theirs. Yet what kind of appeals come from this mouthpiece? What kind of banner do the leaders of China want to hoist over the national liberation movement of the peoples?

The appeals of the Chinese leaders reek strongly of demagogy and adventurism. They want to foist upon the peoples of Asia, Africa and Latin America the idea that the nuclear test-ban treaty and other steps aimed at reducing international tension interfere with the development of their national liberation struggle. Such rantings are a fraud. To stake the fate of the national liberation movement on a worsening of international tension, on pushing humanity to the brink of a thermonuclear world war, as the Chinese leaders are doing, is tantamount to promising the peoples freedom after death.

No, Chinese leaders will not entice anyone on to a road which ends in an abyss. It is not in order to have all their gains threatened with destruction that the peoples of Asia, Africa and Latin America have pressed for independence. They want to live, to strengthen their states, to develop their economies and to create the material foundations for achieving real independence.

The attempts of the Chinese leaders to present matters as if they held a patent for the interpretation of the sentiments and aspirations of the peoples of Asia, Africa and Latin America are not convincing. The incompatibility of the position of the Chinese leaders with the interests of these peoples is best shown by the fact that in spite of their attacks on the nuclear test-ban treaty, states of Asia, Africa and Latin America are acceding to the treaty one after another. On the other hand, it seems that one does not hear of approval by these states of the line taken by the Chinese government.

Is it a fact that the postal services are not functioning efficiently enough or the telegraph has failed and therefore no news is forthcoming about the solidarity of some states with the position of the Chinese government on the question of the nuclear test ban? It seems that this is not the case.

The only thing that remains for the authors of the statements of the Chinese government to do is to use as trump cards the pronouncements of a few apostates who have long since lost any footing in their countries and their parties and whom Peking is trying hard to woo. Oh yes, the Chinese government can also boast of a resolution of the so-called " Fourth International," which unites Trotskyite groups. " Worthy " partners in " proletarian internationalism "—there is no gainsaying that!

The outcry against the nuclear test-ban treaty is being widely utilised in Peking for propaganda for a story, invented in Peking, about a " special " community of interests of the peoples of Asia, Africa and Latin America. Playing on the nationalist sentiments of some leaders in certain countries of Asia, Africa and Latin America, the Chinese leaders are ostentatiously stressing the community of interests of these three continents only, without saying a word about the need for strengthening their solidarity with the peoples of the socialist countries, with the world revolutionary movement of the working class. With such an interpretation of Afro-Asian solidarity, it can serve, not so much as an instrument of struggle against imperialism as a means of isolating the peoples of these continents from the socialist states, as well as from many other peaceloving states. Who, other than imperialists, stands to profit from such a line?

As if foreseeing the present attempts of the Chinese leaders to erect bulkheads within the international communist and national liberation movement, dividing it by the criterion of the colour of the skin, and as if foreseeing their desire to separate the liberation struggle of the peoples from the revolutionary movement of the international proletariat, Lenin wrote: " Anyone who has said ' A ' must say ' B '—anyone who adopts the standpoint of nationalism naturally goes so far as to want to surround with a Chinese wall his nationality, his national working-class movement, undeterred by the fact that it will be necessary to build separate walls in every city, township and village, undeterred by the fact that by his tactics of division and fragmentation he is reducing to naught the great behest of the cohesion and unity of the proletarians of all nations, races and languages." (*Collected Works*, vol. 6, 4th Russian edition, pp. 474–475.)

The Soviet government is far from holding the view that every calumny of the Chinese leadership against the Soviet Union, against its policy of peace and of defending the inalienable right of the peoples to free and independent development, merits an answer from us. But nevertheless it is necessary to touch upon another contention of the Chinese leaders. They declare that it has been their lot to raise still higher the banner of struggle for the complete banning of nuclear weapons, allegedly " discarded " by the Soviet Union. Fine standard-bearers, indeed, are those who conduct a policy of blocking even the first step on the road towards the complete prohibition of nuclear weapons!

We would be only too glad had the government of People's China marched side by side with the Soviet Union, with all the socialist countries in the great struggle for disarmament. Unfortunately that is not the case today.

The banner of the struggle for general and complete disarmament, for the destruction of nuclear weapons, has been raised high and is carefully carried in the hands of all those for whom the word " peace " contains a concrete programme of action to reduce international tension, to ensure conditions for the peaceful co-existence of states with different social systems and to remove the danger of thermonuclear war. Unfortunately the People's Republic of China is not among them today.

In present conditions, while the danger of the most aggressive imperialist forces unleashing a thermonuclear world war still exists, but when at the same time there are mighty forces in the world capable of preventing war and of frustrating the schemes of the aggressive circles, it is especially important for the peoples to have a true orientation in the further struggle for peace.

Just as troops on the battlefield should have a clear idea of the lines they have occupied, of the tasks immediately in hand and of the direction in which they must make a new thrust in order to develop their success, so in the present worldwide struggle to prevent thermonuclear war, people must be armed with knowledge of the practical significance of the successes already achieved, of what they must do further, on what they must concentrate their efforts. And in this respect the Chinese government is doing precisely the opposite of what is expected of the government of a socialist country: it is striving to mislead the peoples, to deprive them of true signposts in the struggle for the strengthening of peace and, therefore, to undermine the offensive drive of the peoples in that struggle.

The Soviet government will continue to spare no efforts to consolidate the unity of the countries of the world socialist system and, on the basis of the monolithic cohesion of the socialist states, on the basis of the common struggle to remove the danger of a thermonuclear world war, for peaceful co-existence, for national independence, democracy and socialism, will fight for the triumph of peace the world over.

The Soviet government does not abandon hope that the leaders of the People's Republic of China will once again weigh up all the consequences of their present policy, which is contrary to the interests of the cohesion of the socialist countries and the interests of peace, and will exert their efforts to ensure that the People's Republic of China again takes its place in the ranks of the states which are engaged in tireless struggle for preventing thermonuclear war, for peaceful co-existence, for the freedom and independence of the peoples.

[*Soviet News*, No. 4885 (August 21, 1963), pp. 103–109.]
Full title: Soviet Government Statement, August 21, 1963 (complete text).

DOCUMENT 9

China Replies to Latest Soviet Attack, September 1, 1963

A COMMENT ON THE SOVIET GOVERNMENT'S STATEMENT
August 21, 1963

On August 21 the Soviet Government issued a statement in reply to the statement made by the spokesman of the Chinese Government on August 15.

This Soviet statement is even less presentable than its fore-runners. It is unable to advance a single logical argument in defence of the Soviet leaders' act of betrayal; it cannot answer any of the questions of substance we raised in our last statement. The only new element in it is its assertion that China wants to gain victory through the launching of thermonuclear war and to bring about the death of half of mankind. With this assertion, the latest slander campaign of the Soviet leaders against China plumbs new depths. Apparently the Soviet leaders have already become so degenerate that they now depend on telling lies for a living.

More and more facts bear witness that on the question of war and peace the Soviet leaders' theory is one of forbidding revolution and their practice is one of moving from adventurism to capitulationism; and the conclusion of the tripartite treaty marks the further development of their capitulationism. To cover all this up they are desperately distorting the Marxist-Leninist line of the Chinese Communist Party and the Chinese Government on the question of war and peace, asserting that China wants to impose its " adventurist programme " on other countries.

The Soviet Government in its statement is insolent enough to say that we are able to criticize them only because China enjoys the protection of Soviet nuclear weapons.

Well, then, leaders of the Soviet Union, please continue to protect us awhile with your nuclear weapons. We shall continue to criticize you, and we hope you will have the courage to argue the matter out with us.

I

In our statements of July 31 and August 15, we demonstrated irrefutably that in signing the tripartite treaty the Soviet leaders betrayed their original stand, sold out the interests of the Soviet people, sold out the interests of the peoples in the socialist camp, and sold out the interests of the people throughout the world.

In its statement of August 3, the Soviet Government erected the shield of state sovereignty against this criticism of ours. Now they are erecting a shield out of national defence secrets. They say that what had changed was circumstances, and not the Soviet leaders. And what were the changed circumstances? Ah! That cannot be divulged because it is a national defence secret.

This is sheer hypocrisy. National defence secret indeed! The simple fact is that after its tests in 1961 and 1962, the Soviet Union came into possession of the technical data which it needed. Who does not know this so-called national defence secret! That took place back in 1962, but as late as June 15, 1963, the Soviet leaders were still saying that the position of the West was unacceptable. How can the 180-degree turn made by the Soviet leaders after June 15, 1963, in betrayal of their original position be explained away by the change which took place in 1962?

With the conclusion of the tripartite treaty, the Soviet statement asserts: At the worst the situation is the same as without the treaty; how can anyone say the treaty has increased the danger of war? The United States may conduct underground nuclear tests, but cannot the Soviet Union do the same?

This assertion can only delude people who do not look beyond the surface or are most naive. The essence of the matter is that the United States is in the lead in the field of underground nuclear testing. Without the tripartite treaty, the United States would have been condemned when it engaged in underground nuclear testing. The tripartite treaty legalizes underground nuclear testing, which precisely helps the United States maintain and improve on its lead.

In the short period since the conclusion of the tripartite treaty the United States has already conducted three underground nuclear tests. On August 24 the U.S. Defence Department submitted a programme to the Senate, proposing a great increase in underground nuclear tests. U.S. Deputy Defence Secretary Gilpatric said,

> "The underground testing programme of the United States will be comprehensive. Therefore, it will be revised to include as many as feasible of the objectives of the tests which we would otherwise do under conditions of unrestricted testing," so as "to ensure the highest practicable rate of progress in nuclear technology."

All this is shocking to people who are truly concerned about peace. How can the Soviet leaders feign blindness?

The whole world knows that the tripartite treaty is designed to manacle socialist countries other than the Soviet Union and all the peace-loving countries, and that it has no restraining effect whatsoever on U.S. imperialism. It does not hinder the United States from using nuclear weapons in time of war, manufacturing and stockpiling nuclear weapons and proliferating nuclear weapons among its allies. Since the conclusion of the tripartite treaty, U.S. imperialism has continuously declared that it is not bound in any way, and the Soviet leaders have not uttered a sound of protest.

The Soviet statement feigns ignorance of all this and maintains that the Soviet leaders' position on the question of preventing the proliferation of nuclear weapons is perfectly reasonable.

The Soviet statement says it would not mean much if one or two more socialist countries came into possession of nuclear weapons, but it would be terrible if one or two more capitalist countries did so; that the Soviet Union cannot on the one hand give nuclear weapons to China and on the other oppose the United States giving nuclear weapons to West Germany; and that if the Soviet Union did so, the United States would surely arm West Germany with nuclear weapons. The Soviet statement boastfully proclaims this to be the Soviet leaders' " principled stand " on the question of preventing nuclear proliferation.

My! A " principled stand "! But let us see what this " principled stand " amounts to.

Anyone having some knowledge of Marxism-Leninism and using his head a little will see

—that it is a cowardly stand which holds the strength of one's own class brothers in utter contempt and holds the strength of the imperialists in awe and veneration;

—that it is an absurd stand which puts the socialist camp and the imperialist camp on a par and makes no distinction between the enemy and ourselves; and

—that it is a reactionary stand which implies that U.S. imperialist nuclear proliferation is not for aggression but for defence and that the aggressive nature of imperialism has already changed.

Even a bourgeois statesman with some commonsense can understand that a commitment undertaken must be premised on a commitment accepted by the other party. The Soviet Union is not giving nuclear weapons to China, but has the United States undertaken an obligation not to arm West Germany with nuclear weapons?

In our view, the dogged adherence by the Soviet leaders to their " principled stand " is a matter of unrequited love. Look how pitiless the U.S. imperialists are! After signing the tripartite treaty, they noisily proceed with building up the NATO " multilateral nuclear force " and continue to ship nuclear weapons to West Germany. Where is there any sign of a commitment?

The tripartite treaty marks the surrender of the Soviet leaders to U.S. imperialism. It is rotten to the core. China of course cannot be a party to it.

The Soviet statement asserts that in refusing to sign this treaty, China is assuming the role of those in the Right-wing of the ranks of the U.S. " madmen," the West German revanchists and the French extremists. If that is the case, do not Chiang Kai-shek, Adenauer and Franco, who have signed, become Left-wing forces of peace? So that is how matters stand! It is indeed a great discovery by the Soviet leaders!

II

Unable to find any reasonable arguments to defend the tripartite treaty, the Soviet leaders resort to slandering China. One slander is that China is opposed to the tripartite treaty because the Soviet Union has denied it the atom bomb. This is a deliberate distortion of China's position.

In our last statement we explained in detail how, as far back as 1959, the Soviet leaders made a gift to the United States of their refusal to provide China with the technical data required for the manufacture of nuclear weapons. But for the sake of larger interests, we never mentioned this before, not even between fraternal Parties. If it were not because the Soviet leaders have colluded with the U.S. imperialists in an effort to force China to undertake not to manufacture nuclear weapons, we would not have wanted to discuss this.

Our exposure has enraged the Soviet leaders, who declare that it amounts to divulgence of confidential documents and information relating to the defences of the countries in the socialist camp, and that they will draw their own conclusions.

Please do not pretend. You know very well that long before we published our last statement you had informed the Americans the secrets between China and the Soviet Union concerning nuclear weapons.

As for drawing conclusions, have you not already done that long ago? Not only have you perfidiously and unilaterally scrapped the agreement on providing China with nuclear technical data, but you have blatantly given more and more military aid to the Indian reactionaries, who are hostile to China and have made incessant armed provocations against it. What is this if it is not drawing your " own conclusions "?

The real point is that the Soviet leaders hold that China should not, and must not, manufacture nuclear weapons, and that only the few nuclear powers, and particularly U.S. imperialism, the enemy of the people of the whole world, are entitled to the continued production of nuclear weapons.

The Soviet statement asserts that China can rely on the nuclear weapons of the Soviet Union and need not manufacture them itself; that if it tries to manufacture them it will result in a great strain on China's economy.

Should or should not China itself master the means of resisting U.S. nuclear blackmail?

True, if the Soviet leaders really practised proletarian internationalism, China might consider it unnecessary to manufacture its own nuclear weapons.

But it is equally true that if the Soviet leaders really practised proletarian internationalism, they would have no reason whatever for obstructing China from manufacturing nuclear weapons.

Is not China very poor and backward? Yes, it is. The Soviet leaders say, how can the Chinese be qualified to manufacture nuclear weapons when they eat watery soup out of a common bowl and do not even have pants to wear?

The Soviet leaders are perhaps too hasty in deriding China for its backwardness. They may or may not have judged right. But in any case, even if we Chinese people are unable to produce an atom bomb for a hundred years, we will neither crawl to the baton of the Soviet leaders nor kneel before the nuclear blackmail of the U.S. imperialists.

The Soviet statement says that if China were to produce two or three atom bombs, the imperialists would aim many more atom bombs at China. This is in effect instigating the imperialists to threaten China with atom bombs.

Of course the fact that the U.S. imperialists may wish to aim more atom and hydrogen bombs at China merits attention and vigilance. But there is nothing terrifying about it. At this very moment the United States has many such bombs already poised against China. It will not make much difference if the United States listens to the Soviet leaders and adds a few more. The Chinese people will not tremble before U.S. nuclear threats. But one must ask: Where do the Soviet leaders place themselves in making such an instigation?

In the eyes of the Soviet leaders, the whole world and the destiny of all mankind revolve round nuclear weapons. Therefore they hold on tightly to their nuclear weapons, afraid that someone might take them away or come to possess them, and so break up their monopoly. They are very nervous. They attribute China's principled criticism of the tripartite treaty to its failure to obtain the atom bombs it desires.

We feel that this attitude of the Soviet leaders is ludicrous. It calls to mind the following ancient Chinese fable:

> Hui Tzu was Prime Minister of the State of Liang. Chuang Tzu was on his way to call on him.
>
> Somebody said to Hui Tzu, " Chuang Tzu is coming with the intention of taking over your place as Prime Minister."
>
> Hui Tzu became afraid and hunted for Chuang Tzu high and low for three days and three nights.
>
> Chuang Tzu appeared before Hui Tzu and said, " Have you heard about the southern bird, the phoenix? It set out from the South Sea to fly to the North Sea. It would not alight except on the Wutung tree. It would eat nothing except the fruit of the bamboo. It would drink nothing except the purest spring water. An owl, which had got hold of a dead rat, looked up as the phoenix flew over and screeched to warn it off. Are you, too, not screeching at me, over your kingdom of Liang?"

The moral of this fable is that different people have different aspirations, and it is improper to measure the stature of great men by the yardstick of small men.

III

The main feature of the Soviet Government's latest statement is its slander that we want socialism to win by means of thermonuclear war and that we would sacrifice 300 million Chinese and a half of mankind in order to create a greater civilization on the corpses and the ruins. Railing at China, the Soviet statement asserts that China is carrying out " an inhuman policy " and following a " bestial conception."

This is really hair-raising stuff. How shocking! The Chinese Communists are nothing but a bunch of bloodthirsty monsters, worse than Hitler, worse than any tyrants past or present, and, needless to say, hundreds of times worse than the U.S. imperialists.

But how is this possible? On what do the Soviet leaders base themselves in making such fantastic charges against China? Their charges, however varied, boil down to two counts:

First, that some responsible Chinese leaders have talked about the possibility that in a war people may die by hundreds of millions;

Second that the Chinese journal *Hongqi* (Red Flag) has made the assertion that the victorious people would create a beautiful future for themselves on the ruins of imperialism.

The references are to certain remarks made by Comrade Mao Tse-tung in his speech at the Moscow meeting of the Communist and Workers' Parties on November 18, 1957, and to a passage in the article " Long Live Leninism! " written by the editorial department of *Hongqi*.

Let us now see what the Chinese Communist Party actually said.

Comrade Mao Tse-tung said:

> It is my opinion that the international situation has now reached a new turning point. There are two winds in the world today, the East wind and the West wind. There is a Chinese saying, " Either the East wind prevails over the West wind or the West wind prevails over the East wind." It is characteristic of the situation today, I believe, that the East wind is prevailing

over the West wind. That is to say, the forces of socialism are overwhelmingly superior to the forces of imperialism.

Proceeding from that estimation, Comrade Mao Tse-tung pointed to the steadily growing possibility of preventing imperialism from launching a new world war.

Comrade Mao Tse-tung then added,

> At present another situation has to be taken into account, namely, that the war maniacs may drop atomic and hydrogen bombs everywhere. They drop them and we act after their fashion; thus there will be chaos and lives will be lost. The question has to be considered for the worst. The Political Bureau of our Party has held several sessions to discuss this question. If fighting breaks out now, China has got only hand-grenades and not atomic bombs—which the Soviet Union has though. Let us imagine, how many people will die if war should break out? Out of the world's population of 2,700 million, one-third—or, if more, half—may be lost. It is they and not we who want to fight; when a fight starts, atomic and hydrogen bombs may be dropped. I debated this question with a foreign statesman. He believed that if an atomic war was fought, the whole of mankind would be annihilated. I said that if the worst came to the worst and half of mankind died, the other half would remain while imperialism would be razed to the ground and the whole world would become socialist; in a number of years there would be 2,700 million people again and definitely more. We Chinese have not yet completed our construction and we desire peace. However, if imperialism insists on fighting a war, we will have no alternative but to make up our minds and fight to the finish before going ahead with our construction. If every day you are afraid of war and war eventually comes, what will you do then? First I have said that the East wind prevails over the West wind and that war will not break out, and now I have added these explanations about the situation in case war should break out. In this way both possibilities have been taken into account.

The passage in " Long Live Leninism! " reads:

> We consistently oppose the launching of criminal wars by imperialism, because imperialist war would impose enormous sacrifices upon the people of various countries (including the people of the United States and other imperialist countries). But should the imperialists impose such sacrifices on them, we believe that, just as the experience of the Russian revolution and the Chinese revolution shows, those sacrifices would not be in vain. The victorious people would very swiftly create on the ruins of imperialism a civilization thousands of times higher than the capitalist system and a truly beautiful future for themselves.

The meaning of these words is very clear:

1. China wants peace, and not war;
2. It is the imperialists, and not we, who want to fight;
3. A world war can be prevented;
4. Even in the eventuality that imperialism should impose a war on the people of the world and inflict tragic losses on them, it is the imperialist system, and not mankind, that would perish, and the future of mankind would still be bright.

In effect, we make the point in these four sentences. These four sentences are interrelated. But the Soviet leaders have seized hold of half the sentence in which we mention the possibility that the people of the world might suffer tragic sacrifice, quoted it out of context and turned the other three and a half sentences inside out. Hence the conclusion: China wants war, and not peace; China, and not imperialism, wants to fight; a world war is inevitable; and China wants to launch a nuclear world war and bring about the death of half of mankind so as to attain a bright future for mankind. It is indeed pitiable that the leaders of a great power, and a great socialist power at that, should resort to such low fabrications.

But the lies told by the Soviet leaders are really too gross and fantastic. Anybody who uses his brains will ask, how can China launch a nuclear war if it does not have a single atom bomb? All revolutionaries throughout the world know that imperialism is the source of war. How can anyone imagine that socialist China will launch a world war? It is inconceivable.

The quoted remarks of Comrade Mao Tse-tung in 1957 were a reply to some people's view that mankind will be annihilated if imperialism unleashes a nuclear war. The Soviet leaders have spread this view over a number of years and are still spreading it. They say that if imperialism unleashes a nuclear war, it will not only scorch but will burn everything to ashes, i.e., the 3,000 million people of the world will all die. We do not agree with this pessimistic and despairing view of theirs. We say that if imperialism should unleash a nuclear war and the worst came to the worst, half of the world's population would be killed. We are optimistic about the future of mankind.

They say, our extreme supposition that half the world's population might die is a bestial conception. Does that not make their oft-repeated view, that all the 3,000 million people of the world would die, doubly bestial?

While propagating the theory of the annihilation of mankind, they say that the people of the world will bury imperialism if imperialism forces a nuclear war on them. For instance, the Open Letter of the Central Committee of the C.P.S.U. of July 14 declared, " It stands to reason, of course, that if the imperialist madmen unleash a war, the peoples will sweep away capitalism and bury it." But people are bound to ask, if according to your theory all the 3,000 million people in the world will die if imperialism unleases a nuclear war, then who would remain to bury imperialism?

As a matter of fact, this lie of the Soviet leaders is not a new one, nor can they claim its authorship.

On October 1 and then on October 8, 1960, Wadsworth, the U.S. delegate to the U.N. General Assembly, quoted out of context the sentences in " Long Live Leninism! " concerning the ruins of imperialism. He slanderously asserted that China " welcomes an atomic war," and wants a world war " fought with hydrogen bombs," " if only that war promises the conquest of the world by communism."

In his book *Socialism and War* published in 1960, Kardelj of the renegade Tito clique also slandered China as wanting to unleash a world war to promote world revolution. On September 2, 1960, the Soviet paper *Pravda* said in criticizing this book that Kardelj was helping the U.S. imperialist big guns and that he, " in substance, repeats the slanders spread by the U.S. imperialists about the ' aggressiveness ' of People's China."

Now the Soviet leaders have simply collected the spittle of the imperialists and the renegades. The U.S. imperialists had a try at this slander but then dropped it when they saw that no one paid it any attention. But the Soviet leaders are endlessly repeating the same lie, toning it up with colour and life, and insisting on making people believe it.

Why do the Soviet leaders continuously repeat this big lie? Do they really believe that the imperialists would not launch another world war? Do they really believe that China wants to launch a world war? Clearly, this is not the crux of the matter.

The crucial point is what should be the policy in face of U.S. imperialist nuclear blackmail and threats—resistance or capitulation? We stand for resistance, and so they say we want to launch a war and bring about the death of half of mankind. They even hold that whoever dares to assume that imperialism may launch a war wants to launch a war himself. In that case, what is the way out? Of course, the only way is capitulation and to capitulate before the imperialists act. In the final analysis, they are racking their brains and telling all these lies for the purpose of covering up their disreputable capitulationist stand.

IV

The Soviet statement declares that " the appeals of the P.R.C. leaders smack strongly of demagogy and adventurism," and that " to link the fate of the national-liberation movement with an aggravation of international tension, with urging humanity to a world thermonuclear war, as the P.R.C. leaders are doing, is like promising the peoples freedom after death."

What the Soviet leaders mean is clear. Possessing nuclear weapons, imperialism must not be resisted. Should the oppressed peoples and nations resist and should the socialist countries support their resistance, that would be pushing mankind into a world thermonuclear war.

The Soviet leaders hold that " no problem of the revolutionary movement of the working class or the national-liberation movement can now be considered in isolation from the struggle to preserve peace and avert a world thermonuclear war."

The Soviet leaders hold that " ' local wars ' in our time are very dangerous, for any small ' local war ' might spark off the conflagration of a world war."

The Soviet leaders hold that if the people of any country dare to wage a revolutionary war against imperialism, all they are doing is hankering after " dying beautifully " and engaging in a " movement for piling up corpses."

The Soviet leaders hold that if a nuclear war should break out, " in the case of many peoples the question of socialism would be eliminated altogether, because they would have disappeared bodily from our planet."

The Soviet leaders even hold that, under the threat of a nuclear war, Kennedy, the chieftain of U.S. imperialism, and people like him have " shown concern for the preservation of peace " and " try on their part to avert a war."

In short, in the opinion of the Soviet leaders, the emergence of nuclear weapons has changed everything, it has changed both the nature of imperialism and the nature of our epoch. Our epoch is no longer one of revolution as defined in the Moscow Statement, but a nuclear epoch, a nuclear century.

In the Open Letter of the Central Committee of the C.P.S.U. dated July 14, the Soviet leaders said, " The nuclear rocket weapons that were created in the middle of our century changed old notions about wars." In reality, this means that, since the emergence of nuclear weapons, war is no longer the continuation of politics, there is no longer any difference between unjust and just wars, imperialism is no longer the source of war, and the people of various countries should no longer wage just wars against imperialist armed aggression and armed suppression by the reactionary regime for such just wars cannot possibly be won but will only bring about the annihilation of mankind.

The conclusion must be: The only thing for all the oppressed peoples and nations and for all countries and people subjected to aggression and oppression to do, if they do not want to court self-destruction, is to capitulate to imperialism which possesses nuclear weapons. Anyone who dares to resist imperialist oppression, aggression and threats and to wage revolutionary war for independence and liberation, and anyone who dares to support such revolutionary war, is guilty of the error of adventurism and will be held responsible for the disaster of the so-called annihilation of mankind. In the opinion of the Soviet leaders, in this nuclear century to remain alive is everything, and there is no other aim in life. This is the philosophy of docile slaves which demands of the people of the world that they should submit to the tender mercies of imperialism. It is a reactionary theory in the service of imperialism. It is a truly bestial conception.

V

The views of the Soviet leaders referred to above are a total betrayal of Marxism-Leninism and are completely contradicted by the facts of history since the end of World War II.

It is clear except to the blind that since the emergence of nuclear weapons, the imperialists have continued to resort to counter-revolutionary wars as a way of carrying out their policies of oppressing and enslaving the peoples of various countries and that the countries and peoples suffering from aggression and oppression have continued to regard revolutionary wars as the way to oppose imperialist aggression and oppression and to win their independence and liberation. The history of the last eighteen years is replete with wars of aggression and wars against aggression, with unjust and just wars. War is still the continuation of politics.

At the end of World War II, after it had dropped two atomic bombs on Hiroshima and Nagasaki in Japan, the U.S. imperialism assumed that armed with this "ultimate weapon" it could ride roughshod over the world and do whatever it pleased. At the time there was a kind of fear-mentality among the Chinese people as well as among the peoples of other countries. U.S. imperialism, possessed of atomic weapons, appeared to them so powerful that they thought it could put down peoples' revolutions at will.

Precisely at that crucial moment Comrade Mao Tse-tung said in his talk with the American correspondent Anna Louise Strong in 1946:

> The atom bomb is a paper tiger which the U.S. reactionaries use to scare people. It looks terrible, but in fact it isn't. Of course, the atom bomb is a weapon of mass slaughter, but the outcome of a war is decided by the people, not by one or two new types of weapon.
>
> All reactionaries are paper tigers. In appearance, the reactionaries are terrifying, but in reality they are not so powerful. From a long-term point of view, it is not the reactionaries but the people who are really powerful.

This Marxist-Leninist thesis of Comrade Mao Tse-tung's was a timely exposure of the U.S. imperialists' plot of atomic blackmail and armed the Chinese people and the revolutionary people of all countries against it. The victory after victory which the people of many countries have won in their revolutionary wars against the aggression and enslavement by the imperialists and their lackeys in the past seventeen years have repeatedly proved the correctness of this thesis.

While the U.S. imperialists still had a monopoly of nuclear weapons, the Chinese people achieved the great victory of their revolution in defiance of U.S. imperialist blackmail and intimidation.

While the U.S. imperialists still retained their nuclear superiority, they were not able to prevent the defeat of their war of aggression in Korea. In November 1950, after the U.S. imperialists had met with serious reverses on the Korean battlefield, Truman, then President of the United States, cried for the use of atomic bombs, and this immediately aroused indignant protests from the people of the whole world and also general panic and opposition from the allies of the United States. Furthermore, U.S. military personnel did not believe that the use of atomic weapons on the Korean battlefield would actually be effective. As a result, throughout the Korean war the U.S. imperialists never dared to use atomic weapons.

Following the armistice in Korea, the people of Viet Nam were victorious in their revolutionary war against French imperialism. Even though it held atomic weapons, U.S. imperialism was unable to realize its plan of increasing its intervention in the war in Viet Nam.

After more than seven years of hard and bitter struggle, the people of Algeria were victorious in their war for national independence.

At the very gate of U.S. imperialism, the people of Cuba won victory in their revolution through armed struggle. U.S. imperialism has never dared to declare that it would use nuclear weapons against the Cuban people.

The people's armed forces in southern Viet Nam are now carrying on a victorious struggle against the U.S. imperialists and their lackey, the Ngo Dinh Diem clique. Although the U.S. imperialists have employed a great variety of new weapons, they have not dared to use nuclear weapons.

U.S. imperialism cannot stop the people's revolutionary struggles in various countries by means of nuclear weapons. The reason is that, politically, recourse to this kind of weapon would place U.S. imperialism in a position of extreme isolation and, militarily, the massive destructiveness of nuclear weapons limits their use, for in civil wars and wars of national independence, where the lines are zigzag and the fighting is at close range, the use of nuclear weapons of mass destruction would inflict damage on both belligerents.

In a speech delivered on December 16, 1959, Kennedy admitted that U.S. nuclear strength "cannot be used in so-called 'brush-fire' peripheral war. It was not used in Korea, Indo-China, Hungary, Suez, Lebanon, Quemoy, Tibet or Laos. In short, it cannot prevent the Communists from gradually nibbling away at the fringe of the free world's territory and strength, until our security is being steadily eroded in piecemeal fashion. . . ."

It is therefore evident that, provided the revolutionary people are not afraid of the imperialists' nuclear blackmail and persevere in their just struggles, they can gain victories in their revolutions. Such struggles and victories have not led to world war, but have constantly weakened and effectively restrained imperialism, and thus have reduced the danger of the imperialists launching a world war and safeguarded world peace.

The interests of the people's revolutions and the interests of world peace are identical. It is a manifestation of the proletarian internationalism of the Chinese Communist Party when it gives full support to the constantly growing national-liberation movements in Asia, Africa and Latin America. The Soviet leaders slander this stand of the Chinese Communist Party as being racist and accuse us of undermining the unity of the national-liberation movement with the international proletariat. As a matter of fact, since you smear the national-liberation movement as a " movement for piling up corpses " and as " promising the peoples freedom after death," what is the need of your talking about this unity? Is there any meaning in uniting with a pile of corpses? Your contempt for the coloured peoples and the oppressed nations is a downright racist and reactionary nationalist viewpoint.

VI

Imperialism, whose doom is sealed, cannot save itself by relying on nuclear weapons, nor can the socialist countries win victory in their struggle against imperialism by relying solely on nuclear weapons.

We have always fully appreciated the important role played by the Soviet Union's possession of nuclear weapons in the struggle of the people of the world against the imperialist policies of aggression and war and for world peace. But there is a limit to everything, and once the limit is exceeded, the thing is reduced to absurdity. It is a pity that in their attiude towards the Soviet Union's possession of nuclear weapons the Soviet leaders have exceeded the limit.

The Soviet leaders keep on exaggerating the role of nuclear weapons and blindly trust in them, despite the masses and have forgotten that the masses are the makers of history, and so they have degenerated into worshippers of nuclear weapons.

In June 1960, during the meeting in Bucharest, the Soviet leader, Khrushchov, remarked that in the past they too had once organized militia but that now they had modern weapons, to them, militia were not troops but just human flesh.

It is crystal clear that in the eyes of the Soviet leaders the 3,000 million people of the world are nothing but rubbish, while the nuclear arms of the Soviet Union and the U.S. imperialists are infinitely powerful magic weapons.

That is why they boast so much about what they call the decisive role of Soviet nuclear weapons in the defence of world peace and completely deny the great significance of the people's anti-imperialist struggles throughout the world.

On July 10, 1962, the Soviet leader said at the World Conference for General Disarmament and Peace in Moscow that " the rocket-nuclear might of the Soviet Union serves as a decisive means of defending peace and has already more than once saved mankind from a world war which the Western imperialist cliques attempted to unleash."

The latest statement of the Soviet Government is even more brazen in asserting that Soviet nuclear weapons played the decisive role in defeating the Anglo-French war of aggression against Egypt in 1956 and frustrating the plot of the U.S. armed threat against Syria in 1957 and the U.S.-British plot to send troops for intervention in Iraq in 1958.

All these defeats suffered by the imperialists resulted primarily from the struggles of the Egyptian, Syrian and Iraqi peoples. The firm support to these peoples by the people of the world, including the Soviet people, also played an important part. How then can all this be credited solely to Soviet nuclear weapons?

It is especially ridiculous that the Soviet statement also gives all the credit to Soviet nuclear weapons for the Chinese people's victory in smashing the armed provocations of U.S. imperialism in the Taiwan Straits in 1958. The Soviet paper *Krasnaya Zvezda* even said on August 25, 1963, " The nuclear might of the Soviet Union, the very country which has now been abused by the slanderers of Peking, had saved millions of Chinese from nuclear death and defended the sovereignty, security and independence of their country."

What were the facts? In August and September of 1958, the situation in the Taiwan Straits was indeed very tense as a result of the aggression and provocations by the U.S. imperialists. The Soviet leaders expressed their support for China on September 7 and 19 respectively. Although at that time the situation in the Taiwan Straits was tense, there was no possibility that a nuclear war would break out and no need for the Soviet Union to support China with its nuclear weapons. It was only when they were clear that this was the situation that the Soviet leaders expressed their support for China.

We have not forgotten and will not forget the support which the Soviet people have given to China on the question of Taiwan over a long period.

Likewise, however, we have not forgotten and will not forget what the Soviet leader, Khrushchov, said about the question of Taiwan after his visit to the United States in October 1959.

He said that the question of Taiwan was an incendiary factor in the international situation and that because the United States supported Chiang Kai-shek and the Soviet Union supported China, there resulted the atmosphere of an imminent great war; but what the Soviet Union stood for was the creation of all conditions to ease international tension and eliminate war.

He further said that there was more than one way to solve every complicated question, depending on what basis you took. For example, after the October Revolution, there was established in the Soviet Far East the Far Eastern Republic, and Lenin recognized it at the time; this was a temporary concession and sacrifice, but later on it was united with Russia.

The meaning of this statement by the Soviet leader was quite clear. To put it bluntly, this was asking China to agree to the U.S. scheme of creating " two Chinas."

This absurd view was of course rebutted and rejected by China, whereupon the Soviet leader made a series of speeches hinting that China was " craving for war like a cock for a fight," and, like Trotsky, wanted " neither peace nor war," etc.

In accordance with the procedure mutually agreed upon by the Soviet Union and the United States, the Chiang Kai-shek clique, swaggering as if it were a sovereign state, has now signed the tripartite treaty. Not only has the Soviet leader asked the Chinese Government to sign the same tripartite treaty along with the Chiang Kai-shek clique spurned by the

Chinese people, and thus to create a two Chinas situation, he has also threatened that, if the Chinese Government opposed this treaty and refused to be bound by it, the United States would help the Chiang Kai-shek clique to manufacture nuclear weapons. It turns out that in order to " save millions of Chinese from nuclear death," one China has to become two Chinas! It is evident that the Soviet leaders will stop at nothing in order to curry favour with the U.S. imperialists. The international position of the German Democratic Republic is beneath their notice and so is China's sovereignty and territorial integrity.

Although the truth has been exposed so fully, they still assert that the nuclear strength of the Soviet Union guarantees China's independence and sovereignty. What effrontery!

VII

Nuclear weapons in the hands of socialist countries should always be defensive weapons against the nuclear threats of the imperialists. In contrast to the imperialists, socialist countries have no need to use nuclear weapons for blackmail or gambling and must not do so. The question of using nuclear weapons concerns the interests of millions upon millions of people; and the socialist countries must be extremely prudent on this question and never act recklessly. In this connection, both adventurism and capitulationism are extremely dangerous.

During the Caribbean crisis, the Soviet leaders committed both the error of adventurism and the error of capitulationism. Instead of criticizing themselves, they have prided themselves on the slap in their face, boasted of their " genuine proletarian internationalism " and proclaimed what they have called a " major victory of the policy of reason, of the forces of peace and socialism." They have wantonly attacked the Chinese Communist Party for the just position it took on this issue, alleging that China hoped for a head-on clash between the United States and the Soviet Union and tried to provoke a nuclear war. This is thoroughly disgusting.

The Soviet leaders never weary of asserting that there was a thermonuclear war crisis in the Caribbean Sea which was averted only because the Soviet leaders firmly pursued the policy of peaceful coexistence.

But the facts are there for everyone to see. Although the tension in the Caribbean Sea stemmed from the U.S. imperialist policy of aggression against Cuba and although there has been a continuing danger of an invasion of Cuba by the U.S. imperialists, nevertheless, before the Soviet Union sent rockets into Cuba, there did not exist a crisis of the United States using nuclear weapons in the Caribbean Sea and of a nuclear war breaking out. If it should be said that such a crisis did arise, it was a result of the rash action of the Soviet leaders.

The Soviet leaders slanderously accuse China of having hoped for a head-on clash between the United States and the Soviet Union. The question is, did we ask you to transport rockets to Cuba? The label of adventurism cannot be pinned on us. If the Marxist-Leninist line we always follow had been acted on, there would never have been a question of shipping rockets to Cuba and the so-called nuclear war crisis would never have existed. How could the question of adventurism have then arisen?

We should like to ask the Soviet leaders, since the transport of rockets to Cuba was a matter of such great importance, did you ever consult the

Soviet people, or the other socialist countries, or the working class in capitalist countries about it? Without consulting anybody you wilfully embarked on a reckless course and irresponsibly played with the lives of millions upon millions of people. The errors were of your own making, and so what ground is there for you to blame others?

There is no need whatsoever to transport rockets to Cuba in order to support the Cuban revolution. That was what the Soviet leaders said in the past, and it is also what they are saying now, and in very beautiful language. For instance, the Open Letter of July 14 of the Central Committee of the C.P.S.U. said that " in case of aggression by American imperialists we shall come to the assistance of the Cuban people from Soviet territory, just as we would have helped them from Cuban territory. True, in this case the rockets would take slightly longer in the flight, but their accuracy would not be impaired by this." That being so, why did you have to ship rockets to Cuba? Was your purpose really to defend the Cuban revolution? Would it not be more correct to say that what you did in the name of defending the Cuban revolution was in reality political gambling?

Anyone with common sense will ask : since the rockets were introduced, why did they have to be withdrawn afterwards? And inasmuch as the rockets were withdrawn afterwards, why had they to be introduced before? According to you, there was a great deal of finesse in first putting them in, and then taking them out. The withdrawal of the Soviet rockets is said to have gained in exchange a guarantee from the United States that it would refrain from invading Cuba. The Americans have said there was no such guarantee. You have said there was. But where is the guarantee? Do you really believe that the United States will not invade Cuba again? Unfortunately, you do not seem to have much confidence in that.

The Soviet leaders have said that China was opposed to the withdrawal of the rockets from Cuba and to the efforts of the Soviet Union to avert a nuclear war. This is a completely groundless statement. As we were totally opposed to your sending the rockets in, why should we oppose their withdrawal? It is understandable you should have tried to extricate yourselves from difficulties of your own creation. But we were resolutely opposed to your acceptance of the completely unjustifiable and humiliating terms which the U.S. imperialists advanced.

The Soviet leaders blame China for not having supported them as an ally should. You had better look up the documents. Was there anything you did right during the Caribbean crisis on which we did not support you? You are dissatisfied, but exactly what did you want us to support?

Did you want us to support you in your decision to accept the inspection of Soviet ships on the high seas by the U.S. pirates? That would not have done! If we had given you support on that, we would have done a disservice to the great Soviet people.

Did you want us to support you in your acceptance of the U.S. imperialists' demand for the " international inspection " of Cuba? That would not have done! If we had given you support on that, we would have done a disservice to the great Cuban people.

In recklessly introducing the rockets into Cuba and then humiliatingly withdrawing them, the Soviet leaders moved from adventurism to capitulationism, and brought disgrace to the Soviet people, the Cuban people, the people of the countries in the socialist camp and the people of the whole world. They have inflicted unprecedented shame and humiliation on the international proletariat. All this has been unalterably written into history. No matter how the Soviet leaders lie or what sleight-of-hand they perform, they can never wash away their shame.

The capitulation of the Soviet leaders has inflated the aggressiveness and arrogance of the imperialists.

After the Caribbean crisis, when the U.S. imperialists saw that their policy of nuclear blackmail had succeeded they concluded that Moscow was more afraid of atomic war than Washington. Just like any fortune hunter who gets a windfall, the U.S. imperialists became overweeningly arrogant. Now that they fully understand the weaknesses of the Soviet leaders, they are using both tough and soft tactics to force them into further capitulation.

The signing of the tripartite treaty is the hallmark of such further capitulation to U.S. imperialism on the part of the Soviet leaders.

VIII

The position and line of the Chinese Communist Party and the Chinese Government on the question of war and peace have always been clear and cannot be distorted.

We resolutely oppose world war and we resolutely defend world peace. Not long after World War II, Comrade Mao Tse-tung stated definitely that a third world war can be prevented. For over a decade, the Chinese people have been firmly persisting in the struggle to oppose the imperialist policies of aggression and war, to prevent a new world war and to preserve world peace. We have consistently held that provided the people of the whole world become united, follow a correct line and persevere in struggle, a new world war can be prevented, a nuclear war can be prevented, and world peace can be preserved.

It is our view that imperialism is the source of modern wars and that U.S. imperialism is the main force of aggression and war. Unless a resolute struggle is waged against the U.S. imperialist policies of aggression and war, defence of world peace is completely out of the question. If one prettifies U.S. imperialism and obscures the targets of this struggle from the people of the world, this will only endanger world peace.

It is our view that in order to strive for world peace, it is necessary to unite in joint efforts all the peace-loving forces of the world, namely, the socialist camp, the national-liberation movement, the revolutionary movement of the people of all countries, and all the peace-loving countries and people. If one despises the force of the masses of the people and blindly trusts nuclear weapons as omnipotent, this will only endanger world peace.

It is our view that in order to strive for world peace, it is necessary to strengthen the unity of the socialist camp and enhance the strength of the national defences of all the countries in the socialist camp. If one splits the socialist camp and weakens its defence forces, it will only endanger world peace.

It is our view that in order to strive for world peace, it is necessary to give full support to the national-liberation movement and the revolutionary struggles of the people of all countries. The more these struggles develop, the more the imperialist forces will be weakened and the greater the possibility of preventing the imperialists from launching world war. If one refuses to support, and even sabotages the national-liberation movement and the revolutionary struggle of the people of all countries, this will only endanger world peace.

We consistently maintain that countries with different social systems should coexist peacefully. It was China which initiated the Five Principles of Peaceful Coexistence. It has made unremitting efforts for peaceful coexistence with countries having different social systems on the basis of the Five Principles. For the socialist countries, peaceful coexistence must in all circumstances be based on principles and must not depart from them. Negotiation is one form of struggle against imperialism. Necessary compromises can be made in negotiations, so long as the principle of upholding the fundamental interests of the people is observed. But if one regards negotiations as the main means, or even the sole means, of striving for peaceful coexistence and does not scruple to sell out the fundamental interests of the people in order to seek compromises with imperialism, that is not peaceful coexistence but capitulationist coexistence. And it will only result in endangering world peace.

We are in favour of general disarmament and hold that the imperialists can be forced to accept certain agreements on disarmament through the unremitting struggle of the people of all countries. We are of the opinion that the complete and thorough prohibition of nuclear weapons can be achieved while imperialism still exists, just as poison gas was prohibited. The reason is that the use of such a weapon of mass destruction is completely contrary to the will of the people and would, moreover, subject the users to destruction. However, universal and complete disarmament can be realized only after imperialism, capitalism and all systems of exploitation have been eliminated. To make propaganda about the possibility of realizing "a world without weapons, without armed forces and without wars" through universal and complete disarmament while imperialism still exists, is to deceive the people of the world and is detrimental to the struggle for world peace.

We hold that while affirming the growing possibility that imperialism can be prevented from launching a new world war, one should also recognize that the danger of a new world war still exists. Necessary preparations must be made against this danger. The better we are prepared, the smaller is the possibility that the imperialists will dare to launch such a war. If anyone stresses only one possibility, the possibility that imperialism will not launch such a war, tries to make the people of the world believe that no other possibility exists, and does not even dare think of the other possibility, that will only lull the vigilance of the world's people, provide opportunities for imperialism to exploit and increase the danger of world war.

In fighting imperialism, we are of the opinion that, strategically and with regard to the whole, one must despise the enemy, dare to struggle against him and dare to seize victory; at the same time, tactically and with regard to each specific struggle, one must take the enemy seriously and be prudent. If one does not take full account of the enemy tactically, and is heedless and reckless, while strategically one dares not despise the enemy, it is inevitable that one will commit the error of adventurism in tactics and the error of capitulationism in strategy.

The position and line of the Chinese Communist Party and the Chinese Government on the question of war and peace are in full conformity with the revolutionary principles of the 1957 Declaration and the 1960 Statement. Ours is a Marxist-Leninist line. Adherence to this line will lead both to victory for the peoples' revolutions and to victory for world peace.

We maintain that the line pursued by the Soviet leaders is an anti-Marxist-Leninist line, one that runs counter to the revolutionary principles of the Declaration and the Statement. Adherence to this line will harm the fundamental interests of the people of all countries, and it will endanger world peace.

Our line on the question of war and peace is indeed the diametrical opposite of that of the Soviet leaders. The Soviet leaders are of course entitled to defend their own line. However, abuse is not debate and misrepresentation is not argument. Communists should always have respect for the facts and talk reason. It is for the Chinese people, the Soviet people and the people of the whole world to judge which line is correct, ours or yours, and which line is wrong. We note that the Soviet papers have published our statement of August 15. We hope you will continue this good practice and also publish our present statement.

[*Peking Review*, VI, 36 (September 6, 1963), pp. 7–16.]

Full title: Statement by the Spokesman of the Chinese Government—A Comment on the Soviet Government's Statement of August 21–September 1, 1963 (complete text).

DOCUMENT 10

The Origin and Development of the Differences Between the Leadership of the CPSU and Ourselves—Comment on the Open Letter of the Central Committee of the CPSU (1) September 6, 1963

ANNOUNCEMENT

On July 14, 1963, the Central Committee of the Communist Party of the Soviet Union published an open letter to Party organisations and all Communists in the Soviet Union.

In a statement on July 19 a spokesman of the Central Committee of the Communist Party of China declared:

The open letter of the Central Committee of the CPSU is an appraisal of our letter of June 14. The Central Committee of the CPC considers that the contents of the open letter do not accord with the facts, and we cannot agree with the views it expresses. At the appropriate time, the Central Committee of the CPC will clarify matters and give its comments.

The open letter of the Central Committee of the CPSU was published in full on July 20 in the *Renmin Ribao* and other national papers and in all provincial and municipal papers throughout China. It was also broadcast in full by Chinese radio stations.

In the Soviet national papers, the open letter was followed by nearly 300 articles attacking China. The *Renmin Ribao* has published extracts from a number of these articles.

Starting today, the Editorial Departments of the *Renmin Ribao* and the journal *Hongqi* are publishing a succession of articles commenting on the open letter of the Central Committee of the CPSU.

Editorial Department of *Renmin Ribao*
Editorial Department of *Hongqi*
September 6, 1963

IT is more than a month since the Central Committee of the Communist Party of the Soviet Union published its open letter of July 14 to Party organisations and all Communists in the Soviet Union. This open letter, and the steps taken by the leadership of the CPSU since its publication, have pushed Sino-Soviet relations to the brink of a split and have carried the differences in the international communist movement to a new stage of unprecedented gravity.

Now Moscow, Washington, New Delhi and Belgrade are joined in a love feast and the Soviet press is running an endless assortment of fantastic stories and theories attacking China. The leadership of the CPSU has allied itself with U.S. imperialism, the Indian reactionaries and the renegade Tito clique against socialist China and against all Marxist-Leninist parties, in open betrayal of Marxism-Leninism and proletarian internationalism, in brazen repudiation of the 1957 Declaration and the 1960 Statement and in flagrant violation of the Sino-Soviet Treaty of Friendship, Alliance and Mutual Assistance.

The present differences within the international communist movement and between the Chinese and Soviet Parties involve a whole series of important questions of principle. In its letter of June 14 to the Central Committee of the CPSU, the Central Committee of the CPC systematically and comprehensively discussed the essence of these differences. It pointed out that, in the last analysis, the present differences within the international communist movement and between the Chinese and Soviet Parties involve the questions of whether or not to accept the revolutionary principles of the 1957 Declaration and the 1960 Statement, whether or not to accept Marxism-Leninism and proletarian internationalism, whether or not there is need for revolution, whether or not imperialism is to be opposed, and whether or not the unity of the socialist camp and the international communist movement is desired.

How have the differences in the international communist movement and between the leadership of the CPSU and ourselves arisen? And how have they grown to their present serious dimensions? Everybody is concerned about these questions.

In our article " Whence the Differences? " (*Renmin Ribao* editorial, February 27, 1963), we dealt with the origin and growth of the differences in the international communist movement in general outline. We deliberately refrained from giving certain facts concerning this question, and particularly certain important facts involving the leadership of the CPSU, and left the leadership of the CPSU some leeway, though we were ready to provide a fuller picture and to thrash out the rights and wrongs when necessary. Now that the open letter of the Central Committee of the CPSU has told many lies about the origin and development of the differences and completely distorted the facts, it has become necessary for us to set forth certain facts in order to explain the matter in greater detail.

In its open letter, the Central Committee of the CPSU dares not state the truth to its Party members and the masses of the people. Instead of being open and above-board and respecting the facts as Marxist-Leninists should, the leadership of the CPSU resorts to the customary practice of bourgeois politicians, distorting the facts and confusing truth and falsehood in its determined attempt to shift the blame for the emergence and growth of the differences on to the Chinese Communist Party.

Lenin once said, " Honesty in politics is the result of strength, and hypocrisy—the result of weakness." Honesty and respect for the facts mark the attitude of Marxist-Leninists. Only those who have degenerated politically depend on telling lies for a living.

The facts are most eloquent. Facts are the best witness. Let us look at the facts.

THE DIFFERENCES BEGAN WITH THE 20TH CONGRESS OF THE CPSU

There is a saying, " It takes more than one cold day for the river to freeze three feet deep." The present differences in the international communist movement did not, of course, begin just today.

The open letter of the Central Committee of the CPSU spreads the notion that the differences in the international communist movement were started by the three articles which we published in April 1960 under the title of *Long Live Leninism!* This is a big lie.

What is the truth?

The truth is that the whole series of differences of principle in the international communist movement began more than seven years ago.

To be specific, it began with the 20th Congress of the CPSU in 1956.

The 20th Congress of the CPSU was the first step along the road of revisionism taken by the leadership of the CPSU. From the 20th Congress to the present, the revisionist line of the leadership of the CPSU has gone through the process of emergence, formation, growth and systematisation. And by a gradual process, too, people have come to understand more and more deeply the revisionist line of the CPSU leadership.

From the very outset we held that a number of views advanced at the 20th Congress concerning the contemporary international struggle and the international Communist movement were wrong, were violations of Marxism-Leninism. In particular, the complete negation of Stalin on the pretext of "combating the personality cult" and the thesis of peaceful transition to Socialism by "the parliamentary road" are gross errors of principle.

The criticism of Stalin at the 20th Congress of the CPSU was wrong both in principle and in method.

Stalin's life was that of a great Marxist-Leninist, a great proletarian revolutionary. For thirty years after Lenin's death, Stalin was the foremost leader of the CPSU and the Soviet Government, as well as the recognised leader of the international Communist movement and the standard-bearer of the world revolution. During his lifetime, Stalin made some serious mistakes, but compared to his great and meritorious deeds his mistakes are only secondary.

Stalin rendered great services to the development of the Soviet Union and the international Communist movement. In the article "On the Historical Experience of the Dictatorship of the Proletariat" published in April 1956, we said:

> After Lenin's death Stalin creatively applied and developed Marxism-Leninism as the chief leader of the Party and the state. Stalin expressed the will and aspirations of the people, and proved himself an outstanding Marxist-Leninist fighter in the struggle in defence of the legacy of Leninism against its enemies—the Trotskyites, Zinovievites and other bourgeois agents. Stalin won the support of the Soviet people and played an important role in history primarily because, together with the other leaders of the Communist Party of the Soviet Union, he defended Lenin's line on the industrialisation of the Soviet Union and the collectivisation of agriculture. By pursuing this line, the Communist Party of the Soviet Union brought about the triumph of Socialism in the Soviet Union and created the conditions for the victory of the Soviet Union in the war against Hitler; these victories of the Soviet people accorded with the interests of the working class of the world and all progressive mankind. It was therefore natural that the name of Stalin was greatly honoured throughout the world.

It was necessary to criticise Stalin's mistakes. But in his secret report to the 20th Congress, Comrade Khrushchov completely negated Stalin, and in doing so defamed the dictatorship of the proletariat, defamed the Socialist system, the great CPSU, the great Soviet Union and the international Communist movement. Far from using a revolutionary proletarian party's method of criticism and self-criticism for the purpose of making an earnest and serious analysis and summation of the historical experience of the dictatorship of the proletariat, he treated Stalin as an enemy and shifted the blame for all mistakes on to Stalin alone.

Khrushchov viciously and demagogically told a host of lies in his secret report, and threw around charges that Stalin had a " persecution mania," indulged in " brutal arbitrariness," took the path of " mass repressions and terror," " knew the country and agriculture only from films " and " planned operations on a globe," that Stalin's leadership " became a serious obstacle in the path of Soviet social development," and so on and so forth. He completely obliterated the meritorious deeds of the Stalin who led the Soviet people in waging resolute struggle against all internal and external foes and achieving great results in Socialist transformation and Socialist construction, who led the Soviet people in defending and consolidating the first Socialist country in the world and winning the glorious victory in the antifascist war, and who defended and developed Marxism-Leninism.

In completely negating Stalin at the 20th Congress of the CPSU, Khrushchov in effect negated the dictatorship of the proletariat and the fundamental theories of Marxism-Leninism which Stalin defended and developed. It was at that congress that Khrushchov, in his summary report, began the repudiation of Marxism-Leninism on a number of questions of principle.

In his report to the 20th Congress, under the pretext that " radical changes " had taken place in the world situation, Khrushchov put forward the thesis of " peaceful transition." He said that the road of the October Revolution was " the only correct road in those historical conditions," but that as the situation had changed, it had become possible to effect the transition from capitalism to Socialism " through the parliamentary road." In essence, this erroneous thesis is a clear revision of the Marxist-Leninist teachings on the state and revolution and a clear denial of the universal significance of the road of the October Revolution.

In his report, under the same pretext that " radical changes " had taken place in the world situation, Khrushchov also questioned the continued validity of Lenin's teachings on imperialism and on war and peace, and in fact tampered with Lenin's teachings.

Khrushchov pictured the U.S. Government and its head as people resisting the forces of war, and not as representatives of the imperialist forces of war. He said, " . . . the advocates of settling outstanding issues by means of war still hold strong positions there [in the United States]," and " . . . they continue to exert big pressure on the President and the Administration." He went on to say that the imperialists were beginning to admit that the positions-of-strength policy had failed and that " symptoms of a certain sobering up are appearing " among them. It was as much as saying that it was possible for the U.S. Government and its head not to represent the interests of U.S. monopoly capital and for them to abandon their policies of war and aggression and that they had become forces defending peace.

Khrushchov declared: " We want to be friends with the United States and to co-operate with it for peace and international security and also in the economic and cultural spheres." This wrong view later developed into the line of " Soviet-U.S. co-operation for the settlement of world problems."

Distorting Lenin's correct principle of peaceful co-existence between countries with different social systems, Khrushchov declared that peaceful co-existence was the " general line of the foreign policy " of the U.S.S.R. This amounted to excluding from the general line of foreign policy of the Socialist countries their mutual assistance and co-operation as well as assistance by them to the revolutionary struggles of the oppressed peoples and nations, or to subordinating all this to the policy of so-called " peaceful co-existence."

The questions raised by the leadership of the CPSU at the 20th Congress, and especially the questions of Stalin and of " peaceful transition," are by no means simply internal affairs of the CPSU; they are vital issues of common interest for all fraternal Parties. Without any prior consultation with the fraternal Parties, the leadership of the CPSU drew arbitrary conclusions; it forced the fraternal Parties to accept a fait accompli and, on the pretext of " combating the personality cult," crudely interfered in the internal affairs of fraternal Parties and countries and subverted their leaderships, thus pushing its policy of sectarianism and splittism in the international Communist movement.

Subsequent developments show with increasing clarity that the revision and betrayal of Marxism-Leninism and proletarian internationalism by the leaders of the CPC have grown out of the above errors.

The CPC has always differed in principle in its view of the 20th Congress of the CPSU, and the leading comrades of the CPSU are well aware of this. Yet the open letter of the Central Committee of the CPSU asserts that the Communist Party of China previously gave the 20th Congress full support, that we " have made a 180-degree turn " in our evaluation of the 20th Congress, and that our position is full of " vacillations and waverings " and is " false."

It is impossible for the leadership of the CPSU to shut out the heavens with one palm. Let the facts speak for themselves.

On many occasions in internal discussions after the 20th Congress of the CPSU, leading comrades of the Central Committee of the CPC solemnly criticised the errors of the CPSU leadership.

In April 1956, less than two months after the 20th Congress, in conversations both with Comrade Mikoyan, Member of the Presidium of the Central Committee of the CPSU, and with the Soviet Ambassador to China, Comrade Mao Tse-tung expressed our views on the question of Stalin. He emphasised that Stalin's " merits outweighed his faults " and that it was necessary to " make a concrete analysis " and " an all-round evaluation " of Stalin.

On October 23, 1956, on receiving the Soviet Ambassador to China, Comrade Mao Tse-tung pointed out, " Stalin deserves to be criticised, but we do not agree with the method of criticism, and there are some other matters we do not agree with."

On November 30, 1956, on receiving the Soviet Ambassador to China, Comrade Mao Tse-tung again pointed out that the basic policy and line during the period when Stalin was in power were correct and that methods that are used against enemies must not be used against one's comrades.

Both Comrade Liu Shao-chi in his conversation with leaders of the CPSU in October 1956, and Comrade Chou En-lai in his conversations on October 1, 1956, with the delegation of the CPSU to the Eighth Congress of the CPC and on January 18, 1957, with leaders of the CPSU, also expressed our views on the question of Stalin, and both criticised the errors of the leaders of the CPSU as consisting chiefly of " total lack of an overall analysis " of Stalin, " lack of self-criticism " and " failure to consult with the fraternal Parties in advance."

In internal discussions with comrades of the CPSU, leading comrades of the Central Committee of the CPC also stated where we differed on the question of peaceful transition. Furthermore, in November 1957 the Central Committee of the CPC presented the Central Committee of the CPSU with a written " Outline of Views on the Question of Peaceful Transition," comprehensively and clearly explaining the viewpoint of the CPC.

In their many internal discussions with comrades of the CPSU, leading comrades of the Central Committee of the CPC also systematically set forth our views on the international situation and the strategy of the international Communist movement, with direct reference to the errors of the 20th Congress of the CPSU.

These are plain facts. How can the leadership of the CPSU obliterate them by bare-faced lying?

Attempting to conceal these important facts, the Central Committee of the CPSU in its open letter quotes out of context public statements by Comrades Mao Tse-tung, Liu Shao-chi and Teng Hsiao-ping to show that at one time the Chinese Communist Party completely affirmed the 20th Congress of the CPSU. This is futile.

The fact is that at no time and in no place did the Chinese Communist Party completely affirm the 20th Congress of the CPSU, agree with the complete negation of Stalin or endorse the view of peaceful transition to Socialism through the " parliamentary road."

Not long after the 20th Congress of the CPSU, on April 5, 1956, we published " On the Historical Experience of the Dictatorship of the Proletariat "; then, on December 29, 1956, we published " More on the Historical Experience of the Dictatorship of the Proletariat." While refuting the anti-Communist slanders of the imperialists and reactionaries, these two articles made an all-round analysis of the life of Stalin, affirmed the universal significance of the road of the October Revolution, summed up the historical experience of the dictatorship of the proletariat, and tactfully but unequivocally criticised the erroneous propositions of the 20th Congress. Is this not a widely known fact?

Since the 20th Congress of the CPSU, the Chinese Communist Party has continued to display the portrait of Stalin along with those of the other great revolutionary leaders, Marx, Engels and Lenin. Is not this, too, a widely known fact?

It needs to be said, of course, that for the sake of unity against the enemy and out of consideration for the difficult position the leaders of the CPSU were then in, we refrained in those days from open criticism of the errors of the 20th Congress, because the imperialists and the reactionaries of all countries were exploiting these errors and carrying on frenzied activities against the Soviet Union, against Communism and against the people, and also because the leaders of the CPSU had not yet departed as far from Marxism-Leninism as they did later. We fervently hoped at the time that the leaders of the CPSU would put their errors right. Consequently, we invariably endeavoured to seek out positive aspects and on public occasions gave them whatever support was appropriate and necessary.

Even so, by stressing positive lessons and principles in their public speeches, leading comrades of the Central Committee of the CPC explained our position with regard to the 20th Congress of the CPSU.

The open letter of the Central Committee of the CPSU asserts that in his political report to the Eighth Congress of the CPC, Comrade Liu Shao-chi completely affirmed the 20th Congress of the CPSU. But it was in this very report that Comrade Liu Shao-chi spoke on the lessons of the Chinese revolution and explained that the road of " peaceful transition " was wrong and impracticable.

The open letter of the Central Committee of the CPSU asserts that in his report to the Eighth Congress of the CPC on the revision of the Party Constitution, Comrade Teng Hsiao-ping completely affirmed the " combat against the personality cult " conducted at the 20th Congress. But it was in this very report that Comrade Teng Hsiao-ping discussed at some length democratic centralism in the Party and the interrelationship between leaders and masses, explained the consistent and correct style of work of our Party, and thus in effect criticised the error of the 20th Congress concerning " combating the personality cult."

Is there anything wrong in the way we acted? Have we not done exactly what a Marxist-Leninist party ought to do by persevering in principle and upholding unity?

How can this consistently correct attitude of the Chinese Communist Party towards the 20th Congress be described as full of " vacillations and waverings," as " false " and as representing " a 180-degree turn "?

In making these charges against us in the open letter, perhaps the Central Committee of the CPSU thought it could deny the criticisms we made because they were known only to a few leaders of the CPSU, and that it could use falsehoods to deceive the broad masses of the membership of the CPSU and the Soviet people. But does this not prove its own falseness?

THE SERIOUS CONSEQUENCES OF THE 20TH CONGRESS OF THE CPSU

The open letter of the Central Committee of the CPSU loudly proclaims the " wonderful " and " majestic results " of the 20th Congress of the CPSU.

But history cannot be altered. People not suffering from too short a memory will recall that by its errors the 20th Congress produced not " wonderful " or " majestic results " but a discrediting of the Soviet Union, of the dictatorship of the proletariat and of Socialism and Communism, and gave an opportunity to the imperialists, the reactionaries and all the other enemies of Communism, with extremely serious consequences for the international Communist movement.

After the congress, swollen with arrogance the imperialists and reactionaries everywhere stirred up a worldwide tidal wave against the Soviet Union, against Communism and against the people. The U.S. imperialists saw the all-out attack on Stalin by the leadership of the CPSU as something that was " never so suited to our purposes," they talked openly about using

Khrushchov's secret report as a "weapon with which to destroy the prestige and influence of the Communist movement" and they took the opportunity to advocate "peaceful transformation" in the Soviet Union.

The Titoites became most aggressive. Flaunting their reactionary slogan of "anti-Stalinism," they wildly attacked the dictatorship of the proletariat and the Socialist system. They declared that the 20th Congress of the CPSU "created sufficient elements" for the "new course" which Yugoslavia had started and that "the question now is whether this course will win or the course of Stalinism will win again."

Those enemies of Communism, the Trotskyites, who had been in desperate straits, feverishly resumed activity. In its *Manifesto to the Workers and Peoples of the Entire World* the so-called Fourth International said, "Today, when the Kremlin leaders are themselves admitting the crimes of Stalin, they implicitly recognise that the indefatigable struggle carried on . . . by the world Trotskyist movement against the degeneration of the workers' state, was fully justified."

The errors of the 20th Congress brought great ideological confusion in the international Communist movement and caused it to be deluged with revisionist ideas. Along with the imperialists, the reactionaries and the Tito clique, renegades from Communism in many countries attacked Marxism-Leninism and the international Communist movement.

Most striking among the events which took place during this period were the incident in Soviet-Polish relations and the counter-revolutionary rebellion in Hungary. The two events were different in character. But the leadership of the CPSU made grave errors in both. By moving up troops in an attempt to subdue the Polish comrades by armed force it committed the error of great-power chauvinism. And at the critical moment when the Hungarian counter-revolutionaries had occupied Budapest, for a time it intended to adopt a policy of capitulation and abandon Socialist Hungary to counter-revolution.

These errors of the leadership of the CPSU inflated the arrogance of all the enemies of Communism, created serious difficulties for many fraternal Parties and caused the international Communist movement great damage.

In the face of this situation, the Chinese Communist Party and other fraternal Parties persevering in Marxism-Leninism firmly demanded repulsing the assaults of imperialism and reaction and safeguarding the socialist camp and the international Communist movement. We insisted on the taking of all necessary measures to smash the counter-revolutionary rebellion in Hungary and firmly opposed the abandonment of Socialist Hungary. We insisted that in the handling of problems between fraternal Parties and countries correct principles should be followed so as to strengthen the unity of the Socialist camp, and we firmly opposed the erroneous methods of great-power chauvinism. At the same time, we made very great efforts to safeguard the prestige of the CPSU.

At that time the leaders of the CPSU accepted our suggestion and on October 30, 1956, issued the Soviet Government's "Declaration on the Foundations of the Development and Further Strengthening of Friendship and Co-operation Between the Soviet Union and Other Socialist Countries," in which they examined some of their own past mistakes in handling their relations with fraternal countries. On November 1, the Chinese Government issued a statement expressing support for the Soviet Government's declaration.

All this we did in the interests of the international Communist movement, and also in order to persuade the leaders of the CPSU to draw the proper lessons and correct their errors in good time and not slide farther away from Marxism-Leninism. But subsequent events showed that the leaders of the CPSU nursed rancour against us and regarded the CPC and its perseverance in proletarian internationalism as the biggest obstacle to their wrong line.

THE 1957 MOSCOW MEETING OF FRATERNAL PARTIES

The 1957 Meeting of Representatives of the Communist and Workers' Parties took place in Moscow after the repulse of the heavy attacks of the imperialists and the reactionaries of various countries on the international Communist movement.

The open letter of the Central Committee of the CPSU says that the 20th Congress of the CPSU played a " tremendous role " in defining the general line of the international Communist movement. The facts show the very reverse. The erroneous views of the 20th Congress on many important questions of principle were rejected and corrected by the 1957 meeting of fraternal Parties.

The well-known Declaration of 1957, adopted by the Moscow Meeting, summed up the experience of the international Communist movement, set forth the common fighting tasks of all the Communist Parties, affirmed the universal significance of the road of the October Revolution, outlined the common laws governing Socialist revolution and Socialist construction and laid down the principles guiding relations among fraternal Parties and countries. The common line of the international Communist movement which was thus worked out at the meeting embodies the revolutionary principles of Marxism-Leninism and is opposed to the erroneous views deviating from Marxism-Leninism which were advanced by the 20th Congress. The principles guiding relations among fraternal Parties and countries laid down in the Declaration are concrete expressions of the principle of proletarian internationalism and stand opposed to the great-power chauvinism and sectarianism of the leadership of the CPSU.

The delegation of the CPC, which was headed by Comrade Mao Tse-tung, did a great deal of work during the meeting. On the one hand, it had full consultations with the leaders of the CPSU, and where necessary and appropriate waged struggle against them, in order to help them correct their errors; on the other hand, it held repeated exchanges of views with the leaders of other fraternal Parties in order that a common document acceptable to all might be worked out.

At this meeting, the chief subject of controversy between us and the delegation of the CPSU was the transition from capitalism to Socialism. In their original draft of the Declaration the leadership of the CPSU insisted on the inclusion of the erroneous views of the 20th Congress on peaceful transition. The original draft said not a word about non-peaceful transition, mentioning only peaceful transition; moreover, it described peaceful transition as " securing a majority in parliament and transforming parliament from an instrument of the bourgeois dictatorship into an instrument of a genuine people's state power." In fact, it substituted the " parliamentary road " advocated by the opportunists of the Second International for the road of the October Revolution and tampered with the basic Marxist-Leninist theory on the state and revolution. The Chinese Communist Party resolutely opposed the wrong views contained in the draft declaration submitted by the leadership of the CPSU. We expressed our views on the two successive drafts put forward by the Central Committee of the CPSU and made a considerable number of major changes of principle which we presented as our own revised draft. Repeated discussions were then held between the delegations of the Chinese and Soviet Parties on the basis of our revised draft before the " Joint Draft Declaration by the CPSU and the CPC " was submitted to the delegations of the other fraternal Parties for their opinions.

As a result of the common efforts of the delegations of the CPC and the other fraternal Parties, the meeting finally adopted the present version of the Declaration, which contains two major changes on the question of the transition from capitalism to Socialism compared with the first draft put forward by the leadership of the CPSU. First, while indicating the possibility of peaceful transition, the Declaration also points to the road of non-peaceful transition and stresses that " Leninism teaches, and experience confirms, that the ruling classes never relinquish power voluntarily." Secondly, while speaking of securing " a firm majority in parliament," the Declaration emphasises the need to " launch an extra-parliamentary mass struggle, smash the resistance of the reactionary forces and create the necessary conditions for peaceful realisation of the Socialist revolution."

Despite these changes, the formulation in the Declaration on the question of the transition from capitalism to Socialism was still unsatisfactory. We finally conceded the point only out of consideration for the repeatedly expressed wish of the leaders of the CPSU that the formulation should show some connection with that of the 20th Congress of the CPSU.

However, we presented the Central Committee of the CPSU with an outline of our views on the question of peaceful transition in which the views of the CPC were explained comprehensively and clearly. The outline emphasises the following:

In the present situation of the international Communist movement, it is advantageous from the point of view of tactics to refer to the desire for peaceful transition. But it would be inappropriate to over-emphasise the possibility of peaceful transition.

They [the proletariat and the Communist Party] must be prepared at all times to repulse counter-revolutionary attacks and, at the critical juncture of the revolution when the working class is seizing state power, to overthrow the bourgeoisie by armed force if it uses armed force to suppress the people's revolution (generally speaking, it is inevitable that the bourgeoisie will do so).

To obtain a majority in parliament is not the same as smashing the old state machinery (chiefly the armed forces) and establishing new state machinery (chiefly the armed forces). Unless the military-bureaucratic state machinery of the bourgeoisie is smashed, a parliamentary majority for the proletariat and their reliable allies will either be impossible . . . or undependable. . . . (See Appendix I.)

As a result of the common efforts of the delegations of the CPC and the other fraternal Parties, the 1957 Declaration also corrected the erroneous views which the CPSU leadership had put forward at the 20th Congress on such questions as imperialism and war and peace, and it added many important points on a number of questions of principle. The main additions were: the thesis that U.S. imperialism is the centre of world reaction and the sworn enemy of the people; the thesis that if imperialism should unleash a world war it would doom itself to destruction; the common laws governing the Socialist revolution and the building of Socialism; the principle of combining the universal truth of Marxism-Leninism with the concrete practice of revolution and construction in different countries; the formulation on the importance of applying dialectical materialism in practical work; the thesis that the seizure of political power by the working class is the beginning of the revolution and not its end; the thesis that it will take a fairly long time to solve the question of who will win—capitalism or Socialism; the thesis that the existence of bourgeois influence is an internal source of revisionism, while surrender to imperialist pressure is its external source; and so on.

At the same time, the delegation of the CPC made some necessary compromises. In addition to the formulation on the question of peaceful transition, we did not agree with the reference to the 20th Congress of the CPSU and suggested changes. But out of consideration for the difficult position of the leadership of the CPSU at the time, we did not insist on the changes.

Who could have imagined that these concessions which we made out of consideration for the larger interest would later be used by the leadership of the CPSU as an excuse for aggravating differences and creating a split in the international Communist movement?

The open letter of the Central Committee of the CPSU constantly equates the resolution of the 20th Congress of the CPSU with the Declaration of 1957 in its attempt to substitute the wrong line of the 20th Congress for the common line of the international communist movement. We have pointed out long ago, and deem it necessary to reiterate now, that in accordance with the principle that all fraternal Parties are independent and equal, no one is entitled to demand of fraternal Parties that they accept the resolutions of the congress of one Party or for that matter anything else; and the resolutions of a Party congress, whatever the Party, cannot be regarded as the common line of the international communist movement and have no binding force on other fraternal Parties. Only Marxism-Leninism and the documents unanimously agreed upon constitute the common code binding us and all fraternal Parties.

THE GROWTH OF THE REVISIONISM OF THE CPSU LEADERSHIP

After the Moscow Meeting of 1957 with its unanimously agreed Declaration, we hoped that the leadership of the CPSU would follow the line laid down in the Declaration and correct its errors. We regret to say that contrary to the expectations we and all other Marxist-Leninist fraternal Parties entertained, the leadership of the CPSU perpetrated increasingly serious violations of the revolutionary principles of the Declaration and the principles guiding relations among fraternal Parties and countries, and departed farther and farther from the path of Marxism-Leninism and proletarian internationalism. The revisionism of the leadership of the CPSU grew. This development aggravated the differences in the international communist movement and carried them to a new stage.

In complete disregard of the common conclusion of the 1957 Declaration that U.S. imperialism is the enemy of all the people of the world, the leadership of the CPSU passionately sought collaboration with U.S. imperialism and the settlement of world problems by the heads of the Soviet Union and the United States. Particularly around the time of the Camp David Talks in September 1959, Khrushchov lauded Eisenhower to the skies, hailing him as a man who " enjoys the absolute confidence of his people " and who " also worries about ensuring peace just as we do." Moreover, comrades of the CPSU energetically advertised the so-called " spirit of Camp David," whose existence Eisenhower himself denied, alleging that it marked " a new era in international relations " and " a turning-point in history."

Completely disregarding the revolutionary line of the 1957 Declaration, in statements by Khrushchov and in the Soviet press the leaders of the CPSU vigorously advocated their revisionist line of " peaceful coexistence," " peaceful competition " and " peaceful transition," praised the " wisdom " and " goodwill " of the imperialists, preached that " a world without weapons, without armed forces and without wars " could be brought into being while the greater part of the globe was still ruled and controlled by imperialism, and that universal and complete disarmament could " open up literally a new epoch in the economic development of Asia, Africa and Latin America," etc., etc.

The CPSU published many books and articles in which it tampered with the fundamental theories of Marxism-Leninism, emasculated their revolutionary spirit and propagated its revisionist views on a whole series of important problems of principle in the fields of philosophy, political economy, socialist and communist theory, history, literature and art.

The leadership of the CPSU actively endeavoured to impose its erroneous views on the international democratic organizations and to change their correct lines. An outstanding case in point was the behaviour of the Soviet comrades at the Peking session of the General Council of the World Federation of Trade Unions in June 1960.

Completely disregarding the principles guiding relations among fraternal Parties and countries which were laid down in the 1957 Declaration, the leaders of the CPSU, eager to curry favour with U.S. imperialism, engaged in unbridled activities against China. They regarded the Chinese Communist Party and its adherence to Marxism-Leninism as an obstacle to their revisionist line. They thought they had solved their internal problems and had " stabilized " their own position and could therefore step up their policy of " being friendly to enemies and tough with friends."

In 1958 the leadership of the CPSU put forward unreasonable demands designed to bring China under Soviet military control. These unreasonable demands were rightly and firmly rejected by the Chinese Government. Not long afterwards, in June 1959, the Soviet Government unilaterally tore up the agreement on new technology for national defence concluded between China and the Soviet Union in October 1957, and refused to provide China with a sample of an atomic bomb and technical data concerning its manufacture.

Then, on the eve of Khrushchov's visit to the United States, ignoring China's repeated objections, the leadership of the CPSU rushed out the TASS statement of September 9 on the Sino-Indian border incident, siding with the Indian reactionaries. In this way, the leadership of the CPSU brought the differences between China and the Soviet Union right into the open before the whole world.

The tearing up of the agreement on new technology for national defence by the leadership of the CPSU and its issuance of the statement on the Sino-Indian border clash on the eve of Khrushchov's visit to the United States were ceremonial gifts to Eisenhower so as to curry favour with the U.S. imperialists and create the so-called " spirit of Camp David."

The leaders of the CPSU and Soviet publications also levelled many virulent attacks on the domestic and foreign policies of the Chinese Communist Party. These attacks were almost invariably led by Khrushchov in person. He insinuated that China's socialist construction was " skipping over a stage " and was " equalitarian communism " and that China's people's communes were " in essence reactionary." By innuendo he maligned China as warlike, guilty of " adventurism," and so on and so forth. Back from the Camp David Talks, he went so far as to try to sell China the U.S. plot of " two Chinas " and, at the state banquet celebrating the Tenth Anniversary of the founding of the People's Republic of China, he read China a lecture against " testing by force the stability of the capitalist system."

The line of revisionism and splittism pursued by the leadership of the CPSU created serious confusion in the ranks of the international communist movement. It seemed as though U.S. imperialism had ceased to be the most ferocious enemy of the people of the world. Eisenhower was welcomed by certain Communists as a " peace envoy." Marxism-Leninism and the Declaration of 1957 seemed to be outmoded.

In the circumstances, in order to defend Marxism-Leninism and the 1957 Declaration and clear up the ideological confusion in the international communist movement, the Communist Party of China published " Long Live Leninism! " and two other articles in April 1960. In our consistent stand of persevering in principle and upholding unity, we concentrated on explaining the revolutionary theses of the 1957 Declaration and the fundamental Marxist-Leninist theories on imperialism, war and peace, proletarian revolution and the dictatorship of the proletariat. The views in these three articles were totally different from the series of erroneous views being propagated by the leaders of the CPSU. However, for the sake of the larger interest, we refrained from publicly criticizing the comrades of the CPSU and directed the spearhead of struggle against the imperialists and the Yugoslav revisionists.

The open letter of the Central Committee of the CPSU spends much energy distorting and attacking " Long Live Leninism! " and the two other articles, but is unable to support its attacks with any convincing arguments. We should like to put this question: In those circumstances, should we have kept silent on the wrong views and fatuous arguments which had become current? Did we not have the right, and indeed the duty, to come forward in defence of Marxism-Leninism and the Declaration of 1957?

THE SURPRISE ASSAULT ON THE CPC BY THE LEADERSHIP OF THE CPSU

A week after the publication of " Long Live Leninism! " and our two other articles, an American U-2 plane intruded into Soviet air space and the United States aborted the four-power summit conference. The " spirit of Camp David " completely vanished. Thus events entirely confirmed our views.

In the face of the arch enemy, it was imperative for the Communist Parties of China and the Soviet Union and the fraternal Parties of the whole world to eliminate their differences, strengthen their unity and wage a common struggle against the enemy. But that was not what happened. In the summer of 1960 there was a widening of the differences in the international communist movement, a large-scale campaign was launched against the CPC, and the leadership of the CPSU extended the ideological differences between the Chinese and Soviet Parties to the sphere of state relations.

In early June 1960 the Central Committee of the CPSU made the proposal that the Third Congress of the Rumanian Workers' Party to be held in Bucharest later in June should be taken as an opportunity for representatives of the Communist and Workers' Parties of all the socialist countries to meet and exchange views on the international situation following the miscarriage of the four-power summit conference caused by the United States. The Chinese Communist Party did not approve of this idea of a hasty meeting nor of the idea of a representative meeting of the Parties of the socialist countries alone. We made the positive proposal that there should be a meeting of representatives of all the Communist and Workers' Parties of the world and maintained that adequate preparations were necessary to make that meeting a success. Our proposal was agreed to by the CPSU. The two Parties thereupon agreed that, in preparation for the international meeting, the representatives of the fraternal Parties attending the Third Congress of the Rumanian Workers' Party could provisionally exchange views on the date and place for the meeting, but not take any decision.

At Bucharest, to our amazement, the leaders of the CPSU went back on their word and unleashed a surprise assault on the Chinese Communist Party, turning the spearhead of the struggle against us and not against U.S. imperialism.

The Bucharest meeting of representatives of fraternal Parties took place from June 24 to June 26. It is a plain lie for the open letter of the Central Committee of the CPSU to describe that meeting as " comradely assistance " to the Chinese Communist Party.

Indeed, on the eve of the meeting, the delegation of the CPSU headed by Khrushchov distributed among the representatives of some fraternal Parties, and read out to those of others, a Letter of Information dated June 21 from the Central Committee of the CPSU to the Central Committee of the CPC. This Letter of Information groundlessly slandered and attacked the CPC all along the line ; it constituted a programme for the anti-China campaign which was launched by the leadership of the CPSU.

In the meeting, Khrushchov took the lead in organizing a great converging onslaught on the Chinese Communist Party. In his speech he wantonly vilified the Chinese Communist Party as " madmen," " wanting to unleash war," " picking up the banner of the imperialist monopoly capitalists," being " pure nationalist " on the Sino-Indian boundary question and employing " Trotskyite ways " against the CPSU. Some of the fraternal Party representatives who obeyed Khrushchov and followed his lead also wantonly charged the CPC with being " dogmatic," " Left adventurist," " pseudo-revolutionary," " sectarian," " worse than Yugoslavia," and so on and so forth.

The anti-China campaign launched by Khrushchov at this meeting also came as a surprise to many fraternal Parties. The representatives of a number of Marxist-Leninist fraternal Parties took exception to the wrong action of the leadership of the CPSU.

At this meeting, the delegation of the Albanian Party of Labour refused to obey the baton of the leaders of the CPSU and firmly opposed their sectarian activities. Consequently the leaders of the CPSU regarded the Albanian Party of Labour as a thorn in their flesh. Whereupon they took increasingly drastic steps against the Albanian Party.

Can this dastardly attack on the CPC launched by the leadership of the CPSU be called " comradely assistance "? Of course not. It was a pre-arranged anti-China performance staged by the leadership of the CPSU; it was a serious and crude violation of the principles guiding relations among fraternal Parties as laid down in the 1957 Declaration; it was a large-scale attack on a Marxist-Leninist party by the revisionists, represented by the leaders of the CPSU.

In the circumstances, the Communist Party of China waged a tit-for-tat struggle against the leadership of the CPSU in defence of the positions of Marxism-Leninism and the principles guiding relations among fraternal Parties as laid down in the Declaration. For the sake of the larger interest, the delegation of the CPC in Bucharest signed the Communique on the meeting, and at the same time, on June 26, 1960, distributed a written statement upon the instructions of the Central Committee of the CPC. In this statement, the delegation of the CPC pointed out that Khrushchov's behaviour at the Bucharest meeting created an extremely bad precedent in the international Communist movement. It solemnly declared:

" There are differences between us and Comrade Khrushchov on a series of fundamental principles of Marxism-Leninism." " The future of the international Communist movement depends on the needs and the struggles of the people of all countries and on the guidance of Marxism-Leninism, and will never be decided by the baton of any one individual." " . . . . our Party believes in and obeys the truth of Marxism-Leninism and Marxism-Leninism alone, and will never submit to erroneous views which run counter to Marxism-Leninism." (See Appendix II.)

The leaders of the CPSU did not reconcile themselves to their failure to subdue the Chinese Communist Party in Bucharest. Immediately after the Bucharest meeting, they brought more pressure to bear on China by taking a number of steps to extend the ideological differences between the Chinese and Soviet Parties to the sphere of state relations.

In July the Soviet Government suddenly unilaterally decided to recall all the Soviet experts in China within one month, thereby tearing up hundreds of agreements and contracts. The Soviet side unilaterally scrapped the agreement on the publication of the magazine *Druzhba* (Friendship) by China in the Soviet Union and of *Su Chung You Hao* (Soviet-Chinese Friendship) by the Soviet Union in China and their distribution on reciprocal terms; it took the unwarranted step of demanding the recall by the Chinese Government of a staff member of the Chinese Embassy in the Soviet Union; and it provoked troubles on the Sino-Soviet border.

Apparently the leaders of the CPSU imagined that once they waved their baton, gathered a group of hatchetmen to make a converging assault, and applied immense political and economic pressures, they could force the

402

Chinese Communist Party to abandon its Marxist-Leninist and proletarian internationalist stand and submit to their revisionist and great-power chauvinist behests. But the tempered and long-tested Chinese Communist Party and Chinese people could be neither vanquished nor subdued. Those who tried to subjugate us by engineering a converging assault and applying pressures completely miscalculated.

We shall leave the details of the way the leadership of the CPSU sabotaged Sino-Soviet relations for other articles. Here we shall simply point out that on the subject of Sino-Soviet relations, the open letter of the Central Committee of the CPSU falsely charges China with extending the ideological differences to the sphere of state relations and with reducing trade between the two countries, while deliberately concealing the fact that the Soviet Government withdrew all its experts from China and unilaterally tore up hundreds of agreements and contracts, and that it was these unilateral Soviet actions which made Sino-Soviet trade shrink. For the leadership of the CPSU to deceive its members and the Soviet people in such a bare-faced way is truly sad.

THE STRUGGLE BETWEEN THE TWO LINES AT THE 1960 MEETING OF FRATERNAL PARTIES

In the latter half of 1960, a sharp struggle developed in the international Communist movement around the meeting of representatives of Communist and Workers' Parties. It was a struggle between the line of Marxism-Leninism and the line of revisionism and between the policy of persevering in principle and upholding unity and the policy of abandoning principle and creating splits.

It had become evident before the meeting that the leadership of the CPSU was stubbornly persisting in its wrong stand and was endeavouring to impose its wrong line on the international Communist movement.

The Chinese Communist Party was keenly aware of the gravity of the differences. In the interests of the international Communist movement we made many efforts, hoping that the leadership of the CPSU would not proceed too far down the wrong path.

On September 10, 1960, the Central Committee of the CPC replied to the June 21 Letter of Information of the Central Committee of the CPSU. In its reply which set forth the facts and reasoned things out, the Central Committee of the CPC systematically explained its views on a series of important questions of principle concerning the world situation and the international Communist movement, refuted the attacks of the leadership of the CPSU on us, criticised its wrong views and put forward to the Central Committee of the CPSU five positive proposals for settling the differences and attaining unity (for the five proposals, see Appendix III).

The Central Committee of the CPC subsequently sent a delegation to Moscow in September for talks with the delegation of the CPSU. During these talks, the delegation of the CPC pointed out that, while prettifying U.S. imperialism, the leadership of the CPSU was actively vilifying China and extending the ideological differences between the two Parties to state relations, and was thus treating enemies as brothers and brothers as enemies. Again and again the delegation of the CPC urged the leaders of the CPSU to change their wrong stand, return to the principles guiding relations among fraternal Parties and countries, and strengthen the unity between the Chinese and Soviet Parties and between the two countries in order to fight the common enemy. However, the leaders of the CPSU showed not the slightest intention of correcting their errors. Thus a sharp struggle became inevitable. This struggle first unfolded in the Drafting Committee, attended by the representatives of 26 fraternal Parties, which prepared the documents for the meeting of fraternal Parties, and later grew to unprecedented acuteness at the meeting of the representatives of 81 fraternal Parties.

In the meetings of the Drafting Committee in Moscow during October, the leaders of the CPSU attempted to force through their own draft statement, which contained a whole string of erroneous views. As a result of principled struggle by the delegations of the CPC and some other fraternal Parties, the Drafting Committee after heated debates made many important changes of principle in the draft statement put forward by the CPSU. The committee reached agreement on most of the draft. However, in their determination to continue the debate, the leadership of the CPSU refused to arrive at agreement on several important points at issue in the draft and, moreover, on Khrushchov's return from New York, even scrapped the agreements which had already been reached on some questions.

The Meeting of the Representatives of the 81 Fraternal Parties was held in Moscow in November 1960. Ignoring the desire of the Chinese and many other delegations to eliminate the differences and strengthen unity, on the eve of the meeting the leadership of the CPSU distributed among the representatives of the fraternal Parties gathered in Moscow a letter of more than sixty thousand words, which attacked the Chinese Communist Party more savagely than ever, thus provoking still sharper controversy.

Such was the most unnatural atmosphere in which the Meeting of the Representatives of the 81 Fraternal Parties was held. By their base conduct, the leaders of the CPSU brought the meeting to the brink of rupture. But the meeting finally reached agreement and achieved positive results, because the delegations of the Chinese Communist Party and some other fraternal Parties stuck to principle, persevered in struggle and upheld unity, and because the majority of the delegations of the fraternal Parties demanded unity and were against a split.

In its open letter, the Central Committee of the CPSU declares that the delegation of the CPC at this meeting " signed the Statement only when the danger arose of its full isolation." This is another lie.

What was the actual state of affairs?

It is true that, both before and during the meeting, the leadership of the CPSU engineered converging assaults on the Chinese Communist Party by a number of representatives of fraternal Parties, and relying on a so-called majority attempted to bring the delegations of the Chinese and other Marxist-Leninist parties to their knees and compel them to accept its revisionist line and views. However, the attempts to impose things on others met with failure, both in the Drafting Committee of the 26 fraternal Parties and in the Meeting of the Representatives of the 81 fraternal Parties.

The fact remains that many of the wrong theses they put forward in their draft statement were rejected. Here are some examples:

The wrong thesis of the leadership of the CPSU that peaceful co-existence and economic competition form the general line of the foreign policy of the Socialist countries was rejected.

Its wrong thesis that the emergence of a new stage in the general crisis of capitalism is the result of peaceful co-existence and peaceful competition was rejected.

Its wrong thesis that there is a growing possibility of peaceful transition was rejected.

Its wrong thesis about opposing the policy of " going it alone " on the part of the Socialist countries, which in effect meant opposing the policy of their relying mainly on themselves in construction was rejected.

Its wrong thesis concerning opposition to so-called " cliquish activities " and " factional activities " in the international Communist movement was rejected. In effect this thesis meant demanding that fraternal Parties should obey its baton, liquidating the principles of independence and equality in relations among fraternal Parties, and replacing the principle of reaching unanimity through consultation by the practice of subduing the minority by the majority.

Its wrong thesis underestimating the serious danger of modern revisionism was rejected.

The fact remains that many correct views on important principles set forth by the delegations of the Chinese and other fraternal Parties were written into the Statement. The theses on the unaltered nature of imperialism; on U.S. imperialism as the enemy of the people of the whole world; on the formation of the most extensive united front against U.S. imperialism; on the national-liberation movement as a significant force in preventing world war; on the thoroughgoing completion by the newly independent countries of their national democratic revolutions; on support by the Socialist countries and the international working-class movement for the national-liberation struggle; on the need for the working class and the masses in certain advanced capitalist countries under U.S. imperialist political, economic and military domination to direct their chief blows at U.S. imperialist domination and also at the monopoly capital and other reactionary forces at home which betray their national interests; on the principle of reaching unanimity through consultation among fraternal Parties; against the revisionist emasculation of the revolutionary spirit of Marxism-Leninism; on the betrayal of Marxism-Leninism by the leaders of the League of Communists of Yugoslavia; and so on—all these theses are present in the Statement as a result of the acceptance of the views of the Chinese and some other delegations.

It is, of course, necessary to add that after the leaders of the CPSU agreed to drop their erroneous propositions and accepted the correct propositions of other Parties, the delegations of the CPC and some other fraternal Parties also made certain concessions. For instance, we differed on the questions of the 20th Congress of the CPSU and of the forms of transition from capitalism to Socialism, but out of consideration for the needs of the CPSU and certain other fraternal Parties we agreed to the inclusion of the same wording on these two questions as that used in the 1957 Declaration. But we made it plain at the time to the leaders of the CPSU that this would be the last time we accommodated ourselves to such a formulation about the 20th Congress; we would never do so again.

From all the above it can be seen that the struggle between the two lines in the international Communist movement dominated the 1960 Moscow Meeting from beginning to end. The errors of the leadership of the CPSU as revealed at this meeting had developed further. From the draft statement of the leaders of the CPSU and their speeches during the meeting, it could be clearly seen that the main political content of the wrong line they were attempting to impose on the fraternal Parties consisted of the erroneous theories of " peaceful co-existence," " peaceful competition " and " peaceful transition," while its organisational content consisted of erroneous, sectarian and splitting policies. It was a revisionist line in fundamental conflict with Marxism-Leninism and proletarian internationalism. The delegations of the Chinese and other Marxist-Leninist parties resolutely opposed it and firmly upheld the line of Marxism-Leninism and proletarian internationalism.

The outcome of the struggle at this meeting was that the revisionist line and views of the leadership of the CPSU were in the main repudiated and that the Marxist-Leninist line gained a great victory. The revolutionary principles embodied in the Statement adopted at the meeting are powerful weapons in the hands of all fraternal Parties in the struggles against imperialism and for world peace, national liberation, people's democracy and Socialism; they are also powerful weapons in the hands of Marxist-Leninists throughout the world in combating modern revisionism.

At the meeting the fraternal Parties which upheld Marxism-Leninism earnestly criticised the erroneous views of the CPSU leadership and compelled it to accept many of their correct views; in doing so they changed the previous highly abnormal situation, in which not even the slightest criticism of the errors of the leadership of the CPSU was tolerated and its word was final. This was an event of great historical significance in the international Communist movement.

The Central Committee of the CPSU asserts in its open letter that the delegation of the CPC was " completely isolated " at the meeting. This is merely an impudent attempt on the part of the leadership of the CPSU to represent its defeat as a victory.

The principles of mutual solidarity as well as independence and equality among fraternal Parties and of reaching unanimity through consultation were observed at the meeting and the mistaken attempt of the leaders of the CPSU to use a majority to overrule the minority and to impose their views on other fraternal Parties was frustrated. The meeting demonstrated once again that in resolving differences among fraternal Parties it is most necessary for Marxist-Leninist parties to stick to principle, persevere in struggle and uphold unity.

THE REVISIONISM OF THE CPSU LEADERSHIP BECOMES SYSTEMATISED

The open letter of the Central Committee of the CPSU asserts that " the CPC leaders were only manoeuvring when they affixed their signatures to the Statement of 1960." Is that really a fact? No. On the contrary, it was the leaders of the CPSU and not we who were manoeuvring.

The facts have shown that at the 1960 meeting the leaders of the CPSU agreed to delete or change the erroneous propositions in their draft statement against their will and they were insincere in their acceptance of the correct propositions of fraternal Parties. They did not care two hoots about the document which was jointly agreed upon by the fraternal Parties.

The ink was scarcely dry on their signature to the 1960 Statement before they began wrecking it. On December 1 Khrushchov signed the Statement on behalf of the Central Committee of the CPSU and 24 hours later, violating what the fraternal Parties had agreed on, the same Khrushchov brazenly described Yugoslavia as a Socialist country at the banquet for the delegations of the fraterna! Parties.

After the meeting of the 81 fraternal Parties, the leaders of the CPSU became more and more blatant in wrecking the 1957 Declaration and the 1960 Statement. On the one hand, they took as their friend U.S. imperialism which the Statement declares to be the enemy of the people of the world, advocating " U.S.-Soviet co-operation " and expressing the desire to work together with Kennedy to " set about building durable bridges of confidence, mutual understanding and friendship." On the other hand, they took some fraternal Parties and countries as their enemies and drastically worsened the Soviet Union's relations with Albania.

The 22nd Congress of the CPSU in October 1961 marked a new low in the CPSU leadership's efforts to oppose Marxism-Leninism and split the socialist camp and the international Communist movement. It marked the systematisation of the revisionism which the leadership of the CPSU had developed step by step from the 20th Congress onward.

The leadership of the CPSU unleashed a great public attack on the Albanian Party of Labour at the 22nd Congress. In his speech Khrushchov went so far as openly to call for the overthrow of the Albanian leadership under Comrades Enver Hoxha and Mehmet Shehu. Thus the leadership of the CPSU established the vicious precedent of a Party congress being used for public attacks on other fraternal Parties.

Another important thing the leadership of the CPSU did at the congress was the renewed concentrated onslaught on Stalin five years after the complete negation of him at the 20th Congress and eight years after his death.

In the final analysis, this was done in order to enable the leaders of the CPSU to throw the Declaration and the Statement overboard, oppose Marxism-Leninism and pursue a systematically revisionist line.

Their revisionism was expressed in concentrated form in the new Programme of the CPSU which that congress adopted.

The open letter of the Central Committee of the CPSU says that the line of the 22nd Congress was " approved at the meetings of representatives of the Communist Parties and reflected in the Declaration and Statement." Is it not very careless of the leaders of the CPSU to make such a statement? How can they describe what happened in 1961 as having been " approved " or " reflected " at the meeting of the Communist and Workers' Parties in 1960, or as far back as that in 1957?

But leaving such silly self-commendation aside for the moment, let us first see the kind of stuff the Programme adopted at the 22nd Congress is made of.

Even a cursory study of the Programme and the report on it made by Khrushchov shows that it is an out-and-out revisionist programme which totally violates the fundamental theories of Marxism-Leninism and the revolutionary principles of the Declaration and the Statement.

It runs counter to the 1957 Declaration and the 1960 Statement on many important questions of principle. Many of the erroneous views of the leadership of the CPSU which were rejected at the 1960 meeting of fraternal Parties reappear. For instance, it describes peaceful coexistence as the general principle of foreign policy, one-sidedly stresses the possibility of peaceful transition and slanders the policy of a socialist country's relying mainly on its own efforts in construction as " going it alone."

The Programme goes a step further in systematizing the wrong line pursued by the leadership of the CPSU since its 20th Congress, the main content of which is " peaceful coexistence," " peaceful competition " and " peaceful transition."

The Programme crudely revises the essence of Marxism-Leninism, namely, its teachings on proletarian revolution, on the dictatorship of the proletariat and on the party of the proletariat, declaring that the dictatorship of the proletariat is no longer needed in the Soviet Union and that the nature of the CPSU as the vanguard of the proletariat has changed, and advancing preposterous theories of a " state of the whole people " and a " party of the entire people."

It substitutes humanism for the Marxist-Leninist theory of class struggle and substitutes the bourgeois slogans of " freedom," " equality " and " fraternity " for the ideals of communism.

It is a programme which opposes revolution on the part of the people still living under the imperialist and capitalist system, who comprise two-thirds of the world's population, and opposes the carrying of revolution through to completion on the part of the people already on the socialist road, who comprise one-third of the world's population. It is a revisionist programme for the preservation or restoration of capitalism.

The Communist Party of China resolutely opposed the errors of the 22nd Congress of the CPSU. Comrade Chou En-lai, who headed the delegation of the CPC to the congress, stated our Party's position in his speech there, and he also frankly criticised the errors of leadership of the CPSU in subsequent conversations with Khrushchov and other leaders of the CPSU.

In his conversation with the delegation of the CPC, Khrushchov flatly turned down our criticisms and advice and even expressed undisguised support for anti-Party elements in the Chinese Communist Party. He openly stated that after the 20th Congress of the CPSU, when the leaders of the CPSU were beginning to take a " road different from that of Stalin " (that is, when they were beginning to take the road of revisionism), they had still needed the support of the fraternal Parties. He said, " The voice of the Chinese Communist Party was then of great significance to us," but " things are different now," and " we are doing well " and " we shall go our own way."

Khrushchov's remarks showed that the leaders of the CPSU had made up their minds to go all the way down the road of revisionism and splitting. Although the Chinese Communist Party has frequently given them comradely advice, they have simply ignored it and shown not the slightest intention of mending their ways.

AN ADVERSE CURRENT THAT IS OPPOSED TO MARXISM-LENINISM AND IS SPLITTING THE INTERNATIONAL COMMUNIST MOVEMENT

In the open letter the leaders of the CPSU try hard to make people believe that after the 22nd Congress they " undertook new attempts " to improve relations between the Chinese and Soviet Parties and to strengthen unity among the fraternal Parties and countries.

This is another lie.

What are the facts?

They show that since the 22nd Congress the leadership of the CPSU has become more unbridled in violating the principles guiding relations among fraternal Parties and countries and in pursuing policies of great-power chauvinism, sectarianism and splittism in order to promote its own line of systematic revisionism, which is in complete violation of Marxism-Leninism. This has brought about a continuous deterioration in Sino-Soviet relations and grave damage to the unity of the fraternal Parties and countries.

The following are the main facts about how the leaders of the CPSU have sabotaged Sino-Soviet unity and the unity of fraternal Parties and countries since the 22nd Congress:

1. The leaders of the CPSU have tried hard to impose their erroneous line upon the international communist movement and to replace the Declaration and the Statement with their own revisionist programme. They describe their erroneous line as the "whole set of Leninist policies of the international communist movement of recent years," and they call their revisionist programme the "real Communist Manifesto of our time" and the "common programme" of the "Communist and Workers' Parties and of the people of the countries in the socialist community."

Any fraternal Party which rejects the erroneous line and programme of the CPSU and perseveres in the fundamental theories of Marxism-Leninism and the revolutionary principles of the Declaration and the Statement is looked upon as an enemy by the leaders of the CPSU, who oppose, attack and injure it and try to subvert its leadership by every possible means.

2. Disregarding everything, the leadership of the CPSU broke off diplomatic relations with socialist Albania, an unprecedented step in the history of relations between Fraternal Parties and countries.

3. The leadership of the CPSU has continued to exert pressure on China and to make outrageous attacks on the Chinese Communist Party. In its letter of February 22, 1962, to the Central Committee of the CPC, the Central Committee of the CPSU accused the CPC of taking a "special stand of their own" and pursuing a line at variance with the common course of the fraternal Parties, and even made a crime out of our support for the Marxist-Leninist Albanian Party of Labour. As preconditions for improving Sino-Soviet relations, the leaders of the CPSU attempted to compel the CPC to abandon its Marxist-Leninist and proletarian internationalist stand, abandon its consistent line, which is in full conformity with the revolutionary principles of the Declaration and the Statement, accept their erroneous line, and also accept as a *fait accompli* their violation of the principles guiding relations among fraternal Parties and countries. In its open letter, the Central Committee of the CPSU boasted of its letters to the Central Committee of the CPC during this period, of Khrushchov's remarks about his desire for unity in October 1962 to our Ambassador to the Soviet Union and so on, but in fact these were all acts for realizing their base attempt.

4. The Central Committee of the CPSU rejected the proposal made by the fraternal Parties of Indonesia, Viet Nam, New Zealand, etc., that a meeting of representatives of the fraternal Parties should be convened, as well as the five positive proposals made by the Central Committee of the

CPC in its letter of April 7, 1962, to the Central Committee of the CPSU for the preparation for a meeting of fraternal Parties. In its reply of May 30, 1962, to the Central Committee of the CPC, the Central Committee of the CPSU went so far as to make the demand that the Albanian comrades abandon their own stand as a precondition for improving Soviet-Albanian relations and also for convening a meeting of the fraternal Parties.

5. In April and May 1962 the leaders of the CPSU used their organs and personnel in Sinkiang, China, to carry out large-scale subversive activities in the Ili region and enticed and coerced several tens of thousands of Chinese citizens into going to the Soviet Union. The Chinese Government lodged repeated protests and made repeated representations, but the Soviet Government refused to repatriate these Chinese citizens on the pretext of the " sense of Soviet legality " and " humanitarianism." To this day this incident remains unsettled. This is indeed an astounding event, unheard of in the relations between socialist countries.

6. In August 1962 the Soviet Government formally notified China that the Soviet Union would conclude an agreement with the United States on the prevention of nuclear proliferation. This was a joint Soviet-U.S. plot to monopolize nuclear weapons and an attempt to deprive China of the right to possess nuclear weapons to resist the U.S. nuclear threat. The Chinese Government lodged repeated protests against this.

7. The leadership of the CPSU has become increasingly anxious to strike political bargains with U.S. imperialism and has been bent on forming a reactionary alliance with Kennedy, even at the expense of the interests of the socialist camp and the international communist movement. An outstanding example was the fact that, during the Caribbean crisis, the leadership of the CPSU committed the error of capitulationism by submitting to the nuclear blackmail of the U.S. imperialists and accepting the U.S. Government's demand for " international inspection " in violation of Cuban sovereignty.

8. The leadership of the CPSU has become increasingly anxious to collude with the Indian reactionaries and has been bent on forming a reactionary alliance with Nehru against socialist China. The leadership of the CPSU and its press openly sided with Indian reaction, condemned China for its just stand on the Sino-Indian border conflict and defended the Nehru government. Two-thirds of Soviet economic aid to India have been given since the Indian reactionaries provoked the Sino-Indian border conflict. Even after large-scale armed conflict on the Sino-Indian border began in the autumn of 1962, the leadership of the CPSU has continued to extend military aid to the Indian reactionaries.

9. The leadership of the CPSU has become increasingly anxious to collude with the Tito clique of Yugoslavia and has been bent on forming a reactionary alliance with the renegade Tito to oppose all Marxist-Leninist parties. After the 22nd Congress, it took a series of steps to reverse the verdict on the Tito clique and thus openly tore up the 1960 Statement.

10. Since November 1962 the leadership of the CPSU has launched still fiercer attacks, on an international scale, against the Chinese Communist Party and other Marxist-Leninist parties and whipped up a new adverse current in order to split the socialist camp and the international communist movement. Khrushchov made one statement after another and the Soviet press carried hundreds of articles attacking the Chinese Communist Party

on a whole set of issues. Directed by the leaders of the CPSU, the congresses of the fraternal Parties of Bulgaria, Hungary, Czechoslovakia, Italy and the Democratic Republic of Germany became stages for anti-China performances, and more than forty fraternal Parties published resolutions, statements or articles attacking the Chinese Communist Party and other Marxist-Leninist parties.

The facts cited above cannot possibly be denied by the leaders of the CPSU. These iron-clad facts prove that the " new attempts " they made after the 22nd Congress of the CPSU were aimed, not at improving Sino-Soviet relations and strengthening unity between the fraternal Parties and countries, but on the contrary, at further ganging up with the U.S. imperialists, the Indian reactionaries and the renegade Tito clique in order to create a wider split in the socialist camp and the international communist movement.

In these grave circumstances, the Chinese Communist Party had no alternative but to make open replies to the attacks of some fraternal Parties. Between December 15, 1962, and March 8, 1963, we published seven such replies. In these articles we continued to leave some leeway and did not criticise the leadership of the CPSU by name.

Despite the serious deterioration in Sino-Soviet relations resulting from the errors of the leadership of the CPSU, the Chinese Communist Party agreed to send its delegation to Moscow for the talks between the Chinese and Soviet Parties, and, in order that there might be a systematic exchange of views in the talks, put forward its proposal concerning the general line of the international communist movement in its letter of reply to the Central Committee of the CPSU dated June 14.

As subsequent facts have shown, the leaders of the CPSU were not only insincere about eliminating differences and strengthening unity, but used the talks as a smokescreen for covering up their activities to further worsen Sino-Soviet relations.

On the eve of the talks, the leaders of the CPSU publicly attacked the Chinese Communist Party by name, through statements and resolutions. At the same time, they unjustifiably expelled a number of Chinese embassy personnel and research students from the Soviet Union.

On July 14, that is, on the eve of the U.S.-British-Soviet talks, while the Sino-Soviet talks were still in progress, the leadership of the CPSU hastily published the open letter of the Central Committee of the CPSU to Party organizations and all Communists in the Soviet Union and launched unbridled attacks on the Chinese Communist Party. This was another precious ceremonial gift made by the leaders of the CPSU to the U.S. imperialists in order to curry favour with them.

Immediately afterwards in Moscow, the leadership of the CPSU signed the treaty on the partial halting of nuclear tests with the United States and Britain in open betrayal of the interests of the Soviet people, the people in the socialist camp including the Chinese people, and the peace-loving people of the world; there was a flurry of contacts between the Soviet Union and India; Khrushchov went to Yugoslavia for a " vacation "; the Soviet press launched a frenzied anti-China campaign; and so on and so forth. This whole train of events strikingly demonstrates that, disregarding everything, the leadership of the CPSU is allying with the imperialists, the reactionaries of all countries and the renegade Tito clique in order to oppose fraternal socialist countries and fraternal Marxist-Leninist parties. All this completely exposes the revisionist and splitting line which the leadership of the CPSU is following.

At present, the " anti-China chorus " of the imperialists, the reactionaries of all countries and the revisionists is making a lot of noise. And the campaign led by Khrushchov to oppose Marxism-Leninism and split the socialist camp and the international communist ranks is being carried on with growing intensity.

WHAT HAVE THE FACTS OF THE PAST SEVEN YEARS DEMONSTRATED?

In the foregoing we have reviewed at some length the origin and development of the differences. Our aim is to clarify the facts which were distorted in the open letter of the Central Committee of the CPSU and to help our Party members and our people and also the Marxist-Leninists and revolutionary people of the world to see the truth.

The facts of the past seven years have amply proved that the differences between the Chinese and Soviet Parties and within the international communist movement have arisen solely because the leadership of the CPSU has departed from Marxism-Leninism and the revolutionary principles of the 1957 Declaration and the 1960 Statement and pursued a revisionist and splitting line in the international communist movement. The process in which the leadership of the CPSU has gone farther and farther down the road of revisionism and splittism is the very process which has widened and aggravated the differences.

The facts of the past seven years have amply proved that the present differences within the international communist movement are differences between the line of adhering to Marxism-Leninism and the line of clinging to revisionism, between the revolutionary line and the non-revolutionary and counter-revolutionary line, between the anti-imperialist line and the line of capitulation to imperialism. They are differences between proletarian internationalism and great-power chauvinism, sectarianism and splittism.

The facts of the past seven years have amply proved that the road taken by the leadership of the CPSU is the course of allying with imperialism against socialism, allying with the United States against China, allying with the reactionaries of all countries against the people of the world, and allying with the renegade Tito clique against fraternal Marxist-Leninist parties. This erroneous line of the leadership of the CPSU has led to a revisionist flood on an international scale, brought the international communist movement face to face with the danger of a split of unprecedented gravity, and brought serious damage to the peoples' cause of world peace, national liberation, people's democracy and socialism.

The facts of the past seven years have also amply proved that the Communist Party of China has constantly striven to prevent the situation from deteriorating and to uphold principle, eliminate differences, strengthen unity and wage a common struggle against the enemy. We have exercised great restraint and done our very best.

The Communist Party of China has always stressed the importance of the Unity of the Chinese and Soviet Parties and the two countries. It has always held in respect the Communist Party of the Soviet Union created by the great Lenin. We have always cherished deep proletarian affection for the great CPSU and the great Soviet people. We have rejoiced over every achievement of the CPSU and the Soviet people, and we have been saddened by every error of the leadership of the CPSU that has harmed the socialist camp and the international communist movement.

It is not just today that the Chinese Communists have begun to discover the errors of the CPSU leadership. Ever since the 20th Congress of the CPSU, we have watched with concern as the leadership of the CPSU took the road of revisionism.

Confronted with this grave situation, our Party has scores of times and for a long period considered: What should we do?

We asked ourselves, should we follow the leadership of the CPSU and suit all our actions to its wishes? In that case, the leadership of the CPSU would of course rejoice, but would not we ourselves then turn into revisionists?

We also asked ourselves, should we keep silent about the errors of the leadership of the CPSU? We believed that its errors were not just accidental, individual and minor errors, but rather a whole series of errors of principle, which endanger the interests of the entire socialist camp and international communist movement. As a member in the ranks of the international communist movement, how could we be indifferent, and keep silent about these errors? If we should do that, would not we be abandoning our duty to defend Marxism-Leninism and proletarian internationalism?

We foresaw that if we criticised the errors of the leaders of the CPSU, they would certainly strike at us vindictively and thus inevitably cause serious damage to China's socialist construction. But should Communists take a stand of national egoism and not dare to uphold truth for fear of vindictive blows? Should Communists barter away principles?

We took into consideration the fact that the CPSU was built by Lenin, that it is the Party of the first socialist state, and that it enjoyed high prestige in the international communist movement and among the people of the whole world. Therefore, over a considerable period of time, we were particularly careful and patient in criticising the leaders of the CPSU, trying our best to confine such criticism to inter-Party talks between the leaders of the Chinese and Soviet Parties and to solve the differences through internal discussions without resorting to open polemics.

But all the comradely criticism and advice given to the leaders of the CPSU by responsible comrades of the Central Committee of the CPC in scores of inter-Party talks did not succeed in enabling them to return to the correct path. The leaders of the CPSU went farther and farther down the road of revisionism and splittism. In return for the advice we gave in goodwill, they applied a succession of political, economic and military pressures against us and launched increasingly violent attacks.

The leaders of the CPSU have a bad habit: they indiscriminatingly stick labels on anyone who criticises them.

They say, " You are anti-Soviet!" No, friends! The label " anti-Soviet " cannot be stuck on us. Our criticism of your errors is precisely for the sake of defending the great CPSU and the great Soviet Union and preventing their prestige from being badly damaged by you. To put it plainly, it is you, and not we, who are really anti-Soviet and who are defaming and discrediting the CPSU and the Soviet Union. Ever since the complete negation of Stalin at the 20th Congress of the CPSU, you have committed innumerable foul deeds. Not all the water in the Volga can wash away the great shame you have brought upon the CPSU and upon the Soviet Union.

They say, "You are trying to seize the leadership!" No, friends! It is not at all clever of you to make this slander. The way you put it, it would seem that some people are contending with you for some such thing as "the leadership." Is this not tantamount to shamelessly claiming that some sort of "leadership" exists in the international communist movement and that you have this "leadership"? It is a very, very bad habit of yours thus to put on the airs of a patriarchal party. It is entirely illegitimate. The 1957 Declaration and the 1960 Statement clearly state that all Communist Parties are independent and equal. According to this principle, the relations among fraternal Parties should under no circumstances be like the relations between a leading Party and the led, and much less like the relations between a patriarchal father and his son. We have always opposed any one Party commanding other fraternal Parties, and it has never occurred to us that we ourselves should command other fraternal Parties, and so the question of contending for leadership simply does not arise. What confronts the international communist movement now is not whether this or that Party should assume leadership, but whether to respond to the baton of revisionism or to uphold the revolutionary principles of the Declaration and the Statement and persevere in the revolutionary line of Marxism-Leninism. Our criticism of the leadership of the CPSU concerns its attempt to lord it over fraternal Parties and to impose its line of revisionism and splittism on them. What we desire is merely the independent and equal status of the fraternal Parties stipulated in the Declaration and the Statement and their unity on the basis of Marxism-Leninism and proletarian internationalism.

It is the leaders of the CPSU who have provoked and extended the present great debate in the international communist movement and forced it on us. Since they have levelled large-scale attacks and all kinds of unscrupulous slanders against us, and since they have openly betrayed Marxism-Leninism and proletarian internationalism and torn up the Declaration and the Statement, they cannot expect us to abstain from replying, from refuting their slanders, from safeguarding the Declaration and the Statement and from defending Marxism-Leninism. The debate is on, and right and wrong must be thoroughly clarified.

We Chinese Communists persevere in principle and uphold unity; we did so in the past, we do so now and we shall continue to do so in the future. While engaging in polemics with the leaders of the CPSU, we still hope they will realize that they have taken a most dangerous road by abandoning revolution, abandoning the revolutionary people of the world, abandoning the unity of the socialist camp and of the international communist movement and eagerly collaborating with the U.S. imperialists, the reactionaries of all countries and the renegade Tito clique.

The interests of Chinese and Soviet peoples, of the socialist camp, of the international communist movement and of the people throughout the world demand that all Communist and Workers' Parties should become united and oppose the common enemy.

We hereby appeal once again to the leadership of the CPSU to correct its errors and return to the path of Marxism-Leninism and proletarian internationalism, the path of the 1957 Declaration and the 1960 Statement.

The international communist movement is going through an important period. The present debate has a vital bearing on the future of the proletarian world revolution and the destiny of mankind. As history will prove, after this great debate Marxism-Leninism will shine forth still more brilliantly and the revolutionary cause of the international proletariat and the people of the world will win still greater victories.

Appendix I

OUTLINE OF VIEWS ON THE QUESTION OF PEACEFUL TRANSITION

November 10, 1957

I. On the question of the transition from capitalism to socialism, it would be more flexible to refer to the two possibilities, peaceful transition and non-peaceful transition, than to just one, and this would place us in a position where we can have the initiative politically at any time.

1. Referring to the possibility of peaceful transition indicates that for us the use of violence is primarily a matter of self-defence. It enables the Communist Parties in the capitalist countries to sidestep attacks on them on this issue, and it is politically advantageous—advantageous for winning the masses and also for depriving the bourgeoisie of its pretexts for such attacks and isolating it.

2. If practical possibilities for peaceful transition were to arise in individual countries in the future when the international or domestic situation changes drastically, we could then make timely use of the opportunity to win the support of the masses and solve the problem of state power by peaceful means.

3. Nevertheless, we should not tie our own hands because of this desire. The bourgeoisie will not step down from the stage of history voluntarily. This is a universal law of class struggle. In no country should the proletariat and the Communist Party slacken their preparations for the revolution in any way. They must be prepared at all times to repulse counter-revolutionary attacks and, at the critical juncture of the revolution when the working class is seizing state power, to overthrow the bourgeoisie by armed force if it uses armed force to suppress the people's revolution (generally speaking, it is inevitable that the bourgeoisie will do so).

II. In the present situation of the international communist movement, it is advantageous from the point of view of tactics to refer to the desire for peaceful transition. But it would be inappropriate to over-emphasise the possibility of peaceful transition. The reasons are:

1. Possibility and reality, the desire and whether or not it can be fulfilled, are two different matters. We should refer to the desire for peaceful transition, but we should not place our hopes mainly on it and therefore should not over-emphasise this aspect.

2. If too much stress is laid on the possibility of peaceful transition, and especially on the possibility of seizing state power by winning a majority in parliament it is liable to weaken the revolutionary will of the proletariat, the working people and the Communist Party and disarm them ideologically.

3. To the best of our knowledge, there is still not a single country where this possibility is of any practical significance. Even if it is slightly more

apparent in a particular country, over-emphasising this possibility is inappropriate because it does not conform with the realities in the overwhelming majority of countries. Should such a possibility actually occur in some country, the Communist Party there must on the one hand strive to realize it, and on the other hand always be prepared to repulse the armed attacks of the bourgeoisie.

4. The result of emphasising this possibility will neither weaken the reactionary nature of the bourgeoisie nor lull them.

5. Nor will such emphasis make the social democratic parties any more revolutionary.

6. Nor will such emphasis make Communist Parties grow any stronger. On the contrary, if some Communist Parties should as a result obscure their revolutionary features and thus become confused with the social democratic parties in the eyes of the people, they would only be weakened.

7. It is very hard to gather forces and prepare for the revolution, and after all parliamentary struggle is easy in comparison. We must fully utilise the parliamentary form of struggle, but its role is limited. What is most important is to proceed with the hard work of gathering the revolutionary forces.

III. To obtain a majority in parliament is not the same as smashing the old state machinery (chiefly the armed forces) and establishing new state machinery (chiefly the armed forces). Unless the military-bureaucratic state machinery of the bourgeoisie is smashed, a parliamentary majority for the proletariat and their reliable allies will either be impossible (because the bourgeoisie will amend the constitution whenever necessary in order to facilitate the consolidation of their dictatorship) or undependable (for instance, elections may be declared null and void, the Communist Party may be outlawed, parliament may be dissolved, etc.).

IV. Peaceful transition to socialism should not be interpreted in such a way as solely to mean transition through a parliamentary majority. The main question is that of the state machinery. In the 1870s, Marx was of the opinion that there was a possibility of achieving socialism in Britain by peaceful means, because " at that time England was a country in which militarism and bureaucracy were less pronounced than in any other." For a period after the February Revolution, Lenin hoped that through " all power to the Soviets " the revolution would develop peacefully and triumph, because at that time " the arms were in the hands of the people." Neither Marx nor Lenin meant that peaceful transition could be realized by using the old state machinery. Lenin repeatedly elaborated on the famous saying of Marx and Engels, " The working class cannot simply lay hold of the ready-made state machinery and wield it for its own purposes."

V. The social democratic parties are not parties of socialism. With the exception of certain Left wings, they are parties serving the bourgeoisie and capitalism. They are a variant of bourgeois political parties. On the question of socialist revolution, our position is fundamentally different from that of the social democratic parties. This distinction must not be obscured. To obscure this distinction only helps the leaders of the social democratic parties to deceive the masses and hinders us from winning the masses away from the influence of the social democratic parties. However, it is unquestionably very important to strengthen our work with respect to the social democratic parties and strive to establish a united front with their Left and middle groups.

VI. Such is our understanding of this question. We do hold differing views on this question, but out of various considerations we did not state our views after the 20th Congress of the Communist Party of the Soviet Union. Since a joint declaration is to be issued, we must now explain our views. However, this need not prevent us from attaining common language in the draft declaration. In order to show a connection between the formulation of this question in the draft declaration and the formulation of the 20th Congress of the Communist Party of the Soviet Union, we agree to take the draft put forward today by the Central Committee of the Communist Party of the Soviet Union as a basis, while proposing amendments in certain places.

Appendix II

STATEMENT OF THE DELEGATION OF THE CPC AT THE BUCHAREST MEETING OF FRATERNAL PARTIES

June 26, 1960

(1) The Central Committee of the Communist Party of China maintains that at this meeting Comrade Khrushchov of the Delegation of the Central Committee of the Communist Party of the Soviet Union has completely violated the long-standing principle in the international communist movement that questions of common concern should be settled by consultation among fraternal Parties, and has completely broken the agreement made prior to the meeting to confine it to an exchange of views and not to make any decision; this he has done by his surprise attack, putting forward a draft communique of the meeting without having consulted the fraternal Parties on its contents beforehand and without permitting full and normal discussion in the meetings. This is an abuse of the prestige enjoyed by the CPSU in the international communist movement, a prestige which has been built up over the long years since Lenin's time, and it is, moreover, an extremely crude act of imposing one's own will on other people. This attitude has nothing in common with Lenin's style of work, and this way of doing things creates an extremely bad precedent in the international communist movement. The Central Committee of the CPC considers that this attitude and this way of doing things on the part of Comrade Khrushchov will have extraordinarily grave consequences for the international communist movement.

(2) The Communist Party of China has always been faithful to Marxism-Leninism and steadfastly adhered to the theoretical positions of Marxism-Leninism. In the past two years and more, it has been completely faithful to the Moscow Declaration of 1957 and has firmly upheld all the Marxist-Leninist theses of the Declaration. There are differences between us and Comrade Khrushchov on a series of fundamental principles of Marxism-Leninism. These differences have a vital bearing on the interests of the entire socialist camp, on the interests of the proletariat and the working people of the whole world, on the question of whether the people of all countries will be able to preserve world peace and prevent the imperialists from launching a world war, and on the question of whether socialism will

continue to score victories in the capitalist world, which comprises two-thirds of the world's population and three-fourths of its land area. All Marxist-Leninists should adopt a serious attitude towards these differences, give them serious thought and hold comradely discussions, so as to achieve unanimous conclusions. However, the attitude Comrade Khrushchov has adopted is patriarchal, arbitrary and tyrannical. He has in fact treated the relationship between the great Communist Party of the Soviet Union and our Party not as one between brothers, but as one between patriarchal father and son. At this meeting he has exerted pressure in an attempt to make our Party submit to his non-Marxist-Leninist views. We hereby solemnly declare that our Party believes in and obeys the truth of Marxism-Leninism and Marxism-Leninism alone, and will never submit to erroneous views which run counter to Marxism-Leninism. We consider that certain views expressed by Comrade Khrushchov in his speech at the Third Congress of the Rumanian Party are erroneous and in contravention of the Moscow Declaration. His speech will be welcomed by the imperialists and the Tito clique and has indeed already been welcomed by them. When the occasion arises, we shall be ready to carry on serious discussions with the CPSU and other fraternal Parties on our differences with Comrade Khrushchov. As for the Letter of Information of the Communist Party of the Soviet Union to the Communist Party of China, which Comrade Khrushchov has distributed in Bucharest, the Central Committee of the CPC will reply to it in detail after carefully studying it; the reply will explain the differences of principle between the two Parties, setting forth the relevant facts, and the Central Committee of the Communist Party of China will hold serious, earnest and comradely discussions with fraternal Parties. We are convinced that in any case the truth of Marxism-Leninism will triumph in the end. Truth does not fear contention. Ultimately, it is impossible to portray truth as error or error as truth. The future of the international communist movement depends on the needs and the struggles of the people of all countries and on the guidance of Marxism-Leninism, and will never be decided by the baton of any one individual.

(3) We, the Communist Party of China, have always striven to safeguard the unity of all Communist Parties and the unity of all Socialist countries. For the sake of genuine unity in the international Communist ranks and for the sake of the common struggle against imperialism and reaction, we hold that it is necessary to unfold normal discussions on the differences and that serious questions of principle should not be settled in a hurry by abnormal methods or simply by vote. Nor should one impose on others arbitrary views which have not been tested in practice or which have already proved to be wrong in such tests. Comrade Khrushchov's way of doing things at this meeting is entirely detrimental to the unity of international Communism. But however Comrade Khrushchov may act, the unity of the Chinese and Soviet Parties and the unity of all the Communist and Workers' Parties is bound to be further strengthened and developed. We are deeply convinced that, as the international Communist movement and Marxism-Leninism develop, the unity of our ranks will constantly grow stronger.

(4) If the relations between our two Parties are viewed as a whole. the above-mentioned differences between Comrade Khrushchov and ourselves are only of a partial character. We hold that the main thing in the

relations between our two Parties is their unity in the struggle for the common cause; this is so because both our countries are Socialist countries and both our Parties are built on the principles of Marxism-Leninism, and are fighting to advance the cause of the whole Socialist camp to oppose imperialist aggression and to win world peace. We believe that Comrade Khrushchov and the Central Committee of the CPSU and we ourselves will be able to find opportunities to hold calm and comradely discussions and resolve our differences, so that the Chinese and Soviet Parties may become more united and their relations further strengthened. This will be highly beneficial to the Socialist camp and to the struggle of the people of the world against imperialist aggression and for world peace.

(5) We are glad to see that the draft communique of the meeting put forward here affirms the correctness of the Moscow Declaration. But the presentation of the Marxist-Leninist theses of the Moscow Declaration in this draft is inaccurate and one-sided. And it is wrong that the draft avoids taking a clear stand on the major problems in the current international situation and makes no mention at all of modern revisionism, the main danger in the international working-class movement. Therefore, this draft is unacceptable to us. For the sake of unity in the common struggle against the enemy, we have submitted a revised draft and propose that it be discussed. If it is not possible to reach agreement this time, we propose that a special drafting committee be set up to work out, after full discussion, a document which is acceptable to all.

Appendix III

The Five Proposals for Settlement of the Differences and Attainment of Unity Contained in the Letter of the Central Committee of the CPC in Reply to the Letter of Information of the Central Committee of the CPSU

September 10, 1960

Striving to settle the differences successfully and to attain unity, we put forward the following proposals in all sincerity:

(1) The fundamental principles of Marxism-Leninism and the principles of the Declaration and the Manifesto of the 1957 Moscow Meeting are the ideological foundation for the unity between our two Parties and among all fraternal Parties. All our statements and actions must be absolutely loyal to the fundamental principles of Marxism-Leninism and the principles of the Moscow Declaration, which we should use as the criteria for judging between truth and falsehood.

(2) The relations among the Socialist countries and among fraternal Parties must strictly conform to the principles of equality, comradeship and internationalism as stipulated by the Moscow Declaration.

(3) All disputes among socialist countries and among fraternal Parties must be settled in accordance with the stipulations of the Moscow Declaration through comradely and unhurried discussion. Both the Soviet Union and China, and both the Soviet and Chinese Parties, bear great responsibilities regarding the international situation and towards the international Communist movement. They should have full consultations and unhurried discussions on all important questions of common concern in

order to have unity of action. If the disputes between the Chinese and Soviet Parties cannot be settled for the time being in consultations between the two Parties, then unhurried discussions should be continued. When necessary, the views of both sides should be presented completely objectively to the Communist and Workers' Parties of all countries so that these Parties may make correct judgments after serious deliberation and in accordance with Marxism-Leninism and the principles of the Moscow Declaration.

(4) It is of the utmost importance for Communists to draw a clear line of demarcation between the enemy and ourselves, between truth and falsehood. Our two Parties should treasure and value our friendship and join hands to oppose the enemy, and should not make statements or take actions liable to undermine the unity between the two Parties and the two countries and thus give the enemy the opportunity of driving a wedge between us.

(5) On the basis of the above principles, our two Parties, together with other Communist and Workers' Parties, should strive through full preparation and consultation to make a success of the meeting of representatives of the Communist and Workers' Parties of all countries to be held in Moscow in November this year, and, at this meeting, should work out a document conforming to the fundamental principles of Marxism-Leninism and the principles of the 1957 Moscow Declaration to serve as a programme to which we should all adhere, a programme for our united struggle against the enemy.

[*Peking Review*, VI, 37 (September 13, 1963), pp. 6–23.]

Full title: The Origin and Development of the Differences Between the Leadership of the CPSU and Ourselves—Comment on the Open Letter of the Central Committee of the CPSU, by the Editorial Departments of *People's Daily* and *Red Flag*, September 6, 1963 (complete text).

DOCUMENT 11

On the Question of Stalin—Comment on the Open Letter of the Central Committee of the C.P.S.U. (2) September 13, 1963

. . . The leaders of the C.P.S.U. have accused the Chinese Communist Party of " defending " Stalin. Yes, we do defend Stalin. When Khrushchov distorts history and completely negates Stalin, naturally we have the inescapable duty to come forward and defend him in the interests of the international communist movement.

In defending Stalin, the Chinese Communist Party defends his correct side, defends the glorious history of struggle of the first state of the dictatorship of the proletariat, which was created by the October Revolution; it defends the glorious history of struggle of the C.P.S.U.; it defends the prestige of the international communist movement among working people throughout the world. In brief, it defends the theory and practice of Marxism-Leninism. It is not only the Chinese Communists who are doing this; all Communists devoted to Marxism-Leninism, all staunch revolutionaries and all fair-minded people have been doing the same thing.

While defending Stalin, we do not defend his mistakes. Long ago the Chinese Communists had first-hand experience of some of his mistakes. Of the erroneous " Left " and Right opportunist lines which emerged in the Chinese Communist Party at one time or another, some arose under the influence of certain mistakes of Stalin's, insofar as their international sources were concerned. In the late twenties, the thirties and the early and middle forties, the Chinese Marxist-Leninists represented by Comrades Mao Tse-tung and Liu Shao-chi resisted the influence of Stalin's mistakes; they gradually overcame the erroneous lines of " Left " and Right opportunism and finally led the Chinese revolution to victory.

But since some of the wrong ideas put forward by Stalin were accepted and applied by certain Chinese comrades, we Chinese should bear the responsibility. In its struggle against " Left " and Right opportunism, therefore, our Party criticized only its own erring comrades and never put the blame on Stalin. The purpose of our criticism was to distinguish between right and wrong, learn the appropriate lessons and advance the revolutionary cause. We merely asked the erring comrades that they should correct their mistakes. If they failed to do so, we waited until they were gradually awakened by their own practical experience, provided they did not organize secret groups for clandestine and disruptive activities. Our method was the proper method of inner-Party criticism and self-criticism; we started from the desire for unity and arrived at a new unity on a new basis through criticism and struggle, and thus good results were achieved. We held that these were contradictions among the people and not between the enemy and ourselves, and that therefore we should use the above method.

What attitude have Comrade Khrushchov and other leaders of the C.P.S.U. taken towards Stalin since the 20th Congress of the C.P.S.U.?

They have not made an overall historical and scientific analysis of his life and work but have completely negated him without any distinction between right and wrong.

They have treated Stalin not as a comrade but as an enemy.

They have not adopted the method of criticism and self-criticism to sum up experience but have blamed Stalin for all errors, or ascribed to him the " mistakes " they have arbitrarily invented.

They have not presented the facts and reasoned things out but have made demagogic personal attacks on Stalin in order to poison people's minds.

Khrushchov has abused Stalin as a " murderer," a " criminal," a " bandit," a " gambler," a " despot of the type of Ivan the Terrible," " the greatest dictator in Russian history," a " fool," an " idiot," etc. When we are compelled to cite all this filthy, vulgar and malicious language, we are afraid it may soil our pen and paper.

Khrushchov has maligned Stalin as " the greatest dictator in Russian history." Does not this mean that the Soviet people lived for 30 long years under the " tyranny " of " the greatest dictator in Russian history " and not under the socialist system? The great Soviet people and the revolutionary people of the whole world completely disagree with this slander!

Khrushchov has maligned Stalin as a " despot of the type of Ivan the Terrible." Does not this mean that the experience the great C.P.S.U. and the great Soviet people provided over 30 years for people the world over was not the experience of the dictatorship of the proletariat but that of life under the rule of a feudal " despot "? The great Soviet people, the Soviet Communists and Marxist-Leninists of the whole world completely disagree with this slander!

Khrushchov has maligned Stalin as a " bandit." Does not this mean that the first socialist state in the world was for a long period headed by a " bandit "? The great Soviet people and the revolutionary people of the whole world completely disagree with this slander!

Khrushchov has maligned Stalin as a " fool." Does not this mean that the C.P.S.U. which waged heroic revolutionary struggles over the past decades had a " fool " as its leader? The Soviet Communists and Marxist-Leninists of the whole world completely disagree with this slander!

Khrushchov has maligned Stalin as an " idiot." Does not this mean that the great Soviet Army which triumphed in the anti-fascist war had an " idiot " as its supreme commander? The glorious Soviet commanders and fighters and all anti-fascist fighters of the world completely disagree with this slander!

Khrushchov has maligned Stalin as a " murderer." Does not this mean that the international communist movement had a " murderer " as its teacher for decades? Communists of the whole world, including the Soviet Communists, completely disagree with this slander!

Khrushchov has maligned Stalin as a " gambler." Does not this mean that the revolutionary peoples had a " gambler " as their standard-bearer in the struggles against imperialism and reaction? All revolutionary people of the world, including the Soviet people, completely disagree with this slander!

Such abuse of Stalin by Khrushchov is a gross insult to the great Soviet people, a gross insult to the C.P.S.U., to the Soviet Army, to the dictatorship of the proletariat and to the socialist system, to the international communist movement, to the revolutionary people the world over and to Marxism-Leninism.

In what position does Khrushchov, who participated in the leadership of the Party and the state during Stalin's period, place himself when he beats his breast, pounds the table and shouts abuse of Stalin at the top of his voice? In the position of an accomplice to a " murderer " or a " bandit "? Or in the same position as a " fool " or an " idiot "?

What difference is there between such abuse of Stalin by Khrushchov and the abuse by the imperialists, the reactionaries in various countries, and the renegades to communism? Why such inveterate hatred of Stalin? Why attack him more ferociously than you do the enemy?

In abusing Stalin, Khrushchov is in fact wildly denouncing the Soviet system and state. His language in this connection is by no means weaker but is actually stronger than that of such renegades as Kautsky, Trotsky, Tito and Djilas.

People should quote the following passage from the open letter of the Central Committee of the C.P.S.U. and ask Khrushchov: " How can they say such a thing about the Party of the great Lenin, about the motherland of socialism, about the people who, the first in the world, accomplished a socialist revolution, upheld its great gains in the bitterest battles against international imperialism and domestic counter-revolution, and display miracles of heroism and dedication in the struggle for the building of communism, honestly fulfilling its internationalist duty to the working people of the world! "

In his article, " The Political Significance of Abuse," Lenin said, " Abuse in politics often covers up the utter lack of ideological content, the helplessness and the impotence, the annoying impotence of the abuser." Does this not apply to the leaders of the C.P.S.U. who, feeling constantly haunted by the spectre of Stalin, try to cover up their total lack of principle, their helplessness and annoying impotence by abusing Stalin?

The great majority of the Soviet people disapprove of such abuse of Stalin. They increasingly cherish the memory of Stalin. The leaders of the C.P.S.U. have seriously isolated themselves from the masses. They always feel they are being threatened by the haunting spectre of Stalin, which is in fact the broad masses' great dissatisfaction with the complete negation of Stalin. So far Khrushchov has not dared to let the Soviet people and the other people in the socialism camp see the secret report completely negating Stalin which he made to the 20th Congress of the C.P.S.U., because it is a report which cannot bear the light of day, a report which would seriously alienate the masses.

Especially noteworthy is the fact that while they abuse Stalin in every possible way, the leaders of the C.P.S.U. regard Eisenhower, Kennedy and the like " with respect and trust." They abuse Stalin as a " despot of the type of Ivan the Terrible " and " the greatest dictator in Russian history," but compliment both Eisenhower and Kennedy as " having the support of the absolute majority of the American people "! They abuse Stalin as an " idiot " but praise Eisenhower and Kennedy as " sensible "! On the one hand, they viciously lash at a great Marxist-Leninist, a great proletarian revolutionary and a great leader of the international communist movement, and on the other, they laud the chieftains of imperialism to the skies. Is there any possibility that the connection between these phenomena is merely accidental and that it does not follow with inexorable logic from the betrayal of Marxism-Leninism?

If his memory is not too short, Khrushchov ought to remember that at a mass rally held in Moscow in January 1937 he himself rightly condemned those who had attacked Stalin, saying, " In lifting their hand against Comrade Stalin, they lifted it against all of us, against the working class and the working people! In lifting their hand against Comrade Stalin, they lifted it against the teachings of Marx, Engels and Lenin!" Khrushchov himself repeatedly extolled Stalin as an "intimate friend and comrade-in-arms of the great Lenin," as " the greatest genius, teacher and leader of mankind " and " the great, ever victorious marshal," as " the sincere friend of the people " and as his " own father."

If one compares the remarks made by Khrushchov when Stalin was alive with those made after his death, one will not fail to see that Khrushchov has made a 180-degree turn in his evaluation of Stalin.

If his memory is not too short, Khrushchov should of course remember that during the period of Stalin's leadership he himself was particularly active in supporting and carrying out the then prevailing policy for suppressing counter-revolutionaries.

On June 6, 1937, at the Fifth Party Conference of Moscow Province, Khrushchov declared :

> Our Party will mercilessly crush the band of traitors and betrayers, and wipe out all the Trotskyist-Right dregs. . . . The guarantee of this is the unshakable leadership of our Central Committee, the unshakable leadership of our leader Comrade Stalin. . . . We shall totally annihilate the enemies—to the last man—and scatter their ashes to the winds.

On June 8, 1938, at the Fourth Party Conference of Kiev Province, Khrushchov declared :

> The Yakyirs, Balyitskys, Lyubchenkys, Zatonskys and other scum wanted to bring Polish landowners to the Ukraine, wanted to bring here the German fascists, landlords and capitalists. . . . We have annihilated a considerable number of enemies, but still not all. Therefore, it is necessary to keep our eyes open. We should bear firmly in mind the words of Comrade Stalin, that as long as capitalist encirclement exists, spies and saboteurs will be smuggled into our country.

Why does Khrushchov, who was in the leadership of the Party and the state in Stalin's period and who actively supported and firmly executed the policy for suppressing counter-revolutionaries, repudiate everything done during this period and shift the blame for all errors on to Stalin alone, while altogether whitewashing himself?

When Stalin did something wrong, he was capable of criticizing himself. For instance, he had given some bad counsel with regard to the Chinese revolution. After the victory of the Chinese revolution, he admitted his mistake. Stalin also admitted some of his mistakes in the work of purifying the Party ranks in his report to the 18th Congress of the C.P.S.U. (B) in 1939. But what about Khrushchov? He simply does not know what self-criticism is; all he does is to shift the entire blame on to others and claim the entire credit for himself.

It is not surprising that these ugly actions of Khrushchov's should have taken place when modern revisionism is on the rampage. As Lenin said in

1915 when he criticized the revisionists of the Second International for their betrayal of Marxism, " In our time when words previously spoken are forgotten, principles are abandoned, world outlook is discarded and resolutions and solemn promises are thrown away, it is not at all surprising that such a thing should happen." . . .

[*Peking Review*, VI, 38 (September 20, 1963), pp. 8–15, at pp. 10–12.]

Full title: On the Question of Stalin—Comment on the Open Letter of the Central Committee of the CPSU (2), by the Editorial Departments of *People's Daily* and *Red Flag*, September 13, 1963 (excerpts).

DOCUMENT 12

Soviet Government Statement, September 21, 1963

Another " statement by a spokesman of the Chinese government " against the treaty banning nuclear weapon tests in the atmosphere, in outer space and under water was issued in Peking on September 1, 1963.

On acquainting oneself with its contents, one immediately notices that on this occasion, too, a government statement is being used mainly in order to slander the Communist Party of the Soviet Union (C.P.S.U.) and the other Communist Parties in connection with a wide range of questions on which the leadership of the Communist Party of China (C.P.C.) has differences with the international communist movement.

In the new statement the government of the People's Republic of China actually leaves aside all the arguments put forward by the Soviet government and the governments of other socialist countries in favour of signing this treaty. The Chinese leaders apparently have nothing to say in justification of their opposition to the banning of nuclear tests and therefore make up for the lack of arguments with abuse and slander against the Soviet Union and its peaceloving foreign policy.

At the same time they again elaborate on their erroneous and adventurist platform on questions of war and peace, a platform which has been emphatically rejected by the peace-loving peoples. In addition, the Chinese leaders have openly attacked the agreed views and positions of the international communist movement and, instead of stepping up the struggle against imperialism, have turned the front against the fraternal socialist states and the Marxist-Leninist parties.

The Chinese government's statement of September 1, like the whole of the big propaganda campaign which was launched recently by the Chinese leadership, no longer constitutes comradely discussion between communists, but actions by persons who have set themselves the aim of discrediting the C.P.S.U. and the Soviet Union at all costs and of splitting the communist movement and undermining the unity of the anti-imperialist forces.

Being aware of the weakness of their ideological positions, the Chinese leaders are trying to drag the discussion on the principal questions of our times down to the level of a vociferous exchange of angry words and unfounded accusations. The Soviet government and the Communist Party of the Soviet Union will never set out on such a road—a road unworthy of communists.

We shall not trade abuse for abuse. At the same time we find it necessary to return once again to a detailed examination of the questions touched upon in the Chinese government's statement of September 1 and to declare our own position. This is all the more necessary since in this, the third statement, the policy of the Soviet Union is grossly distorted time and time again, facts which are common knowledge are misrepresented, and documents are even being falsified.

1

In its statement the Chinese government asserts that the treaty on the prohibition of nuclear tests in the atmosphere, in outer space and under water is a " deception," a " betrayal " of the interests of the socialist countries and of the peoples of the whole world.

Nothing could be more absurd than these claims. The reason the nuclear test-ban treaty has received such wide support throughout the world is that it meets the interests of all peaceloving peoples and is the first, though limited success, but a real success, for the struggle of the broad masses of the peoples of the whole world against the danger of nuclear war—a struggle which has been going on for many years. This success, far from lulling the vigilance of the peoples against the intrigues of imperialism, as the Chinese leaders assert, has infused new strength in the fighters for peace and strengthened belief in the possibility of forcing the imperialists to make concessions.

The peoples of the world see the practical significance of the treaty in the fact that its signing stops the contamination of the atmosphere with radioactive materials (strontium-90, caesium-137, etc.), which are dangerous to the health of the people, not only of the present but also of future generations. It is an open secret that the nuclear weapon tests held in the atmosphere, the total yield of which equals hundreds of millions of tons of T.N.T., have increased the level of radioactivity on our planet. Scientists have estimated that every new series of nuclear tests in the atmosphere places the health and the lives of hundreds of thousands of people in jeopardy.

It can be said with complete conviction—and the experience of the past years fully corroborates this—that if this treaty had not been signed, then this year or in the very near future, nuclear weapons tests would again have been held in the atmosphere, spreading to new geographical areas and, undoubtedly, increasing the danger of radioactive contamination. Further nuclear tests in the atmosphere would have increased the harmful influence of radioactivity on human beings, as well as on the animal and vegetable world.

The signing of the nuclear test-ban treaty is directly beneficial to the cause of peace and the interests of the peoples in other respects as well. Assuming that the treaty is observed by all countries, it will, to a certain extent, slow down a further increase of the nuclear arms race.

Yet it is not only in this that the positive significance of the treaty lies. The fact that the Soviet Union, on the one hand, and the United States and the United Kingdom, on the other, have succeeded in agreeing on the prohibition of nuclear tests in three environments, creates prerequisites for increasing trust between states with different social systems and, thus, also for new steps towards easing international tension.

It follows from what has been said above that the nuclear test-ban treaty is a good and useful thing for the people.

Of course, it would have been better if agreement had been reached, already at the present time, on the prohibition of all nuclear tests, including underground tests. It would have been still better to have arrived at the general prohibition and destruction of nuclear weapons. And it would have been extremely good for mankind to have achieved general and complete disarmament already today. Precisely such a proposal was made by the Soviet

427

government at the 15th session of the United Nations General Assembly in 1960. It is for this that the socialist countries, all the peaceloving forces, are striving. The nuclear test-ban treaty is precisely one of the links in this important struggle.

The attempts of the Chinese leaders to present matters as though the signing of the nuclear test-ban treaty tends to weaken the defence potential of the socialist community are absolutely untenable. Is it not a fact that the test-ban treaty imposes identical obligations on all the parties to it?—None of the states that have signed this document obtains any unilateral military advantages. Try as they may, the Chinese leaders are quite unable to prove that the nuclear test-ban agreement has given any unilateral advantage to the United States of America. In the latest statement, for instance, they argue that the United States has superiority, so they allege, as regards underground testing and that this is the main point. Yet it is precisely this that exposes the completely lame character of the arguments of the Chinese leadership, because in reality the essence of the matter is quite different.

It is no secret that the core of the nuclear power of the Soviet Union which deters the imperialists from aggression, is by no means composed of those types of nuclear weapons which are perfected by means of underground tests, but precisely of those with regard to which the balance is in favour of the Soviet Union, as many American leaders are compelled to admit. That is the first point.

Secondly, the treaty that has been signed does not prevent the Soviet Union from carrying out underground nuclear tests, should this be necessary in order to ensure the security of our country, the security of all the socialist states. If we were to speak at all about who has lost and who has gained from the conclusion of the treaty, it might be definitely stated: It is the forces of aggression and war that have lost, and it is the cause of peace and progress, it is all mankind that has gained.

The most diverse forces are coming out in support of the test-ban treaty. Over 90 states have signed it already. Among them, together with the socialist countries, are all the major powers of the world, with the exception of France, whose ruling circles have embarked on a plan for nuclear armament that has nothing to do with the interests of peace.

The overwhelming majority of the states of Asia, Africa and Latin America which have achieved national liberation, have acceded to the treaty. The treaty has been favourably assessed by international democratic organisations, trade unions, political parties and many progressive public organisations. Every day that goes by brings more and more reports of worldwide support for the treaty.

Fearing political isolation, even those for whom the treaty definitely goes against the grain have felt themselves compelled to join in the treaty. For want of anything better, the Chinese leaders are grasping at this fact in their hopeless attempts to compromise the treaty. Yet has the cause of peace suffered from the fact that the treaty has been signed, for instance, by the government of Western Germany, or by the government of Franco Spain? The fact that even those governments, hostile as they are to the cause of peace, have not dared to evade signing the treaty, shows its tremendous power of attraction for the masses of the people, which the ruling circles of the capitalist countries are compelled to take into account.

The worldwide referendum which has swept all continents following the conclusion of the treaty, has demonstrated that by coming out against the prohibition of nuclear tests, the Chinese leaders have suffered a serious moral and political defeat.

The unseemly attitude of the Chinese government with regard to the nuclear test-ban treaty does not have the support of the peoples, a fact which was amply demonstrated at the recent meeting of the executive committee of the Afro-Asian Solidarity Organisation in Nicosia. Hard as the Chinese delegates tried to induce those who took part in that meeting to refrain from passing a resolution approving the Moscow treaty, they had no success.

So as not to find themselves completely isolated and also in order to " save face," the Chinese representatives were compelled to dodge and wriggle in every way. They did not dare to vote against the resolution which voiced support for the Moscow treaty, although behind the scenes they conducted all kinds of intrigues against the treaty, and before they left Nicosia made a special statement on this question. An unenviable situation for those who try to pose as the only exponents of the views of the peoples of Asia and Africa!

The attempts of the Chinese leaders to appeal to the international communist movement and allege that their obstruction of the nuclear test-ban treaty follows from the documents of the Moscow meetings of Communist and Workers' Parties (!), are completely untenable. One can easily satisfy oneself that the position of the Chinese government amounts to complete apostasy from the common, collectively-formulated line of the communist movement on these questions. As is well known, the 1957 Moscow meeting of Communist Parties, together with the Declaration, approved a Peace Manifesto, which solemnly appealed to all people of good will, urging them to demand " prohibition of the manufacture and use of atomic and hydrogen weapons, and, *as a first step, an immediate end to the testing of these weapons.*" Under this document there is also the signature of the leader of the delegation of the Communist Party of China, Comrade Mao Tse-tung.

Is it a fact that the events of the subsequent period have compelled the world communist movement to change its attitude to the problem of banning nuclear weapon tests and drop from the agenda the task of struggling for the implementation of this demand? By no means—life itself has confirmed that this task confronts the peoples just as sharply as before, and this found expression in the decisions of the second international meeting of Communist and Workers' Parties in 1960.

The Statement adopted at the meeting of representatives of 81 parties says:

> " *The meeting considers that the implementation of the programme for general and complete disarmament, put forward by the Soviet Union, would be of historic importance for the destinies of mankind.* To realise this programme means to eliminate the very possibility of waging wars between countries. It is not easy to realise, owing to the stubborn resistance of the imperialists.
>
> " Hence it is essential to wage an active and determined struggle against the aggressive imperialist forces with the aim of carrying this programme into practice. It is necessary to wage this struggle on an increasing scale and to strive perseveringly to achieve tangible results—the *banning* of the *testing* and manufacture of nuclear weapons, the abolition of military blocs and war

bases on foreign soil and a substantial reduction of armed forces and armaments, all of which should pave the way to general disarmament."

That document also bears the signature of the delegation of the Communist Party of China.

This shows that the leadership of the Communist Party of China was coming out a short time ago, together with all the fraternal parties, in favour of banning nuclear weapon tests, regarding this as a first and necessary step towards general and complete disarmament.

Three years have gone by since then and the struggle of the peoples against nuclear weapon tests has mounted more and more. And now that it has been crowned with success, now that the first step has been taken and a test-ban treaty has been signed, the Chinese leaders have turned completely round and declared it to be "deception," "treason," "a conspiracy of the imperialists." What is the logic of this, may we ask?

Isn't it clear that we have here a complete renunciation by the Chinese leaders of decisions adopted by the fraternal parties, a complete departure by them from the jointly co-ordinated positions and commitments?

The Chinese leaders can issue a thousand and one more statements on the nuclear test-ban treaty, but they will not be able to whitewash their treachery and hypocrisy in the eyes of communists, in the eyes of all mankind.

Mankind's age-old dream of ruling out war from the life of society has been expressed by Marxist-Leninists in the slogan: "A world without armaments, a world without wars." The communists are consistently fighting for this great goal, rallying round their banner the broadest masses of the people of the entire world. This struggle does not at all signify, as the Chinese leaders claim, a departure from class positions but, on the contrary, fully accords with the class interests of the proletariat and all the working people, with the tasks of the social and national liberation of the peoples. This struggle strengthens the positions of the anti-imperialist forces and weakens imperialism.

Imperialism props up its domination by force of arms. To achieve disarmament means to deal a blow against the forces of imperialist aggression. It is not difficult to understand why the struggle for disarmament, for a world without armaments, is one of the most important directions of struggle against imperialism and against the aggressive policy it pursues.

The Chinese leaders pretend not to understand this. They deliberately present the struggle for disarmament as pacifism, thereby depriving it of its class essence and ignoring the fact that the broadest masses of the working people, above all, are interested in the solution of the problem of disarmament.

As a matter of fact, the arguments of the Chinese theoreticians place them right in a vicious circle, from which there is no way out. According to their logic, wars can be done away with and disarmament achieved only after imperialism has been abolished. At the same time the abolition of imperialism is directly linked with the need for the working class and all the masses of the people to undermine its militarist foundation. But this is precisely a struggle which the Chinese leaders denigrate in an arrogant way, calling it pacifism.

The fallacy of this position stems from the inability or unwillingness of the Chinese leaders to see the realistic ways of struggling against imperialism which are opening up in the present epoch. Their bombastic revolutionary phrases about the need to put an early end to imperialism, really cover up their lack of confidence in the forces of world socialism, in the forces of the working class and the national liberation movement, and their fear of difficulties in the struggle.

It should not cause surprise when such points of departure lead the Chinese leadership to capitulation on the most important questions of foreign policy, including the possibility of solving the problem of disarmament.

The world communist movement maintains that in our day the solution of the disarmament problem is a realistic and feasible goal. The possibility of achieving disarmament was already foreseen by the founders of scientific communism and, what is more, in an epoch when capitalism dominated the entire world. For instance, in describing the conditions in Europe at the end of the last quarter of the last century, Engels wrote in 1893 about the mad arms race, about the desire of every great power to outstrip the others in military preparedness. " Is it a fact that there is no other way out of the blind alley than a devastating war, the like of which has not been seen by the world?" he asked, and he replied: " I insist: disarmament, and thereby a guarantee of peace, is possible. . . ."

On the basis of what premises did Engels proceed in reaching this conclusion? Primarily on the basis of the fact that " in all countries the broad sections of the population with whom the obligation to supply the mass of the troops and to pay the bulk of the taxes almost exclusively lies, are calling for disarmament." (Marx and Engels, *Works,* second Russian edition, vol. 22, p. 387.)

It will be seen from what has been said above that Engels regarded disarmament as a problem with a most direct bearing on the interests of the broad masses of the people, and, if only because of this fact, as a profoundly political and, therefore, a class problem. This, of course, is a far cry from what the Chinese " theoreticians," who are so prone to pose as the most righteous of Marxists, have to say about disarmament.

In our day the prerequisites for success in the struggle for disarmament and peace have increased immeasurably.

The appearance of weapons of mass destruction has made disarmament a truly vital task of the broadest masses of the people. The forces of the international working class, the forces of the fighters for disarmament and peace have increased many times over. These forces now lean for support on the might of the world socialist system; they are led by the most influential political force of our times—the international communist movement. Their demand for disarmament is supported by dozens of peaceloving states, by peoples fighting for national liberation, by trade unions and by many political parties and democratic organisations.

Clearly, in such conditions, the question of whether or not there is to be war, whether or not it will be possible to achieve disarmament, depends to an increasing extent on the peoples themselves, on the peaceloving forces throughout the world, on the activity and scale of their struggle, and not on the imperialists.

It is a truism that as long as imperialism exists, it will retain its aggressive nature, its contradictions; it is fraught with war. Proceeding on this basis, the Chinese leaders claim that war is inevitable. Communists cannot adopt such a fatalistic attitude. We realise that the struggle against a new world war and for disarmament is not an easy task. But we clearly see the possibility of accomplishing this historic task, and we have done and are doing everything necessary to mobilise the peoples for the struggle against the arms race, the struggle to prevent a new world war.

Nor is it possible to ignore the fact that the leaders of the People's Republic of China have recently been attempting to use questions of disarmament for an unseemly political game.

Together with the other fraternal parties, the Chinese leaders signed the Statement of the 1960 Moscow meeting, which expresses support for the Soviet proposals for general and complete disarmament. But only a short time later they declared disarmament to be an illusion and launched a campaign against those proposals—a campaign which they have already been waging for some years. Suddenly, on July 31, 1963, the Chinese government loudly and solemnly proclaimed a programme for the complete prohibition and destruction of nuclear weapons and all means of delivering them to their targets. It was with a feeling of surprise that the public throughout the world saw that this programme had actually been compiled from earlier Soviet proposals, which had only recently been described in Peking as " illusions."

The question naturally arose: For the sake of what aims has the Chinese government come out with this programme now? It is not difficult to see that the Chinese leaders carried out this manoeuvre in the hope of setting up the demand for the prohibition and destruction of nuclear weapons in opposition to the nuclear test-ban treaty. But this manoeuvre has failed because everyone, even persons who are not well-versed in politics, realises that the ending of tests of nuclear weapons is not in contradiction with, but on the contrary, facilitates the task of entirely prohibiting and destroying those weapons.

In its new statement of September 1, however, the Chinese government is, in actual fact, again sounding a retreat.

It is leaving aside the solemnly-proclaimed programme of nuclear disarmament which was copied from Soviet proposals, and is narrowing things down merely to a prohibition of the use of nuclear weapons " just as the use of poison gases was prohibited." It is thus going back on its previous demand for the stopping of the production of nuclear weapons and for destroying the stockpiles of those weapons and the means of delivery.

The raising of the question of prohibiting the use of nuclear weapons is not new, either, of course. This proposal has been put forward and upheld by the Soviet Union and many other states for many years already. As much as two years ago, thanks to the joint efforts of the socialist countries and states of Asia, Africa and Latin America, it was possible to achieve the adoption by the United Nations General Assembly of a resolution on the need to conclude an international agreement prohibiting the use of nuclear weapons. The conclusion of such an agreement would undoubtedly be useful. One cannot, however, set up the task of achieving such an agreement in opposition to the nuclear test-ban treaty which has already been concluded, any more than one can reduce the entire struggle for disarmament to this—also partial—measure.

And so it is seen that the Chinese leaders do not have any programme for disarmament: they are not waging and do not want to wage a struggle for this great aim and if they do sometimes talk about disarmament, they do so only in order to cover up their real intentions.

2

The Chinese government statement says that in "justifying" the nuclear test-ban treaty (as though this treaty needs any justification?), the Soviet Union has put forward "slanderous inventions" of some sort about China. What is all this about? It has transpired that our statement of August 21 exposed the real motives guiding the Chinese leaders in their opposition to the nuclear test-ban treaty—it revealed their desire to acquire their own atom bomb at any cost. The Chinese leaders do not agree with this conclusion. In their statement of September 1 they even call it "ludicrous," and in order to make their reply more biting, they quote a Chinese legend with the following moral: "Everyone has his own ideals and it is not for dwarfs to measure with their own yardstick the deeds of giants."

It will be necessary to return once again to the motives that prompted the Peking "giants" to rush into battle against the nuclear test-ban treaty. What is said about this in their new statement? It actually confirms the conclusion we have drawn and proves once again that the negative attitude of the Chinese government to the nuclear test-ban treaty is explained precisely by their desire to make their country a nuclear power. The Chinese statement again repeats the allegation that the treaty perpetuates the three-power "monopoly" of atomic and hydrogen weapons and is aimed at "tying the hands of socialist countries, with the exception of the Soviet Union, and tying the hands of all peaceloving countries."

In the first place it is profoundly provocative that the Chinese leaders should have posed the question of a "monopoly" of nuclear weapons in such a way that the Soviet Union, a socialist state, is placed on the same footing as imperialist states—the United States of America and Britain. The peoples of the countries of the socialist community and all the peoples of the world know full well whom the nuclear weapons at the disposal of the Soviet state serve, and whom the nuclear arsenal of the imperialists serves.

But this is not the only point. The Chinese leaders also found it necessary to talk about "monopoly" in order to justify their right to nuclear weapons. But in vain do the authors of the statement try to speak for the socialist and all peaceloving countries. As is well known, not one of them has proclaimed that it is its intention to obtain nuclear weapons. Far from that, the governments of socialist states have more than once made statements to the effect that they do not intend to create their own nuclear weapons, being convinced that the nuclear rocket shield at the disposal of the Soviet Union offers them reliable protection.

This time, however, the Chinese government revealed its intentions even more openly, proclaiming for everyone to hear that in spite of all the economic difficulties experienced by its country, it was prepared to work, even if it took 100 years, to create its own atomic weapons. So we see that the schemes of the Peking "giants" are quite transparent.

Naturally, the question of whether or not China is to develop nuclear weapons is one for the People's Republic of China itself to decide. But the other socialist countries are entitled to say what they think about the Chinese government's attitude, which obstructs the nuclear test-ban treaty that has the unanimous support of all peoples. It is a fact that the international consequences of such an attitude directly affect all the socialist countries.

Their desire to provide themselves with the atom bomb at all costs and regardless of everything, cannot fail to give rise to serious doubts regarding the aims of the foreign policy of China's leaders.

It is a fact that they cannot prove that this is necessary in the interests of the defence of China and of the whole socialist camp. It is well known that the U.S.S.R.'s nuclear power is sufficient to wipe from the face of the earth any state or coalition of states that might encroach on the revolutionary gains of the socialist countries. Even the imperialists have no illusions on that subject.

In these conditions, need there be Chinese atom bombs, too, for the defence of the socialist camp? Of course not. The Chinese leaders themselves not so long ago admitted that inasmuch as the Soviet Union had achieved great successes in the production of nuclear weapons, China clearly " need not organise the production of such weapons, especially considering the fact that they are very costly." That was said by none other than Mao Tse-tung in September 1958.

What has changed since then? Has the nuclear rocket power of the U.S.S.R. become weaker since that time? On the contrary, the whole world is aware of our country's tremendous successes in this field. If anything has changed, it has been the policy of the government of the People's Republic of China, its attitude towards the Soviet Union, towards the whole socialist community.

In recent times much has been said about the fact that the spreading of nuclear weapons is not in the interests of peace. An increase in the number of socialist countries possessing nuclear weapons would immediately lead to a chain reaction in the imperialist camp, and the atomic cancer would spread throughout the entire globe, greatly increasing the threat of nuclear war.

The authors of the statement hint that the Soviet Union could, if it wanted to, present nuclear weapons to China with one hand and, with the other, could struggle against the United States giving nuclear weapons to Western Germany. However, such recipes, so to speak, have a nasty smell.

Indeed, what would have happened if the Soviet Union had, on the one hand, started arming its allies with atom bombs and, on the other, had poured forth declarations against similar actions on the part of the United States? What would have been the consequences of that? They would have been most deplorable.

If the United States imperialists have not agreed up to now to the atomic arming of Western Germany, Japan and their other allies, that is explained above all by the fact that they have not dared to act contrary to the position of the socialist countries and to the unanimous demand of the public in their own and other countries.

And what would happen if we were to follow the insistent advice from Peking? The aggressive circles in the United States and in the other imperialist countries would immediately make use of this in order to step up the nuclear arms race and involve more and more countries in it. That could only hinder the resistance of the masses of the people to the nuclear arms race in the capitalist countries. We consider that such a development of events would be very dangerous to the cause of peace.

The Chinese government believes that the atomic arming of Western Germany, Japan and the other imperialist powers could allegedly be compensated for by the appearance of nuclear weapons in China. Yet if we recognise that imperialism is the source of war, it is also necessary to recognise that the danger of war will increase in proportion to the number of imperialist states that receive nuclear weapons, especially so when they are countries where aggressive, revenge-seeking elements are so strong.

It is common knowledge that the rulers of Western Germany, for instance, are not only allies of American imperialism, but also have their own aggressive plans with regard to the German Democratic Republic, and with regard to Poland, Czechoslovakia and the Soviet Union as well, and are striving to secure the revision of frontiers. Revenge-seeking schemes are also being harboured by the Japanese reactionaries.

The reason why the imperialists of Western Germany and other countries are trying to acquire nuclear weapons for themselves can easily be explained: they need them in order to pursue their predatory, aggressive foreign policy. But it is inconceivable that people who call themselves Marxists should, by their policy, help revenge-seekers and other reactionaries to carry out their schemes. Giving revenge-seekers a chance to get hold of nuclear weapons is tantamount to putting a torch into the hands of a madman who is dancing on a keg of gunpowder.

Common sense indicates that in the interests of peace it is necessary to refrain from increasing the number of nuclear powers and to wage a struggle for the banning and complete elimination of nuclear weapons.

Unfortunately, common sense is far from being the strong point of the Chinese leaders. Otherwise they would at least have taken into account the interests of the economic development of their own country and would have been grateful to the Soviet Union for shouldering the difficult task of manufacturing nuclear weapons for the defence needs of the whole socialist camp. It is well known that China does not have surplus resources, and it takes enormous resources to produce nuclear weapons.

We have told the Chinese leaders all this honestly and frankly. But the authors of the statement have even tried to reproach us for this. Clearly wanting to play upon the national feelings of the Chinese people, they are presenting things as if the Soviet Union were gloating over China's poverty and backwardness. And they say this about the Soviet people, who themselves experienced tremendous privations in overcoming the age-old backwardness of tsarist Russia. We do not consider ours to be a poor country, but even we have much to do in order to put an end to those material difficulties which still exist for the time being and about which we speak openly.

Our party and the Soviet government have full understanding and full sympathy for the difficulties experienced by other peoples, by the great Chinese people. We know that the basic cause of those difficulties is China's grim past, the aftermath of imperialist domination, the many years of war, the iniquity of the feudal-bureaucratic rulers.

Soviet people sincerely rejoiced when, as a result of the heroic work of the Chinese people, China's face began to change, new factories and mills appeared, irrigation facilities were built and agriculture was being reconstructed in accordance with socialist principles. Comrade Nikita Khrushchov had this to say about that on November 29, 1956:

"Soviet people view with admiration the victories of the Chinese people, the victories of the glorious fraternal Communist Party of China, under whose leadership the Chinese people are successfully building socialism."

The Soviet people not only rejoiced at the successes of fraternal China, but also helped the Chinese people to overcome more quickly the dire legacy of the past, to develop successfully their national economy, to create new branches of industry, to carry out a technical revolution, to train national cadres and to put an end to poverty and want.

For some reason or other the Chinese leaders do not like it when we recall this. But we speak of our assistance not in order to boast about it, but in order to show other nations that the Soviet people honestly fulfil their international duty to the fraternal Chinese people. It is not our fault that the leaders of the People's Republic of China have curtailed economic co-operation with the Soviet Union and thereby deprived the Chinese people of a chance to benefit from the Soviet Union's unselfish help.

Precisely because the interests of the Chinese people are dear to us, we were upset by the turn which became apparent in the development of the Chinese national economy in 1958, when the leaders of the People's Republic of China proclaimed their line of the " Three Red Banners," announced the " Great Leap " and began setting up People's Communes. Our party saw that this was a road of dangerous experiments, a road of disregard for economic laws and for the experience of other socialist states. For instance, we could not help feeling doubts about the plan to increase steel output in the People's Republic of China from five million to 80–100 million tons in five years, and to increase total industrial output six and a half times over and agricultural production two and a half times over. These plan targets were not corroborated by any sound economic calculations. We could not fail to feel alarmed when, with every step they took, the leaders of the People's Republic of China began to pour abuse on the Leninist principle of material incentive, abandoned the principle of remunerating labour, and went over to equalitarian distribution in People's Communes.

Our party did not find it possible to come out with open criticism of this line of the Chinese leadership. At the same time we could not conduct propaganda for those unjustified experiments either, because we would thereby have been doing a poor service to the Chinese communists and would have been misleading other fraternal parties. We regarded it as our duty to tell the Chinese leaders in a comradely way as early as 1958 about our doubts concerning such " innovations."

This was said by Nikita Khrushchov personally to Mao Tse-tung in the summer of 1958. The head of the Soviet government pointed out in those conversations that many things which the Chinese comrades regarded as the very latest in Marxism, as a method of speeding up the building of communism, had already been tried out in practice by our own people during the first years of the revolution. In our day we learned that such a form of organising peasant production as the commune did not justify itself for many reasons. Our party accomplished the task of the socialist trans-formation of agriculture on the basis of Lenin's co-operative plan.

The Chinese leaders turned a deaf ear to our considerations and did not take into account the experience of our party and state. Moreover, people in China began calling us conservatives, believing that the " Great Leap " and the People's Communes would permit the People's Republic to skip a whole stage in the building of a new society and go over to communism straight away.

Everyone now knows what really came of all this. The industry and agriculture of China have been seriously upset and the leaders of the People's Republic have been compelled already for some years to work on so-called "adjustments" of the national economy, which actually means recognition of the utter failure of the line of the "Three Red Banners."

Today the leaders of China are trying to explain their country's serious economic difficulties by various objective reasons. What is more, they are striving to put the blame for these difficulties on the Soviet Union, alleging that failures in the Chinese economy occurred because the Soviet Union broke the existing agreements and recalled its specialists.

The Soviet government has already explained on more than one occasion the reasons why it was compelled to recall from China its specialists, who were placed by the Chinese authorities in conditions which ruled out the possibility of doing normal work and which were humiliating to their human dignity. And we do not consider it necessary to dwell at length on this question here.

The attempts of the Chinese leaders to justify difficulties in the development of the Chinese economy by references to the recall of Soviet specialists are absolutely artificial, all the more so since not a single Soviet specialist is known to have worked in Chinese agriculture or in many branches of industry. No matter how the Chinese leaders manoeuvre, they will have to admit, sooner or later, that the real reason for the dire state of the Chinese economy lies in the fact that Leninist principles of managing the socialist economy were flagrantly violated there and grave mistakes were made, for which the Chinese people are now having to pay.

In striving to justify their stand on the question of nuclear weapons, the leaders of the People's Republic of China have gone to such lengths as to say that the Soviet Union became, as from a certain time, an unreliable ally, that it cannot be relied upon now and this is why China, you see, should make her own nuclear weapons. In order to make this version, so to speak, look more trustworthy, they misrepresent the universally-known stand of the U.S.S.R. with regard to Taiwan * and accuse the Soviet Union of having agreed to recognise the existence of "two Chinas."

What "proofs" are brought forward to confirm this? Primarily that the Chiang Kai-shekites have signed the American copy of the nuclear test-ban treaty. In this connection the Chinese government hastened to declare: You accuse us of linking up with the American "wild men," the French extremists and the West German revenge-seekers, while you yourselves by signing the treaty, have landed in the same company with Chiang Kai-shek.

What a proof! As if the Chinese leaders did not know that the Chiang Kai-shekites have signed the treaty precisely for the purpose of speculating on the political miscalculations of the government of the People's Republic of China, on its irresponsible attitude with regard to the treaty, and thereby creating the impression that, as distinct from the People's Republic of China, they are allegedly in favour of the easing of international tension. American propaganda is using this in order to further its own ends in every possible way.

* Formosa.

It is not the Soviet Union that is to be blamed for the fact that the Chiang Kai-shek dregs and American propaganda have received material for such speculation, but the Chinese government, which is alone responsible for this. There can be no doubt that the imperialists will strive to avail themselves further of every such opportunity in their own interests. Nothing else can be expected of them.

As for our attitude to the Chiang Kai-shek clique, it is well known. We have not recognised and do not recognise the signature of a Chiang Kai-shek representative under any international documents. The Soviet government did not invite the Chiang Kai-shekite to sign the treaty and did not give its consent to this. Moreover, the Soviet government warned the United States government already during the talks on the conclusion of the treaty, that it would not recognise the signature of a representative of the Chiang Kai-shek clique and that the only legitimate signature of China under the treaty could be that of a representative of the People's Republic of China.

It can only be regretted that precisely this signature is lacking under the test-ban treaty.

The statement of the Chinese government also contains another nonsensical invention to the effect that the Soviet Union " wants China to agree to the shady schemes of the United States, aimed at setting up ' two Chinas.' " What is more, it refers to a statement of Comrade Nikita Khrushchov, made in October, 1959, during a conversation with leaders of the People's Republic of China. During this talk Nikita Khrushchov said, touching on the Taiwan question, that different ways to solve it were possible—not only military ways, but peaceful ways, too. Now the Chinese leaders, distorting the meaning of those pronouncements, strive to present the case as though the Soviet Union, in allowing for the possibility of a peaceful settlement of the Taiwan issue, thereby recognised a " two Chinas " situation.

But this, of course, is utter nonsense. It was none other than the government of the People's Republic of China that in its day put forward the idea of the peaceful reunification of Taiwan with the rest of the territory of China and was even ready, according to reports, to give Chiang Kai-shek a responsible post in the Chinese government. Did it thereby also want to legalise a " two Chinas " situation?

The whole world knows that the Soviet government has always shared and supported the stand of the People's Republic of China on the question of Taiwan.

The Soviet Union has never agreed, and never will agree to the wresting of Taiwan from China and it resolutely rejects the conception of "two Chinas." In the course of the talks with the United States President in 1959, the head of the Soviet government, Nikita Khrushchov, resolutely stressed that Taiwan was an inalienable part of China and that the Chinese people had every right to liberate Taiwan.

The message from the head of the Soviet government to the President of the United States of October 12, 1959, said:

" The so-called question of Taiwan is a question of relations between Chinese and Chinese, a purely internal matter for China. The extension to Taiwan of the system of government now existing on the rest of China's territory will, in actual fact, be the final stage of the revolutionary liberation process which has been going on in China for many years.

" No international complications would have arisen over Taiwan in general, had it not been for foreign interference in the civil war in China, had it not been for the situation artificially created in Taiwan as a result of the United States' military support and protection for Chiang Kai-shek."

Addressing the session of the United Nations General Assembly in 1960, the head of the Soviet government, Nikita Khrushchov, declared:

" It is not secret from anyone that the idea of ' two Chinas ' is actually a poorly-disguised diversion aimed at partitioning the territory of great China and at annexing one of the parts of that country—the province of Taiwan. It has long been clear that the provocative plans for creating ' two Chinas ' are doomed to failure and the sooner certain politicians in the United States realise this, the better it will be for the cause of world peace."

The Soviet Union has more than once proved by deeds its loyalty to its duty as an ally in relation to fraternal countries, including China. Who does not remember, for instance, that when a dangerous situation arose in the area of the Taiwan Strait in 1958, the Soviet government warned the President of the United States that it would regard an attack on the People's Republic of China as an attack on the Soviet Union and that if the aggressor used nuclear weapons, the Soviet Union would use its own nuclear rocket weapons to defend China.

During those anxious days the Chinese leadership was grateful for the effective Soviet support and duly appreciated the role of the Soviet Union in ensuring the security of the People's Republic of China. A letter from the central committee of the Communist Party of China of October 15, 1958, signed by Mao Tse-tung, said:

" We are deeply touched by your boundless devotion to the principles of Marxism-Leninism and internationalism.

" On behalf of all the comrades who are members of the Communist Party of China, I convey heartfelt gratitude. . . ."

After that, the letter continued as follows:

" We are fully confident that should the events on Taiwan resolve themselves into a war between China and the United States, the Soviet Union will unfailingly render assistance to us with all its strength. Actually, in our struggle with the Americans we have already now received powerful support from the Soviet Union."

The newspaper *People's Daily* wrote in the same vein (September 11, 1958):

" The statement of the Chairman of the U.S.S.R. Council of Ministers to the effect that an attack on the People's Republic of China would be tantamount to an attack on the Soviet Union and that the U.S.S.R., together with China, would do everything to uphold the security of both states and the interests of peace in the Far East and throughout the world, constitutes effective and powerful support for the people of China in their struggle against American armed provocations. This is a serious warning to the American rulers."

Now that the critical days of the Taiwan crisis are behind us, the Chinese government is claiming the direct opposite.

" A still greater absurdity," it says, in its statement of September 1, " is the fact that the Soviet statement also credits Soviet nuclear weapons with the victory of the Chinese people in smashing the armed provocation of American imperialism in the Taiwan Strait in 1958. . . . Although the situation in the area of Taiwan Strait was tense, nevertheless the possibility of nuclear war did not arise and there was no need to render support to China with Soviet nuclear weapons. When all that became clear to the Soviet leaders, they came out in support of China."

The Chinese leaders, it seems, have short memories. They think that facts can be assessed in one way today and in another tomorrow, and in yet another way the day after tomorrow. Unfortunately, such treatment of facts has become a usual method of struggle of the leaders of the People's Republic of China against the Communist Party of the Soviet Union and the other Marxist-Leninist parties. But slander and deceit only undermine their own authority and give rise to still greater doubts about the political aims of the Chinese leadership.

Matters, however, are not confined to this. Now that the United States imperialists are well aware of the strength of the Soviet nuclear rocket shield, which is reliably guarding the security of all socialist countries, the Chinese leaders are less afraid of the possibility of American aggression against China. In this situation they believe they can permit themselves to jeer at those very measures of the Soviet Union during the Taiwan crisis for which, at that time, they themselves warmly thanked us. The Chinese leaders now say cynically in their statement of September 1: "Well, Soviet leaders, protect us with your nuclear weapons, but we shall still criticise you."

In this connection one cannot but recall the old Russian proverb: "Don't foul the well; you may need its water!"

The statement of the Chinese government also contains the following amazing conclusion which deserves to be quoted:

"It is true that if Soviet leaders really adhered to the principles of proletarian internationalism, then China would not have had to ponder over the need to produce nuclear weapons. However, it is also true that if Soviet leaders really adhered to the principles of proletarian internationalism, they would have had no grounds whatsoever for preventing China from producing nuclear weapons."

There is also another proverb: "People who live in glass houses should not throw stones." The Chinese leaders, who are occupying a more than doubtful position, would do better to be careful in raising the question of proletarian internationalism and of who is violating its principles. The stones thrown by them are bouncing back, breaking to pieces their flimsy logical contrivances. Indeed, if the leaders of China follow the principles of proletarian internationalism, why are they trying so hard to get hold of their own atom bomb? After all, persons who are stopping at nothing in their desire to acquire new types of devastating weapons should, after all, have some motives? What is behind this desire?

From our point of view, the very idea of a need to acquire their own nuclear weapons can be conceived by the leaders of a country whose security is guaranteed by the whole might of the socialist camp, only when they have developed special aims and interests of some kind which cannot be supported by the military strength of the socialist camp. But only people who are renouncing proletarian internationalism, departing from socialist positions on questions of foreign policy and discarding the Leninist principles of peaceful co-existence, can develop aims and interests of such a kind.

Plans for developing nuclear weapons in order to increase, for instance, one's influence in countries of Asia, Africa and Latin America, or to create for oneself a "position of strength" on disputed international issues, or to increase international tension—such plans cannot possibly be made to accord with the peaceloving course in foreign policy pursued by the countries of the socialist system. We will be frank: we would not like to think that the government of the People's Republic of China is guided by such motives.

We are convinced that the prestige of any socialist country is measured by the example it sets the peoples in the struggle for the fulfilment of their aspirations, in the creation of a better life, in the development and strengthening of the economy and culture, improving the wellbeing of the working people and developing socialist democracy, in the struggle for peace on earth. That is what really increases the international authority of socialist countries in the eyes of the peoples throughout the world. And it is such a policy that was bequeathed to the communists by Marx, Engels and Lenin.

3

The Chinese leaders have had to justify themselves very often recently with regard to the just accusations, advanced by the world public, that, by their policy, they are leading matters to an aggravation of world tension and are pushing the world towards a thermonuclear war.

In the statement of September 1 the Chinese leaders try to prove that they have never come out against the policy of peace and peaceful co-existence, but, on the contrary, are the most fervent supporters of the prevention of war.

This statement by the Chinese leadership could be welcomed if it indeed signified a turning point in the views of the Chinese leaders on the question of war and peace and in their policy on the world scene.

In reality, however, we see that they are not even considering such a turning point, but, as before, are upholding their erroneous conception on the question of war and peace which is fraught with serious consequences for the security of nations. The difference between their present statements and the previous ones consists only in the fact that they are now trying still harder to screen their real position and to hide it behind words about peaceful wishes and their desire to preserve peace.

By resorting to denial and self-justification, however, the authors of the statement become still more confused and create new doubts with regard to the true attitude of the Chinese leadership to the problem of war and peace.

Indeed, what are they trying to prove? They allege that quotations from statements by Mao Tse-tung that not all, but half, of mankind would perish in a future war and from his well-known article *Long Live Leninism!* published in the magazine *Red Flag* on the "wonderful prospects" which allegedly would open up before mankind after a thermonuclear war, have been torn from the text and misinterpreted in Soviet documents.

Well, we are ready to examine the question of who is distorting and who is misinterpreting both quotations. We shall dwell on this below.

But don't the authors of the statement see that in this way they are giving themselves away lock, stock and barrel, that they are refuting but only once more confirming the grave fears of the world communist movement and the progressive public with regard to the position of the

Chinese leaders on the questions of war and peace? What are they arguing about? In effect, they are arguing about what part of mankind will perish in the event of a new world war—all or only half.

The statement says:

" The words of Mao Tse-tung, used by him in 1957 and quoted above, were addressed to those people who allege that in the case of a nuclear war being unleashed by imperialism mankind will perish.

The statement goes on to say,

" We do not agree with this view of theirs, so pessimistic and full of despair. We say that if imperialism unleashes a nuclear war, it will bring on the death of at least half of the world's population." And in conclusion it says: " We are confident of the bright future of mankind."

This is, indeed, monstrous talk! What " wonderful future " can one speak of in view of the prospect of the annihilation of half of mankind! No less dangerous is another fact, that the Chinese leaders are making their forecasts regarding the possible consequences of war not simply because they want to penetrate into the future with the eye of the mind, but in order to justify a definite policy.

The authors of the statement themselves do not deny this. Summing up the argument on how many people would perish in the flames of thermo-nuclear war, they write: " Essentially the question is what policy, after all, should be followed in the face of the nuclear blackmail and nuclear threat of the American imperialism—to offer resistance or to surrender?"

It goes without saying that no Soviet leader ever posed, or could pose, the question of surrender. It is not for surrender that the Soviet Union has created and is perfecting its enormous nuclear might. There is no doubt— nor can there be any—that if the imperialist aggressors attack the socialist camp, they will receive a crushing rebuff.

The question has to be posed differently: must we, seriously and with all our strength, fight for peace, must we adhere to the principles of peace-ful co-existence between states with different social systems as the general line of foreign policy, or take our cue from the " wild men " and compete with the imperialists in building up international tension? It is in solving this question that the Chinese leaders deliberate whether a half or all of mankind would be destroyed in the flames of a new war. If it would be " only " half, then a war may be risked because a " wonderful future " is in store for the other half!

That this is exactly how the question is being posed is evident also from the pronouncement by Mao Tse-tung even in the altered form in which it is given in the statement of the Chinese government of September " . . . if the worst came to the worst and half of mankind died, the other half would remain, while imperialism would be razed to the ground and the whole world would become socialist."

No less eloquent in this sense is the quotation from the magazine *Red Flag* which they are trying to deny, to the effect that in case of war the victorious peoples " will very quickly create a civilisation a thousand times higher on the ruins of destroyed imperialism."

We consider that it is absolutely impermissible for communists to argue from such positions and to determine a policy on the basis of how many people would perish in a thermonuclear holocaust: half of mankind or the whole of mankind.

We Marxist-Leninists hold the destinies of all the peoples close to our hearts. We realise full well what modern nuclear weapons are, and we therefore consider forecasting the scale of casualties in a future war to be absurd and irresponsible, and this is what the Chinese leaders are doing instead of concentrating their efforts on the struggle to prevent a new world war.

If communists, if the peace fighters, if all the peaceloving forces allow atomic bombs to start falling, then the question of how many people will perish and how many will survive will no longer be controlled by governments and political parties.

It will be decided by military technology, by the logic of the development of war and by the number of countries and peoples which will find themselves in the sphere of direct or indirect effects of nuclear weapons.

Trying to distort the clear-cut position of the C.P.S.U. on the question of atomic war and its consequences, the Chinese leaders ascribe to the C.P.S.U. leadership, to Comrade Nikita Khrushchov, a statement allegedly made by him at the Bucharest meeting of fraternal parties, to the effect that now that nuclear weapons exist, " an organised militia is not an army but cannon fodder." Having invented this absurdity, the authors of the statement immediately draw a staggering conclusion from it: " in the eyes of the Soviet leaders the entire 3,000 million people of the world are nothing but worthless rubbish."

Can there be anyone who knows the noble humanitarianism of Soviet foreign policy, and who is aware of our struggle for the future of the peoples, who would believe this invention? This is what Nikita Khrushchov actually said:

" Let the Chinese comrades take no offence. Of course you have a great experience of war, but chiefly of guerrilla war, while we fought a more serious, so to say classic, war against Hitler Germany. The imperialist strategists now regard divisions as cannon fodder. What counts with them now is who has hydrogen bombs and combat planes and how many. Whereas formerly the enemy had to be put out of action with the bayonet, now they will be dropping bombs."

This is what was said in Bucharest. What evil intent do the Chinese leaders read into this?

The Chinese theoreticians have tackled the task of substantiating their recipes for a " wonderful future " in earnest; they are even trying to substantiate some law according to which the more people perish, the better for the cause of the revolution.

" Reactionaries of all colours have sought to destroy the revolution by means of terror," says a Chinese publication entitled *Imperialism and All Reactionaries are Paper Tigers.*

" They thought that the more people were killed, the smaller would be the forces of the revolution. Contrary to such reactionary subjective wishes, the facts show that the more people that are killed by the reactionaries, the greater are the forces of the revolution, the nearer reaction is to its doom. This is an inexorable law."

The Chinese leaders are urging the socialist countries and communists to become fatalists and to accept the inevitability of sacrificing a half—if only a half!—of the population on the altar of a new war. It is clear that the losses of the countries with great density of population which would find themselves in the centre of hostilities would be even greater, and their peoples might cease to exist altogether.

As a matter of fact, they have spoken about this with the utmost frankness and on more than one occasion. For instance, when a Czechoslovak journalist pointed out in a conversation with Tao Chu, a member of the central committee of the Communist Party of China, that in Czechoslovakia with her population of 13 million, the entire nation might perish in a thermonuclear war, he was told:

> " In the case of a war of annihilation, the small countries belonging to the socialist camp would have to subordinate their interests to the common interests of the entire camp as a whole."

Another high Chinese official in a conversation with Soviet representatives contended that Comrade Togliatti, secretary-general of the Italian Communist Party, was mistaken when, expressing concern for the destiny of his people, he said that in the case of a thermonuclear war the whole of Italy would be destroyed.

> " But other peoples would remain," said that official, " and imperialism will be destroyed. . . ."

Such, in essence, is the point of view of the Chinese leaders on the questions of thermonuclear world war. They refuse to take into consideration the tremendous casualties that war would bring. They refuse to take scientific data into consideration and, with a stubbornness which is worthy of a better cause, keep repeating that one should not exaggerate the dangerous consequences of a world war, even if half of the population of our planet would die.

But even if part of humanity, whether more than half or less than half, survives, who can seriously believe that the survivors would be able rapidly to build a new high civilisation in conditions when cities and economic and cultural centres would have been reduced to radioactive rubble, when whole countries would have been consumed by nuclear fire and when the earth's atmosphere would have been poisoned with lethal radioactive matter.

In politics one must proceed not from Utopias but from the fact that thermonuclear war would entail disastrous consequences for all peoples and for the whole world. All countries, even those which survived the war, would be set back in their development by decades, perhaps even by centuries.

Neither will the picture of the birthrate in a world after a thermonuclear war look the way the Chinese leaders are trying to present it: half the people will perish but—who cares?—mothers will give birth to new ones and the human race will be none the worse for that.

The Chinese leaders refuse to take all these facts into consideration; in essence they preach that thermonuclear war is permissible. What is this, after all, a special brand of heroism or some new-fangled humanitarianism? Is such a position compatible with the noble duty of leaders of the working class, of working people?

Did they stop to ponder the question in Peking as to who, in point of fact, is destined to perish in the flames of a thermonuclear war if it does break out? The imperialists and monopolists? Not they alone, unfortunately. They will touch off the war, but it is the tremendous masses of working people—workers, peasants and intellectuals—that would perish in it.

Not a single Marxist party which has a responsibility to the people will ever accept the Chinese propositions as the basis of its policy.

This is how matters stand with regard to the substance of the argument. Let us now return to the question of quotations.

The authors of the statement quote a corrected version of Mao Tse-tung's pronouncement at the 1957 Moscow meeting which differs substantially from the genuine text. For the sake of truth we shall quote from the records of the meeting the words actually uttered by Mao Tse-tung in the presence of those taking part in the meeting. This pronouncement reveals most nakedly the erroneous views of the Chinese leadership.

"Can one guess," he said, "how great the toll of human casualties in a future war will be? Possibly it would be a third of the 2,700 million inhabitants of the entire world, i.e., only 900 million people. I consider this to be even low, if atomic bombs should actually fall. Of course it is most terrible. But even half would not be so bad. Why? Because it was not we that wanted it but they. It is they who are imposing war on us. If we fight, atomic and hydrogen weapons will be used. Personally I think that in the whole world there will be such suffering that half of humanity and perhaps more than a half will perish.

"I had an argument about this with Nehru. In this respect he is more pessimistic than I am. I told him that if half of humanity is destroyed, the other half will still remain but imperialism will be destroyed entirely and there will be only socialism in all the world, and within half a century, or a whole century, the population will again increase by even more than half."

The substance of this pronouncement is fully confirmed in the statement of September 1, but the version of the text cited in that document contains words and phrases which clearly betray a desire to veil its genuine meaning. For instance, the statement lays special emphasis on the words:

"Here in China we are engaged in construction, we want peace. However, if the imperialists, notwithstanding anything, impose a war we shall have to clench our teeth, postpone construction, to resume it after the war."

The point is, however, that these were not at all the words that were uttered at the 1957 meeting. This is what Mao Tse-tung actually said:

"In China construction has not got under way in earnest. If the imperialists impose a war on us, we shall be prepared to terminate the construction; let us first have a trial of strength, and then return to construction."

It will be clear to everyone that this pronouncement has an absolutely different meaning. What does the call "let us first have a trial of strength and then return to construction" mean? Is this a call for peace, for the struggle for peaceful co-existence? In essence, this means exactly an orientation towards an armed conflict, towards a military solution of the contradictions between socialism and capitalism. And no one could succeed in presenting this orientation as a slip of the tongue.

The Chinese leaders are displeased when they are reminded of this statement by Mao Tse-tung, and they claim that what was involved was the case of the imperialists thrusting war on the peoples. In this connection, we would like to ask: where and when did they speak of any other prospect of victory over capitalism? Where and when did they specifically declare that the socialist countries could defeat capitalism by the course of peaceful competition with it?

The Chinese press and the documents of the Chinese Communist Party systematically and stubbornly preach the idea that " peaceful economic competition is not a real means of struggle against imperialism," and that " peaceful co-existence cannot be recognised as the general policy of the socialist countries."

The facts show that instead of the policy of peaceful co-existence, the Chinese leaders are lavishly praising the " cold war " and a situation of world tension.

As far back as 1958, when the view concerning the supposed benefits which the cold war situation offered to the interests of the revolution was apparently only taking shape in Peking, the head of the People's Republic of China advanced the following ideas: The West thinks that it will profit from the cold war. However, the cold war " is more profitable to our countries." Later the Chinese leaders developed this kind of belief into a whole " theory."

> " In the talks on the questions of international policy," runs the resolution of the 3rd plenary meeting of the central committee of the Costa Rica People's Vanguard Party, " the Chinese leaders told our comrades that the ' cold war is a good thing ' and that the ' situation of tension is a good situation ' for the development of the revolutionary struggle."

These ideas are being extensively put forward in the Chinese press. Here are some examples. In one of its issues in December, 1962, the newspaper *People's Daily* said:

> " As to the assertion that it is possible to create ' a world without war,' this is certainly absolute nonsense."

Liao Cheng-chih, member of the central committee of the Communist Party of China, at the session of the World Peace Council in Stockholm in December, 1961, tried to prove that those who think that it is possible to reach agreement with the imperialists and ensure peaceful co-existence are deceiving themselves.

Let us analyse the real meaning of these propositions.

On the one hand, the Chinese leaders assert that war is inevitable as long as imperialism exists, and put forward the view that international tension and the cold war are a boon. On the other hand, they say that if world war does break out, nothing terrible will happen, because half mankind will remain alive anyway, and will build an even more wonderful future.

If you couple these views together, you will see clearly that they do not deal at all with what will happen if the imperialists unleash war, in spite of all the efforts of the forces of peace. Nothing of the kind, such talks are only a means of camouflage. In reality the stand of the Chinese leadership looks quite different. The war variant of the development of events is regarded by it as inevitable and even more desirable than the peaceful variant.

With all this in the background, it is hard for the Chinese leaders to present themselves as the champions of peace and of peaceful co-existence.

The core of the matter, however, is not only in quotations and statements, but in the fact that in recent years the Chinese leaders have been carrying out in practice a policy which leaves no doubts of their desire to undermine peaceful co-existence between states with different social systems.

Having no faith in the possibility of preventing a thermonuclear world war, the Chinese leaders are putting obstacles in the path of carrying out the measures proposed by the Soviet Union and the other socialist countries to lessen international tension. Every time that, thanks to the efforts of the socialist countries and peaceloving peoples, a relaxation of tension has taken place in recent years, the Chinese leadership has left no stone unturned in order to undermine such a relaxation.

No doubt remains now that one of the reasons for the attack by the Chinese leaders on the policy of the world communist movement was the lessening of international tension, which took place in 1959, when there was a definite relaxation in the cold war between the Soviet Union and the United States, especially after Comrade Khrushchov's trip to the U.S.A.

It cannot be considered as accidental that at that actual period the Chinese leaders got themselves involved in an armed clash on the Indian-Chinese border, and this besides creating an acute situation in that part of the world, was ultimately aimed at torpedoing the relaxation of international tension which had taken place.

Already at the time when the Chinese-Indian conflict began in 1959, the Soviet leaders told the Chinese government frankly that the aggravation of the dispute in connection with frontier territories in the Himalayas, territories inherited by China and India from the old days, and the development of this dispute into a large armed conflict was undesirable and fraught with negative consequences, not only for Chinese-Indian relations but for the whole international situation.

We consider that in frontier disputes, especially in a dispute of the type of the Chinese-Indian clash, one should adhere to the Leninist views according to which it is possible to settle any frontier problems without resorting to armed force, granted that both sides desire to do so.

Everyone can now see that the Chinese-Indian conflict in the Himalayas had the most negative consequences for the cause of peace, inflicted great harm on the unity of the anti-imperialist front in Asia and placed the progressive forces in India in an extremely difficult position.

As could be expected, China herself did not benefit in any way. And her prestige in the eyes of the peoples of the world, and especially of the Afro-Asian peoples, has certainly not grown.

It was with a feeling of bewilderment and bitterness that the peoples saw one of the socialist countries, which had recently become independent and served as a model to them, get itself involved in a military conflict with a young neutralist state and, using its military superiority, endeavour to gain for itself in that way a favourable solution of the problem of a certain part of territory.

The Chinese leaders ignored the comradely advice of other socialist and fraternal countries. Moreover, they saw in this an unwillingness to support them in the international arena and considered this comradely advice a great injury to themselves.

In the article *What is the Cause of the Dispute?*, the Chinese comrades directly link the beginning of their differences with the fraternal parties with the fact that the Soviet Union and other socialist countries failed to give unconditional support to China's stand in the conflict on the Indian-Chinese border.

The actions of the Chinese leaders, which undermine the policy of neutralism, in effect help the imperialist powers to increase their influence in the emancipated countries and especially in India.

All this can, of course, hold up the development of the struggle for national independence and have a negative effect on the balance of forces in the world arena: This attitude to a neutral country is all the more obscure in view of the fact that the government of the People's Republic of China has in every way been making overtures to the blatantly reactionary régimes in Asia and Africa, including countries which belong to the imperialist military blocs.

The Chinese leaders often use the question of the Soviet Union's aid to India for anti-Soviet purposes. However, they do not tell their people the truth of the fact that Soviet aid to the peoples of the emancipated countries is imbued with the desire to strengthen their economic and political positions in their struggle for independence and against imperialism.

That policy is also to be seen clearly in our relations with India. The Soviet Union helped the Indian people, who had shaken off the yoke of British imperialism, to gain a footing in neutral positions and to oppose the attempts of the imperialists to impose an economic yoke on India. We have always considered this policy to be correct, for it conforms to the interests of peace and socialism.

It would not be amiss to recall the fact that before 1959 the People's Republic of China pursued the same kind of policy with regard to India. We were glad to see the development of good-neighbourly relations between Asia's two largest states, their support of one another in the struggle for peace and against the aggressive designs of imperialism. We met with approval the friendly contacts between Chinese and Indian leaders, their joint statement in favour of peace, and especially, the Pancha Shila principles proclaimed by Premiers Chou En-lai and Nehru. In the light of all this, the Chinese-Indian armed conflict came as a complete surprise both to the Soviet people and to the whole world public.

The Chinese leaders are now making accusations, stating that India is waging war on China and using Soviet armaments. First of all, this is essentially not true to the facts; secondly, if one were to follow this kind of logic, the Indian government has a great deal more reason to declare that the Chinese troops are waging war on India and are using Soviet armaments—because everyone knows of the tremendous military aid which the Soviet Union gives to China.

In helping socialist China and peaceloving India, we have been prompted by the best of sentiments. We were proceeding from these friendly feelings and in the interests of strengthening the peace and unity of the anti-imperialist forces when we declared that the Chinese-Indian conflict evoked our deep regret. We still consider that the solution of that conflict in a peaceful way, through negotiations, would be in the interest of both the Chinese and Indian peoples and in the interests of world peace.

In recent years, on her borders with neighbouring states, the Chinese side has been stooping to acts of a nature which gives us reason to think that the government of the People's Republic of China is departing, on this question, more and more from Leninist positions. The leaders of the People's Republic of China are deliberately concentrating the people's attention on frontier problems, artificially fanning nationalist passions and dislike for other peoples.

Since 1960, Chinese servicemen and civilians have been systematically violating the Soviet frontier. In the one year of 1962, more than 5,000 violations of the Soviet frontier from the Chinese side have been recorded. Attempts are also being made to "develop" some parts of Soviet territory without permission.

One Chinese citizen who crossed the border had written instructions from the People's Committee of the Heilun Ch'iang province, which said:

> "When fish are being caught on the disputed islands of the Amur and the Ussuri, the Soviet border guards often demand that our fishermen leave these islands. We propose that the catching of fish on the disputed islands be continued and that the Soviet border guards be told that these islands belong to China, and that the border is being violated by them, not by us."

And further:

> ". . . our fishermen are not to be removed from these islands in any circumstances. We imagine that, in view of the friendly relations between our states, the Soviet side will not resort to force to remove our fishermen from the islands."

The Soviet government has already proposed many times to the government of the People's Republic of China that consultations be held on the question of the demarcation of specific sections of the frontier line, so as to exclude any possibility of misunderstanding. However, the Chinese side evades such consultations, while at the same time continuing to violate the border.

This cannot but make us wary, especially in view of the fact that Chinese propaganda is giving clear hints alleging that there has been unjust demarcation of some sections of the Soviet-Chinese border in the past.

However, the artificial creation, in our times, of any territorial problems —especially between socialist countries—would amount to entering on a very dangerous path. If, today, countries begin making territorial claims on one another, using as arguments certain ancient data and the graves of their forefathers, if they start fighting to revise the historically developed frontiers, this will lead to no good, but will merely create feuds among all peoples, to the joy of the enemies of peace.

It should not be forgotten that questions of territorial disputes and claims have often in the past been the source of acute friction and conflict between states, a source inflaming nationalist passions. It is common knowledge that territorial disputes and frontier conflicts have been used as pretexts for wars of conquest. That is why communists consistently work for the solution of frontier problems through negotiation. The socialist countries, guided in their relations by the principle of proletarian internationalism, should show other peoples an example in the friendly solution of territorial problems.

The Soviet Union has no frontier conflicts with any of her neighbouring states. And we are proud of this, because this situation is in line not only with the interests of the Soviet Union, but also with the interests of all the socialist countries and the interests of world peace.

The petty methods the Chinese leaders use in fighting against the Leninist course in foreign policy taken by the socialist countries can be particularly clearly seen in their pontifications on last year's crisis in the Caribbean. Quite a lot of space is devoted to this question in the September 1 statement. You can find there assertions that the cause of the crisis was the "reckless" behaviour of the Soviet leaders and that it was "adventurism" to install Soviet rockets on Cuba. There are also wordy allegations that the evacuation of those rockets from Cuba meant "capitulation." There is only one feature lacking from all these things discussed in the statement of the government of the People's Republic of China—and that is the truth.

Listening to the Chinese leaders, you would think that it was not the aggressiveness of American imperialism that placed the world on the brink of thermonuclear catastrophe in October 1962; it appears that American imperialism was not to blame, for it had not even thought of threatening Cuba!

This, however, is a flagrant lie, which Peking needs now in order to vilify the Soviet government's actions in retrospect—actions taken at a critical moment for the defence of the Cuban revolution from the threat of America's military intervention.

Neither the Cuban leaders nor the Soviet government had any doubts that this threat existed, and that the clouds were closing down over Cuba virtually day by day. The fact that the U.S. government and the Cuban counter-revolutionaries had reached an understanding for the invasion of Cuba, and that it was only left to select the moment for that invasion was confirmed, six months later, by a statement by Miro Cordona, leader of the Cuban counter-revolutionaries. In April 1963, he made public the fact that the Cuban counter-revolutionaries had signed an agreement with the U.S. government on the organisation of an invasion of Cuba.

In these conditions the Soviet Union, acting in the spirit of proletarian internationalism, supplied without hesitation its nuclear missile weapons for the defence of Cuba's revolutionary gains. The determination of the Cuban people and the Soviet rockets did their job. The American imperialists did not venture to attack Cuba, and the invasion plan was foiled. Moreover, assurance was received from the U.S. President that the U.S.A. would not undertake an attack on Cuba and would keep her allies from doing so in the future.

All this is well known to the entire world. And here is how Comrade Fidel Castro has assessed the role played by the Soviet Union in those grim days, its might, its policy in safeguarding the integrity of revolutionary Cuba. He said:

"Shining in eternal glory will be the country which, to protect a small people thousands of miles away from it, put in the balance of thermonuclear warfare its wellbeing, forged by 45 years of creative labour and at the price of tremendous sacrifices!

"The Soviet Union, which lost more people in the great patriotic war against the fascists than there are in the whole of Cuba in order to uphold its right to existence and to the development of its tremendous wealth, did not hesitate to assume the risk of a terrible war and the defence of our small country. History does not know such an example of solidarity.

"This is internationalism!

"This is communism!"

Need we add anything to those words of Comrade Fidel Castro? That is how the Soviet Union acted, guiding itself by the principles of proletarian internationalism. It acted—brushing aside the inflammatory "advice" which emanated from Peking during the Caribbean crisis—advice which would assuredly have plunged the world into the cauldron of thermonuclear war if we had followed it instead of the Leninist course of our foreign policy.

For, in effect, the Chinese leaders then tried to prod us into an extremely dangerous gamble and convert Cuba into a field where the concept formulated for the small peoples in Peking—to sacrifice themselves "for the sake of the wonderful future of mankind"—would have been tried out for the first time.

Now, when a year has passed since the Caribbean crisis, it is becoming even more clear that the Chinese leadership sabotaged the agreed actions of the socialist countries for ensuring the security of the island of freedom, and thereby played into the hands of the aggressive forces of imperialism.

The imperialist circles of the West do not conceal their satisfaction at the present line of the People's Republic of China, frankly declaring that the policy of the government of the People's Republic of China facilitates their actions in maintaining tension in the Caribbean. Can this line of the Chinese leaders be described otherwise than as a betrayal of the interests of the Cuban people, betrayal of the interests of the peoples of the socialist countries?

The policy of the Soviet government, directed towards a peaceful resolution of the Caribbean crisis, towards protecting the peaceful labours of the Cuban people, has been warmly and unanimously approved by the whole Soviet people, by all peaceloving people in the world. Only the extreme rancour of the Chinese leadership can explain the fact that they are still trying to speculate on the difficulties which existed during the solution of the Caribbean crisis, time and again advancing a provocative version of the policy of the U.S.S.R during that period.

4

This is not the first time that we have had to deal with statements by Chinese leaders alleging that the struggle to ease international tension, for the peaceful co-existence of states with different social systems, conflicts with the tasks of the world revolution and of the national liberation movement.

In their latest document, that of September 1, the Chinese leaders are again using a government statement to raise this question once again. They contend that the struggle of the Soviet Union for peace and peaceful co-existence is nothing else but a "ban on revolution," and forgetting the interests of the liberation struggle of the peoples.

Because a correct understanding of the problems of war, peace, and revolution in our time has assumed the utmost importance for working out the correct political line of the socialist countries and of the whole communist movement, we must demonstrate once more the falseness of the views and actions of the Chinese leadership on these questions, and set our own position.

Does the policy of peace and peaceful co-existence favour the development of revolutionary class struggle in the capitalist countries? Does it favour an upsurge of the national liberation movement? Is it in the interests of the working class, of the working masses—i.e. of the overwhelming majority of the population of the earth—to strengthen peace, to impose upon imperialism a policy of peaceful co-existence of states with different social systems? It is on the answer to these questions that the strategy and tactics of the working class and the communist movement in a large measure depend.

The entire experience of the working class and the national liberation movement in the postwar years shows convincingly that the struggle for socialism is closely interwoven with the struggle for peace, that not a single problem of any magnitude of the people's revolutionary and liberation struggles can now be regarded out of the context of the struggle for peace and peaceful co-existence.

Summing up this experience, the 1960 meeting of representatives of the Communist and Workers' Parties pointed out in its statement that it is exactly " in conditions of peaceful co-existence that favourable opportunities are provided for the development of the class struggle in the capitalist countries and the national liberation movement of the peoples of the colonial and dependent countries. In their turn, the successes of the revolutionary class and national liberation struggle promote peaceful co-existence."

Peace is the prime condition for strengthening and expanding the positions of socialism in the world arena. Socialism does not need war. In conditions of peace, the socialist system has the best chance of displaying its superiority over capitalism, of achieving successes in economic development, of developing democracy, raising the welfare and culture of the people. And this, as Lenin taught, is the principal medium through which the socialist countries have a revolutionary influence on other peoples.

In conditions of the peaceful co-existence of the two systems, an upsurge is taking place, an upsurge of the economic and political struggle of the working class, of the broad masses of the workers of the highly-developed capitalist countries against imperialism, for their vital interests, for socialism. In the 15 postwar years in the capitalist world, two-and-a-half times as many factory and office workers have taken part in strikes as in the 20 prewar years. The tide of the strike movement is rising higher and higher. Whereas 13,800,000 people took part in strikes in 1956, the figure rose to more than 60,000,000 in 1961. The international communist movement has grown into the biggest political force of our time.

Life shows that, far from impeding an upsurge of the national liberation movement, the policy of peace and of strengthening peaceful co-existence stimulates it. It is in the conditions of peaceful co-existence of states with different social systems that the peoples of more than 50 countries have achieved national independence.

Conditions of peace presented them with favourable opportunities for consolidating their political independence, for achieving economic independence, for overcoming age-old backwardness. The national democratic forces have a chance to press for the realisation of social reforms in the interests of the broad masses of the peoples. The countries which have freed themselves from colonial oppression are now becoming an increasingly important political factor in the international arena.

Not a single world problem can be decided any longer without their participation.

Peace is the true ally of socialism, of the international working class movement of the peoples fighting for national liberation, and time is working for socialism and progress, against imperialism.

And what would have happened if the socialist countries, the international communist movement, had accepted the line of the Chinese leaders on the issues of war and peace?

For the socialist countries, this would mean that they would have to curtail peaceful construction, to slow down the rate of development of the productive forces and of raising the living standards of the masses of the people, because it would be necessary for them to divert very substantial quantities of additional resources to military requirements.

Reactionary circles in the capitalist countries usually take advantage of an atmosphere of international tension to resort to violent repressions against the working class and democratic organisations, to decimate the communist parties and drive them underground, to attack the vital interests, the democratic rights and freedoms of the working people.

To countries that have freed themselves from colonialism, the stepping up of tension would complicate the solution of the task of creating a national industry, the task of ousting the imperialist monopolies from their economies, the task of the carrying out of social reforms by their progressive forces; it would have diverted their resources, scanty as they are, towards military preparations. That would have delayed the liberation of peoples still held in colonial bondage.

If the viewpoint of the Chinese leaders had come out on top, if, instead of fighting for peace, the communists had themselves adopted the road of aggravating international tension, if they had conceded that world war was fatally inevitable, then mankind would have been plunged into the thermonuclear holocaust. In vain do the Chinese leaders delude themselves and others into thinking that this would bring nearer the triumph of world revolution.

When the C.P.S.U. and the fraternal parties of other countries say that imperialism would be destroyed in the flames of a new world war, they proceed from the assumption that the working people themselves would overthrow the ruling, exploiting class of their countries on whom would lie the grave responsibility for the monstrous annihilation of millions upon millions of people. But if the communists, following the line of the Chinese leaders, lowered the banner of peace and—more than that—themselves helped to unleash war, would the masses of the people entrust their destinies to such inglorious communists?

No, the peoples would never forgive those who, in one way or another, pushed mankind into thermonuclear war, no matter with what revolutionary phrases this fact was camouflaged.

It will be easily seen that the policy of the Chinese leaders is directed against the fundamental interests of the masses of the people of all countries. In reality it is tantamount to a betrayal of world socialism, of the working class and the national liberation movement, to treason to the cause of world revolution.

Revising the teaching of Marxism-Leninism, revising the general line of the communist movement, the Chinese leaders are trying to impose on the international working class and the national liberation movement the theory of speeding revolution by means of " revolutionary wars."

They believe that only in this way can the socialist countries advance the cause of the revolution in the capitalist countries.

Here we are dealing with a violation of the Leninist thesis that revolution is the domestic affair of the working people of each country and that revolution cannot be imported from abroad. Having adopted the policy of speeding up revolution, the leaders of the People's Republic of China irresponsibly proceed from the assumption that revolutions are possible always, everywhere and under all conditions. They ignore the real balance of class forces, ignore the question of the existence of a revolutionary situation in any particular country and disregard the international situation.

The Chinese theoreticians deliberately make a hotch-potch of a multitude of different questions: world war, local wars, national liberation and civil wars, popular uprisings, peaceful and non-peaceful ways of revolution. They need to do this so as to distort the position of the C.P.S.U. and the other fraternal parties, to present matters as if the communist movement, by adopting a policy of defending peace, is by this very fact opposing revolution.

But the position of the C.P.S.U. and of the fraternal parties is clear. We are most resolutely opposed to world war, just as we are opposed in general to wars between states. Only the imperialists need a world war—so as to seize foreign territories, to enslave and plunder the peoples, to wage struggle against the socialist countries.

We maintain, firmly and consistently, that there is no justification—nor can there be any—for touching off a new world war which, in view of the destructive nature of modern weapons, would be a real disaster for the peoples. There need, of course, be no doubt that if the imperialists were to unleash war, the peoples would sweep capitalism away and bury it. But the communists, who represent the peoples, are called upon to do everything in their power to prevent a new world war.

At the same time, the C.P.S.U. and the other Marxist-Leninist parties consider it necessary to display the maximum vigilance with regard to all the local wars and conflicts engendered by the imperialists' "policy of strength." The facts show that, faced with an abrupt change in the balance of strength in favour of world socialism and fearing that a world war would end in complete collapse for the imperialists, some imperialist circles place their hopes on touching off local wars, striving in this way to achieve their aggressive designs.

It is the task of all democratic and peaceloving forces to give the most determined rebuff to the imperialist fomenters of local wars. This is all the more important since local wars might be the spark igniting the flames of world war. The Chinese leaders make a serious error by contending that local conflicts would under no conditions lead to universal thermonuclear war. The logic of this reasoning leads to the recognition of local wars as an acceptable and desirable political method for the socialist countries, too —in particular for the " export " of revolution.

But the entire experience of the postwar years—the experience of such crises as, for instance, the Suez crisis, caused by the Anglo-Franco-Israeli aggression against Egypt—shows how great is the threat in our days of local wars growing over into a universal war.

The danger of thermonuclear weapons being used in local wars also becomes very real, if they involve countries possessing such weapons, or the countries bound by relevant alliances to the nuclear power.

There is a difference of principle in our attitude towards national liberation civil wars—popular uprisings. Peoples fighting, arms in hand, for their freedom and independence, for socialism, are waging a just war and we support them, as we have always done.

Like civil war, a war of liberation is usually fought within one country. The question of the use of nuclear weapons does not arise with regard to it. So far they have not been used in such a war. This is quite comprehensible, because in such cases there is very often no clearly defined front line dividing the adversaries. So it has been in Viet Nam, Cuba, Algeria and other countries.

Soviet communists welcome the struggle of the peoples who are waging wars for national and social liberation and render them every possible assistance.

As to the question of peaceful and non-peaceful forms of national liberation struggle and the struggle for socialism, here, too, the position of the Communist Party of the Soviet Union and the fraternal parties is absolutely clear and fully accords with the interests of the peoples.

We proceed from the premise that various forms of struggle exist, that revolutionary forces must master all these forms—both peaceful and non-peaceful—and be able to apply them skilfully in conformity with concrete situations. Such a position is the genuinely Leninist and only correct one. It has been recorded in the most important documents of the international communist movement.

It is not the C.P.S.U. or the communist movement, but the Chinese leaders who are departing from these theses. They are directly linking the victory of the revolution with war.

Mao Tse-tung says outright that " the world can be reorganised only with the help of a rifle " and that " war can be destroyed only through war." War, to quote Mao Tse-tung, is precisely the bridge over which " mankind will pass to the new historic epoch."

The theory of " revolutionary war " for the purpose of accelerating the revolutionary process is by no means a new one. It has been extracted from the dusty Trotskyite archive. This pseudo-revolutionary theory was smashed to smithereens in his time by Lenin. And now, many years later, there are people who wish to make this scheme universal and foist it on the revolutionary forces.

What did Lenin say about the so-called theory of accelerating revolution, preached by Trotsky and the " Leftists "? He called it an " itch for revolutionary phraseology." Lenin said that any moujik would have told the author of such a theory:

> " You know, my lord, it's best you leave off governing a state and enlist as a verbal clown or go and have a hot bath to wash off the itch." (*Works, Russian edition, vol. 27, p. 18.*)

Lenin used to tell such people:

> " Perhaps the authors believe that the interests of international revolution require its *prodding* on which would result only in war, and by no means in peace which could give the masses the impression that imperialism is sort of ' legalised '? Such a ' theory ' would utterly contradict Marxism, which has always rejected the idea of ' prodding on ' revolutions, which develop as the class contradictions which engender revolutions grow increasingly acute. Such a theory would be tantamount to the view that an armed uprising is a form of struggle which is compulsory always, and in all conditions." (*Works, vol. 27, p. 49.*)

Lenin fought implacably against revolutionary phrasemongers. He made the behest to communists:

> " We must fight against the revolutionary phrase, we have to fight, fight without fail, so that no one at any time can utter the bitter truth about us: ' the revolutionary phrase about the revolutionary war killed the revolution.' "

(Works, Russian edition, vol. 27, *p.* 10.)

The Chinese theoreticians, who repeat the sorry anti-Soviet slander about a " ban on revolution," cannot, of course, be ignorant of the fact that revolution does not take place on orders from Moscow or Peking, and that once it is ripe, no " ban " can stop it. And if they seriously believe in the possibility of starting a revolution by the incantation of a left revolutionary phrase, then they are very far from Marxism-Leninism.

Marxist-Leninist teaching on revolution is now known to all educated people. Marxism-Leninism teaches that definite objective and subjective prerequisites are necessary for the victory of the revolution. The struggle for revolution in the capitalist countries is the internal matter of the working class of each country. Only the working class of this or that country and its communist vanguard can determine revolutionary tactics, the forms and methods of their struggle, and determine the time and form of the revolution.

The victory of the cause of socialism and the national liberation movement is inevitable. This is an objective process proceeding from the development of human society. Just as in its time capitalism replaced feudalism, socialism in the same way will inevitably defeat capitalism. Neither Washington, nor London, nor Paris, nor Bonn can avert the process of the collapse of capitalism.

The question is not whether " to carry on or not to carry on the revolution " as it is posed by the Peking theoreticians. Only naïve people can think that should some leaders suffering from " the itch of the revolutionary phrase " wish it, then a revolution will immediately flare up in any part of the world. The authors of this theory would do better to ponder over the fact that, despite all their incantations, life is passing them by.

Indeed can the experience of revolution in the post-war epoch be confined to any pattern? The Chinese leaders, for instance, believe that all the post-war years were years of " revolutionary wars," that all the peoples have achieved liberation or can achieve it exclusively by way of war.

But this is an attempt to distort reality, to squeeze it into the narrow limits of dead patterns. In reality the national liberation of the peoples was achieved in a struggle which included a complex interweaving of the most diverse methods and means, both peaceful and not.

The Chinese leaders accuse the Soviet people of pacifism, and of striving to disarm the liberated countries. Perhaps the Chinese leaders have facts in their possession to prove this? No, they do not have a single fact, no matter how long their statements may be. They have never given concrete examples.

That is why they have to resort to groundless declarations. There is quite a number of them in the latest Chinese government statement, too. It is alleged there that our policy in respect of the national liberation movement boils down to the following:

> " One should not resist the imperialists who possess nuclear weapons; if the oppressed peoples and oppressed nations resist and if the socialist countries support their resistance, that means pushing mankind into world thermonuclear war."

Every word here is a lie, intended to delude and deceive uninformed people. The idea of this political subversion is clear: to smear the Soviet Union, to sow among the peoples of Asia, Africa and Latin America mistrust in the policy of the Soviet Union.

The struggling peoples, however, well know that the Soviet Union has always come out and will come out against colonialism, that it has supported and will support the sacred struggle of the oppressed nations.

"The Soviet Union's position is precise and clear-cut," Comrade Nikita Khrushchov declared, " in Asia, in Africa, in Latin America, in no area of the world should there be a single people living in the chains of colonialism. All peoples should be free."

The Soviet Union is doing everything necessary to prevent a nuclear hurricane from sweeping our planet, from searing continents and leaving behind millions and millions of corpses, not excluding countries that have become free from colonialism.

Is there anything bad in this? Every sensible person will reply: " This is good. I am grateful to the Soviet Union." But the Chinese government for some reason is not satisfied with this struggle by the Soviet Union. Since they do not dare state this openly, however, they have decided to resort to falsifications, attempting to pass off black for white.

In its desire to smear the policy of the Soviet Union, the Chinese government allows itself to produce rude concoctions which sometimes reach the point of absurdity. They allege, for example, that the Soviet leaders have called the national liberation movement a " movement for piling up corpses."

The Chinese leaders apparently think that all means are good, provided they lead to the aim that they have set. But one may ask: What do such methods have in common with the morality of communists? The Soviet Union believed and believes that to uphold their independence in modern conditions the newly independent countries must not disarm but strengthen their defences, and is helping them in this righteous cause.

The Soviet Union is supporting the young newly independent countries, and is helping them not only in words but also in deeds to defend their national interests. In rendering this aid, our people sees its internationalist duty. Why do the Chinese leaders keep absolutely silent about this aspect of the question? Why are they so irritated by every mention of the concrete practical aid rendered by our country to the peoples who are in difficulty because of the aggressive intrigues of the imperialists or are experiencing serious economic difficulties in the strengthening of the independence of their countries?

The answer to these questions is not in doubt. The Chinese leaders have set themselves the aim of making a breach in the relations of friendship and co-operation between the U.S.S.R. and other countries of socialism with the national liberation movement. They are pressing for this for the sake of their special vanguardist aims which dominate their entire present-day political course.

In promoting this course, the Chinese leaders are trying to shout as loudly as possible about their revolutionariness. No one, however, has ever heard of a single case when shouts have brought down even a flimsy structure. This is all the more true for the capitalist system. A wise Eastern saying is: " If one hears *Khalva, Khalva,* it will not make it any sweeter in his mouth." The victory of the revolution does not need hysterical appeals, but the firm advance of the working masses and their good organisation; it needs the greatest possible number of practical deeds in the struggle against imperialism, for peace and socialism.

*   *   *

When you take a closer look at the theories of the Chinese leaders, and especially their practical activities in the world arena in recent times, you cannot help wondering: Are they really such zealous revolutionaries as they pretend to be? Are they really so concerned for the fate of the world revolution, the struggle of the peoples of other countries for socialism? Their acts show that, far from putting the interests of the peoples fighting for socialism and national liberation first, the Chinese leaders are pursuing their own great power aims.

Were the Chinese leaders concerned for the fate of the Cuban revolution in the period of the Caribbean crisis? No, they occupied a provocative position, adding fuel to the glowing embers of the conflict, and strove for only one thing, regardless of the consequences this might have for the Cuban people—to exploit the crisis for their factional ends.

And did they reckon, in the Sino-Indian border dispute, with the consequences their policy might have for the revolutionary forces of India, for the Communist Party, the working class of that country, for the entire national liberation movement? No, in this case, too, they pursued their own special aims.

Do they care now about the consequences it would have for the world, when they urge them, in their statement, to ignore the realities of the existing situation, to leave out of consideration the possibility of thermonuclear war?

Everything shows that the true objectives of the Chinese leaders are becoming increasingly removed from the interests of the struggle for the victory of socialism in all the countries of the world.

*   *   *

The recent events—a special place among which belongs to the Chinese leaders' active struggle against the test-ban treaty and their vehement attacks upon the Soviet Union, most evident in the latest statement of the government of the People's Republic of China—cannot but arouse deep concern.

The statements and concrete practical actions of the Chinese leaders on questions of war, peace and peaceful co-existence, on the strategy and tactics of the world communist movement, on the unity of the socialist camp, and on Chinese-Soviet relations show that the government of the People's Republic of China is departing further and further from the common co-ordinated line of the countries of the socialist community, from the programme, provisions and principles of the world communist movement.

The C.P.S.U. central committee and the Soviet government have stated repeatedly that they are ready to do everything in their power to strengthen unity between the Communist Party of the Soviet Union and the Communist Party of China, between the Soviet and the Chinese peoples. On our part, these statements have been backed by the necessary practical actions. Unfortunately, however, all our appeals to our Chinese comrades, urging them to take the road to settling differences, so as to develop our relations on the basis of what unites us, have remained unheeded. None of our practical steps in that direction have met with support.

While the C.P.S.U. and the Soviet government have striven and still strive earnestly to strengthen the unity of the socialist camp and the world communist movement, the leaders of the Communist Party of China are going farther along the road of division. The disagreements which have arisen between the leaders of the C.P.C. on the one hand, and the C.P.S.U. and the world communist movement on the other, are increasingly being transferred by them to inter-state relations. The Chinese government has resorted to openly hostile acts against the Soviet Union.

Its foreign policy steps more and more contradict the peaceloving policy of the U.S.S.R. and the other countries of the socialist community.

The latest statements of the Chinese leaders aimed against the C.P.S.U. and the other Marxist-Leninist parties give rise to apprehensions in yet other respects. They have not only outdone all previous statements of the Chinese leaders in the quantity of abuse and irate expressions, but they have revealed to the imperialists the internal affairs of the communist movement—confidential correspondence between the governments and parties of the socialist countries, international talks and meetings of the fraternal parties.

Not being scrupulous about their choice of words and expressions, the leaders of the Communist Party of China acrimoniously slander the central committee of the Communist Party of the Soviet Union and its leadership and the government agencies and officials of other communist and workers' parties—and especially Comrade Nikita Khrushchov. Judging by everything, they have set themselves the special task of discrediting the outstanding leaders of the world communist movement who are waging a principled and consistent struggle against the splitting line of the Chinese leaders.

All this shows that the leaders of the C.P.C. have transcended the boundaries of comradely party discussion and are now waging an open political struggle against the C.P.S.U. and the other Marxist-Leninist parties, a struggle for their special goals. The impression is more and more strongly created that the Chinese leadership regard those Marxist-Leninist parties which disagree with them, and their leaders, as political opponents.

The Soviet people reject with angry indignation this unworthy campaign against the Soviet Union and the other socialist countries, against the world communist movement.

The whole Soviet people and the entire Communist Party of the Soviet Union are rallied more closely than ever around the C.P.S.U. central committee, headed by Comrade Nikita Khrushchov. The feelings and thoughts of our party and of the whole Soviet people were expressed by the June plenary meeting of the C.P.S.U. central committee.

It declared in its resolution:

" The plenary meeting of the central committee of the Communist Party of the Soviet Union entirely and unanimously approves the political activity of the presidium of the C.P.S.U. central committee and the first secretary of the C.P.S.U. central committee, Chairman of the U.S.S.R. Council of Ministers, Comrade Nikita Sergeyevich Khrushchov, in further rallying the forces of the world communist movement, and also all the concrete actions and measures undertaken by the presidium of the C.P.S.U. central committee in the mutual relations with the central committee of the Communist Party of China."

Our country and our party are linked to the great Chinese people and the Communist Party of China by a long standing unselfish friendship. " The

Soviet people," Comrade Nikita Khrushchov has declared, "treat the Chinese people as their brother, friend and ally." Our fraternal attitude to the Chinese people remains unchanged. The Soviet government declares that it will go on doing everything in its power to eliminate the present difficulties, that it will stint neither energy nor time to strengthening unity with China on the basis of the principles of Marxism-Leninism and proletarian internationalism.

The Soviet government would like to stress the impermissibility of transferring differences on ideological questions, disagreements arising among parties, to relations between socialist states, of using them as the pretext for fanning nationalism and chauvinism, mistrust and dissension between the peoples of these states.

There is no justification, nor can there be any, for the fact that the leaders of the People's Republic of China, instead of considering the existing differences in the course of friendly discussion as befits like-minded communists, have started along the road of hostile, anti-Soviet attacks and slanderous *démarches* against our party.

We are deeply convinced that, in the existing situation, the question of ending open polemics between the governments of the People's Republic of China and the U.S.S.R., between the Communist Party of China and the Communist Party of the Soviet Union, remains just as urgent as before. It is common knowledge that, even before the meeting of the delegations of the two parties in Moscow and during the meeting itself, the C.P.S.U central committee put forward a proposal that open polemics should be ended so that the existing disputes could be discussed calmly and in a businesslike way and that ways of overcoming the existing differences could be found.

Now, too, we believe that those who really strive to strengthen the camp of socialism, those who desire to strengthen the unity of the world communist movement, must come out for the ending of open polemics, because they only stir up and deepen disagreements. Only persons who pay lip service to unity while actually pursuing a splitting policy can refuse to end polemics.

The meeting of representatives of the C.P.S.U. and the C.P.C., held in Moscow from July 5–20, 1963, has not been ended—it was suspended on the motion of the Chinese delegation and agreement was reached to continue it later. It should be pointed out that the latest actions of the government of the People's Republic of China and the C.P.C. leadership and the campaign of open hostility against the C.P.S.U. and the Soviet Union does not provide evidence of their intention to resume the meeting.

Our readiness to avail ourselves of every opportunity in an effort to overcome existing disagreements is dictated by sincere concern for the interests of the countries of the socialist community and the world communist movement, for the consolidation of the peace and security of all nations. We have taken and are taking all steps that depend on us to achieve unity with China to strengthen the unity of the communist ranks.

However, it would be a grave mistake for the Chinese leaders to interpret our good will wrongly. If they intend to continue with their hostile actions against the Soviet Union, to continue slandering our party and the other fraternal parties, to step up their factional activities in the world communist movement, they must clearly realise that along that road the most vigorous rebuff awaits them from the C.P.S.U. and from the Soviet people.

We shall not retreat an inch from the principles of Marxism-Leninism. We shall not be moved by any adventurist attacks on our policy—after all, the vital interests of the Soviet people and of all peoples, new successes of the world revolutionary process and the fate of peace and socialism, depend on the Leninist line of our party and of the whole communist movement. Our party has fought and will continue to fight against all attempts to divert us from this correct Leninist road.

[*Soviet News*, Nos. 4896 and 4897 (September 23–24, 1963), pp. 159–174.]

Full title: Soviet Government Statement—Reply to Statement Made by the Chinese Government, September 21, 1963 (complete text).

DOCUMENT 13

Is Yugoslavia a Socialist Country?—Comment on the Open Letters of the Central Committee of the C.P.S.U. (3) September 26, 1963

The open letter of the Central Committee of the C.P.S.U. asserts that for a time " the C.P.C. leaders had no doubts as to the nature of the socialist system in Yugoslavia," and that now the Chinese leaders " have drastically changed their position on the Yugoslavian question."

True, Yugoslavia was once a socialist state. For a time the country advanced along the path of socialism.

But soon after, owing to the Tito clique's betrayal, the Yugoslav social system began to degenerate step by step.

In 1954, when Khrushchev proposed to improve relations with Yugoslavia, we agreed to treat it as a fraternal socialist country for the purpose of winning it back to the path of socialism and watching how the Tito clique would develop.

We did not entertain very much hope for the Tito clique even then. In its letter of June 10, 1954, to the Central Committee of the C.P.S.U., the Central Committee of the C.P.C. pointed out that the fact should be taken into account that as the leaders of Yugoslavia had already gone quite far in their dealings with imperialism, they might reject our effort to win it over and refuse to return to the path of socialism; " but even though this should occur, it would not involve any political loss to the camp of peace, democracy and socialism—on the contrary, it would further expose the hypocrisy of the Yugoslav leaders before the people of Yugoslavia and of the world."

Unfortunately, our words have proved all too true! Indeed the Tito clique has flatly rejected our effort to win it over and gone farther and farther along the path of revisionism.

After it refused to sign the 1957 Declaration, the Tito clique put forward its out-and-out revisionist programme in 1958 and set this banner of modern revisionism against the 1957 Declaration which is the common programme acknowledged by all Communist and Workers' Parties. The process of restoring capitalism in Yugoslavia has been realized step by step. And internationally, the Tito clique is serving more and more energetically as a counter-revolutionary special detachment of U.S. imperialism.

In these circumstances, the attitude every Marxist-Leninist party should take towards the Tito clique is no longer the one it should take towards a fraternal Party or a fraternal country, nor should it be that of winning the Tito clique over, but it should be one of thoroughly exposing and firmly combating this gang of renegades. The 1960 Statement has given its clear conclusion on this point.

The open letter of the Central Committee of the C.P.S.U. has deliberately evaded the series of important events which occurred after the meeting of the fraternal Parties in November 1957 and also the conclusions unanimously reached at the meeting of the fraternal Parties in 1960, and tries to defend the erroneous stand of the leadership of the C.P.S.U. by quoting a sentence

462

from the editorial on Yugoslavia in the *Renmin Ribao* (People's Daily) of September 12, 1957. This is futile.

The facts prove that our position with regard to the Tito clique conforms with reality, is a principled position, and is in accord with the common agreement of the meeting of the fraternal Parties in 1960. On the other hand, the leaders of the C.P.S.U. have tried in a thousand and one ways to reverse the verdict on the Tito clique, which testifies to their betrayal of Marxism-Leninism, their abandonment of the 1960 Statement, and their rendering of assistance to the U.S. imperialists and their lackeys in deceiving the people of Yugoslavia and of the whole world.

Khrushchev says that the Yugoslav leaders have removed very much of what was considered erroneous. But the Titoites do not admit that they have committed any errors, much less removed them. The Titoites say that they have " no need " to correct any error and that " it would just be a waste of time " and " simply superfluous and ridiculous " to expect them to do so.

Let us look at the facts. Have the Titoites changed their revisionist programme? No, they have not. Have they accepted the 1957 Declaration and the 1960 Statement? No, they have not. Have they changed their revisionist domestic and foreign policies? Again, no.

The new constitution adopted by the Yugoslav Federal People's Assembly in April 1963 most clearly shows that the Tito clique has not in the least changed its revisionist stand. The constitution is the legal embodiment of the out-and-out revisionist programme of the Tito clique. Edvard Kardelj said in his report on the draft of the new constitution that it is the " legal-political and organizational embodiment " of the concepts of the programme of the L.C.Y.

Khrushchev is warmly fraternizing with the Tito clique not because it has corrected any of its errors but because he is following in Tito's footsteps.

Consider the following facts:

1. Tito denounces Stalin in order to oppose Marxism-Leninism in its very fundamentals. Khrushchev completely negates Stalin for the same purpose.

2. Both Tito and Khrushchev repudiate the fundamental theories of Marxism-Leninism, both malign as dogmatists the Chinese and other Communists who firmly uphold Marxism-Leninism, and both describe their own revision of Marxism-Leninism as a " creative development " of Marxism-Leninism.

3. Both Tito and Khrushchev laud the chieftains of U.S. imperialism. Tito says that Eisenhower " is a man who persistently defends peace," and that Kennedy's effort " will be helpful to the improvement of international relations and to the peaceful settlement of pressing world problems." Khrushchev says that Eisenhower " has a sincere desire for peace," and that Kennedy " shows solicitude for the preservation of peace."

4. Both Tito and Khrushchev play up the horrors of nuclear war in order to intimidate the people of the world into abandoning revolutionary struggle. Tito says that once a nuclear war breaks out, it will be the " annihilation of mankind." Likewise, Khrushchev says that once a nuclear war breaks out, " we will destroy our Noah's Ark—the globe."

5. Both Tito and Khrushchev preach that a world without weapons,

without armed forces and without wars can be brought into being while imperialism still exists.

6. Tito proclaims that " active peaceful coexistence " is the cornerstone of Yugoslavia's foreign policy, while Khrushchev declares that peaceful coexistence is the " general line of the foreign policy " of the Soviet Union.

7. Both Tito and Khrushchev proclaim that the possibility of peaceful transition from capitalism to socialism has increased. The Tito clique says that " mankind is irresistibly entering a long way into the era of socialism through different ways." Khrushchev says that the road of the October Revolution can be replaced by the " parliamentary road."

8. Tito advocates the introduction of " political and economic integration " of the world through " peaceful competition." Khrushchev also advocates " all-round co-operation " with imperialism through " peaceful economic competition."

9. The Tito clique sabotages the national-liberation movement and national-liberation wars in every way. Khrushchev opposes the national-liberation movement and national-liberation wars on the pretext that " any small ' local war ' might spark off the conflagration of a world war."

10. The Tito clique has renounced the dictatorship of the proletariat. Under the slogan of " the state of the whole people," Khrushchev also renounces the dictatorship of the proletariat.

11. The Tito clique denies that the Communist Party should be the vanguard of the working class. Likewise, Khrushchev says that the C.P.S.U. " has become the party of the entire people."

12. The Tito clique, flaunting the " non-bloc " label, is opposing the socialist camp. Khrushchev also says that " expressions like blocs, etc., are temporary phenomena." They both want to liquidate the socialist camp.

From these facts one must conclude that, both in domestic and foreign policy, Khrushchev really regards Tito as his teacher and is sliding down the path of revisionism hard on Tito's heels.

Khrushchev has abandoned Marxism-Leninism, scrapped the 1960 Statement and wallowed in the mire with the renegade Tito clique, in complete violation of the interests of the Soviet Union, the Soviet people and the people of the whole world. This will not be tolerated by the great Soviet people, the overwhelming majority of the members of the C.P.S.U. and cadres at various levels, all of whom have a glorious revolutionary tradition.

The great Soviet people and the membership of the C.P.S.U. will never agree with Khrushchev's collusion with the Tito clique in opposition to the fraternal Parties which uphold Marxism-Leninism.

The great Soviet people and the membership of the C.P.S.U. will never agree with Khrushchev's collusion with the Tito clique and collaboration with imperialism in opposing socialist China, Albania and other fraternal countries and in disrupting the socialist camp.

The great Soviet people and the membership of the C.P.S.U. will never agree with Khrushchev's collusion with the Tito clique and collaboration with the reactionaries of all countries in opposition to the people of the world and to revolution.

The great Soviet people and the membership of the C.P.S.U. will never agree with Khrushchev's efforts to follow the example of the Yugoslav revisionists, change the nature of the Party and the state and pave the way for the restoration of capitalism.

Khrushchev has caused dark clouds to overcast the Soviet Union, the first socialist country in the world. But this can only be an interlude in the history of the C.P.S.U. and of the Soviet Union. People who are deceived and hoodwinked for a time will gradually wake up in the end. History has confirmed, and will continue to confirm, that whoever wants to turn back the Soviet people in their advance is like the grasshopper in the fable which wanted to stop the chariot. He will never succeed in his aim.

The restoration of capitalism in Yugoslavia provides a new historical lesson to the international communist movement.

This lesson shows us that when the working class has seized power, struggle continues between the bourgeoisie and the proletariat, struggle for victory continues between the two roads of capitalism and socialism, and there is a danger that capitalism may be restored. Yugoslavia presents a typical example of the restoration of capitalism.

It shows us that not only is it possible for a working-class party to fall under the control of a labour aristocracy, degenerate into a bourgeois party and become a flunkey of imperialism before it seizes power, but even after it seizes power it is possible for a working-class party to fall under the control of new bourgeois elements, degenerate into a bourgeois party and become a flunkey of imperialism. The League of Communists of Yugoslavia typifies such degeneration.

It shows us that the restoration of capitalism in a socialist country can be achieved not necessarily through a counter-revolutionary coup d'état or armed imperialist invasion and that it can also be achieved through the degradation of the leading group in that country. The easiest way to capture a fortress is from within. Yugoslavia provides a typical case in point.

It shows us that revisionism is the product of imperialist policy. Old-line revisionism arose as a result of the imperialist policy of buying over and fostering a labour aristocracy. Modern revisionism has arisen in the same way. Sparing no cost, imperialism has now extended the scope of its operations and is buying over leading groups in socialist countries and pursues through them its desired policy of " peaceful evolution." U.S. imperialism regards Yugoslavia as the " bellwether " because it has set an example in this respect.

The leaders of the C.P.S.U. proclaim that they have already eliminated the danger of the restoration of capitalism and are building communism. If this were true, it would of course be heartening. But we see that in fact they are imitating Yugoslavia in every way and have taken a most dangerous road. This deeply worries and pains us.

Out of our warm love for the great Soviet Union and the great C.P.S.U., we would like sincerely to appeal to the leaders of the C.P.S.U.: Comrades and friends! Do not follow the Yugoslav road. Turn back at once. Or it will be too late!

[*Peking Review*, VI, 39 (September 27, 1963), pp. 14–27.]

Full title: Is Yugoslavia a Socialist Country?—Comment on the Open Letter of the Central Committee of the CPSU (3), by the Editorial Departments of *People's Daily* and *Red Flag*, September 26, 1963 (excerpts).

DOCUMENT 14

Marxism-Leninism is the Basis for the Unity of the Communist Movement, *Kommunist*, October 18, 1963

A current has appeared in the world Communist movement that is moving farther and farther away from Marxism-Leninism, from the general position of the Communists of the whole world.

The now widely known serious differences between the Chinese leaders and the Communist movement are being used in Peking to unfold a campaign against the fraternal Parties, unprecedented in its scope, that is sharply hostile in tone and whose methods have nothing in common with a discussion between like-minded people. Political and public organisations and leaders of the Chinese People's Republic, the press, the entire propaganda apparatus and state agencies both within the country and abroad have been drawn into the campaign. In other words, all the resources at the disposal of a large state have been set in motion to wage a struggle within the Communist movement. This has aggravated the situation to the extreme.

Enormous harm is being done to the cause of socialism and of the entire revolutionary movement, and every Communist, in whatever country he lives and in whatever setting he is fighting for his ideals, is obliged to fulfil his internationalist duty—to do everything possible to stop the development of events in the direction Peking wants to give them. If this is not done in time, the consequences for the entire Communist movement may be extremely grave.

Every true Communist understands that the situation can be corrected only from the position of persistent defence of Marxist-Leninist teaching and its creative spirit. . . .

The bankruptcy and political harm of the Chinese leaders' present course consists primarily in that it contradicts Marxism-Leninism and the programme documents of the international Communist movement. The special " general line " they have placed in opposition to the general line of the international Communist movement is in its ideological content nothing other than a departure from Marxism-Leninism, a failure to understand the essence of the new stage of world history. And the intensified attempts to thrust this line upon others reflect the eagerness of the Chinese leaders to take advantage of the authority and force of the world Communist movement in order to turn historical development in a direction that would reinforce their positions—not caring how this affects the world revolutionary movement. These calculations, based on subjective convictions, that it is possible to solve problems of world history by the " volitional method " and in spite of objective logic are, of course, doomed to failure. However, this does not mean that they cannot seriously harm the whole cause of socialism if they are not rebuffed in time.

What are the chief features of the actual content of the special platform that has been created in Peking?

In the area of theory—rejection of the Marxist-Leninist principle of concrete analysis of the concrete situation, subjectivism in treating urgent questions of social development, and juggling with quotations taken out of context from the classical writings of Marxism-Leninism to prove their case; distortion of Marxist-Leninist principles under the pretext of adapting them to national conditions (in this case, the " Sinification " of Marxism-Leninism).

In the country's public and political life—a regime of the cult of the individual, a striving to take advantage of the devotion of the broad working masses to the cause of socialism in order to impose arbitrary schemes in deciding internal and international problems.

In the area of foreign policy—an orientation towards maintaining international tensions, which is regarded as a favourable atmosphere for implementing hegemonistic plans, masked in the slogan " world revolution." If one follows the course that is being imposed from Peking concerning the world thermonuclear war that might be provoked, it would seem that this is not a hindrance but, on the contrary, a good thing for the revolution.

In the area of relations with socialist countries—rejection of the orientation toward the socialist camp as the chief force of modern world development, for such orientation presupposes reckoning with general laws in using this force in the interests of socialist victory throughout the world. Membership in the socialist commonwealth entails strengthening this commonwealth in a Leninist manner through comprehensive development of the economy, intensifying successes in all areas of the life of socialist society and thereby increasing the attractive force of its example for the peoples of the nonsocialist world.

The laws of development of the socialist camp " do not suit " the Chinese leaders now. Therefore they are pleading a case for curtailing the economic, scientific, cultural and other ties within this camp, for undermining its solidarity. They oppose the many-sided cooperation of the socialist countries, the international socialist division of labour, and they favour enclosed national economies, basing all this on allusions to " equality."

This arbitrariness in the approach toward the mutual relations of the socialist countries becomes more graphic if one recalls that only a few years ago a version of " equality " directly opposite to the present one was intensively disseminated from Peking. Namely, it was asserted that the obligation of socialist countries that had moved forward in their economic development allegedly consisted in " waiting for " the lagging ones and giving them everything that had been created by the forward-moving countries, as distinct from the lagging ones. This parasitical understanding of the principles of proletarian internationalism with regard to the relations between socialist countries was in radical contradiction to Leninism, in particular to Lenin's principle of material interest, and could do no less harm to the cause of socialism than the present emasculation of these principles to such a formal bourgeois and, in essence, nationalistic understanding of " equality."

Because it is hopeless to seek support from the socialist camp as a whole and among the international working class with such views and postulates, the Chinese leaders are striving to assume the position of leader in the zone of the national-liberation movement, in order to obtain an opportunity to act in its name in the international arena and take advantage of it in their interests. Hence the various demagogic theories about "the zone of revolutionary storms," theories that the contradiction between imperialism and the national-liberation movement is the decisive contradiction and that precisely this movement, and not the working class itself, will save the working class from capitalism, and so on. Hence the racist notes in the Chinese propaganda and actions in the international arena.

Basically, such is the ideological platform and true sense of Peking's special line.

And what are the methods by which they are striving to thrust it upon the world Communist movement?

In order to achieve their ends, the Chinese leaders have, to judge by their actions, decided to tear down the international Communist movement and create some kind of new movement under their aegis. They see the shortest route to this in discrediting the CPSU. The logic of apostasy from Marxism-Leninism has thus led them to the old, well-trodden path of anti-communism. They have made the Communist Party of the Soviet Union itself the prime target of their attacks on the Communist movement and its general line, for the CPSU which has put the course of the 20th Congress at the foundation of its activity, is convincingly demonstrating in practice the vital force of Leninist methods, striving for the successful forward movement of the Soviet Union toward communism and furthering the development of the revolutionary process throughout the world.

People begin to indulge in revolutionary phrasemongering when they are not in harmony with the cause of revolution. The Chinese leaders have proved to be in just this situation today. Representing themselves as super-revolutionaries, they have in fact thrown all their energies not into the struggle against imperialism but into a struggle against the CPSU and the other Marxist-Leninist parties, which through their concrete deeds are promoting the winning of one position after another from capitalism and the development of the world revolutionary process. . . .

The Chinese propagandists have invented the theory about a certain " special " community of interests of the peoples of Asia, Africa and Latin America. This theory completely contradicts Marxism-Leninism. Playing on the growth of national self-awareness among the peoples of Asia, Africa and Latin America, the CPC leaders constantly emphasise the community of interests of the peoples of these three continents alone. Chinese representatives at many conferences of international public organisations also reduce the matter at hand to a certain historical and geopolitical community of the destinies of the Afro-Asian and Latin American countries. In these arguments China is acting not like a socialist country, but only like an Asian country and a former semicolony. Given this interpretation, Afro-Asian solidarity serves less as a weapon for the struggle against imperialism than as a means for isolating the peoples of these continents from the socialist states.

The Chinese leaders do not limit themselves to proclaiming incorrect views. They are now striving wherever possible to isolate the democratic public organisations of the above-mentioned three continents, to create separate, enclosed confederations and actually to oppose them to the international confederations of the working people: The World Federation of Trade Unions, the Women's International Democratic Federation, the World

Federation of Democratic Youth, the International Student Union, organisations of journalists and others. The attempt to create a separate organisation for journalists of the Afro-Asian countries, which they undertook at the Jakarta conference, serves precisely this purpose. At the Tanganyika conference the Chinese representatives went as far as outspoken racist attacks. They told the representatives of the Afro-Asian countries, referring to the Soviet delegation and the delegations of other socialist states, as well as to the representatives of the European Communist Parties: "These are whites; it is impossible to come to agreement with them on the struggle against imperialism." It is characteristic that the representatives of the African and Asian countries spoke with indignation about such assertions, impermissible and shameful for Communists, thereby showing that they dissociated themselves from such racist preaching.

Neither concern for the world revolution nor concern for the further upsurge of the national-liberation movement lies at the basis of this course. Arguments about the "special place" of the national-liberation movement can deceive no one. They are simply attempts to earn cheap popularity among the peoples of Asia, Africa and Latin America through flattering words, to establish their hegemony over them and use them for egotistical, great-power goals. They are thereby actually proposing that the peoples of the national-liberation zone leave the path of rapprochement with the socialist countries and the international workers' movement, the path of uniting these great anti-imperialist forces for the struggle against the common enemy—imperialism. They are trying to thrust upon the national-liberation movement ideas, schemes and dogmas that are in contradiction with its objective role in the world revolutionary process, its real needs and its historically conditioned tasks—in other words, its vital interests. But this would be a path of defeat for the young national states and for the entire national-liberation struggle of the peoples. . . .

The political and ideological concepts of the CPC theoreticians largely coincide with those of the Trotskyites.

This is a fact. What was the essence of the Trotskyite "theory" of permanent revolution? Its cornerstone was a lack of faith in the possibility of solving internal contradictions and difficulties after the victory of the revolution, in the possibility of victory for socialism and communism in individual countries (or groups of countries) without a victory over imperialism throughout the world. Hence the slanderous Trotskyite thesis about the allegedly inevitable "rebirth" and "restoration of capitalism" if revolutions in other countries "do not come in time."

The Trotskyites saw the chief task of the victorious proletariat to lie not in building socialism and communism, thereby first rendering support to the international working class and furthering the successful development of the world revolutionary process as a whole, but in waging a "revolutionary war" against world capitalism, "prodding" the revolution in other countries. Have those in Peking departed far from this point of view?

Further. The Chinese theoreticians announce that the postulate concerning the possibility of averting a war in conditions when imperialism still exists is an illusion. The Trotskyites preach the same views. Wars between countries, says the "Manifesto" of the Fifth Congress of the Fourth International, are possible but not inevitable, while war between imperialism and the workers' movement is inevitable and may break out at any time (as is known, the Trotskyites include the "worker states," as they express it—that is, the socialist countries—in their concept of the workers' movement). Just as the Chinese leaders do, the Trotskyites place peaceful coexistence in opposition to the revolutionary struggle, holding that the struggle for peace harms the cause of revolution. . . .

The Chinese leaders are conducting their schismatic activity within the ranks of the international Communist movement more and more openly. They have created a special " theory " on the interrelations between the Communist Parties that is in radical contradiction to Marxism-Leninism— the theory of the " temporary minority," which supposedly has truth on its side, and the " temporary majority," which is in error. This thoroughly anti-Leninist " theory " has been called upon to justify freedom of fractional activity; it rejects international proletarian discipline, about the need for which Lenin spoke, and completely revises the relevant postulates of the 1960 Statement.

Chinese propaganda is stubbornly silent on the principle, reinforced in this document, of the need for " solidarity in the observance by each Communist Party of the evaluations and conclusions concerning the general tasks of struggle against imperialism and for peace, democracy and socialism jointly worked out by the fraternal parties at their conferences." Another important postulate of the Statement—on the impermissibility of " any actions that could undermine [this] unity "—is assiduously ignored. All this is done because the Statement stipulates a strict ban on fractional activity within the Communist movement. . . .

The history of the Communist movement has known many different forms of struggle, but it is now for the first time encountering methods and measures in which the positions of other parties are completely distorted and views are ascribed to them that they have never expressed and never shared.

The Chinese press and radio propaganda is not striking against the common enemy, imperialism, but has turned the front against the socialist countries and against the international Communist movement.

In the capitalist countries, Chinese propaganda materials aimed against the Marxist-Leninist parties are sent not only to these parties themselves but to other political parties, to various political and public figures, to journalists and the editors of bourgeois newspapers and wire services, including the most reactionary ones. Paid advertisements have appeared in the bourgeois newspapers of a number of capitalist countries announcing what Chinese literature is for sale in the bookstores of these countries and where such literature can be ordered.

This undermining propaganda is greeted with delight in the camp of reaction. Imperialist, Trotskyite and other anti-communist organisations seize upon it as a weapon. The American authorities, for example, not only failed to put any obstacles in the path of the distribution of a Jenmin Jihpao article directed against the U.S. Communist Party but even encouraged its distribution. The Argentine Ministry of the Interior and post office department, which had long maintained the strictest control over materials arriving from the U.S.S.R., admitted Chinese materials directed against the CPSU and the whole international Communist movement without interference. The same thing has been observed in the F.R.G. and many other capitalist countries.

The Chinese leaders have assumed the right of impudently interfering in the internal affairs of fraternal parties, stubbornly thrusting their views and tactics upon them. In articles directed against the Communist Parties of France, Italy, India and the U.S.A., filth is poured on the guiding figures of these and other fraternal parties. The authors of these articles arbitrarily and subjectively evaluate the activities of fraternal parties, direct Communists to activities and conditions for which they are not ready and belittle the programme documents of the parties.

Passing themselves off as champions of the equality of the Communist Parties, the Chinese leaders are in fact shamelessly trampling on their rights and interests, slanderously representing the fraternal parties, which are independently working out and implementing their own policies, as some kind of obedient crowd that allegedly " turns " left and right at the command of the " baton from Moscow." At the same time, they are trying to issue directives to the Communist movement from Peking. Chinese articles and documents are gaudy with such turns of phrase as: " Communists living in the capitalist world must . . .," " The proletariat in the capitalist countries of Europe and America must . . .," " The proletarian parties in the imperialist mother countries are obliged to . . .," " Socialist countries absolutely must . . .," and so on.

For a long time the Peking leaders have not restricted themselves merely to subversive propaganda that is anticommunist in nature. They have been carrying out direct schismatic activity in other countries, inspiring and supporting various antiparty factional groups that have unloosed a filthy campaign against the CPSU and against the leadership of the Communist Parties of these countries themselves.

In the U.S.A. they have intensified their support for the antiparty " Progressive Labor " and " Hammer and Sickle " groups in which adventurists of the Homer Chase and Milton Rosen type, who have been expelled from the U.S. Communist Party, are active. In their publications these renegades furiously attack the leadership of the U.S. Communist Party and propagandise the idea of creating a " new Marxist party " in the U.S. However, not one of these organisations has been able to attract new supporters to its side from the ranks of the U.S. Communist Party, although their actions are doing definite damage and preventing the solidarity of all progressive forces in the common struggle for peace, democracy and social progress.

Chinese representatives have undertaken an attempt to develop factional activity within the Italian Communist Party. A small group of Italian Communists in the city of Padua issued a series of brochures in which the tactical postulates of the Italian Communist Party are subjected to criticism from the Chinese positions. Shortly thereafter, the obviously incited " Italy-China Society " was created in the city of Perugia, with branches in a dozen other cities, including Rome, Milan and Palermo. This society's activity immediately showed that it was conceived as the embryo of a new leftist party, the task of which was to struggle against the policies of the Italian Communist Party and its leaders. Antiparty elements that had been expelled from the Communist Party for revisionist activity came together under the " Italy-China " sign. This whole fuss, aimed at undermining the authority of the Italian Communist Party, failed ignominiously. Italian Communists severly denounced the factionalists, and those who refused to return to the party's position (literally a handful) were expelled from its ranks.

The schismatic activity of the Chinese emissaries to Italy gave impetus to the galvanisation of various provocateur groups: In Rome, for example, there arose a certain "Association of Friends of People's China," which declared its intention of holding a "revolutionary congress" in December and which inserted want ads in the bourgeois newspapers for people to distribute Chinese materials. Groups of Trotskyites and other riffraff have become more active.

Chinese representatives are developing active schismatic activity against the Communist Party of Australia, using, in particular, E. Hill, a former member of the leadership of this party. After he was removed from the Central Committee of the Australian Communist Party, he was demonstratively invited to visit China, where he was accorded high honours. Upon returning from China, Hill openly set about creating a schismatic group.

In the spirit of anti-Leninist concepts, the Chinese representatives have also cultivated the Belgian J. Grippa. Trading on certain of his personal weaknesses, they have in every way encouraged Grippa's pretensions to the leadership of the Communist Party of Belgium and have rendered him and his supporters every kind of support. The Grippa schismatic group which was about to build a nest for itself in the Brussels Federation of the Communist Party of Belgium, was exposed and thrown from the party in disgrace. Now the schismatics are openly seeking support from their spiritual fathers overseas. Grippa himself headed a delegation to Albania in the summer of 1963, and one of his associates—Masso—led one to China, where he was received by Mao Tse-tung.

The Chinese are even striving to create "our Communist Party" in Switzerland; in a month this "party" recruited exactly five people.

In Brazil the Chinese representatives are supporting the groups of Amazonas, Grabois, Pomar and other factionaries who have been expelled from the Communist Party. The newspaper *Clase Operaria* that is put out by this group publishes all the main Chinese and Albanian articles directed against the international Communist movement. Another channel through which the Chinese schismatics in Brazil are now operating is the Trotskyite and other press organs—the newspaper *Frente Operaria* and the magazine *Politica Operaria*.

Chinese representatives are conducting active schismatic activity in Chile. Their major activity has been the creation of the Spartacus publishing house and then an "Information Bureau," which engages in the distribution of Chinese propaganda materials. Trotskyite elements and renegades of the Reinos group have been enlisted in preparing these materials, directed against the Communist Party of Chile. Still another factional group, calling itself the Marxist People's Vanguard, has appeared in Chile as a result of the schismatic activities of the Chinese leaders.

The "ideological platform" of all these minor factional groups consists in unrestrained praise for the Chinese leaders' concepts. They shout from the rooftops that they rely on the Peking leaders and are inspired by their ideas in the strugle against the Communist movement.

An obvious attempt is being made in Peking to knock together an international bloc out of groups and groupings of this sort, consisting largely of people who have been expelled from the Communist Parties and all possible unprincipled and corrupt elements. No longer shy, the Chinese leaders admit they support and will continue to support these people, whom they call " true revolutionaries "; in other words, they will openly place them in opposition to the world Communist movement. They are already gathering all these renegades under their aegis, regarding them as their agents in the struggle against Marxist-Leninist cadres that have been tempered in class battles against imperialism.

The fraternal Communist Parties have angrily censured the so-called " general line " the Peking leaders are attempting to thrust upon them, and their schismatic, undermining activities in the Communist movement.

Up to the present time 65 Communist Parties have condemned the views and actions of the Chinese schismatics in official decisions by their guiding agencies and have expressed complete solidarity and support for the principled CPSU position in its struggle for the ideological purity of revolutionary theory and unity within the Communist ranks. . . .

It may be asked: Why do they now need a renaissance of the ideology and practice of the cult of the individual?

Primarily because the line of the 20th CPSU Congress, which yielded such remarkable results for the entire world liberation movement, is undermining the internal policy of the Chinese leaders, which is based on preserving the regime of the cult of the individual.

Further, it is because they needed Stalin's name for the struggle against the CPSU Central Committee and its Leninist policy, in order to attempt to drive the international Communist movement from the Marxist-Leninist path and subordinate it to the nationalist, dogmatic line of Peking.

At the same time, the Chinese leaders' statements against the overcoming of the Stalin cult are a campaign against the method of collective leadership, are an appeal to support the idolisation of Mao Tse-tung in which Chinese propaganda is intensively engaged. This preaching of the Mao Tse-tung cult has been actively conducted within the ranks of the Chinese Communist Party and among broad sections of the Chinese people for a number of years. It can be said with complete certainty that the Communist movement is confronted with an attempt to replace Leninism with " Mao Tse-tungism."

In Peking they are shouting loudest of all about fidelity to Marxism-Leninism, but they are in fact trying to destroy its heart, its creative spirit, to undermine the ideological basis of the Communist movement, rob it of its ability to utilise favourable conditions to struggle for the cause of socialism, for a real attack on imperialism. We are witnessing a campaign against the very foundations of Marxism-Leninism that is unparalleled since the time of Trotskyism.

True, it is now impossible in the ranks of the international Communist movement to oppose Leninism openly. Leninism has become the banner of millions-strong masses throughout the world, including China. Those who openly lift a hand against Leninism will inevitably alienate themselves from the broad masses. This is why the Chinese leaders swear allegiance to Marxism-Leninism in words. In fact, they are trying to replace the general international nature of Leninism with a so-called national, or " nationalised," " Sinified," Marxism.

Soon after the 1960 Moscow conference, at which the representatives of the fraternal parties condemned a policy that signified, in effect, the substitution of Maoist tenets for Marxism-Leninism, Chinese propaganda began to circulate throughout the world an interview that Liu Shao-chi had given at one time to Anna Louise Strong, in which he declared: " Marx and Lenin were Europeans: They wrote about European history and problems, rarely touching upon Asia or China. . . . Mao not only applied Marxism to new conditions but developed it further. *He created the Chinese, or Asiatic, form of Marxism.*" *

Developing this thesis, Chinese propaganda has gone even farther. The magazine *Sinkiang Hungchi* writes: " Mao Tse-tung's ideas are the creative development of Marxism-Leninism in a new historical period. This creative development not only has specific importance for the Chinese revolution but also has general importance for the modern epoch of world revolution. We have every right to say that Mao Tse-tung's ideas are the Marxism-Leninism of the epoch of socialist revolutions and socialist construction."

Another magazine of the Chinese party asserts that " Marx and Engels gave scientifically based reasons for the inevitability of the appearance of socialism, although they could not formulate the laws of development of socialist society itself, while Lenin, although he did speak about this question, barely touched on it. And only when the new historical period, the period of socialist revolutions and socialist construction, arrived, did Mao Tse-tung give a complete systematic picture."

The attempt to replace Marxism-Leninism with the ideas of Mao Tse-tung is evoking a decisive protest from all Communists. Our banner has been and will continue to be Marxism-Leninism. We have fought and will continue to fight for the purity of the ideals of Marxism-Leninism. . . .

The entire international Communist movement condemns the line, practice and methods of struggle used by the Chinese leaders against the Marxist-Leninist parties. The Chinese leaders, unloosing an attack upon the common positions of the Communist movement, have again, as at the 1960 Moscow conference, found themselves before the solid front of the Marxist-Leninist parties. . . .

[*Kommunist*, No. 15, October 1963, pp. 13–47; *The Current Digest of the Soviet Press*, XV, 43 (November 20, 1963), pp. 3–14.]

* [This same quotation appears, in slightly different form, in V. Kudryavtsev's *Izvestia* article " Africa in One Formation " (Current Digest of the Soviet Press, Vol. XV, No. 41, pp. 20–21), where it is identified as taken from a letter written to Anna Louise Strong by Liu Shao-ch'i and published in the June, 1947, issue of Amerasia.—CDSP note.]

Full title: Marxism-Leninism Is the Basis for the Unity of the Communist Movement, October 18, 1963 (excerpts).

DOCUMENT 15

Apologists of Neo-Colonialism—Comment on the Open Letter of the Central Committee of the C.P.S.U. (4) October 21, 1963

The history of the eighteen years since World War II has shown that wars of national liberation are unavoidable so long as the imperialists and their lackeys try to maintain their brutal rule by bayonets and use force to suppress the revolution of oppressed nations. These large-scale and small-scale revolutionary wars against the imperialists and their lackeys, which have never ceased, have hit hard at the imperialist forces of war, strengthened the forces defending world peace and effectively prevented the imperialists from realising their plan of launching a world war. Frankly speaking, Khrushchev's clamour about the need to " put out " the sparks of revolution for the sake of peace is an attempt to oppose revolution in the name of safeguarding peace.

Proceeding from these wrong views and policies, the leaders of the CPSU not only demand that the oppressed nations should abandon their revolutionary struggle for liberation and " peacefully co-exist " with the imperialists and colonialists, but even side with imperialism and use a variety of methods to extinguish the sparks of revolution in Asia, Africa and Latin America.

Take the example of the Algerian people's war of national liberation. The leadership of the CPSU not only withheld support for a long period but actually took the side of French imperialism. Khrushchev used to treat Algeria's national independence as an " internal affair " of France. Speaking on the Algerian question on October 3, 1955, he said, " I had and have in view, first of all, that the USSR does not interfere in the internal affairs of other states." Receiving a correspondent of *Le Figaro* on March 27, 1958, he said, " We do not want France to grow weaker, we want her to become still greater."

To curry favour with the French imperialists, the leaders of the CPSU did not dare to recognise the Provisional Government of the Republic of Algeria for a long time; not until the victory of the Algerian people's war of resistance against French aggression was a foregone conclusion and France was compelled to agree to Algerian independence did they hurriedly recognise the Republic of Algeria. This unseemly attitude brought shame on the socialist countries. Yet the leaders of the CPSU glory in their shame and assert that the victory the Algerian people paid for with their blood should also be credited to the policy of " peaceful co-existence."

Again, let us examine the part played by the leaders of the CPSU in the Congo question. Not only did they refuse to give active support to the Congolese people's armed struggle against colonialism, but they were anxious to " co-operate " with U.S. imperialism in putting out the spark in the Congo.

On July 13, 1960, the Soviet Union joined with the United States in voting for the UN Security Council resolution on the dispatch of UN forces to the Congo; thus it helped the U.S. imperialists use the flag of the United

Nations in their armed intervention in the Congo. The Soviet Union also provided the UN forces with means of transportation. In a cable to Kasavubu and Lumumba of July 15, Khrushchev said that " the United Nations Security Council has done a useful thing." Thereafter, the Soviet press kept up a stream of praise for the United Nations for " helping the Government of the Congolese Republic to defend the independence and sovereignty of the country," and expressed the hope that the United Nations would adopt " resolute measures." In its statements of August 21 and September 10, the Soviet Government continued to praise the United Nations, which was suppressing the Congolese people.

In 1961 the leaders of the CPSU persuaded Gizenga to attend the Congolese parliament, which had been convened under the " protection " of UN troops, and to join the puppet government. The leadership of the CPSU falsely alleged that the convocation of the Congolese parliament was " an important event in the life of the young republic " and " a success of the national forces."

Clearly these wrong policies of the leadership of the CPSU rendered U.S. imperialism a great service in its aggression against the Congo. Lumumba was murdered. Gizenga was imprisoned, many other patriots were persecuted, and the Congolese struggle for national independence suffered a setback. Does the leadership of the CPSU feel no responsibility for all this?

Having used up all their wonder-working weapons for opposing the national-liberation movement, the leaders of the CPSU are now reduced to seeking help from racism, the most reactionary of all imperialist theories. They describe the correct stand of the CPC in resolutely supporting the national-liberation movement as " creating racial and geographical barriers," " replacing the class approach with the racial approach," and " playing upon the national and even racial prejudices of the Asian and African peoples."

If Marxism-Leninism did not exist, perhaps such lies could deceive people. Unfortunately for the manufacturers of these lies, they live in the wrong age, for Marxism-Leninism has already found its way deep into people's hearts. As Stalin rightly pointed out, Leninism " broke down the wall between whites and blacks, between Europeans and Asiatics, between the ' civilized ' and ' uncivilized ' slaves of imperialism." (Stalin, op. cit., Vol. VI, p. 144.) It is futile for the leaders of the CPSU to try and rebuild this wall of racism.

In the last analysis, the national question in the contemporary world is one of class struggle and anti-imperialist struggle. Today the workers, peasants, revolutionary intellectuals, anti-imperialist and patriotic bourgeois elements and other patriotic and anti-imperialist enlightened people of all races—white, black, yellow or brown—have formed a broad united front against the imperialists, headed by the United States, and their lackeys. This united front is expanding and growing stronger. The question here is not whether to side with the white people or the coloured people, but whether to side with the oppressed peoples and nations or with the handful of imperialists and reactionaries.

According to the Marxist-Leninist class stand, oppressed nations must draw a clear line of demarcation between themselves and the imperialists and colonialists. To blur this line represents a chauvinist view serving imperialism and colonialism.

Lenin said:

This is precisely why the central point in the Social-Democratic programme must be the distinction between oppressing and oppressed nations, which is the *essence* of imperialism, which is *falsely* evaded by the social-chauvinists, and by Kautsky. (Lenin, *Selected Works,* New York, Vol. V, p. 284.)

By slandering the unity of the people of Asia, Africa and Latin America in the anti-imperialist struggle as being " based on the geographical and racial principles," the leaders of the CPSU have obviously placed themselves in the position of the social-chauvinists and of Kautsky.

When they peddle the " theory of racism," describing the national-liberation movement in Asia, Africa and Latin America as one of the coloured against the white race, the leaders of the CPSU are clearly aiming at inciting racial hatred among the white people in Europe and North America, at diverting the people of the world from the struggle against imperialism and at turning the international working-class movement away from the struggle against modern revisionism.

The leaders of the CPSU have raised a hue and cry about the " Yellow Peril " and the " imminent menace of Genghis Khan." This is really not worth refuting. We do not intend in this article to comment on the historical role of Genghis Khan or on the development of the Mongolian, Russian and Chinese nations and the process of their formation into states. We would only remind the leaders of the CPSU of their need to review their history lessons before manufacturing such tales. Genghis Khan was a Khan of Mongolia, and in his day both China and Russia were subjected to Mongolian aggression. He invaded part of northwestern and northern China in 1215 and Russia in 1223. After his death, his successors subjugated Russia in 1240 and thrity-nine years later, in 1279, conquered the whole of China.

Lu Hsun, the well-known Chinese writer, has a paragraph about Genghis Khan in an article he wrote in 1934. We include it here for your reference as it may be useful to you.

He wrote that, as a young man of twenty,

I had been told that " our " Genghis Khan had conquered Europe and ushered in the most splendid period in " our " history. Not until I was twenty-five did I discover that this so-called most splendid period of " our " history was actually the time when the Mongolians conquered China and we became slaves. And not until last August, when browsing through three books on Mongolian history, looking for history stories, did I find out that the conquest of " Russia " by the Mongolians and their invasion of Hungary and Austria actually preceded their conquest of China, and that the Genghis Khan of that time was not yet our Khan. The Russians were enslaved before we were, and presumably it is they who ought to be able to say " When our Genghis Khan conquered China, he ushered in the most splendid period of our history." (Lu Hsun, *Collected Works,* Chinese ed., Vol. VI, p. 109.)

Anyone with a little knowledge of modern world history knows that the " theory of the Yellow Peril " about which the CPSU leadership has been making such a noise is a legacy of the German Emperor William II. Half a century ago, William II stated, " I am a believer in the Yellow Peril."

The German Emperor's purpose in propagating the "theory of the Yellow Peril" was to carry the partition of China further, to invade Asia, to suppress revolution in Asia, to divert the attention of the European people from revolution and to use it as a smoke screen for his active preparations for the imperialist world war and for his attempt to gain world hegemony.

When William II spread this "theory of the Yellow Peril," the European bourgeoisie was in deep decline and extremely reactionary, and democratic revolutions were sweeping through China, Turkey and Persia and affecting India, around the time of the 1905 Russian Revolution. That was the period, too, when Lenin made his famous remark about "backward Europe and advanced Asia."

William II was a bigwig in his day. But in reality he proved to be only a snow man in the sun. In a very short time this reactionary chieftain vanished from the scene, together with the reactionary theory he invented. The great Lenin and his brilliant teachings live on for ever.

Fifty years have gone by; imperialism in Western Europe and North America has become still more moribund and reactionary, and its days are numbered. Meanwhile, the revolutionary storm raging over Asia, Africa and Latin America has grown many times stronger than in Lenin's time. It is hardly credible that today there are still people who wish to step into the shoes of William II. This is indeed a mockery of history.

The policy of the leadership of the CPSU on the national-colonial question is identical with the bankrupt policy of the revisionists of the Second International. The only difference is that the latter served the imperialists' old colonialism, while the modern revisionists serve the imperialists' neo-colonialism.

The old revisionists sang to the tune of the old colonialists, and Khrushchov sings to the tune of the neo-colonialists.

The heroes of the Second International, represented by Bernstein and Kautsky, were apologists for the old colonial rule of imperialism. They openly declared that colonial rule was progressive, that it "brought a high civilisation" to the colonies and "developed the productive forces" there. They even asserted that the "abolition of the colonies would mean barbarism."

In this respect Khrushchov is somewhat different from the old revisionists He is bold enough to denounce the old colonial system.

How is it that Khrushchov is so bold? Because the imperialists have changed their tune.

After World War II, under the twin blows of the socialist revolution and the national-liberation revolution, the imperialists were forced to recognize that " if the West had attempted to perpetuate the status quo of colonialism, it would have made violent revolution inevitable and defeat inevitable." The old colonialist forms of rule " on the contrary . . . are likely to prove ' running sores ' which destroy both the economic and the moral vigour of a nation's life." Thus it became necessary to change the form and practise neo-colonialism.

Thus, too, Khrushchov singing to the tune of the neo-colonialists flaunts the " theory of the disappearance of colonialism " in order to cover up the new colonialism. What is more, he tries to induce the oppressed nations to embrace this new colonialism. He actively propagates the view that " peaceful co-existence " between the oppressed nations and civilized imperialism will make "the national economy grow rapidly" and bring about an "unlift of their productive forces," enable the home market in the oppressed countries to "become incomparably greater" and "furnish more raw materials, and various products and goods required by the economy of the industrially developed countries" and, at the same time, will "considerably raise the living standard of the inhabitants in the highly developed capitalist countries."

Nor has Khrushchov forgotten to collect certain wornout weapons from the arsenal of the revisionists of the Second International.

Here are some examples.

The old revisionists opposed wars of national liberation and held that the national question "can be settled only through international agreements" and "advance in all the arts of peace." On this question, Khrushchov has taken over the line of the revisionists of the Second International; he advocates a "quiet burial of the colonial system."

The old revisionists attacked the revolutionary Marxists, hurling at them the slander that "Bolshevism is in essence a warlike type of socialism" and that "the Communist International harbours the illusion that the liberation of the workers can be achieved by means of the bayonets of the victorious Red Army and that a new world war is necessary for the world revolution." They also spread the story that this position had "created the greatest danger of a new world war." The language Khrushchov uses today to slander the Chinese Communist Party and other fraternal Marxist-Leninist parties is exactly the language used by the old revisionists in slandering the Bolsheviks. It is hard to find any difference.

It must be said that in serving the imperialists' neo-colonialism, Khrushchov is not a whit inferior to the old revisionists in their service of the imperialists' old colonialism.

Lenin showed how the policy of imperialism caused the international workers' movement to split into two sections, the revolutionary and the opportunist. The revolutionary section sided with the oppressed nations and opposed the imperialists and colonialists. On the other hand, the opportunist section fed on crumbs from the spoils which the imperialists and colonialists squeezed out of the people of the colonies and semi-colonies. It sided with the imperialists and colonialists and opposed the revolution of the oppressed nations for liberation.

The same kind of division between revolutionaries and opportunists in the international working-class movement as that described by Lenin is now taking shape not only in the working-class movement in capitalist countries but also in socialist countries where the proletariat wields state power.

The experience of history shows that if the national-liberation movement is to achieve complete victory it must form a solid alliance with the revolutionary working-class movement, draw a clear line of demarcation between itself and the revisionists who serve the imperialists and colonialists, and firmly eradicate their influence.

The experience of history shows that if the working-class movement of the capitalist countries in Western Europe and North America is to achieve complete victory, it must form a close alliance with the national-liberation movement in Asia, Africa and Latin America, draw a clear line of demarcation between itself and the revisionists, and firmly eradicate their influence.

The revisionists are agents of imperialism who have hidden themselves among the ranks of the international working-class movement. Lenin said, ". . . the fight against imperialism is a sham and humbug unless it is inseparably bound up with the fight against opportunism." (Lenin, *Selected Works,* Moscow, Vol. I, Part 2, p. 566.) Thus it is clear that the present fight against imperialism and old and new colonialism must be linked closely with the fight against the apologists of neo-colonialism.

However hard the imperialists disguise their intentions and bestir themselves, however hard their apologists whitewash and help neo-colonialism, imperialism and colonialism cannot escape their doom. The victory of the national-liberation revolution is irresistible. Sooner or later the apologists of neo-colonialism will go bankrupt.

Workers of the world and the oppressed nations, unite!

[*Peking Review*, VI, 43 (October 25, 1963), pp. 6–15.]

Full title: Apologists of Neo-Colonialism—Comment on the Open Letter of the Central Committee of the CPSU (4), by the Editorial Departments of *People's Daily* and *Red Flag,* October 21, 1963 (excerpts).

DOCUMENT 16

**Two Different Lines on the Question of War and Peace
Comment on the Open Letter of the Central Committee
of the C.P.S.U. (5) November 18, 1963**

The Marxist-Leninist line is the correct line conducive to the winning of world peace. It is the line consistently upheld by all Marxist-Leninist parties, including the Communist Party of China, and by all Marxist-Leninists. The revisionist line is a wrong line which serves to increase the danger of a new war. It is the line gradually developed by the leaders of the CPSU since its twentieth Congress.

On the question of war and peace many lies slandering the Chinese communists have been fabricated in the open letter of the Central Committee of the CPSU and in numerous statements by the leaders of the CPSU, but these cannot conceal the essence of the differences. . . .

The U.S. imperialists are the wildest militarists of modern times, the wildest plotters of a new world war, and the most ferocious enemy of world peace.

It is thus clear that the U.S. imperialists have not become beautiful angels in spite of Khrushchev's bible-reading and psalm-singing; they have not turned into compassionate Buddhas in spite of Khrushchev's prayers and incense-burning. However hard Khrushchev tries to serve the U.S. imperialists, they show not the slightest appreciation. They continue to expose their own peace camouflage by fresh and numerous activities of aggression and war, and thus they continue to slap Khrushchev in the face and reveal the bankruptcy of his ridiculous theories prettifying imperialism. The lot of the willing apologists of U.S. imperialism is indeed a sorry one.

THE QUESTION OF THE POSSIBILITY OF PREVENTING A NEW WORLD WAR

It is a fact that the imperialists headed by the United States are actively preparing a new world war and that the danger of such a war does exist. We should make this fact clear to the people. But can a new world war be prevented?

The views of the Chinese communists on this question have always been quite explicit. After the conclusion of World War II, Comrade Mao Tse-tung scientifically analysed the postwar international situation and advanced the view that a new world war can be prevented. Back in 1946, in his well-known talk with the American correspondent, Anna Louise Strong, he said: But the fact that the U.S. reactionaries are now trumpeting so loudly about a U.S.-Soviet war and creating a foul atmosphere, so soon after the end of World War II, compels us to take a look at their real aims. It turns out that under the cover of anti-Soviet slogans they are frantically attacking the workers and democratic circles in the United States and turning all the countries which are the targets of U.S. external expansion into U.S. dependencies. I think the American people and the peoples of all countries menaced by U.S. aggression should unite and struggle against the attacks

481

of the U.S. reactionaries and their running dogs in these countries. Only by victory in this struggle can a third world war be avoided; otherwise it is unavoidable. (Mao Tse-tung, *Selected Works*, Foreign Languages Press, Peking, 1961, IV, p. 100.)

Comrade Mao Tse-tung's remarks were directed against a pessimistic appraisal of the international situation at the time. The imperialists headed by the United States, together with the reactionaries in various countries, were daily intensifying its anti-Soviet, anti-communist, and anti-popular activities and trumpeting that " war between the United States and the Soviet Union is inevitable " and that " the outbreak of a third world was is inevitable." The Chiang Kai-shek reactionaries gave this great publicity in order to intimidate the Chinese people. Frightened by such blackmail, some comrades became fainthearted in the face of the armed attacks launched by the Chiang Kai-shek reactionaries with U.S. imperialist support and dared not firmly oppose the counter-revolutionary war with a revolutionary war. Comrade Mao Tse-tung held different views. He pointed out that a new world war could be prevented provided resolute and effective struggles were waged against world reaction. His scientific proposition was confirmed by the great victory of the Chinese revolution.

The victory of the Chinese revolution brought about a tremendous change in the international balance of class forces. Comrade Mao Tse-tung pointed out in June 1950: The menace of war by the imperialist camp still exists, the possibility of a third world war still exists. But the forces thwarting the danger of war and preventing a third world war are rapidly developing, and the political consciousness of the broad masses of the people of the world is rising. A new world war can be prevented provided the communist parties of the world keep on uniting and strengthening all the forces of peace and democracy that can be united. (*People's Daily*, June 13, 1950.)

In November 1957 at the meeting of fraternal parties Comrade Mao Tse-tung made a detailed analysis of the changes in international relations since the end of World War II and showed that the international situation had reached a new turning point. He vividly depicted the situation with a metaphor from a classical Chinese novel, " The East Wind Prevails Over the West Wind." He said: " It is characteristic of the situation today, I believe, that the East wind is prevailing over the West wind. That is to say, the forces of socialism are overwhelmingly superior to the forces of imperialism." (*On Imperialism and All Reactionaries Are Paper Tigers*.)

He arrived at this conclusion by an analysis of international class relations. He explicitly placed on the side of " the East wind " the socialist camp, the international working class, the communist parties, the oppressed peoples and nations, and the peace-loving people and countries, while confining " the West Wind " to the war forces of imperialism and reaction. The political meaning of this metaphor is very lucid and definite. The fact that the leaders of the CPSU and their followers are twisting this metaphor into a geographical or ethnical or meteorological concept only shows that they want to squeeze themselves into the ranks of the " West " in order to placate the imperialists and to stir up chauvinism in Europe and North America.

Comrade Mao Tse-tung's main aim in stating that " the East wind prevails over the West wind " was to point to the growing possibility that a new world war could be prevented and that the socialist countries would be able to carry on their construction in a peaceful environment. These propositions of Comrade Mao Tse-tung have been and are the consistent views of the CCP. It is thus clear that the leaders of the CPSU are deliberately concocting a lie in alleging that the CCP does "not believe in the possibility of preventing a new world war."

Again, it is clear that the thesis on the possibility of preventing a third world war was advanced by Marxist-Leninists long ago; it was not first put forward at the twentieth Congress of the CPSU, nor is it Khrushchev's "creation."

Is it then true that Khrushchev has created nothing at all? No. He has created something. Unfortunately, these "creations" are by no means Marxist-Leninist, but revisionist.

First, Khrushchev has wilfully interpreted the possibility of preventing a new world war as the only possibility, holding that there is no danger of a new world war.

Marxist-Leninists hold that while pointing to the possibility of preventing a new world war we must also call attention to the possibility that imperialism may unleash a world war. Only by pointing to both possibilities, pursuing correct policies, and preparing for both eventualities can we effectively mobilise the masses to wage struggles in defence of world peace. Only thus will the socialist countries and people and other peace-loving countries and people not be caught unawares and utterly unprepared should imperialism force a world war on the people of the world.

However, Khrushchev and others are against exposing the danger of a new war which the imperialists are plotting. According to them, imperialism has actually become peace-loving. This is helping the imperialists to lull the masses and sap their fighting will so that they will lose their vigilance against the danger of the new war the imperialists are plotting.

Second, Khrushchev has wilfully interpreted the possibility of preventing a new world war as the possibility of preventing all wars, holding that the Leninist axiom that war is inevitable so long as imperialism exists is outmoded.

The possibility of preventing a new war is one thing; the possibility of preventing all wars, including revolutionary wars, is another. And it is completely wrong to confuse the two.

There is soil for wars so long as imperialism and the system of exploitation of man by man exist. This is an objective law discovered by Lenin after abundant scientific study.

Stalin said in 1952 after indicating the possibility of preventing a new world war: "To eliminate the inevitability of war, it is necessary to abolish imperialism." (Stalin, *Economic Problems of Socialism in the USSR,* FLPH, Moscow, 1952, p. 41.)

Lenin and Stalin are right and Khrushchev is wrong. History shows that, while the imperialists have succeeded in launching two world wars, they have waged numerous wars of other kinds. Since World War II by their policies of aggression and war the imperialists headed by the United States have brought about ceaseless local wars and armed conflicts of every description in many places, and especially in Asia, Africa, and Latin America.

It is clear that national liberation wars are inevitable when the imperialists, and the U.S. imperialists in particular, send their troops or use their lackeys to carry out sanguinary suppression of the oppressed nations and countries fighting for or upholding national independence. . . .

In summing up the lessons of the Paris Commune in his speech commemorating the seventh anniversary of the founding of the First International in 1871, Marx mentioned the conditions for the elimination of class domination and class oppression. He said: ". . . before such a change can be consummated, a dictatorship of the proletariat is necessary, and its first premise is an army of the proletariat. The working class must win the right to its emancipation on the battlefield." (Marx and Engels, *Works*, German ed., Verlag Dietz, Berlin, 1962, Vol. 17, p. 433.)

In accordance with Marxist-Leninist theory, Comrade Mao Tse-tung advanced in 1938 the famous thesis that "political power grows out of the barrel of a gun," when discussing the lessons of the Russian and Chinese revolutions. This thesis, too, has now become a target of attack by the leaders of the CPSU. They say it is evidence of China's being "warlike."

Respected friends, slanders like yours were refuted by Comrade Mao Tse-tung as far back as 25 years ago: "according to the Marxist theory of the state, the army is the chief component of state power. Whoever wants to seize and retain state power must have a strong army. Some people ridicule us as advocates for the omnipotence of war. Yes, we are advocates of the omnipotence of revolutionary war; that is good, not bad, it is Marxist." (Mao Tse-tung, *Selected Military Writings*, FLPH, Peking, 1963, p. 273.)

What is wrong with Comrade Mao Tse-tung's remark? Only those who reject all the historical experience gained in the bourgeois and proletarian revolutions over the last few hundred years would reject this view of his.

With their guns, the Chinese people have created a socialist political power. All except imperialists and their lackeys can readily understand that this is a fine thing and that it is an important factor in safeguarding world peace and preventing a third world war.

Marxist-Leninists never conceal their views. We wholeheartedly support every people's revolutionary war. As Lenin said of such revolutionary war, "Of all the wars known in history it is the only lawful, rightful, just, and truly great war." (Lenin, *Collected Works*, FLPH, Moscow, Vol. 8, p. 107.) If we are accused of being warlike simply because of this, it only goes to prove that we genuinely side with the oppressed peoples and nations and are true Marxist-Leninists.

The imperialists and revisionists always denounced the Bolsheviks and revolutionary leaders like Lenin and Stalin as being "warlike." The very fact that today we are likewise abused by imperialists and revisionists shows that we have been holding aloft the revolutionary banner of Marxism-Leninism.

Khrushchev and others vigorously propagate the view that all wars can be prevented and "a world without weapons, without armed forces, and without wars" can be brought into being while imperialism still exists. This is nothing but Kautsky's theory of "ultra-imperialism," which has long been bankrupt. Their purpose is all too clear; it is to make the people believe that permanent peace can be realised under imperialism and thereby abolish revolution and national liberation wars and revolutionary civil wars against imperialism and its lackeys, and in fact to help the imperialists in their preparations for a new war.

NUCLEAR FETISHISM AND NUCLEAR BLACKMAIL ARE THE THEORETICAL BASIS AND GUIDING POLICY OF MODERN REVISIONISM

The heart of the theory of the leaders of the CPSU on war and peace is their thesis that the emergence of nuclear weapons has changed everything and has changed the laws of class struggle.

The open letter of the Central Committee of the CPSU says: " The nuclear rocket weapons that were created in the middle of our century changed the old notions about war." In what way were they changed?

The leaders of the CPSU hold that with the appearance of nuclear weapons there is no longer any difference between just and unjust wars. They say: " The atomic bomb does not adhere to the class principle," and that " the atomic bomb does not distinguish between the imperialists and working people; it hits big areas and therefore millions of workers would be destroyed for each monopolist."

They hold that with the appearance of nuclear weapons the oppressed peoples and nations must abandon revolution and refrain from waging just popular revolutionary wars and wars of national liberation, or else such wars would lead to the destruction of mankind. They say: ". . . any small local war might spark off the conflagration of a world war," and " Today, any sort of war, although it may break out as an ordinary non-nuclear war, is likely to develop into a destructive nuclear missile conflagration." Thus, " we will destroy our Noah's Ark—the Globe."

The leaders of the CPSU hold that the socialist countries must not resist but must yield to imperialist nuclear blackmail and war threats. Khrushchev said: " There can be no doubt that a world nuclear war, if started by the imperialist maniacs, would inevitably result in the downfall of the capitalist system, a system breeding wars. But would the socialist countries and the cause of socialism all over the world benefit from a world nuclear disaster? Only people who deliberately shut their eyes to the facts can think so. As regards Marxist-Leninists, they cannot propose to establish a communist civilisation on the ruins of centres of world culture, on land laid waste and contaminated by nuclear fallout. We need hardly add that in the case of many peoples, the question of socialism would be eliminated altogether because they would have disappeared bodily from our planet."

In short, according to the leaders of the CPSU, with the emergence of nuclear weapons, the contradiction between the socialist and the imperialist camps, the contradiction between the proletariat and the bourgeoisie in the capitalist countries, and the contradiction between the oppressed nations and imperialism have all disappeared. The world no longer has any class contradictions. They regard the contradictions in the contemporary world as boiling down to a single contradiction; that is, their fictitious contradiction between the so-called common survival of imperialism and the oppressed classes and nations on the one hand and their total destruction on the other.

As far as they are concerned, Marxism-Leninism, the Declaration and the Statement, and socialism and communism have all been cast to the winds.

How frankly *Pravda* puts it! " What is the use of principles if one's head is chopped off?"

This is tantamount to saying that the revolutionaries who died under the sabres of the reactionaries for the victory of the Russian revolutions, the October Revolution; the warriors who bravely gave up their lives in the anti-fascist war, the heroes who shed their blood in the struggle against imperialism and for national independence, and the martyrs to the revolutionary cause through the ages were all fools. Why should they have given up their heads for adherence to principle?

This is the philosophy of out-and-out renegades. It is a shameless statement, to be found only in the confessions of renegades.

Guided by this theory of nuclear fetishism and nuclear blackmail, the leaders of the CPSU maintain that the way to defend world peace is not for all existing peace forces to unite and form the broadest united front against U.S. imperialism and its lackeys but for the two nuclear powers, the United States and the Soviet Union, to co-operate in settling the world's problems.

Khrushchev has said: " We (the United States and the USSR) are the strongest countries in the world and if we unite for peace there can be no war. Then if any madman wanted war, we would but have to shake our fingers to warn him off."

It is thus apparent to everybody how far the leaders of the CPSU have gone in regarding the enemy as their friend.

In order to cover up their error, the leaders of the CPSU have not hesitated to attack the correct line of the CCP by lies and slanders. They assert that by advocating support for the people's wars of national liberation and revolutionary civil wars the CCP wants to provoke a nuclear world war. This is a curious lie.

The CCP has always held that the socialist countries should actively support the people's revolutionary struggles, including wars of national liberation and revolutionary civil wars. To fail to do so would be to renounce their proletarian internationalist duty. At the same time, we hold that the oppressed peoples and nations can achieve liberation only by their own resolute revolutionary struggle and that no one else can do it for them.

We have always maintained that socialist countries must not use nuclear weapons to support the people's wars of national liberation and revolutionary civil wars and have no need to do so.

We consistently hold that in the hands of a socialist country nuclear weapons must always be defensive weapons for resisting imperialist nuclear threats. A socialist country absolutely must not be the first to use nuclear weapons, nor should it in any circumstances play with them or engage in nuclear blackmail and nuclear gambling.

We are opposed both to the wrong practice on the part of the leaders of the CPSU of withholding support from the revolutionary struggles of the peoples and to their wrong approach to nuclear weapons. Instead of examining their own errors they accuse us of hoping for a " head-on clash " between the Soviet Union and the United States and of trying to push them into a nuclear war.

Our answer is: No, friends. You had better stop your sensation-mongering calumny. The CCP is firmly opposed to a " head-on clash " between the Soviet Union and the United States, and not in words only. In deeds too, it has worked hard to avert direct armed conflict between them. Examples of this are the Korean war against U.S. aggression, in which we fought side by side with the Korean comrades, and our struggle against the United States in the Taiwan Strait. We ourselves preferred to shoulder the heavy sacrifices necessary and stood in the first line of defence of the socialist camp so that the Soviet Union might stay in the second line. Have the leaders of the CPSU any sense of proletarian morality when they concoct such lies?

In fact, it is not we but the leaders of the CPSU who have frequently boasted that they would use nuclear weapons to help the anti-imperialist struggle of one country or another.

As everyone knows, the oppressed peoples and nations have no nuclear weapons and they cannot use them to make revolutions, nor is there any need for them to do so. The leaders of the CPSU admit that there is often no clear battleline between the two sides in national liberation wars and civil wars and therefore the use of nuclear weapons is out of the question. We should then like to ask the leaders of the CPSU: What need is there for a socialist country to support the people's revolutionary struggles by nuclear weapons?

We should also like to ask them: How would a socialist country use nuclear weapons to support the revolutionary struggle of an oppressed people or nation? Would it use nuclear weapons in an area where a war of national liberation or a revolutionary civil war was in progress, thereby subjecting both the revolutionary people and the imperialists to a nuclear strike? Or would it be the first to use nuclear weapons against an imperialist country which was waging a conventional war of aggression elsewhere? Obviously, in either case it is absolutely impermissible for a socialist country to use nuclear weapons.

The fact is that when the leaders of the CPSU brandish their nuclear weapons it is not really to support the peoples' anti-imperialist struggles.

Sometimes, in order to gain cheap prestige, they just publish empty statements which they never intend to honour. At other times, during the Caribbean crisis for instance, they engage in speculative, opportunistic, and irresponsible nuclear gambling for ulterior motives. As soon as their nuclear blackmail is seen through and is countered in kind, they retreat one step after another, switching from adventurism to capitulationism, and lose all by their nuclear gambling.

We wish to point out that the great Soviet people and Red Army have been and remain a great force safeguarding world peace. But Khrushchev's military ideas based on nuclear fetishism and nuclear blackmail are entirely wrong.

Khrushchev sees only nuclear weapons. According to him, "the present level of military technique being what it is, the air force and the navy have lost their former importance. These arms are being replaced and not reduced."

Of course, those units and men having combat duties on the ground are even less significant. According to him, "In our time, a country's defensive capacity is not determined by the number of men under arms, of men in uniform . . . . a country's defence potential depends in decisive measure on the firepower and the means of delivery that country commands."

As for the militia and the people, they are still more inconsequential. Khrushchev has made the well-known remark that for those now having modern weapons at their disposal, the militia is not an army but just human flesh.

Khrushchev's whole set of military theories runs completely counter to Marxist-Leninist teachings on war and the army. To follow his wrong theories will necessarily involve disintegrating the army and disarming oneself morally.

Obviously, if any socialist country should accept Khrushchev's erroneous military strategy, it would inevitably place itself in a most dangerous position.

Khrushchev may confer on himself such titles as "a great peace champion," award himself a peace prize and pin heroes' medals on himself, but no matter how much he may praise himself, he will not be able to cover up his dangerous practice of recklessly playing with nuclear weapons or his fawning before imperialist nuclear blackmail.

FIGHT OR CAPITULATE?

World peace can be won only through struggle by the people of all countries and not by begging the imperialists for it. Peace can be effectively safeguarded only by relying on the masses of the people and waging a tit-for-tat struggle against the imperialist policies of aggression and war. This is the correct policy.

Tit-for-tat struggle is an important conclusion drawn by the Chinese people from their prolonged struggle against imperialism and its lackeys.

Comrade Mao Tse-tung said: Chiang Kai-shek always tries to wrest every ounce of power and every ounce of gain from the people. And we? Our policy is to give them tit for tat and to fight for every inch of land. We act after his fashion. (Mao Tse-tung, *Selected Works*, IV, p. 14.)

He added: He always tries to impose war on the people, one sword in his left hand and another in his right. We take up swords, too, following his example. (*Ibid.*)

Analysing the domestic political situation in 1945, Comrade Mao Tse-tung said: "How to give 'tit for tat' depends on the situation. Sometimes not going to negotiations is tit-for-tat, and sometimes going to negotiations is also tit-for-tat . . . if they start fighting, we fight back, fight to win peace. Peace will not come unless we strike hard blows at the reactionaries who dare to attack the liberated areas." (*Ibid.*, p. 56.)

He drew the following historical lesson from the failure of China's revolution of 1924–27: "Confronted by counter-revolutionary attacks against the people, Chen Tu-hsiu did not adopt the policy of giving tit for tat and fighting for every inch of land; as a result, in 1927, within the space of a few months, the people lost all the rights they had won." (*Ibid.*, p. 16.)

The Chinese communists understand and adhere to the policy of giving tit for tat. We oppose both capitulationism and adventurism. This correct policy insured the victory of the Chinese revolution and the Chinese people's subsequent great successes in their struggle against imperialism.

All revolutionary people approve and welcome this correct fighting policy put forward by the Chinese communists. All imperialists and reactionaries fear and hate it.

The policy of giving tit for tat as put forward by the CCP is virulently attacked by the leaders of the CPSU. This only goes to show that they do not in the least want to oppose imperialism. Their sole purpose in attacking and smearing the policy of tit for tat is to cover up their wrong line of catering to the needs of imperialism and surrendering to it.

The CPSU leaders assert that a tit-for-tat struggle against imperialism will lead to international tension. How terrible! According to their logic, the imperialists are allowed to commit aggression and make threats against others, but the victims of imperialist aggression are not allowed to fight; the imperialists are allowed to oppress others, but the oppressed are not allowed to resist. This is a naked attempt to absolve the imperialists of their crimes of aggression. This is a philosophy of the jungle, pure and simple.

International tension is the product of the imperialist policies of aggression and war. The peoples should of course wage a firm struggle against imperialist aggression and threats. Facts have shown that only through struggle can imperialism be compelled to retreat and a genuine relaxation of international tension be achieved. Constant retreat before the imperialists cannot lead to genuine relaxation but will only encourage their aggression.

We have always opposed the creation of international tension by imperialism and stood for the relaxation of such tension, but the imperialists are bent on committing aggression and creating tension everywhere and that can only lead to the opposite of what they desire.

Comrade Mao Tse-tung said: " The U.S. imperialists believe that they will always benefit from a tense situation, but the fact is that tension created by the United States has led to the opposite of what it desires. It serves to mobilise the people of the whole world against the U.S. aggressors." (*People's Daily,* September 9, 1948.)

Further: " If the U.S. monopoly groups persist in their policies of aggression and war, the day is bound to come when the people of the world will hang them by the neck." (*Ibid.*)

The Declaration of 1957 rightly says: " By this policy, these anti-popular, aggressive imperialist forces are courting their own ruin; creating their own gravediggers."

This is the dialectic of history. Those who revere the imperialists can hardly understand this truth.

The CPSU leaders assert that by advocating a tit-for-tat struggle the CCP has rejected negotiations. This again is nonsense. We consistently maintain that those who refuse negotiations under all circumstances are definitely not Marxist-Leninists. The Chinese communists conducted negotiations with the Kuomintang many times during the revolutionary civil wars. They did not refuse to negotiate even on the eve of nation-wide liberation.

Comrade Mao Tse-tung said in March 1949: Whether the peace negotiations are overall or local, we should be prepared for such an eventuality. We should not refuse to enter into negotiations because we are afraid of trouble and want to avoid complications nor should we enter into negotiations with our minds in a haze. We should be firm in principle; we should also have all the flexibility permissible and necessary for carrying out our principles. (Mao Tse-tung, *Selected Works,* FLPH, Peking, IV, p. 372.)

Internationally, in struggling against imperialism and reaction, the Chinese communists take the same correct attitude toward negotiations.

In October 1951 Comrade Mao Tse-tung had this to say about the Korean armistice negotiations. " We have long said that the Korean question should be settled by peaceful means. This still holds good now. So long as the U.S. Government is willing to settle the question on a just and reasonable basis and will stop using every shameless means possible to wreck and obstruct the progress of the negotiations as it has done in the past, success in the Korean armistice negotiation is possible; otherwise it is impossible." (*People's Daily*, October 24, 1951.)

Resolute struggle against the U.S. imperialists compelled them to accept the Korean armistice agreement in the course of negotiations.

We took an active part in the 1954 Geneva conference and contributed to the restoration of peace in Indochina.

We are in favour of negotiations even with the United States, which has occupied our territory of Taiwan. The Sino-U.S. ambassadorial talks have been going on for more than eight years now.

We took an active part in the 1961 Geneva conference on the Laotian question and promoted the signing of the Geneva agreements respecting the independence and neutrality of Laos.

Do the Chinese communists allow themselves alone to negotiate with imperialist countries while opposing negotiations by the leaders of the CPSU with the leaders of the imperialist countries?

No, of course not. In fact, we have always actively supported all such negotiations by the Soviet Government with imperialist countries as are beneficial and not detrimental to the defence of world peace.

Comrade Mao Tse-tung said on May 14, 1960 : We support the holding of the summit conference whether or not this sort of conference yields achievements, or whether the achievements are big or small. But the winning of world peace should depend primarily on resolute struggle by the people of all countries. (*People's Daily*, May 15, 1960.)

We favour negotiations with imperialist countries. But it is absolutely impermissible to pin hope for world peace on negotiations, to spread illusions about them and thereby paralysing the fighting will of the peoples, as Khrushchev has done.

Actually, Khrushchev's wrong approach to negotiations is itself harmful to negotiations. The more Khrushchev retreats before the imperialists and the more he begs, the more the appetite of the imperialists will grow. Khrushchev, who poses as the greatest devotee of negotiations in history, is always an unrequited lover and too often a laughing-stock. Countless historical facts have shown that imperialists and reactionaries never care to save the face of capitulationists.

To sum up, our difference with the leaders of the CPSU on the question of war and peace is one between two different lines—whether or not to oppose imperialism, whether or not to support revolutionary struggles, whether or not to mobilise the people of the world against the imperialist war plots and whether or not to adhere to Marxism-Leninism. . . .

Peking Review, VI, 47 (November 27, 1963), pp. 6–16.]

Full title: Two Different Lines on the Question of War and Peace— Comment on the Open Letter of the Central Committee of the CPSU (5), by the Editorial Departments of *People's Daily* and *Red Flag*, November 18, 1963 (excerpts).

SELECTED BIBLIOGRAPHY

Communist China and the Soviet Bloc (*The Annals*, Vol. 349, September 1963).
Philadelphia: American Academy of Political and Social Science, 1963.
A symposium on Chinese Communism and the rift.

Communist Strategies in Asia. A. DOAK BARNETT, ed. [New York: Frederick A.
Praeger, 1963.]
An excellent symposium on Asian Communist parties and their roles in the rift.

The Soviet Bloc: Unity and Conflict. ZBIGNIEW K. BRZEZINSKI. Rev. ed. [New
York: Frederick A. Praeger, 1961.]
The standard work on bloc politics through 1960, with an excellent epilogue
on the rift in the revised edition.

"Threat and Opportunity in the Communist Schism." ZBIGNIEW K. BRZEZINSKI.
Foreign Affairs, Vol. XL, No. 3 (April 1963), pp. 513–526.
An excellent estimate, with policy recommendations.

"The Dismissal of Marshal P'eng Teh-huai." DAVID A. CHARLES. *The China
Quarterly,* No. 8 (October-December 1961), pp. 63–76.
The basic and reliable account.

The New Cold War: Moscow v. Pekin. EDWARD CRANKSHAW. [Harmondsworth,
Eng.: Penguin, 1963.]
Valuable, as are his articles, for disclosure of unpublished Sino-Soviet exchanges,
particularly at the November 1960 81-party meeting.

"Long Divisions and Fine Fractions." ALEXANDER DALLIN. *Problems of Communism,* Vol. XI, No. 2 (March-April 1962), pp. 7–16.
The best analysis of the situation in international Communism at the beginning
of 1962.

Diversity in International Communism. ALEXANDER DALLIN, ed., with JONATHAN
HARRIS and GREY HODNETT. [New York: Columbia University Press, 1963.]
A voluminous documentary study, covering all Communist parties, from the
Twenty-second Party Congress and up to April 1963.

Albania and the Sino-Soviet Rift. WILLIAM E. GRIFFITH. [Cambridge, Mass.:
M.I.T. Press, 1963.]
Detailed analysis, with documents, of Albania in the rift, through November
1962.

"The November 1960 Moscow Meeting: A Preliminary Reconstruction." WILLIAM
E. GRIFFITH. *The China Quarterly,* No. 11 (July-September 1962), pp. 38–57;
reprinted in Laqueur and Labedz, *Polycentrism* (New York: Frederick H.
Praeger, 1962), pp. 107–126.
Now needs to be supplemented; see p. 19, ftn. 14, *supra.*

The Sino-Soviet Dispute. GEOFFREY HUDSON, RICHARD LOWENTHAL and RODERICK
MACFARQUHAR. [New York: Frederick A. Praeger, 1961.]
Analyses and documents of the rift up to early 1961.

Polycentrism. WALTER LAQUEUR and LEOPOLD LABEDZ, eds. [New York: Frederick
A. Praeger, 1962.]
A symposium as of 1961

Unity and Contradiction. KURT LONDON, ed. [New York: Frederick A. Praeger,
1963.]
A 1962 collection of essays by leading authorities on the rift and its background.

"The Rise and Decline of International Communism." RICHARD LOWENTHAL.
Problems of Communism, Vol. XII, No. 2 (March-April 1963), pp. 19–32.
Among the best analyses of the rift and its effects.

"The World Scene Transformed." RICHARD LOWENTHAL. *Encounter,* Vol. XXI,
No. 4 (October 1963), pp. 3–10.
The best overall analysis of the effect of the rift and of the Cuban crisis.

Communism in North Vietnam. P. J. HONEY. [Cambridge, Mass.: M.I.T. Press, 1963.]

" Der Zweifrontenkampf der KPdSU." BORIS MEISSNER. *Osteuropa,* Vol. XIII, No. 9 (September 1963), pp. 577–604.

Particularly good for the interaction of domestic Soviet developments and the rift.

Problems of Communism, Vol. XI, No. 3 (May-June 1962). 64 pp.

A symposium on the state of international Communism.

" The Great Schism." HUGH SETON-WATSON. *Encounter,* Vol. XV, No. 5 (May 1963), pp. 61–70.

One of the best brief analyses.

The Sino-Soviet Conflict. DONALD S. ZAGORIA. [Princeton: Princeton University Press, 1961.]

The best detailed book-length treatment, up to the Twenty-second CPSU Congress; now needs to be supplemented by material which has since become available. See p. 19, ftn. 14, *supra.*

A detailed study of the North Vietnamese party's role in the rift.

Peking and Moscow. KLAUS MENHERT. [New York: G. P. Putnam, 1963.]

The best historical background of the rift.

The most useful regular analyses of current Sino-Soviet and international Communist developments are produced in Munich by analysts of Radio Free Europe, notably Richard Rockingham Gill, Joseph C. Kun and Kevin Devlin, and of Radio Liberty, particularly Christian Duevel.

INDEX

THE M.I.T. PRESS PAPERBACK SERIES